exam

me:
- what does enthusiastic worship do re ms. & world
① takes up time might spend on other things
② creates stronger social boundaries twsen insiders +
    outsiders - a la Whitehouse (23)

me: reverse the causal direction between ~~relation~~ social
    relations + ~~content~~ religious content -

- argument: ① Variations in extent to which religion is social/collective
            ② examples at various levels
            ③ might use this variation as DV
            ④ might also use it as IV
            ⑤ can do ④ w/ NCS, conceptualizing worship ~~as~~
                these terms

- 3 key vars: - time in worship ⌐111,103   } I'm saying:
              - ~~#~~ social boundaries ⌐111   enthusiasm ──+──→ social
              - enthusiasm in worship   ↗+↗ time +   boundaries
11 - these
connections more or
less explicitly   ↓ -
recognized   civic
                                                              engagement
⌐54
99 - a ratcheting
113 - no seniors in   - time + enthusiasm connected
early services   because boringness sets in --
                         same reason we use more class.
                         discussion in longer class periods
                       - this ~~also~~ makes time the key IV -> if going to
                         keep people occupied religiously for long periods,
                         enthusiasm is very likely to develop -

- maybe ~~time~~/enthusiasm two indicators of same underlying
                                part a byproduct of time (+

vice versa : $E = t \# social\ boundaries^2 = E = t s^2$
                         density? $t\frac{E}{t} = s^2$
                                               $t = \frac{E}{s^2}$

is the obv. st
is more at football
+ basketball but not ?   - at given level of social density, increasing
waves at football   time spent together will increase enthusiasm
+ basketball games   or: higher the enthusiasm to time ratio, ~~more~~
                    (but why no E at movies?)   stronger the
                                                         boundaries
                              ↳ because product isn't human actor?, then
                                why not live theatre → because no
                       - maybe only holds where $E > \emptyset$ relevant
                                                                   social
                                                                   boundaries

n. $E = S_i t^2$: social boundaries & time together generates
  this activity (time-squared because 2 hours will mean far
  more... double amount of E over 1 hour
-D. only ran this one way: C.E. generates boundaries
  also, D. didn't break C.E. down into time and content
  dimensions

$S = \frac{E}{t^2}$: enthusiasm/time ratio measures boundary strength

NB: if boundary strength is miniscule, can increase time
  quite a lot w/o increasing E.

$t^2 = \frac{E}{S}$: at given E, increase S will decrease t spent
  together -- as in Jewish participation in
  weekly services v. Xtian -- similar kinds of
  services, done much less frequently
  attended

E/t^2 either eats 0 or 1, flipping back + forth between 0, 1

t_i = amount of time spent in identity-specific behavior to event
          f = frequency of events

E_i = amount of time in enthusiastic identity-specific behavior

S_i = strength of boundary around specific identity

→ for some i, $E_i = t_i$, since no such thing as t_i that's not
  E_i -- nationalist behavior? -- in these cases, solidarity an inflexible switch

NB: if increase t_i w/o increasing E_i, will necessarily reduce S_i

- but clearly are is in which $E_i < t_i$: school, concerts, sports,
  church -- basically anything where is performance - audience
  aspect

- can imagine situation in which people constantly focused
  in i, in which case t_i can't increase -- then,
  increasing S_i has to increase E_i & one form of E_i
  is violence -- if t_i not at limit, increasing S_i
  can increase t_i w/o increasing E_i -- wear veils, one
    e.g.
  others read more Koran, do more charity -- in secular
  society, S_i has room to expand w/o turning violent,
  but there's a limit -

Enthusiasm = Minutes & Community

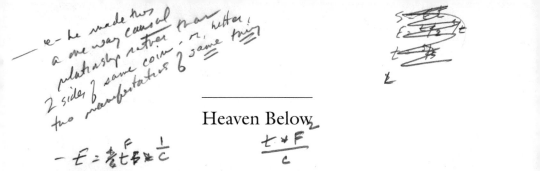

re - he made this a one way causal relationship rather than 2 sides of same coin, or better, two manifestations of same thing

Heaven Below

$$-E = \frac{F}{t} \# \frac{1}{c}$$

$$\frac{t \# F}{c}$$

---

135 - on music + sociability in lengthy worship services

224 - on how limited social services were

251 - self-consciously a _new_ form -- no history

11/07 - w/ ritual-sincerity theme in mind.

71 - < 50% of early converts spoke in tongues - co-variation in the practice -- some did; some didn't

42 & 43 - tongues necessary for high status in community (also 44)

56 - on sincerity -- a backslider's tongues interpreted as fake

69 - on testimony as strengthening collective identities, esp. by solidifying a person's position as a member in good standing in the group

Heaven Below

Early Pentecostals and American Culture

Grant Wacker

Harvard University Press

Cambridge, Massachusetts, and London, England | 2001

Library of Congress Cataloging-in-Publication Data

Wacker, Grant, 1945–
    Heaven below : early Pentecostals and American culture / Grant Wacker.
      p. cm.
    Includes bibliographical references and index.
    ISBN 0-674-00499-X (alk. paper)
    1. Pentecostalism—United States—History—20th century.
  2. Pentecostal churches—United States—History—20th century.
  3. United States—Church history—20th century.   I. Title.

 BR1644.5.U6 W33   2001
289.9′4′097309041—dc21   00-054221

For Laura
light of my life

Contents

Preface   *ix*

Acknowledgments   *xi*

Introduction   *1*

1. Temperament   *18*

2. Tongues   *35*

3. Testimony   *58*

4. Authority   *70*

5. Cosmos   *87*

6. Worship   *99*

7. Rhetoric   *112*

8. Customs   *121*

9. Leaders   *141*

10. Women   *158*

11. Boundaries   *177*

12. Society   *197*

13. Nation   *217*

14. War   *240*

15. Destiny   *251*

Epilogue   *266*

Appendix: U.S. Pentecostal Statistics   *271*

Notes   *273*

Index   *355*

Preface

This book describes the contours of pentecostal culture in the United States from 1900 to 1925, the place and time of the movement's birth and early development. We all know, however, that books do not tumble from the sky like sacred meteors. They have a history of their own. So it may be helpful to say a few words about the story behind the story, how this study came to be written and the assumptions that inform it.

The following pages might be described as an essay that got out of hand. Some twenty years ago the late Professor Timothy L. Smith of The Johns Hopkins University asked me to write an article on pentecostals for an anthology he was putting together on the evangelical mosaic in America. I balked, knowing that several fine monographs already existed. What more could be said about the subject? But Tim persisted, characteristically pressing me to go back to the primary sources and read them for myself. I soon discovered that the surface barely had been scratched. Early pentecostals were furious writers, churning out thousands of pages of text—mostly in periodicals—in the first few years of the revival's life. Some of that material had not been read at all, and much of it not read with cultural questions in mind. I also soon discovered that if otherworldly aspirations marked the surface of those texts, thisworldly shrewdness marked the underside. No one, it seemed, had paid much attention to the significance of that doubleness. So it was that I heard the call, if not from on high, at least from my friends, to try to tell my own version of the story.

It is time now to explain my own relation to the pentecostal tradition. In one sense this bit of self-disclosure should not matter at all, for my intent is to offer an account that can be discussed in the general marketplace of ideas without regard to confessional commitments. But since antiseptic impartiality is impossible, and probably not desirable anyway, it seems only fair to acknowledge the perspective from which I write. In brief, I was reared in a pentecostal home and attended a pentecostal church once or twice a week until I left for college. My father, grandfather, aunts, uncles, and cousins in all directions were pentecostal ministers or missionaries. Until adulthood I simply assumed, as they did, that all mature Christians would speak in tongues and expect miracles of divine healing. A secular college and graduate school fostered changes. In time I came to identify myself simply as an evangelical Christian, and that is where my head, at least, remains. For many years now a small United Methodist Church, evangelical though not charismatic, has served as a congenial abode, both theologically and culturally.

Yet in many ways my heart never left home. Pentecostals continue to be my people. I embrace many of their values. I understand their jokes and, what is worse, I usually think they are funny. To be sure, I cringe when I watch pentecostal flamethrowers on television. But I grow defensive when outsiders take swipes at them, not because they do not deserve it, but because most outsiders have not earned the right. More important, perhaps, my pentecostal upbringing continues to influence my deepest assumptions about what is and is not possible in a world allegedly governed solely by natural processes. Miracle stories, which play a large role in this book, never appear with qualifying terms like "alleged" or "so-called." That is partly because I try to see the world through my subjects' eyes, and partly because I remain unsure where their view ends and mine begins. I have long imagined, in other words, that God must have missed class the day they covered the Enlightenment. Clearly the Almighty did not get the word that He was not supposed to transform persons' lives in miraculous ways day after day.

So I guess that the most honest way to explain my relation to the pentecostal tradition is to say that I am a pilgrim with one leg still stuck in the tent. I hope that being 50 percent outsider and 50 percent insider is an asset that enables me to combine the cool eye of the critic with the warm heart of the believer. Whether I have done a decent job of describing that distant world others will have to judge. But I suspect that the posture of being half out and half in, though awkward, defines the fate of many religious historians. Sooner or later most of us end up writing autobiography anyway. The challenge is to make it more than that.

Acknowledgments

My colleague David Steinmetz once wrote that the historian's task is to resurrect the dead and let them speak. As it turns out, that is the easy part. The hard part is finding the means adequately to thank the friends who helped along the way.

First come the research assistants at the University of North Carolina and then at Duke University. Many have now graduated to thriving careers of their own. They include Chris Armstrong, Lee Carter, Russ Congleton, Bill Durbin, Jane Harris, Margaret Kim, Susie Mroz, Conrad Ostwalt, Larry Snyder, and David Zercher. Betsy Flowers tamed my prose and prepared the index. Jay Blossom took valuable days from his own dissertation writing to work through the manuscript with exceptional care. Dan Ramirez opened my horizons to the richness of the Latino and the Oneness pentecostal traditions, though for the most part their stories remain his to tell. One of my teachers used to say that graduate students were not so much students as junior colleagues. He was right.

Numerous colleagues provided encouragement and astute (sometimes too astute) criticism. Comrades at the Institute for the Study of American Evangelicals rank among the faithful. So does the late George Rawlyk. Edith Blumhofer, Bob Cooley, Russ Spittler, and Skip Stout wrote recommendation letters at crucial junctures. David Bundy, Joe Creech, Gary McGee, Mel Robeck, Roger Robins, Jeanette Scholer, W. C. Turner, and Wayne Warner shared hard-won primary sources. Perennial conversation partners Don Argue, Dan Bays, Jim Bratt, Gus Cerillo, Liz Clark, Murray Dempster, David Hackett, Mike Hamilton, Richard Heitzenrater, Hans Hillerbrand, Richard Hughes, Mike Lienesch, Laurie Maffly-Kipp, George Marsden, Bruce Mullin, Ron Numbers, Russ Richey, David Steinmetz, Tom Tweed, and especially Peter Kaufman helped me think about problems of perspective, method, and fairness to historical subjects no longer able to speak for themselves. They also assured me that there was a story to tell at a time in the writing when I had grown doubtful. Phil Barlow, Marc Chaves, Chris Smith, and

Bob Woodberry assisted with the Appendix. David Daniels, Jim Goff, Peter Kaufman, Mel Robeck, W. C. Turner, and Wayne Warner read portions of the manuscript. Randall Balmer, Edith Blumhofer, Joel Carpenter, and Mark Noll ploughed through it all, from "kiver to kiver," as we say in the South. The book's main thesis emerged many years ago from conversations with Everett Wilson, as we daily navigated the harrowing commute to school together over the Santa Cruz mountains. My deans, first Dennis Campbell and later Greg Jones, said yes to every request. Peg Fulton, editor, and Bill Hutchison, mentor, mixed critique and inspiration in perfect measure. In more ways than one, Nat Hatch made the project possible. Of course I bear sole responsibility for the flaws that remain.

The Assemblies of God's Flower Pentecostal Heritage Center, expertly directed by Wayne Warner, extended research facilities and sequestered writing space on numerous occasions. Archivists Glenn Gohr, Joyce Lee, Brett Pavia, and Faye Williams helped immeasurably. The Assemblies of God Seminary, Bethany College, Emmanuel School of Religion, Miami University, University of Wisconsin–Madison, Vanguard University, Wake Forest University, Westmont College, and the American religious history colloquia at Harvard and at Duke–UNC gave me chances to try out ideas. Scott Kelley and Ray Woody, friends forever, made research trips to Springfield, Missouri, more like retreats than work.

As always family members offered resources of another sort. My mother-in-law, Geneva Bowman, and my mother, Merian Zeller, let me hole up in spare bedrooms for extended periods, free of phones and chores. My long-departed gram, a single missionary to Africa at nineteen, taught me what all pentecostals are supposed to know by instinct: that most rivers are crossable. More than once my wife, Katherine, led the way. My younger daughter, Julia, broadened my horizons more than I bargained for—and in the process helped me better appreciate the diversity of life situations early pentecostals represented. This book is dedicated to my older daughter, Laura. My personal library contains hundreds of photocopies of rare pentecostal periodicals catalogued in the loopy handwriting of a twelve-year-old who tagged along to help. Now a history teacher herself, Laura has filled my life with joy for a very long time.

Two grants from the Pew Charitable Trusts, one from the Independent Scholars Program, the other from the Evangelical Scholars' Initiative, funded the research and writing of much of this book. Some paragraphs in Chapter 1 appeared in "The Functions of Faith in Primitive Pentecostalism," *Harvard Theological Review*, 77 (1984); "Caring and Curing: The Pentecostal Tradition," in *Caring and Curing: Health and Medicine in the Western Faith Tra-*

ditions, ed. Ronald L. Numbers and Darryl W. Amundsen (New York: Macmillan, 1986); and "Searching for Eden with a Satellite Dish: Primitivism, Pragmatism, and the Pentecostal Character," in *The Primitive Church in the Modern World,* ed. Richard T. Hughes (Urbana: University of Illinois Press, 1995). Portions of Chapter 13 appeared in "Early Pentecostals and the Almost Chosen People," *Pneuma: Journal of the Society for Pentecostal Studies,* 19 (Fall 1997). Some paragraphs in Chapter 15 appeared in "Playing for Keeps: The Primitivist Impulse in Early Pentecostalism," in *The American Quest for the Primitive Church,* ed. Richard T. Hughes (Urbana: University of Illinois Press, 1988); and I presented parts of this chapter at the Sixth German-American Historical Symposium, "Visions of the Future," Krefeld, Germany, May 1999. In every case the presentation has been revised for this book.

We have no need of organs or pianos, for the Holy Ghost plays the piano in all our hearts . . . It is so sweet. It is heaven below.

UNSIGNED, *APOSTOLIC FAITH*, DECEMBER 1906

Introduction

It started in the American heartland, in the twilight of the nineteenth century. First hundreds, then thousands, then tens of thousands of Baptists and Methodists, along with a smaller number of Quakers, Mennonites, and Presbyterians, left their natal fellowships to join one of the great religious migrations of modern times. Some pulled out and some were kicked out, but most just drifted away. However separated, all sought new communions more visibly filled with the New Testament church's supernatural power. These spiritual adventurers went by a variety of names—including premillennialists, holiness folk and, from the lips of outsiders, holy rollers. But we might call them all radical evangelicals, for they commonly insisted that the only true gospel was the "four-fold" gospel of personal salvation, Holy Ghost baptism, divine healing, and the Lord's soon return. In the span of two decades, roughly 1885–1905, they formed numerous sects bearing such defiantly "come-outer" labels as Shiloh, Pillar of Fire, Fire-Baptized Holiness Association, Christian and Missionary Alliance, and Missionary Bands of the World.[1]

To outsiders the turbid emotionalism of radical evangelical meetings, or at least those that marked the most leftward wing of the movement, seemed paramount. And with good reason. In the fire-baptized holiness services of the late 1890s, one leader remembered, the "people screamed until you could hear them for three miles on a clear night, and until the blood vessels stood out like whip cords."[2] A newspaper reporter visiting Maria Woodworth-Etter's divine healing rallies in Oakland in 1889 wrote that her services produced "mental debauchery" and that those who attended did so "at their own risk." Another said that her prayer meetings sounded like the "female ward of an insane asylum."[3]

Nonetheless, raw emotion never made up the whole of the story. A long tradition of ideas lay behind the apparent pandemonium. We might picture those ideas as four distinct though frequently confluent streams that had been flowing across the American religious landscape for many decades. Each eventually constituted a part of the four-fold gospel. The first stream, both theologically and historically, emphasized heartfelt salvation through faith in Jesus Christ. This notion dated back to the Great Awakening in the mid–eighteenth century (if not earlier), when it was commonly called the new birth. Late-nineteenth-century radical evangelicals perpetuated both the ideology and the experience of the new birth with little change. Like their forebears, they made it the nonnegotiable marker that divided Christians from non-Christians.[4]

The second stream constituting the four-fold gospel—Holy Ghost baptism—flowed from three closely related though historically distinct tributaries. One started in England in the eighteenth century with John Wesley's notion of entire sanctification. Though the new birth signaled the true beginning of the Christian life, he preached, corrupt desires persisted. This "inbred sin" needed to be eradicated in a lifelong process of moral cleansing. "He breaks the power of canceled sin," ran one of the most beloved lyrics in Charles Wesley's signature hymn, "O For a Thousand Tongues to Sing." But in mid-nineteenth-century America holiness Wesleyans, led by evangelist Phoebe Palmer, came to view entire sanctification less as a process than as a state one entered by faith at a definable moment in time. In this state—commonly dubbed the second blessing—Christians found themselves miraculously enabled to rise above sin's terrible power.[5]

Another tributary emerged from the teachings of Oberlin president Charles G. Finney and other Reformed (or broadly Calvinist) writers just before and after the Civil War. Like Palmer, these Oberlin perfectionists, as they were known, emphasized a definable, life-transforming experience after conversion. Unlike Palmer, however, they understood it primarily as an on-going process, defined by the ability to consecrate one's life wholly to Christ's service.[6]

Still another tributary flowed across the Atlantic from the annual "higher life" conferences at Keswick, England. Higher life teachers urged that the second experience in the order of salvation was properly understood as a series of experiences that equipped believers for extraordinary feats of witness and service. They called it an enduement of power. "Baptism with the Spirit," American higher life preacher Reuben A. Torrey testily remarked, "is not primarily intended to make believers happy nor holy, but to make them useful."[7]

By the end of the century Christians in each of these three tributary traditions had come to label the postconversion experience (or experiences) the "baptism with the Holy Ghost." But where holiness Wesleyans spoke of purity, Oberlin perfectionists and Keswick higher life advocates more often spoke of power. Grass-roots believers typically blurred those lines and talked about purity and power in a single breath.[8]

Divine healing and anticipation of the Lord's soon return constituted the third and fourth streams comprised by the four-fold gospel. Divine healing was as old as Christianity itself, but the distinctive form that it took in American radical evangelical circles emerged from mid-nineteenth-century developments in Switzerland, Germany, and Britain. This pattern departed from historic Christian doctrine (which had enjoined elders to anoint and pray for the sick) by insisting that Christ's atonement on the cross provided healing for the body just as it provided healing for the soul. Penitent faith won the former just as readily as it secured the latter. In the United States many voices popularized the atonement-healing idea, including most notably A. B. Simpson, founder of the Christian and Missionary Alliance.[9] In the same years anticipation of the Lord's soon return expressed itself in the language of dispensational premillennialism, which called for an imminent secret rapture of the saints, immediately followed by seven years of terrible tribulation, the second coming of the Lord, the millennium, and final judgment. This scheme, initially articulated by the Plymouth Brethren in Britain, received influential statement on the American side by *Missionary Review of the World* editor A. T. Pierson and Christian Zionist William E. Blackstone.[10]

Partisans channeled each of these theological streams—personal salvation, Holy Ghost baptism (in Wesleyan holiness, Oberlin perfectionist, and Keswick higher life forms), divine healing, and dispensational premillennialism—through a vast institutional network. That network included conferences, summer camps, books, magazines, colleges, Bible institutes, and a web of national, regional, and local associations. In particular the numerous "faith homes" established throughout the Northeast and Midwest in the 1880s and 1890s facilitated the theology and practice of divine healing. Some of the better known ones involved Charles Cullis's Faith Cure House in Boston, A. B. Simpson's Berachah House in New York City and, most notably, John Alexander Dowie's healing homes in Chicago and Zion City, Illinois. Spectacular healing revivals also started in the late 1880s and 1890s as Dowie and Woodworth-Etter separately crisscrossed the country with their independent deliverance meetings.[11] Dense networks of personal friendships, especially among leaders, facilitated spreading the word in ways that are only beginning to come to light.[12]

Other broadly evangelical influences, though harder to track, helped to define the range of available assumptions and practices. A restorationist yearning to recover the supernatural power and miracles of the New Testament church complemented the four-fold gospel, more as a premise than as an explicit affirmation. Many radical evangelicals expected that the "former rain," the signs and wonders described in Acts, would soon be fulfilled by the "latter rain," a final outpouring of the Holy Spirit's glory at the close of history. The exact origins of this influence are hard to pin down, but nineteenth-cen-

tury Protestantism brimmed with restorationist impulses that strongly affected other indigenous groups including the Churches of Christ and the
Latter-day Saints.[13] Religious outlooks and practices initiated in West Africa,
and mediated through black evangelical Christianity in the United States,
also may have played a formative role.[14]

The sectarian and more widely Christian aspirations of the age also shaped
the radical evangelical ethos. Though few direct ties linked Adventists, Mormons, Spiritualists, Christian Scientists, and Jehovah's Witnesses with radical
evangelicals, it is significant that all of these groups emerged in the same cultural milieu. More important, each of the former shared one or more of the
latter's interests in the immediacy of the supernatural, the healing of the
physical body, and the imminent apocalyptic ending of history—all portended in a special reading of a sacred text.[15] And though a vast gulf, both
cultural and theological, separated the Holy Ghost revival from the emerging
liberal-modernist impulse in mainline Protestantism, both traditions distinguished themselves by emphasizing the nearness and salvific power of God's
Spirit in history. Roman Catholics too evinced unprecedented interest in the
Holy Spirit's sanctifying presence in contemporary life. It would be risky to
make too much of these contextual influences, but obtuse to ignore them altogether. Like everyone else, radical evangelicals worked with the common
fund of ideas and assumptions provided by late Victorian culture.[16]

Influences from the secular popular culture also shaped the radical evangelical ethos. Most conspicuous, perhaps, was the surging interest in physical
health. The presumption that a long-lived, pain-free body should be normative for all people spurred the growth of recreational sports, fitness regimens,
and institutional expressions of a muscular Christianity such as the YMCA
and YWCA. Popular culture also fostered a fascination with millennial
schemes. Some texts, like Edward Bellamy's best-selling *Looking Backward*
(1888), envisioned a utopia engineered through purely human efforts of social planning. Others, like Charles Sheldon's best-selling *In His Steps* (1896),
envisioned a utopia engineered through partly divine and partly human self-
sacrifice. Still others yearned for the renovating power imagined to reside in
distant ages and faraway places. Though variously conceived, millions saw a
new day coming.[17]

Finally, it is important to remember that radical evangelicals arrayed themselves along a dual spectrum of social class and worship style. Though systematic research remains to be done, present evidence suggests that those who
came from the Wesleyan holiness tradition typically represented the stable
working class and evinced a sharply counterestablishment style. At the same
time those who came from the Oberlin perfectionist and Keswick higher life
traditions typically represented the lower middle class and evinced a less

confrontational style.[18] Though autobiographical allusions in the earliest pentecostal periodicals suggest that a majority of first-generation converts hailed from Wesleyan holiness groups, a sizable minority came from the other bodies.

As the nineteenth century drew to a close a small number of radical evangelicals increasingly longed for more than the four-fold gospel. Though their prescriptions varied, all sensed the possibility of a spiritual experience more intense, more palpable than anything they had yet known. So it was that just after the turn of the century one tiny band, meeting in a Bible school in Topeka, Kansas, grew particularly interested in the miracles described in the New Testament's Acts of the Apostles. Led by an itinerant Methodist healer named Charles Fox Parham, the seekers read that on the Day of Pentecost Jesus' followers experienced Holy Ghost baptism and "began to speak with other tongues, as the Spirit gave them utterance." This simple story, which had fascinated Christians for nearly 1900 years, raised a question as disturbing as it was provocative. If speaking in tongues accompanied Holy Ghost baptism on the Day of Pentecost, why not now? Indeed, if then, why not always and everywhere?

For the Kansas zealots the answer presented itself with the force of an epiphany: speaking in tongues *always* accompanied Holy Ghost baptism, first as an audible sign of the Holy Ghost's presence, second as a tool for evangelism. This claim, unique in the history of Christianity, defined a relatively rare, relatively difficult physical activity or skill as a nonnegotiable hallmark of a fully developed Christian life. Not incidentally, it also defined believers who did not speak in tongues as second-class Christians. By definition they had not received the coveted baptism experience.

Though speaking in tongues, or glossolalia, probably had existed off and on for centuries, no one knows when the practice first appeared in radical evangelical circles. After the pentecostal movement was well under way, many claimed to have spoken in tongues in worship meetings in the 1880s and 1890s.[19] But there is reason for hesitation about those claims, for few were reported at the time they occurred. It is possible, of course, that glossolalic outbursts took place but were not reported because the religious culture had not yet invested the experience with clear theological meaning. Either way, Parham probably knew about tongues by 1898, and personally heard it in 1900 at Frank W. Sandford's Holy Ghost and Us divine healing compound in Maine.[20] The fact that Parham soon connected Holy Ghost baptism with tongues was hardly surprising in itself, since every time Acts mentioned the former it spoke of the latter too, either explicitly or implicitly. Still, to insist, as Parham did, that tongues *always* accompanied Holy Ghost baptism and that the baptism–tongues experience formed a third distinct event in the order of salvation (following conversion and sanctification) marked a dramatic development in the radical evangelical tradition.

From these inauspicious beginnings the pentecostal message spread slowly but steadily, mainly among old-stock whites—hard-working, plain folk. Initially it made news in the Kansas press, then shriveled and nearly died. In 1903 Parham salvaged the revival by returning to a divine healing ministry. Two years later he took the Apostolic Faith—as he called it—to Houston. There a black evangelist named William J. Seymour embraced the message and carried it to Los Angeles, where his preaching sparked the now famous Azusa Street revival in the spring of 1906. In the meantime Parham's disciples bore the Apostolic Faith to Chicago, and then to urban centers of the Northeast, especially New York City. By the early 1910s the revival had reached most parts of the United States, Canada, and northern Mexico, claiming 50,000—possibly 100,000—converts.[21] Though old-stock whites would remain preponderant, after 1906 the movement acquired a conspicuously multi-ethnic face.[22]

While some partisans of the Holy Ghost revival—probably a large minority—resisted all efforts toward organization beyond the local congregation, many others soon formed themselves into identifiable denominations. Between 1906 and 1911 reports from Azusa prompted a cluster of thriving Wesleyan sects in the Southeast to adopt the pentecostal message. These included, among others, the predominantly black Church of God in Christ, led by C. H. Mason, the Church of God (Cleveland, Tennessee), led by A. J. Tomlinson, and the Pentecostal Holiness Church, led by J. H. King. After a slow start the good news caught fire among radical evangelicals of Reformed (particularly Baptist and Presbyterian) background in the central and south-central states. In 1914 several thousand of these folk coalesced to form the Assemblies of God. In the late 1910s evangelist Aimee Semple McPherson broke from that fellowship to establish her own following in Los Angeles, incorporated in 1927 as the International Church of the Foursquare Gospel. One significant theological difference separated the older pentecostal bodies of Wesleyan origin from the younger ones of Reformed origin. Where the former called for three distinct steps in the order of salvation (conversion, sanctification, and Holy Ghost baptism), the latter stipulated only two (conversion-sanctification and Holy Ghost baptism).

In 1916 a dispute arose in the Assemblies of God over the nature of the Trinity. That controversy contributed to the formation of several Oneness organizations, as they came to be called. The latter held, among other things, that God was one (not triune), and that He had fully revealed Himself in Jesus Christ. In time the largest of the Oneness bodies would include the mostly white United Pentecostal Church and the mostly black Pentecostal

Assemblies of the World. Another important Oneness body, the largely Latino Apostolic Assembly of the Faith in Christ Jesus, emerged independently on the West Coast in the 1910s.[23]

Denominational formation fostered numerical growth and social respectability. By the end of the twentieth century more than 200 distinct pentecostal sects had established themselves on the American landscape.[24] Most were pocket-sized, yet the two largest, the Assemblies of God and the Church of God in Christ, claimed millions of members apiece. Several others—including the Church of God, the International Church of the Foursquare Gospel, the International Pentecostal Holiness Church, the Pentecostal Assemblies of the World, and the United Pentecostal Church—claimed hundreds of thousands apiece. Precise figures remained elusive, but 10 million adherents in the United States alone seemed plausible.[25] Social status followed numbers. By the 1950s the pentecostal movement had started to capture the attention of mainline theologians and national news magazines.[26] In 1978 the *Christian Century* judged healing evangelist Oral Roberts one of the ten most influential religious leaders in the United States. Two decades later *Christian History* magazine ranked Azusa pioneer William J. Seymour one of the ten most influential Christians of the twentieth century.[27] At the beginning of the new millennium the high-profile careers of Admiral Vern Clark, Chief of Naval Operations, and John Ashcroft, U.S. Attorney General, both publicly identified pentecostals, left little doubt that the tradition had become a permanent and respected fixture of American life.

After World War II events grew complicated in two ways. First, pentecostal or pentecostal-like teachings and practices overflowed their historic boundaries in the radical evangelical tradition and penetrated the Roman Catholic Church and some of the older Protestant denominations, especially the Protestant Episcopal Church and the Lutheran Church in America. Pentecostal impulses also prompted the formation of parachurch organizations, such as Women's Aglow and Full Gospel Business Men's Fellowship International, as well as independent megachurches bearing upbeat names like Highway Assembly and Abundant Life Center.[28] These newer converts proved casual about labels. Sometimes they called themselves pentecostals, sometimes charismatics, sometimes just Spirit-filled Christians. They also proved flexible about the necessity of speaking in tongues. Though all esteemed the practice, not all required it as the older pentecostal groups had done (and continued to do).[29] But the family resemblance remained unmistakable. A 1978 Gallup survey reported that 19 percent, or 29 million, of adult Americans considered themselves pentecostal or charismatic Christians. About one-third came from the older or "classical" pentecostal sects, and the others from mainstream denominations and independent fellowships.[30]

The second complication of the post–World War II years involved the dramatic growth of pentecostal or pentecostal-like teachings and practices outside Europe and North America. Though Holy Ghost missionaries had carried their glad tidings around the world in the first decade of the revival's life, the international movement (like the North American one) advanced slowly. But then, in the 1960s and 1970s, expansionist impulses in the United States, indigenous revivals elsewhere, and capitalist and postcapitalist transformations everywhere spurred the extension of the pentecostal message, especially in Latin America, sub-Saharan Africa, and southeast Asia.[31] At the end of the century, according to demographers David W. Barrett and Todd M. Johnson, nearly 525 million persons considered themselves pentecostals or charismatics, making them the largest aggregation of Christians on the planet outside the Roman Catholic Church. Those numbers may have swelled in the telling, yet other studies consistently showed that within a hundred years of its beginnings the pentecostal-charismatic movement claimed an immense following, both at home and abroad.[32]

This book seeks to explore a small but important slice of this vast—and vastly complicated—global religious phenomenon. My topic is the cultural terrain sculpted by first-generation pentecostals in the United States. I harbor no illusions that the movement's founders were moral giants, nor do I suppose that their successors were moral midgets. Cranks and scoundrels along with many manifestly saintly souls turned up in all generations, and the first was no exception. But the founders sparked the effervescent period of rapid symbol formation. The ideas, practices, and institutions they set in motion persisted long after their deaths and, to a great extent, continued to define pentecostal patterns in America at the end of the twentieth century. From them later adherents learned what questions to ask of life and, perhaps more important, what questions not to ask. By the 1930s the guiding lights of that first generation were dimming with the trials of old age. Energetic young leaders were surging forward, eager to take over. The fire from heaven would continue to fall, but never again, it seemed, with that same awesome power.

Aims

Sometimes it appears that the only thing growing faster than the worldwide pentecostal-charismatic movement is the flow of scholarly books and articles about it. No wonder. The revival's size, angularity, and historical proximity have made it an attractive specimen for testing every conceivable theory about ecstatic experience, sect formation, and religious evolution. Charles Edwin Jones's multivolume bibliographic *Guide*(s) to the holiness, pentecostal, black perfectionist, and charismatic movements contain literally thousands of entries. Most refer to primary sources written by partisans, but many hundreds record secondary treatments by theologians, historians, religionists, and social scientists.[33]

Much the same can be said for the early history of pentecostals in the United States, the subject of this book. Generalists have mapped the broad contours of the story, and specialists have tracked the emergence of all of the major denominations and some of the smaller ones too. Missiologists have examined the revival's aggressive outreach programs. Biographers have traced the careers of prominent leaders, including Charles Fox Parham, Maria Woodworth-Etter, and Aimee Semple McPherson. Theologians have excavated the movement's ideational roots in the rich sectarian loam of the nineteenth century. Some of these scholars have moved beyond the early years and ably traced the narrative into the later decades of the twentieth century. Taken together, their work adds up to an impressive amount of scholarly attention.[34]

So why the present study? Remarkably, few have provided what early pentecostals themselves surely would have considered most important: a close description of their everyday lives, and especially the religious aspects of their everyday lives. Once we start this line of inquiry, the questions tumble forth in dizzying profusion. How did believers interpret their religious experiences? Structure their worship? Choose their leaders? Regulate their leisure? Perceive other Christians? Function in the workplace? Relate to the nation? In brief, what did the world look and feel like in that first intense burst of enthusiasm just before and after World War I?

In seeking answers to these questions I have listened less to formal theological debates and more to the conversations that took place around the kitchen table. Literary critic Lionel Trilling once urged students of the past to pay particular attention to the "hum and buzz of implication," the part of culture that "never gets fully stated, coming in the tone of greetings and the tone of quarrels, in slang and humor and popular songs, in the way children play, in the gesture the waiter makes when he puts down the plate, in the very nature of the food we prefer."[35] This book seeks to follow Trilling's advice. I try to catch the "hum and buzz of implication," the multitudinous whispers of everyday life that the other studies have tended to overlook.

Though the book's primary goal is simply to register the sounds of the pentecostal past as fully as possible in a single volume, a closely related secondary aim is to understand why the movement survived at all. In 1910 few outsiders believed that it would last another decade, let alone another century. Internal dissension met external ridicule every day of the week. So why did this new mix of old ingredients prove so viable? In brief, what made it work?

In the last twenty-five years scholars have offered numerous explanations for pentecostalism's persistence. Most fit into one of three categories. The first might be called the compensation model. In this perspective the movement is best understood as a substitute for the material comforts and social esteem that converts wanted but could not obtain. In the words of one thoughtful proponent of this position, enthusiasts sought to relieve their distress by losing themselves in the "almost wholly otherworldly, symbolic, and psychotherapeutic" benefits of supernaturalist religion.[36] The second explanation might be called the functional model. In this perspective the pentecostal revival seems less an effort to escape adversity than a creative resource for dealing with it. In the face of wrenching social changes, the argument runs, the Holy Ghost movement provided an island of stability in a sea of chaos. It offered respite from toil, release from loneliness, and comfort in the face of death.[37] The third explanation might be called the mobilization model. In this perspective pentecostal leaders functioned as creative agents in their own right. They loomed large on the religious landscape when they established the institutional structures that made their emergence possible, and tumbled into obscurity when they failed to keep those structures intact. Simply stated, energetic leaders first created a need, then moved people and material resources to meet it.[38]

All three of these explanations for pentecostalism's vitality have much to commend them, but all reveal two shortcomings. First, they tend to sidestep troublesome data that do not fit the scheme. Second, they tend to relegate religious motives to a secondary role. In this study, therefore, I try to address those needs by frankly acknowledging the angularity of the data and by giving religious motives their proper due. I do not suppose that my interpretation displaces the others, but I do think that it adds an enriching perspective.

My main argument can be stated in a single sentence: *The genius of the pentecostal movement lay in its ability to hold two seemingly incompatible impulses in productive tension.* I call the two impulses the primitive and the pragmatic. The nuances of each will become apparent in due course, but for now we might simply think of them as idealism versus realism, or principle versus practicality. Sociologist James Mathisen once remarked that the main challenge most religious movements face is figuring out how to capture lightning in a bottle.[39] Pentecostals' distinctive understanding of the human encounter with the divine, which included both primitivist and pragmatic dimensions, enabled them to capture lightning in a bottle and, more important, to keep it there, decade after decade, without stilling the fire or cracking the vessel.

Because supporting this thesis constitutes the interpretive burden of the following chapters, it may be helpful briefly to explain how it arose in the course of my research, and why it seems a useful framework for understanding the movement's remarkable tensile strength.

Primitivist and Pragmatic Impulses

Stepping back in time, quietly slipping into early pentecostals' kitchens and parlors, I heard, first of all, a great deal of talk about Holy Ghost baptism. I heard how God's Spirit entered their bodies, took control of their tongues, and gave advice on life's most mundane decisions. I also heard about the Bible, its power, its beauty, and the way it served as the final authority on all questions of daily living as well as human salvation. And I heard about signs and wonders—drunkards delivered, eyes restored, unlettered folk speaking foreign languages they had never studied. The more I listened to those discussions, however, the more I realized that most of them were really about something else. And that something else, of course, was God. Occasionally the longing to touch God bordered on mysticism, a craving to be absorbed into the One or even to obliterate one's own identity into the identity of the All. But typically it suggested a yearning simply to know the divine mind and will as directly and as purely as possible, without the distorting refractions of human volition, traditions, or speculations.

An incident in the life of Church of God general overseer A. J. Tomlinson shows how forcefully the desire for immediate contact with God could shape pentecostals' outlook. The event took place in the winter of 1913. Striding forward to address his Tennessee mountain faithful, Tomlinson announced that on this particular occasion he would read his remarks out loud, word for word. The hearers must have been stunned. Pentecostal preachers never read their sermons out loud as seminary-trained ministers did—indeed they prided themselves on their ability to speak extemporaneously so that the Holy Spirit could rule their tongues. But this day would be different. Tomlinson dared not leave anything out. "This that I am about to produce," he began, "was principly prepared at the midnight hour when alone with God that it might not be a second-handed production but purely first-handed."[40] That single sentence captured the movement's deepest aspiration. The words that the mountain preacher proposed to speak that day would not be "second-handed," not derivative, not passed through the distortions of human imagination or traditions. Rather they would come directly from God Himself, "purely first-handed."

The yearning to know God directly sometimes bore a dark side. Outsiders often said that pentecostals seemed more bent on destroying other people's traditions than proclaiming their own. And they were partly right. Converts frequently supposed that they had to destroy before they could build. Again Tomlinson spoke for many when he declared, on the front page of his fortnightly *Evening Light and Church of God Evangel:* "Creeds, articles of faith, systems, false churches are even now quivering, almost ready to fall."[41] Or so he hoped. In Tomlinson's mind the interpretations of Scripture produced by denominational churches, no less than the ones produced by godless secularists, all suffered from the same fatal flaw. All represented humanly fabricated—and therefore error-riddled—structures that had to be torn down so that true churches of God could be erected in their place.

In this book I describe this longing for direct contact with the divine in a number of ways. Sometimes I dub it otherworldliness, sometimes heavenly mindedness. Most often, however, I call it *primitivism,* for that term seems most precisely to register the impulse's exact texture. Primitivism suggests, in accord with its Latin root *primus,* a determination to return to first things, original things, fundamental things. It denotes believers' yearning to be guided solely by God's Spirit in every aspect of their lives, however great or small. With this term I hope to connote not so much an upward reach for transcendence as a downward or even backward quest for the infinitely pure and powerful fount of being itself.

If my explorations into the materials of early pentecostalism had ended there, with the manifestations of the primitivist impulse, this book would have been shorter (and finished sooner). But the research took an unexpected turn, as it often does. Almost immediately I began to hear—off in the distance—other words, other sounds, not anticipated. I heard about mundane realities like budgets and schedules and financial accountability. I heard about adjusting doctrine to the needs of the moment, the value of a carefully trained leadership, the importance of working hard and getting ahead. I heard respected leaders calling for good common sense in the conduct of the revival. I even heard heated arguments about power of the human kind, who had it and who did not (or should not). Before long it became clear that pentecostals, though primitivists, were never purely so. For all of their declarations about living solely in the realm of the supernatural, with the Holy Spirit guiding every step of their lives, they nonetheless displayed a remarkably clear-eyed vision of the way things worked here on earth.

Martha Wing Robinson's diary illustrates the astuteness of pentecostals' practical instincts. In 1910 Robinson, Elder Eugene Brooks, and their spouses founded the zealously pentecostal Zion Faith Home in Zion City, Illinois. We first need to note that no Holy Ghost leader exemplified the *primitivist* impulse more forcefully than Robinson. Her diary entries show her constantly—outsiders would have said obsessively—seeking to lose her consciousness in the Holy Spirit's.[42] Nonetheless, however wonderful those experiences may have been, they never seemed too wonderful to keep Robinson from tending to business. And there lay the key. As we read ahead in the diary, we find a woman prone to labor forty-eight hours at a stretch without food or sleep because of the press of business.[43] We also encounter a woman admonishing her guests never to "wake up and doze" but to get busy at once. If they ran out of useful things to do, they could always go back to their rooms and study the Bible. Then the knockout punch: "The Lord abomi-nates that pokey time that does nothing, a sort of easy-goingness."[44] Robin-son's determination to mind the store, even as she minded her soul, would have made any banker proud.

I must admit that for many months I resisted the plain import of this sec-ond body of evidence, large and clamorous though it was. For one thing, it contradicted what pentecostals said about themselves in their almost-nightly testimony meetings. Everyone knew—did they not?—that Christ alone guided their actions, whatever the personal or social cost. It also contradicted what they claimed about themselves in their polemical literature. Other Christians behaved pragmatically, according to a calculus of self-interest, not Holy Ghost folk. Though pentecostals freely acknowledged the rewards of the Holy Spirit-filled life in the here and now, they insisted that all mundane benefits came directly from the Lord. Saints themselves arranged nothing.

The tenacity and stridency of pentecostals' insistence that they never acted in their own interests or, if they did, that they did so only in temporary and inconsequential ways, was the tip-off that their story was not as simple as they wanted outsiders to believe. The more I probed the more I realized that if there was an official set of minutes to be read on public occasions, there was also an unofficial set to be read on private occasions. These nested in the mar-gins of their course notes, in the pages of their diaries, in the debates over-heard by neighbors. Sometimes the unofficial minutes developed over time, as when pentecostals gradually abandoned their principled pacifism during World War I. More often, however, they existed from the beginning—a si-lent, forceful reminder that social survival exacted its price. Older Christian bodies had resolved the grace-versus-nature problem through a fulsome doc-trine of incarnation, or a mystic appreciation of the sacraments, or a rich sense of divine immanence in all of history. But pentecostals, who were determined to eliminate the natural side of every equation, had no choice but to camou-flage the countless tiny compromises that made life possible.

This book describes this second body of evidence with various terms. Sometimes I use words like "realism" or "practicality," especially when pen-tecostals' willingness to accommodate themselves to the limits of everyday life seems foremost. Other times I use words like "sagacity" or "shrewdness," especially when their eagerness to make do and get ahead appears paramount. But the one term that seems best to capture all of these meanings, and thus the one I use most often, is *pragmatism*. This word suggests that at the end of the day pentecostals proved remarkably willing to work within the social and cultural expectations of the age. Again and again we see them holding their proverbial finger to the wind, calculating where they were, where they wanted to go and, above all, how to get there. That last instinct, the ability to figure the odds and react appropriately, made them pragmatists to the bone.

There it was, then, in pairs: the primitive and the pragmatic. If Tomlinson's determination to know God "first-handed" captured the former, Robinson's determination to avoid that "pokey time" captured the latter. Various metaphors come to mind. We might think of the two impulses as alternating voices in a dialogue, or as contrasting threads in a tapestry, or as complementary plots in a story. The Old Testament's portrait of the alien and the resident, or the New Testament's image of the pilgrim and the citizen, offer additional possibilities. We might even picture the two impulses as official and unofficial versions of the same meeting. The list of possible metaphors does not end here, but by now the point should be clear. No effort to describe the world of early pentecostalism can be complete without accounting for both impulses and the way they worked together to secure the movement's survival.

It is now possible to refine this book's argument a bit. Throughout the period of our concern (and in many ways to the present) the primitive and the pragmatic impulses balanced each other. In some spheres the former predominated, in others the latter predominated, but overall they compensated one another as needed. Viewed from one angle it is clear that the two impulses stood in tension, partly because the logic of the primitive excluded the pragmatic, and partly because pentecostals almost always denied that the pragmatic existed at all. Yet viewed from another angle it is equally clear that the two impulses creatively complemented each other. Pentecostals' primitivist conviction that the Holy Spirit did everything, and that they themselves did nothing, bore grandly pragmatic results. It freed them from self-doubt, legitimated reasonable accommodations to modern culture, and released boundless energy for feats of worldly enterprise. At the same time, this vigorous engagement with everyday life stabilized the primitive and kept it from consuming itself in a fury of charismatic fire.

A peek ahead may be helpful. The following chapters offer interlocking essays on different aspects of pentecostal life. First and foremost these chapters seek to serve as travel reports, field notes describing the revival's cultural landscape. But they might also be read as a modest defense of the thesis stated above. In each, the focus moves from practices that served mainly primitivist aims to practices that served mainly pragmatic ones. The key term here is "mainly." In the "hum and buzz" of daily life any given practice (such as speaking in tongues) undoubtedly served multiple purposes. I am simply suggesting that on balance some practices mainly helped the community relate to the divine, while others mainly helped it navigate the hard complexities of modern life.

Qualifications

Two brief but important qualifications are now needed. The first is almost but perhaps not quite too obvious to require comment. In short, the contrast between the primitive and the pragmatic was not by any means unique to early pentecostals. Saint Luke's story of the sisters Mary and Martha—Mary sitting at the Lord's feet listening to his teaching, Martha dutifully worried about the meal—suggested that the difference was as ancient and as universal as Christianity itself. One might actually say that the two sisters defined and legitimated distinct approaches to the Christian life that had persisted in varying combinations for two millennia—and nowhere more clearly than in late-nineteenth-century America. So it was that the Oneida Perfectionists, fired by a potent mix of arcane Scripture readings and charismatic authority, implemented systematic work habits and commercial imagination that led to the redoubtable Oneida, Ltd., silver plate company. Later, premillennialist missionaries circled the globe heralding the fiery climax of history—fully armed, of course, with the most up-to-date means of transportation, publication, recruitment, and fund-raising available. A strange compound of "profound mysticism" and "fiercely practical common sense" was the way that novelist Pearl Buck described her China missionary mother.[45] Or to take an example closer to home, the early-twentieth-century divine healing community of Zion City, Illinois, banned physicians and manufactured medicines on scriptural grounds, yet welcomed state-of-the-art factories and farsighted city planning. The point is simple: virtually every definable group in the history of Christianity, or at least every group that enjoyed significant longevity and numerical success, found ways to weave heavenly aspirations with everyday realities.

Nonetheless, every group wove that tapestry in its own distinctive way, and so did early pentecostals. Saints drew threads from the historic Christian tradition and from the environing culture but fashioned them into a pattern that struck many contemporaries as refreshingly—or alarmingly—new. On one hand pentecostals' conviction that God's Spirit literally took up residence inside their physical bodies authorized tongues, healings, visions, resurrections, and other miraculous phenomena that had largely disappeared from American Protestant culture, especially mainline groups. On the other hand that same conviction also authorized a kind of swashbuckling entrepreneurialism that left many observers amazed when they were not appalled.[46] In the moral universe of early pentecostalism, then, it was never entirely clear whether heaven had invaded earth or earth had invaded heaven. And the results proved predictable. The very word *pentecostal* soon came to connote a recognizable style or way of doing things as much as anything else.

For partisans, the label suggested commitment. For friends, ardor. For foes, excess: excessive zeal, excessive shrewdness, excessive everything. One of Aimee Semple McPherson's contemporary critics may have said more than he realized when he quipped that the flamboyant evangelist embodied the "pulchritudinous pinnacle of pseudo-Pentecostalism."[47] One suspects that the most pertinent term in that slam was neither pulchritudinous nor pentecostalism, but pinnacle.

The other major qualification is that the scope of this book is limited by four strategic decisions. The first is to treat the founding generation, roughly 1900–25, more or less as a single moment in time. Obviously changes took place every hour of every day, and I seek to honor those changes when they mattered. But in that first intense burst of fervor the continuities proved more important than the changes. Broad patterns of social and cultural evolution—always dear to historians' hearts—are hard to document until the third and fourth generations. Even then, as I argue in the Epilogue, the underlying impulses—the fundamental cultural arrangements—remained remarkably persistent and helped account for the movement's growth in the Third World. The second decision is to focus on the United States, which I know best by training and availability of primary materials. Canadian and British sources occasionally turn up, as well as reports from missionaries and converts in other parts of the world. But I do not claim that the present study necessarily illumines the pentecostal experience in other settings (though I suspect that it does, since Holy Ghost religion, like most sectarian ideologies, readily transcended political boundaries). The third decision is to view early pentecostalism in the United States as a cultural whole. I pay little attention to regional, ethnic, and gender differences, and almost none at all to the doctrinal distinctives of the three main theological subgroups (Wesleyan trinitarians, Reformed trinitarians, and Oneness believers). In some contexts all of those differences counted—sometimes a great deal—but not for my analysis. The fourth decision is to define the relevant sources broadly rather than narrowly. That means that I draw on several small, nearly pentecostal bodies when they helpfully illustrate the point at hand.[48]

It remains finally to say a word about terminology. Though not free of complications, I use the terms *ethnic* and *racial* in a historical sense to refer to the differing social experiences of culturally Anglo and non-Anglo pentecostals and of white and black pentecostals. Partisans always used the masculine pronoun capitalized to refer to persons of the Trinity, including the Holy Spirit. I follow their practice. But if labels for the deity were fixed, labels for the Lord's humble followers were not. The word *pentecostal* did not come into common usage until the 1910s, and did not win the day until the 1920s. The souls who eventually called themselves pentecostals initially went by a variety of terms, most often saints, apostolics, or just workers. From time to time they also identified themselves with adjectives such as full gospel, full salvation, latter rain, Holy Ghost, Holy Spirit, or Spirit-filled. I use all of these terms interchangeably, just as they did—with one exception. They also called themselves holiness people. I avoid that term since in the late 1910s holiness came to denote its theological "opposite": antipentecostals in the Wesleyan wing of the radical evangelical tradition.

Significance

The question of significance must finally be addressed. Why should anyone want to know about the culture of early pentecostals? In short, so what?

The movement's stunning numerical size at the end of the twentieth century might offer justification enough for this inquiry, but two additional reasons also present themselves. One is intrinsic interest. The conceptual world of first-generation pentecostals was as exquisitely complex as the conceptual world of a Ralph Waldo Emerson or of an Emily Dickinson. Both the premises and the conclusions of saints' thinking were, to put it mildly, different from such elites, but the intricacy of the consciousness that created them was not. Second, the story of the early pentecostals casts grave doubt on the glib use of secularization theory. The revival changed in countless ways, but long-term, evolutionary progression from otherworldly saintliness to thisworldly secularity was not one of them. Believers juggled those forces from the outset, hour by hour, day by day. Charting their behavior may help us understand the successes and failures of religious eruptions in other times and places.[49]

To say that early pentecostals merit our attention is not to say that the task is always pleasant. Even by their own standards they often proved petty and mean-spirited. In a way, though, that is precisely the point. As classicist Peter Brown once put it, to the honest historian the dead "appear exactly as they were—every bit as odd as we are, as problematical, as difficult of access. To explore such people with sympathy, with trained insight, and with a large measure of common cunning, is to learn again to appreciate . . . [that] 'Man is a vast deep.'"[50] In these pages I do not aim to spare pentecostals from criticism when they deserve it, nor exempt them from praise when they deserve that too, but simply to follow the golden rule: to write about them as fairly as I hope they would have written about me.

1

Temperament

Perry Miller charted the path. In 1939 the Harvard historian opened his landmark study of the seventeenth-century New England mind by saying that he would begin, not with Puritans' theological ideas, but with something deeper, something more fundamental. He would start, he said, with the Puritan mood. He called it the "Augustinian strain of piety"—an outlook so deeply ingrained that the subjects scarcely knew it existed. The Puritan mood functioned like a pair of tinted spectacles, coloring and shaping Puritans' view of social reality before they rationalized it in a formal, speculative theology.[1]

We might say much the same about early pentecostals' outlook—though the word *temperament* seems more apt than *mood*. Pentecostals too saw the world in a manner so habitual, so deeply ingrained, that they scarcely knew it existed. Our journey into the realm of Holy Ghost religion properly begins, then, not with theology, nor even with ritual, but in that almost inaccessible zone of impulse and attitude that preceded self-conscious rationalization. One quickly discovers, however, that the pentecostal temperament was a rather messy thing (it was a rather messy thing for Puritans too). If believers sometimes seemed lost in clouds of timeless truths and heavenly delights, other times they appeared remarkably clear-eyed about how to make do and get ahead in modern America. This chapter recovers a small slice of that complexity.

But first a caveat is needed. The following pages do not claim to disclose a pentecostal personality type (or types). The revival claimed a cross section of the population, which meant that it undoubtedly had its fair share of free spirits on one side and melancholics on the other and everything in between. But that is not our concern. Nor do these pages plunge into the murky waters of intentionality, let alone subliminality. Our sole topic rather is the way that pentecostal culture publicly encouraged certain recurring attitudes toward the other world, and this one, and the creative complementarity between them.

Piety

If outsiders knew nothing else about early pentecostals, they knew that saints sought to live their days and especially their nights in a heavenly city glittering with the signs and wonders of the New Testament church. In that holy space the timeless truths and universal values of Scripture would reign uncontested. And to a remarkable extent they succeeded too. When believers entered the realm of daily affairs, they considered themselves aliens at best, pilgrims passing through foreign territory. G. K. Chesterton once said that Christians could be defined as persons who felt "homesick at home." Whether he spoke for the mass of modern Christians may be debated, but clearly he spoke for pentecostals.[2]

Examples of this relentless heaven-mindedness surfaced everywhere. One Chicago partisan put it as plainly as the English language permitted: "Those who speak in tongues seem to live in another world."[3] Living in another world took many forms. For some, it engendered something like a sixth sense, a fundamentally new way of seeing even the natural landscape around them. "It seemed as if human joys vanished," one Florida advocate wrote. "It seemed as if the whole world and the people looked a different color."[4] A Wesleyan Methodist pastor in Toronto spoke of a surge of feelings she had never known, describing it as "overwhelming power," "absence of fleshly effort," a sensation of walking "softly with God."[5] Some devotees entered a sacred zone where time itself seemed calibrated by divine rather than human standards. Looking back to the first blush of the revival from the vantage point of the 1920s, evangelist Frank Bartleman judged that he would "*rather live six months at that time than fifty years of ordinary time.*"[6] Partisans commonly spoke of spending hour after hour, sometimes entire days, in prayer and singing without thought of food[7] or awareness that night had fallen or that daylight had dawned.[8] In their nightly prayer meetings, one Webb City, Missouri, devotee wrote, "it seemed impossible to distinguish between the earthly and the heavenly anthems . . . [Some] could scarcely endure the 'weight of glory' that rested upon them."[9] Another recalled that when he underwent the baptism experience, "the fire fell and burned up all that would burn and what would not burn was caught up into heaven . . . My spirit long[ed] to be free from a sin-cursed world and be at home with Jesus."[10] One pentecostal historian touched an essential chord when he wrote that many onlookers believed that saints were "either insane over religion, or drunk on some glorious dream."[11] All told, it was a breathtaking vision of history, where the old experiences were swept away and new ones erected in their place.

If the other world of timeless truths and universal values served as an all-consuming center of concern, it is hardly surprising that pentecostals betrayed little interest in earthly affairs such as presidential elections or local political controversies. Their response to the world war raging in Europe was instructive. Though I later probe this question more deeply, here it suffices to say that most professed no opinion at all until the iron hand of the Selective Service finally left them no choice. Even then many tried not to think about it at all. In the midst of the conflict one prominent editor promised that his periodical would never "take part in the heated discussions about the war."[12] Others made plain that non-Christian soldiers risked more than physical danger. "War is a feeder of hell," stormed the *Church of God Evangel*. "This last awful struggle has been the cause of millions of mother[s'] boys dropping into the region of the damned where they are entering their eternal tortures."[13] The current world war mainly reminded evangelist Aimee McPherson that biblical prophecies about the "Signs of the Times" were coming true with "astounding" exactness.[14]

Holy Spirit–filled believers not only lost interest in politics but also proved oblivious to many of the day-to-day recreations that most people considered simple and legitimate pleasures of life. I am not speaking here of a pipe by the fireplace on a winter's night or a frosty beer on a summer afternoon. Enjoyments of that sort, which all radical evangelicals shunned, remained inconceivable. The point rather is that even commonly sanctioned satisfactions such as dropping a fishing line or watching a parade faded in the glow of the heavenly light. Consider, for example, the diary of Pentecostal Holiness Church leader George Floyd Taylor. Besides a daily weather report, the document speaks almost entirely of sermons preached, Bible passages pondered, church classes taught, and prayer meetings attended. The entry for August 27, 1908, taken virtually at random, proclaims, "My soul is a sea of glass . . . Glory! Glory! . . . My soul secretly cries out for God to hide me away in His presence."[15] One would never suspect that this husband and father of four—a man perennially troubled by a serious physical handicap—had ever paused to appreciate the world pulsating around him. And then there was Walter Higgins, who received a directive from the Lord to launch a revival in Poplar Bluff, Missouri. "We were out of groceries in the house and I hated to leave my wife alone in that condition," the young evangelist lamented. Nonetheless he went.[16]

Predictably, otherworldly impulses emerged with special force in times of death and mourning. When the end approached for Church of God founder Richard G. Spurling, Jr., he asked not to be buried facing east, as his Tennessee mountain people normally were. Rather Spurling wanted to be buried facing west, toward his homeplace. With that gesture he wished to signal that he had spent too much time caring for his family and not enough doing the only thing that really mattered, preaching the gospel.[17] Eulogies spoke volumes. Dead at twenty-four, China missionary Cora Fritsch's obituary made clear what her colleagues considered the defining moments of her life:

Born	Oct 23, 1888
Born of the Spirit	July 1905
Baptized in the Spirit	March 1907
Ordained as Missionary	Sept 1907
Married	Feb 1, 1912
Went to be with Jesus	Dec 7, 1912

Fritsch undoubtedly knew other joys, other landmarks of the spirit, but of them the record remains mute.[18]

Enthusiasts subordinated even courtship and romance to a calculus of otherworldly rewards. Neither the wedding nor the wedding night could be accepted as events memorable for themselves. The notice of an Inglewood, California, ceremony reported, for example, that a time of "rejoicing and praise before God" preceded the wedding. Happily, many souls were saved as well.[19] A newspaper published by a pentecostal band in San Francisco observed that when two of its members married, the ritual concluded with an "exhortation for sinners to seek the Lord."[20] The same intentional pattern turned up in Britain. In the Welsh hamlet of Llandilo, one paper reported, the celebrants partitioned the wedding home into a food room and a prayer room. Likely to everyone's delight, a "brother received the baptism of the Holy Ghost" in the prayer room, while the others presumably received mundane nourishment in the food room.[21] Back in Arkansas evangelist Howard Goss primly recorded that his bride Ethel spent their wedding night preaching a requested sermon at a local church—with telling effect, one assumes.[22] A brother from Canada asked the readers of the *Christian Evangel* to pray that God would give him the young woman of his choice—"a baptized saint"—for a wife. Why? For romance? For family? Perish the thought! If they married, he solemnly explained, they could start a rest home for missionaries.[23]

If pentecostals discountenanced the routine pleasures of life, they were equally prepared to forgo the bonds that tethered them to earth. That outlook helps explain why one could dismiss digging a storm cellar as a "habit . . . of the flesh."[24] It also helps explain why another, who worried about the eternal fate of her loved ones, could become anxious about it. If a mother were *truly* heaven-bound, it seemed, she would not be compromised by any earthly interest, even a concern for the souls of her offspring.[25] Night after night enthusiasts lustily sang, "Take the world, but give me Jesus." But there really was not much to take. Most were already living on that distant shore.

Certitude

Piety fostered certitude. Indeed for early pentecostals the two traits seemed directly correlated: the more intense the former, the more intense the latter. Converts commonly acknowledged that the baptism experience had dispelled all doubts about the reality of the supernatural and the truth of their distinctive theological claims. Lewi Petrus, founder and for many years pastor of the largest pentecostal church in Sweden, illustrates the pattern. Before he received the Holy Spirit, Petrus wrote, he found himself constantly tormented by an "enormous army of doubts." But no longer. "Without exaggerating I can say that I have found it just as *impossible to doubt,* as at times I formerly found it *impossible to believe,* the truths of the Bible."[26] The "Trinity-filled" Christian, wrote one editor, was not troubled with a "ghost of doubt, or paralyzing agnosticism."[27] Evangelist Aimee McPherson similarly remembered that Holy Spirit baptism had freed her of incipient atheism in her adolescence.[28] One suspects that outright atheism was never much of a threat for the young Aimee, given her Salvation Army upbringing, but self-perceptions counted.

For pentecostals the essence of certitude was not narrowness but irreversibility. Once committed to an item of belief, there was no turning back. Even to discuss received doctrine with the idea of rethinking it was, according to E. N. Bell, the movement's best educated leader, "to waste time thrashing over the old straw."[29] When William H. Durham, a widely respected firebrand, died prematurely in 1912, the strongest tribute his friend and fellow leader Bell could pay him was to say that he had been "no compromiser."[30] The secular culture might consider a willingness to mull over the options and weigh various points of view a mark of virtue. Not pentecostals.

If certitude precluded critical analysis of one's cherished convictions, it also precluded objective disconfirmation by external events. Saints had an answer for everything. If something bad happened to a gainsayer, they trumpeted the doubter's misfortune as a sign of God's retribution. If one of their own suffered the identical fate, they saw it as a test.[31] Believers' interpretation of the 1906 San Francisco earthquake proved typical. What could the rumbling possibly mean except imminent judgment on a wretched civilization? When someone pointed out that worse disasters had taken place in other parts of the world, pentecostals mounted a quick and easy retort: the Bible had *predicted* that skeptics would come along in the Last Days saying things like that.[32] Or again, news that three missionaries had been killed by "dangerous beasts" in Africa prompted the happy rejoinder that *only* three had died. "How wonderfully this shows God's protecting care!" exulted the *New Acts.*[33] The leader of Los Angeles' Upper Room Mission summed up pentecostals' determination never to let their schemes be affected by adverse events: "We praise Go[d] . . . for the blessings that have come to us in the disguise of . . . trials."[34] If outsiders came away scratching their heads, insiders remained unfazed, for they knew the assurance of certitude.

In the 1950s, Church of God historian Charles W. Conn observed that in an age filled with "discordant and capricious theological sounds," the Holy Ghost movement provided a "retreat from the turbulence of doubt and denial."[35] Conn, a veteran of the tradition, rightly sensed that the movement had been steeled by a profound sense of certitude in matters of mind as well as heart.

Absolutism

If piety fostered certitude, certitude fostered absolutism—a propensity to see life in moral extremes. Differently stated, pentecostals' world often lacked ambiguities or shadings of gray. Disagreements that most folk, even most evangelical folk, interpreted as honest differences of opinion, pentecostals saw as vast differences of judgment, shadowed with eternal consequences. To some extent absolutism stemmed from apocalypticism. After all, one who constantly looked for the Lord's return in the clouds of glory could hardly afford to be lax about things that really mattered.[36] But the absolutist outlook cropped up too automatically and in too many contexts to be attributed to apocalypticism alone. The trait ran deeper, suggesting that it served more as the wellspring than as the consequence of their principles.

Zealots never tired of rehearsing tales of individuals who had spoken ill of the movement—and suffered torment or even death as a consequence. In Ohio one young person attended a Holy Ghost meeting, mimicked tongues speech in mockery, and suddenly was stricken dumb by the power of God.[37] In Shawnee Town, Illinois, a woman made the fatal mistake of ridiculing Walter Higgins as he tried to preach his first Holy Ghost sermon. Several days afterward she was killed on the highway.[38] In California the president of a "denominational college" hindered the boys in his charge from hearing God's truth about the pentecostal blessing. Though he was in vigorous health at the time, he died shortly afterward, eaten up, doctors said, by worms.[39]

Unfortunately retribution for impeding the progress of the pentecostal revival was not limited to this life. Those who said that tongues constituted a work of the devil (as some radical evangelicals did) committed the Unpardonable Sin. Opposition equaled blasphemy, pure and simple. Founder Charles Parham put the matter plainly: "Anyone attributing the work of the Holy Spirit . . . to the Devil, commits the unpardonable sin and will not be forgiven in this or the next world."[40] The rank and file proved equally quick to equate opposition with blasphemy. One nameless sister from the Azusa Mission dropped by another church where the "evangelist denounced the works of grace." That very evening she had a vision in which she witnessed the hapless congregation's eternal fate: an "open hell just back of the pulpit, with the awful, lurid flames coming up, and people sitting around the altar with their feet hanging over into the open hell, unconscious of their condition."[41] One did not need openly to deny the truth of pentecostals' favorite beliefs to trigger their judgment. A simple failure to accept their point of view provoked rejoinders carrying ultimate sanctions. Invariably such persons came to some terrible fate—run over by a street car, mutilated in an industrial accident—and usually sooner rather than later.[42] Spiritual slackers who failed to seek Holy Ghost baptism learned that they would miss the soon-coming Rapture of the saints.[43]

A conflict that erupted in Pasadena, California, in the summer of 1906 shows how easily questions of common courtesy could swell into confrontations of ultimate value. The antagonists were a newly pentecostalized sect called the Household of God versus the proverbial neighbors next door. It all started when the Household's leader, a one-time Baptist preacher named A. H. Post, received Holy Spirit baptism and decided to hold forth in a tent on a vacant lot in a residential section. The services ran every day from 10 A.M. until the wee hours of the morning. One Mrs. West, owner of the Globe Boarding House adjacent to the lot, filed a complaint with the city council asking the worshipers to move because they were disturbing her guests. Post refused, stating that he would not comply unless God Himself authorized it. The city council suggested that the Household at least move to the back of the property. Post refused. A benefactor offered to pay all expenses if the sect would transfer to another part of town. Post turned him down too.[44] Losing patience, the city council finally hauled Brother Post into court. He declined both a jury trial and the aid of sympathetic witnesses, stating only, "God is my defense." Post acknowledged that he was undoubtedly disturbing the neighbors, yet insisted that the source of the noise was not really himself but the "spirit of God" inside him. When asked one more time by the judge if he would move the tent so that the neighbors could get some sleep, Post responded predictably: "I get my orders from Heaven . . . This is not the contest of man versus man, but the battle of God versus the devil."[45] The judge gave Post a suspended sentence and the police forcibly removed the tent.[46]

Pentecostals' propensity to frame decisions in absolute terms defined relationships within the community as well. When disagreements arose, comrades on the inside found themselves subjected to ultimate sanctions just as quickly as gainsayers on the outside. In the winter of 1900, for example, several residents at Frank Sandford's quasi-pentecostal Shiloh community in Durham, Maine, questioned his autocratic rule. The prophet countered by pointing out that the Almighty had chosen "the leaders whom He chooses to lead His hosts." Critics were not simply misguided but evil. They would be "set aside and sent reeling down to hell."[47] After smallpox had taken several lives at the compound three years later, Sandford made clear that remorse was out of place. "We have not the slightest doubt that each one of these people were cut down directly or indirectly by the judgment hand of God"—then added, lest anyone needed it, that such judgment was just "a little foretaste of what is [coming to] the entire world."[48]

A potpourri of instances, drawn almost at random from a variety of life situations, shows how absolutism functioned at the level of everyday life. In the entire town of Falcon, North Carolina, an advertisement for the Falcon Holiness School boasted, one could not buy tobacco, or "dope drinks" (presumably Coca Cola), or find "Theaters, Circuses, Moving Picture Shows, Base Ball Games, Social Parties and Dances"—all "agencies of evil" hurling young people to their "eternal destruction."[49] The *Church of God Evangel* similarly warned that "[t]obacco users, whiskey drinkers, dope gulpers, labor unioners, socialists, lodgers, adulterers, fornicators, politicians . . . murderers, and all liars" were equally exposed to the "awful wrath" to come.[50] *From Ballroom to Brothel*, a popular pentecostal tract, made clear that all exits from the ballroom led straight to the Lake of Fire.[51] That it might be possible to dance with one's spouse in a ballroom and not automatically end up in a brothel eluded the pentecostal mind. When someone smirked at evangelist Elizabeth Sisson for dancing up and down the aisles "under the power," she retorted, in classic Holy Ghost fashion, "It's amusing to you now, but it won't be so funny when you drop into hell."[52] Or when Sarah Parham said that holding a deck of playing cards was the same as holding a rattlesnake, there is every reason to believe that she meant exactly what she said.[53]

Converts readily interpreted outsiders' accounts of their revival as hostile at best, blasphemous at worst. At the Azusa mission one partisan told fellow worshipers about a vision the Lord had given him. In that vision a non-pentecostal woman, a Wesleyan holiness "professor," stumbled over a precipice into the yawning jaws of hell below. As she fell into the flames, a "shout went up from the demons, with . . . roars of laughter."[54] And why not? If the stakes were ultimate, surely the sanctions should be ultimate too. In a binary world constituted by up or down choices, considerations of context or gradations of value simply did not enter the picture.

Prevailing Prayer

Absolutism, finally, fostered prevailing prayer. By this I mean the conviction that prayer could bend nature to one's interests. It is important to be precise here. Adherents did not endorse magic. They did not think that prevailing prayer by itself influenced nature, as if by telekinesis. All would have said that they influenced nature only through God's power. But in practice the line between saints' entreaties and divine assistance blurred. Primitivists to the core, saints instinctively held that prevailing prayer, rightly executed, worked exactly like gravity or sunlight.

Prevailing prayer manifested itself in many contexts, ranging from the trivial (making a lost pen appear)[55] to the amazing (driving mosquitoes from a prayer meeting)[56] to the momentous (forcing the weather to change).[57] But the clearest and most persistent manifestation lay in pentecostals' abiding conviction that prevailing prayer—sometimes called the prayer of faith— would automatically bring healing to the body. Holy Ghost people inherited from their radical evangelical parents an elaborate theology of healing, based on the covenantal promises in Exodus 15:26, the Great Commission in Mark 16:17–18, the gifts of healing in 1 Corinthians 12:9, the healing ministry of the church's elders in James 5:14, and, above all, the promise of healing in Christ's atonement on the cross. The last stemmed from the radical evangelical reading of Isaiah 53:5: "He was wounded for our transgressions . . . and with his stripes we are healed." But where most Christians and a majority of radical evangelicals had considered prayer for healing a petition for God's favor, pentecostals effectively considered it a causal agent in itself. God had promised to respond positively to all genuine prayers, therefore He would.[58]

In plain truth pentecostal writers turned healing grace into a healing contract. "Getting things from God is like playing checkers," said F. F. Bosworth, the most respected healing evangelist of the 1910s and 1920s. "Our move is to expect what he promises . . . before we *see* the healing . . . He always moves when it is His turn."[59] E. W. Kenyon, a quasi pentecostal with possible early connections to New Thought, produced numerous works that both influenced and represented the infant movement.[60] According to Kenyon, genuine faith did not even acknowledge the existence of disease. To do so was to "sign for the package" Satan had left. Indeed, said Kenyon, "it is not good taste to ask [God] to heal us, for he has already done it. He declared that we are healed; therefore we are."[61] In a popular tract of 1920, healing evangelist Maria Woodworth-Etter would make the same point without flinching: "In reality we are healed when we believe . . . We must cling to the promises of Jesus instead of looking at our feelings . . . for our senses are false witnesses."[62] Oakland's Carrie Judd Montgomery, one of the most prolific and articulate figures in the movement's early history, articulated the case with memorable clarity: "I have never failed to receive according to my faith."[63]

Emotional health no less than physical health fell under the same stricture. Optimism was not optional. One leader simply and typically commanded his readers to take hold of themselves and think straight: "[The Christian] is never to be sorrowful for a moment, but to be ALWAYS REJOICING."[64] In the pentecostal temperament, the genuineness of one's faith equaled one's ability to get up and subdue the afflicting disease. Nothing less would do.

In these matters leaders spoke for, not to, the masses. In upstate New York, for example, Edith Shaw explained that she had prayed for healing from diphtheria, but a "raging fever" and continued suffering tempted her to doubt that her healing had actually taken place. Then the Lord spoke: "These are not symptoms of diphtheria, for I healed you of that last night . . . I healed you when you prayed . . . I want you to act just as you would if you felt perfectly well, *because* you *are* well." Shaw captured the essence of prevailing prayer in a single, revealing sentence: "I saw that God's Word was true and the symptoms were the devil's lie."[65] One now-nameless grandmother, who had worn eyeglasses for twenty years, tossed them out when she decided to pray for restoration of her eyesight. From that point on she forced herself to read ten chapters of her Bible each day without glasses because God had promised that he would answer the prayer of faith. "Why, salt water is good for the eyes," she wrote, tears tumbling down onto the page.[66]

Given the premise that God always responded to prevailing prayer, the persistence of illness could be explained only two ways: either one's life was impure or one's faith was shallow. Either way, sufferers caused their own infirmities. The propensity to blame the victim had been implicit in the work of A. B. Simpson and other radical evangelical writers of the late nineteenth century, but early pentecostals made it painfully explicit: "[W]hose fault is it if you stay sick?" demanded Lilian Yeomans, a former physician and prominent convert. "Not the fault of the Lord . . . [I]f we are not healed we must look for the cause of it in ourselves."[67] Since God had promised to mend the body if one prayed with genuine faith, the only possible result was immediate and complete restoration of the body.

How did the ideology work out in actual practice? The evidence predictably suggests a variety of responses. Some failed. Though editors proved reluctant to say much about failures in print, the early periodicals hinted that many believers who were unable to drop their crutches at the altar either drifted away or fell into a permanent underclass of spiritually second-rate citizens.[68] Some trimmed. Testimonies typically began by admitting that the author had first consulted a worldly doctor, but the latter had failed to cure the illness or injury (frequently adding, following biblical precedent, that the doctor had been baffled or even angered when patients returned to show off their healing.)[69] Some rationalized. They interpreted their plight as a mark of divine favor for allowing them to be tested.[70] Some fell into excessive zealotry, even by the movement's own standards. We know that a few died or allowed their children to die rather than resort to worldly means.[71] Indeed one of the persistent problems for the more responsible denominational officials involved grass-roots extremism, which they defined as refusal to cooperate with nature by washing a wound, wearing eyeglasses, or seeing a dentist.[72] And some—thousands, if the testimony literature can be trusted—found relief, at least for a while.[73] However varied the responses, the basic aim of prevailing prayer held fast through the first generation, and reappeared with a vengeance in the late twentieth century, at least among a large minority of pentecostals, as the secret of financial health.[74] The formula worked every time if one just possessed the grit to put it into practice.

Early pentecostals held no franchise on any of these culturally reenforced traits—piety, certitude, absolutism, or prevailing prayer—but all of them marked Holy Ghost believers in conspicuous ways. They structured the first thought in the morning and the last one at night. Yet somewhere between sunrise and sunset, in the clamor and clatter of everyday life, another cluster of traits also forced its way to the surface. These traits were not entirely different from the former—they mingled in all sorts of ways—but on the whole they drew their sustenance from earthly affairs, where the oxygen was richer and the water more plentiful.

Independence

Contrary to the official portrait, an independent spirit flowed through pentecostals' veins. "With all handles knocked off I could be free in Christ," was the way that Joel Adams Wright, a New Hampshire realtor, explained his migration from the Free Baptists to the Free Methodists to the First Fruit Harvesters, a Holy Ghost sect of his own creation.[75] Timothy L. Smith once wrote that nineteenth-century holiness come-outers proved "unable to accept much real discipline save their own."[76] That characterization fit early pentecostals equally well, perhaps even better, for they were mavericks at heart, careless of tradition, willing to drop old allegiances at the first hint of strain.

For one thing, the independent spirit recoiled at the specter of regularization. "We must break loose from the yoke of bondage we have gotten into by tradition and custom," Overseer A. J. Tomlinson declared.[77] When the Assemblies of God broke apart in 1916 in a dispute about the Trinity, young David Lee Floyd rushed to raise the banner of the Oneness cause in a periodical symptomatically called the *Blessed Truth*. Predictably Floyd did not seek anyone's advice, let alone anyone's permission. "I didn't ask none of them to take no responsibility," was the way that he recalled those events years later.[78] The evangelist Frank Bartleman spoke for many others. "Don't marry a movement. Only the free man can hope to get God's perfect mind and will."[79] What Tomlinson, Floyd, and Bartleman articulated, each in his own raw-boned way, was a classically American sentiment, memorialized in the best of populist traditions.

In the early years probably the majority of pentecostal periodicals were actually launched, edited, and run as one-man or one-woman operations. Many of these editors continued to publish and jealously guard their subscription lists long after they had joined a pentecostal sect with its own official publication. At least a score of elementary and secondary academies and Bible institutes, also launched as more or less one-person operations, persisted long after the founder had joined a body with its own centrally sponsored institutions. Such independent operations irked denominational bureaucrats, but in their heart of hearts they knew that the movement had been born of a defiant temper. In later years patriarch Howard Goss, a denominational bureaucrat himself, acknowledged that the very "foundation for the vast Pentecostal Movement" had been laid by loners and free lancers, by missionaries without board support and pastors without degrees or salaries or—listen closely— "restful holidays."[80]

The fear of imposed conformity ironically prompted the formation of new groups designed to fight imposed conformity. Consider, for example, the Pentecostal Assemblies of the U.S.A, a tiny, fiercely independent sect that organized itself in Chicago in the winter of 1919. In one sense there was really no need to do so. The Assemblies of God had been well established in that area for a half-dozen years, and virtually no doctrinal or sociological differences separated them. But the new band found the old one too confining. The Chicago delegates insisted that the younger organization's purpose was "neither to legislate laws of government, nor to usurp authority over the various local Assemblies, [n]or to deprive them of their scripturally recognized local rights and privileges."[81] Nor would they countenance "laying down any creed as a basis of fellowship other than the Word of God entirely free from all human interpretation."[82]

This stormy independence formed part of a larger complex of assumptions emphasizing the autonomy of individual choice in all affairs of life, including the order of salvation. Conversion, sanctification, and Holy Spirit baptism started with the individual, skirted the institutional church, downplayed the ordinances, and ended with the individual. Lines melted: in the bright light of day the willfulness evident in prevailing prayer readily turned itself inside out and served a different master. Everything centered, they imagined, in a sovereign, rational decision of the unfettered self. Once the disabling effects of sin had been stripped away by the conversion experience, anyone should be able to take their life in hand and set things straight. For first-generation converts living long enough to watch the television shows of the late 1950s, one suspects that the series of choice might well have been *The Hour of Decision*—followed, of course, by *The Lone Ranger*.

Independence of spirit, a willingness to pick up and leave the old behind, marched hand in hand with boldness of mind, an eagerness to fashion something new in its place. Thumbing through the biographical data, one is struck not only by saints' cavalier attitude toward the conventions of the past, but even more by their propensity to strike out in fresh directions whenever the situation seemed to offer it. They professed to work within the historic traditions of evangelical Christianity, but to a remarkable degree they simply proceeded by their own lights. Indeed the revival's cardinal doctrinal distinctive—that speaking in tongues constituted the sole authentic sign of Holy Spirit baptism—stood unprecedented in the entire history of the Hebrew and Christian traditions. Standing alone like that may have taken a toll at some deep psychological level. But, at least on the surface, believers apparently suffered not a twinge of self-consciousness, let alone embarrassment, about their theological inventiveness.

The point I wish to emphasize here is not so much the singularity of pentecostals' theological ideas as the go-for-broke frame of mind that they brought to their formulation. To take one of countless examples, only a tiny minority ever shared Charles Fox Parham's doctrine of conditional immortality (annihilation of the wicked). But the way that he came to that conclusion was altogether typical. Parham had been schooled as an old-fashioned holiness Methodist. After marrying, Parham's wife's grandfather, a Quaker with conditional immortality leanings, challenged the young man to read the Bible without commentaries in hand or creeds in mind. Parham did, and soon reached the same position himself, which he stubbornly maintained the rest of his life despite relentless vilification from other pentecostals.[83]

The independence that characterized much of pentecostals' thinking also characterized much of their behavior. Consider the case of M. L. Ryan, pastor of a flock in Spokane, Washington, founder of Pacific Holiness College, and editor of an influential weekly called *Apostolic Light*. In the summer of 1907 Ryan led a band of eighteen missionaries to Japan without knowing any of the Asian languages, without the endorsement of any board or denomination, and apparently without any certain destination in mind or clear notion of how they would support themselves after they got there. When the expedition reached Tokyo, Ryan discovered they would have to pay high customs fees. Undeterred, he immediately offered his typewriter and tent as collateral, somehow secured a two-masted lifeboat and proceeded to sail around Tokyo harbor preaching the pentecostal message (presumably with an interpreter in tow). Within days Ryan had managed to turn out two issues of an English and Japanese edition of *Apostolic Light*.[84]

Ryan's freewheeling instincts reappeared in the lives of thousands. Mother Elizabeth R. Wheaton, widely known as the prison evangelist, waved aside any hint that her work with inmates stemmed from "morbid sentimentalism or enthusiasm." Such impulses, she urged, "would have worn off when the novelty was gone."[85] Though Wheaton acknowledged the Holy Spirit's enabling power—as well she might, for her own sanctification experience in the 1880s had been as luxuriant as anyone's—she also made clear that tough work required tough people.[86] If "holy boldness" required the probity of a saint, it also required the grit of a soldier, and apostolics considered themselves ready to deliver on both fronts.[87]

Outsiders often said that pentecostals were anti-intellectual, but they missed the point. Typically the driving motivation was not anti-intellectualism but simple impatience, a determination to get on with the job rather than waste time on pointless theorizing. Tomlinson excoriated those who squandered precious moments in "deep tiresome thinking" when the age called for something else: "holy zeal and undaunted courage." The fainthearted might lament the rush of technological progress, but not this mountain preacher. Why, he wondered, should Christians let others, "by going hungry and arising early . . . win the prize for energy, wit, long-suffering, perseverance, grit and determination?"[88] Evangelist Howard Goss probably revealed more than he intended when he declared that "God made *grappling hooks* of His Pentecostal preachers rather than bookworms."[89] Granted, not everyone was a grappling hook. Common sense tells us that the movement attracted its share of bookworms too. But no one thought to preserve their memory because they did not fit the ideal. Rather we read about stalwarts remembered for proving themselves "vivid, magnetic . . . incisive,"[90] or "erect, clear-eyed, tense and enthusiastic,"[91] or "strong," "domineering," and "severe."[92] In pentecostal culture these words functioned almost as compliments.

Independence fired stamina. The evidence is too spotty to warrant confident generalizations about the rank and file, but we know that the leaders, at least, proved remarkably vigorous. Examples readily surface. One evangelist remembered that if workers could not afford trains or carriages, "they rode bicycles, or in lumber wagons; some went horseback, some walked . . . Often men removed their clothes, tied their bundles above their heads and swam rivers" to get to the next night's meeting.[93] At one point in 1908 Winnipeg pastor A. H. Argue casually remarked that he had led nine services per week every week for the previous nine months.[94] About the same time Mary Mother Barnes achieved local notoriety for shepherding a revival in Thayer, Missouri, from 9 A.M. until midnight, seven days a week, for eight months straight.[95] In 1912 E. N. Bell proudly grumbled that as sole editor of *Word and Witness* he had mailed out 19,000 copies of the paper each month, personally answered 600 to 700 letters each month, and held down a full-time pastorate in Malvern, Arkansas, where he preached five times a week and maintained a regular hospital visitation ministry.[96] The diary of A. J. Tomlinson stands as a chronicle of tireless travel on foot, mule, train, auto, ship—whatever was available—and the preaching of, on the average, one sermon a day for nearly forty years. The entries for a July 1925 weekend were typical. At age sixty-five, between Thursday and Sunday, he reported delivering ten sermons amid swarming mosquitoes and drenching humidity. "The only rest I got," Tomlinson added in a telling postscript, "was while the saints were shouting, dancing and talking in tongues."[97]

Even allowing for a bit of self-varnishing, it seems a remarkable record of exertion for men and women who liked to say that God did everything. Early pentecostals may have held little in common with Manhattan ward boss George Washington Plunkitt, but like him, writes historian Roger Robins, "they were men and women of action who could say, 'I seen my opportunities and I took 'em.'"[98]

Canniness

Finally, it is worth asking how independence of spirit and mind coalesced to form canny, worldly wise personalities. A little-noticed stretch in the life of Aimee Semple McPherson reveals a great deal.

McPherson told her own story (many times, actually). Born in 1890 near the hamlet of Salford, Ontario, the young Aimee Kennedy seemed destined for nothing much except a quiet life on a Canadian farm. But then, at the age of nineteen, she embraced the full gospel message preached by handsome Irish evangelist Robert Semple. Soon married, the young couple headed for Hong Kong as missionaries. After a mere ten weeks in China, Robert died, leaving Aimee with an infant daughter and nothing to live on. The stranded widow returned to the United States where she took a series of odd jobs just to survive. These misfortunes left her in a frame of mind to accept a marriage proposal from a Rhode Island businessman named Harold McPherson. But Aimee settled into her new role of a modestly respectable New England housewife with great difficulty. The independence so characteristic of the pentecostal temperament, which led her to China in the first place, started asserting itself again. After two years, Aimee temporarily left Harold and headed out onto the revival circuit. She immediately found her life's calling. Harold came and went but that did not matter. Having put her hand to the "Gospel plow," she later wrote, she could not turn back.[99] We can see, perhaps more clearly than she herself did, that this move not only marked her liberation from the confines of smalltown domesticity but also introduced her to the buzzing marketplace of twentieth-century life.

We miss an important part of McPherson's story—and early pentecostalism's too—if we overlook the large element of rollicking self-promotion in these narratives. At the callow age of twenty-seven McPherson concluded that her life had been so packed with important events it warranted an autobiography. As an advertisement for *The Personal Testimony and Life of Sister H. S. McPherson* put it, the volume recounted her youthful spiritual infidelity, salvation, baptism, healing, and divine calling. All this was now available for only ten cents—although one should buy immediately since the supply was nearly exhausted.[100] McPherson puffing McPherson proved a lifelong calling. Years later, in a cemetery scheme that never quite got off the ground, the noted preacher tried to sell burial plots near her own anticipated burial site. She marketed them to her premillennialist followers under the logo, "Go Up with Aimee!"[101] One observer quipped that when she carried the Foursquare Gospel ball for a touchdown, "Jesus ran interference."[102] Given Sister's gifts, it comes as no surprise that she erected the fifth religious radio station in the United States, KFSG (Kall Four Square Gospel),[103] and made herself the first woman in the radio business anywhere in the world.[104]

Nonetheless, the most interesting part of this story has largely escaped notice. When McPherson put up KFSG she immediately ran into conflict with Secretary of Commerce Herbert Hoover for refusing to broadcast on a prescribed frequency. "Please order your minions of Satan to leave my station alone," she barked to Hoover. "You cannot expect the almighty to abide by your wave length nonsense. When I offer my prayers to Him I must fit into His wave reception." That much was standard pentecostal absolutizing, the tendency to ratchet every issue into one of ultimate morality. Less noticed but equally important, however, was the confrontation's outcome: after an appropriate display of outrage, McPherson readily backed down in order to achieve her larger goals. She not only agreed to broadcast on an assigned frequency but hired a trained engineer to make sure it was done properly.[105] In the end she prevailed, too. In the early 2000s the station was still flourishing, long after she—and Hoover—had gone to their heavenly rewards.

The conventional image of Holy Ghost leaders as bumpkins fumbling around in the modern world may have held a speck of truth, but typically they knew exactly where the bodies were buried. This shrewdness about the real world turned up everywhere we look in the tradition. In later years Kathryn Kuhlman, Oral Roberts, Jimmy Swaggart, and Pat Robertson would exemplify the same innovative, take-charge inclinations that prevailed from the beginning. A world of significance lay in one early stalwart's comment that the "Holy Ghost does not put us out of business; he puts us in business."[106] Others agreed, probably without fully realizing what they were saying. "We are proving by every-day experience," wrote A. E. Street, editor of

Fort Wayne's *Intercessory Missionary*, "that the gift of TONGUES DOES NOT UNFIT ONE FOR AN ORDINARY SENSIBLE LIFE."[107] If there was a wallflower in the bouquet, no one could tell.

In sum, pentecostal culture encouraged certain ways of thinking and behaving that seemed so deep seated they almost preceded self-conscious articulation. Some of those ways looked backward, toward first things, toward timeless truths and universal values. From that viewpoint most of life's decisions seemed freighted with everlasting consequences. At the same time, however, other ways of thinking and behaving looked forward toward the hustle of twentieth-century life. From that viewpoint most decisions seemed manageable ones, with negotiable consequences to be accepted or rejected as the moment dictated.

2

Tongues

When early pentecostals wanted to explain themselves to the outside world—indeed when they wanted to explain themselves to each other—they usually started with the experience of Holy Ghost baptism signified by speaking in tongues. Their priorities dictate ours. The goal of this chapter is to try to appreciate what it felt like when God's own Spirit entered the human body, took command of the speech organ, "and spoke a language of ineffable purity, simplicity, and power."[1] In time we shall see how tongues served as a practical instrument for the revival's propagation, and also explore modern scholars' theories about the phenomenon's origins. But the first task is to describe the event's inner contours.

Experiencing Tongues

Four autobiographical accounts, each exceptionally rich with detail, illumine the tongues event. We start with the formidable A. J. Tomlinson, general overseer of the Church of God and one of the most dynamic figures in the movement's history. Sunday morning, January 12, 1908, Cleveland, Tennessee, marked the day of days. As barnstorming evangelist G. B. Cashwell was holding forth on the subject of Holy Ghost baptism with the evidence of tongues, Tomlinson felt himself "almost unconsciously" slip off his chair into a heap. "My mind was clear," he wrote, "but a peculiar power so enveloped and thrilled my whole being that I concluded to yield myself up to God and await results." The results were not long in coming. First his feet started shaking uncontrollably and "clatter against the wall." Then his arms and head began to jerk. The overseer's jaws seemed frozen but his lips "moved and twisted about as if a physician was making a special examination." Soon, he recalled, "my body was rolled and tossed about beyond my control . . . my feet were raised up several times, and my tongue would stick out of my mouth in spite of my efforts to keep it inside my mouth." Tomlinson felt himself enveloped in a great sheet, in which he was "literally lifted up and off

35

the floor several inches." While enclosed in the sheet, "floods and billows of glory" surged through his body, followed by "excruciating pain and agony . . . similar to that of my Savior and Mount Calvary."[2] The overseer reported that his mind's eye saw Central America and the "awful condition of the people there." He endured a "paroxysm of suffering." The Holy Spirit then used his "lips and tongue" to speak the language of the Indian tribes of Central America. After a little rest, the Lord directed his eye to Brazil, where the sequence of extreme suffering and speaking the native tongue repeated itself. The cycle continued, fixing next on Chile, then Patagonia, Africa, Jerusalem, Japan, northern Canada, back to his present home town of Cleveland, Tennessee, on to Chattanooga, then over to his natal town of Westfield, Indiana, and finally to the Indiana villages of Hortonville and Sheridan. There it all ended. At each point in the journey Tomlinson experienced new agonies, followed by torrents of tongues, always speaking the language of the people involved.[3] Throughout the experience he felt that he was engaged in a "terrible conflict" with the devil. Three times in the next five years he went through a similar train of events, and each time "truthful witnesses" saw streaks of fire "resting" near his head.[4]

Not much is known about Glenn A. Cook's early years except that he was born in 1867, probably in Indiana. The spring of 1906 found him working in Los Angeles as a newspaper reporter and part-time preacher with radical evangelical sympathies. After visiting the Azusa Mission, Cook rejected the Holy Ghost message, not because he saw too much "fleshly demonstration and noise" but because the teaching seemed "heretical." Soon Cook determined to lay aside "all doctrine, all pre-conceived ideas." Almost immediately Holy Ghost power started shooting through his body like "electric needles." At first he resisted, but then became "limp as a piece of cloth." Five times in five weeks the now middle-aged reporter underwent the same experience, each time feeling "sweet and clean," as in a "washing machine." One Saturday morning Cook awoke, stretched his arms toward heaven, and felt his body "shaken violently by a great power." It seemed that his head was removed, a "large pipe" fitted onto his neck, and Holy Ghost power surged into his body. Cook stressed the inadequacy of words to capture the experience. All he could say, he wrote, was that it felt like the "action of a pump under terrific pressure, filling me with oil." The oil seemed to engorge his toes, then other parts of his body, until his whole torso seemed about to burst. His own spirit appeared to leave his body and "float in the air just above," while his body felt "hard and metallic like iron." At that point Cook deliberately terminated the experience (a point worth noting) because he had to go to work. But thirty hours later, while attending a service at the mission, he sensed his "throat and tongue begin to move" involuntarily. Soon, he wrote,

"I began to stutter and then out came a distinct language which I could hardly restrain. I talked and laughed with joy far into the night." In later years Cook gained a reputation for aggressive advocacy, but not before carrying the Holy Ghost message back to the Indianapolis area, and then to C. H. Mason's Church of God in Christ congregation in Memphis.[5]

William H. Durham was, like many pentecostal leaders, intense, self-taught, and fiercely combative for correct doctrine. He wrote about his baptism experience within days of its occurrence in March 1907, and elaborated it several times thereafter. In the spring of 1906, while serving as pastor of the North Avenue Mission in Chicago, Durham heard about the revival events in Los Angeles. Initially he considered them spiritually benign but doctrinally dubious. By fall he had changed his mind, partly on scriptural grounds and partly because of the renewed "joy, power and glory" he witnessed among pentecostal converts. Though the Chicago pastor determined to receive the baptism himself, success proved elusive. Weeks of intense prayer yielded only helplessness. In February 1907 Durham journeyed to Azusa. His despair deepened as he attended service after service without success. Finally, three friends helped him see the problem. "[C]ease trying to do anything," they urged, just surrender to God. Instantly, Durham recalled, every pore of his body opened and a "*current of electricity*" seemed to flow in from every side. He felt as if the "physical life" had been drawn from his torso till he "literally grasped for breath, and fell in a heap on the floor." He was transparent. Lying on the floor two hours, helpless but fully conscious, Durham enjoyed the Holy Spirit's "sweetness," even as revelations "impossible . . . to tell" swept over him. Still, no tongues. In the next two days the scenario reoccurred several times. On the third night (significantly) Holy Ghost power finally fell. "My body was worked in sections," he recalled. "Even the skin on my face was jerked and shaken." Durham's jaw began to quiver, his throat and voice box swelled, and finally his tongue and lips started to articulate "strange sounds." For a "long time" thereafter—the exact period he never specified—the young pastor could speak only in tongues. An intense consciousness of the Holy Spirit's presence never left him, he wrote.[6]

The final autobiographical account for us to consider reenforces themes we have already observed and introduces several new ones. It came from T. B. Barratt, who enjoyed wide respect in pentecostal circles as the patriarch of the revival in Scandinavia. Born in 1862, Barratt had served Methodist churches in Norway, eventually founding the Oslo City Mission in 1902. A search for funds for that mission led him to New York City where, in the fall of 1906, he read about the Los Angeles revival in a stray copy of the Azusa Mission's *Apostolic Faith*. Convinced of the revival's validity, Barratt sought the "full Bible evidence" up to twelve hours a day, day after day. Then, on November 15, he awoke from a nap to find his "jaws working on their own account"—which could only mean that the "physical sign . . . had . . . commenced." The fire fell just after midnight. At the New York City mission where he was staying a Canadian sister laid hands on him, causing him to fall to the floor, helpless. Eventually Barratt asked Lucy Leatherman also to lay hands on him—even though, he later admitted, the "devil taunted" him by pointing out the irregularity of asking a woman for prayer. At that moment bystanders reported tongues of fire and a supernatural light over his head. "Immediately," Barratt continued, "I was filled with light and such a power that I began to shout as loud as I could in a foreign language." Now physically invigorated and "strong as a lion," he stood erect. In the next four hours Barratt held forth in seven or eight distinct foreign languages. The sermon—so loud that "10,000 might easily have heard"—was interspersed with a "baritone solo" in perfect "rhythm and cadence." Barratt said that at times his body felt "on fire inside."[7]

These four accounts reflect important commonalities. First, it should be noted that the subjects resolved all doctrinal doubts about the validity of the baptism experience before anything else took place. Indeed I know of no instance in which a person held reservations about the authenticity of Holy Spirit baptism but experienced it anyway. Second, resolving doctrinal doubts about the blessing constituted the necessary but not the sufficient condition for receiving it. Later we shall see that many, perhaps half, who sought the experience never gained it, and many who did struggled for weeks or months before success. Third, another person often initiated the experience by laying on hands. Frequently the initiator was someone like Lucy Farrow, widely esteemed in Holy Ghost circles for that form of ministry. Fourth, the event usually took place in a setting where others also were seeking and receiving the baptism (although sometimes, as in Cook's case, the actual eruption or completion came later, in a moment of quiet). Fifth, tongues typically involved an initial verbal explosion, at stentorian volume, followed by a sense that one was speaking multiple distinct foreign languages. Finally, many said that they found themselves able to speak *only* in tongues for hours and or days afterward. (One servant woman who could speak only in tongues frightened her employer so much that she was required to take a week's vacation.)[8]

Looking beyond these four accounts to scores of others, we find them all bound by additional threads of common experience. Most striking, perhaps, was the intensity of the physical sensations accompanying the event. Partisans frequently reported electrical shocks in various parts of the body. Zion City evangelist John G. Lake said that "shocks of power increased in rapidity and voltage," first entering his head, then rushing through his body, finally passing through his feet into the floor. Later, confronting a demon-possessed man, God's Spirit surged through his body "like a flash of lightning."[9] When Aimee McPherson received the baptism, she too shook as if "holding the positive and negative handles of the electric battery in the school laboratory."[10] Images involving fire, heat, or hot coals appeared almost as frequently as electrical metaphors. Patriarch Howard Goss, a hardy soul who later boasted that he never lost a day's work in fifty years, recalled that when he received the baptism the "fire of God flamed hotter and hotter, until I thought that I must be *actually* on fire."[11] Many others used liquid similes. McPherson spoke of "ripples, waves, billows, oceans, cloudbursts of blessing" flooding her body.[12] Jenny Moore—almost certainly the Jenny Moore who would later marry William J. Seymour—employed similar language: "[I]t seemed as if a vessel broke within me and water surged up through my being, which when it reached my mouth came out in a torrent of speech in the languages which God had given me."[13] Many experienced muscle spasms. Tomlinson's recollection that his tongue shot in and out of his mouth against his will was unusual, but rapid jerking or queer feelings in the legs, arms, and neck were not.[14]

Holy Ghost baptism often involved ecstatic activities closely related to tongues. Occasionally believers described outright levitation,[15] but more often they remembered looking at their own body from a distance.[16] For example one Los Angeles sister felt called to proclaim the pentecostal message in Oakland but lacked money for a train ticket. After much travail in prayer, she was "caught away in the Spirit." When the Lord brought her back He assured her, "If I can carry you around Los Angeles without a body, I can take you to Oakland without a fare."[17] While Canadian evangelist Ella M. Goff was listening to another minister preach, the Holy Spirit physically lifted her from her seat and carried her "to the front of the hall" where she "fell under the mighty power of God."[18] Some broke into spasms of laughter.[19] T. B. Barratt's experience of singing in tongues in a beautiful baritone voice he had never known was unusual but far from unique. Jenny Moore, for example, reported that when she received the baptism she also received a miraculous ability to play the piano so that she could accompany her own singing in tongues.[20] Others claimed to be able to recite rhyming poetry in tongues,[21] carry on conversations with each other in tongues,[22] transliterate tongues into Roman script,[23] write tongues in a supernatural orthography,[24] enter into ecstatic silence beyond tongues,[25] sketch as the Holy Spirit directed the hand,[26] and do deaf-mute signing of tongues. One observer said that Owen Lee, a Catholic converted at Azusa, made "deaf and dumb signs . . . with such rapidity that the eye could not trace or record the different signs given."[27]

An event pentecostals called the heavenly chorus or anthem constituted one of the most frequent and puzzling forms of ecstatic expression. We examine this phenomenon more closely later. Here it suffices to say that it probably involved a number of persons singing in tongues at the same time in perceived harmony.[28] Occasionally rhythmic sounds of supernatural origin accompanied the heavenly chorus.[29] Firsthand observers used terms like "unearthly," "ravishing," or "weirdly sweet" to describe the music they heard on those occasions.[30]

Finally, we should note that bystanders commonly served as foils. The baptism experience itself may have been an individual transaction between the believer and God, but the recounting of the experience almost always involved others—especially nonpentecostal or non-Christian others. Patterns varied. Some, taken up in a vision, saw specific geographic regions or vast aggregations of humanity that urgently needed to hear the full gospel message before the Lord's return.[31] Others reported that eyewitnesses, including skeptics, had seen miraculous phenomena in the vicinity such as doves or angels or tongues of fire.[32] Still others said that the experience was ineffable or (more often) unrevealable—both notions ironically presupposing an absent interlocutor.[33] In sum, bystanders almost always stayed well in view, whether as objects of evangelism, or as corroborators of the supernatural, or as implied readers of the text. The experience may have been personal, but rarely private.

Centrality of Tongues

In principle salvation should have come first and sanctification second, but in practice Holy Ghost baptism, signified by speaking in tongues, took priority. Spiritual, psychological, and social factors dictated this emphasis. The spiritual was simplest. Most who joined the movement already considered themselves saved and sanctified, so they naturally fixed their attention on the next and, in their view, final rung on the ladder of Christian experience. The psychological factor too was simple, or at least fairly so. Holy Ghost baptism could not be heard, but tongues could. Once theological writers made a connection between baptism and tongues, it seemed inevitable that earnest Christians would seek tongues as an audible proof of baptism (which also meant proof of their right standing with God). The social factor proved most complex. To a significant extent pentecostals, like most people, fashioned their beliefs and practices in response to outsiders' views of them. Since outsiders dismissed tongues as a speck in the Christian tradition at best, or demonic at worst, saints reacted predictably. They stoutly defended the practice that formed their main reason for existing as an identifiable movement in the first place. The process spiraled: the more strident the critique, the more determined the reaction. By 1907 in many places—by 1910 in most—saints' apology for tongues had acquired a momentum of its own, often functioning like a runaway train displacing everything else on the tracks.

To be sure, several important qualifications to the claim that tongues came first are needed. The most obvious is that theory and practice frequently parted ways. Though hard data are impossible to come by, knowledgeable contemporaries estimated that fewer than half of first-generation converts actually spoke in tongues (a figure paralleling estimates of modern adherents as well).[34] That fact alone suggests that the richness of pentecostal culture could not be reduced to tongues any more than the richness of, say, Roman Catholic culture could be reduced to devotion to the Blessed Virgin.

Second, at various times and places other hallmarks of the radical evangelical tradition seemed almost as important as tongues, including, of course, divine healing and the Second Coming. The Church of God in Christ periodical, *Whole Truth,* for example, spoke a great deal about miracles of spiritual and physical healing but very little about tongues. Similarly the Atlanta-based *Bridegroom's Messenger,* which represented a cluster of independent groups in the southeast, offered many articles about healing, missions, and the Lord's return but few about tongues. From time to time less obvious traits vied for prominence too. J. G. Campbell, editor of the Goose Creek, Texas, *Apostolic Faith,* argued that reliance on God for all financial needs formed one of the most distinctive features of Charles Parham's Bible school in Topeka.[35] In 1912 Parham himself declared that conditional immortality (annihilation of the wicked) equaled the "most important tenet" in the "whole fabric of Christian doctrine."[36] And as late as 1922 the Church of God's *Faithful Standard* ranked baptism by immersion along with healing and tongues as necessary tenets of the movement.[37]

These two qualifications lead to the third and most important one. In short, to say that tongues took priority in pentecostal culture is not to say that Charles Parham's idea that tongues constituted the necessary initial evidence of Holy Ghost baptism won immediate or universal approval. Famed India missionary Minnie Abrams, for example, insisted until her death in 1910 that tongues formed the normal but not the invariable evidence of Holy Spirit baptism.[38] For that matter Elizabeth V. Baker, a leading pentecostal editor and a founder of the Rochester Bible Institute, initially denied that tongues served as the necessary evidence. To say that stalwarts like Huss and Wesley did not have the baptism, she countered, was the "same as to say that one can live the most Christ-like life, bringing forth all the fruits of the Spirit, *without the Holy Spirit.*"[39] Even A. J. Tomlinson—soon the straightest of the straight on this question—did not mention tongues in his diary until June 1907,[40] did not experience tongues himself until January 1908,[41] and did not define tongues as the evidence of Holy Ghost baptism until August 1910.[42] Finally, it is important to remember that even after the initial evidence teaching took hold, a small but worthy minority of voices vigorously insisted that the gift should never be confused for the Giver, the Holy Spirit Himself.[43]

Still, these qualifications formed the exceptions that proved the rule. From the outset tongues, more than any other belief or practice, defined pentecostals' religious identity, both in their own minds and in the minds of outsiders. Tongues was the Shekinah glory in their midst. The periodicals' testimony columns bulged with accounts of the experience, which they breathlessly called by many names—baptism, blessing, evidence, fullness, gift, pentecost, power, witness or, simply, the tongues. Letters to editors discussed its theological meaning with monotonous regularity. Polemical literature shouldered tongues' defense as though it were the centerpiece of the entire history of Christian doctrine.

The evidence for this argument should become apparent in due course, but a glance at the Azusa Mission's (more or less) bimonthly *Apostolic Faith,* issued fourteen times between September 1906 and June 1908, offers a preview of the terrain ahead. A computer-based word search of the first twelve issues (now digitized) reveals 175 references to the Second Coming, 179 to healing, 200 to sanctification, 418 to salvation, and 1,103 to speaking in tongues—more than all the others combined.[44] This finding is significant, for despite its brief life span, this eight-page paper might well be christened the revival's flagship periodical. Each issue contains hundreds of news items, testimonies, letters, and editorial asides. Quickly reaching a circulation of 40,000, perhaps 50,000, *Apostolic Faith* turned up in homes, street cars, and mission stations in all parts of the continent and many parts of the world.[45] If any one text spoke for the movement as a whole, it was *Apostolic Faith.*

What the Azusa periodical intimated, leaders' memories' confirmed. In one of the earliest historical reflections on the movement's beginnings, penned in 1915, Japan missionary M. L. Ryan judged that its "chief characteristic was the revival of speaking in tongues."[46] Ryan was not alone. Kansas preacher Charles Fox Parham, a theological architect of the revival, later explained how things had started back in 1901. "Having heard so many different religious bodies claim different proofs as the evidence of . . . the Pentecostal baptism," he remembered, he and a band of seekers determined to discover the answer "that was indisputable because it tallied absolutely with the Word." And that answer, of course, was tongues, as described in Acts 2. Those events probably did not take place quite as neatly as Parham recalled, but in this respect his memory served him accurately.[47]

Given early pentecostals' preoccupation with tongues, it is hardly surprising that they soon tried to make the practice a prerequisite for full acceptance within the community. Parham's initial evidence teaching caught on quickly and spread widely. In the first column of the first issue of *Apostolic Faith,* published in September 1906, William J. Seymour went out of his way to distinguish himself from other radical evangelical preachers in the Los Angeles area. Seymour was the pastor of the Apostolic Faith Mission and, with Clara E. Lum, co-editor of the paper.[48] In his account, the Los Angeles preachers supposed that "sanctification was the baptism with the Holy Ghost." But they were wrong, they did not have "the evidence of the second chapter of Acts."[49] Nine months later *Intercessory Missionary* editor A. E. Street echoed Seymour's words from his listening post in the Midwest: "Tongues and the Interpretation of tongues are the ONLY WORKS THAT WERE PECULIAR TO PENTECOST and the age it ushered in." In Street's mind, what history made clear the plain teachings of the Bible rendered indisputable: "According to the BIBLE THERE IS ONLY ONE ACT THAT ANY MAN CAN PERFORM TO PROVE THAT HE HAS HAD THE TRUE PENTECOSTAL EXPERIENCE AND THAT IS TO SPEAK IN TONGUES."[50] Less than six months after the full gospel message arrived in India, missionary Albert Norton declared—more than a little defiantly—that God had made tongues "integral" to the revival.[51] By 1913 A. J. Tomlinson too had gained both clarity and certainty on the question. Speaking from his redoubt in the eastern Tennessee mountains, the general overseer left no question about the orthodox position on tongues: "The red flag of truth and uncompromising boldness and undaunted courage and holy zeal must float over every nation and clime, declaring emphatically that no one ever has or ever will receive the baptism with the Holy Ghost without the speaking in other tongues accompanying as the evidence."[52] In 1918 another writer—almost certainly Elder G. T. Haywood, the black editor of the Oneness periodical *Voice in the Wilderness*—would feel so strongly about the matter he would issue a warning on the editorial page. "BEWARE of any so-called Pentecostal preacher who will tell you that it is not necessary that speaking in tongues accompany the baptism of the Holy Ghost. He either has never received the Holy Ghost, or has back-slidden in heart."[53] Haywood may not have represented all pentecostals, but he certainly represented the vast majority by the time of World War I.[54]

Institutional prescriptions and proscriptions sheathed the initial evidence doctrine in the hard steel of church discipline. With few exceptions, by the mid-1910s only those who had experienced or were wholeheartedly seeking baptism with tongues found themselves eligible for ordination as pastors or endorsement as missionaries.[55] Doubters were first drowned out then drummed out. In 1918 the Assemblies of God excluded even F. F. Bosworth, one of the most beloved of the first-generation healing evangelists, for refusing to bend to the official position.[56] William J. Seymour's steady tumble into obscurity after 1912 probably stemmed from several sources, including white racism and his own lack of leadership inclinations. But Seymour's decision to renounce his earlier insistence on tongues as the initial evidence of Holy Spirit baptism surely contributed to his eclipse.[57]

By far the most telling indication of tongues' centrality in pentecostal culture lay in outsiders' choice of labels. Scanning the secular and theological newspapers of the day, one quickly discovers that bystanders typically denoted the upstarts down the street not by dubbing them salvationists, sanctificationists, premillennialists, or healing enthusiasts—all of which might have worked well enough—but by calling them "Tongue people."[58] Other favorite labels included "tongues movement,"[59] "'tongues' craze,"[60] "tongues delusion,"[61] "tongues heresy,"[62] and "tongues sorcery."[63] The *Topeka Daily Capital* jauntily but perceptively renamed Charles Parham's Bible school "The Parham School of Tongues."[64] In one of the earliest booklet-length critiques of the "'Speaking with Tongues' Revival," British Plymouth Brethren writer Sir Robert Anderson remarked that "the special gift which is the boast of this new 'revival' is that of tongues."[65] In 1914 University of Southern California historian Charles William Shumway agreed, saying that the stirring was popularly known as the "Tongues Movement" or as "Holy Rollers."[66] Though these monikers were more than a little unfair, the recurring reference to tongues should tell us where the gold lay.

Finally, it should be noted that pentecostals soon refined their tongues teaching in a significant way. Specifically, in the beginning they simply talked about tongues as the Holy Ghost speaking through the believer's lips, first as a sign of the baptism experience, second as a means for edifying the faithful and winning the faithless. But by 1907 many leaders were cleaving tongues speech into two distinct forms: the *sign* and the *gift*. They deemed the former normative for all Christians, saying that its main purpose was to signify that the Holy Spirit had filled the believer's very body with His power (based on Acts 2:4, 10:44–46, and 19:1–6). In contrast they deemed the latter a special gift that God bestowed selectively, according to His will and believers' willingness (based on 1 Cor. 12 and 14). Whatever its exegetical merits, this sign–gift distinction proved a stroke of sociological genius, for it combined structure with flexibility. Though no one seemed to notice it, this teaching paralleled the Roman Catholic Church's teaching that there was no salvation outside the Church. The sign–gift doctrine effectively said that all Christians were expected to enter the House of the Holy Ghost by manifesting the sign of tongues at least once. But once in, each would find that the House contained as many different rooms as their gifts and graces made possible.[67]

Missionary Tongues

Though born in the heavenlies, ecstatic phenomena connected with the real world of workaday affairs in countless ways. Mastery of ecstasy brought status within the community, provided boundaries in a religious ecology of growing complexity, and offered meaning for lives caught in humdrum routine. The list of such connections could be extended at length, but it may be more helpful to examine one ecstatic behavior pattern in detail. The aim is to see how pragmatic impulses first helped to bring it into existence and then, just as surely, dictated its demise.

Our subject is missionary tongues: the ability to speak an actual though unstudied foreign language at will (technically called xenolalia or xenoglossy).[68] Belief in missionary tongues dated from the 1830s in Scotland, and constituted a minor though persistent element of radical evangelical missionary strategy on both sides of the Atlantic throughout the late nineteenth century.[69] But the concept came to serve as a veritable cornerstone of Charles Parham's theological system, for he taught his followers that *all* authentic tongues involved extant foreign languages.[70] For the first five or six years most saints likely shared his view. Shortly we shall see that most writers soon gave up the notion that all tongues consisted of actual languages, yet almost all continued to believe that *some* did.[71]

Belief tutored practice. The early literature contained hundreds if not thousands of reports of missionary tongues at home and abroad.[72] A. W. Frodsham, a British convert making a tour of American pentecostal missions in 1911, commented on the tenacity of saints' belief in the phenomenon. Frodsham reported that leaders permitted public messages in tongues to proceed even without vernacular interpretation (contrary to Paul's rule in 1 Cor.) lest they contain a message for a foreign-language speaking soul in the congregation.[73] Though the evidence remains sketchy, there are good reasons to believe that between 1906 and 1909 more than a dozen zealots journeyed to remote outposts on the mission field armed only with the conviction that they would be empowered to speak the native language when they arrived.[74] The diversity of the languages routinely noted in the primary accounts—Russian, Spanish, African, Armenian, Syrian, Hebrew, Chinese, Zulu, Assyrian, and the like—bespeaks the cosmopolitan range of saints' linguistic ambitions.[75]

The literary structure of the missionary tongues accounts tells us a great deal about how the practice functioned in pentecostal culture. For one thing, the vast majority of reports were second- or thirdhand. The narrator normally had heard about a xenolalic incident taking place at a meeting in another town, or among friends, and related it as factual. Most proved imprecise about the dialect of the language spoken and the identity of the speakers and hearers. The vagueness of the following account typified most: "A girl of twelve years preaches and sings in the Indian language," announced Azusa's *Apostolic Faith* in 1906—without any sense that additional details or corroboration might be desirable.[76] Or again, in 1914 one J. E. Simmons, pastor in

Factoria, Kansas, casually commented that his eight-month ministry in that little mining town had seen notable successes: "Now 46 are saved and 33 have received the baptism. One brother as he spoke in the Spirit was understood in 4 languages."[77] Exactly who the brother was, or which languages he spoke, or how anyone would know, went unsaid.

Though most xenolalia accounts were short on details, a few offered just enough specifics to arouse outsiders' curiosity, both then and now. The Azusa *Apostolic Faith* reported, for example, that the "gift of the English language with the understanding of the words" had been given to one Jennie Jacobson, a Swedish sister who had lived in the United States for only two months.[78] Englishman George B. Studd noted that at the Los Angeles Upper Room Mission a German-speaking woman had uttered a message in the Basuto language, which a Basuto man in the congregation understood.[79] Or again, Josie Ellis of Neek City, Missouri, claimed to speak "over twenty different languages," including Italian, Mexican, Delaware Indian, German, Dutch, and "a few words in Norwegian."[80] In these accounts the languages involved were specific enough, but the means of testing them were not.

Only a tiny fraction of the xenolalia accounts involved believers who had personally heard *and* held good credentials for knowing the language in question. But a few did. In 1907, for example, veteran India missionary George E. Berg, attested that at one service the Holy Spirit spoke through another sister sitting next to him in a "language of India."[81] Harriette Shimer, a Quaker missionary to China, declared that she had heard editor Carrie Judd Montgomery sing in Chinese at an Oakland prayer meeting in 1908.[82] Albert Norton, another long-time India missionary, claimed that at Pandita Ramabai's orphanage at Mukti he had heard a humble Indian girl, who knew no English, proclaim in tongues: "O Lord, open the mouth; O Lord, open the heart . . . O the blood of Jesus."[83] Though not unique, Norton's account proved unusual in that he specified the exact words he heard.

I have discovered only one first-generation pentecostal who claimed a permanent gift of missionary tongues—but, like the medieval monk who reportedly placed his decapitated head in his hands and walked home, one is significant. Her name was Sophie Hansen. Not much is known about Hansen except that about 1907 she was called to China as a missionary. On July 26, 1908, six months after arriving in Shanghai, she found herself suddenly able to preach a sermon in Chinese—so she reported in 1911 in the Atlanta-based *Bridegroom's Messenger.* Hansen said that an English-speaking Chinese man substantiated the event.[84] In a 1916 letter posted to the Oakland-based *Triumphs of Faith* Hansen affirmed that she had traveled all over China, using her gift of Chinese at will, but proved able to use it for speaking the "Gospel only," not "earthly things."[85] In 1921 she again stated in *Bridegroom's Messenger* that the "Holy Spirit still speaks Chinese through me from heaven, without learning it, just as clearly as when I received the gift. Can speak it any time, but the Gospel only."[86] Though a 1917 communique to the home front from Sophie's husband George said nothing about Sophie or missionary tongues, there is evidence that her reputation for being able to speak Chinese at will persisted in pentecostal circles at least into 1919.[87]

Where did the idea of missionary tongues come from? Though radical evangelicals had reported miraculous linguistic phenomena from time to time, none made it a staple of everyday discussion and practice as pentecostals did. The question of origins is particularly intriguing since severe questions of credibility afflicted all reports of missionary tongues, including Hansen's. Granted, Hansen cited a corroborator, but all that survived was Hansen's statement, not the corroborator's. (Moreover we may reasonably assume that after six months of living in China Hansen might well have unconsciously picked up more of the language than she realized.) I have not located any instance in which a person affirmed that they heard their *own* natal language spoken at length through xenolalic means.[88] In 1914 the historian Charles William Shumway, likely the first outside scholar seriously to study the practice, spent six months trying to track down and verify missionary tongues reports. He came to the conclusion that all rested on chains of hearsay, with little or no foundation.[89] My aim here is not to debunk missionary tongues but to understand why the practice became so firmly rooted in pentecostal culture despite the absence of corroborating evidence. The most fantastic healing claims were normally subjected to verification tests of some sort. So why not missionary tongues?

Several possibilities present themselves. One, of course, is that pentecostals were simply fibbing in the interests of a higher cause. Christians had done worse. But to suppose that hundreds of earnest souls who prided themselves on their probity would have intentionally lied seems more improbable than the phenomenon it seeks to explain. Another more likely possibility is that in the din of the revival setting saints honestly mistook tongues utterances for actual languages. Given that a significant minority of converts came from non-English speaking backgrounds, and given that tongues likely reflected the intonation and phonological patterns of the speaker's natal language, many utterances undoubtedly sounded like actual foreign languages. Still another possibility may have involved cryptomnesia: the ability to vocalize portions of a language one had casually encountered—say, on a playground or in a neighborhood restaurant—but never consciously mastered. There are in fact a number of perplexing cases on record of nonpentecostals who acquired the ability partially to speak an unstudied language presumably in this way.[90]

Either of the latter two explanations may be sufficient, but another, more persuasive possibility beckons. In a word, ideology dictated behavior. This is not exactly to say that the wish fathered the belief, but it is to say that everything in the culture conspired to encourage pentecostals to find ways first to birth and then to legitimate the practice. Specifically: the Lord was coming soon, the heathen were perishing for want of the gospel, thus the Holy Spirit had given missionary tongues to the church as a speedy and practical means for meeting that need. Missionary tongues would hasten world evangelization by enabling partisans to bypass years of arduous language study. Given the urgency of the situation and the difficulty and inaccessibility of traditional means of language acquisition, it seems virtually inevitable that pentecostals would have found such a resource in their cultural tool kit.

It is hard to imagine a strategy more clearly born of pragmatic inclinations. One patriarch argued that the supernatural gifts of speaking and writing in foreign languages were equipping God's children "to cross at once the chasms which they hitherto have had to cross by years of study and practise."[91] Another, an elderly home missionary to the Florida swamplands, exulted that the Holy Spirit was giving "the language of every nation and tribe of people in all the earth." With that gift in hand, he explained, they would not have to "take the time to learn the languages, but [could] enter upon their work of teaching the people immediately."[92] One is tempted to suggest that only a pentecostal could have turned otherworldly convictions into thisworldly implementations so easily—and so adroitly.

But if pragmatic considerations nurtured the birth of missionary tongues, they also dictated its demise. As early as the summer of 1907, for example, we find one Japan missionary writing home, expressing frustration with the slowness and difficulty of learning Japanese, wishing that he might somehow overcome that hurdle, nowhere intimating that he expected a xenolalic gift.[93] The formidable Carrie Judd Montgomery, who believed with all her heart that she had heard the phenomenon with her own ears,[94] nonetheless took Chinese language lessons before visiting that land in the spring of 1909.[95] Most pentecostal sects soon established rigorous and well-respected language training programs for their foreign missionary candidates. Indeed by 1917 the Assemblies of God, the largest and strongest of the pentecostal groups, had determined that all missionary candidates must provide proof of two years of foreign language instruction before departing.[96] Five years later India missionary Fred Merian wrote home about the appalling need for a Christian witness in the villages, significantly adding that he and his wife Lillian were "longing for the day" when they would be able to speak the native language fluently.[97]

Two brief stories, one drawn from the life of a general in the pentecostal army, the other from a private, show how convictions about the ready availability of missionary tongues for world evangelization underwent modification in the face of real life battles.

In the jargon of the revival, A. G. Garr was not a "comp"—not a man to compromise his beliefs. Born in Kentucky in 1874, Garr suffered recurring bouts of religious anxiety until he found salvation at age fifteen on a mountain trail near his home. Later he attended (Presbyterian) Centre College and (Wesleyan) Asbury College but apparently did not graduate from either. At Asbury he married Lillian Anderson, daughter of a Methodist bishop. Garr next turned up in Los Angeles in 1906 serving a Burning Bush congregation. When he heard about the revival blazing at the Azusa Mission, he visited and experienced Holy Spirit baptism on June 14. Tradition holds that Garr thus became the first pastor of an established sect to embrace the full gospel message. That was not exactly true, since the Burning Bush, not wanting fanatics to tarnish their image, had already forced him out. Nonetheless, Garr felt certain the Holy Spirit was calling him and Lillian to India as missionaries. He also felt certain that the Holy Spirit had miraculously enabled him to speak Bengali and Hindustani and Lillian to speak Tibetan and Chinese. Reportedly the Azusa faithful raised $1,200 in fifteen minutes to speed the young couple on their way. They left within a month, some said within a week. Garr's admiring biographer described a thousand other pentecostals when he remarked that "Garr's principal rule was to get started."[98]

The couple arrived in Calcutta in January 1907. The funding arrangements may have been adequate but Garr's language preparation was not. A resident missionary who knew Hindi told him that his gift of Bengali (a cognate language) was unintelligible. Garr refused to believe him and proceeded to preach to the Bengalis anyway. Failing, presumably after several tries, the couple moved to Hong Kong in October 1907, where they buckled down to the arduous task of learning the language the hard way. In time Garr found success as a missionary leader, but the personal cost was high. The couple lost one daughter and their black helper to bubonic plague, and another daughter in childbirth. Evincing the peripatetic ways so characteristic of pentecostal missionaries, the Garrs moved to Japan in the spring of 1908, returned to Hong Kong in the fall of 1909, took a year's furlough in the United States (roughly spring 1910 to spring 1911), and finally settled back in the United States for good in December 1911. In 1931, after two decades as a successful itinerant evangelist at home, Garr founded and ably served a large independent pentecostal church in Charlotte, North Carolina, until his death in 1944.

To the end, Garr never doubted the truth of the full gospel message, nor that tongues might embody actual languages, but he did soon relinquish the conviction that he could speak unstudied languages at will. That admission came hard. Between 1907 and 1909 Garr published at least a half-dozen items in American pentecostal periodicals, but never mentioned missionary tongues. In 1908 he told the British magazine *Confidence:* "So far I have not seen anyone who is able to preach to the natives in their own tongue with the languages given with the Holy Ghost. Here in Hong Kong, we preached the word to the natives through an interpreter."[99] By 1911 Lillian Garr would write that she was investing six hours each day studying Chinese, even crying over it at night. When Charles Shumway interviewed Garr in 1912, he reported that by then Garr had come to doubt that anyone, including the apostles, had ever spoken foreign languages by miraculous means. In a 1914 autobiographical sermon Garr still insisted that when he received Holy Spirit baptism back in 1906 he had spoken Hindustani (confirmed, he said, by a Hindu bystander)—but he significantly did not claim that he had ever been able to speak the language at will. Many years later two of Garr's closest friends, Frank Ewart and A. G. Osterberg, separately reported that Garr privately admitted he had been forced to use interpreters from the outset.

What does this brief vignette say about pragmatism in pentecostal culture? Briefly put, saints started their journeys in the heavenlies but they usually knew when it was time to return to *terra firma.* Garr sailed halfway around the world, his young family in tow, fired by a dream of expeditiously evangelizing heathen peoples through the miracle of an unstudied foreign language. Yet equally important for present purposes is the fact that he modified that dream when hammered by contrary evidence. If the modification came painfully, it is not hard to imagine why, given the cost of backing down, retooling, and starting over.

One more story, briefly told, shows that a person too uncelebrated to leave even a name to history knew how to accept the verdict of daily experience. The narrative survives in an obscure news account printed in a 1907 issue of the *Baptist Missionary Review.* According to the report, Mabel E. Archibald, a Baptist missionary to the Near East, met three pentecostal missionaries—two American women and a Swedish man—at Gibraltar in the fall of 1906. All four were headed for mission work among Arabic-speaking Jews in Palestine. One of the pentecostal women, who had lived in Palestine seven years, already knew the Arabic language. The other pentecostal woman and man did not, they expected the Lord to give it to them on arrival. Our subject, the unnamed pentecostal woman who did not speak Arabic, tried to converse with some Moors at Gibraltar. When she found that she could not, she decided to return to Los Angeles to warn the others of their mistake. "I feel so happy since I have made this decision!" she declared to Mabel Archibald. That decision proved costly, however. The Swedish man proceeded to excoriate both women because, he said, "Satan was keeping them from going on to Palestine to do the Lord's work."[100] That was all. We do not know the outcome of this tale of hope, disillusion, reassessment, and animosity over the meaning of missionary tongues. But if we can take the narrative at face value, it well symbolizes the blending of primitivist determination and pragmatic calculation in a single representative life.[101]

Fairness dictates caution. Taken whole, the evidence does not suggest that pentecostals always bent themselves to practical considerations with ease, let alone grace, as if ideology readily subjected itself to prudential negotiation. Garr did not back down until experience clubbed him in the face and the angel of death took two daughters and a trusted helper. The Swedish man ignored his colleague's (and presumably his own) inability to converse with local Moors. And though no pentecostal sect ever made missionary tongues an official point of doctrine, none ever repudiated it either.[102] All of this is to say that elements of the old invincible certitude lingered, bloodied but never wholly defeated.

Nonetheless, by the beginning of the second generation the concept of missionary tongues had receded into the hazy realm of pentecostal mythology. It remained too much an artifact of first-century signs and wonders to be given up as an item of faith, yet too unreliable to be taken seriously as a prescription for working policy.

Sources of Tongues

Tongues phenomena almost certainly precede the modern pentecostal revival, though probably not as frequently within Christian history,[103] nor as rarely outside Christian history,[104] as Holy Ghost folk liked (and still like) to believe. The evidence for glossolalia among Irvingites in Britain in the 1820s, Mormons in the United States in the 1830s and 1890s, and psychics in the United States at the turn of the century is compelling.[105] Moreover trance speaking by women in the Spiritualist tradition seemingly involved many of the supranormal features of glossolalia, such as preternatural facility with language.[106] The key point here is that in the absence of tape recorders, video cameras, and on-site ethnologists asking impertinent questions, it is hard to know exactly what those speech acts really were, or what they meant to the people who uttered or heard them.

If the pre-twentieth-century materials remain murky, what can be learned from the findings of modern social scientists in general, and linguists in particular? Nonpentecostals, especially those who have never heard tongues, often suppose that glossolalia is only gibberish, made-up words thrown together at random. Mature pentecostals and professional linguists both know, however, that the real thing is a baffling and awesome phenomenon precisely because it is not gibberish. Cross-cultural investigations have shown that a glossolalic utterance is drawn from the basic sounds or phonemes of a speaker's native language. These phonemes erupt in patterns resembling the patterns of one's vernacular tongue. That is why glossolalia is easily mistaken for language: it sounds like it, especially in real-life situations where it competes with other noises and is cued by gestures and facial expressions.

Linguists argue, however, that glossolalia is not a real language. Specifically, glossolalia reveals no grammar or syntax. It has no past, present, or future tenses, no means for distinguishing verblike actions from nounlike entities, and no ability to specify singular versus plural agents and objects. Moreover glossolalia carries no semantic value. In other words, the sound units of glossolalic speech bear no predictable relationship to their natural or social context. Glossolalic sound units may, of course, connote a purely private meaning for the speaker, and they may convey a specifiable meaning for hearers in tightly structured or repetitive situations (such as worship services in which the same persons utter the same message under the same conditions). But on the whole they seem content empty.

So where does glossolalia come from? Many social scientists believe that speaking in tongues is, despite superficial variations, an easily identifiable form of speech because it arises from an underlying physiological function (or malfunction) called dissociation. In dissociation the higher speech control center in the cerebral cortex of the brain is cut off from the lower motor control center in the medulla. Aborted language results, sounds that bear some of the phonological characteristics of ordinary language but lack the structure, intricacy, and nuance of ordinary language. Many theories have been offered for why this short-circuiting takes place, ranging from the hypothesis that glossolalia represents regression to infantile speech to speculation that it somehow symbolizes pentecostals' marginal social status. Whatever the trigger, the crucial point here is that according to this point of view glossolalia stems from an underlying physiological process.[107]

The early primary sources offer considerable support for this physiological interpretation. They show that ecstatic states sometimes overtook believers unaware and, once initiated, contorted their bodies in ways they did not anticipate and sometimes did not even desire. For example, evangelist Frank Bartleman described a 1908 Indianapolis revival during which he glanced at the other preachers on the platform and discovered they were all prostrate. "One of them had his feet tangled up in a chair . . . My body began to rock . . . and I fell over onto the piano and lay there."[108] It stretches credulity to suppose that either the "other preachers" or Bartleman himself actually desired to find themselves in these positions. The elderly Howard Goss similarly remembered that in the earliest pentecostal meetings many who had been slain in the Holy Spirit seemed "unaware that they had fallen . . . [T]here was seemingly no way we could curb it, for they were out like a light . . . and nothing brought them to."[109] When partisans threw self-interest to the wind for no discernible reason, theological or otherwise, we might reasonably suspect that involuntary physiological processes were involved. During a July 1906 Pasadena revival, for example, the local newspaper reported that one vendor "cracking ice in a tub outside the tent . . . received an attack of the tongues and danced and shouted around the tub, using the strange language while the ice melted."[110] Given the cost of ice in a Pasadena summer, one doubts that the vendor deliberately chose to let his product evaporate.

Striking changes in daily behavior also implied dissociation. Consider the behavior of Mabel Smith at a 1914 Houston rally. According to one eyewitness—probably Charles Parham—Smith was normally a "timid, refined lady." But on this occasion she suddenly jumped up and performed an "Indian stomp dance all over the meeting house." Smith's gesticulations and imitations of "Indian jargon" created such an uproar that bystanders called a policeman to quell the disturbance. Smith thereupon "whirled him around" and literally pummeled and kicked him from the tent. Shortly afterward Smith quieted down and, according to Parham, "never again in all her beautiful ministry" repeated that behavior. Though the writer attributed Smith's behavior to "an Indian spook-spirit," the aberrational nature of her actions suggested involuntary prompting.[111]

As late as 1922 A. J. Tomlinson recounted with obvious satisfaction the "manifestations" that took place under his own preaching. Sometimes, he said, the Holy Spirit would "operate on the women to pull the hair of others, snatch men's neckties, and women's pins or ribbons or lace on their dresses. So many were injured and bruised by these manifestations that people got afraid to attend the meetings."[112] On one occasion, Tomlinson nostalgically recalled, seekers "flounce[d] about similar to a chicken when its head is cut off. . . . A man was lying on his back on the straw, and a woman walked up to him and kicked him in the side several times . . . A little later [she] struck him a hard blow on his head with her hand." Eventually, Tomlinson dryly added, "the power of God seemed to subside and people got back more to the normal state again."[113]

These stories seem persuasive enough in their own right, but other indications of cognitive dissociation corroborate them. For one thing, pentecostals themselves often acknowledged that they had gone without sleep, food, and water for extended periods before receiving baptism.[114] Their own statements about the uncontrollability and arbitrariness of their experiences proved especially telling. Many found themselves unable to return to vernacular English for hours or days after breaking out in tongues, and others said they could not stop the process nor even reduce the speed and volume of the verbal torrent once it started.[115] Some freely linked the baptism experience to physically discernible sensations in their foreheads. "[M]y forehead became sealed," Africa missionary John G. Lake wrote in his diary in October 1907. "[M]y brain in the front portion of my head became inactive, and I realized the Spirit speaking of His seal in their foreheads."[116] It is hard to imagine a more explicit statement of dissociation.

Having said this, a significant body of evidence, both secondary and primary, suggests another interpretation. Some scholars believe that glossolalia is not distinctive enough to mark it off as a definable, discrete physiological activity at all. They contend rather that the linguistic evidence is so slippery we stand on safer ground if we think of tongues as culturally rather than physiologically prompted and defined. By this reckoning, converts spoke in tongues when they and their hearers *thought* they were. What counted, in other words, was not what took place in the synapses of the brain but what took place in the environing culture. This second position bypasses the problem of trying to figure out whether ancient Montanists or modern Spiritualists really did or did not speak in tongues. Rather the point is that glossolalia did not possess any inherent meaning outside the meaning that speakers and hearers ascribed to it. So for Irvingites, Mormons, and Spiritualists the crucial question was not whether they uttered sounds similar to the sounds voiced by pentecostals, but whether the folks who heard those sounds regarded them as signs of divine presence.[117]

This second or cultural (rather than physiological) way of conceiving the origins of ecstatic speech also draws on solid evidence from first-generation pentecostals. The most radical stream within the radical evangelical tradition—the stream that gave birth to the Holy Ghost revival—had actively encouraged ecstatic weeping, laughing, jerking, dancing, prostration and, on rare occasions, even tongues. "Every artery, vein, nerve, muscle, and fiber of my being is thrilling, throbbing and pulsating with the fiery current," exulted one nameless partisan in 1896, pointedly adding, "This is now my daily experience."[118] Pentecostals inherited these cues and intensified them by making tongues and other forms of ecstatic behavior normative. In short, the momentum and direction of radical evangelical *culture* effectively predetermined that Holy Ghost ecstasy would emerge sooner or later.

Three anecdotes, chosen almost at random among scores of possibilities, show that in the 1880s and 1890s something very close to the baptism-tongues experience was rapidly becoming normative. Consider for example the experience of J. H. King, for many years general superintendent of the Pentecostal Holiness Church. King described his 1885 sanctification experience as a Methodist circuit rider in words more suggestive of ecstasy than the ones he would use twenty-two years later to limn his baptism experience: "[M]y heart was filled with light, love and glory . . . I seemingly was taken out of myself and thought I was within a few feet of the gates of Heaven . . . [I]t was utterly indescribable."[119] Or consider the experience of Frank Bartleman, the influential first-generation historian of the revival. Long before he became pentecostal, Bartleman recalled, he had experienced "electric shocks" at radical evangelical camp meetings in Pennsylvania so intense that he fell to the floor unconscious.[120] Or consider the record of healing evangelist Maria Woodworth-Etter, whose 1880 anointing experience rivaled in ecstatic intensity any pentecostal experience she would undergo in later decades. "My body was light as the air . . . There was liquid fire, and the angels were all around in the fire and glory," she wrote shortly afterward.[121]

One additional example shows, in a somewhat different way, how thoroughly radical evangelical culture had prepared the soil for the tongues experience. Healing evangelist Elizabeth Sisson penned the narrative sometime in the late 1890s.[122] Born in New England in 1843, the globe-trotting evangelist experienced conversion at age twenty in a Congregational church. In the next quarter century Sisson served as a Congregational missionary in India, experienced the healing of an "incurable disease" at W. S. Boardman's Bethshan Faith Home in London, and finally ended up as a "Holy Ghost" worker in the Chicago area. But as time passed (exact dates elude us) Sisson felt a "wordless groan" in her soul for a more vivid experience of God's presence. Finally, at a morning camp meeting her "whole being let go to God"— whereupon she found herself "imbedded in God." Within seconds, she wrote, "heaven opened above my soul, and from the throne of God came flowing down great streams of love in hot tides." Sisson proceeded to deliver the morning sermon, but afterward remembered none of what she said. "As I staggered about the platform, filled with unutterable glory," she recalled, "I could but say to myself, 'Oh, this is the Holy Ghost *and fire*. Why, I am drunk—drunk with God and glory." She felt herself wrapped in the Holy Ghost as the "atmosphere the folded bud, but now that same blessed Holy Ghost atmosphere had warmed every petal to unfolding, till it lay a full blown rose, luxuriating in the heavenly atmosphere, its very heart all response to God."[123] All of the elements of the classic pentecostal baptism experience can be found in Sisson's account of her conversion, sanctification, anointing, and baptism of fire—all, that is, except tongues. The point is inescapable. The radical evangelical environment *prepared* some men and women to look for an experience deeper, more powerful than anything they had yet known. Thus prepared, they knew when to let it happen or, to use their own language, they knew when to let the Holy Spirit have His own way.

The cultural-origins interpretation gains persuasiveness when we note how important the environmental cues proved. Indeed, if the setting was not right, the whole performance could be discounted as false or even demonic. So in one instance the saints interpreted a message in tongues as curses against God uttered in Chinese.[124] The record left no hint why that particular ejaculation seemed blasphemous, but clearly the community's lack of ratification played a crucial role. San Francisco's *Glad Tidings* told a similar story. In 1927 one Seattle woman landed on the mission floor "under the demon power," where she began to speak in devil tongues, "each one distinct and cruelly hideous." In most instances anyone so smitten would have been regarded as slain in the Holy Spirit and praising God in tongues. Why not in this case? It is impossible to know for sure, of course, but a revealing clue can be found in a stray comment that the woman was a "backslider."[125] The details varied from case to case but, taken together, they make clear that subtle communal cues helped to distinguish legitimate from illegitimate ecstasy.

So where does all this leave us? Was the tongues experience mainly prompted by disassociative processes in the brain? Or by inducements from the broader culture? Clearly the primary literature supports both interpretations. But it also supports a third possibility, which I find the most compelling.

Specifically, partisans almost certainly fell into physiologically disassociative states but—and this is the key point—they also knew exactly how and when to enter and leave those states. That meant that the baptism experience undoubtedly involved some form of dissociation, yet cues from the culture taught them when dissociation was appropriate, how to control the depth of the process, and when to exit. Consider the words of Danish actress Anna Larssen, who remembered that her "inside seemed to be on fire" when she broke into a distinct foreign language, yet stressed her mastery of the situation: "I was in no kind of ecstasy. I had full control of my senses."[126] Another first generation pundit—not named but likely A. J. Tomlinson—proved even more astute. This writer sensed that the experience presented itself as inherently two-sided. To receive Holy Spirit baptism, he urged, "we must fully surrender the tongue to [the Holy Spirit's] control." And then the telling codicil: "It takes some time for most people to learn how to do this."[127]

This interpretation, stressing the simultaneously physiological and cultural character of the tongues event, brings us back to the main argument of this book. The disassociative nature of tongues embodied the primitivist impulse with striking precision, for it involved the abandonment of the finite, self-interested will in obedience to a directing force from the outside. So too the environmentalist nature of tongues embodied the pragmatic impulse with striking precision, for it involved a willingness to respond to cues provided by the external culture at appropriate times and places.

By now no one should be surprised. If early pentecostals had sat down and self-consciously tried to weave the two strands that constituted their ecstatic experiences—the otherworldly and the thisworldly—into a grand religious tapestry, it is hard to imagine how they could have done the job more adroitly.

— nice discussion, but missing the boundary creation / maintenance function of tongues (+ other intense collective exp)

3

Testimony

Like countless Christians before them, early pentecostals assumed that their personal faith stories bore normative implications for others. Consequently they devoted much of the time in their worship services—maybe a third of the total—to public testimonies about their spiritual journeys. At this distance it is impossible to know exactly what they said in those boisterous meetings since no one thought to write things down. Journalists occasionally dropped by and reported snippets of what they heard, but nothing substantial has survived. Even so, all is not lost. Several book-length memoirs from the first generation exist, along with scores of theological articles containing autobiographical asides. There are good reasons to believe that the words partisans wrote about themselves in these literary texts at least roughly paralleled the words they spoke about themselves in communal settings. More important, the early periodical literature bulged with letters from the rank and file. Numbering in the thousands, many seemed woven from the threads of personal spiritual experience.

Interpreting these autobiographical texts involves two problems. The first is the relentlessly stylized, three-step sequence they reflected. The initial step explained the problems that drove converts to seek a life-transforming spiritual experience in the first place. The second detailed the event itself. (Normally this second step should have entailed analytically distinct components—conversion, sanctification, baptism—but converts usually blurred them all into one.) The third step elaborated the benefits received. This three-step pattern gives pause, since most converts penned their testimonies long after they had passed through the first two steps and were heartily enjoying the third. From that vantage point, they cast their words in a dramatic before-and-after framework in which the pentecostal experience marked a transition from darkness into light. We simply never find an admission that things might have been the same, let alone better, before the transition (except among apostates, whose countertestimonies were equally predictable). Conversion probably did mark an improvement in believers' lives, certainly in their own estimation, and probably in objectively verifiable ways too, but not as uniformly as they wanted others to believe. I am not suggesting that writers self-consciously fabricated, nor that editors deliberately distorted, their stories. But Peter I. Kaufman properly reminds us that autobiography involves an artful arrangement of the narrative to make things come out right.[1] The present task is to accept that reality and try to correct for it.

The second interpretive problem is that the texts before us have been shorn of their real-life context. We know nothing of the nods of affirmation that hastened the tempo or the yawns that impeded it. And we know nothing of the gestures that added nuances of meaning as the words tumbled forth. "Christians are shouting, devils howling, and hypocrites growling," thundered one convert.[2] "Let us saw off our shot guns, shorten our sermons, and we will do the devil more damage," barked another.[3] If this is the part that remains, how much richer was the original? Still, common sense suggests that with a bit of empathy we should be able to restore at least some of the human and material context that those literary traces imply.

Multiple Lives, Multiple Journeys

Many, perhaps most, spiritual memoirs began by referring to years of intense yearning for an "enduement of power." The exact meaning of that ubiquitous phrase varied. For some it meant the ability to perform apostolic miracles of healing and exorcism, for others the ability to witness for Christ with extrahuman boldness and effectiveness. Given the radical evangelical air most converts still breathed, neither goal was particularly surprising. What is surprising is the large number who admitted starting out with no clear idea of what they were looking for—except a spiritual experience deeper or fuller or more palpable than anything they had known.[4] If the exact content of the goal remained murky, the path for reaching it often seemed even more murky. The testimonies painted a consistent picture of struggle. The English vicar A. A. Boddy, for example, had sought spiritual boldness for years. In 1904 he traveled from his home in Sunderland to Wales where he heard that radical evangelical fires were burning—but left as cold as he came. He then sailed 1,500 miles to Norway where he heard that pentecostal fires were burning—yet again left unfulfilled. Boddy eventually received the baptism back home in Sunderland, but not without a major expenditure of time, effort, and money.[5] C. H. Mason, founder of the Church of God in Christ, reported a similar struggle. A husband for only a few months, Mason journeyed from Memphis to the Azusa Mission in Los Angeles where, he declared, "I want[ed] the baptism so bad that I did not know what to do."[6] A list of such examples could be extended at length. But these two, drawn from dramatically different traditions and social locations, show that the road from darkness into light was strewn with boulders. At least in memory.

If a growing desire for an enduement of power, whatever the cost, formed the deep background of most baptism accounts, what formed the proximate background? Differently stated, what factors precipitated the decision to go ahead and act? Some enthusiasts insisted that nothing triggered their move except a free, rational decision to embrace the truth. But most memoirs disclosed a more complex process. Both positive and negative influences came into play. By far the most frequently mentioned positive influence was an agreeable relationship with pentecostal friends and relatives.[7] Again and again saints said they converted because others whom they trusted or loved had done so.[8] Negative influences seemed more diverse. Some spoke of financial and occupational reverses. Others recalled painful experiences at home. Fire-Baptized leader B. H. Irwin traced a recognizable trajectory when he said that he accepted the pentecostal message just after his young daughter's death.[9] Still others seemed unable to pinpoint any one factor but found life chronically disappointing. Agnes Ozman, reputedly the first person to receive baptism with tongues, offered a classic example. "At times," she wrote, "I longed for the Holy Spirit to come in more than for my necessary food and at night a desire was felt more than for sleep and I know it was the Lord."[10] At that point Ozman was thirty, unmarried, unsettled, drifting from one experimental community to another. The pentecostal experience provided a desperately needed mooring—at least for a while, for Ozman, like others, apparently wandered in and out of the movement for years before making a firm commitment.[11]

At this point a brief digression may be helpful. Testimonies of this sort—detailing what might be called compensation conversions—abound. However, lest we too quickly categorize such conversions as reflex reactions to life crises, two points should be remembered. First, the compensation model likely says more about the observer than the observed. It simply never occurred to adherents to interpret their new allegiance as reparation for the loss of something else. They invariably construed the disappointments that preceded conversion as God's way of arousing them from their hell-bent smugness. Second, compensation explanations ignore the obvious. Converts made a change in their lives when the prevailing answers seemed inadequate and more attractive ones presented themselves. Under the circumstances, adhering to the old would have required more explanation than embracing the new.[12]

Whatever the precipitating factors, the testimonies show that the pilgrim almost always faced one final test—the Terrible Test, we might call it—before plunging. The Terrible Test took various forms. Some recalled acute fear of financial loss. Successful pastors worried that if they cast their lot with the un-washed pentecostals they might lose their jobs. What then? "It was in the midst of winter," Chicago parson William H. Piper remembered. "I had a wife and six children to support, but no income and no bank account."[13] Then, too, many fretted about falling into a trap set by Satan. When Holy Ghost fires reached southern Illinois, evangelist Carl O'Guin recollected, he fought it because he had heard that pentecostals "mesmerized" people.[14] J. H. King's problem was more intellectual. By his own admission this seri-ous-minded leader of the Pentecostal Holiness Church had fallen into rank fanaticism back in the 1890s—and "suffered awful agonies in getting out from [that] satanic snare." Determined not to make the same mistake twice, King admitted that he resisted the pentecostal message until careful study of the Scripture eventually persuaded him of its truth.[15] And then there was the will, the ever-prideful will, always determined to go its own way. C. Beruldsen of Edinburgh, Scotland, revealed the insidious ways that the will could deceive. Beruldsen resisted a divine call to accept tongues. Shortly afterward an evil hindrance in the form of a young lady rose and left the room. At last, Beruldsen felt freed of her self-protecting pride. "When the door closed my tongue loosened and I spoke in New Tongues for about two hours."[16] We do not know the outcome of the story, but it was not the first time in the history of Christian testimony literature that the devil had come to town as pride.

"Faith measured in tears" is the way one historian describes Elizabethan pi-ety.[17] He might well have said the same about early pentecostals. Even after the Terrible Test had been passed, baptism with tongues often did not come easily or quickly. The memoirs suggest that thousands "tarried" for days, weeks, even years. Frank Ewart, a Baptist pastor from Australia, probably re-flected the norm when he said that he sought the experience for twenty-one days with "insatiable hunger."[18] For some the ordeal bordered on despera-tion.[19]

Yet the testimonies never ended there, at least not the ones that survive in print. When we turn the page we invariably find that the yearning for the sweet taste of divinity, as Jonathan Edwards put it, found extravagant satisfac-tion at the pentecostal altar rail.[20] If the price of seeking Holy Spirit baptism proved high, the payoff proved immeasurably higher, and in ways both spiri-tual and mundane.

Spiritual Rewards

Assurance of salvation came first, both logically and experientially. Pentecos-tals' radical evangelical parents had said that the best evidence of divine favor was a renewed heart freed of self-love. The children found that answer too flimsy. They needed proof, hard palpable proof, of their right standing before God—and tongues met that need with lapidary precision. One North Carolina convert spoke for most when he declared that in the pentecostal revival he had found a "know-so salvation, not a reckon so, hope so, think so, guess so, may be so, nor anything of the kind."[21] Admittedly, boastful notes occasionally marred the chorus, and should not be discounted. A Baptist divine was drawn in when he heard that pentecost had everything else in the religious world "backed clean off the map."[22] But in their better moments, at least, converts sounded a gentler note. Holy Spirit baptism offered wondrous evidence that the Lord had saved, sanctified, and filled them with His blessed Holy Spirit.

Spiritual power (the much-desired "enduement of power") followed assurance. Spiritual power referred to leverage over the forces of Satan, never to clout in secular affairs. A writer for the Azusa *Apostolic Faith* put the matter plainly: the full Gospel gives "power to heal our bodies, and . . . power to raise us from the dead."[23] Partisans intended both points literally, as the thousands of references to miraculous physical healings and scores of references to resurrections from the dead in the early literature attested.[24] The ability to bring lost souls to faith in Christ was promised too. A British monthly aptly titled *Flames of Fire* spoke for all: "With this 'Fire' cold dead congregations will be galvanized." Ministers will know the "thrill of power . . . The universal chorus [is] 'we need power.'"[25]

Chest-thumping declarations of that sort assumed a more nuanced character in the context of actual lives. The joint testimony of Africa missionaries Samuel J. and Ardella Mead proved as typical as it was illuminating. The Meads had served as Methodist missionaries in Africa since 1885, operating primarily as school teachers and farmers. By all external measures of such things they had enjoyed a successful ministry. Their bishop, William Taylor, lionized them in *The Flaming Torch in Darkest Africa* (1898) as model servants of the Lord. And by internal measures too their ministry seemed successful. In 1906 Samuel wrote that both he and his wife had been justified, sanctified, anointed, and the "joy of heaven" filled their souls. Yet they felt an acute "lack of power" in their lives. The Meads returned to the United States in 1904. What they did next is not known, but in the fall of 1906 they heard about the Azusa Mission in Los Angeles, traveled there, and received the coveted baptism experience.[26] They also claimed to recognize numerous African dialects in the mission's ecstatic worship.[27] The couple sailed back to Africa in January. The last known trace of their lives beamed brightly in a communique posted from Caconda, Benguella, in the spring of 1907. "There is a goodness in God's mercy like the wideness of the sea," they wrote, slightly changing the words of a beloved hymn.[28] For the Meads, as for countless others, spiritual power equaled the fullness of the Gospel.

It is important not to sentimentalize these testimonies. Many of the old problems persisted. The letters—thousands of letters—sent by men and women who left no trace of themselves except their names suggested the intractability of the problems they faced. "I am so lonely," wrote Mattie Mason. "I have no one to talk to me about . . . the baptism with the Holy Ghost and I am the only one here."[29] "[T]he devil is going to kill me," Reanie Hancock feared.[30] Lilah Peppers grimly acknowledged that she had nearly succumbed to "temptations, doubts, fears, and trials."[31] And if little children felt heavy in the hand, grown ones lay heavy on the heart. "Please pray for my son who is in France that he may come home safely," pleaded one Mrs. E. M. T. Away in the army, "R. B.'s" son had not written for some time. "[Pray] that he will give his heart to God, and that I may soon hear from him."[32] Already there were memories of better days gone by. By 1918 Brother Pittman was thinking back to the "good old camp meeting times of ten years ago . . . when there were about thirty or forty hungry souls praying through to God."[33] Old habits, including old habits of spiritual inertia, died hard.

But if the former problems persisted, the revival provided powerful resources for coping with them. The patterns that Russell E. Richey discerned in the testimonies of early American Methodists reappeared among early pentecostals: the essential equality of persons before God, the availability of grace for all, the responsibility they bore for one another in the unity of this new community, the love that brothers and sisters in the faith accorded one another regardless of status.[34] "I've crossed over Jordan to Canaan's fair land, And this is like heaven to me."[35] So ran one of the choruses, worn smooth by use.

Rewards More Mundane

The thick piety of the rhetoric sometimes prevents us from seeing clearly what converts themselves always knew: that the pentecostal experience made daily life better. One of the more surprising features of the testimonies is how often they described Holy Ghost baptism as physically invigorating. "[N]ew blood pulsated through my veins like a mountain stream," exulted a pastor from Australia.[36] So too the wealthy and rather tony Carrie Judd Montgomery found that the "quickening life of the Holy Spirit" energized her body after a "very busy day."[37] Such physical benefits extended to plain folk too. Da-

— would like more attention to us + arts — —
did no one ever leave the movement?

vid Faulkner lamented that for nearly all of his ninety-nine years he had been a Baptist (a *mere* Baptist he almost seems to have said), but when the Lord saved him he "felt about like a boy sixteen years old."[38]

Descriptions of physical invigoration readily shaded into descriptions of physical pleasure. Unlike later generations, which proved squeamish about such matters, the first generation was remarkably frank about the agreeableness of the sensations that sometimes accompanied the baptism experience. Different ones spoke of "agony . . . so pleasant,"[39] or of "ecstatic rapture,"[40] or "at times he thrilled us as by an electrical surcharging."[41] Metaphors that suggested a feeling of being overwhelming by a divine power, with connotations of bliss, appeared often. For example, one Harriet Gravelle of London, Ontario, remembered the night that a fire—a real flame—entered her window and filled her soul with warmth and joy. Later Gravelle saw stripes of fire and the Holy Spirit as a dove descending upon her. "The fire went through me," she exulted, "the Spirit of the Lord filled my tabernacle."[42] It is hard to know how to interpret such accounts. On one hand in many cases the baptism experience undoubtedly felt pleasing to the senses. On the other hand the English language offers only a limited repertoire of words for expressing acute enjoyment of any sort, so it is not surprising that enthusiasts periodically used a vocabulary of physical delight to denote religious ecstasy.

The testimonies described more ordinary rewards too. Many spoke of clearing up old debts. Whether Holy Ghost saints were any more or less inclined to pay their bills than others is impossible to say. But the evidence certainly suggests that the baptism experience and subsequent integration into an ethically rigorous community led to heightened financial responsibility.[43] Indeed, several of the sects organized in the heat of the revival included a plank about financial restitution in their statements of faith.[44] Memoirs detailed other forms of restitution as well, including patching things up with one's mother-in-law.[45] Many ran painfully true to life. Some souls discovered that the baptism made defiant teenagers tolerable and irascible spouses lovable—though it was never clear whether the change took place in the family member or in the beholder.[46]

The pentecostal blessing could also bring about, for lack of better terms, a focusing of the personality. Healing evangelist John G. Lake told a down-home story that represented many. An Indianapolis man, while tarrying at the altar of a pentecostal mission in that city, fell victim to a demon that drove him insane. The man ended up in an asylum, leaving his family destitute. Lake wrote, "[I put] my hands on his head and rebuked, bound, and cast the devil out. He was instantly delivered." Three days later the asylum discharged the patient who went home and returned to work at a grain elevator.[47] Even allowing for some stylization in the account, the baptism experience surely helped this hapless soul clarify his sense of direction. Though converts sometimes acknowledged a temporary loss of interest in workaday affairs, on balance the experience provided means for doing what needed to be done.

Hundreds spoke of deliverance from debilitating addictions, including alcohol, tobacco, morphine, and swearing. The testimony of F. C. Morton, a Church of God stalwart, proved more colorful than most but representative. Morton allowed that he had chewed for twenty-two years, smoked for eighteen, tried to "drink up all the whiskey and beer in town," and won a reputation for cussing. Morton's next sentence helps us grasp the appeal of the full gospel message: "[B]ut from the day God saved me, never did another oath come out of my mouth."[48] The four-line testimony of one Brother Lee, who visited the Azusa Mission in the fall of 1906, spoke volumes in another way. "It settles a man when he gets the baptism," Lee declared. "It gives you a sound mind. This salvation keeps me out of the saloons and jails and [the] red light district."[49] Lee's words boiled down to a simple admission: all of his previous affiliations had failed him. They had not provided the structure and discipline he needed to live successfully either as a Christian or as a productive member of society.[50]

Then too the baptism experience helped saints come to terms with the bitter pill of racism in their hearts. The experiences of Jonathan Perkins and of A. G. Osterberg proved revealing, albeit in different ways. At first Perkins, a white Methodist minister in Kansas, had recoiled from the pentecostals because, he said, they failed to keep blacks in their place. But then he converted to the movement in a predominantly black revival in Wichita in 1923. "I had to wade through a whole camp meeting of them when I got the Baptism," Perkins wrote. "God surely broke me over the wheel of my prejudice."[51] Osterberg, a young Swede with Baptist roots, recalled that the spring of 1906 found him serving a holiness church in Los Angeles. When three of his deacons decided to visit a household prayer meeting where pentecostal fires were burning, he chose to tag along. Yet somehow he had missed a key part of the story, for he did not know that the folk in the cottage were African Americans. When they arrived Osterberg was taken aback, thinking, "What kind of a mess are we getting into here?" But the Holy Spirit prevailed and the scales fell from his eyes. Osterberg came away convinced that his new "colored" friends were "upper class . . . very refined, and particularly humble."[52] Osterberg's testimony reflected a change less dramatic yet perhaps more culturally significant precisely because paternalism marched with manifest good will.

And finally, there was healing, not just the natural mending of the body as acknowledged by all Christian traditions, but pentecostal healing—the miraculous, inexplicable restoration of bones broken and organs ravaged. From first to last, divine healing remained central to the movement's self-understanding. One enthusiast's description of a 1903 Galena, Kansas, revival revealed both the throbbing energy and the healing focus of a typical Holy Ghost meeting: "[A]ll about the tent were empty cots and wheelchairs, and numerous discarded canes and crutches were hung round about the tent, while those who had been delivered from using the same leaped and shouted and rejoiced."[53] In all parts of the country the story ran the same. The premier issue of *Apostolic Faith,* published in Los Angeles in 1906, overflowed with healing stories. The cover of the initial issue of *Latter Rain Evangel,* published in Chicago in 1908, declared that its aim was to proclaim the message of "Jesus the Redeemer, Jesus the Healer." The lead article of *Pentecost,* launched in Indianapolis in 1908, bore the headline: "Broken Arm Healed." In the mountains of eastern Tennessee the first issue of *Evening Light and Church of God Evangel* brimmed with narratives describing the Lord's assault on the "strongholds of the Devil," the cause of sickness.[54] For that matter many of the most prominent leaders, including Charles Fox Parham and Maria Woodworth-Etter, had earned their keep primarily as itinerant healing evangelists before joining the revival, and continued to do so long afterward.

First-generation healing testimonies tallied in the thousands. They detailed every conceivable form of restoration, ranging from runny noses dried up to dead bodies raised to life—and everything in between. Most were cast in the symbol-rich vocabulary of the New Testament (threes, sevens, and twelves predominated), but a surprising number resembled the straightforward prose of a medical report. For present purposes it suffices briefly to examine two examples, both drawn from the August 28, 1907 issue of *Apostolic Light,* an internationally circulated weekly published in Spokane, Washington, by pastor M. L. Ryan.[55] I have chosen these examples partly because they are typical and partly because they show, contrary to stereotype, that pentecostal fires burned brightly in the sparsely settled Pacific Northwest.

We begin with E. J. Page of 1020 Helena Street, Spokane, who won front-page coverage with his account of the Lord's protection and healing. A well digger by trade, Page had been seeking the "baptism of the Holy Ghost and fire" for about three months. One July day, twenty-six feet down, the well bucket broke loose and hit him. Though the bucket contained sixty pounds of curbing, Page went back to work unharmed. Eighty feet down the same thing happened, but Page was neither hurt nor frightened for he knew that God would take care of him. Minutes later, at ninety feet, several "large rocks" big enough to kill a man somehow broke free and came crashing down. Though Page suffered a "very sore head" for several weeks, no serious harm was done. He went home and asked God what the accidents meant. God promised to protect him. Elated, Page prepared to go to the Holy

Ghost meeting that night. To his great surprise he found that the Lord had healed his head enough that he could comb his hair over the sore spot. Sunday, August 6, Page not only received the "witness" of the Holy Spirit but spoke in multiple languages. Later that month the Lord healed him of the "stomach trouble" that had been plaguing him for seven years.[56]

Eula Wilson's resurrection from the dead did not warrant front-page coverage with E. J. Page's recovery—perhaps because it was not a local story—but her experience did win two columns on the inside. In the summer of 1907 Eula was a schoolgirl, almost blind in one eye, living with her mother at 1226 Cleveland, Wichita, Kansas. Eula told her own story. "I died a[t] eight o'clock Wednesday night. I was thoroughly conscious of an ascending motion and was borne to heaven in a white cloud attended by two [angels]." Eula's mother confirmed the account, adding that Eula gained consciousness at 2:00 A.M. Thursday but died again Friday night. At 10:00 P.M. Saturday she returned to life, "arose from the bed and walked across the room cured from all disease," her eyesight restored as well. Dr. A. O. Burton, Eula's physician, was not willing to say that she had literally died, but he did admit bafflement: "I never saw anything like it in my practice; I do not understand how she revived." Eula's neighbor, Mrs. C. E. Skelley, harbored no doubts whatsoever. "God performed a miracle," Skelley insisted. "I and others saw her die. We laid her out and prepared her for the grave. God sent her back to earth to spread his word and those who disbelieve are sitting in the seat of the scornful."[57] At this point Eula Wilson quietly disappeared from the historical record.

The granular details of these accounts—culled virtually at random among thousands of possibilities—reveal the mundane benefits, as well as the extramundane awesomeness, of the Holy Spirit-filled existence. If tongues defined the movement, healing gave it life.

And then there was joy—not necessarily happiness, a passing emotion—but joy, the quiet, deep-seated conviction that one's life made sense. Stalwarts described the satisfaction they experienced in the revival in various ways. Some exhibited thoughtful analysis. Texas attorney W. F. Carothers said that the movement gave him deep insight into the things of God, precious fellowship, and rigorous ethical expectations to help structure his personal life.[58] If Carothers spoke for the cautious intellectuals of the pentecostal world, Amanda Smith (probably not the famous black evangelist of that name) spoke for the exuberant activists: "This blessed way never gets old; always new and juicy, never dry. Hallelujah!"[59] Joy transcended social location as readily as personal disposition. Matriarch Elizabeth V. Baker, as well fixed as any, came away from her own Elim Faith Home meeting feeling that "one could hardly tell whether one was in the body or out for the melting sweetness and the unspeakable joy that filled our hearts."[60] Age seemed to make no difference either. When the *Pentecostal Holiness Advocate* was founded in 1917, young Walter Brack, all of eighteen, breathlessly wrote in to declare that after "enjoying salvation" nearly three years, he still possessed the "old time Holy Ghost religion"—and expected to "stand true till Jesus comes."[61] However experienced, the fundamental mood of the revival found timeless expression in the words of A. D. Bayer: "[T]he love is still burning in my heart . . . How good the Lord has been to me."[62]

Such examples tumble forth from the primary accounts by the hundreds, indeed by the thousands. The songs expressed it best of all.

> It is joy unspeakable and full of glory,
> Full of glory, full of glory;
> It is joy unspeakable and full of glory,
> Oh, the half has never yet been told.[63]

If primitivist premises fostered pragmatic results, one of the most enduring surely proved to be the sheer delight saints found in the revival's life. "You have endured your religion long enough, now begin to enjoy it," declared San Antonio pastor L. C. Hall.[64] He spoke for a generation.

Forms of Identity

Pentecostal testimonies described a long spiritual pilgrimage, one that typically began in the deep recesses of the divine holiness but somehow ended up smiling and stretching broadly in the warm sunlight of modern life. Those testimonies served at least three very practical functions.

First, they strengthened personal identity by narrating God's wondrous handiwork in individual lives. In 1918 young Ralph M. Riggs had just graduated from the Rochester Bible Institute, commonly known as Elim. In time Riggs would become general superintendent of the Assemblies of God, but in 1918 he was an untested stripling preparing for a ten-year stint as a missionary in South Africa. Reflecting on his years at Elim, Riggs said their value lay less in the intellectual training he had received than in the discovery he could be released from the "narrow confines" of his own mind. What he learned was not how to prepare himself for the Lord's work, but how to "open up" so that the Lord could work through him.[65] Convinced that his will had been melted down and then refashioned to serve as a hardened instrument in the Almighty's hands, Riggs, like others of his generation, steeled himself for herculean feats of spiritual conquest.

Second, the testimony strengthened collective identity by sealing the link between the individual and the group. Once spoken in public, or disseminated in print, the testimony helped to dispel any remaining ambivalence the convert might have felt about the decision to join. Just as important, it helped to dispel any remaining ambivalence the group might have harbored about its decision to receive the new member into its ranks. At the same time, the testimony raised the cost of defection by making the commitment public. It amplified one person's triumphs by making them everyone's triumphs. Speakers rarely spoke of failures, either their own or their group's, but when they did, the failure was mitigated because it was shared.

Finally and most important, the testimony clothed individual lives with timeless significance. No one wanted to believe that their own life bore no meaning larger than itself. The testimony forcefully asserted that the believer's passage on this earth formed part of a magnificent drama in which cosmic good vanquished cosmic evil. One anonymous devotee attending an Apostolic Faith convocation near Baxter Springs, Kansas, in 1916, spoke for thousands: "In streams of living fire the Word of God fell . . . like as at Sinai . . . [A]lready a Heaven-born soldiery are treading their way to the various battlefields to spread the flames."[66] Though the folk who journeyed to that little mining town in southeastern Kansas in the winter of 1916 might have looked like farmers and washer women and postal clerks, they really were not. They formed a heaven-born soldiery, linked in a continuous line with those who had waited at the base of Mount Sinai to receive the Word of the living God. Believers' incessant talk of skirmishes and sieges and bloodied warriors of the faith erased the boundary between the petty realities of the present and the ultimate realities of the eternal. Each person's private struggles somehow soared above the merely private and reappeared in a framework that spanned the millennia.

Such talk was heady stuff. If it fueled pentecostals' eagerness to do important things for the Lord, it also fueled their ability to do important things for themselves.

— did no one ever unconvert? what did they say about it?

4

Authority

Pentecostals' daily lives unfolded within a coherent set of assumptions about the sources of authority. This is not to say of course that everyone manifested the same level of self-consciousness about such matters. But if an outsider had asked what they thought about authority—where it came from and how it worked—virtually all converts would have said that legitimate authority rested finally in the Bible, in the doctrines the Bible contained, and in the Holy Spirit's direct communication of biblical and doctrinal truths. The key point here is that all three sources of authority—Bible, doctrine, and Holy Spirit—served as interlocking components in a single mechanism not subject to historical change. Even so, saints invariably modified their formal convictions about authority in the face of daily experience. To them those acts never amounted to much—just a minor concession to common sense, they would have said. But viewed from afar, we can see that their tinkering produced major results, for it kept the mechanism in balance, like the flywheel of a finely tuned engine.

The Bible

In the beginning was the Word. Assemblies of God leaders articulated that point with succinct force at their organizing meeting in 1914. The event's purpose, they said, was "to recognize Scriptural methods and order for worship, unity, fellowship, work and business for God, and to disapprove of all unscriptural methods, doctrines and conduct."[1] Pentecostal writers often used carpentry metaphors (also favored by Masons) to reenforce the notion that the Bible came first. All private visions or inspirations by the Holy Spirit, they said, must be "plumb-lined by the Word," placed on the "square of God's Word."[2] With that premise firmly in place, the rest followed naturally.

For one thing, the Bible contained all the information one needed to know in order to navigate life's tough decisions. We might call this idea the principle of plenary relevance. Whenever serious questions about God's purpose for humans arose, the obvious recourse was to open the Book and "see what

God Himself says on this subject."[3] Pentecostal Quaker Levi Lupton illustrated the trait well. When a follower asked if a Christian might wear jewelry, Lupton responded that there was "but one way" to find out: check the "Christian Dictionary."[4] If readers wanted the Bible to function as a real dictionary, it had to be accepted entirely, not selectively, as if it were true in some places and not in others. One leader warned that a believer could not accept the Bible "in spots" and hope to keep Holy Ghost baptism.[5] Another darkly noted that there was "just as much condemnation for taking from God's word as there [was] for adding to [it]."[6] Azusa pioneer William J. Seymour said it concisely: "[S]tay within the lids of God's word."[7] In a score of ways, then, the early literature revealed the breadth and depth of the conviction that the Bible offered a compendium of answers for all significant questions. It needed only to be read, believed, and obeyed.[8]

The principle of plenary relevance helps explain why, throughout the first decade of the movement's life, virtually all pentecostal educational programs used the Bible as the sole textbook.[9] It also helps explain why until mid-century most Holy Ghost schools were called Bible Institutes. Adherents proudly noted that the full gospel message had first emerged in a school in Topeka, Kansas, where no book except the Bible—the King James Authorized Version to be precise—had been used. Their motive for making the Bible the main if not the sole source of reading was neither intellectual narrowness nor cultural parochialism, though that may have been the effect. Rather they simply felt certain that no other resource of significant information existed. *Tongues of Fire,* the organ of the Holy Ghost and Us Bible School in Maine, belied its seemingly antinomian orientation by making clear to all observers that it stood for the "*Word of God in its entirety and that without adulteration.*"[10] If looking to other texts invited error, why do it?

The importance of Scripture as the first and final authority can be seen in pentecostals' pervasive restorationism. Latter rain folk determined to make the Bible in general and Acts in particular the blueprint for the modern church. If God had expressed His will with clarity in the apostolic age, and if God had not changed, then twentieth-century Christians were obliged to fashion their own lives according to that blueprint. "[T]here was not one gospel for the apostles and early church and another for us," wrote ex-Presbyterian minister Joseph Hutchinson. "[T]he same gifts and powers [are] still in the church."[11] Hutchinson spoke for many. One said that the movement's only aim was to see the "book of Acts re-enacted,"[12] another that they sought to restore the apostolic faith in "every way,"[13] still another that the pentecostal revival was "completing the circle" of history.[14] Saints sang their restorationist convictions, both literally and figuratively. "Spiritual signs follow saints of God," ran the words of one popular tune, "Who in apostolic footsteps trod."[15] When converts were asked what they believed, said a reporter visiting the Union Holiness Mission in New York City in 1906, they quoted St. Paul: "The faith once delivered to the saints."[16]

Pentecostals' restorationism represented more than a merely rational effort to mine the Good Book for blueprints. They yearned physically to enter the apostolic world, to breathe its air, feel its life, see its signs and wonders with their own eyes. So they gave biblical names to their meeting houses and to the streets in their retreat grounds.[17] All across the country stalwarts evangelized from Gospel Cars.[18] Visitors to Shiloh were picked up in a Gospel Carriage and pulled back to the compound by white steeds named Grace and Glory.[19] When Church of God leader A. J. Tomlinson was baptized in water, he heard a voice saying, as Jesus did, "This is my beloved son, in whom I am well pleased."[20] Zealots commonly described their experiences in terms of threes, sevens, twelves, and forties. Summer encampments lasted forty days,[21] converts "came through" in groups of forty.[22] Zion Faith Home leader Martha Wing Robinson underwent her most memorable spiritual experience on her thirty-third birthday, following three days and nights of continual prayer, at which time the Holy Spirit spoke three words through her lips.[23] While sitting in his missionary bungalow in India, Brother Schoonmaker heard a "mighty rushing wind." Hurrying out to locate the source, he discovered, not surprisingly, a nearby church with "twelve people praying under the spirit and soon three were talking in tongues."[24]

Though a list of such examples could be extended at length, it may be more useful to spend a moment or two with founder Charles Parham, who honed numerological restorationism into a high art. When Parham sketched the initial falling of divine power at his Kansas Bible school, which enrolled forty students, he wrote that he had received Holy Spirit baptism three days after his student Agnes Ozman first received it, in an upper room of the school, in the midst of twelve ministers also seeking the experience. When Ozman felt the baptism, a halo surrounded her head, while biblical "tongues of fire" danced above the heads of the twelve ministers. Parham reported that Ozman had been unable to speak in English for three days.[25] When Parham sought the baptism experience for himself the next day, he waited on the Lord from 9:00 A.M. until 3:00 P.M.—the very hours Christ had "spent on the cross."[26] To be sure, these events fell 1,900 years and many thousands of miles outside the New Testament world. But that fact did not bother pentecostals a bit, for they construed their own lives as transparent appropriations of the New Testament pattern.

Interpreting the Bible

Saints vested ultimate authority in the Bible because they knew exactly how the Bible came into existence. In brief, great men of old heard God's words and wrote them down. Scripture thus embodied God's thoughts, pure and simple. The Anglican convert A. A. Boddy said it as succinctly as any one: the Holy Spirit "dictated the whole Bible."[27] That simple but momentous fact meant that the Old and New Testaments addressed the historical setting in which they were written but they were not influenced by that setting in any substantial way. The same point held for the Bible's clear messages: they were exempted from the taint of time and place. When Professor D. Wesley Myland of the Gibeah Bible School in Plainfield, Indiana, offered a series of arcane lectures on the origin and destiny of the human race at Chicago's Stone Church, the pastor, William H. Piper, ponderously observed: "No man could have *thought* these lectures out; they bear the imprint of heaven's teaching."[28] Such assumptions set the tone for decades. One third-generation pentecostal (who eventually earned a Ph.D. in biblical studies at Harvard) remembered that he had grown up in the tradition believing that the Bible had "dropped from heaven as a sacred meteor."[29]

This assumption—what we might call the "sacred meteor" theory of biblical origins—fostered an abiding conviction that the Bible had been preserved from errors of any sort—historical, scientific, or theological. Granted, the earliest statements of faith normally spoke of Scripture's reliability as the "all-sufficient rule for faith and practice," not factual accuracy.[30] The crucial question therefore is what the absence of explicit discussion about the Bible's perfection really meant. Did it mean that early pentecostals harbored doubts about the Bible's plenary accuracy? Or did it mean that they presupposed it so completely it never occurred to them to raise the question?

The evidence, taken in context, strongly suggests the latter explanation. First-generation leaders did not know much about the intricacies of biblical higher criticism, nor modern theories of biblical inspiration, but they knew enough to rebuke them all. "I believe in the plenary inspiration of the Scriptures," trumpeted B. H. Irwin, founder of the Fire-Baptized Holiness Church. "I detest and despise . . . this higher criticism, rationalism, and this seeking on the part of ungodly professors to do away with objectionable parts of the Word of God, and as fire-baptized people we stand on the whole Book, hallelujah!"[31] Worldly men might consider the Bible a "fairy tale," wrote D. W. Kerr, one of the better educated leaders, but Holy Spirit-filled believers knew the truth: "Holy men . . . wrote as they were moved by the Holy Ghost . . . The Word of God [contains] the truth, the whole truth, and nothing but the truth."[32] One Church of God writer summed things up as crisply as the language permitted: "[The Bible's] precepts are binding, its histories are true, and its decisions are immutable."[33]

This point brings us to the role of literalism. If God's word tumbled from His hand without taint of error, then it should be read as literally as reasonably possible. To outsiders, of course, pentecostals' rendering of Scripture appeared anything but literal. Their ability to divine the most intricate details of contemporary European history in Daniel,[34] airplanes in Isaiah,[35] automobiles in Nehemiah,[36] and the operating rules of the Russian navy in Revelation[37] seemed preposterous at best. But saints themselves thought they were reading—not interpreting, but simply reading—the Holy Book strictly literally. Scriptures should be taken "just as they are written," said one Azusa *Apostolic Faith* commenter.[38] The Portland *Apostolic Faith* echoed that view: "You absolutely lose your own judgment in regard to the Word of God. You eat it down without trimming or cutting, right from the mouth of God."[39] One pentecostal faction insisted that the New Testament did not sanction the use of real wine at the Lord's Supper because the text did not specify fermented drink. An opposing faction argued the opposite because the text did not specify unfermented drink.[40]

Rigorous literalism—hard and unforgiving—served as an ethic for daily life. The perennial problem of divorce and remarriage offers a case in point. The leaders of the Pacific Coast Apostolic Faith Mission initially allowed those who were divorced and remarried to preach with the Mission's endorsement if those events had taken place before they became Christians. "But after searching the Scriptures," they explained, "we found it was wrong . . . We found no scripture where the preacher could be engaged in this blessed Gospel ministry with two living companions."[41] The same attitude governed speculations about the future. "Divine predictions regarding the course and end of this age," asserted a San Francisco pastor, will be fulfilled with a "literalness that is at once hopeful and alarming."[42] Strict honesty allowed no conclusion except the plain meaning of Scripture: the United States itself would soon be attacked and defeated by a reunited Roman Empire. The Christian's allegiance was to God's Word, not to personal whims or patriotic desires.[43] The practice of handling poisonous snakes, drinking poison, and holding hot coals, which persisted for many years among pentecostal groups in the southern Appalachians, stemmed from a similarly straightforward reading of Mark 16:18.[44]

The conviction that tongues always accompanied Holy Spirit baptism, which quickly became the movement's hallmark, likewise grew from a forthright reading of the New Testament, in this case Acts 2:4, 10:44–46, and 19:1–7. In those passages the Holy Spirit and tongues seemed linked, and that was good enough for pentecostals. In the first sustained text of pentecostal theology, George Floyd Taylor urged his readers not to get "hung up" just because stalwarts like Charles G. Finney, Jonathan Edwards, and Hudson Taylor had never professed to speak in tongues. They were "great and good men," he allowed, "but unless they had the Bible evidence of Pentecost, we can not Scripturally say that they had the Baptism of the Holy Ghost."[45] After sixteen allegedly unsuccessful years as a missionary in China, W. W. Simpson's life and ministry seemed to turn around when he decided to accept the "Word of God at its simple face value" and seek baptism with tongues.[46]

How did apostolics come to think this way? What cultural factors prompted them to suppose that "theory is no good" because "the Bible is self-explanatory,"[47] or that understanding God's Word required only a "clean heart, a surrendered will and an open mind,"[48] or that it was possible to grasp Scripture "entirely unbiased . . . by preconceived notions or interpretations"?[49] In short, how did pentecostals move from the assumption that the Bible was wholly truthful to the dramatically different assumption that the Bible should be read literally—which was to say, without any special preparation or interpretive principles?

Situations varied. Most converts undoubtedly simply presupposed that truthfulness required literalism. That equation hung low in the radical evangelical air they breathed. For those who thought about the matter a bit more, however, two rationales emerged. The first was moral: a literal reading of Scripture implied a humble willingness to bend before the plain meaning of God's own words.[50] The second was intellectual: since God's rules for the world were clear, God's Book must be equally clear. Literalism produced clarity, allegorism produced confusion.[51] Though few saints seemed to realize it, this notion—or tissue of closely related notions—had a name and a history. Philosophers and theologians called it common sense realism (often, just realism). It emerged from universities in Scotland in the eighteenth century, overran American colleges in the early nineteenth century, and spread widely among ordinary evangelical Protestants in many parts of the United States in the late nineteenth century.[52] Beloved radical evangelical writers like W. D. Godbey and Reuben Torrey mediated realist assumptions to pentecostals. Torrey's influential 1898 *What the Bible Teaches* made the point plainly: "The method of the book is rigidly inductive . . . Exactness of statement is first aimed at in every instance, then clearness of statement. Beauty and impressiveness must always yield to precision and clearness."[53] Therefore, except in rare and explicitly stated instances of allegorization, the Bible's words served as transparent conveyers of meaning. Founder Charles Parham spoke for most when he declared that "there are a thousand contradictions, if you read the Scriptures thru the creed's spectacles, but cleansed by the blood from false doctrines and traditions . . . the Bible stands out clear and bold, without a possible contradiction."[54] The biblical writers said what they meant and meant what they said.

One final matter merits attention when thinking about the role of literalism in pentecostal culture. Saints did not produce much of a systematic theology until the 1950s or later. Undoubtedly several factors discouraged partisans from such endeavors, including the general absence of seminary training and lack of rewards for investing one's time that way. Still, the principal reason was the supposition that the Bible's words explained themselves. All they needed was a good set of eyes, an open mind, and a willing heart.

Doctrine

If the Bible tumbled down from outside time and space, and if it taught only truth, and if it was supposed to be read literally, then it followed that the Bible's teachings should be articulated carefully and defended vigorously. True Christianity began not in the froth of exuberant emotion but in the bedrock of correct thinking. The priority that zealots placed on getting things straight, doctrinally straight, can be seen in numerous ways.

Consider periodical titles. The great majority bore names that captured the movement's key ideas. *Apostolic Faith* was the favorite, topping the masthead of at least five of the earliest publications. Other favorites included *Apostolic Witness, Glad Tidings, Latter Rain Evangel, Midnight Cry,* and *Pentecostal Testimony.* All of these titles heralded a point of doctrine. Important periodicals bearing a purely devotional notion, such as *Trust,* proved few and far between (and in actual practice *Trust* proved as insistently doctrinal as any). Still more revealing for present purposes are the titles that affirmed the priority of the word *truth.* One thinks, for example, of *Apostolic Truth, Blessed Truth, Gospel Truth, Grace and Truth, Present Truth, Truth for the Times,* and *Whole Truth.* Even *Gold Tried in the Fire,* a devotionally oriented title if there ever was one, bore the revealing subtitle: *Holiness without Carnality Truth without Error,* as did *Tongues of Fire . . . The Ground of the Truth.*[55]

Labels spoke volumes. Truth Bible School, probably the first pentecostal Bible college in China, founded in Chihli in 1924, significantly chose a name that would highlight the accuracy of its beliefs.[56] A huge gilt-lettered sign reading "THE TRUTH" adorned the entrance to the Holy Ghost and Us Bible School in Durham, Maine. The premier issue of Seattle's *Midnight Cry* proclaimed that it would never publish a "particle of error; but only the truth, the whole truth and nothing but the truth."[57] At least three of the most prominent sects affixed a definite article in front of their official names: The Church of God, The Church of God of Prophecy, and The Apostolic Faith. Pentecostals repeatedly employed metaphors heralding the completeness of their message. That notion bore the connotation of spiritual fullness, to be sure, but it also suggested that they alone possessed the entire truth. In the 1890s the mostly black, holiness-oriented Churches of God in Christ called its periodical *Truth.* Its pentecostal offspring, the Church of God in Christ, significantly changed the name to *Whole Truth.* Zealots commonly called their meeting houses Full Gospel Assemblies or Full Gospel Tabernacles. The title was intentionally invidious: they preached the *full* gospel, while other traditions preached only a partial one. "We are the only people in the world that are prepared to carry a FULL GOSPEL," the *Church of God Evangel* crowed. "This statement may seem a little egotistical and selfish, but when the matter is simmered down to the cold facts it is too true to be sneered at."[58] The same logic led Aimee McPherson to dub the denomination she created the International Church of the Foursquare Gospel. Christian and Missionary Alliance founder A. B. Simpson had spoken of a four-fold gospel back in the 1890s, but it would take a pentecostal to change four-fold into four-square, denoting hermetic completeness as much as anything else.

The evidence for pentecostals' determination to exact goose-step conformity in matters of doctrine is so voluminous it is hard to understand how the contrary notion ever arose. We might well begin with William J. Seymour himself, to challenge the myth that the man with the big heart was casual about doctrinal regularity. Though Seymour could speak quite movingly about the importance of charity in the Christian life, his own Azusa Mission issued a formal creedal statement on the inside front page of the first issue of the Mission's paper, *Apostolic Faith*.[59] Shortly afterward the paper affirmed that all who honored the blood of Christ were brothers, yet warned: "[W]e are not willing to accept any errors, it matters not how charming and sweet they may seem to be."[60] The periodical reiterated the point time after time. Those who supposed that it was possible to be one in spirit without being one in doctrine were sadly mistaken. "Impure [d]octrine," Seymour insisted, equaled "spiritual fornication."[61] Other pentecostal writers followed *Apostolic Faith* in linking doctrinal irregularities with sexual license, among the gravest of sins. Elmer K. Fisher, head of the Upper Room Mission a few blocks down the street, shackled "false doctrine" with "spiritual adultery," solemnly warning that anyone so defiled would be driven out.[62]

The coercive attitudes that prevailed in the Los Angeles missions reigned elsewhere as well. Mrs. W. H. Finley, writing for Charles Parham's newspaper in Kansas, made the point as plainly as words permitted: "love is the soul and doctrine [is] the back-bone."[63] A leader of the Christian Workers Union near Boston asserted that the union would not put up with any "sickly, sentimental idea of a love and unity" if it meant any "sacrifice of truth."[64] Even George Floyd Taylor, a pioneer of the pentecostal message in the Southeast and widely regarded as one of the most thoughtful figures in the movement's early history, refused to make concessions for mistaken opinions, however sincerely held. Anyone who wanted to receive Holy Spirit baptism, he warned, would have to "lay aside any erroneous theory, no matter how long [he may] have believed or preached it."[65]

Unconventional beliefs invited instant rebuke. Without love one ranked as an inadequate brother, without correct doctrine one ranked as no brother at all. The large number of schisms between 1915 and 1935, which typically began as disputes over seemingly minor points of belief, suggested that pentecostal groups held little interest in compromise and none at all in theological pluralism.[66] The proper form of church government, the timing of sanctification, the proof of Holy Spirit baptism, the morality of seeking a physician, the possibility of universal salvation—all issues that most evangelicals considered more or less open for discussion—triggered lockouts, personal denunciations, and an iron-fisted determination always to speak one's mind, regardless of the human cost.

The evidence bulges with examples. Fights about the timing of the sanctification experience—did it coincide with or did it follow the conversion experience?—illustrate the point. In 1911 William H. Durham, who held the former view, found himself literally locked out of the Azusa Mission by his one-time friend William J. Seymour, who held the latter view.[67] Durham tangled with Charles Fox Parham on the same issue, but Parham did more than lock the door. He asked God to smite whoever was wrong, then boasted about it when Durham died six months later at thirty-nine.[68] At a 1913 Los Angeles camp meeting small-time evangelist J. C. Seibert discovered that big-time evangelist Maria Woodworth-Etter had come to accept Durham's view. Seibert judged that Woodworth-Etter had willfully associated herself with such "damnable doctrine" because she was "utterly deluded and believed a lie."[69] Animosity about the precise timing of the sanctification experience toxified the air for years. A decade later a difference of opinion on the matter prompted J. H. King, general superintendent of the Pentecostal Holiness Church, personally to order Aimee McPherson off the platform of one of the churches in his jurisdiction in Virginia.[70] Unflinching adherence to theological rectitude knew no political borders. In East London, Ontario, B. L. Fitzpatrick reported that a cottage discussion about the nature of the Godhead—a perennially and peculiarly intrapentecostal concern—led to an invitation to settle the issue "in . . . the back." At that juncture, said Fitzpatrick, "[a]nother man ran across the room and put his fist in my face."[71] The quest for regularity cut across ethnic lines too. "Truth is truth," thundered a leader of the interracial Pentecostal Assemblies of the World. "[I]t matters not who proclaims it."[72]

Pentecostal leaders sometimes worried about the effects of so much snarling over correct doctrine.[73] At one point the *Weekly Evangel* warned the faithful that its "Question and Answer" column was "run for the edification of our readers, not to be a prize ring to thrash out the fine points of doctrines and to split hairs over controverted points."[74] But split hairs they did. Frank

Bartleman, one of the most perceptive of the early insider historians (and something of a theological brawler himself) rued the ceaseless fighting, even at Azusa. "The doctrinal issue has also been a great battle," he lamented. "Many were too dogmatic at 'Azusa' . . . Much harm was done the work in the beginning by unwise zeal."[75] Nor was the problem limited to the Azusa Mission. By 1909, Bartleman reported, the other missions in the southern California area had grown "very zealous for doctrine, as usual . . . The missions had fought each other almost to a standstill. Little love remained."[76] In 1911 T. B. Barratt, a Norwegian Holy Ghost leader visiting new works in the United States, issued "An Urgent Plea for Charity and Unity." He was, he said, dismayed by the "sad spirit of division and separation which the enemy has introduced among earnest Pentecostal people in many centres."[77] The following year A. A. Boddy, an Anglican vicar visiting the Los Angeles missions, sadly noted that one wealthy and well-educated leader had stopped attending church altogether, apparently because he was miffed about some doctrinal irregularities. "The great trouble in this work," the good parson concluded, "seems to have been the severe condemnation of those who did not in all points see alike."[78] After three decades as head of the Pentecostal Holiness Church, J. H. King sadly confessed that "strife, contentions, divisions, judicial trials, and confusions" had brought him to the "point of almost complete helplessness."[79]

It might be supposed that what pentecostals did officially, as representatives of an institution, or as members of church, was one thing, while what they did unofficially, as friends and co-laborers in the Lord's vineyard, was another. Not so. Doctrinal differences soured personal friendships too. For years A. G. Garr and Frank Ewart had toiled together, pioneering the message in southern California. When Ewart, along with scores of pentecostal leaders, adopted the "New Truth" of God's Oneness just before World War I, Garr stuck with the traditional Trinitarian formulation. Though they continued to love one another, Ewart said, personal fellowship was no longer possible. "This [disagreement] caused the very painful parting between us," he lamented years later. Ewart looked forward to the time in heaven when they would "all see eye to eye, and doctrinal differences [would] never again intrude."[80] Ewart's manifest genuineness underscored the poignancy of the break. The wedge that drove these old friends apart for the remainder of their earthly lives was not a personal slur, not an unrequited debt, but a difference of opinion about the Godhead. Though pentecostals occasionally minimized the importance of doctrine, their behavior belied their words.

Still, not all of the brawling over correct doctrine stemmed from dogmatism or from a determination to enforce social conformity. Early pentecostals, as much as any group on the American landscape, desired to know the truth for its own sake and to chart their lives accordingly. The doctrinal struggles that many went through before joining—or finally deciding not to join—bespoke the integrity of their motivations. Many wedded the movement because they had come to *believe,* even unwillingly, that its theological claims were biblically irrefutable. Repeatedly we see men and women dragged in by their minds, as if against their wills. A surprising number recalled they had preached the truth of the pentecostal message, including the necessity of Holy Spirit baptism, for months and in some cases for years before they themselves had experienced tongues.[81] In other words, they embraced the message in their heads long before they felt the Holy Spirit stirring the chords in their throats.

J. H. King's pilgrimage illustrates the process. This particular soldier of the cross was well named, for he comes across as an autodidact of imposing standards. At the turn of the century King headed the Fire-Baptized Holiness Church (before it became pentecostal). As the leader of that sect King had long believed that the conversion and sanctification experiences must be followed by a third landmark event known as baptism with fire. Like everyone else in that tradition he also believed that supernatural signs and wonders typically accompanied baptism with fire. During a trip to Winnipeg in the fall of 1906 King picked up a copy of the Azusa *Apostolic Faith.* There he read about the California revival, which he deemed genuine. But he balked at the notion, preached at Azusa, that baptism with fire and baptism with the Holy Ghost were different things and that tongues always signified the latter. Yet King was hooked. A haunting suspicion that the Azusa stalwarts might be biblically correct drove him into an extended period of study with Bible commentaries in hand. Five months later he capitulated. "I was convinced against my will," he admitted.[82]

Things were not always so serious, however. Some partisans obviously loved to play with religious ideas for their own sake, almost as a hobby. The labyrinthine prolixity of Charles Parham's eschatological ponderings, or of A. S. Copley's biblical typologies, or of Andrew Urshan's ruminations on the Oneness of the deity, or of D. Wesley Myland's reconstructions of God's Plan of the Ages, or of George S. Brinkman's musings on the Ten Lost Tribes of Israel revealed worlds within worlds of complexity. Numbers proved especially fascinating for some. Working from the information supplied in Revelation 21:15, for instance, A. J. Tomlinson calculated that heaven contained 469,793,088,000,000,000,000 cubic feet—minus 124,198,272,000,000,000,000 cubic feet for the "dwelling places of the angels."[83] Though the British fundamentalist Ivan Panin was not pentecostal himself, saints liked to cite his numerological findings because they helped to prove that Scripture's veracity could be "scientifically demonstrated." Pentecostals proudly rehearsed Panin's discovery that the first seventeen verses of the New Testament contained: "49 words, or 7 sevens, of which 42, or 6 sevens, are nouns. Of the 42 nouns, 35, or 5 sevens, are proper nouns, and 7 are common nouns. Of the 35 proper names, 28, or 4 sevens, are male ancestors of Jesus, and 7 are not."[84] Sometimes such speculations grew so complicated they had to be graphed on paper just to keep it all straight.[85] There is no way to know how many ordinary folk invested their evenings in intellectually arcane pursuits, but the frequent appearance of such materials in the most widely circulated periodicals suggested that editors knew what subscribers wanted.

The goal then was precision—first, last, and always, precision. Authors rarely acknowledged, let alone took pleasure in, the possibility that language might bear multiple meanings. There was, in other words, no pentecostal version of the influential nineteenth-century Congregational pastor Horace Bushnell, who reveled in the polysemic possibilities of theological language. When in 1914 A. J. Tomlinson warned his mountain followers to remember that the "standard of truth is fixed and any deviation from that standard is error,"[86] he happened to be referring to New Testament polity. Yet that declaration revealed as much about his preference for conceptual exactness as for any particular form of church organization. I do not wish to overstate the point. Pentecostals never supposed that divine things were perfectly knowable. But they did suppose that all of the truly important points that human beings needed to know for their salvation could be stated in the same declarative, straightforward language one might use to order bolts at the dry goods store.

Holy Spirit

If ultimate authority rested on the hard rock of Scripture and the plain doctrines it contained, it also rested on the Holy Spirit's directives. For the pentecostal mind there was no point talking about a ranked order among the three. All represented co-existent and perfectly equal expressions of the same divine mind. The last, no less than the first two, conveyed the finality of Being itself, untouched by human contrivance.

The Holy Spirit communicated with believers in three distinct ways. The first, both rare and intriguing, materialized in extracanonical literary texts resembling the Book of Mormon in genre if not in content. One of the best known involved a set of booklets, variously called *Yellow Books, God's Newspapers,* or *Letters from Jesus,* written by zealots in the Chicago area about 1910. No copies have survived, but we know they existed because rival factions condemned them. These booklets, containing word-for-word transcriptions of supernatural revelations, apparently addressed mundane matters such as the reason for the sinking of the *Titanic* and not-so-mundane matters such as the location of angels.[87] Other extracanonical texts have survived. One was a devotional pamphlet cast in the orotund cadences of King James English, replete with "thees" and "thous" and "hearken untos."[88] As noted, the early records also contain numerous instances of grapholalia, illegible letters scribbled by the Holy Spirit using the hand of a baptized believer. Pentecostals believed that these letters were of divine origin and occasionally sought to translate them or have them translated by learned men or natal speakers of the language in which they were written.[89]

The second mode of direct Holy Spirit communication involved disclosures directly to believers' consciousness. For example Harvard graduate Nathan Harriman, a member of the quasi-pentecostal Shiloh community in Maine, urged disciples not to waste their time searching for a "'systematic theology'" but to seek to "*absorb* the Word through their spiritual pores."[90] Mystical or almost mystical transmissions of this sort assisted sound exegesis. E. N. Bell, first chairman of the Assemblies of God, urged his readers always to keep their "skylights open" for "any new light God may throw upon the old Word."[91] Bell meant what he said too. At one point new light on the Godhead prompted him nearly to jump ship and join the Oneness faction, which was threatening to split the infant sect down the middle. Thus the Holy Spirit transmitted ideas as pure and clear as sunlight directly into believers' minds, brightening the dark corners of Scripture and spotlighting verities long obscured by man-made creeds and traditions.

The interpretation of tongues constituted the third and most common means of direct Holy Spirit instruction. The practice quickly acquired a quasi-inspired status comparable, perhaps, to Ellen White's vision-inspired teachings among the Seventh-day Adventists. At this distance it is impossible to know how many adherents actually possessed the gift of interpretation. But if present experience can be taken as a guide, in any given meeting probably two or three sought to render their own or others' tongues messages in the vernacular in accord with 1 Corinthians 14. Moreover pastors undoubtedly nurtured the gift for themselves, for it served as an effective means for regulating the tempo and direction of the service.[92]

Interpretations of tongues messages normally took one of two forms. The more frequent one aimed simply to edify the hearers, typically warning against spiritual indifference and encouraging the faithful, for example, to plunge "into the depths of His power."[93] Most were couched in King James English, which bore the effect if not the intent of heightened solemnity.[94] The vacuousness of those utterances meant, of course, that they could be neither confirmed nor disconfirmed by empirical events. Indeed one zealot groused that he did not expect to attend any more camp meetings precisely because participants wasted too much time waiting for "mysterious revelations" and "vague and pointless messages."[95] The gift of interpretation, exercised in this hortatory mode, occupied a hazy borderland between noncognitive and cognitive forms of authority. Though straightforward declarative sentences were involved, they did not readily lend themselves to the practical language of everyday life.

The second, less common form of interpretation, invoked the Holy Spirit's guidance for the affairs of daily life. Communicating in this mode, the divine voice spoke in specific, down-to-earth ways. His advice specified where to lodge, when and where to travel, how to pack one's bags, where to find lost keys.[96] From time to time He would single out the right person to marry,[97] specify the corner where a meeting hall should be built,[98] or even make clear that the Lord wanted to be praised as pentecostals normally did, with "uplifted hands."[99] Bible school instructors encouraged both tongues and interpretations of tongues in their classrooms to confirm the veracity of their teaching.[100] Believers particularly coveted such supernatural validation when "deeper truth was unveiled."[101]

The Holy Spirit seemed usually to sanction what hearers wanted to hear, especially when troublemakers threatened to disrupt the smooth operation of plans well laid. For example when a group of workers gathered in Chicago in January 1914 to protest the formation of a Pentecostal Missionary Union, the divine voice made clear that He agreed with the protesters, not with their rivals.[102] That same month the Holy Spirit approved the organizational efforts of the young Church of God in the Tennessee mountains, assuring its assembled ministers: "I directed this thing. I'm at the back of it."[103] The planning meeting of the Assemblies of God, gathered in the face of intense grass-roots opposition, gratefully adjourned after hearing the Holy Spirit say, "I have guided in all this, and my approval rests upon it."[104] If saints worried about the perils of self-deception, they rarely let on.

Lest we assume too quickly, however, that the Holy Spirit always confirmed what believers wanted to hear, it should be remembered that the Third Person sometimes conveyed unwelcome news. For example in September 1906 the Azusa community learned that Los Angeles would soon suffer a devastating earthquake.[105] No one hinted that Christians would escape the devastation. That same month another Angeleno, Brother Thomas Mahler, received heavenly instructions to pack up and head for Africa as a missionary, where he would "suffer martyrdom." Remarkably, he obeyed, and as far as we know he lost his life on the mission field, exactly as predicted.[106] Brother

Mahler's story suggests that sometimes we need to pause and simply appreciate the integrity that unified these ordinary—and sometimes not so ordinary—lives.

Experience

Finally, daily practice taught its own lessons too. The "grave mistress of Experience," as Pilgrim governor William Bradford called it, provided early pentecostals another source of authority, a source more flexible and more workable than the otherworldly dictates of Scripture, doctrine, or Holy Spirit inspiration. It would be inaccurate to suggest that these earnest believers intentionally relativized, let alone historicized, the Holy Book or holy doctrine or the Holy Spirit in order to fit their own practical ends. But they did find ways to make those angular demands more responsive to mundane events.

For one thing, pentecostals instinctively acknowledged that sometimes they had to make small compromises today in order to achieve large aims tomorrow. Consider the way that the goal of effective evangelism subtly and sometimes not so subtly structured their daily behavior. The desire to win souls often induced saints to overlook ideological distinctions. So Maria Woodworth-Etter, the most prominent healing evangelist of the era, would boast that in her meetings she never permitted "any doctrinal points; no 'isms,' no antagonistic points to be aired . . . nothing but Christ."[107]

The same goal—effective evangelism—led enthusiasts to express their ideas in tracts, songbooks, newspapers, and devotional booklets, all being cheap, handy to use, and easy to memorize. If lengthy creeds, catechisms, and multivolume works of systematic theology proved ineffective for their supposed purposes, why use them? Pentecostals sensed that effective evangelism required concise statements of faith.[108] At the same time, when Holy Ghost folk felt challenged, either by dissenters on the inside or critics on the outside, they proved capable of unleashing torrents of words. The way that the men and women who organized the Assemblies of God in 1914 approached the question of an official creed is instructive. No one suggested, let alone drafted, anything like a statement of faith at the initial meeting. Why should they? Everyone already knew what they believed. But when a dispute arose the following year over the Godhead, leaders commissioned a closely reasoned defense of their position. When that body adopted a formal "Statement of Fundamental Truths" in 1916, the section on the Trinity was nearly as lengthy as all of the other "Fundamental Truths" combined. In sum, when practically possible, Holy Ghost believers sensibly preferred concise articulations over windy ones. But when the situation called for other responses, they acted accordingly.

The "grave mistress of Experience" taught pentecostals other, equally important lessons not found in the Bible, or in received doctrine, or in the Holy Spirit's whisperings. One was the unpleasant fact that elites, even Holy Spirit-filled elites, could use doctrinal regularity as a tool for building institutions, which would include some and exclude others. "I believe 'fundamental fences' have been the curse of all denominations," wrote Edgar C. Steinberg to the interracial Oneness periodical, *Voice in the Wilderness,* in 1920. This was code language. Steinberg almost certainly was referring to the "Statement of Fundamental Truths" that the rival Assemblies of God had recently issued specifically to exclude Oneness adherents like himself from its ranks. "Paul says we are known in part, and if so, then we continually have things to learn."[109] Through his hurt Steinberg sensed that the Assemblies of God had mistaken zeal for commitment, conformity for rigor. Such fears were understandable in light of the long history of real and perceived abuses that pentecostals had known in their parent denominations, where, as one patriarch bitterly recalled, "a lot of preachers had got their whiskers singed."[110]

Finally, pentecostals freely admitted that good sense and sound judgment represented a kind of authority that could not be gainsaid. Faces lined by years of struggling to make ends meet, or to turn irresponsible kids into responsible adults, spoke volumes. "An ounce of testimony," wrote one of the most thoughtful of the initial leaders, "is often more helpful to hungry hearts than a pound of doctrinal teaching. The weight and value of healthful testimonies are sometimes incalculable because of their Scripturalness, simplicity, depth, brevity and intensity."[111] At this distance it is impossible to know exactly what the speaker had in mind. But one senses that other criteria involving the ability successfully to negotiate daily affairs were coming into play. Consider an otherwise obscure resolution, passed by the Pentecostal Assemblies of the World in 1920, stipulating that "young or inexperienced workers" must be credentialed by their "Local Body," not by the "General Body." Though no formal explanation appeared, the reason was easy to figure. Paper credentials easily could lie, while personal credentials—the kind won in face-to-face interaction at the local level year after year—could not. And when that sect urged a mother who planned to go "out into the work of the Lord" not to leave her children for more than thirty days, "except by consent of her husband," one senses a voice of wisdom speaking. One also senses that the voice grew not from study of the Book, nor from special illumination by the Holy Spirit, but from communal experience hard won.[112]

M. L. Ryan's missionary expedition to Japan revealed similar assumptions about the authority of good sense and sound judgment. For the better part of a year, from the fall of 1906 through the fall of 1907, this Spokane, Washington, pastor spearheaded the Holy Ghost revival in the Pacific Northwest.

In September 1907 Ryan assigned himself the task of leading a dozen men and women to that storied land to herald the pentecostal tidings. Apparently no one in the group had ever been to Japan, no one spoke the language, and no one had secured support from an established board. They departed amid great rejoicing (and tears), certain that God would miraculously equip them with the needed connections, languages, and funds.[113] Nonetheless, just before leaving, Ryan's *Apostolic Light* assured supporters that most of his followers were not "novices." They were not "rushing off" to the foreign field simply because they had received a "great blessing" and "spoken in the tongues of those nations." To the contrary, the paper carefully explained, they had been endorsed by "experienced workers." That meant, among other things, that they had proved themselves "worthy of the money of the people who are standing by them with their prayers and their means." Lest any doubt remained, the author then played the trump card: each volunteer had been "accepted in the Holiness movement for years." Accepted in the holiness movement? Since when did acceptance in any human organization, holiness or otherwise, matter? But this was business. And in business, especially the missions business, stability counted. The very title of the news item describing these events said it all: "Staunch Workers Going."[114] There it was, a world of meaning in a word. Staunch.

If authority grew from supernatural signs and wonders, it also grew from a life well lived, from a life that manifested the fruits of Christian grace in day-to-day affairs. Early pentecostals never wavered in the insistence that tongues constituted a nonnegotiable hallmark of Holy Spirit baptism. But once that point was acknowledged, they quickly moved on to insist, with equal vigor, that tongues was not enough. The *Apostolic Light* spoke for all: "real baptism with the Holy Ghost comes upon a life that is already melted, tender, and patient toward opposers." Harshness, austerity, and bluster belonged to the flesh, not to those who walked after the Holy Spirit.[115] Holy Ghost people took considerable pride in the sweetness of their character, even if outsiders often saw things differently. One Oakland convert wondered if it was reasonable to suppose that the "most spiritual ones in the church . . . should be deceived, while worldly professors, or those far less saintly . . . be correct?"[116] In the earliest known attempt to put together a history of the "Tongues Movement," Seeley Kinne based the truthfulness of the message on the fact that it had been advocated by "[p]eople of untarnished character."[117]

Most who joined the revival undoubtedly did so because of the supernatural signs and wonders they had witnessed, or at least hoped to witness. At the same time, most who stayed undoubtedly did so because the revival offered resources for stabilized and transformed lives. That kind of authority shone bright when others dimmed in the dark hours of the night.

— no institutional authority?

5

Cosmos

This chapter begins with a Sunday school story, undoubtedly as old as the hills. As the tale goes, a little boy visiting his faraway grandparents found himself in a strange bedroom. All of the reassuring sights and sounds of his own room were gone. As night fell and the house grew silent, the lad began to hear the alarming creaks and groans of an unfamiliar place. He tried to be brave but, fearing the worst, finally called his grandmother to his side. Grandma whispered, "Don't worry. God is everywhere." To this bit of homespun wisdom, the young fellow responded, "Yes, I know, but sometimes I need a God with skin."

This pocket-sized story captures a central feature of pentecostals' view of the cosmos. Briefly put, traditional boundaries separating the invisible world from the visible world blurred beyond recognition. However much saints aspired to worship the unseen creator God of Genesis, or the unseen Logos of John, in actual practice they worshipped a God with skin. By the same token, ordinary visible things readily blended with the extraordinary invisible things. In early pentecostal culture, then, the boundary between the two realms dissolved to the touch. Systematic theologians plying their trade in ivy-walled seminaries might have judged pentecostals' cosmos less than orthodox. But for saints such mingling came as easily as breathing.

Jesus

God the Father came first, of course, but only technically. The omniscient, omnipotent, omnipresent God of the Protestant Reformers took a curtain bow now and then, in official theological texts and printed Sunday School lessons, but in actual practice, in the daily devotional life of ordinary believers, Jesus Christ the Son readily upstaged God the Father. One historian's assertion that early pentecostalism, like all modern revival movements, was a Jesus cult, may have been too strong, yet Jesus' predominance in grass-roots piety is hard to deny. One study of 700 early pentecostal hymns revealed, for example, that Jesus the Son was mentioned three times more often than God the Father.[1] Indeed one might plausibly argue that the large Oneness faction, which largely broke from the main body of Trinitarian pentecostals in the mid 1910s, represented one of the movement's deepest theological instincts.[2] Oneness testimonials brimmed with accounts of saints being baptized in water in Jesus Name and then surfacing speaking in tongues. When Oneness leader G. T. Haywood spoke of the "sweet songs of the blood of Jesus," he spoke of longings too deep for ordinary words.[3]

For lay folk, Jesus' functions proved multifaceted. His blood-based vicarious atonement for the sins of the world came first. Though this notion had informed Christian thinking for centuries, by 1900 most mainline and many evangelical Protestants had reduced the vicarious atonement to an abstraction.[4] Not pentecostals. In their preaching the doctrine still flourished, drenched in sanguine imagery. Holy Ghost people constantly talked about the salvific efficacy of Jesus blood,[5] sometimes claiming they had joined the revival precisely because of the revival's special emphasis on that precious truth.[6] For that matter, they often spoke as if Jesus' blood possessed restorative powers beyond its role in the scheme of salvation. When a band of saints in Durham, Maine, asserted that they had been able to raise one Olive Mills from the dead just by shouting, "The blood! The blood of Christ[!],"[7] no one, it seemed, raised an eyebrow of dissent.

And then there was the power of Jesus' very name. It could shield believers from evil and physical danger like a verbal iron curtain.[8] When Satan afflicts, one zealot exulted, the Comforter says, "Jesus! Jesus! Jesus!"[9] The Lord's name held so much power demons recoiled when someone uttered that single, potent word. "It is one thing to command a demon . . . to come out of a man," an Ohio evangelist dryly noted, "but it is quite another to see the body writhe and roll on the floor when the command is given in the Name of Jesus." Indeed, when demon-possessed persons tried to say the name Jesus, their throats choked and eyes glared with "devilish hate and fear."[10]

Even so, the greatest privilege of pentecostal baptism was not that Jesus might do good things for the convert, but that he proved intrinsically satisfying in Himself. Many believed that true worship ought to seek one goal: to make Jesus' presence real. For Arthur S. Booth-Clibborn, son-in-law of Salvation Army founders William and Catherine Booth, the "office of the Spirit" aimed only to "reveal Jesus . . . JESUS ONLY. REALITY."[11] For others it was "Jesus in justification, Jesus in sanctification and Jesus in the baptism of the Holy Ghost."[12] The periodical literature overflowed with sentimental anecdotes and lush poems about the Son,[13] whom writers commonly called their "Elder Brother," both in prayers addressed to him and in daily conversation.[14] Though apostolics rarely displayed mystical tendencies, occasionally their love for Jesus broached the trancelike intensity of Moravian Savior piety. Jesus "entered my body, pushing His head up into my head, His hands into my hands, His feet into my feet, taking full possession of me . . . the organs of the body as well as the spirit and soul,"[15] was the way one convert remembered the experience in 1910.

Again, well-worn hymns bore layers of meaning that formal theological texts could intimate but not replicate.

> Take the world, but give me Jesus;
> All its joys are but a name.
> But His love abideth ever,
> Through eternal years the same.[16]

Jesus reigned, not always with theological precision, but with religious force. The sheer number of the songs about Jesus that drifted out from their meetinghouses night after night surely offered a hint of some of their most deeply cherished values.

Holy Spirit

If in daily devotional practice God the Father receded into the background and Jesus the Son stepped to the fore, the Holy Spirit readily displaced both. This claim gains special force if references to Holy Ghost baptism, as well as to the Holy Spirit Himself, are taken as an index.

Remarkably the Holy Spirit's character proved both variable and sometimes even of dubious orthodoxy. Despite pentecostal theologians' strenuous insistence that the Holy Spirit was a person, not an impersonal power, in actual practice the lines blurred. Some of the best-loved songs were symptomatic: "Old-time Power," "Pentecostal Power," "When the Power Fell on Me," "Bring Your Vessels Not a Few ('He will fill your heart to overflowing, With the Holy Ghost and power')." Insiders might have objected that such references simply denoted the Holy Spirit's life-giving energy. Perhaps so, yet pentecostal writers themselves occasionally intimated that at some deep, almost precognitive level they conceived the Holy Spirit more as a material force than as a living personality. The inanimate subject in the title of the well-worn hymn, "Let It Breathe on Me," written by the influential evangelist William Booth-Clibborn, may have revealed more than he realized. Enthusiasts sometimes described the Holy Spirit's presence in worship gatherings as "liquid fire"[17] or as a "blue smoke"[18] or as a "blue vapor"[19] that seemed literally to hover over the group. A 1926 tract likened the Third Person's operations to the laws of electricity, noting that recruits would be "shocked and destroyed" if they attempted "to use this mighty force without adjusting [them]selves to the laws which govern it."[20] A respected pentecostal theologian in England described the Holy Spirit as a "felt power" emanating from the Bible like "invisible rays eddying in irresistible arcs." To him the latter resembled a "rose plot that emits delicious perfume."[21]

When pentecostals spoke of being filled with the Holy Spirit, they meant exactly what they said: the Third Person literally filled their physical bodies.[22] Oregon pastor M. L. Ryan discerned, for example, that Jesus, speaking through the Holy Spirit, was left-handed. The reason was simple: the normally right-handed Ryan found himself mysteriously impelled to write the Holy Spirit's words with his left hand.[23] Similarly Joel Adams Wright, a wealthy businessman in northern New England, remembered the divine power welling up within. "All at once," he recalled, "something inside of me seemed to be rolling up toward my throat. I opened my mouth and the Holy Ghost shouted through me and I was free."[24] The ancient connection between the Holy Spirit and human breath captured pentecostals' imagination with special force. One British writer carefully explained, however, that converts should not on that account too quickly assume that the Holy Ghost resided only in the "upper part of the body, viz. the lungs and heart." To the contrary, the Bible said, "Out of the *belly* shall flow rivers of living water."[25]

From time to time the Holy Spirit became too much of a person, unpredictable and petulant, very much like a child, easily "grieved."[26] With disconcerting frequency the Holy Ghost seemed to take offense and withdraw, leaving believers wondering why. Two Saskatchewan brothers realized too late that they had "checked the Spirit" when they allowed themselves to shiver after being baptized in a nearby river.[27] Once in 1908 pastor Martha Wing Robinson somehow failed to understand exactly what the Holy Spirit wanted her to do. Predictably, she soon fell into extreme illness and depression. Mistakes of this sort, however inadvertent, demanded a penalty. Robinson saw the demon of death enter her bedroom window and literally fasten itself on her body until the Lord told her to command it to go away.[28] Worse, the stakes were higher than just mortal death. Matthew 12:31 and Mark 3:29 taught that the Unpardonable Sin, the sin for which there was no forgiveness in this life or the next, equaled blasphemy against the Holy Spirit.[29] God the Father and Christ the Son might forgive, but not the Holy Spirit, who punished offenders everlastingly. When pioneering evangelist Mary Bryant grimly declared that it was "a more grievous thing to reject the Holy Ghost than to reject Jesus," she expressed one of the revival's deepest convictions.[30]

Fear of grieving the Holy Spirit often took another form: trepidation that one might unwittingly mistake the work of an evil spirit for the work of the true one, or vice versa—and then be held eternally accountable for the error. Agnes Ozman ruefully remembered that just after she and others at Parham's

Bible school had received Holy Spirit baptism in January 1901, they set out for the Shiloh community in Maine. Even though these earnest pilgrims had prayerfully sought the Holy Spirit's direction, they later came to the grim conclusion that the "voice" they heard and followed was not the Lord's.[31] The Holy Spirit's inscrutability compounded the problem. The *Latter Rain Evangel* explained that when seekers first sought His direction, they ordinarily received an ambiguous response. Seekers needed to keep pressing until the response became specific and incontrovertible. Altogether the Holy Spirit often seemed a potent mix: playful yet petulant child, loving yet frightening father.

Other Spirits

In the first blush of the revival the cosmos also seemed to include—besides Father, Son, and Holy Ghost—a large, indeterminate realm inhabited by angels and other supernatural or quasi-supernatural beings. One partisan explained that there were "three realms of law—the Natural and Supernatural, and between these comes a strange middle realm called Preternatural." The latter constituted the home of "clairvoyance, second-sight, hypnotism, mind-reading, insanity, and abnormal passions."[32] While some enthusiasts considered angels entirely beneficial,[33] others warned that Christians should not try to become familiar with them because the supernatural realm teemed with demonic as well as angelic forces.[34] On balance the preternatural proved more ominous than not. As South Africa missionary John G. Lake put it in 1910, "the air is full of murder and suicide."[35] Some things were better left alone.

In the pentecostal cosmos Satan and his demon functionaries proved palpably real and, like the Holy Ghost, always and everywhere present, or at least potentially so. According to Memphis pastor L. P. Adams, Satan occupied a throne "located up in the atmosphere." From that locale "his edicts are issued."[36] One zealot likened demons to "swarms of asteroids" filling the earth's atmosphere,[37] another to "herds" hovering over certain buildings within cities.[38] Demons even lurked in church services, including Holy Ghost church services and camp meetings.[39] They attached themselves to the human body "like ticks on cattle,"[40] where they liked to live in the "juices in human blood, or . . . absorb to themselves some of the natural affections."[41] Sometimes demons proved so numerous they had to be fought off in "a hand to hand fight."[42]

No one should think that demons were all alike, however. Saints constructed charts detailing the types, functions, and correct names of the various species.[43] As founder Charles Parham saw it, they were "greater in diversity than human beings," and they always sought to possess a person "congenial to them in some characteristic."[44] That meant that there were demons of witchcraft, of fortune telling, of insanity, of drunkenness, of gluttony, of idleness, and of wonder working. The dark pantheon also included despotic demons, theological demons, and yelling and screeching demons.[45] At a 1908 camp meeting in Elkland, Pennsylvania, evangelist Frank Bartleman encountered a child burdened by a "whining demon" and a dog "possessed with barking."[46] Sometimes demon-possessed persons could be detected because they manifested a "certain wildness in the eye and harshness in the voice."[47]

Demons enjoyed the ability to torment Holy Spirit–baptized believers along with non-Christians. Sometimes they disrupted pentecostal meetings by prompting erroneous or even vile messages in tongues. On occasion "religious demons" caused "professors of holiness" to do nonsensical things such as running around the house screaming or climbing trees for no good reason.[48] Sometimes saints speaking in prayer found that a demon had slipped in and taken control of their jaws.[49] Everyone knew that evil spirits caused most illnesses. Therefore in many cases divine healing involved exorcism of the tormenting spirit,[50] which required placing one's hand on the "afflicted part" and in the name of Jesus commanding the demon to depart.[51] Dramatic contests ensued. When George Floyd Taylor's wife came down with a "dreadful cough," he stayed up with her through the night. "We keep praying it off," he scribbled in his diary. "God stops it and the devil brings it back. God shall have the victory."[52]

By far the most fearsome aspect of the netherworld lay in Satan's ability to fake the Holy Spirit's deeds—and sometimes it was nearly impossible to tell which was which. Working through the influence of these imps, individuals could speak in bogus tongues, perform bogus miracles, and initiate bogus healings.[53] (One helpful test, however, was to see if the demon-influenced person could say "Jesus is Lord.")[54] Given the apparent similarity of the manifestations produced by the two kinds of spirits, holy and unholy, pentecostals invested much energy attacking Spiritualist mediums, whom they perceived, logically enough, as deadly rivals. For many, the conversion of a Spiritualist medium ranked as the most prized trophy of all.[55]

Miracles

Just as the invisible realm consisted of different kinds of entities, so too the visible realm consisted of different kinds of entities: nature and humans. To be sure, pentecostals said little about nature as such. The primary literature showed scant interest in nature either as a philosophical concept or as a source of aesthetic enjoyment (except in occasional moments of patriotic pride in the American landscape). One might almost say that for saints nature existed only in order to be negated by antinature—by miracle. But that was saying a lot.

First-generation writers never worried much about the exact form of miracles. All they knew was that signs and wonders came directly from God (or occasionally from Satan), and they happened all the time and in all manner of places. Some miracles transpired in the more or less private context of worship (trance, dancing, prostration, screaming, laughing, weeping, jerking, healings, and speaking in tongues), and some in the more or less public context of everyday life. Our present concern is only with the latter.

The first point to notice is that virtually all of the wonders that pentecostals witnessed in nature involved biblical motifs. Referring to other groups, Catherine Albanese argues that nature religion (worship of mountains, rivers, trees, and the like) focused not on nature per se, but on nature as seen through a thick filter of culturally constructed meanings.[56] The same pattern held true for pentecostals. Just as the primal elements of blood, fire, water, and light figured prominently in biblical miracle stories, those same elements reappeared with monotonous predictability in pentecostal miracle stories. Consider, for example, the experience of an unnamed woman attending an all-night prayer meeting at Glad Tidings Tabernacle in New York City in 1929. At 2:00 A.M. everyone present saw blood splatter onto her fresh white dress. The stains remained (significantly) for three days, then disappeared.[57] Or again, in 1924 biblical fire fell on a New Year's Eve Watch Night service at Hempolia Station, Massachusetts. On this occasion a supernatural blaze appeared directly above the meetinghouse—just as tongues of fire, as related in Acts, had marked the room where the disciples gathered for prayer. The flame was so spectacular that the neighbors called out the fire department.[58] Or again, at a Portland, Oregon, camp meeting in 1910, one brother saw "great crystal drops" of "'latter rain'" falling inside the tabernacle, just as readers of the Old Testament book of Joel might expect.[59]

Biblical precedents took less conventional forms too. For example enthusiasts reported seeing Jesus' face on a meeting room wall,[60] or bloodstained crosses floating across the night sky,[61] or angels fluttering about the moon,[62] or victuals multiplied before their very eyes in order to feed a waiting crowd.[63] Predictions about the future mixed biblical motifs with natural forces. Zealots foretold that natural calamities, usually earthquakes, reminiscent of the one that followed Christ's crucifixion, would befall particular cities or regions, invariably to be followed by terrible suffering and loss of life.[64] On those rare occasions when pentecostals witnessed uncanny phenomena that did not rest on an obvious scriptural precedent, such as a snowstorm in

Costa Rica,[65] they nonetheless construed them as curiosities presaging the imminence of the Second Coming. Sometimes the process worked the other way around: preternatural phenomena helped to explain the import of the Bible. For example Alice Garrigus, a one-time Mount Holyoke student who pioneered the pentecostal message in Maritime Canada, tried to teach her Bible school classes how to read the stars in order to decode the meaning of obscure Scripture passages.[66]

Another class of miracles, one that modern anthropologists might call sympathetic magic, also touched converts' daily lives. These events involved the transfer of divine energy from one specially gifted believer to another. Healer-missionary John G. Lake disclosed, for example, that when he prayed for a sick person he could literally "feel the Spirit flow" down his arm into his hand and then into the subject's body.[67] Zealots commonly acquired the ability to speak in tongues the same way: by being touched by someone who already possessed the gift and could convey it to others. As noted, certain individuals, such as evangelists G. B. Cashwell and Lucy Farrow, found themselves in high demand partly because of their talent for transferring the baptism experience through the laying on of hands.[68]

Pentecostals also believed that material objects could serve as vehicles for healing or for other manifestations of miraculous power. In accord with biblical precedent, the most frequently used item was an anointed handkerchief, which apostolics laid or pressed on the afflicted portion of the body.[69] The English healing evangelist Smith Wigglesworth declared that he had used the same cloth more than 200 times.[70] Periodicals sometimes functioned the same way. Converts told how particular issues of newspapers such as *Apostolic Faith* or *Upper Room* brought relief when applied like a balm to the site of the infirmity.[71] Indeed adherents sometimes proved so respectful—or fearful—of the supernatural power embedded in their periodicals that persons who had not received Holy Spirit baptism were not allowed to touch them.[72]

But if ordinary believers experienced miracles daily, did those events therefore cease to be miraculous? Pentecostals themselves would emphatically have said no. The cosmos constituted a vast battlefield on which cosmic forces struggled for supremacy. In prayer meetings at the Shiloh community in Maine, for example, N. N. Harriman boasted that one could literally feel the "fury of mortal combat."[73] The same perception turned up almost everywhere. In the Pacific Northwest, Oregon *Apostolic Faith* editor Florence Crawford warned her troops always to remember: "We don't fight against flesh and blood now. This is a greater fight—and the greater fight comes far greater power."[74] Globe-trotting preacher Frank Bartleman spoke of the exhaustion of daily entering into "spiritual conflict, the centering of spiritual opposing forces in each battle, and the constant, awful pressure of the forces of evil."[75] Saints lived on a planet swept by gales of good and evil. It resembled a scene from the Old Testament book of Ezekial, a page torn from time and brought to life in twentieth-century America.

But lurking deep within this portrait of the world was another being also limned in the Old Testament. His name was Adam, and though he had fallen from favor, he seemed able to reach up and touch the sky at will.

Humans

To outsiders it probably looked like the pragmatic impulse had ridden into town on a stallion. For sheer breathtaking audacity pentecostals' view of humans found few rivals in the annals of traditional Christianity. No group on the American religious landscape was more convinced that unregenerate souls could think straight, discount bad doctrine, and accept Christ's offer of salvation if they would just stand up and do so. And that step marked only the beginning. After conversion, sanctification, and Holy Spirit baptism, saints could quite literally become vessels of the Almighty's power on earth. Whether this process denoted the supernaturalization of the natural or the naturalization of the supernatural seemed moot.

To be sure, Holy Ghost people would have deplored this characterization. Like other radical evangelicals, they supposed that unregenerate humans arrived in the world defiled by original sin. The children of Cain feasted on the "bread of demons," growled Toronto pastor S. S. Craig. Indeed, if humans possessed the "feeblest spark" of natural good, Calvary would be reduced to "wanton ostentation."[76] Even after conversion, the soul remained bound in the chains of temptation. "Oh, there is much of the flesh, of self, left in one when one is cleansed of sin," muttered faith home director Martha Wing Robinson.[77] And sin blighted everyone, including the least of God's children. When one convert asked Assemblies of God chairman E. N. Bell if children too young to give their heart to Jesus would go up in the Rapture, Bell's reassuring answer was significant, but so was the anxiety that produced the question in the first place.[78]

Even so, pentecostals' working anthropology, the assumptions they actually lived by most of the time, proved dramatically different. St. Louis pastor S. D. Kinne would say that people fell prey to demons, sin, and evil, not because of any innate moral frailty, but because they *chose* to live in "some sin, being wilful, failing to keep humble and teachable, believing some false doctrine, or [believing a] teaching that has some error mixed with truth."[79] And if unregenerate souls could lift themselves by their spiritual bootstraps, regenerate, Holy Spirit-filled souls rode so tall in the saddle that no one, not even the Enemy, could bring them down. Though all persons started life as miserable denizens of the dust, the full gospel message promised that Holy Spirit–baptized souls could serve as pure vehicles for the Lord's plans here on earth. When saints trumpeted that "sanctification makes us holy as Jesus is,"[80] or said that they had not entertained an evil thought for years,[81] or claimed "continual victory all the time, on every possible line, on every occasion, without any exception,"[82] it was easy for outsiders to raise an eyebrow of disbelief. An exhilarating anthropology it was—but one fraught with unforeseen complications.[83]

The problem here was that saints had backed themselves into a corner. Freed from earthly temptation, they remained vulnerable to sinful pride about their freedom from earthly temptation. California evangelist Frank Bartleman unwittingly exemplified the problem. When one preacher opined in the *Way of Faith*, "Rev. Frank Bartleman [is] perhaps the most humble and saintly person with whom I ever came in contact," Bartleman carefully reproduced that happy comment in his own book—adding, with a dutiful blush, "I record the above with humility and shame."[84] Perhaps a bit *more* humility and shame might have prompted him to let the compliment pass, like a desert flower its bloom unseen.

If humility begat pride, self-emptying begat power—but with a difference, of course. The former process believers condemned, the latter they encouraged as a desirable consequence of the spiritual life. The movement's devotional literature brimmed with condemnations of the self-life. An anonymous writer for the little monthly published by Los Angeles' Upper Room Mission made the point with memorable brevity: "Death and life are relative terms . . . the degree of death determining the degree of life."[85] Though no friend of pentecostals, the radical evangelical author Hannah Whitall Smith (whom saints nonetheless admired) expressed their sentiments precisely when she insisted that the higher Christian life required "entire surrender" of the self to Him, "submit[ting] fully to His possession and His control."[86] Holy Ghost enthusiasts used songs to remind themselves that the self had to step aside in order for Christ to step in.

> Not I, but Christ, in ev'ry look and action;
> Not I, but Christ, in ev'ry tho't and word.[87]

And here—precisely here—lay the essence of pentecostals' view of humans, in all its triumphant glory. Though Christ alone reigned, He used His special Holy Spirit–filled children to implement His will on earth. "To the man or woman who is willing to be emptied of the last vestige of self," one enthusiast wrote, "no power of hell or earth can possibly [prevail]."[88]

Converts had stumbled on psychological dynamite. Despite their self-effacing, self-abnegating intentions, they had come up with a formula that armed the self with an iron cloak of moral and, through the ideology of divine healing, even physical invincibility. Once again a beloved hymn inscribed the movement's day-to-day working assumptions. First, the premise.

> I am prostrate in the dust,
> I with Christ am crucified.

Then the conclusion, astounding by most measures of historic Christian thinking:

> Jesus comes! He fills my soul;
> Perfected in Him I am.[89]

The perfected soul spoke with divine authority. So Charles Fox Parham, a leading architect of the revival, would insist that he alone had received a "God-given commission to deliver to this age the truths of a restored PENTECOST." Frequently resorting to the prophetic voice, the Kansas healer claimed to represent God Himself as he excoriated rivals and predicted future events.[90] The same sense of holy rectitude animated faith home leader Martha Wing Robinson, who proffered much advice to her guests, usually as the Lord's thoughts, not her own. Indeed the Holy Ghost sometimes directed Robinson to put His advice in writing—"teaching letters," she called them.[91] Some stalwarts saw themselves playing a pivotal if not determinative role even in the salvation or damnation of bystanders. In the early days, recalled evangelist Howard Goss, "each of us fully realized . . . that the eternal fate of some soul depended upon our personal conduct."[92] If outsiders marveled at the temerity of it all, insiders seemed too preoccupied with their own critical role in the grand scheme of things to take notice.

To be sure, partisans feared the perils of holy pride, but usually in others, not themselves. We know little about Cora Harris MacIlravy, for example, but we do know that she had established the Elbethel Faith Home in Chicago in 1912 specifically to counteract the spiraling arrogance of another local pastor—though she had the good taste not to name the rival.[93] A. A. Boddy, the pentecostal vicar of Sunderland parish in northeastern England, expressed grave reservations after touring Finis Yoakum's Pisgah Home and Gardens near Los Angeles in 1912. Boddy denounced Yoakum's refusal to submit to an audit, his eagerness to take on titles like bishop and overseer, and his habit of exaggerating healing stories, a trait Boddy memorably dubbed "optimania."[94] Even William J. Seymour, widely revered in the beginning for his gentleness of spirit,[95] later felt the sting of rebuke for spiritual arrogance. Glenn A. Cook, an early co-worker at Azusa, charged that Seymour's fame eventually went to his head. When Seymour and other stalwarts at the mission "awakened to the scope of the work," Cook lamented some years later, "God could not use them longer."[96] We can only wonder what Seymour thought of Cook, who left his own legacy of combativeness.[97]

Early pentecostals rarely recognized how close their anthropology—their understanding of humanness—positioned them to the precipice of self-apotheosis. Armed with the conviction that the Holy Spirit–filled self represented a purely passive instrument for the transmission of divine power, they marched out to subdue themselves, the devil and, not incidentally, anyone who got in their way. Since every deed that pentecostals undertook was for the Lord, and since they bore only penultimate responsibility anyway, saints could well afford to risk total loss for total gain. That was a cosmos worth defending.

6

Worship

If early pentecostals' explicit reflections on worship constituted the sole topic of this chapter, there would not be much to discuss. In their minds worship was something one did, not something one theorized about. After all, had not the Holy Spirit delivered them from all that Romish nonsense? Fortunately we are not left to twist in the wind. The record contains numerous clues about saints' worship behavior and, better yet, the motivations that prompted it. Outsiders who stopped to observe their services sometimes left bemused, sometimes incredulous, but rarely indifferent. Insiders too revealed a good deal about their own worship habits, however inadvertently. Though disinterested ethnographic description was the last thing on their minds, their detailed accounts of what took place in their meetings offer a wealth of data about the revival's cultural landscape. Taken together, the two kinds of reports—outsiders' and insiders'—coalesce to show that pentecostal worship oscillated between antistructural and structural impulses. Planned spontaneity, we might call it. Though few saw it at the time, from this distance it is evident that the spontaneity part served primitivist aims, the planned part pragmatic ones. More important, the interplay between those tensions provided resources that enabled adherents first to survive and then to flourish in modernizing America.

Freedom in the Spirit

In the public eye the Holy Ghost revival epitomized the uninhibited expression of raw religious emotion. Of course saints held no monopoly on that trait. For the better part of two centuries American evangelicals had countenanced public weeping as a sign of remorse before God. Methodists in the early nineteenth century had gone further, sanctioning various forms of involuntary motor behavior as normal by-products of strong religious feelings.[1] Radical evangelicals in the late nineteenth century ratcheted up the intensity even more, endorsing leaping, screaming, and deathlike prostration. Azusa pioneer Frank Bartleman rightly remembered that there had been a "tremendous lot of fanaticism in the Holiness movement."[2] What distinguished pentecostals, at least in public perception, was not so much the presence of uninhibited emotion as its centrality. "The common heartbeat of every service," David Edwin Harrell writes of a somewhat later era, "was the miracle—the hypnotic moment when the Spirit moved to heal the sick and raise the dead."[3]

Any service—indeed any part of any service—that looked like it had been planned seemed a sure sign of nominal Christianity. When India missionary Jacob Mueller decided to take a day off and visit an Episcopal church in 1921, he came away disgusted. "All form and therefore little or no reality," was the best he could muster.[4] Mueller's thinking rested on the assumption that the Holy Spirit moved autonomously, therefore unpredictably, with no regard for denominational traditions or conventional expectations about decorum. As late as 1932, the Englishman Donald Gee, one of the movement's best-read and most worldly wise leaders, would insist that a "[p]entecostal meeting where you always know what is going to happen next is backslidden."[5] Armed with these assumptions, it is little wonder that Holy Ghost services were not so much started as "launched."[6]

Even after we allow for the tendentiousness of many of the sources, there can be little doubt that pentecostal meetings can be aptly described with two words: chaotic and deafening.[7] It would be hard to exaggerate the apparent disorder that prevailed through the 1910s and, in many places, through the 1920s (and sometimes to the present). The first known newspaper account of a pentecostal meeting spoke of the men and women at Charles Parham's Bible school in Topeka, Kansas, in January 1901, "racing about the room" for the better part of thirteen hours, all the while "jabbering a strange gibberish."[8] Topeka foreshadowed things to come. Journalists witnessed similar phenomena when the revival made its way to Los Angeles in 1906. "The night is made hideous . . . by the howlings of the worshipers," wrote the *Los Angeles Times* reporter who first described the newborn Azusa Mission. "[T]he devotees of the weird doctrine practice the most fanatical rites, preach the wildest theories and work themselves into a state of mad excitement."[9] Several blocks away at Burbank Hall, a *Los Angeles Daily Times* journalist observed a "cultured young woman" holding forth in a language she claimed to be Arabic, but "sounded like the rapid chattering of a frightened simian."[10]

The revival fanned out from southern California to all parts of the country, and anarchic worship followed. A meeting in Salem, Oregon, in the fall of 1906 produced so much "writhing and groaning" and "hideous noise" that the local newspaper editor called for sanctions against the zealots so the neighbors could get some rest. Where in the New Testament, he demanded, is it recorded that on the Day of Pentecost people "spoke in tones loud enough to be heard several blocks away?"[11] Just before Christmas of that year a *New York American* correspondent visited the Union Holiness Mission at 40th Street. Though the congregants seemed to include individuals of "refinement and culture," said the reporter, they lost themselves in "heights of frenzy" appearing to transcend the "limits of normal physical endurance."[12] Several months later a Birmingham, Alabama, reporter wandered into a tent revival in that city. He found the worshipers twisting and turning in states of ecstasy. "Each one writhed in a different manner," he observed, "and as they writhed they would moan, scream and speak unintelligible words." By the end of the service the place looked like a "jumping jack factory."[13] An Iowa correspondent used similar language to describe a 1907 rally in Des Moines: "[T]he devotees writhe on the floor like epileptics, leap into the air, chatter, scream, gnash their teeth, or beat themselves over the head . . . all the time uttering strange, unintelligible gibberish."[14] An Ohio newspaper bore the headline, "Men Lying Prostrate on Straw as Sisters Brush the Flies Away." The attached story described a 1907 encampment near Cleveland by saying, "It was a perfect bedlam and pandemonium reigned supreme."[15] At Levi Lupton's World Evangelization camp meeting near Alliance, Ohio, one newspaperman spotted believers racing from tent to tent to watch new enthusiasts receive Holy Spirit baptism and speak in tongues.[16]

Later accounts read very much the same, belying claims of rapid routinization, let alone secularization. By 1909 the revival had been surging for eight years when Frederick Henke, a Northwestern University theology professor, visited a Chicago mission. The scene appeared chaotic. Henke observed "some shouting, some manifesting violent jerks, some screaming, and some laughing aloud . . . Arms move frantically, heads jerk so violently that some of the women are unable to keep their hats on, and speaking in tongues is heard in nearly every testimony."[17] Four years later Doremus A. Hayes, a New Testament professor at Garrett Biblical Institute, visited Chicago's North Avenue Mission. Throughout the service, Hayes recorded, members were "affected with nervous paroxysms that made them shudder and writhe." Their habit of rapidly sucking air through their teeth created a hissing sound like a serpent.[18] About the same time an Ottumwa, Iowa, newspaper judged that Billy Sunday services in that city did not approach the "fervor and strain and soul exultation" that pentecostals manifested. Besides an unsuccessful attempt to raise a corpse, it said, the "Faithists" proved notable for their "laughing, high-trebled, piercing exclamations," followed by "strange lapses into the unconscious."[19]

A Bridgeport, Connecticut, journalist repeatedly used the word *cataleptic* to depict the worshipers at a Maria Woodworth-Etter meeting in 1913. "The interior of the tent resembled a veritable madhouse," he observed. Some of the faithful lay on the ground for hours without moving a muscle, some continually embraced and kissed, some shook "to and fro in a 'tango' movement," and some executed what looked like a "'turkey-trot' sway" as if they were in a "cabaret or hootchy-kootchy show." All together, he judged, the "scene in the tent resembled the fabled confusions of Bedlam."[20] Charles W. Shumway, a University of Southern California student who was writing a research thesis on speaking in tongues, visited pentecostal missions in the Los Angeles area in 1913 and 1914. At those meetings, he averred, "pandemonium" reigned. Saints seemed to "take pride in disorder." He found people jumping up and down on their chairs, "barking like dogs, hooting like owls," shouting in such "stentorian tones" that "many times people a half block away" would stop to listen—and ridicule.[21] When a Frenchman, Jules Bois, visited a half-dozen apostolic missions in Brooklyn in 1925 he found similar scenes. Rapid music quickly gave way to exultant chanting and convulsive jerking of body limbs—followed by trance and, not surprisingly, abundant perspiration.[22]

Pentecostal meetings overseas followed the same script. Though the British might have preferred to think they remained free of such excesses,[23] they did not. A reporter visiting a tent revival at Merrington Green in Shropshire in 1907 wrote of partisans falling into "paroxysms of horrible, unnatural laughter," making sounds like ducks quacking, lambs bleating, and dogs barking.[24] Under the headline, "Weird Chants and Frenzied Appeals," a Welsh newspaper spoke of the "sobs, sighs, groans, and table-thumping" that resembled the "mourning chants" of an Irish wake.[25] Throughout Britain, newspaper banners told the same story. "Men and Women Writhe in Religious Frenzy," trumpeted a *Daily Chronicle* headline about a 1910 Bedford meeting.[26] In Peckham, a service run by Holy Brother Wilson featured enthusiasts who "lost all control of themselves, and went swaying, shrieking mad." Witnesses saw a tall girl "wriggle and gasp and jerk," while a grey-haired woman tap-danced, cracked her fingers, and cried out in a "shrill, unhuman treble: 'Bub-bub-bub, bub-bub-bub, bubble-bubble-bubble-booo!'"[27]

In India things looked very much the same. When William T. Ellis, a correspondent for the *Chicago Daily News* visited a pentecostal mission school in that country in 1907, he found "a scene utterly without parallel." The occupants of the mission, adolescent women, were "crying at the top of their lungs." One woman moved around the mission on her knees, violently swinging her arms, while another fell over "fainting from sheer exhaustion." To Ellis's eye the contortions of the young women's faces bespoke "extreme agony."[28]

Just as pentecostals seemed to ignore conventional notions of decorum, they also downplayed conventional notions of when and where it was appropriate to worship. Meetings took place at all hours of the day and night. The literature brims with accounts of services that began at 5:00 A.M., or lasted till 5:00 A.M., or ran for ten or twelve hours at a stretch.[29] Azusa pioneer A. G. Osterberg remembered that in the salad days of the revival, time meant nothing. Days passed into weeks and weeks into months without any clear reckoning of the date.[30] Place too seemed irrelevant. Saints reported that they received Holy Spirit baptism wherever the fire fell—while praying in the belfry, sitting on the porch, shoveling coal at home, sitting on a coal pile at work, talking on the phone, resting in bed, doing dishes.[31] Zealots preached anywhere they could find a hearing: on trolleys and trains, in depots, abandoned saloons and tobacco warehouses, in open fields and of course on street corners.[32]

Leaders cultivated a sense that Holy Ghost worship occurred according to divine, not mundane, rules by highlighting the supernatural signs and wonders that accompanied the event. Years later patriarch Howard Goss said that when he visited William H. Durham's North Avenue Mission in Chicago, a "thick haze" resembling blue smoke "filled the top third of the Auditorium." People fell to the floor before they could even reach their seats.[33] On at least two occasions A. J. Tomlinson described a similar phenomenon, one occurring in August 1908 in Chattanooga, the other the following month in Cleveland, Tennessee. When he came to the pulpit, Tomlinson wrote regarding the meeting in Cleveland, "I seemed to see a kind of blue vapor, or mist, settle down on the congregation, and people turned pale."[34] Canada's Alice Garrigus enjoyed a reputation for the comparative decorum of her services. Still, in one of her meetings in Victoria, Newfoundland, she reported that a "white mist was seen filling the atmosphere." Some of the worshipers fled the meeting house in fear.[35] Though Goss, Tomlinson, and Garrigus clearly meant to describe physical phenomena they had witnessed with their own eyes, their accounts carried a larger import. They told the faithful that the Almighty had lifted their worship out of ordinary time and place and sanctioned it, just as Yahweh of old had sanctioned Israelite worship in the Holy of Holies.

Holy Ghost Order

If pentecostals proved unwilling to order worship by the protocols of the mainline Protestant denominations, they were equally unwilling to limit the right to speak in worship to socially respectable white male adults. In the heat of the revival traditional social barriers crumbled. Later we shall see that the egalitarian ideal did not eradicate gender and racial distinctions across the board, but in the specific context of worship striking equality prevailed.

First consider the role of women in pentecostal meetings. Outsiders' reports underscored their prominence.[36] Though insiders' reports did not seem especially concerned either to highlight or to obscure women's participation in the worship services, many nonetheless make clear that women played a conspicuous part, approaching parity with men.[37] Women freely testified of their spiritual experiences, especially healing, Holy Spirit baptism, and witnessing for Christ. And as long as no one inquired too closely into exactly what they were actually doing, women also preached. One of countless examples, chosen for its typicalness, was the entry for Sunday, April 23, 1922, in the diary of the United Holy Church bishop Henry L. Fisher: "Conducted Services at Mt Zion Holy church all day Sisters Delk of Norfolk Va and Harper of Kinston NC did the preaching Had a very large crowd attending."[38] What should be noted here is the unselfconscious interaction among the three leaders in this black denomination. Fisher, a man, ran the service, while Delk and Harper, both women, apparently preached back-to-back sermons—and no one seemed to think anything amiss.

Perhaps the most revealing index of female authority in the worship context was men's grudging willingness to subordinate themselves to women in spiritual matters. Brother Adolph Rosa, pastor of a Methodist People's Church in Los Angeles, revealed the abasement that such a step involved. "I was too proud . . . to humble myself in a lowly mission and let ladies pray over me . . . [W]hat [would] people . . . think of me[?]"[39] The testimonial of the Norwegian pentecostal pioneer T. B. Barratt betrayed similar qualms. When a sister in New York offered to lay hands on him so that he might receive the coveted baptism, Barratt stiffened. "The devil taunted me by saying: 'The idea of a minister going to ask a woman to pray for him!'" Significantly, Barratt relented.[40]

The relation between whites and blacks in the worship setting also suggested equality before God, albeit less marked than that between males and females. Though external social relations continued to be structured by the segregationist proscriptions of the Jim Crow era, inside the church the two groups mixed frequently and amicably.[41] In that context they spoke highly of one another. G. B. Cashwell, a white Holiness Church evangelist from North Carolina, journeyed to Azusa in the fall of 1906 to receive the pentecostal blessing in an interracial setting.[42] Returning to North Carolina, Cashwell talked of the "colored people" who were baptized in his meetings, exulting, "All the people of God are one here."[43] In Memphis, Cashwell met C. H. Mason, founder of the mostly black Church of God in Christ. Mason impressed Cashwell as a "precious brother," one "filled with the blessed Holy Ghost."[44] Mason in turn reported that "white people" in Newport News, Virginia, asked him to come and preach the gospel to them.[45] Perhaps the most striking manifestation of reversal of prevailing norms was the willingness of whites, including southern whites, to subordinate themselves to blacks in the worship context. When the Anglican vicar A. A. Boddy visited the Azusa mission in the fall of 1912, he saw white southerners receiving the baptism through the ministry of black preachers and—this is the crucial part—they went home and said so.[46]

Finally, we should note that the early periodicals contained scores of references to children testifying to Holy Spirit baptism and exhorting others. Most sources failed to specify their exact age, but those that did normally spoke of boys and girls about ten to fourteen. In these settings saints did not treat children as children but as adults endowed with special spiritual authority. Like adults, they not only spoke in tongues but reportedly spoke intelligible languages such as Spanish and Latin. Sometimes adults asked children to deliver the principal address of the meeting. The records never suggest that children prepared their talks as they might have done for a designated "children's Sunday" in a mainline church. Rather in the course of an otherwise routine worship service, a youngster would unexpectedly receive the baptism, speak in tongues, and then assume leadership of the meeting. Children displayed their newfound powers in various ways—by testifying, by admonishing strangers of their evil ways, by singing in ecstatic speech, by visiting local hospitals where they exercised their gifts of healing, and by leading full-scale revival services.[47] A few, such as Uldine Utley, went on to become professional child evangelists.[48] In more routine ways too children enjoyed equality in the worshipping community. "If you had knees," one matriarch remembered, "you were old enough to pray."[49]

It should be stressed that women, blacks, and children assumed a visible role in public worship, not because pentecostals suddenly came to believe that Galatians 3:28 ("In Christ there is neither Jew nor Greek, male nor female") formed the core of the Gospel, nor because they suddenly grew politically progressive. Rather these otherwise disenfranchised groups spoke freely and commanded respect in these settings because saints assumed that the Holy Spirit spoke through them. It ill-behooved anyone to interfere with the Lord's chosen vessels.

Yet there lay the clue that things may have been more scripted than they first seemed. The Almighty was unpredictable, but never arbitrary.

Explicit Regularization

The omniscient direction of God's Holy Spirit formed the balancing assumption that restored order to disorder, reason to unreason. This premise helps to explain many data that otherwise seem bizarre, even by pentecostal standards.

Three brief examples taken from widely scattered sources between 1905 and 1910 illustrate the pattern. Speaking of a meeting he conducted in the fall of 1905, the Church of God leader A. J. Tomlinson recorded in his diary that "people fell in the floor and some writhed like serpents . . . Some fell in the road, one seemed to be off in a trance four or five hours." That much was standard fare. It is the next sentence that gives pause: "The church seemed to be greatly edified and blessed." Edified? Blessed? No, not if one assumed that the flesh prompted such behavior. But yes, if one assumed, as the hard-driving, worldly wise Tomlinson clearly did, that God's Spirit orchestrated everything.[50]

Then again N. J. Holmes, principal of the Holmes Bible and Missionary Institute near Greenville, South Carolina, carefully described the coming of the divine power to his school in the summer of 1907. Students spoke and sang in tongues and danced and played the organ "under the power of the Holy Spirit," he wrote. The fervor grew so intense that they forgot to pause for dinner and supper. An outsider probably would have described the scene as chaotic. Yet to Holmes, "there was no confusion and no disorder, [because] the harmony and freedom of the Holy Spirit prevailed."[51]

Three years later at a camp meeting in Omaha, Nebraska, Agnes Ozman— purportedly the first to speak in tongues at Parham's Bible school—fell into another ecstatic experience. "[T]he Holy Ghost filled my soul and body and my feet danced in the Spirit and I was carried in the Spirit up the aisle to the pulpit," was the way she remembered the event. Again, this recollection might pass as standard fare till we read the next sentence: "I knew fanaticism was not to be feared."[52] No one, and certainly no pentecostal, wanted to be known as a fanatic. They had problems enough without that moniker hanging around their necks. But it takes only a bit of empathy to see that Ozman had redefined the term *fanatic* so that it meant abandonment to the Holy Spirit's superintendence, not human caprice.

Even so, leaders differed about what the Holy Spirit wanted. If crashing breakers held a special beauty for some, calm waters attracted others, especially the ones responsible for navigating the ship. A small but vocal minority mustered the courage to say that unruly worship displeased the Lord. Charles Fox Parham proved most notable in this respect. In the first onrush of the revival he apparently welcomed ecstatic manifestations. But by 1907 Parham had changed his mind and, by 1912, had become a voice for restraint.[53] He distinguished authentic from inauthentic operations of the Holy Spirit. "Anything the Holy Spirit inspires is edifying," he warned, but "[j]erking, trembling, falling to the floor, jabbering, screaming and other disorders have been denounced by us."[54]

Others echoed Parham's misgivings. In 1914 a *Word and Witness* manifesto—almost certainly written by E. N. Bell, the first chairman of the Assemblies of God—admonished churches not to tolerate enthusiasts who insisted on rolling back and forth across the floor of the church.[55] Elizabeth V. Baker, the no-nonsense founder and director of a faith home in Rochester, New York, similarly made clear that she would not put up with "fleshly activity." The latter included "[u]nnatural sounds imitating barn-yard fowls, or the starting of motor cars, or steam-whistles, [and] unseemly and indelicate postures."[56]

The pressure for regularization soon included the most sacred of all worship activities, speaking in tongues. Though the fear of offending the Holy Spirit by prematurely cutting off a tongues message never left pentecostals,[57] they soon regarded some practices to be clearly contrived. For example some zealots had fallen into the habit of chanting "Blood, Blood, Blood"[58] or "Glory! Glory! Glory! Glory!"[59] faster and faster until the tongue tumbled into ecstatic speech. A writer for the avuncular *Word and Witness* decried this habit, saying that the movement would not tolerate onlookers' coaxing seekers to repeat a single word, "until their tongue is so tired they cannot talk, and they begin to 'jab, jab, jab; jib, jib, jib' and then cry out 'you got it.'"[60] The Norwegian pastor T. B. Barratt likewise condemned nonsensical chanting as a trick, doubly pernicious because one might actually learn to speak in tongues that way without being truly baptized by God's Spirit.[61]

The gifts of prophecy and interpretation also required attention. Most utterances of this sort stirred no waves because nothing substantive—that is, nothing empirically confirmable or disconfirmable—was said. But not always. From time to time earnest seekers interrogated the Holy Spirit's vessels for desperately desired advice. In this practice, known as "inquiring of the Lord," an individual would pose a mundane question, such as whom to marry or what job to take, and wait for the answer. Indeed, in the first blush of the revival, one "precious brother," newly endowed with the ability to predict weather conditions two weeks or more in advance, invited inquiries.[62] But responsible pastors and editors almost immediately dropped the hammer on such practices for obvious reasons: too often wrong answers came back. Marriages prescribed by the Holy Spirit crashed on the rocks of divorce. Recommended jobs turned out to be dead ends.[63] The unwashed presumed to give advice to the washed. Children berated adults. "We have seen some . . . very disgusting scenes, of fleshly impassioned rebuke in the assemblies," growled one elder. "God's children are being driven from our meetings by these abuses."[64] On one occasion the Holy Spirit even seemed to instruct a young man to go out and murder his uncle with an ax—which he allegedly did.[65]

Given these concerns, it is not surprising that worship gradually settled into loose patterns. To call it a prescribed order of worship would be an exaggeration. But singing, testimonies, prayer, sermon, and the call to come forward for salvation, healing, and baptism took a predictable sequence—though the order and length of each part of the meeting varied considerably.[66] Yet that kind of explicit regularization represented only the tip of the berg. A little probing shows an array of devices, more instinctive than self-conscious, that imposed real order on apparent disorder.

Implicit Regularization

Implicit forms of regularization were harder to see yet equally effective. Denied the rich liturgical life of the historic denominations, saints regained many of the same benefits through the disciplined use of ecstasy. The result was to reintroduce the traditional sacraments of the church, albeit in veiled form, in all of their vivifying power. Even allowing that glossolalic words were not quite as material as bread, wine, or oil, it is hard to think of any entity that better fit the definition of a holy emblem. Holy Ghost people instinctively sensed that too. In 1916 the Assemblies of God initially asserted in its Statement of Fundamental Truths that the "full consummation" of Holy Ghost baptism was "indicated by the initial sign of speaking in tongues." The following year that body significantly amended that statement to read "initial physical evidence."[67]

Then too the Holy Spirit occasionally flowed out beyond the tongue, transforming the entire human body into a living sacrament. Consider for example A. J. Tomlinson's comment that sometimes the "Spirit wants to laugh . . . He laughs through [a] person till He is satisfied."[68] Or consider Agnes Ozman LaBerge's recollection that in a 1910 Omaha revival the "Holy Ghost filled my soul and body and my feet danced in the Spirit and I was carried in the Spirit up the aisle."[69] Little realizing what they were doing, perhaps, believers effectively sacramentalized the divine power by locating it within their own bodies, within time and space.

In prostrate trance, which pentecostals called being "slain in the Spirit," the entire torso became a holy emblem. In those situations Christ's physical death and resurrection was re-embodied—not just reenacted but literally re-embodied—night after night, before the very eyes of believers and nonbelievers alike. In one account after another we read that prostrate worshipers covered the floor.[70] The stories sometimes stated and often implied that no one was left standing, which suggested that prostration gained a ritualistic significance comparable, perhaps, to kneeling or genuflecting in liturgical church traditions. Men and women lying facedown throughout the service provided a variation on the theme.[71] Unlike the prostrate, who presumably were smitten in trance, these latter individuals positioned themselves on the floor or ground as an act of reverence. But their behavior also represented a self-consciously ritualized act, possibly echoing similar instances in Scripture (for example Moses in Deuteronomy 9:18).[72]

Other regularizing activities involved synchronized behavior. Many services featured "glory marches" in which believers joined hands and paraded around the perimeter of the meeting hall in a manner reminiscent of Shaker dances.[73] In one of his revival meetings, A. J. Tomlinson proudly recalled, a dozen of the faithful were "leaping, dancing, and all keeping perfect time."[74] The sources repeatedly mention worshipers on their knees. Sometimes they knelt on a Bible.[75] More often we read of entire congregations spending most of the service on their knees, or walking on their knees to or across the altar area.[76] At the founding meeting of a Church of God association in Alabama in 1911 (a precursor of the Assemblies of God), controversy erupted over the practice of praying with hands upturned while standing. Was it optional or required? Soon an interpreted tongues message settled the matter once and for all: it was required.[77] Any reasonably impartial outsider surely saw what saints did not: that the Holy Spirit Himself had just turned a seemingly spontaneous act of praise into a prescribed ritual.

Predictably cues defining and regularizing ritual contact between the sexes developed very quickly. Though the movement unquestionably owed some of its success to converts' willingness to comfort each other with the warmth of physical touch, abuses arose, and responsible leaders moved immediately to stop them. Protocols for the laying on of hands required careful specification. When the ill seek to be "anointed with oil in the seat of the particular malady," Kansas' *Apostolic Faith* editorially advised, "women must in every case anoint women, and men must anoint men."[78] Likewise holy kisses required disciplining. Men should kiss only men and women only women, insisted the editor of *Word and Witness,* and "NOT IN THE MOUTH."[79] "Combustible materials are found at times where least expected," said the Anglican editor of *Confidence,* primly implying that the holy kiss needed some steadying in Britain too.[80]

And then there was congregational singing, one of the most notable and remarked on features of pentecostal worship. The ever-astute Frank Bartleman noted the centrality of singing in pentecostal meetings, as did others.[81] "Curious people came to hear the sa[i]nts sing," wrote one matriarch of the early days in Texas. "[E]ven skeptics knew they experienced, from a super[natural?] power, and would be convicted."[82] Music offered leaders a ready means for managing the intensity of the service. They could ratchet up the tempo until worshipers broke into ecstatic praise, or tone it down when things seemed to be getting out of hand. Either way, music gave leaders a tool for regularizing the expression of emotion. Further, and perhaps more important, musical harmony induced social harmony. Potential conflict was averted, as singing required the concerted action of many in a common and manifestly pleasurable endeavor.[83]

As noted, one of the most observed (although, in actual practice, probably fairly rare) ritualized activities involved the "heavenly anthem" or "heavenly chorus" as converts called it. This behavior consisted of singing in tongues by a number of persons at the same time. At this distance it is hard to know exactly what the heavenly chorus sounded like, but pentecostals repeatedly described the event as one of unearthly beauty.[84] I know of no outsider account of this activity, although journalists' sometimes spoke of eerie chanting in Holy Ghost meetings.[85] What is clear is that everyone was expected either to harmonize or at least cooperate by keeping quiet.

A variety of initiation rituals, which pentecostals used with greater or lesser degrees of self-awareness, also steadied the community. The effect, although surely not the intent, of such practices was to make the transition from the outside to the inside so memorable, and thus so emotionally expensive, that turning back became unthinkable. Stalwarts baptized converts in icy streams and lakes and boasted about it in the local press. In Davis City, Iowa, the evangelist Burt McCafferty—a grizzled soul not afraid to protect his revival tent by shooting at vandals—cut through fourteen inches of ice to immerse one convert in subzero weather. (McCafferty dryly added that he almost let him slip under the ice.)[86] Pastors rarely took time to jot down formal membership lists, but they hardly needed to since, as one eyewitness later put it— we can almost see the grin—everyone already knew who belonged and who did not.[87] And if anyone seriously considered leaving the fold, they found the price of defecting high. One opponent said that pentecostals subjected waverers to intense pressure, telling them that anyone who left, after knowing the truth, risked the Unpardonable Sin.[88] In all of these devices, one suspects, apostolics sensed more about the dynamics of human nature than they could clearly explain to themselves. But however clearly or dimly understood, they helped to secure the community's boundaries.

Finally, if pentecostals seemed to subvert mainline conventions about the timing of worship by holding services at all hours of the day and night, closer inspection reveals a more subtle picture. The key point is that they worshipped *all of the time,* and there lay the genius. Through the 1910s, most mission halls maintained multiple services on Sunday—usually morning, afternoon, and evening. Enthusiasts commonly gathered every night of the week except one, and many met for a morning or noon prayer meeting during the day as well.[89] Sister Hilda Reeder's eulogy in 1932 for Bishop G. T. Haywood of the Pentecostal Assemblies of the World undoubtedly represented the aspirations if not the practices of most Holy Ghost pastors. Never content with two services on Sunday and another midweek, she intoned, the bishop held meetings every night of the week save one.[90]

Though no one explicitly said so, and probably few realized it, the sheer frequency of these gatherings served at least three functions beyond worship. Knowing who was really in and really out constituted the first. Nonbelievers, mainline Protestants, and radical evangelicals who attacked the infant movement were, in a sense, no issue since everyone already knew where they stood. The problem lay with the fair-weather friends. David D. Hall writes about this phenomenon among New England Puritans. He calls them "'horse-shed'" Christians—adherents who participated but kept their distance.[91] Frequent meetings helped to identify the horse-shed Christians by making clear who was—and was not—willing to invest the requisite hours. Once those hours had been invested, dropping out grew more costly.

Frequent worship also provided a steady source of support for believers' encounters with the hostile world outside, and that support formed a second function. Powerful communal bonds developed during the meeting's heat and confusion. Those bonds thickened during the testimony times when feelings were shared and hurts assuaged. Moreover frequent meetings facilitated information exchange about secular as well as religious matters. Given pentecostals' suspicion of secular newspapers, they likely gained most of their news about the outside world from each other in Holy Ghost meetings.[92] Information filtered this way not only contributed to the saints' sense of swelling numbers but also their feeling of invincibility in the face of external opposition.

Adherents only dimly grasped the third and possibly most important survival function of frequent meetings: the reconfiguring of family relationships. Sometimes the process surely impacted families negatively. Gathering with one's comrades almost every night of the week and all day Sunday left little time for anything else. Emotional needs that the family once satisfied now found satisfaction within the confines of the worship meeting. Yet here we must be careful. The evidence suggests that more often than not pentecostals actually strengthened their families by subordinating them to the discipline and social life of the church. That reinforcement occurred precisely because believers' deepest values were rooted in ideals more enduring than the contingencies of the moment.[93]

Pentecostal worship was more than it seemed. Outsiders saw only fanaticism, but insiders saw more. They discerned order within disorder, reason within unreason. Not a bad bargain for saints heaven bound.

7

Rhetoric

The physical setting intimated the structure of the rhetoric. To the casual observer Holy Ghost meeting places must have looked like scenes from a Currier and Ives lithograph: rickety tents, backwoods huts, storefront halls needing paint. With few exceptions pentecostals studiously disregarded society's notions of aesthetic attractiveness.[1] Contemporary descriptions of their buildings emphasized the bareness of the walls, the lack of windows, the absence of heat and flooring, the general messiness, even the determined obscurity of the location.[2] Leaders boasted that their buildings ranked among the humblest in the land, and with good reason. "[B]arn" or "barn-like" was the way stalwarts described the Azusa Mission, the revival's most heralded meeting place.[3] After comparing simple pentecostal structures to the elaborate edifices of the mainline churches, one British partisan predictably found the latter sadly lacking. "Nowhere in the New Testament do we find the Apostles getting subscriptions for the erection of buildings, or spending their time in the building of sanctuaries."[4] In saints' minds a worship place needed to provide shelter and a modicum of heat, but not much else.

Close inspection would have shown, however, that pentecostals rarely fashioned their worship dwellings as haphazardly as first appeared. Outsiders may have seen only bare walls, but insiders saw something else: banners heralding the Lord's soon return, posters proclaiming the full gospel, hand-lettered Scripture verses promising divine healing, discarded crutches, trusses, wheelchairs, eyeglasses, and other paraphernalia of once-broken bodies—all trophies won in the war against Satan's scourge.[5] The same squint-eyed intentionality governed even the use of rooms within the meeting place. Zealots frequently set apart a specific area, preferably an "Upper Room" for prayer, Holy Spirit baptism, and impartation of supernatural gifts.[6] They particularly liked to take over the devil's warehouses—vacant saloons and dance halls ranked high on the list—and turn them into houses of worship.[7] Few of these actions were accidental. Converts were affirming their ability to transform disordered zones into ordered ones. No medieval cathedral could have spoken more forcefully of its builders' vision.

Observers who knew how to read the cues embedded in the revival's architectural settings would have known something else too. They would have discerned that the stormy preaching that took place in those settings was more intricately structured than first met the ear. But that structure acquired meaning only in the context of inspired exhortation.

Holy Ghost Preaching

If in principle pentecostals' architecture originated in the skies, so did their preaching—when there was preaching, that is. In the very beginning many services lacked a sermon, consisting entirely of songs, prayers, testimonies, and corporate praise, repeated over and over, hour after hour. At times the Almighty's power seemed so overwhelming that a sermon appeared to be an irreverent attempt by mere humans to intrude on the solemnity of the Holy Spirit's workings. When the Lord finally did lead one or another to stand up and preach, they tried to keep the Holy Spirit in the foreground and themselves in the background. In principle and often in practice worshipers simply waited for the Almighty to choose a vessel for the evening. No one knew who would speak until the moment for the sermon arrived and someone volunteered. Moreover, as at a ballroom dance, protocol dictated that the main exhorter should let another saint cut in and present their own sermon if the latter felt inspired for the task.[8] Other preachers or lay persons in the congregation also felt free to mount the platform and add their own commentary to the main speaker's sermon if the Holy Spirit so led.[9]

Unfortunately the Lord sometimes seemed to prompt two or more individuals to try to talk at the same time. Controversy erupted. The prominent evangelist Frank Bartleman remembered that at a Los Angeles tent revival he wanted to deliver the evening's sermon, but another soul "jumped up" ahead of him and "rattled like an empty wagon for a half hour, saying nothing." Exasperated, Bartleman arose and proceeded to preach, but was forced to fend off renewed efforts by the original speaker to regain control of the pulpit. Bartleman apparently learned a lesson from this contest. On a later occasion, when a "fanatical preacher" tried to cut him off, he publicly rebuked the challenger and stood his ground. Yet Bartleman knew when to take his turn. At a Sunday morning worship service in Pasadena, the Holy Spirit prompted him to jump up and race across the platform shouting at the top of his lungs. But then he thought better of it and sat down, reflecting, "I did not want to interfere with the one speaking."[10] Manners counted too.

Planned or not, all preachers sought to make themselves mouthpieces for the Holy Spirit's very own words. Worldly standards of pulpit eloquence meant nothing. An advertisement placed in the March 17, 1917, issue of the *Pentecostal Evangel,* for example, called for an assistant with specified credentials: "A young man who can lead singing, hold prayer meetings, visit the sick, work at the altar, and take a preaching service now and then. Need not be a great preacher but must be faithful and filled with the Spirit." Translated: good preaching was fine but not necessary. J. D. Wells of San Jose, California, did not wait to be asked. He went ahead and advertised his own qualifications, the foremost of which seemed to be a "Gospel tent, 40' x 60', wired for electric lights, seating 500, ready for summer campaign."[11] If Brother Wells's portfolio included homiletic skills, he did not think it important enough to say.

If native preaching talent counted little, prepared sermons counted even less. The issue here was not whether it was permissible to write the sermon out and read it (obviously not), nor whether it was all right to rely on an outline (generally not). Rather the question was whether God sanctioned humanly constructed sermons at all. Charles Fox Parham boasted that he never prepared a sermon nor even thought about what he would say until the moment arrived. Even then, he did not think much about what he was saying, for the Holy Spirit supplied the words.[12] No one commanded greater awe in pentecostal circles than healing evangelist Maria Woodworth-Etter. And no one insisted more strenuously that until the moment she started to speak, she had no idea what she would say. Invariably the "power came," she avowed. "[A]ll I had to do was to open my mouth."[13] The Holy Spirit not only dictated what exhorters said, but also where in the meeting hall they would hold forth. According to one approving report, the featured speaker for a 1906 Ohio camp meeting "preached all over the tent, up and down the aisles, upon the benches [until he] fell prostrate in the straw."[14] High praise that was.

Pulpit Artistry

Though the pentecostal preaching ideal emphasized direct and spontaneous inspiration by the Holy Spirit, saints nonetheless quickly discovered that the Lord worked in predictable ways—and many of them proved both remarkably effective and, well, practical.

First came platform charisma, magnetism behind the pulpit. Apostolic preachers cultivated an almost legendary ability to capture an audience's interest and move it to action. Aimee McPherson's style offers a classic case in point. Descriptions of Sister's ministry were legion. Almost no one, except the most ardent partisan, ever thought to attribute her success to the conceptual weight of her sermons (described by one reporter as a "mass of commonplaces, melodrama, tawdriness, and cheap emotionalism").[15] Yet virtually all acknowledged her platform prowess. A writer for *Harper's Monthly*

Magazine thus spoke of McPherson's "electrical quality" and "inexplicable . . . magnetism," adding that she evinced an "uncanny" aptitude for sensing the waning of attention. Observers of all persuasions commented on Sister's singular ability first to tickle her listeners' funny bones and then to pull their heart strings.[16]

And then there was verbal agility. Ann Rowe Seaman writes of the "blowtorch" preaching style of pentecostal television evangelist Jimmy Swaggart.[17] With one deftly chosen word, Seaman isolates a key feature of the movement's homiletic tradition. In the beginning, Charles Parham achieved regional notoriety for his facility with language. One visitor clocked his delivery at 250 words a minute. If there was any doubt about Parham having the gift of tongues, the visitor dryly added, "he has at least the gift of one, for . . . he never stumbles for a word."[18] Parham's biographers have emphasized his rhetorical agility on the platform, saying that he readily switched back and forth between traditional evangelical theology and dense asides on Zionism, dispensational premillennialism, British Israelism, the fate of the Ark, and local politics—all washed down with much humor and varieties of gospel music.[19] Parham represented many. When William H. Durham mounted a three-week assault on sin in New York City in the spring of 1911, (likely) Robert H. Brown, the host pastor, breathlessly reported the results: "this man of God poured fiery shot and shell into the ranks of the enemy, dealing death to sin and striking terror to everything that savored with compromise."[20] Brown did not directly comment on Durham's facility with the language. But then he hardly needed to. Anyone who could assail the enemy with "fiery shot and shell" for three weeks running must have possessed uncommon mastery of the mother tongue.

Platform charisma did not place a premium on delicacy. A single letter, now brittle and yellowed with age, made that point effectively. Bearing only the date "Friday," posted from the village of Banbridge, England, the note succinctly stipulated what the Banbridge church members most wanted: "a good rousing *Holy Ghost Preacher*."[21] We can reasonably guess that stentorian volume formed a large part of rousing. Russell E. Richey observes that early Methodists were never afraid of the voice[22]—and neither were their pentecostal heirs. So it was that Charles W. Carter, an otherwise unknown preacher, made the apostolic message reverberate along the streets of Pasadena in the fall of 1906. Though Carter claimed the "'gift of tongues,'" allowed a local reporter, he certainly had the "gift of gab"—powered by a "voice like the call of the wrath to come."[23]

Gusto required plainness. Though pentecostal preachers fell into arcane discussions from time to time, on the whole they sought ordinary words for ordinary people. Again McPherson represented hundreds. The logo of her periodical, *Bridal Call,* said it perfectly. "We endeavor to set forth in simple words . . . the plain message of Salvation."[24] Apostolic preachers prided themselves on the commonsense forthrightness of their sermons. "God wants men and women that will preach this Gospel square from the shoulder," declared a California zealot.[25] No one wanted to be patronized, but the profundity of simplicity was another matter altogether.

Platform charisma also needed dramatic tension, which the effective pentecostal preacher found in opposition. Sometimes opposition lay wholly outside the movement's boundaries, in the secular world or in the established denominations—what A. J. Tomlinson scorned as "modern churchanity."[26] More often, however, the antagonistic force resided squarely within the movement itself. One example suffices. The premier issue of *Latter Rain Evangel,* published in the fall of 1908, recounted the proceedings of a typical Sunday afternoon worship service in the Stone Church in Chicago (probably the first pentecostal congregation to own a comparatively large, architecturally impressive building). The young pastor, William H. Piper, bore a reputation in Holy Ghost circles as a thoughtful and forceful speaker. Early in the morning, the article tells us, the Holy Spirit descended on Piper and told him what to preach that day. Piper proceeded to preach about Old Testament dispensations, tithing, and missions. At regular intervals tongues messages erupted. Translated, they confirmed the validity of Piper's teachings. But then, halfway through the meeting, demonic forces entered the sanctuary. Piper abruptly stopped: "I feel Satan is opposing this service." Then the Holy Spirit spoke through an interpreted tongues utterance: "Our Father in heaven . . . rebuke every power of Satan in this room . . . [B]id every demon depart from this room, every oppressing power of Satan." Shortly afterward the Holy Spirit spoke words of thanksgiving: "Oh, our Father, we praise Thee that Thou hast overcome all."[27] The events that transpired that Sunday afternoon proved symptomatic. Besides revealing the supernaturally charged atmosphere of early pentecostal worship (even at its most formal), they show how Piper heightened the tension of the service by pitting the powers of evil against the powers of righteousness. He did this not abstractly, not in some far-off heathen land, but right there, deep within the sacred space of the sanctuary itself. That Piper almost certainly acted without design made the regularizing function of his preaching style all the more significant.

Like evangelicals in general, especially in the South, apostolic preachers rendered their words both cogent and memorable in yet another way, and this time the Holy Spirit received none of the credit (or blame). In a word, parsons instinctively grasped that things went better with sugar. Admittedly, hardly any of the published sermons contain much levity, but that fact likely reflects the sanitizing hand of editors rather than what was actually said. Indeed, Frank Bartleman, perennial watchdog of pastoral mores, went out of his way to condemn the prevalence of "wise-cracking" in the pulpit—a sure indication that it took place.[28] What follows may not have originated in the pulpit, but most of it can be traced to pastors and evangelists, who likely preached as they wrote.

That much pentecostal rhetoric equaled pure corn stands beyond dispute. Homer L. Cox expressed gratitude for a friend receiving the Holy Ghost's "embalming fluid from the great 'Undertaker' in the skies."[29] Brothers Dave Givens and Bert Doss reported back to Apostolic Faith headquarters that they had gone "hunting with the Gospel gun in the woods of Carterville, MO."[30] Not to be outdone, the problem with Billy Sunday, shot back one Kansas *Apostolic Faith* partisan, was that his converts too often "hit the saw dust trail, but not the solid rock."[31] Corn or not, Holy Ghost preachers loved to lace their sermons with down-home stories. The Holiness Church leader A. B. Crumpler—a near-pentecostal—remarked that if people wanted to attack him for his radical views that was fine. He said it reminded him of the man who let his wife pummel him: "It don't hurt me, and it does her a heap of good."[32] Charles Parham enjoyed telling of the young man who received a dollar for six months preaching. When someone remarked that it was very poor pay, the fellow replied, "True but it was poorer preaching."[33] Judging from the saccharine piety of Carrie Judd Montgomery's *Triumphs of Faith*, one would surmise that a more earnest soul never lived. Yet even Montgomery could reprint the story of a Mississippi steamboat pilot who said he did not know where the river snags lay. "I reckon I know where the snags ain't, and that's where I expect to do my sailing."[34]

Saints proved surprisingly capable of finding ironic humor in their own foibles—though usually with a hortatory end in view. One missionary, hoping to dispel Western parochialism, told a story about herself. When she visited a cloth factory in China in the 1920s, all of the women and girl workers shielded their eyes with their hands. The missionary later learned that they did so because they found the sight of a person with blue eyes and light hair so repulsive they were nearly "incapacitated" for work.[35]

Occasionally pentecostals' humor could be dignified as wit, and classic by any measure. When the Presbyterian pastor S. A. Jamieson converted to the movement, he lamented that all of his old sermon texts had burned. "They were very dry," he deadpanned.[36] The Massachusetts pastor Albert Weaver liked to tell of the woman who found herself in the midst of a severe storm at sea. Rushing up to the ship's captain, she demanded, "'Captain, is there any hope?' 'Only in God, madam,' said he. 'Oh, my, has it come to that?' was her reply."[37] An Ohio pastor, T. C. Leonard, acquired a reputation for his Irish wisecracks, as barbed as they were quick. Distrustful of things Californian, he traced the divisive Oneness teaching (that God was one, not triune) to the region of "lost angels." Borrowing from St. Paul, Leonard went on to characterize the views of Oneness rival G. T. Haywood as "Haywood and stubble," and his paper, *Voice in the Wilderness,* as *Voice from the Wilderness.*[38]

Pentecostals also used sarcasm to gouge their enemies. Parham led the way, challenging a local Baptist antagonist who routinely tagged his name with Ph.D., D.D., and LL.D. to come by and spend a week at Parham's school. When God was finished with him, Parham promised, he would want to add "A.S.S." to the list.[39] William Welch, likely editor of the Seattle-based *Midnight Cry,* honed the art of sarcasm to a fine point. In a series of articles on the pretensions of other sects, Welch began by nailing the "cunning Fox" of the Quakers and the "Camel" of the Disciples. He found Phineas Bresee of the Nazarenes "not quite large enough for an M. E. Bishop but plenty large enough to take the place of Christ." Welch considered the Methodist Episcopal Church, South, an improvement over its northern cousin, but "one being north of Christ and the other south of him He must be some where between the two." If they merged, as rumored, said Welch, "we are wondering if they will be to the east or west of Christ but we are guessing . . . that they will travel to the east and thus miss him altogether."[40]

Not surprisingly, people who knew how to deploy humor in their cause also knew how to use public advertising. The latter genre revealed, as no other body of texts, how instinctively—not to mention how effectively—pentecostals leavened Holy Spirit ideology with dollops of down-to-earth shrewdness. Saints gave the recipe away when they decided to advertise their meetings in newspapers, posters, and mass distribution flyers. Consider this broadside for a Memphis summer encampment.

The Summer Campmeeting!

IN MEMPHIS

JULY 7TH TO 18TH, OR LONGER . . .

We are expecting the following workers to be in the Meeting: Harry E. Bowly, M. Allen Weed, J. S. Tally, C. Holt, Z. D. Simpson, W. P. Mims, J. H. Duke, and others whom the Lord shall send . . .[41]

Several points merit comment here. First, the ending date remained unspecified, as befitted a pentecostal encampment. It would have been presumptuous to say exactly how long the Holy Spirit would move among the saints. Second, the promised speakers were not identified as evangelists, pastors, or missionaries—that is, men with a specifiable vocation—but only as "workers," undefined toilers in the Lord's vineyard, free to go and do as the Holy Spirit directed. Third, the roster of speakers remained open-ended. There was no way to tell in advance whom the Lord might send. But then—and this is the key point—the advertisement prudently went on to *name* the instruments that the Holy Spirit would be using on this particular occasion. Though some of those names are now lost to obscurity, others (Bowly, Holt, and Mims) are remembered as gifted evangelists. All had been tried and tested out on the kerosene circuit—seasoned speakers, definitely worth coming to hear, the ads effectively said.

In truth, the Memphis flyer well represented most texts of this sort, for many of the early advertisements heralded speakers' pulpit skills without apology. Readers were assured that J. S. McConnell and his wife would prove "Fearless, Eloquent, Biblical"; that Pastor Harvey McAlister would acquit himself as an "Able Bible Expositor"; that W. R. Croson's listeners would hear the "Word of God preached as it is written"; that B. E. Lasater would speak on subjects of "Great Prophetic Importance"; that W. H. Merrin, the "'Cyclone Evangelist'" would not disappoint; that R. G. "Preach It" Cockerell would live up to his reputation as the "Texas Whirlwind Evangelist." Advance billing promised a great deal to those who traveled to hear 84-year-old ex-Congressman William D. Upshaw.

NOBODY SLEEPS WHILE HE SPEAKS
HIS SERMONS ARE BIBLICAL
HIS STORIES ARE GRIPPING
HIS MANNER IS MAGNETIC.[42]

Pentecostals' perennial fondness for bigness brought out their best (or worst) advertising instincts.

WORLD'S GREATEST PENTECOSTAL CONVOCATION
A Nation Wide Union Revival Meeting
Evangelists with World-Wide Reputation will speak[43]

Seven Days in Portland!
By a Unanimous Vote of Great
Spiritual Mass Meeting the
Well Known
Beloved Evangelist
Mother Kennedy
continues
Revival Services . . .
Great throngs are attending every service . . .
MOTHER KENNEDY can be heard all over the tabernacle
as she preaches in a clear, pleasant, voice
imbued by the Holy Spirit.[44]

Admittedly, not everyone measured pulpit artistry by flamboyance. A few counted careful preparation the mark of a truly successful sermon. The respected Assemblies of God Bible teacher Frank M. Boyd, for example, excoriated young men who substituted zeal for knowledge. All too often, he charged, they fell back on personal testimony rather than solid biblical exposition. They shouted "'Glory to God!'" and "'Hallelujah!'" and performed a few "gymnastic stunts" when they ran out of something solid to say. Boyd left his mark by insisting that inspiration presupposed rather than replaced thorough preparation and orderly presentation.[45]

Saints did not define good preaching as homiletics professors in the mainline seminaries would have defined it, but the criteria were just as real. Success tasted just as sweet, and failure just as bitter. The diary of Pentecostal Holiness Church editor George Floyd Taylor detailed weary months of itinerating through dusty North Carolina hamlets. It might be read as a chronicle of soldiering behind the pulpit for uncertain money and few results.[46] Still others simply flubbed as preachers. Taylor's boss, J. H. King, made a similar confession near the end of his own life. "If a large audience is the criterion by which to judge the importance, value and worth of the work done, then I am an utter failure."[47] Preaching was a hard dollar under any circumstances, but it became harder when speakers found themselves unable to measure up to their hearers' expectations.

In sum, speakers brought a wide variety of tools to the pulpit and skillfully put them to work (or felt the sting of reproach when they failed). Platform charisma, loquacity, timing, drama, humor, expansiveness and, sometimes, even study, paid off. Several decades passed before pentecostal Bible training schools offered courses in homiletics. But that hardly mattered. The faithful already knew what they liked and rewarded it accordingly. Artists of preaching like McPherson, Parham, and Durham embodied the ideal. And when the ideal found voice, no one thought to ask for a refund.

8

Customs

If early pentecostals behaved in recognizable ways at worship, they behaved in equally recognizable ways at work and play. Expectations inherited from the radical evangelical tradition and then adapted to new needs governed a large part of each day. This chapter analyzes those protocols—the largely un-self-conscious yet clearly discretionary codes of eating, dressing, playing, and personal deportment that helped to define saints' lives and mark their place on the American religious landscape.

Holy Ghost customs bore multiple dimensions, ranging from the primitivist to the pragmatic. The first prompted believers to defy many of the behavior patterns normative in the established churches and in respectable, middle-class American society. Sometimes that defiance stemmed from biblical prescriptions, sometimes from a desire to follow the Holy Ghost's direct instructions, and sometimes, it seemed, from nothing loftier than a sectarian fondness for angularity. At the same time, the pragmatic impulse tempted converts to embrace activities that can only be described as accommodationist in function if not in intent. They owed less to scriptural or spiritual imperatives than to the insistent demands of social survival in twentieth-century America.

Stand Up for Jesus

Over the centuries the Christian church had forbidden many activities that the general population found enjoyable—and therefore pursued regardless of the clergy's displeasure. But culture-denying impulses defined some Christian traditions more than others. In the late nineteenth century British and North American evangelicals distinguished themselves by resisting many of the customs prevalent in respectable society.[1] The most radical among them moved considerably further, single-mindedly denouncing all but the most basic comforts of life.

The British Anglican C. T. Studd never quite became pentecostal himself, but he merits brief examination because his teachings and personal example influenced saints' ideals about the demands of the separated life. Renowned in England in the 1880s for his prowess on the Cambridge University cricket team, Studd later served as a missionary to China, India, and central Africa. He inherited a fortune when his father died, but promptly donated almost all of it to independent ministries such as George Mueller's Bristol orphanage. Studd lived as he gave. As a missionary he allowed himself no needless comforts. The one-time athlete routinely slept on the floor, sat on backless chairs, dressed in coarse cloths, and ate the plainest foods available. When he grew old and his teeth rotted, he refused to buy false teeth in order to save the Lord's money. He lived in native-built houses, never took a holiday, and avoided recreation. Routinely working eighteen-hour days, Studd persisted in his Bible translation work even when he was too weak to sit up. And he expected his co-workers on the mission field to do likewise. Studd dismissed conventional Christianity as worse than useless—equivalent to "shooting lions with a pea-shooter." What the age demanded, he insisted, was a "*red hot, unconventional, unfettered Holy Ghost religion,*" one that would generate "*reckless sacrifice and heroism.*" The supposedly innocent pleasures offered by contemporary culture evoked his contempt. Studd called for a "fiery baptism of the Holy Ghost" that would transform "soft, sleek Christians into hot lively heroes for Christ, who will advance and fight and die." In words that would reverberate through decades of missionary lore, Studd insisted that the church required "forked-lightning Christians"—or none at all. "A lost reputation," he judged, served as the "best degree for Christ's service."[2]

Saints aimed to follow Studd's example. To be sure, the standard evangelical taboos on dancing, gambling, cards, tobacco, alcohol, and immodest apparel received little attention, not because anyone doubted their evil, but because they remained too inconceivable to require explicit condemnation. Believers focused their scorn, rather, on a wide range of recreational activities that most evangelicals—not to mention most respectable men and women of the age—considered the innocent pleasures of God's creation. We can organize these proscriptions into categories pertaining to the mouth, eyes, ears, body, and genitals.

Mouth taboos began with forbidden foods and drinks. They included meat in general and shellfish and hog products in particular, soft drinks in general and Coca Cola in particular. Mouth taboos also included coffee, tea, ice cream, chewing gum and, of course, medicinal drugs. Both the definition and the enforcement of these proscriptions varied from time to time and from group to group. At the Assemblies of God's 1914 organizing meeting, for example, elders decided that eating meat was so controversial that they would leave it to individuals to decide for themselves.[3] Though no Holy

Ghost sect ever endorsed the use of tobacco, Church of God elders wrangled for years about the scope of the evil. Was it moral to grow tobacco if that was the only way to earn a living? Was it permissible to work in a store that sold cigarettes?[4] Whatever the variations, the main point is that pentecostal leaders sought to outlaw many consumables other Christians quietly tolerated or simply took for granted.[5]

Some went a good deal further. In the early days many stalwarts fasted regularly.[6] The students at Charles Parham's Bible school in Topeka reportedly had gone without food for six days before Agnes Ozman (and then others) spoke in tongues on January 1, 1901.[7] The black saints who received Holy Spirit baptism at the Bonnie Brae house on April 9, 1906, just before the Azusa Mission outpouring, had been fasting for ten days before "Pentecost fell."[8] The diary of Henry L. Fisher, the founding patriarch of the United Holy Church in North Carolina, revealed that he often fasted on Friday, apparently in preparation for the evening service.[9] In 1910 three zealots in the "Western" part of the United States reputedly starved themselves to death by trying to go without food for the biblically sanctioned forty days.[10] Such deprivation represented many things, some of them prudential. But the most obvious included a primitivist yearning for direct contact with God, regardless of social conventions. "Fast days carried people out of ordinary time—or out of time's decay—back to that moment when all things were 'new'" is how David D. Hall describes the practice's aims in colonial New England. He might well have said the same about early pentecostal culture.[11]

Mouth taboos extended to what came out of the mouth as well. Again, the appropriateness of lying, swearing, and telling racy stories never arose. Pentecostals treated such behaviors as they treated cannibalism: too obviously evil to require explicit condemnation. But they did worry about the frivolous use of the tongue. The latter included idle talk, foolish talk, jesting with friends, and telling tall tales. Aimee McPherson—never at a loss for words herself—scored the practice of reciting limericks at a grade school play. A child of God, she insisted, should not utter "one idle word (let alone foolish words)."[12] Faith home director Martha Wing Robinson chastised herself for indulging in "general conversation" when she could have been better occupied in prayer.[13] The same proscriptions applied at the grass roots. One sister's congregation in Alamo, Texas, rebuked this otherwise faceless soul for using tobacco and "carrying on foolish & gesting."[14] A Chicago correspondent allowed that a Christian should be "cheerful, light-hearted, free and sunny, but not overtalkative." Too much prattling, she explained, "interrupts the spirit of devotion."[15] The ban on inappropriate speech extended even to euphemisms, what one earnest partisan called "Sugar-Coated Swearing." Offending terms included "My goodness, good gracious, Sakes alive, Gee whiz."[16] A Lytham, England, newspaper reported in 1913 that a local missioner placed "foolish talking and jesting" on the same plane with fornication and idolatry.[17] In this context we can appreciate A. J. Tomlinson's otherwise inexplicably dour insistence that much of the friction within the church "germinate[d] in lightness and frivolous conversation around the fireside."[18]

The basic issue here was clear. A flapping tongue was controlled by the self, not the Holy Ghost. When believers completely yielded themselves to the Lord, explained the English vicar A. A. Boddy, the Lord took command of the organ's muscles. On those occasions true worship became, in Boddy's telling words, "almost involuntary."[19] Contrary to stereotype, women no less than men were determined to see the tongue regulated. *Triumphs of Faith* editor Carrie Judd Montgomery warned believers to heed James 3:6: "The unsanctified tongue is called a 'fire,' which is able to defile the whole body and to set on fire the whole course of nature . . . 'IT IS SET ON FIRE OF HELL.'"[20] That the prolific Montgomery herself wrote—and presumably spoke—incessantly raises the suspicion that she was flailing her own demons as much as others'.

The misuse of the eyes and ears seemed just as bad. At one time or another partisans censured the reading of novels, newspapers, and comic books.[21] They attacked "worldly music" with vehemence. The latter included ragtime, tunes played on the fiddle, and classical violin.[22] The British firebrand Stephen Jeffreys dismissed tony music in church as "nothing but rubbish."[23] Admittedly, if the number of inquiries directed to editors of the various publications can be taken as a reliable index of the way many among the faithful felt, the laity seemed reluctant to give up music with a snappy rhythm. But leaders insisted. So it was that one questioner, who asked if it was all right to play waltzes on the piano at home, learned that it was better to play "sacred music" at all times.[24] Another leader allowed that temperance and patriotic songs might be acceptable under certain circumstances, but in general one should stick with Christian tunes.[25]

The way that a true child of God clothed and adorned the body also fell under the wary eye of pentecostal watchdogs. This issue was more complicated than one might suspect. Several sources suggest that the earliest partisans actually displayed a measure of openness to secular clothing styles. According to Howard Goss, a founder of the Apostolic Faith movement in the Southwest, "lady workers" in particular adopted the styles of the day. Bedecked with silks, satins, and jewels, they were, he remembered, "very smartly turned out."[26] But things soon changed. By 1910 or 1915 at the latest pentecostals had largely adopted the "POOR-DRESS-GOSPEL," as one writer put it.[27] Elders particularly worried about superfluous items of adornment, including watches, rings, hat pins, neckties, and brass buttons. At the

Azusa mission, one writer declared, God's Spirit literally grabbed the hands of converts and compelled them to pull the rings from their fingers and hat pins from their hair.[28]

Alluring clothing warranted repeated condemnation—which suggests, of course, that the problem would not go away. Neckties and abbreviated sports attire for men earned occasional rebuke,[29] but, predictably, writers found women's attire more worrisome. The main problem was the plain fact that women's clothing—or the lack of it—attracted men's attention. An unnamed writer for the Kansas *Apostolic Faith* assailed "scant attire, peekaboo waists, hobble skirts and flimsy silken stockings." Brushing aside any possibility that men might be responsible for the rise in sexual misdeeds, the author placed the blame squarely on the heads of "mothers and daughters themselves."[30] Females shared males' concerns. "Women who want to please Jesus," asserted one Church of God matriarch, "will never make their clothes so attractive as to draw the attention of men."[31] Pentecostal Bible schools went out of their way to regulate female students' dress. The Peniel Bible Institute in Dayton, Ohio, for example, required female students not to cut or curl their hair, to forgo cosmetics, and to wear uniforms.[32] Items of adornment could be almost as dangerous as beguiling clothing. For the Quaker pentecostal Levi Lupton, no Holy Spirit-filled woman would degrade herself with any form of adornment, however innocuous by worldly standards. "What does that gaudy ribbon . . . on your dress say? . . . TAKE CARE! [Y]ou might just as well write on your clothes: 'No truth in religion.'"[33]

Pentecostals' determination to articulate and enforce behavioral codes based on biblical or direct Holy Spirit prescriptions rather than convenience or convention emerged with particular force in the realm of sexual behavior. In order to understand this process of self-definition, we first need to ask how the contrary image arose in the popular imagination.

The stereotype of pentecostals as libertines on the lam is almost as old as the revival itself. Saints themselves bore much of the blame, for they used charges of immoral sexual activities as a club for thumping each other in intramural power struggles. Charles Parham, for example, claimed that lewd behavior had disgraced Holy Ghost missions in the Midwest and southern California. "The wild, weird prayer services in many of these fanatical meetings, where the contact of bodies in motion is as certain and damning as in the dance hall, leads to free-love, affinity-foolism and soul-mating." Parham asserted—without a trace of evidence, one might add—that some leading Chicago workers had found themselves in a "delicate condition" because unorthodox views of sanctification had eroded their moral standards.[34] *Word and Witness* repudiated Parham himself for unspecified "sins."[35] Still more damaging was the charge or implication by some factions that others espoused free love teachings and practices. This indictment cropped up in the early issues of the Azusa *Apostolic Faith,* reappeared in periodicals throughout the United States and in Britain, and troubled black as well as white fellowships.[36]

Outsiders added fuel to the fire. Radical evangelicals perennially claimed that Holy Ghost folk engaged in sexual practices too vile to detail in polite company.[37] Novelists and movie producers soon joined in, shrewdly sensing that pentecostals—who lacked the financial and legal resources to fight back—offered a lucrative source of sizzling plot lines. So it was that John Steinbeck would forever typecast apostolics as poor, illiterate, and licentious in his 1939 classic, *The Grapes of Wrath.* "I used ta get the people jumpin' an' talkin' in tongues and glory-shoutin' till they just fell down an' passed out," said the Reverend Casy, a one-time Holy Ghost preacher. "An' then—you know what I'd do? I'd take one of them girls out in the grass, an' I'd lay with her. Done it ever' time."[38] So too the adultery, cruelty, and hypocrisy of a black "Fire Baptized" preacher formed one of the main narrative threads in James Baldwin's 1952 classic, *Go Tell It on the Mountain.* When the protagonist—significantly named Gabriel Grimes—finally found the strength to resist sexual temptation, dance hall women laughed at him. "[T]hey knew a long brown girl who could make him lay his Bible down. He fled from them; they frightened him." A pentecostal holy man, it seemed, never escaped vulnerability.[39]

By the 1990s Hollywood had gone to great lengths to avoid any hint of racial, ethnic, or sexual stereotyping. Yet in *Cape Fear* Robert DeNiro played a cigar-smoking, pentecostal "cracker" turned psychopathic rapist-murderer. DeNiro's villainous character, tattooed with Bible verses and a cross, met his violent demise babbling in tongues. Reviewers, tasting a bit of blood themselves, rushed in for the kill on this overwrought remake of a 1962 thriller. Yet none intimated that the main character himself—described by one as a "homicidal genius . . . gone hillbilly and Pentecostal"—might have been wildly improbable.[40] Admittedly Robert Duvall's *The Apostle,* released in 1998, offered a more textured portrait of a fireball preacher as a man of integrity struggling with his own demons. But even if Duvall's character was pentecostal, which may be debated, he still emerged as violent, poorly educated and, of course, a womanizer.[41]

Fact or fiction? Common sense tells us surely some of both, but the preponderance of evidence supports the latter. First, hard proof of sexual misconduct by first-generation leaders is virtually impossible to come by. Unquestionably some notables were careless of appearances, but that is not the same as proof. Second, perceived strayers faced discipline in church tribunals or found themselves abandoned by the rank and file (with the notable exception of Aimee McPherson, whose alleged misconduct made great press copy but was never substantiated). Third, no measurable faction ever tried to rede-fine the boundaries of normative sexual behavior, as the Mormons and the Oneida Perfectionists had done. Those who said that pentecostals practiced free love invariably said it about someone else and, except for Charles Fox Parham, never seemed able to name actual sites.[42]

Viewed from afar, then, the most reasonable explanation for the licentious-ness stereotype was self-interest. Insiders' claims that other insiders had strayed into gross immorality helped establish the accusers' own doctrinal and moral purity. Likewise outsiders' claims helped establish the doctrinal and moral integrity of the outsiders—or lined their pockets with ready cash. Moreover pentecostals brought much of the problem on themselves in a way not yet noted. From the beginning they proved eager to flaunt their recti-tude. When conversion, sanctification, and Holy Spirit baptism did not turn them into saints, but left them ordinary Christians subject to the same fail-ings that bedeviled everyone else, the rest of the world noticed.

This analysis brings us back to the question of prescribed sexual norms within the community. (The crucial word here is *prescribed,* for the evidence is too sketchy to warrant hard conclusions about actual behavior.) Writers said little about sex outside marriage, almost certainly because the idea re-mained too morally preposterous to merit serious attention. But "excess in the conjugal relation" was another matter.[43] One leader after another lined up to call for marital purity (sometimes called soul mating, or spiritual separa-tion, or the clean sheet principle). The central problem, they made clear, was the "burning fever of *lust,*" which Oregon pastor Earnest Hanson depicted as the most heinous of sins.[44] Many, perhaps most, partisans did not discrimi-nate between marital and nonmarital forms of that sin either. "Lust wars against the soul both before and after marriage," declared the Los Angeles pastor Elmer K. Fisher. God permitted the marriage bed so that immature Christians might have an outlet for their urges, but He expected mature Christians to rise above them. "God surely does require us to know how to possess our vessels in sanctification and honor. The fire can be put out in our members."[45] If Fisher expected marital restraint, the Los Angeles-based *Glad Tidings* went further, calling for sexual continence except for procreation. Christian husbands and wives who engaged in sex for any other reason low-ered themselves to the level of animals and birds. "If licentiousness on the part of those that are unmarried deserves punishment . . . does not the same law hold just as binding in the sight of God on those that have been granted a legalized marriage certificate by man?"[46] Lust was lust, whatever the context.

But what about procreation? Did any apostolics forbid sexual relations en-tirely, as the Shakers had done? The answer is possibly yes but probably no. The problem is that some preachers said that other preachers called for marital celibacy in preparation for Christ's second coming.[47] But this charge, like the free love indictment, invariably applied to someone else—someone with no name. With characteristic bluntness, E. N. Bell, editor of *Word and Witness,* dismissed marital celibacy as a "*woman-made theory* . . . hatched by some dried up old maid."[48] Most leaders clearly believed that sex for procreation was necessary and proper because childbearing remained a Christian responsibility. Yet even here, in the scriptural injunction to multiply, pentecostals flew their colors high. Thomas Myerscough, for example, leader of the Pentecostal Missionary Union in Britain, rebuked women who avoided sex because of their "*antipathy* to or fear of the responsibilities of motherhood." If a woman feared the ordeal of childbirth, he judged, the scriptural solution was not celibacy but faith that the Lord would deliver her from the pain. "The child of God must use no means to prevent child-bearing . . . Let us be in true submission to our God."[49] Outsiders might embrace marital sex for love or pleasure, or avoid it for the same reasons, but not pentecostals. Their norms came from above.

The same renunciative pattern held true when the faithful fashioned standards of recreation. Once again the standard evangelical sins of smoking, drinking, dancing, and gambling were too obviously heinous to require much denunciation. For latter rain folk, like the most radical of their radical evangelical parents, the hammer fell on seemingly inconsequential acts. The list was extensive. At one time or another saints forbade or strongly discouraged (in alphabetical order) bands, baseball, boating, bowling, circuses, fireworks, football, loitering, parades, skating, valentines, and zoos. They also denounced amusement parks, beach parties, big dinners, chatting on the telephone, Christmas trees, crossword puzzles, home movies, ice cream socials, kissing bees, scenic railroad trips, and visiting relatives and going on automobile joyrides on Sundays.[50] These were not idle threats either. Minutes of disciplinary proceedings are extremely hard to come by, but the few that have survived show that members were scolded or excluded for a wide range of offenses. The latter included going to picnics and drinking Coca-Cola (thought to contain cocaine), as well as, of course, the more usual evangelical sins of dancing, cussing, chewing, fighting, drinking, smoking, adultery, heresy, and falling into a "disorderly walk."[51]

Pentecostal schools went out of their way to highlight the recreational activities they prohibited. The promotional literature of the Holiness School in Falcon, North Carolina, seemed typical. As noted in Chapter 1, in the entire town one could not buy tobacco or "dope drinks" or attend "Theaters, Circuses, Moving Picture Shows, Base Ball Games, Social Parties and Dances"—all "agencies of evil" sending young people to their "eternal destruction."[52] The China missionary E. May Law boasted that she had transported several

Chinese boys to the Falcon institution precisely because no tobacco products or "deadly picture shows" could be found within that community.[53] The cultural disruption those small children surely experienced seemed a small price to pay when measured against the evils they were spared.

Recreation's near-cousin, purposeless merriment, earned rebuke too. "One of the principal things that our race is running after today [is] pleasure, or fun. FUN! FUN!! FUN!!!" was the way Ohio Quaker Levi Lupton measured the temper of the times.[54] Pastor A. W. Burpee of Massachusetts expressed similar dismay, especially about believers' inclination to eat in restaurants. "Why is it that people have such a mania for a 'good time?'"[55] The songwriters Herbert and Lillie Buffum declared with evident pride that their paper, *Gold Tried in the Fire,* carried "no secular advertisements, no column for nonsense."[56] Pentecostals outside North America, no less than their American counterparts, had no toleration for easy living. One British zealot scorned fire-baptized pastors for looking for prosperous churches and easy positions. "It seems God's Children are *looking for good times,*" he glowered.[57] At a mission school for girls in Mukti, India, one stalwart boasted that the "light minded and frivolous" were "sternly rebuked."[58] In this context it is possible to believe that patriarch Howard Goss may have spoken a measure of truth, or at least desired truth, when he said that the revival's early days saw "almost no teasing or joking, no relating of amusing anecdotes . . . little ordinary visiting."[59]

If the outside world seemed to pursue pleasure for its own sake, the mainline churches bore much of the blame. According to H. W. Schermer, a frequent contributor to the Kansas-based *Apostolic Faith,* outsiders wallowed in "frivolity and vanity." They offered "charity in small doses and society in large chunks." He challenged his readers to imagine Christ "stuffing himself with ice cream, cake and punch, sitting at a card table gambling for a hat pin or cuff button, romping over the green with a half-naked girl, indulging in silly flirtations."[60] Schermer spoke for many. A popular tract of the World War I era, aptly dubbed *The Cook-Stove Apostasy,* attacked church suppers. What the Body of Christ needed, said the tract, was "less *ham* and *sham* and more heaven. Less *pie* and more *piety.* Less use for the cook and more use for the Old Book."[61] Of course pentecostals themselves held church dinners—they called them fellowship suppers—but they distinguished their own affairs, which were spiritually purposeful, from the others, which were merely occasions for entertainment.

Saints never formulated much of a justification for their blanket denunciations of most conventionally accepted pastimes. If pressed, their first response likely would have been to rehearse Bible verses about the body being the temple of the Lord. Their second response would have been to say something about the way such taboos set them apart from the God-ignoring folk around them. Either way, the driving impulse was to lose themselves in another time and place where life was simpler, purer, and, above all, directly ordered by God's will. They desired, in other words, to reenter the New Testament church—or better yet, Eden before the Fall.

Going Out on Faith

Primitivist aspirations emerged with particular clarity when it came to money. For pentecostals, George Mueller's orphanage in Bristol, England, which ran for decades solely on the free will offerings of the faithful, seemed to define the Holy Spirit's ideal. Until the 1920s—and in many places long afterward—a pastor's willingness to serve without guaranteed support formed a prerequisite for employment. W. F. Carothers' 1909 book *Church Government,* the earliest systematic treatment of polity, specified that the only biblically sanctioned pattern of remuneration was to take whatever the Lord and the people chose to provide week by week.[62] Some believers went further, claiming that *all* money-raising devices, including church suppers and auctions, earned God's condemnation because they involved human planning.[63] In brief, saints yearned to depend on God alone for all of their daily material needs. They called it going out on faith.

The principle of radical dependence on the Lord extended to support for one's dependents no less than oneself. Again A. J. Tomlinson's diary proves especially revealing. Just after the turn of the century Tomlinson established an orphanage deep in the western North Carolina mountains. Though the details remain murky, apparently he was the sole source of maintenance for the twenty-one souls who lived at the institution (including his own family). The diary recounted the constant ordeal of securing money for food and fuel. Three or four dollars would arrive in the mail each day, three or four would be expended each day. Taking April 10, 1901, virtually at random, there was no corn for the horses. After Tomlinson spent $4.20 for food for the children, only 72 cents remained for postage for mailing his periodical, *Samson's Foxes* (a noteworthy point in itself). Time passed, nothing changed. Or so it appeared. But then on April 15 "some friends in Ohio" sent $8.95, more than enough for present needs—and the cycle began all over again.[64]

Living by faith functioned as a badge of spiritual status. Anyone who did otherwise, Howard Goss remembered, was considered "hopelessly backslidden."[65] Indeed, in Levi Lupton's mind, a gospel worker needed to transcend even the *desire* for a fixed salary. If saints worried about how they were going to make ends meet, he implied, they would be like other folks seeking "luxury."[66] Missionaries lived by the same standard. Periodicals brimmed with stories of men and women rushing to the foreign field without promise of financial support from the folks at home. According to the accounts, many embarked without sufficient train or freighter fare even to reach their destination. Some left without enough change in their pockets to travel from the mission hall to the trolley station.[67]

The faith principle worked both ways. If pastors and missionaries received only what their followers cared to give, devotees gave only what the Holy Spirit directed. The notion of an annual pledge remained inconceivable.[68] Many assemblies refused even to take up a collection, preferring instead to leave a box at the back of the meeting room for people to contribute as they saw fit.[69] Most of the early periodicals set no subscription price. They asked readers to pay what they could afford or what the Holy Spirit directed.[70] Some periodicals declined advertising because it implied financial dependence on a predictable earthly revenue source.[71] Many of the early camp meetings operated the same way. Believers paid for their food and bedding only as they felt directed.[72] The evidence intimates that more than a few showed up without return train fare, trusting the Lord to get them home again.[73] At the Azusa Mission and probably elsewhere no financial records were kept. Pastor Seymour disbursed funds to outgoing missionaries as he wished. If the absence of bookkeeping reflected a measure of laxness in the glow of the revival, it also reflected a conviction that the Lord kept books and therefore no one else needed to.[74]

The disinclination to countenance the financial protocols of the established churches in particular, and of middle-class life in general, showed up in indirect ways too. Some believers disparaged life insurance. "We still believe in the insurance company of heaven," said one, "that insures against the fire of hell and gives an eternal policy of life everlasting."[75] Throughout the first generation most refused to borrow money. Portland's Apostolic Faith sect, for example, did not permit anyone to preach under its auspices who was known to owe anything to anyone.[76] One editor bluntly informed his readers that the periodical would appear when, but only when, God had provided all the requisite funds for printing and mailing since there would be no indebtedness on his watch.[77] Though Azusa pastor William J. Seymour and some other leaders apparently felt no scruples about using their clergy status for railroad discounts,[78] other, more primitivist-thinking pentecostals would have none of it. Charles Parham and like-minded pastors in the Old Apostolic Faith declared that their God was able to provide full fare whenever it was needed.[79]

Apostolics loved to recount stories showing how the Lord always provided—if one's faith was strong enough. The most common theme might be called the Return Fare Test. In these narratives the Lord directed the partisan to go to a particular place, often far away, with only enough money to get there but no hint of how they would return. So it was that in the summer of 1905 Levi Lupton and an entourage of helpers embarked on a missionary tour of the "Dark Continent." They possessed sufficient funds to journey from Alliance, Ohio, to an unnamed destination in Africa, and then back as far as Liverpool, England—but no farther. In England, Lupton reported, they simply waited until the rest of the fare turned up. Hours before they were scheduled to depart, an envelope arrived containing $486, the exact sum needed. In this account Lupton significantly omitted all sorts of details we might desire, but those mundane matters were beside the point. The story's import lay in another line: "It is splendid to . . . know that you are in the centre of God's will."[80] The following year the evangelist G. B. Cashwell enjoyed similar divine favor. He was working as a Wesleyan holiness preacher in North Carolina in the fall of 1906 when he heard about the Holy Ghost revival blazing in Los Angeles. He determined to go and see it for himself. Apparently Cashwell had enough money to travel from North Carolina to California, but not a dime for the return trip. Yet he trusted the Lord. After receiving Holy Spirit baptism at Azusa, the writer explained, the Lord supplied the return fare with enough left over to buy a suit of clothes.[81]

Shortly after these events, the Holy Spirit prompted evangelists John and Hattie McConnell to travel from Spokane, Washington, to the Stone Church in Chicago to attend a Holy Ghost convention. Their experiences exemplified another common theme, which might be called The Lord Knows Tomorrow Test. Though Hattie was four months pregnant, and they were nearly broke, the McConnells went anyway, trusting that God would meet their temporal needs. A church member provided a place to stay, but no food. Soon their meager funds ran out. With hunger cramping her body, and literally not one penny in hand, Hattie fell on her knees, reminding the Lord that He had promised to supply their needs. At that very moment an anonymous donor slipped three dollars into her hand. A few days later a millionaire church member took them in and generously provided hospitality. Again, we search in vain for concrete details. Who? Where? How much? But Hattie included the only detail that mattered to her: "We were rejoicing in Gods faithfulness."[82]

To what extent can such narratives be taken at face value? Like most stories pentecostals told about their spiritual journeys, there is no way to confirm or disconfirm the factual details. But financial faith narratives had little to do with money and everything to do with faith. The point was to make oneself entirely dependent on the Lord for all of one's daily needs. We simply never read of believers who threw themselves on the Lord's mercy and ended up starving and destitute. All stories were success stories.

That said, many pioneers clearly did sacrifice a great deal—and never thought twice about it. Not a few went hungry in the cause, while others used all of their own resources to rent a tent or a meeting hall.[83] F. M. Britton's pattern may not have been typical, but neither was it rare. Born in 1870, Britton, like many of the founding figures, seemed naturally possessed of a steel spinal column. (We can almost visualize him as the male protagonist in Grant Wood's *American Gothic*.) First Southern Methodist, then Fire Baptized Holiness, then Pentecostal Holiness, Britton crisscrossed Georgia and northern Florida preaching the full gospel message. He supported his first wife when she "stood true to God and died without drugs." At least two of his fourteen children also died without resorting to drugs or, presumably, medical doctors. In this context Britton's recollections of relentlessly itinerating on foot across the southern lowlands seem believable. When there was no money, he ate wild huckleberries and persimmons. He thought nothing of hiking to his destinations and preaching three times a day. On one occasion, which seemed to typify most, Britton found himself sixty miles from home and without train fare. With the matter-of-factness of a weather forecast, he reported that he hoofed the distance in two days, slept on a church bench, used his Bible and songbook as a pillow, and somehow squeezed by on ten cents worth of crackers. "When I got in sight of home," the footsore pilgrim intoned, "I saw my good patient sweet wife look and see me, and she and the children came running to meet me. Oh, how glad I was no mortal tongue can tell."[84]

Early pentecostals, like all Christian groups, were a mixed lot. But few could doubt that Britton, at least, was the genuine article.

Practical Holiness

Denying worldly conventions provided more than spiritual satisfactions, however. Such denials also afforded very tangible real-life benefits. Tobacco ruined health and wasted money. Alcohol destroyed jobs and families. Gambling wrecked savings. Immodest dress dehumanized both men and women. Circuses turned freaks into commodities. Fireworks endangered the lives of producers and spectators alike. Drugs and manufactured medicines (believers saw no distinction between the two) harmed the body, often irreparably. Trashy novels degraded common discourse. Fatty ham, ice cream, and soft drinks led to obesity. The list could be extended but the point should be clear. Taboos that originated in primitivist yearnings for transcendent purity almost always improved health and longevity in the here and now. As long as everyone understood that saints' authority was fundamentally otherworldly, and that their motives were fundamentally holy, they freely touted the prudential benefits of the pentecostal ethic.

Less obvious but equally important for present purposes was the way that pentecostals redefined worldly conventions for their own uses. Consider, for example, their attitude toward secular notions of attractiveness for women. In later years one Church of God matriarch would carefully explain that true comeliness did not reside in the latest fads but in the "beauty of holiness displayed in her face."[85] Saints sensed that the accidents of birth and erosions of time limited natural glamour. But the beauty of holiness was available to anyone and did not require deep pockets. As the *Faithful Standard* pointed out, Holy Spirit women did not need to adorn themselves with worldly fashions since they could buy "[b]etter clothes for the same money" at pentecostal-owned stores.[86] Though saints never managed entirely to extricate themselves from worldly notions of attractiveness—their lionizing of beauty queen convert Edith Mae Pennington being a case in point—the ideal of true versus sham loveliness remained clear.

Then too we might consider the norms for relaxation. Baseball was out, but faith homes were in. The fact that pentecostals set up (or perpetuated) these institutions in all parts of the country proved that they knew how to take time off and enjoy themselves, even if they could not bring themselves to admit it. Residents typically stayed for several days or weeks at a time, paid as they were able, passed the time in singing and prayer and—almost certainly—a good deal of small talk laced with laughter. Edith L. Blumhofer argues that women in particular found opportunities for self-expression in faith homes, many of which were founded and run by women. A stay in those settings fulfilled many of the recreational purposes of a more traditional week at the beach.[87]

Or consider food rituals. If victuals denied served otherworldly needs, victuals enjoyed served thisworldly needs beyond nutrition. Indirect but persuasive evidence suggests that pentecostals, like most culturally or ethnically definable groups, found that eating together acted as a social lubricant, something like alcohol in secular social gatherings. Recalling his first pastorate in Leith, Scotland, the theologian Donald Gee remembered the culinary delights of the church parties with particular fondness.[88] The rotundity of the young Aimee McPherson and photographs of any number of first-generation leaders suggest that he was not alone. An extended account in *Apostolic Faith* of an all-day birthday celebration for Charles Fox Parham in 1912 asserted, with predictable solemnity, that the day was spent in "earnest devotions to God." Perhaps so, but a close reading reveals more. "The day broke forth with beautiful sunshine," we read, and soon the campground was "filled with baskets containing the fat of the land." One participant even described Parham's sermon as "a feast with the Lord."[89] Though the metaphors were of course biblical in origin, the choice of metaphors was as pentecostal as apple pie.[90]

Or consider the sheer fun of the meetings themselves. Patriarch Howard Goss admitted that the revival owed much of its success to its music. Unlike the "slow, dragging and listless" tunes that the established churches offered, apostolics featured "fast music" and singing "at almost break-neck speed."[91] In his study of Depression-era pentecostal sharecroppers, Dan Morgan shows how an enterprising Fresno pastor used the musical talents and tastes of ordinary folk to build a successful church. Moving from storefront missions and turkey sheds, the pastor made a point to fill the front of the new church with souls who could play accordions, guitars, banjos, saxophones, harmonicas, trombones, and trumpets. The sounds of a fiddle, a saw, and a washboard filled the meetings. On that rock that particular church—and presumably many others—was built.[92] Predictably, apostolics preferred the catchy, easy-to-memorize, easy-to-sing songs of Fanny Crosby, Thoro Harris, and Herbert and Lillie Buffum over the historic hymns of the church. The latter required trained musical skills, the former mainly a warm heart.

Or consider the camaraderie of the gatherings, the laughing and crying and sharing of common experiences. Coming together for worship with one's closest friends helped pass many a long winter evening.[93] The few surviving diaries and autobiographies intimate that Holy Ghost folk commonly attended church five or six times a week, and did so at least partly because it offered a time of intensely rewarding fellowship.[94] The pleasures of almost daily church attendance illumine the pages of the journal that Los Angeles leader George B. Studd kept for the year 1908. Studd—younger brother of C. T., whom we met at the outset of this chapter—might be called a mission buff. Nearly every day of the year we find him visiting one meeting or another, occasionally speaking, sometimes offering a public prayer, but usually just showing up, singing, and then going on to a member's house afterward for additional prayer, singing, and—not incidentally—victuals.[95] If enthusiasts like Studd went often, they also went long. Two visitors to a Simcoe, Ontario, revival happily reported that the services had run all day Sunday with only a twenty-minute intermission between them.[96] What could be better?

The sociability always present but discretely denied in the regular worship meetings turned unabashedly explicit at the camp meetings. Descriptions of those affairs customarily highlighted the scheduled services—typically one before breakfast, one in midmorning, one after lunch, and another starting after supper and lasting till the wee hours of the morning. But they also betrayed, however inadvertently, the picnics, the plentiful edibles, the songfests, and the "warm Christian fellowship" interspersed along the way.[97] When the Church of God promised that its Eighth Annual Assembly would not be like a "camp meeting where we go just to have a good time getting blest; where we have shouting, leaping and dancing for joy," the band probably revealed more about itself than it intended.[98] The revival never had much of a social program, but it was profoundly and joyfully communal from first to last.

God's Rule for Prosperity

Common sense manifested itself in subtler and, in the long run, more important ways than securing the health and temporal welfare of individuals or even the movement at large. Simply stated, common sense prompted saints to measure their hours, to husband their energies, and thus prepare themselves to function effectively within the increasingly industrialized, rationally organized rules of modern society. We may reasonably doubt that Holy Ghost believers knew much about Max Weber's *Protestant Ethic and the Spirit of Capitalism,* but deep down they exemplified everything he wrote about.[99]

First of all, time counted. A potpourri of brief examples makes the point. In the 1920s and 1930s Raymond T. Richey achieved national repute as a divine-healing evangelist. Portions of a volume Richey published in 1922 under the title *Helps to Young and Old* might have passed for an updated version of Benjamin Franklin's *Poor Richard's Almanack.* Rise early. Never be unemployed. Never trifle. Never allow your thoughts to wander. Never speak without thinking. Stay busy.[100] According to one editor, saints had "'gone crazy over'" crossword puzzles. That many were trying to solve *Bible* crosswords made no difference. The habit induced them to "waste valuable time"—precious moments that could have been spent in "profitable service."[101] When an inquirer asked E. N. Bell in 1922 about proper hair styles for women, the new Assemblies of God chairman rehearsed the usual litany of advice. But when all was said and done, one of the main reasons for avoiding elaborate braiding was the sheer amount of time it took. The point was clear. They had more productive things to do.[102]

The early twentieth century saw the advent of efficiency studies conceived by researchers like F. W. Taylor and implemented by can-do entrepreneurs like Henry Ford. Pentecostals absorbed that spirit better than they imagined. Time counted, not just for the preaching of the gospel, but for everything. "Laziness is one of the most lamentable diseases that any one can be afflicted with," declaimed the Los Angeles-based *Good Report.* "Nothing but the grace of God is sufficient to deliver one from this dreadful malady."[103] Perhaps so, but a bit of humanly devised structure would surely help, as evident from the military academy atmosphere of many Holy Ghost schools. At the Glad Tidings Bible Institute in San Francisco, for example, students found their schedule prescribed from early morning until late at night, six days a week, Tuesday through Sunday. Monday, allegedly their day off, centered on "washing and thorough house cleaning." Lest prospective students be put off by too much structure, the materials did note that they were allowed one free hour each day—from 10:00 to 11:00 P.M.[104] It is hard to believe that all of the resident adolescents actually saluted this schedule. But the ideal remained clear. The Holy Spirit expected saints to prove themselves not just holy but productive too.

The prudent use of time called for the prudent use of financial resources. The Los Angeles revival was still whimpering in its cradle when an Azusa Mission leader warned the flock that the Lord expected them to carry on with the ordinary affairs of life in a responsible way. They should not "run ahead of the Holy Spirit" by quitting their jobs or by selling their homes or their businesses.[105] Rather they should promptly pay all of their bills: "grocery bills, water bills, furniture bills, coal bills, gas bills, and all honest bills."[106] Even foreign missionaries fell under the same strictures. The South Africa missionary John G. Lake exploded with anger as enthusiastic recruits stepped off the boat without a dime in their pockets and no clue what they would do for support. Trusting the Lord, Lake insisted, did not preclude sensible preparation.[107]

Saving wisely dictated spending wisely. On the eve of the Depression, in an essay aptly titled, "God's Rule for Prosperity," *Pentecostal Evangel* editor Charles E. Robinson averred that prosperity did not mean wealth and ease, but it did mean a sufficient share of the world's goods to make oneself and one's family comfortable. Saints never tired of pointing out that the money spent for tobacco and alcohol for oneself and for one's friends (the latter a key point in itself) could be used in more useful ways. High on the list of needless expenditures was wasted food. Many families cooked more than they ate, a practice "hateful to God." And why—we can feel Robinson really warming to the theme—why devote one's hard-won resources to physicians and drugs? Divine healing provided superior and, significantly, free health care. To waste money on physicians and drugs was "dishonoring to God."[108] The true Christian would not squander money on frivolous gifts either. "Turn the extravagant custom of Christmas giving to good account," urged Quaker pentecostal Levi Lupton. Preferably give to the church, but if you must exchange presents, give books.[109]

If financial prudence behooved Holy Spirit-filled individuals, it also behooved Holy Spirit-filled fellowships. In 1914, Assemblies of God chairman E. N. Bell urged his colleagues to be as watchful of the movement's wallet as of their own. "I personally know one man who has $40,000 he wants to leave to missions," Bell dryly observed, "but he wants us to manifest some *business sense*." There were plenty of potential donors out there, but it was unrealistic to think that any would contribute to a movement "administered by irresponsible individuals."[110] The cat was out of the bag.

Saving wisely, spending wisely. Both presupposed resources to work with in the first place. On that score pentecostals differed sharply among themselves. If some worried about materialism, others sought prosperity without a trace of guilt. For the latter, self-imposed penury betokened not humility but spiritual arrogance. For every F. M. Britton who retreated from any hint of cultural accommodation, there was an L. P. Adams who rushed to embrace the brawniest expressions of American capitalism.

Adams, a one-time attorney, served a White Church of God in Christ congregation in Memphis just before and after World War I. His periodical, *Grace and Truth,* carried all the usual theological fare. But it also carried more worldly fare, including an array of Christian ephemera, all for sale—picture calendars festooned with Scripture verses (just twenty-five cents apiece), a replica of Jesus' cross (just ten cents), and many books. Though Adams hawked the usual evangelical standbys—Blackstone, Riley, Scofield, Seiss, and Simpson—he pushed his own the hardest. "The orders are still coming in from almost every state," Adams breathlessly declared in the October 1915 issue. "[B]ut we are not yet satisfied, because we yearn deeply that [our books] go into the hands of every person." If the Memphis pastor acted locally, he thought globally. "We are not content to reach only a few hundreds, but we want to reach the thousands." Of course reaching thousands required inducements—hence discounts for bulk orders. And for those who purchased before Christmas, there was a special reduction, a "Christmas gift to you." *Grace and Truth,* alas, did not accept checks, and all orders had to be paid in cash in advance.[111]

Adams appropriated Madison Avenue tactics more flagrantly than most, but he was hardly alone. Early pentecostal periodicals promoted reduced-rate Bibles ("When we say this is a great bargain we are prepared to prove our statement"),[112] Precious Promise Boxes (thirty-five cents), Christian Hero books detailing thrilling tales of heroism, adventure, love, triumph, and dangers among cannibals (seventy-five cents) and, for Christmas, "The Leak-Proof Wigglesworth Anointing Bottle," available postpaid for one dollar.[113] The interracial Pentecostal Assemblies of the World marketed Tabernacle Charts for fifty cents apiece, "While They Last," that is, along with Bridegroom Envelopes, fifty cents per hundred. Given the imminence of the end, promptness counted: "Order at once. Supply limited."[114] The idea that the Holy Spirit owned the copyright on pentecostal music apparently did not impress songwriter and publisher R. E. Winsett. When the Gospel Publishing House asked him for permission to use his work, Winsett dickered. Though the songs were worth $10 a piece, the GPH could have them twenty for $100, or ten for $60—but only if they paid cash on the barrel. Otherwise the price went up. "Don't forget also," Winsett added, "that the G. P. H. owes me $195.00 for books."[115]

No one noticed any ironies here, least of all founding theologian Charles

Parham. The Kansas preacher boasted—assuming he wrote the editorials in his monthly *Apostolic Faith*—that he received no salary, took no collections, charged nothing for his periodical, billed students nothing for board, room, or tuition in his Bible school, and allowed visitors at his faith home to stay free until they were healed.[116] He lived by faith alone. Even so, living by faith allowed one to accept a golden opportunity when it was offered. When in the winter of 1912 Parham decided it was time to publish the *Apostolic Faith* in a more regular way, it seemed prudent to secure a reliable printing press. Such printing machinery, one of his associates pointed out, could be purchased—but only if readers acted immediately. "Send in contributions at once," urged the advertising flyer, "in order to take advantage of unparalleled opportunities."[117]

Where financial prudence left off and financial covetousness began was sometimes hard to tell. I have discovered only one instance of alleged outright theft in pentecostal circles: George Studd's overcoat disappeared from the Azusa mission.[118] But in other ways pentecostals ventured, or were perceived to venture, close to the edge. The most common charge was that they manipulated hearers' emotions in order to extort bigger donations.[119] Responsible leaders occasionally acknowledged as much. Pastor M. M. Pinson of Phoenix excoriated the "fakes" who lived like demons yet told their "pitiful story" to gain money.[120] A writer for the Kansas *Apostolic Faith* assailed itinerant evangelists for trying to extort funds from the faithful. Unscrupulous whiners, they spent "most of their time like paupers—by the wayside, begging piteously, crying out their divers needs and infirmities."[121] Envy may have tinged the moral outrage of whistle-blowers, yet the primary literature intimates that some apostolics really did betray a propensity to deal very closely. A nameless correspondent to the *Weekly Evangel* in 1918 wondered, "Is it a sin to tell the neighbors and the Lord our land is worth $100 per acre, but tell the tax assessor it is worth $25?"[122] Obviously the writer's conscience had declared war on his pecuniary interests.

Institutions could evince the same watchful eye when it came to the ledger book. The *Latter Rain Evangel* started life in 1908 with the Holy Spirit as the sole editor, according to the front page of the premier issue.[123] Three years later that organ absorbed another periodical, *New Acts*. Since the former was bigger and more expensive, *New Acts* subscribers now learned, they would receive the new paper only half as long. Moreover any material copied from the new *Latter Rain Evangel* had to be properly credited.[124] All of this was ethical, but surely incongruous for a periodical edited solely by the Holy Spirit.

Once started down this path, the prospect—or temptation, according to one's point of view—of living well seemed inevitable. William J. Seymour seemed an otherworldly soul, yet he insisted that those who labored in the

Lord's vineyard should be "nicely carried, for they are worthy of it."[125] Nor was Seymour alone. In 1913 New York City physician Arthur L. Slocum received Holy Spirit baptism. Soon called to India as a missionary, Slocum reported that he and his wife automatically assumed that the Lord expected them to sail second class. Not so. Just before departing the Lord told them to travel first class and enjoy the best of accommodations. Lest he worry about the propriety of that extravagance, the Lord assured Slocum that "He died for the well-to-do just as much as for the poor."[126]

Slocum's close friend Elizabeth V. Baker also showed that ethereal spirituality could waltz arm in arm with material comfort. Baker was married to a Chicago physician when the Lord directed her to establish a church, a faith home, and a Bible and missionary training institute in Rochester, New York. The marriage did not prosper, but Baker's comfortable life-style did. In Baker's mind, "to be poorly clothed or fed is *lack of faith,* except at special times when God may choose to prove and discipline His children."[127] Later the Holy Spirit directed her to visit Pandita Ramabai's famed orphanage in India. At the time, there was not sufficient money for the trip, and Baker's wardrobe needed "much replenishing." But the Lord amply provided: "gift after gift kept pouring in." Shortly before the scheduled debarkation date, a "dressmaker kindly offered her service, and in a few days all was ready; money, clothing, every little needful thing, till I could truly say, 'I lacked nothing.'"[128] Baker articulated her monetary philosophy clearly: "A religion that does not unlock our pocket-books as well as our hearts is not the religion of the Christ who gave Himself to poverty that we might be rich."[129] In these moments heavenly and earthly horizons blended seamlessly.

None of the early leaders would have put things quite this way, but many saw a direct and obvious connection between a full gospel conversion and upward economic mobility. Thomas Hezmalhalch, a missionary to the Mojaves in the California desert, thus attributed the Indians' economic degradation to the superstitiousness of their religion. "But when they get converted," he primly observed, "they at once begin to clean up and build themselves homes, and cease from the evil practices and habits of the tribe life."[130] A. J. Tomlinson witnessed the same process among ragged mountain folk in the Great Smokies. On visiting a family that had entered the church eighteen months previously, Tomlinson came away elated. "Want and penury had given way to (I could not say plenty, but) comfort. Ignorance and discouragement had given way to intelligence and industry."[131]

Early pentecostals knew as well as any that the Lord demanded a separated life. But they also knew as well as any that He appreciated good common sense.

9

Leaders

Some of the chapters in this book would have pleased early pentecostals and some would have concerned them, but this one would have puzzled them. After all, when it came to leaders, what was there to write about? In their minds they had none, or at least none worth mentioning. The Holy Ghost ran everything. Of course certain men and women *seemed* to manage things. But appearances were deceiving. In reality the figures who stood behind the pulpits, or edited the periodicals, or planned the meetings were only yielded instruments—vessels, they liked to call themselves—awaiting the Lord's bidding. In saints' eyes autocrats and bureaucrats filled the ranks of other traditions, but not theirs. The revival had come into existence without human direction and, thankfully, operated that way ever since.

Here as elsewhere we dare not take pentecostals solely at their word. Considered whole, the evidence makes clear that strong, determined, clear-eyed leaders orchestrated the revival from first to last. And they did it just as Christian orchestrators had always done: by inspiring the cooperative, squeezing the uncooperative, and cajoling the undecided. Moreover—and this is the key point—Holy Ghost officials knew how to transform coercive power into moral authority. If the essence of leadership was the ability to persuade people to do what needed to be done, the essence of effective leadership was the ability to persuade them to do it of their own accord. And in this respect the revival's torchbearers proved skillful beyond their grandest dreams.

A recurring scenario in Aimee McPherson's ministry illustrates the very real yet delicate tension that separated pentecostals' primitivist yearning to keep themselves free from earthly guides and their pragmatic willingness to create and heed them as needed. The closing section of *This Is That*, McPherson's autobiography, consisted of verbatim transcripts of "Visions, Prophecies, Messages in Tongues and Interpretation. Given by Sister McPherson." A disclaimer, printed at the beginning, stipulated that "Sister McPherson claims no authorship, as when these messages were spoken through her, she was completely under the power of the Holy Spirit." The disclaimer further averred that McPherson exercised no control over her tongue or voice. The Holy Spirit alone spoke through her.[1] That much was standard pentecostal fare. The point that seemed to escape notice was that a very human stenographer with a freshly sharpened pencil was on hand, eager to record the Holy Spirit's words—not once, but meeting after meeting. Believers instinctively recognized, even if they did not explicitly admit, that the Holy Spirit almost always spoke through the same vessels.

One qualification about the terrain ahead is needed. In brief, our subject is leaders, not clergy. Though most leaders were clergy, and many clergy were leaders, the overlap was never exact, especially for women. Even if it had been, the subjective authority associated with leaders almost always authenticated the objective authority associated with clergy, not the reverse. The priority of subjective over objective modes of authority meant that a contemporary who wanted to know how pentecostal leadership really worked needed to start, not with the formal decrees of ecclesiastical councils, but with the subtle, almost indecipherable cues of daily life. And that is where our own examination of the geography of leadership most naturally begins, in that rich zone of gesture and response that appeared on no organizational flowchart.

Visions of Innocence

When saints looked at their own beginnings they were pleased to discover that they had no founders—no Martin Luther, no John Wesley, and certainly no Joseph Smith. Just like the Bible itself, the pentecostal revival had come directly from the divine hand, in all essential points already fully formed. One Azusa pioneer made the point with memorable simplicity: "The source is from the skies."[2] Even pentecostal historians, who of all people should have known better, fell into step. In 1915, in one of the earliest attempts to survey the movement's history, the China missionary M. L. Ryan put the point as plainly as possible: "This great world-wide movement did not originate with man. It has no great earthly leader. It is not a religious organization. It will not be organized."[3] As late as 1961 pentecostal historian Carl Brumback published *Suddenly . . . from Heaven: A History of The Assemblies of God.* Brumback's main title exemplified one of the revival's deepest assumptions.

If in pentecostal eyes the movement lacked mortal founders, it also lacked mortal managers. The Lord Himself had guided it from beginning to end. In a reminiscence significantly titled, "The Holy Spirit Bishop of the Church," Azusa leader William J. Seymour averred that every assembly's first action was to make sure that the "Holy Ghost [was] installed as the chairman." Whenever a group of worshipers lost their spiritual effectiveness, he charged, it was because humans tried to direct their own affairs.[4] Such views were not restricted to individuals either. Organized sects said the same. For example the congregated divines of the first General Council of the Assemblies of God trumpeted that they remained free of earthly directors. "[T]his great movement of God has no man nor set of men at the head of it but God to guide and mold it into clean cut Scriptural paths by the Holy Spirit."[5]

It should be noted that pentecostals were not simply saying that they lacked a single dominant leader. Rather they had no leaders at all. A complete "absence of human machinery" was the way that the Rochester Bible Institute teacher Elizabeth V. Baker described the revival's structure.[6] Kansas City's A. S. Copley, among the most thoughtful of first-generation writers, similarly asserted, without a trace of irony, that the "Apostolic Faith movement is not an organization or controlled by man in any way, but is under the direct control and supervision of the Holy Ghost."[7] This conviction explains why some periodicals refused to list a human editor. As the premier issue of the *Latter Rain Evangel* made plain in October 1908, no person's name would appear on the masthead because the magazine would contain nothing of human origin.[8]

The vision of leaderlessness marked all pentecostal groups, but the Church of God in the southern highlands and the Apostolic Faith Church in Wales and southwestern England—two of the most hierarchical and authoritarian sects—were most vocal about it. In 1908, without a trace of self-criticism, the elders of the Church of God insisted, for example, that none of their deliberations had been humanly constructed. All decisions, bylaws, and doctrinal pronouncements had been articulated by "Christ and His disciples."[9] The general overseer A. J. Tomlinson acknowledged that the Church of God seemed to be administered by humans, but in reality it was "government by the immediate direction of God."[10] Or as William Oliver Hutchinson, the founder of the Apostolic Faith Church put it, the only truly valid instructions were those that came directly from the Holy Spirit without human intermediaries. When divinely ordained persons spoke, they talked with the same infallible authority as the Apostle Paul. Their words carried the very "Voice of God" into the meeting hall.[11]

Converts sustained the vision of leaderlessness in a number of ways. First and foremost was their habit of addressing each other as if they were all members of a single extended family. Adults normally called each other Brother or Sister. Though some sects eventually adopted status-rich titles for top administrators (General Superintendent, Bishop), in daily discourse all were called Brother or Sister. A fair number of women and several men—especially venerated because of age, accomplishment, or saintliness—went by the familial titles of Mother or Daddy. Saints reserved Mr. and Mrs. for outsiders, partly to make clear that they *were* outsiders, and partly to avoid the outside world's social stratifications. Occasionally a stray Rev. or Elder roamed the literature, but the more formal and grammatically correct The Reverend never appeared, probably because it raised the image of a seminary-trained dandy. We need not assume that this labeling process was self-conscious in order to appreciate how it both camouflaged and shaped social reality.

Converts also sustained the vision of leaderlessness by emphasizing the social equality of the men and women who constituted the movement. Granted, saints were not above a little name-dropping when it suited their purposes, but on the whole they preferred to tout the revival's egalitarianism. "No instrument that God can use is rejected on account of color or dress or lack of education," said one earnest partisan.[12] These words, published in the Azusa Mission's *Apostolic Faith* in the fall of 1906, served as one of the earliest and most quoted lines in the corpus of first-generation literature. The most ardent partisan knew, of course, that the revival was not free of social stratification. One former Baptist pastor admitted that the revival embraced the "refined and cultured American," the "Hindu wrapped in . . . superstition," and the "African scarcely above the level of savagery." But that fact hardly mattered. Once converted and baptized with the Holy Spirit, he went on, all alike responded with the same tongues, saying, "Get ready, for the Lord is coming."[13] Though modern readers cringe at the racism and ethnocentrism embedded in such remarks, the underlying message of essential equality in Christ remained fast.

Finally, pentecostals sustained the vision of leaderlessness by refusing to set up accredited seminaries until the 1960s. Shortly we shall see that education per se was not the issue, for they esteemed education of the right kind. What they resisted, rather, was a degreed clergy, preachers with artificial marks of social distinction, all puffed up and self-absorbed with their own importance. Latter rain folk were neither the first nor the last sectarians to mock the men in black by saying that D.D. stood not for Doctor of Divinity but Dumb Dog.[14]

Nonetheless the ideal of a leaderless movement, however genuinely held, did not square with social reality. The plain truth is that the pentecostal sky was studded with stars, luminaries of the flesh-and-blood variety, and their trajectories both illumined and ordered the world around them. Together they defined the movement's identity more than most imagined.

Torchbearers

No one wanted to be remembered as an administrator, let alone a bureaucrat, but many of the best-known leaders were in fact administrators, and very good ones too. The standard accounts of the main pentecostal sects make clear (either explicitly or implicitly) that men and women like E. N. Bell of the Assemblies of God, Florence Crawford of the Apostolic Faith, G. T. Haywood of the Pentecostal Assemblies of the World, J. H. King of the Pentecostal Holiness Church, C. H. Mason of the Church of God in Christ, Aimee McPherson of the International Church of the Foursquare Gospel, and A. J. Tomlinson of the Church of God all ran their bodies with a benign but firm hand.[15]

But if the role of denominational administrators did not decisively put to rest the fantasy that no line separated leaders from followers, the role of celebrities did. The career of the most heralded pentecostal of all, Aimee Semple McPherson, offers a ready example. Sister, as she liked to be called (a fact not free of irony), held multiple leadership roles at once: a denominational head and administrator, a local pastor in Los Angeles, a radio personality, and an itinerant evangelist and divine healer. Probably the first pentecostal to win wide recognition outside the camp of believers, McPherson ranked as one of most conspicuous figures of the interwar years. In fact both of her recent scholarly biographers suggest that in the public eye she competed favorably with the likes of Mary Pickford, Douglas Fairbanks, Babe Ruth, Charles Lindberg, even presidential candidate William Jennings Bryan. Everywhere Sister traveled she drew people—first to secondhand tents, later to imposing uptown churches, eventually to the largest civic auditoriums and outdoor arenas in the country.[16]

The statistics pile up like snowdrifts. One evangelistic tour stretching from 1919 to 1922 purportedly drew more attenders than any road show or whistle stop circuit in American history, including those by P. T. Barnum, Harry Houdini, or Teddy Roosevelt. When she reappeared from her claimed kidnapping on a sweltering afternoon in the summer of 1926, 50,000 of the faithful thronged the Los Angeles train depot while an additional 100,000 lined the route back to Angelus Temple. Another burst of barnstorming in 1933 and 1934 led Sister personally to address more than 2 million persons, 2 percent of the U.S. population. The 5,000 seats of Angelus Temple filled, emptied, and filled again three times every Sunday, and often weeknights too, for twenty years running. Millions more followed her activities in the papers and on the radio. On average, she hit the front page of America's biggest dailies three times a week throughout the 1920s. On the radio the very sound of her voice, said one secular biographer, triggered an excitement in crowds "bordering on hysteria." When she died, 60,000 mourners filed past her bier. Until Oral Roberts strode out of the Oklahoma prairie in the late 1940s, no other enthusiast came close to rivaling Sister's visibility outside pentecostal circles.

Inside those circles, however, plenty of contenders jostled for pride of place. Healing evangelist Maria Woodworth-Etter easily qualified as the most prominent challenger. Woodworth-Etter's turbulent career played itself out in the kerosene lantern world of small towns, steamy tents, and ecstatic preaching. Born near Lisbon, Ohio, in 1844, she entered full-time itinerant ministry in 1880 under the auspices of the United Brethren and then the (Winebrenner) Churches of God. Soon men and women attending her meetings started inexplicably falling to the floor in a trancelike state that she initially regarded as a sign of Holy Ghost baptism. Before long the "Trance Evangelist," as she was called, introduced divine healing as well. Invitations poured in to hold meetings in churches of all denominations (including the Reorganized Latter Day Saints) throughout the Midwest and on both coasts. In time Woodworth-Etter found favor in all parts of the nation and among many constituencies. Though she habitually exaggerated the results of her ministry, contemporary newspaper accounts confirmed that year after year thousands of gawkers, true believers, and plain folk seeking healing—often as a last resort—jammed her meetings. On one occasion nearly 20,000 showed up. Woodworth-Etter's services became synonymous with the most unrestrained forms of revivalist emotion long before pentecostal fires swept the Midwest. After 1904 speaking in tongues, along with trances and healings, regularly punctuated the evangelist's work.[17]

Like moths drawn to a flame, it was only a matter of time until Woodworth-Etter and pentecostals would find each other. Initially she kept her distance, apparently because of pentecostals' reluctance to ordain women. But when she finally joined forces with Holy Ghost believers in 1912, they loved her. The faithful paid no attention to her marital difficulties, inaccurate prophecies, scrapes with the law, or weakness for plagiarism. Her numerous books sold tens of thousands and achieved a semicanonical status during her lifetime. All that was required to draw a crowd was to promise that Woodworth-Etter would be present.[18] One soul wrote that she wanted only to touch the evangelist's wrist.[19] Woodworth-Etter never managed to be very precise about the theological meaning of the events that took place in her meetings, but she amply proved that Aimee McPherson was certainly not the first and in some ways not even the most important evangelist to preach down the latter rain.

After McPherson and Woodworth-Etter, several scores of men and women angled for public recognition. One or two, such as Smith Wigglesworth, enjoyed perennial attention on both sides of the Atlantic. A barely literate plumber from Bradford, England, Wigglesworth won a soaring reputation for his ability successfully to pray for the healing of the sick.[20] More typically, however, pentecostal celebrities gained regional prominence. C. H. Mason, bishop of the Church of God in Christ, for example, found himself highly sought after as a special speaker for both white and black gatherings throughout the South.[21] Some rose as luminaries only within their own denominational families. A. J. Tomlinson probably proved too combative to be desired by many but his own Church of God folk, but among his own, he reigned as king of the traveling pulpit.[22] The same regional prominence marked the ministries of Florence Crawford in the Pacific Northwest and Ida Robinson in the urban Northeast.

Pentecostal celebrities represented a variety of social locations. Some, like Danish actress Anna Larssen and American beauty queen Edith Mae Pennington, enjoyed special status because of glittery positions they had held before joining the movement. Some served, or at least used, a local congregation as a base of operations, but many others, perhaps a majority, made their entire living as traveling evangelists. The special glamour attached to the careers of itinerants can be inferred from the acid comments of local pastors annoyed by their lack of responsibility for the day-to-day work of the church.[23] And then there were the missionary heroes. Like countless evangelicals before them, pentecostals elevated missionaries to near beatific rank. The mere mention of the name of Victor Plymire, who toiled for forty-one years on the Tibetan–Chinese border with only a handful of converts to show for his life's work, or of Lillian Trasher, who founded a sprawling orphanage complex outside Assiout, Egypt, was enough to moisten the eyes and open the wallets of any number of believers. The list of such heroes could be extended at length. The point here is simply to suggest that many individuals enjoyed a prominent place in the pentecostal pantheon, very much as George Whitefield or Dwight L. Moody had known in the longer and broader evangelical tradition.[24]

The line that distinguished leaders from followers was always shifting and permeable, but it was there, and everyone knew it. When the Oneness controversy ripped apart the Assemblies of God in 1916, young Frank Ewart proudly reported that the distinctive claims of the Oneness faction had found particular favor not among the rank and file, but among the "elite of the Pentecostal movement"—among luminaries like E. N. Bell, L. C. Hall, and William E. Booth-Clibborn.[25] The substantive accuracy of Ewart's claim is irrelevant just now. The point to notice is that by speaking of a pentecostal "elite" he implicitly admitted significant stratification *within* the ranks. Or to take an example of a quite different kind, a 1922 advertisement for a Bible training school in Cleveland, Tennessee, spotlighted the gulf that separated leaders from followers. "WHY DON'T YOU BE A PREACHER?" blazed the headline. "You sorta have a feeling that every next year is going to find you flashing out as something important. You wouldn't have figured five years ago today that you would be just what you are today . . . Why don't you be a preacher?"[26] The advertisement told the tale. Preachers held the reins.

Holy Spirit Gifts

At some instinctive level everyone knew that definable qualifications helped to divide pentecostals into discrete orders of leaders and followers. Most notably, the possession of Holy Spirit gifts facilitated leadership status, while their absence made leadership not impossible but certainly less likely. (That Holy Spirit gifts themselves seemed purely supernatural in origin only enhanced their practical usefulness in the scramble for leadership.)

Specifically, those who could speak in tongues eclipsed those who could not. Though pentecostal theology specified that everyone was supposed to speak in tongues at the moment of baptism, recurring streams of data suggest that many, probably a large minority, never could. As a consequence they found themselves locked out of leadership positions altogether. Evidence suggests for example that A. B. Simpson, the longtime head of the Christian and Missionary Alliance, sought the baptism-tongues experience for at least five years without success. In time Simpson not only gave up but also distanced himself and his own thriving sect from the revival.[27] One suspects that other sympathetic onlookers who never made a commitment, such as the Southern Baptist biblical scholar A. S. Worrell, may have remained outside for the same reason. Similar difficulties plagued many who did join the revival. We know from autobiographical accounts that numbers of men and women who eventually achieved prominence in Holy Ghost ranks had struggled for months and sometimes years to acquire tongues.[28] These stories suggest that the ability to meet the ideal helped to qualify a person for leadership status precisely because many of their brothers and sisters could not.

If only a slight majority or, more likely, only a minority of pentecostals spoke in tongues at all, we might reasonably infer that the ability to do so well—that is, volubly, articulately, and fluently—distinguished a much smaller minority. But distinguish them it did. Indeed particular authors went out of their way to stress the grandness of their glossolalic abilities. The Norwegian evangelist T. B. Barratt's narration of his baptism experience in New York in the fall of 1906 exemplifies scores of others. We encountered Barratt's testimony in Chapter 2. Here the point to notice is his emphasis on the sheer magnificence of the gift. "Immediately I . . . began to speak clearly and distinctly with a great volume of voice in a foreign tongue," he began. A verbal torrent poured forth without interruption for fourteen hours, running from noon until four the following morning. "I must have spoken about eight different languages during that time." Barratt went on to describe the tonalities of each of the languages that rushed through his lips. One was guttural, another nasal, still another resembled the roar of a cataract. He remembered lapsing into a "rapturous . . . baritone solo," using one of the "most pure and delightful languages" he ever heard. Barratt recalled speaking so forcibly that several thousand persons easily could have heard him.[29] It is worth noting how carefully Barratt dissected and then presented and re-presented the experience for public consumption, publishing at least three differing though compatible versions.[30] The import is clear. Men and women who could speak in tongues, and especially those who could do so skillfully, even flamboyantly, held an advantageous position in the race for leadership.

The possession of other Holy Spirit endowments lent standing as well. Most obvious, perhaps, was the ability to heal the physical body. Indeed it would be hard to find a first-generation leader who did not claim the capacity to heal through the Lord's power. Yet the power to transmit Holy Spirit gifts to others may have constituted a more significant leadership credential precisely because it was less obvious. This skill betokened a double measure of divine blessing: first for the gift itself, and then for the capacity to kindle it among the faithful. The black evangelist Lucy F. Farrow showed how the process worked in actual practice. Farrow, the niece of abolitionist Frederick Douglass, was serving as pastor of a holiness band in Houston in 1905 when Charles Fox Parham engaged her to work as a governess in his home. Though the details remain fuzzy, Farrow apparently received the baptism experience at Parham's hands in that city. In the fall of 1906, after another stint in Los Angeles, Farrow carried pentecostal embers back to Texas and Virginia, and later to Liberia. Historians know next to nothing about the details of her life, not even the date of her birth or death. No evidence survives to tell us that she was a good preacher or a sound biblical expositor or even a caring pastor. But her aptitude for igniting the supernatural gifts among others saved her from obscurity. As one typical report put it, at a 1906 camp meeting near Houston some twenty-five seekers stood lined up in a row in front of her. When Farrow "laid hands upon them . . . many began to speak in tongues at once."[31] Among the faithful, such talents counted as credentials beyond price.

Yieldedness

Another important credential for leadership status stemmed, ironically, from seeming not to want it. Simply put, only pristine vessels unblemished by any taint of personal ambition qualified for leadership. Martha Wing Robinson, the fiercely assertive leader of Zion Faith Homes near Chicago, represented many. "To know the mind of God," she declared, "we must be free from our own mind. He literally has to think through us." Only then, in response to a "*blank* mind," did God speak.[32] Ramrods like Robinson did not think twice about imposing their norms of yieldedness on others. Robinson's warning to her readers about the fate of a Mr. Marlett typified the genre. Unable to pay his rent, and no prospects in sight, Marlett understandably felt a twinge of anxiety when an eviction notice turned up in his mailbox. Yet Marlett's disquiet about ending up on the street provoked the Lord's displeasure. Only when he learned to yield even that concern to the Lord did the desperately needed funds appear.[33]

The yieldedness ideal seems clear enough at the devotional level, but how did it serve the movement's leadership needs? Rather than trying to examine an array of essentially similar examples, it may be more helpful to focus on the way that it functioned in one specific context: Bible training schools. Most schools claimed to make the Bible the sole textbook. But the plain truth is that pentecostal students usually did not study the Bible by itself. Instead, singularly commanding teachers led them through it, motivated by the conviction that they were imparting only the Holy Spirit's thoughts. That clearly was the case with Frank W. Sandford and Charles Fox Parham, both of whom boasted that their schools in Maine and in Kansas offered no courses, no subjects, no grades, no textbooks and, most significantly, no faculty—except themselves.[34] At D. Wesley Myland's well-respected Gibeah Bible School in Plainfield, Indiana, one student happily recalled that the Holy Spirit alone— albeit the Holy Spirit working through the lips of Brother Myland—illumined the Book of Life.[35] Or again, at Mount Tabor Bible Training School in Chicago, as the promotional literature explained, "The Textbook is the Bible, and the ENTIRE BIBLE." To be sure, a human teacher, Brother Andrew L. Fraser, would help make the Bible's meaning clear, but he played no substantive role, for the "Teacher recognized above all others is the Divine Author of the Text-Book—the Holy Spirit."[36] This pattern, in which one or at most a handful of strong personalities not only taught Scripture but also functioned as the final authority on its meaning, may have become even more entrenched in the 1920s. One historian of pentecostal education has drawn attention to the exceptional influence of figures such as Robert and Mary Craig at Glad Tidings Bible Institute in San Francisco, P. C. Nelson at Southwestern Bible Institute in Enid, Oklahoma, W. I. Evans at Central Bible Institute in Springfield, Missouri, and Ivan Q. Spencer at Elim, in Rochester, New York.[37]

We need not doubt the sincerity of these powerful teacher-leaders in order to see that their efforts drew students deep into own interpretive framework. Given the centrality of a divinely normative book expounded by divinely guided instructors, how could it have been otherwise? One pioneer sized up the reality of the situation with shrewd precision. Pastor William H. Durham of Chicago assailed all "Bible Schools and Training Homes" (except those sustained within local assemblies) because they served as a base for the self-aggrandizement of the instructors. "[E]very man who wants to build himself up goes to work and starts a 'Home,' 'Training Home,' or 'School'," Durham judged. Soon they become "little, petty Theological Seminaries" indistinguishable from all other seminaries.[38] Durham himself was not the most humble man who ever trod the earth, but he grasped the psychological dangers that beset strong teacher-leaders and receptive students. He saw that leaders became most powerful when they seemed most completely divested of self-interest. Durham's complaint went unanswered and his warning unheeded. Eager students wanted to believe that certain of their leaders possessed such rare insight into divine matters that it was neither necessary nor prudent to seek a second opinion. And honest men and women, working from the best of intentions, discovered that yieldedness provided sinecures of extraordinary influence.

Learning

If Holy Spirit gifts and yieldedness served as leadership credentials, so did more mundane attributes. Education ranked especially high. Not worldly education, of course, but mastery of the King James text of the Bible and the body of Christian doctrine peculiar to the radical evangelical and pentecostal traditions.

Admittedly, any claim that Holy Ghost enthusiasts esteemed learning, however qualified, would have struck most contemporaries as perverse. For example a writer for the *Nation*, visiting a "Holy Roller" meeting on Shin Bone Ridge outside Dayton, Tennessee, in 1925—the place and the summer of the famous Scopes trial—purportedly heard the following.

"I ain't got no learnin' an' never had none," said Preacher Joe Leffew. "Glory be to the Lamb! Some folks work their hands off'n up 'n to the elbows to give their young-uns education, and all they do is send their young-uns to hell."[39]

Though pentecostals themselves rarely published anything as strident as the real or alleged Shin Bone Ridge diatribe, it is undeniable that they said and did just enough uninformed things to give the image of anti-intellectualism an aura of truth. In the first generation none of the organized bodies erected any standard of education as a prerequisite for ordination. Worldly schools provoked suspicion at best, hostility at worst. Former Campbellite minister T. K. Leonard sneered about the results of a secular education.

"Time is too precious, Jesus is coming too soon, and education has proven too futile."[40] Quaker pentecostal Levi Lupton assailed outsiders' academies as nearly worthless, cradles for "football, baseball, cards, the dance hall [and] theatre going."[41] In England, too, formal education fell under the gun. The only preparation a man or woman needed for ministry, sniffed one editor, was an "upper-room experience."[42] A list of such comments could be extended at length.

Still, there is more to the story. If some pentecostals disparaged formal education, most rushed to defend it, at least education of the right kind. A. C. Holland, editor of the Pentecostal Holiness Church's *Apostolic Evangel,* likely spoke for most when he argued that the twin evils of the day were education for its own sake (what a later generation would call secular humanism), and no education at all. The solution lay in training conducted under Christian auspices with Christian purposes.[43] So it was that pentecostals immediately set out to establish schools of all sorts and grade levels.[44] They rarely tried to erect alternatives to the rapidly growing public school system (except in Newfoundland), but short- and long-term Bible training institutes for adolescent and adult students soon dotted the map from coast to coast. In 1917 the General Council of the Assemblies of God urged all Holy Spirit–filled young people to enroll in "some properly and scripturally accredited Bible Training School."[45] Scanning the standard denominational histories, one is struck by the sheer number of educational enterprises that every one of the major bodies launched within months or years of their founding.[46] By 1914 ten were up and running, by 1930 at least twenty flourished.[47] That their curricula remained untouched by critical and scientific procedures, and that their teaching methods entailed heavy doses of rote memorization and pious uplift, seems certain.[48] But the more pertinent fact is that pentecostals, like most sectarians, scrupulously sought to articulate and preserve the information that seemed relevant to the definition of their own identity.

This observation brings us back to the main point. Whether such education was acquired through formal means or through self-tutoring, believers almost always treated it as an obvious qualification for leadership. The cases of D. Wesley Myland and G. T. Haywood can be taken as typical.

Like many of the better-educated men and women in the revival, Myland started off with the Christian and Missionary Alliance (CMA). By 1912, however, the initial evidence doctrine, which Myland embraced but the CMA did not, left him without a denominational home. Though Myland never formally affiliated with any of the major pentecostal bodies, he remained one of the most influential figures in their ranks. He served as an editor, Bible school teacher, prolific writer, and author of one of the most widely circulated defenses of the movement, *The Latter Rain Covenant* (1910). Seekers undoubtedly experienced Holy Spirit baptism and healing under Myland's ministry, yet those abilities never functioned as his calling card. Myland's fame rested squarely on his reputation for detailed exposition of the Scripture and especially his ready command of the intricacies of dispensational premillennial theology.[49]

Erudition served the leadership aspirations of black pentecostals with equal effectiveness, as G. T. Haywood's career made clear. An Indianapolis foundry worker with two years of high school, Haywood converted to the movement in 1908 and soon took over the pulpit of a struggling pentecostal mission in that city. Eventually he adopted the Oneness position, joined the Pentecostal Assemblies of the World (PAW), and played a key role in making that group the leading Oneness body in the United States at that time. He steadily rose through the ranks of the PAW to become its presiding bishop in 1925. As with Myland, adherents undoubtedly experienced baptism and healing under Haywood's ministry, but those were not the gifts for which he was (and remains) most widely and proudly remembered. Instead, contemporaries and biographers emphasized his astonishing mastery of the King James text of the Bible, including his ability to fire biblical passages like bullets from a Gatling gun. They spoke of his voracious reading habits, his skill as an architect and newspaper cartoonist, and his fascination with new technology, including (at the price of controversy) compact movie cameras.[50]

The aim here is not to try to prove that either Myland or Haywood, or for that matter scores of others we might have focused on, were learned men as measured by the standards of the old-line divinity schools. My hunch is that they could have held their own with the best in an IQ test or in a debate on the content of the King James Bible, but that is irrelevant. The point to notice rather is that individuals who possessed or were perceived to possess exceptional learning, and who demonstrated an ability to integrate that learning with daily life, found honor among their fellow believers.[51]

Organizational Skills

Effectiveness behind the desk constituted one more factor that propelled individuals into positions of leadership. Of course pentecostals themselves never admitted that. That the aptitudes that served men and women well in the secular marketplace might serve them equally well within the church marketplace was unthinkable—or at least unpublishable. But pious obfuscation notwithstanding, saints admired men and women who knew how to get things done.

W. W. Simpson illustrates the point as well as any. Born in White County, Tennessee, in 1869, Simpson served a rural Congregational church but soon felt called to carry the gospel to the "'uttermost'" part of the world. He arrived in Shanghai in 1892, and the remote China–Tibet border region three years later. In 1912 Simpson experienced Holy Spirit baptism. Feeling uncomfortable in the CMA, he united with the Assemblies of God about 1915. Except for brief furloughs, Simpson toiled in Tibet and northwest China for fifty-seven years. In that span he married twice, fathered nine children, introduced potato and rye farming to the Kansu region, founded and ran three large orphanages, cofounded Truth Bible School in North China and, like many mainline missionaries (but unlike most pentecostal missionaries) became deeply involved in local politics. When the great famine struck in the 1920s, he credited seed potatoes, which resisted drought, with saving more than 1 million lives in Kansu province alone. Simpson received no aid from the Chinese International Relief Commission (apparently because of his faith mission status), yet managed to raise sufficient funds from independent donors back home to support some 500 children in his orphanages.[52]

Simpson, like many pentecostal leaders, displayed an additional skill that is commonly overlooked: the ability to identify others who could do the things they themselves could not do. One scholar perceptively suggests that saints' leaders were "people managers."[53] The evidence is too spotty to substantiate this claim broadly, but much of it points that way. Simpson, the country boy from the hills of east Tennessee, did not have to know how to manage an orphanage of 500. It was enough that he knew how to enlist those who did. For that matter Aimee McPherson, the farm girl from the plains of Ontario, did not have to know much about accounting in order to set up and manage a sprawling broadcasting and publishing complex. She knew people who did.[54]

There is an old saw that believers should pray as if everything depended on God but work as if nothing did. Off the top of their heads pentecostals would have dismissed that aphorism as irreverent. But in their heart of hearts they knew better. Sometimes the evidence for this claim gently taps us on the shoulder, as when the radically primitivist evangelist Frank Bartleman remarked, almost as an aside, that it was better to "wear out than rust out."[55] But sometimes the evidence smacks us in the face, as when veteran Africa missionary John G. Lake proclaimed that Africa had no room for teachers with a "sentimental gospel." What that continent needed, rather, was "real practical, hard-headed, strong, clear Christian teachers." Though Lake never minimized the importance of supernatural manifestations of the Holy Spirit, he revealed a good deal about his working assumptions when he added that the South African government liked missionaries who were able to "get something done."[56]

Final Thoughts

In this concluding section two refinements of the argument are now needed. The first is that the pentecostal movement, like virtually all popular religious stirrings, required strong leadership if it was to survive at all. Almost by definition the revival impulse remained highly unstable. In recent years historians of eighteenth- and nineteenth-century religious stirrings have demonstrated the critical role of forceful leadership, thrusting up from the grass roots, when other institutional structures had grown weak.[57] By this measure pentecostal pastors, editors, evangelists, missionaries, and denominational officials served, in David Martin's words, as real leaders, not just "enablers."[58] They gave the movement definition and direction. Without them there would be nothing to write about today except perhaps a relic or two in the museum of sectarian curiosities.[59]

The second refinement can be simply stated: there were limits. If the pragmatic side of pentecostal culture fostered strong, aggressive leaders, it also curbed them when they threatened to career out of control. Partisans proudly noted that their revival included no figures comparable to Joseph Smith among Latter-day Saints, or Ellen G. White among Seventh-day Adventists, or Mary Baker Eddy among Christian Scientists, all of whom built their extraordinary power on claims of recurring, infallible, extrabiblical revelation. To be sure, plenty of Holy Ghost leaders said that they too had received direct revelations. But those revelations were episodic in duration, restricted in scope, and subject to severe communal scrutiny. The aborted careers of aspiring prophets John Alexander Dowie and Frank W. Sandford show how decisively pentecostal culture could shackle men and women who pushed the edges too hard.

Of the two, Dowie proved more successful in attracting a following, partly because he possessed more business sense. This Australian émigré first founded the Christian Catholic Apostolic Church in Chicago in the 1890s, and then the communal theocracy of Zion City fifty miles north of Chicago just after the turn of the century. Blessed with boundless energy, he never lacked confidence in his calling or in his abilities to fulfill it. In 1899 Dowie designated himself the Messenger of the Covenant foretold in Malachi. Two years later he declared himself the third and final manifestation of the prophet Elijah, the sole person authorized by God to reinstate the form, authority, and power of primitive Christianity. By 1904 Dowie had come to believe that he personally incarnated "THE FIRST APOSTLE OF THE LORD JESUS, THE CHRIST" and the "High Priest on Earth . . . of that High Priest in Heaven." From that point until his untimely death in 1907, Dowie signed his name,

"John Alexander, First Apostle." He even tried, with limited success, to co-erce his lieutenants publicly to endorse those nearly messianic claims.[60]

During those same years Frank W. Sandford embarked on a similar though independent path in northern New England. Just before the turn of the century this Yankee prophet established the Holy Ghost and Us Bible School in Durham, Maine, and sparked a widespread healing movement popularly known as Shiloh. In time Sandford, like Dowie, reached the conclusion that he alone was the Messenger of the Covenant[61] and the reincarnation of the prophet Elijah.[62] He even compelled his followers to acknowledge that their standing in God's eyes depended on the perfection of their obedience both to Jesus Christ and to himself.[63] As far as the public record showed, Sandford articulated those claims without a trace of self-doubt. In 1911 federal author-ities finally jailed him on manslaughter charges, following a missionary ven-ture gone fatally awry. Until then, however, the prophet promoted himself, in the words of one sympathetic follower, as the bearer of the "blackness of other people's transgressions," and regularly offered intercessory prayers on their behalf.[64]

Though Dowie and Sandford both fell from favor among their own fol-lowers after 1905, the key point is that neither man ever gained credibility in the pentecostal revival (which was gathering steam as the Zion City and Shiloh movements were declining). In one sense this failure is curious. Both Dowie and Sandford were enormously talented and mysteriously gifted. Both heralded a message that prefigured pentecostals' full gospel teaching in every respect except for the initial evidence of tongues. Though the latter point should not be minimized, one quickly senses that the real problem lay else-where: Dowie and Sandford had lurched wildly out of control. Indeed Holy Ghost writers repeatedly held up both men for ridicule, saying that they epit-omized everything that could go wrong.[65] People voted with their feet. The evidence is sketchy, but we know that between 1905 and 1910 scores, possi-bly hundreds, drifted from Zion City and from Shiloh into Holy Ghost fel-lowships in all parts of the country.[66]

If Dowie's Zion and Sandford's Shiloh did not work, what did? A. J. Tomlinson's tightrope career demonstrated, as precisely as any, how an indi-vidual might use primitivist premises to establish and maintain leadership sta-tus—but never going too far. This one-time Quaker ruled over the Church of God as a benign autocrat for the better part of two decades. Without ques-tion his voluminous (and by all reports voluble) utterances under the power of the Holy Spirit helped to secure his position. He insisted that the Holy Spirit Himself had appointed him general overseer. That very fact, he claimed, made the overseer's position more exalted than president of the United States or king of England. "[T]his is a government and position under God, for the Holy Ghost has placed me in it as you all know."[67] The Lord even worked through others to establish Tomlinson's authority. When a question arose at the 1913 Annual Assembly about the wisdom of reelecting Tomlinson general overseer year after year, the Holy Spirit stepped in and, speaking through an unidentified zealot, settled the matter once and for all: "Brother Tomlinson is in his place. I placed him there and I will take him away when I am ready."[68] Nonetheless, despite such extraordinary command over the loyalties of his people, there is no evidence that Tomlinson ever dreamed of penning a corpus of extrabiblical canonical texts, or deviating from the sexual mores of the community, or justifying any of his decisions on grounds other than scriptural ones. Though Tomlinson's people eventually drove him from office, no one ever intimated personal dishonesty, just mismanagement.[69] Year after year this tough mountain preacher trekked the high country of the supernatural without mishap. Like most pentecostal leaders, or at least most who survived long enough to tell about it, he knew exactly where the path lay.

Viewed from afar, the pattern emerges clearly. Holy Ghost folk encouraged strong leaders. They put up with autocrats when they had to, but loose canons they would not tolerate. Knowing the limits was part of pragmatism's text too. In the parlance of a later generation, pentecostals constructed a level playing field where men and women of native talent got a chance to show their stuff. If that was the American way, it was also the pentecostal style.

10

Women

This subject, as few others, sparks arguments. Those who know nothing else about American religion often know one thing for sure: Holy Ghost religion offered a hospitable home for women in general and for women preachers in particular. Bring up speaking in tongues and they are likely to think of Aimee McPherson. Say healing evangelism and they are almost as likely to think of Kathryn Kuhlman as of Oral Roberts. Such views are not limited to casual observers either. Scholars of women's religious history also have urged that the pentecostal revival afforded opportunities for women that they did not enjoy in most denominational contexts.[1] Recently, however, other students of the revival have started to paint a less roseate portrait of women's place. Though they admit that the picture was mixed, they have emphasized the resistance that talented and assertive females encountered. In their view the vast majority of pentecostal women faced formidable theological and sociological hurdles. High-profile figures like McPherson and Maria Woodworth-Etter were the exceptions that proved the rule.[2]

Both views are partly right. The data can lead, quite legitimately, to dramatically different conclusions depending on which body of evidence one chooses to emphasize. Things grow even more complicated when we realize that often the most serious confrontations lay not between factions but within the hearts and minds of individuals, men and women alike. In this chapter, therefore, the first task is to understand how the primitivist impulse emboldened some women to flout conventional restrictions in order to pursue a vocation of active public ministry. The second task is to see how the pragmatic impulse, the need for an orderly accommodation to American social expectations, simultaneously dictated a more traditional reading of Scripture and a more judicious hearing of what the Holy Spirit was saying.

Two method problems snarl any effort to chart the contours of women's place in pentecostal culture, and they should be at least acknowledged if not resolved at the outset. The more obvious one is that the question of women's place in the revival is somewhat anachronistic. Today's readers are more in-

terested in it than early pentecostals themselves were. Even the handful of female leaders who staked out a firm position on women's prerogatives ranked
it fairly low on their list of their concerns, at least if the amount of attention
they gave it in their writings and sermons was any indication. To state the obvious, wringing answers from data not designed to provide such answers creates distortions.

A second, more gnarly problem is that men wrote most of the relevant
texts. It is true that manuscript materials and letters to the editors of the earliest periodicals seem evenly split between male and female authors. Yet males
penned most of the official denominational publications and virtually all of
the published historical accounts. The possibility of a distinctly male bias becomes evident when we measure the "standard" early histories of the Azusa
revival written by Bennett F. Lawrence, Frank Bartleman, Thomas R. Nickel,
and A. C. Valdez against a brief recounting, written in 1939, by Mother
Emma Cotton, pastor of a large Church of God in Christ congregation in
Los Angeles. In all of the male-authored accounts, William J. Seymour was
the principal player while other men—including Charles Fox Parham, Joseph
Smale, Richard Asberry, and Edward S. Lee—assumed important supporting
roles. Though those accounts did mention Julia Hutchins, Lucy Farrow, and
Neely Terry, they uniformly relegated them to bit parts. Cotton reversed the
scale of importance. In her ordering of the past, women orchestrated the key
events. Lucy Farrow, not Seymour, emerged as the central prophet igniting
Holy Ghost fires in Southern California.[3] I am not arguing that Cotton was
right and the others wrong, but I am suggesting that male authors made assumptions that women did not necessarily share.

Keeping these caveats in mind, the task before us now is to appreciate the
subtleties of women's role in pentecostal culture and try to see how they
played out in the revival's daily life.

Women's Predominance

To some extent, pentecostals' desire to heed the Holy Spirit's directives
emerged from the broader culture. After the Civil War women saw a rapid expansion of opportunities in legal, business, and professional spheres. In state
after state the barriers to suffrage crumbled, culminating in the adoption of
the Nineteenth Amendment in 1920. Similar trends marked the radical evangelical subculture. Pentecostals inherited the public ministry roles of British
Christians such as Catherine Booth, Christabel Pankhurst, and Jesse Penn-
Lewis, along with Americans like Phoebe Palmer, Amanda Berry Smith, and
Hannah Whitall Smith. The theological justification for women's ministry articulated by radical evangelical theorists such as the Boston pastor A. J.

Gordon proved equally important. As far back as 1894 he had argued that Joel's prophecy, "*Your sons and your daughters shall prophesy,*" partially realized on the Day of Pentecost, served as the "*Magna Charta* of the Christian Church." Gordon excoriated timeworn conventions that reduced women to "church drudge[s]" whose only role was to prepare "sandwiches and coffee" for socials.[4]

Pentecostals pressed these trends. Let us begin with women in clerical or quasi-clerical positions. Statistics can conceal as much as they reveal, but on the face of it the statistical tale catches our attention. Consider the Assemblies of God, the Church of God, and the International Church of the Foursquare Gospel, three of the oldest and largest pentecostal bodies. The first group organized itself in 1914. Clergy rolls published shortly afterward show that women constituted nearly one-third of its ministers. To be sure, by 1925 the percentage had dropped to slightly less than a fifth, yet two-thirds of the overseas missionaries were women, and few would doubt that missionaries ranked as the true celebrity-heroes of the movement.[5] A similar pattern turned up in the Church of God. Five of the eight stalwarts who gathered in the eastern Tennessee mountains in 1886 to form the precursor "Christian Union" were women.[6] When that body reconstituted itself in 1906 as the Church of God, women comprised nearly one-third of the founding members.[7] When Aimee McPherson incorporated the International Church of the Foursquare Gospel in 1927, single women were serving eighteen of the fifty-five branch churches as pastors—one-third of the total. Married couples oversaw another sixteen congregations as copastors.[8] McPherson's own meteoric career, though hardly characteristic of anyone except herself, at least said something about believers' readiness to salute a woman leader.

Women's leadership roles crossed racial, ethnic, and geographic boundaries. While the Azusa revival was still cooking at full steam, Florence Crawford pulled out and established a sturdy little sect of her own in Portland, Oregon, known as The Apostolic Faith. Two decades later, on the other side of the country, Ida Robinson led a group out of the black United Holy Church to form the Mount Sinai Holy Church of America, which featured a prominent place for women bishops and elders. In these and other pentecostal groups, women occasionally served as the sole pastors of churches, especially if they had planted them in the first place. More commonly, however, they functioned as copastors with their husbands. Considered whole, the primary evidence suggests that something like half of the traveling evangelists, divine healers, and overseas missionaries were women. Dozens single-handedly set up and ran Bible institutes and orphanages. Scores more staked out influential careers as tract writers, hymn writers, and newspaper editors.[9]

What about the grass roots? How numerous were women at that level? To begin with, we know with fair certainty that the majority of first-generation converts were female. The evidence remains sparse, but virtually all of it points in the same direction. The 1916 *Census of Religious Bodies* showed that women constituted 59 percent of the members of the three pentecostal groups that submitted membership data. That figure only slightly exceeded the 56 percent average for all denominations (and actually trailed the 59.8 percent average for five large mainline bodies). But over the next ten years the gap widened considerably. The seven reporting pentecostal sects listed an average of 64 percent female members versus a steady 56 percent for all denominations. Another decade passed and the gap yawned wider still. The 1936 census showed eleven pentecostal sects with an average female membership of 65 percent, measured against a steady 56 percent for all denominations. All together, then, in the pews and probably on the street corners too, pentecostal women consistently outnumbered men, not dramatically, but visibly.[10]

Literary evidence tells a similar story of conspicuous female participation. Newspaper reporters repeatedly noticed that women made up the majority of worshipers.[11] Opponents fixed on the movement's appeal to women in general and, they said, to hysterical women in particular.[12] One of the most prominent matriarchs, interviewed in the 1970s, remembered that women usually received Holy Spirit baptism first, their husbands coming along later.[13] And then there was the matter of salience. Holy Ghost folk, like most churchgoing Christians, arrayed themselves along a spectrum of commitment, ranging from those who merely showed up once in a while to those consumed by the revival's goals. So the question becomes not simply the percentage of women involved, but the percentage of women who were highly involved. Who prayed? Who cared for the sick? Who typed the letters? The data remain too spotty to warrant firm answers. But if recent studies of pentecostal women's participation can be retrofitted on the past, women clearly counted as high as men on most commitment scales.[14]

Though it would be risky to press this point too hard, one might also say that the pentecostal movement revealed feminine imagery at some deeply symbolic level. Adherents insisted, for example, that the Holy Spirit filled seekers with a surrendered heart, evoking stereotypes of women's compliant nature. Then too, zealots applied the submission ideal especially to the tongue, the most defiant of members, and also one conventionally associated with women—chatty, long-winded women. The early pentecostal movement resonated with stereotypically female norms, if not imagery, in one additional way. Historians of nineteenth-century religion have shown that when evangelical men gave their hearts to Christ, they readily relinquished brawling, drinking, swearing, gambling, and philandering. They proudly replaced, or at least tried to replace, those habits with stereotypically female ones of gentleness, peaceableness, sobriety, and fidelity.[15] Pentecostals did all that and more. They made public weeping—scorned among men, esteemed among women—not simply acceptable but a criterion of the success of a Holy Ghost meeting. So it was that the men who gathered in Little Rock in 1922 to organize the Southern Bible Conference were unable to transact business for seven days running. Consumed in a "delirium of tears," said founder William E. Booth-Clibborn, "the spirit of weeping would break forth until none could speak."[16] But speak he did, and for many.[17]

In a variety of ways, then, women maintained a conspicuous place in the early pentecostal movement. But how did all of this come about? Differently asked, how did the broader pentecostal subculture define women's role in the home, church, and society?

Prophesying Daughters

Agnes Ozman's story offers some clues. The fire fell on January 1, 1901, making her, by most accounts, the first person to experience Holy Ghost baptism with the evidence of tongues.[18] Like Mary Magdalene at the tomb, she also seemed to be the first to herald the message to a waiting world. Recalling the event twenty years later, Ozman averred that the very next evening she and several others ventured out into a frigid Topeka night to witness to others at a downtown mission. Soon she, with a score of colleagues, all "baptized men and women," took the word to nearby Lawrence where they went out "by twos over the city calling and praying with people." Ozman's account drifts. We pick up the thread again in the summer of 1906 in Lincoln, Nebraska, where she was once more fervently preaching the message. On to Omaha, over to Council Bluffs, back to Topeka, down to Cherryvale, and on through every burg of the Midwest, it seems, stopping only long enough to preach, heal, organize a mission—and then move on.[19] Ozman's story bears significance precisely because she was not trying to make a point about women's ministry. The sole issue was that she, no less than the men who experienced the Holy Spirit's touch, felt called to proclaim what she knew.

The early literature bulges with scraps of evidence about women like Agnes Ozman. For a few, such as Marie Burgess, who helped to found Glad Tidings Hall in New York City, we have substantial information. For several score, such as the black evangelist Lucy Farrow, who took the message from Azusa to Portsmouth and then to Liberia, we possess several paragraphs at most.[20] For the vast majority, we know virtually nothing. They were anonymous souls who just packed up, moved out, and did what needed to be done. If any worried about the formalities of women in ministry, few let on. We read, for example, a routine news item in the December 1906 Azusa *Apostolic Faith* concerning the mission in Woodland, California: "Sisters Sophie and Reece from Oakland, whom God has been using, are at present in charge."[21] That was all, just "in charge." Where Sisters Sophie and Reece came from or where they ended up or even what "in charge" meant, no one knows. And no one knows precisely because no one thought their activities exceptional enough to require comment, much less justification. With minor variations this story replayed itself over and over. Reading almost at random in the early periodicals, we learn of a Mrs. Whitford and of a Mrs. Smith handling the meetings near Rochester,[22] of a Mrs. Fannie Dobson running the assembly in Galena,[23] of a Mrs. L. M. Hedge preaching down the fire at St. Joseph, Missouri,[24] of a fourteen-year-old "sister" going out from Azusa and leading a revival in which "one hundred and ninety souls were saved."[25] We hear young Halcy Tomlinson—A. J.'s daughter—confiding in her diary about a Mrs. McCanless: "There is a lady preacher . . . preaching here now and she is certainly a fine preacher . . . no mistake."[26]

This kind of immediate, un-self-conscious activity may have been the norm, but some enthusiasts did pause a bit, just long enough to come up with a rationale for doing what they had already determined to do. Explanations varied. The most famous of pentecostals simply brushed aside Saint Paul's apparent ban on women preaching with a two-sentence rejoinder: Paul, said Sister Aimee, was referring to noisy, uncouth women in the local congregation in Corinth, not us.[27] Besides—now coming to the real point— God had called her, and from that moment forward she determined to go, "live or die, sink or swim."[28] Florence Crawford felt the same way. "The Lord told me yesterday to go into all the world and preach His Gospel," she announced to her friends at the Azusa Mission in the fall of 1906. With squared shoulders Crawford soon quit Los Angeles and headed for Portland, Oregon, where she launched her own work.[29] Elizabeth Sisson, once a mainline missionary to India, later an itinerant Bible teacher known for her leather lungs and multicolored petticoats, stiffened at the idea that she should have to justify her ministry to anyone. In a vision the Lord's "Empowering Hands" had enfolded her and declared: "I have ordained you." From that day forward, Sisson glowered, "all human ordination shriveled into utter insignificance."[30]

Insofar as pentecostals' offered a self-consciously theological justification for women's public ministry, it stemmed from their understanding of the Day of Pentecost. Before then, said Azusa's *Apostolic Faith*, women had been denied the coveted anointing oil. But the prophet Joel affirmed that everything would change on the Day of Pentecost when the Lord would pour out His Spirit on all flesh, sons and daughters alike. So it was that on that fateful morning, "All the women received the anointed oil of the Holy Ghost and were able to preach the same as the men."[31] Full acceptance of women's right—indeed obligation—to preach thus arose from pentecostals' philosophy of history. Over the centuries women had occupied a "subordinate place of servitude and of silence in the house of God," said New York City undertaker Stephen Merritt. But no longer. "Woman under the anointing and imbuing of the Holy Ghost is to be a great factor in the preparatory work of these latter days."[32] Other men, or at least some other men, agreed. Charles Fox Parham took it as self-evident that anyone, male or female, who received the gift of tongues automatically bore the responsibility to herald the Lord's return at home and abroad. To be able to preach in an unstudied foreign language was, after all, the main purpose of the gift, and since women received the gift, they manifestly shared the obligation.[33]

For many women (and some men), women's ministry symbolized something larger than itself. If to preach was to testify to the Holy Spirit's life-changing power, not to preach was to succumb to humanmade rules at best, open sin at worst. When Bible school founder Elizabeth V. Baker yielded her life to the Lord, He demanded: "Will you go into pulpits and preach for Me?" Feeling "great aversion" to seeing women in a pulpit, Baker replied: "O, I cannot, I cannot." But the Lord persisted. Eventually Baker came to see that it was not piety but "[p]rejudice, pride, cowardice"—that is, mere convention—that held her back. Baker got off easy, once she understood that she was being torn between the voice of the Living Lord and "human logic."[34] But for other women, dread of standing up before a crowd and defying centuries-old customs stirred fear. Maria Woodworth-Etter's battle with family, friends, and, most of all, herself, spoke volumes. Woodworth-Etter's call aroused excruciating self-doubt. "[M]y whole nature shrunk from going to stand as a gazing-stock for the people," she recalled. Woodworth-Etter's husband and adolescent daughter scorned her ministerial ambitions. Satan flooded her with anxiety, reminding her that audiences would only "make sport" of her. Shrinking in "darkness and despair," seeing no way out, Woodworth-Etter hoped only to die. But that was not to be, for the Lord mightily "qualified" her for the work ahead by baptizing her with the "Holy Ghost, and fire, and power."[35] Though her account followed the Old Testament pattern of hearing, resisting, and yielding, only the most callous could fail to feel the turbulence of the emotions involved. More important, Woodworth-Etter came to interpret opposition to women preaching not simply as thoughtless habit by folks who should have known better, but as the work of the devil himself. Resistance to female ministry was sin, and it merited righteous rebuke.

In its purest form, then, the primitivist impulse pulled men and women away from inherited assumptions and thrust them outward. It endowed them with a new and exhilarating freedom to preach the truth, save the lost, heal the lame. Like a kettledrum echoing up from the deep, God's call beckoned women to herald the Word wherever the Holy Spirit directed.

Obedient Daughters

But real life intruded, as it always did. Getting along day by day eroded the loftiest of aspirations. Almost immediately converts of both sexes started imposing restrictions on women's ministry opportunities.

We begin with context. Just as certain trends in the broader culture reenforced the liberating import of the primitivist impulse, so too other trends in the broader culture reenforced the restricting, accommodating import of the pragmatic impulse. To some extent the inclination to batten down the hatches should be seen as a predictable response to frightening changes rumbling through American society in the Progressive Era. In the realm of labor, for instance, women were entering the work force in unprecedented numbers, competing with men and sometimes displacing them. Women seemed especially visible as the public carriers of new and looser standards of dress, recreation, and sexual behavior.[36] Moreover the norms provided by the radical evangelical subculture, from which pentecostals initially took most of their cues, were acquiring an increasingly conservative cast. The reasons for these sea changes need not detain us. It suffices to note that where Phoebe Palmer and friends had once served as powerful role models for ordinary evangelical women, after the turn of the century, and especially after World War I, such women were increasingly seen as exceptional, not normative.[37]

We also need to look closer to home, at tensions brewing within the Holy Ghost subculture itself. In a perceptive study of the spread of pentecostalism around the world in recent decades, Harvey Cox notes that in Sicily opponents sometimes call Holy Spirit baptized women "witches" and "whores." At first glance these terms appear inexplicable. Sicilian pentecostal women have nothing to do with witchcraft, and they maintain impeccable standards of sexual behavior. Yet on reflection, Cox argues, the terms make sense. Witch denotes one who connects with a higher power and deploys it in unsanctioned ways. Whore denotes not sexual promiscuity, but a woman who operates freely, outside the control of a governing man.[38] Cox's insights apply to the revival's formative years in North America. They help us see that in the minds of first-generation zealots, the primitivist liberation of women, left to itself, might well have careened out of control.

The tortured story of women's credentialing as ministers in the infant Assemblies of God illustrates the anxiety that both men and women felt about these matters. To jump ahead in the story, that process ended with women's gaining clergy recognition and privileges, yet only after navigating many twists and turns both sharp and painful. The final outcome was checkered at best. What happened?

When delegates gathered in Hot Springs, Arkansas, in the spring of 1914 to set up a barebones organization, they legislated two matters pertaining to women. First, voting privileges would be restricted to men. Second, women would be ordained as evangelists and as missionaries, but *not* as elders. The delegates did not define elder, presumably because everyone knew what the term denoted. It probably meant local pastors charged with responsibility for preaching and sacred duties such as officiating at the Lord's Supper. Clearly the overall intent was to encourage women in some forms of public ministry but to exclude them from the most powerfully symbolic and publicly authoritative forms.[39] (The records do not show whether women participated in this decision to restrict their own ministry.)

In the later years of the founding decade the tale grew more complex—and more interesting. The second General Council, which met in the fall of 1914, stipulated that sisters who were "mature believers" would be received as advisory members of the Council. No one said anything about mature men.[40] Women's status did not arise in the third and fourth Councils, though at the fourth, three women—all, significantly, foreign missionaries—addressed the delegates.[41] At the fifth General Council, held in 1917, Elizabeth Sisson, a woman of exceptional force, delivered the keynote address. (The General Council has never been opened and rarely addressed by a woman since then). The minutes recorded that delegates spent "[s]ome time"—one sniffs a euphemism here—discussing whether the sisters would be permitted to vote. After much deliberation the brethren decided that it was better to leave things as they were, with women serving as advisory members only.[42] The sixth General Council, gathered in 1918, marked a quiet but significant development. A roster of pastors, evangelists, missionaries, and home missionaries appended to the minutes added a new category, assistant pastors. Half of the assistant pastors named were women (twelve of twenty-four), yet all served churches with their husbands, who were listed as pastors.[43] Two years later the minutes started referring to the right of women to be ordained as evangelists, in which capacity they might serve as assistant pastors or missionaries as well as evangelists.[44] In the meantime the voting issue refused to die. In 1919 the chairman reiterated that women would not be permitted to vote, though they could speak from the floor.[45]

In the 1920s the General Council persisted in the same zigzag path it would follow for the rest of the century. At the beginning of the decade women received permission to vote and speak on "all questions" in business meetings (the same year, it is worth noting, that women gained suffrage rights under the U.S. Constitution).[46] Even so, the head preceded the heart. According to one eyewitness, Chairman J. W. Welch disapproved of Aimee McPherson speaking to the denomination's 1920 convention because he disliked the idea of a woman preaching (she did it anyway, reportedly with great panache).[47] In a key decision handed down three years later, the sect's Credential Committee acknowledged that ordained women enjoyed the right to administer the ordinances, perform weddings and funerals, and of course preach. Whether this decision originated from above or closer by in Washington, D.C. may be debated. The U.S. Clergy Bureau had threatened to withhold clergy discounts on the railroads unless women's ordination certificates specified that they performed all of the customary clergy duties. Nonetheless, the Credential Committee cautioned that it did not wish to encourage women in this direction. The brethren said they meant to permit women to perform those tasks "only when ordained men are not present to do them or when some such real emergency makes it necessary for them to do so."[48] Apparently practice followed prescription. Two aging leaders interviewed in 1977 readily remembered that in the early days women officiated at the Lord's Supper only in emergencies and rarely served as senior pastors.[49]

The 1930s witnessed two important developments—the first temporary, the second permanent. In 1931 the Council partially reversed earlier policies by stating that women were to be ordained only as evangelists (not pastors) and by removing the authorization to officiate at Holy Communion, even when no man was available.[50] In 1935 the Council reinstated the earlier policy of granting women full ordination as evangelists or pastors, including the right to administer the ordinances "when such acts are necessary." The Council offered this opportunity to "[m]atured women of not less than twenty-five years of age"—restrictions not applied to males.[51] In 1947 the Council limited ordination for both men and women to persons twenty-three or older, but never changed the recommendation that women administer the ordinances "when such acts are necessary."

The twisting path of women's ordination in the Assemblies of God's early decades typified pentecostalism as a whole (the Mount Sinai Holy Church of America forming a notable exception). At first glance, the Church of God, the second largest white body, rapidly progressed from considerable openness toward women in 1906 to considerable restriction on them by 1912. Yet David G. Roebuck, the principal scholar of women's role in that tradition, argues that the initial openness to women's ministry was not really as inviting as it seemed. The operative assumption was not that women should hold office equally with men, but that the Holy Spirit, who ministered through their lips, must not be denied.[52] In another variant of the pattern, the largely black Church of God in Christ barred women from ordination, probably from the outset. Even so, in some congregations the "church mothers" enjoyed a degree of authority unparalleled in white bodies, and a pastor's widow sometimes carried on his ministry.[53] The large minority of Oneness pentecostals differed from Trinitarian pentecostals in key respects, but not here. Like the Trinitarians, they seemed never quite able to decide if they wanted to give women ministry opportunities or not. In 1919 the founders of the Pentecostal Assemblies of the World, a body distinguished both by its Oneness theology and its interracial constituency, permitted women to serve as evangelists and missionaries, but not as pastors or elders.[54] The following year those same founders said that women evangelists could officiate at church functions, including marriages and Holy Communion—though only in "cases of emergency."[55]

Vignettes revealing the pervasiveness of this ambivalence toward the role of women, which women shared with men, pop up everywhere. For example partisans commonly called certain matriarchs, black and white alike, Mother—"Mother" standing in place of their given name. Indeed, for some, that appellation became so firmly fixed that modern researchers have to work hard even to find the given name.[56] How should we interpret this practice? As noted, the Mother label served multiple purposes, including endearment. Yet it also underscored that these women leaders were *female* leaders (unlike male leaders who rarely were called Dad or Father). In brief, the title "Mother," like the title "Lady" in southern genteel culture, both elevated and restricted women.

Where ambiguity left off and contradiction began was anyone's guess. Two anecdotes show, however, how easily the first devolved into the second. The first involved the actions of the [North] Eastern District of the Assemblies of God in 1917. By then most of the younger ministers in that district had been or would be educated in one of the four main pentecostal Bible institutes operating in that region (Zion in Providence, Bethel in Newark, Metropolitan in North Bergen, and Elim in Rochester). All of those institutions had been founded and run by women. Yet the minutes of the first District Council contained this remarkable clause: "Resolved, that we regard it unscriptural for a woman to be head of a Bible school for the training of ministers and missionaries."[57] Why? Common experience tells us that some of the delegates must have been reacting to bad experiences at the hands of authoritarian matriarchs. But could that have been true of all of them? Still more puzzling was Aimee McPherson's attitude toward other women. Sister insisted that all clergy functions in the sect she founded must remain open to women. Yet she herself appointed only men as elders of Angelus Temple, baptized converts only in the presence of a male elder, and refused to share her platform with another woman.[58]

However we account for such puzzles, there is little question that they inflicted pain on individuals. The story of Eleanor Frey, an obscure evangelist based in the Northeast, represented the perplexities and hurts borne by many. In 1928 Frey sent a long letter to J. R. Evans, general secretary of the Assemblies of God. Frey began by noting how privileged she felt to be a pentecostal worker, out on the "firing line" for the Lord. For eighteen years she had preached under Baptist colors with manifest success—and *"full ordination,"* she pointedly added. Even so, in pentecostal ranks Frey had found a "blessed fellowship" unparalleled among the Baptists. At the moment, she was filling in for a pentecostal pastor in Montreal away on vacation, preaching twice a day every day, visiting the sick, burying the dead, administering the ordinances and, above all, seeing souls saved and baptized with the Holy Spirit.[59]

Then Frey came to the point. Because of her husband's failing health, she desired a settled pastorate in southern California. But that was the rub. At the most recent Southern California District Council, "they"—presumably "they" meant the district's male elders—"brought up their foolish women question again . . . and thrashed it and thrashed it pro and con, until one felt like asking God to forgive us for being women." After rehearsing the customary scriptural precedents for women serving in public ministry, Frey unleashed a bitter retort: "God Almighty is no fool . . . Would He fill a woman with the Holy Ghost—endow her with ability—give her a vision for souls and then tell her to shut her mouth?"[60] Secretary Evans responded evasively. Though the California officials had debated the issue, he allowed, nothing had come of it, and Frey remained free to serve a church in that region—"if one is open to you."[61]

"If one is open to you." Frey never found a permanent appointment. In the meantime she continued to make a living as a traveling evangelist, precisely what she did not want to do.[62] Male obstructionism did not, of course, stop charismatic fullbacks like Aimee McPherson and Maria Woodworth-Etter, who just rammed their way up the middle. But women who were less driven, less gifted, or less fortunately situated than they fared differently. They found themselves barred from forms of ministry that men readily enjoyed. And women sometimes helped to restrict their own options. Offered a pastor's position in the young International Church of the Foursquare Gospel in California, Eleanor Frey held back. Why? Because her husband did not approve. "As I always have made it a point in my life to do nothing my husband objected to," she sighed, "I just let the matter rest."[63] Being filled with the Holy Spirit may have made life more fulfilling, but not necessarily easier.

The ideas of W. F. Carothers, a Houston attorney who penned one of the earliest and most systematic analyses of the gender question, offer a window into the theological assumptions that both informed and limited Frey's world. Since Carothers dominated the pentecostal scene in the Southwest for the better part of a decade, his views merit close attention.

Carothers began in typical evangelical fashion by rehearsing, line for line, all of the New Testament passages that bore on the subject. Given that the meaning of those passages was so transparent, he noted a bit wearily, additional comment was hardly "worth while." Nonetheless duty impelled him to go ahead and comment.[64] In Carothers's view the biblical record suggested two reasons for restricting women's work—one historical, the other natural. As for history, in the New Testament "pastors, elders or bishops" were always men. As for nature, the structure of creation itself dictated that man and woman would forever occupy separate spheres in the church's life. But what about Galatians 3:28, which forcefully attested that in Christ there was neither male nor female? Those words had nothing to do with public ministry, Carothers retorted. They meant only that the woman enjoyed "absolutely equal access to salvation with the man."[65] Though the task at hand was to exegete ancient Scripture, not to proffer social criticism, the Houston attorney could not resist the temptation to add his personal gloss. He looked around at southern mores and liked what he saw. The "heavenly" distinction between man and woman, he boasted, was most sincerely observed in the "old chivalrous Southland, and nothing is more of a monstrosity than modern efforts to obliterate and disregard the differences between the sexes as we observe it in many quarters."[66]

Considered whole, the evidence leaves the impression that Carothers spoke for most men and many women as well. E. N. Bell, for example, the first chairman of the Assemblies of God and a man with a solid education, took a somewhat different path but reached the same destination. Though Scripture certainly authorized women to testify, Bell allowed, there was "no instance of any woman being put in a place of authority to rule, govern or teach . . . by the authority of their office." Two reasons presented themselves. One was man's greater physical strength. Those who spoke from the authority of an office were obliged to enforce their words, and men were "better adapted through their natural inheritances" to impose their wills on others. The other reason was Christian charity. Simple kindness dictated that men should *"take these heavy responsibilites off their shoulders."*[67] Whether Bell intended to exclude women only from administrative chores, or whether he also meant to exclude them from full ministerial responsibilities, remains unclear. He conceded that a qualified woman could step in when a qualified man could not be found, but only temporarily, only as an exception, and only if the local assembly agreed.[68] Yet even this much flexibility was not countenanced by many male pentecostal leaders. More typical probably was the posture of A. J. Tomlinson, leader of the Church of God in the Appalachians, who prohibited women from church government functions, and later William J. Seymour, leader of the Apostolic Faith on the West Coast, who said that women could be ministers but not "Baptize and ordain."[69]

We can summarize the story to this point as follows. When the primitivist impulse surged, both Scripture and the Holy Spirit seemed to authorize nontraditional roles for women. But when due regard for the dictates of prudence—the pragmatic impulse—began to take over, pundits of both sexes started calling for a more thoughtful reading of Scripture and a more judicious hearing of what the Holy Spirit really was saying. In this latter mode everyone agreed that women enjoyed the right to speak in public, as long as they testified to what the Lord had done for them personally, or as long as they restricted themselves to serving as a mouthpiece for the Holy Spirit. What most saints doubted, at least when they sat down and began to think about it, was the right of women to speak officially, by virtue of a prescribed position. Though few if any came right out and said so, it was easy to see what the problem was. The authority to speak officially carried with it the right to exposit Scripture, which meant teaching men; the right to vote in business meetings, which meant adjudicating disputes among men and between men and women; and the right to administer Holy Communion, which meant putting men in a recipient role.

Other Scriptures

If a more considered reading of the New Testament produced warrants for circumscribing women's ministry, that was partly because pentecostals, like everyone else, brought extrabiblical assumptions to their work. Class antagonism was one of them. Though middle- and upper-middle-class men did not escape criticism, pentecostals, or at least pentecostal men, found the snootiness of upper-crust women especially repellent.[70] The true church, grumbled H. W. Schermer in the Kansas *Apostolic Faith,* should suffer no "gaudily attired Jezebel in her gilded pew . . . bestowing mother-love and affection upon poodle dogs and her admiration on titled dudes."[71] The inordinate amount of time that women spent fixing their hair and adorning their bodies with jewelry and fine clothing particularly offended E. N. Bell.[72] The record does not show that Bell or any other leader worried about the time that men spent trimming their beards or preening before a mirror, however. One does not have to be especially cynical to suspect that it was the class of women who were financially able to bedeck their bodies with jewelry and fine clothing that prompted Bell's aspersions.

The materials imply that murkier fears about authoritarian women intruded too. William Welch, likely the editor of Seattle's *Midnight Cry,* gallantly allowed that he held no objection to women preaching. It was simply a question of "usurped authority." Well, maybe there was a little more to it than that. "If you would mention 'subjection to husbands' to one of these heady female critics," he groused, "you would hear from the pit at once."[73] Others agreed. George Floyd Taylor, long the editor of the *Pentecostal Holiness Advocate,* had consistently distinguished himself among top echelon male leaders for his forthright defense of women's right to preach. Yet even he recoiled at the prospect of women bossing men. "I think [the New Testament] means for woman to have the proper respect for man," Taylor opined, "and not try to take his place, or show herself equal with man in the church."[74] Men worried about other men who fell in step behind the "petticoat brigade," as Elder G. T. Haywood of the Pentecostal Assemblies of the World put it. "Women," he judged, "are to be helpers and not leaders and usurpers of authority."[75] Men were not alone in these apprehensions. Women too seemed to shrink from the prospect of other women holding too much power. "No woman that has the Spirit of Jesus wants to usurp authority over the man," cautioned Azusa's *Apostolic Faith.* Though unsigned, this article surely carried the endorsement of co-editor Clara E. Lum.[76]

If bossy women were bad enough, unregulated women were even worse. An unnamed writer for *Word and Witness* deplored the "harm" created by single women going out on the mission field, wandering from station to station, unsupervised, "bringing reproach" wherever they traveled.[77] The disturbing presence of such women threatened the well-being of a restored New Testament church.

If female pushiness worried some, treading on the time-honored prerogatives of the male household head offended others. In San Jose, California, Pastor Max Freimark—a German Jewish convert—worried that women who were bobbing their hair, leaving their homes, and plunging into the world of business competition were snookering men at their own game. "Man should be the head of the woman," he warned. "You can go into many houses and it is hard to tell who is the head."[78] In Maine, Shiloh leader Frank W. Sandford muttered about willful women, purportedly Christians, who pretended to obey their husbands yet harbored rebellious thoughts. Such a woman was a "monstrosity, a two-headed person in charge." The result? "God's order reversed, angels astonished, the church shamed, hell rejoicing."[79] Being head of the house meant being head of one's children too. In Joplin, Missouri, the editor of *Walker's Gospel Messenger* urged both parents to chum with their children—the father with the boys, the mother with the girls. Even so, the father remained the key to the Christian home. No matter how upright the mother, he warned, the child "secretly . . . determines to do as his father."[80]

Men complained with particular bitterness about the way that women provoked them sexually, imperiling their immortal souls. A New York City editor judged that multitudes of men owed their "eternal damnation to the boldness of women's attire."[81] A Kansas writer targeted women, including so-called church women, who "indulge in slander and vulgar conversation [and] flirt and play with the male sex, and expose their persons in the same hideous manner." At church parties and picnics the fellows could be seen "romping over the green with a half naked girl, indulging in silly flirtations."[82] While males clearly bore some responsibility for this outrage, women bore more. An unnamed writer for the Kansas *Apostolic Faith*—likely the editor Charles Fox Parham—challenged the common assumption that men misled women. More often the reverse held true. Respectable mothers and daughters "enticed" men with their alluring and revealing clothing.[83] Women joined the chorus of lament, attacking other women for tempting their husbands. One matron traced the "poisonous breath" of corruption sweeping the country back to its source: the scantiness of feminine apparel. The problem was not the temptress down the street, but the mother, the married woman, "who knows the evil and still indulges in her short dresses."[84]

Deep if not wholly subterranean presuppositions about the fixity of gender roles fueled these attacks on female and female-inspired licentiousness. Examples appeared in various guises. Pentecostals rarely spoke of matters so delicate as unmarried teenage pregnancy, yet when they did, their assumptions came through loud and clear. The *Pentecostal Rescue Journal* worried, for instance, about daughters who had suffered the "terrible misfortune of being robbed of [their] virtue," as well as "girls now living a regular life of shame."[85] Though apostolics never countenanced a sexual double standard for men and women, they imperceptibly slipped into the prevailing notion that premarital pregnancy was the young woman's special "shame." Or to take a case of a different sort, a writer for the North Carolina–based *Holiness Advocate* (soon to become pentecostal) somberly warned "Christian young men" not to choose a "giddy, frivolous girl [for a wife] simply because she is pretty, vivacious, and perhaps a ready conversationalist." Instead, they should seek a companion of "sense, judgment, health, piety."[86] Apparently it never occurred to the author, and probably not to the *Advocate*'s readers either, that young women should scrutinize young men for the same traits.

All of these concerns about the validity of women's ministry, which bubbled up from a wide range of biblical, theological, and cultural wellsprings, flowed together in a singularly trenchant document published about 1920 by California evangelist Frank Bartleman. He called it, aptly enough, *Flapper Evangelism: Fashion's Fools Headed for Hell*. Bartleman ranked as one of the most prolific writers and widely traveled speakers of the early days. The booklet is difficult to peg. On one hand it represented a fiercely primitivist attack on the artificiality of modern society, for which women were both the principal culprits and principal victims. The sole purpose of the cosmetic industry, for example, was to deceive, to make women look different from how they really looked, and women paid the price, both physically and financially. Expensive fur pelts draped over bare backs was bad enough, but what about high-heeled shoes? "It is a common sight to see women standing on one foot in the street car, from pain from too tight shoes. What Fashion's Fools!"[87] Modern businesses proved even worse, filling newspapers and magazines with advertisements featuring "semi-naked women."[88] It should be noted that this portrait of female nudity as a commodified tool of women's exploitation came not from feminist political ideology, but primitivist religious fervor.

At the same time, however, Bartleman reproduced some of the oldest and cruelest stereotypes about women, thus showing how firmly tradition continued to grip him. Exceptions aside, modern women proved contemptible because they were weak. Acting from impulse, impatient with sound doctrine, easily unbalanced and highly strung, females predictably accounted for the bulk of the inmates in insane asylums. No wonder God never ordained "petticoat government."[89] The acid-tongued preacher feared women more than he disdained them. Women first withheld their affections from men, then tormented them with skimpy clothing.[90] Females flaunted their freedom by smoking, drinking, and cursing in public. Indeed the modern man rightfully feared marriage, knowing that the woman often won her way in divorce courts with her "wicked charms, corrupting the officials."[91] If women provoked Bartleman's contempt because they were inferior and his fear because they were dangerous, they provoked his loathing because they blurred the fundamental orders of creation. Specifically, they befogged the race's sexual identity. Sporting bobbed hair and wearing men's breeches, modern women turned themselves into "a kind of 'What is it.'"[92] They stood as an insult to God, who made no "third sexers."[93] Worse, these sexually confused women promoted sexually confused men, who seemed as weak and effeminate as the women they emulated. It all portended the imminent end of history.

If Frank Bartleman is hard to peg on a cultural map, it is even harder to situate some of the strong women who articulated a conventional or at least a semiconventional position that, if taken seriously, would have prevented them from doing the very things they were doing. One thinks, for example, of Marie Brown, copastor of Glad Tidings Tabernacle in New York City; Emma Cotton, copastor of Azusa Temple in Los Angeles; Mrs. Crisp, principal of the Women's Training Home of the Pentecostal Missionary Union in London; Minnie T. Draper, president of the Bethel Missionary Society and

Bible School in Newark, New Jersey; Virginia E. Moss, founder and principal of the Beulah Heights Bible and Missionary Training School in North Bergen, New Jersey; Martha Wing Robinson, head of Zion Faith Homes in Zion, Illinois; and Elizabeth Sexton, longtime editor of *Bridegroom's Messenger* in Atlanta. All preached. All built and ran institutions. All left legacies of notable accomplishments. Yet to my knowledge none explicitly challenged the assumptions of male clerical and social privilege, let alone received ordination as elders.[94] In words that the feminist theologian Mary McClintock Fulkerson applied to a later generation of pentecostal women, they simultaneously resisted and reenforced the canonical system.[95]

How do we explain this combination of assertion and compliance? For one thing, some women, especially older ones, prospered in the established system just as it was, and most likely saw no reason to change things. Consider the case of Julia Delk. Virtually all ordained clergy of the black United Holy Church were male, yet Delk weaves in and out of the early convocation records, apparently preaching at will and obviously functioning as a matriarch of considerable authority. Especially pertinent here is a 1929 minute showing that she urged the assembled saints not to give "so many young women Preachers License."[96] One suspects a timeless pattern here: an older, well-established figure trying to make certain that upstarts proved their mettle before entering public ministry.

Then too the price of assertion proved steep. Marriage casualty figures for female leaders told their own story. Though Aimee McPherson's first husband died on the mission field, her second husband divorced her for desertion and the third for mental cruelty.[97] Similar marital breakups befell others in the limelight. Bible institute matriarch Elizabeth V. Baker divorced one husband and spent most of her life separated from the second. Healing evangelist Maria Woodworth-Etter's first union ended in divorce; her biographer describes the marriage as "stormy."[98] Florence Crawford, founder of the Apostolic Faith, permanently separated from her husband of sixteen years following her baptism experience and entry into public ministry. We also find the opposite phenomenon: many of the most widely respected women leaders, especially on the mission field, never married at all, including Minnie Abrams, Susan C. Easton, Alice Belle Garrigus, Alice Luce, Elizabeth Sisson, Lillian Trasher, and Lilian B. Yeomans. People elected to marry or remain single for all sorts of reasons, yet given that virtually all of the front rank male leaders married one woman for life,[99] one can only surmise that public eminence dictated different options for females.

Finally, many women undoubtedly believed that the traditional side of the pentecostal message actually made their lives more, not less, secure. The evidence is spotty, but it is there. As biblical literalists, pentecostals knew that if they preached the hard words of 1 Timothy 2:11 they also had to preach the soft words of Ephesians 5:28 as well. It is difficult to imagine anyone more patriarchal than W. F. Carothers or Frank Bartleman. Yet both insisted, vigorously and without qualification, that God expected husbands to love their wives as they loved their own bodies, as Christ had loved the church.[100] The same animus informed saints' denunciations of divorce which, they said, only harmed families. An unnamed writer for Azusa's *Apostolic Faith* exulted that the pentecostal experience had changed her brother. Once a rounder, he had gone back to live with his wife. "This Gospel," the author smiled, "surely is building up homes"—a sentiment that needed no explanation.[101]

One more factor undoubtedly helped to maintain conventional attitudes. In brief, for most women, as for most men, politics simply was not life's fundamental category.[102] The experience of Efraim Sandblom, a Swedish missionary to India, said something important about the rhythms of ordinary affairs. Almost as soon as the pentecostal message reached India, he recalled, the Holy Spirit baptized him. Sandblom and his unnamed spouse (a significant point in itself) determined that they would not sleep until the Lord baptized her too. They prayed together hour after hour until she at long last received the fire from heaven. "[B]illows of joy rolled over us," he recalled. "We were simply *filled* with the joy of the Lord, and . . . went peacefully to sleep."[103] Such stories, disarming in their lack of pretense, suggest that for many men and women other priorities eclipsed self-conscious gender concerns of any sort—traditional, progressive, or otherwise.

In this chapter I have tried to show that women in early pentecostalism, as in most of conservative Protestantism,[104] suffered conflicting pressures, but that still leaves us with the task of explaining why. Some students of the revival, following Max Weber, have argued that the process represented a predictable evolution from prophetic to priestly modes of leadership.[105] What these observers rightly see is that by the end of the first generation, women were facing serious restrictions on public ministry. What they fail adequately to see is that pentecostal women faced these restrictions virtually from the beginning. If the primitivist impulse drove them to defy worldly conventions, the pragmatic impulse reminded them that defiance was costly. Everywhere the struggle raged back and forth, between traditions, within traditions, and inside the hearts and minds of individuals. First-generation saints rarely admitted to themselves, let alone to outsiders, that conflicting attitudes battled for dominance. But if the egalitarian author of Galatians 3:28 and the patriarchal author of 1 Timothy 2:11 could not get things entirely harmonized, perhaps early pentecostals should not be judged too harshly for failing to do so either.

11

Boundaries

Rancor—bitter, partisan rancor—formed one of the most salient features of the pentecostal movement's early history. Robert Anderson correctly observes that "fratricidal brawling" marred converts' relations with each other, and much the same could be said about their relations with outsiders.[1] Though I have discovered no evidence of loss of life, sometimes their conflicts with outsiders became so heated one side or the other (or both) landed in court. So the question before us in this chapter is a simple one. Why did saints have such a hard time getting along with their neighbors? Why could they not rest content to leave the final sorting out in God's hands? In brief, why did they invest so much energy in drawing boundaries?

The answer stems from both the primitivist and the pragmatic impulses of their culture. The first fostered the conviction that Holy Spirit-filled believers had come to know, either through inerrant Scripture or through direct revelation, exactly what God wanted them to think and to do. Undue sensitivity to the way others might see the world was taken as a sign of weakness, not strength. The second impulse worked its own parallel damage. At first glance one might suppose that pragmatism would have prompted pentecostals to make compromises with the folk around them—prompted them, in other words, to get along by going along. And occasionally it did. But the determination to make a mark on the world frequently outweighed the capacity for negotiation. We should not assume that thisworldliness always spurred pentecostals to behave effectively, let alone wisely. Often it fostered a confrontational attitude toward strangers, especially those who seemed to be standing in their way and blocking their opportunities for advancement. Pragmatic motives, in other words, proved capable of producing dramatically unpragmatic results.

The primitive and the pragmatic impulses generated conflicts with different groups of people. Otherworldly aspirations provoked quarrels with a wide array of religious bodies, men and women who crossed pentecostals' deepest convictions about matters of faith and church practice. None possessed the right to hold, let alone propagate, erroneous views, however sincerely held. Thisworldly aspirations, on the other hand, provoked conflicts with professional groups and with large or impersonal organizations. Those bodies earned saints' scorn by seeming to obstruct their progress on the social ladder. Pentecostals were too determined to make a go of things than to put up with such barriers without a long, hard fight.

Theological Foes

Like most Americans, early pentecostals considered themselves good neighbors—friendly, open minded, generous to a fault. If we listened only to the pronouncements they aired for public consumption, we would almost think that the divine fire had burned up all traces of self-centeredness. Though converts never used the word *ecumenism,* that is exactly what they believed the full gospel message offered: a new dispensation in which the old divisions would be erased. In this End Times stirring, the Azusa *Apostolic Faith* declared in the fall of 1906, God "recognizes no man-made creeds, doctrines, nor classes of people."[2] Six months later the paper warned partisans about the perils of arrogance. "The moment we feel we have all the truth or more than anyone else, we will drop."[3] To an inquirer who wanted to know if the revival should be regarded as a sect or a denomination, the paper answered forcefully: "No; it is undenominational and unsectarian."[4] Warmly expansive sentiments of that sort arrived early and stayed late. As recently as the mid-1920s a new latter rain periodical emerged bearing the expansively ecumenical title: *Herald of the Church: An Advocate of the Scriptural Unity of the People of God in One Body.*[5]

At first glance these sentiments appeared heartfelt, but a shark lurked just beneath the surface. Pentecostals' ecumenism was the ecumenism of the carnivore. Everyone was welcome as long as they were willing to be devoured. Let us go back to Azusa. The mission's warning about the perils of arrogance fell on the heels of another declaration, one that succinctly captured the limitations of pentecostal openness: "We that have the truth should handle it very carefully."[6] Those first five words are worth noting again: "we that have the truth." Virtually every pentecostal affirmation of universalizing intent carried, in one way or another, this same qualification, this same double edge. Occasionally saints saw, or almost saw, the irony of it all. Elmer K. Fisher, pastor of Los Angeles' Upper Room Mission, acknowledged that the movement had produced "division and unhappy dissension" in the church. Yet he remained unapologetic. Among "true Christians" some would always prove "more ready and quick to press on into the new light which God is shedding forth."[7]

Given their premises, pentecostals had reason to be wary. They saw theological enemies everywhere they looked and—to steal a line from Martin E. Marty—they looked everywhere. Some of the most dangerous enemies were ostensible colleagues in other parts of the Holy Ghost camp. We noted some of those intramural conflicts in Chapter 4. Here it suffices to say that such fights often turned into grudge matches over seemingly minuscule differences of doctrine. Friendships dissolved and erstwhile brothers and sisters in Christ were driven from the fold. Significantly, pentecostals were not able to forge any kind of cooperative fellowship among themselves until 1948, despite much talk and several abortive attempts to do so in the 1920s.[8] Granted, sociological differences may have played a role in those tensions. Robert Anderson makes a persuasive case that some of the friction in the infant Assemblies of God, for example, stemmed from status differences between men and women who came from the Christian and Missionary Alliance on one hand and those who came from the (Texas–Arkansas) Apostolic Faith on the other.[9] Nonetheless, the evidence leaves little question that a large part of the wrangling grew from each faction's conviction that it alone knew God's mind.

Much the same can be said about pentecostals' perennially strained relationships with radical evangelicals—those holiness Wesleyans and higher life fundamentalists who stood closest to them on the cultural and theological landscape. That story is so rich, and so symptomatic of larger patterns of sectarian rivalry in America, it requires a separate study in itself.[10] For now it is enough to note that both pentecostals and radical evangelicals used all available weapons, apparently including arson and physical violence, to defend their positions. Though once again sociological differences may have played a role, the main precipitator was the conviction, held by both sides, that they alone knew God's mind without the distortions of human pretense.

If primitivist assumptions prompted pentecostals to fight with siblings and cousins, those assumptions also prompted them to assail a large company of men and women who might be called symbolic foes. By symbolic foes I mean the religious folk that saints usually encountered indirectly, either on paper or by word of mouth. They included off-brand sects, name-brand Protestants, and Roman Catholics.

Off-brand sects consisted of the historically diverse groups that most evangelical Protestants thoughtlessly lumped together and dismissed as cults. Over the years sociologists have used the term *cult* in a measured way to describe a religious group that emerged, yet sharply distinguished itself, from the primary religious tradition of the culture. Pentecostals used the label both loosely and pejoratively to describe any group that had, in their view, willfully chosen to deny the essential doctrines of Christianity, especially the vicarious atonement of Jesus Christ.[11] The danger list included Theosophy, Spiritualism, New Thought, Buddhism, Father Divineism, Bahai, hypnotism, witchcraft, fortune telling and, above all, their American-born rivals—Christian Scientists, Mormons, and Jehovah's Witnesses.[12]

Each of these last three groups posed its own distinct danger. Christian Science seemed to demand serious theological refutation. This is not to say that pentecostals' attacks on Christian Scientists were either fair or persuasive. But it is to say that they found the Scientists' message credible enough to warrant an avalanche of proof-texts and first-person testimonials of deliverance. Pentecostals went to great lengths to distinguish their own form of healing, based on faith in God's power, from Christian Scientists' form, based on faith in the power of humans to heal themselves.[13] Mormons posed a different kind of threat—sexual seduction. They drew young girls and women into their trap as a fly into amber. One broadside, symptomatically titled "Mormonism! A Survey of Its Blasphemous Pretensions and Evil Practices," betokened both the kind of discourse and the depth of fear that the Mormons aroused.[14] "Polygamous, murderous, lying, secret-society Mormons" was the way that the Saint Louis pastor S. D. Kinne described them. Rumors that Mormons had practiced speaking in tongues could not be taken seriously.[15] If Mormons exploited sexual frailty, Jehovah's Witnesses exploited intellectual gullibility. Their message, which denied Christ's literal resurrection, represented the "greatest heresy of the ages."[16] Pentecostals never managed to explain why Witnesses—then called Russellites—proved so adept at winning converts, including converts from pentecostal ranks. But whatever the reason, saints explained Witnesses' attractiveness by saying that many persons were just too weak minded to be able to name a fraud when they saw one.[17]

Mainline Protestants constituted another frightful though largely symbolic adversary. In pentecostals' view, nominalism—Christianity in name only—bedeviled all of the mainline churches.[18] Sometimes nominalism presented itself as dry formalism, a chronic emptiness of spirit. "A bastard Christianity, pale, sickly, powerless, the offspring of a backslidden church, and a fallen world," was how the English preacher H. Mogridge detailed it.[19] Mogridge spoke more colorfully than most but reflected rank-and-file opinion accurately enough. Consider for example the sentiments of C. H. Fredericks, a Mississippi preacher affiliated with Parham's Apostolic Faith. In Fredericks's mind, God could only pity the "fractional part of the gospel" that the mainline churches hawked. The latter were filled with unanointed pastors, men who bore much of the blame for the "spiritual desolation" of the age.[20]

Going through the motions of Christian practice was bad enough, lapsing into frivolity even worse. Again Fredericks spoke for many. Instead of focusing on the pressing needs of the hour, he charged, the mainline churches featured entertainments, "fairs, festivals, concerts, tableaux, amateur theatricals . . . grabbags and ring cakes."[21] H. W. Schermer, a Kansas *Apostolic Faith* regular, scored them for dishing up "charity in small doses and society in large chunks." In his view they majored in "ice cream socials, card parties, kissing bees . . . frivolity and vanity—a conglomeration of silly talk."[22] In New England, the popular tract writer Abbie C. Morrow assailed the modern church's preference for "free and easy fellowship." In the dispensation of the Holy Spirit, she warned, "frolicking and mirth" would cease.[23]

If lassitude gnawed at mainline Protestantism's heart, theological liberalism gnawed at its mind. No first-generation pentecostal leader attempted a serious, systematic engagement with the theological establishment, but they hurled plenty of epithets, pitched low and fast, against the peril of "rationalism."[24] Ohio Quaker Levi Lupton expressed the prevailing attitude as forcefully as any: liberals "plunged a multitude of inquiring souls into hell."[25] Pentecostals never imagined, let alone acknowledged, that liberals might be honorable men and women trying to refurbish an ancient creed for modern needs. Instead they fastened on liberals' perceived duplicity, their habit of purporting to be orthodox even as they fostered doubt. "Infidels masquerading as men of God," was the judgment of Santa Cruz, California, pastor J. N. Hoover. What liberals had to offer, he snapped, was "atheism in small doses."[26] Bertha Pinkham Dixon, a Quaker missionary, told of her experience at an unnamed "Eastern university." Her Old Testament professor's "peculiarly reverent manner" and call for "utmost charity" for those who still clung to the old traditions made his attacks on the Bible all the more pernicious.[27]

The denominations and groups that fell within the institutional shadow of mainstream Protestantism were many—actually, almost everyone except radical evangelicals (who had their own grievous faults). Pentecostals routinely spoke of seeking to win converts from other Protestant communions, including broadly evangelical ones like Friends, Brethren, Lutherans, Missionary Baptists, Salvation Army, and Plymouth Brethren.[28] They crowed about individuals' converting from those traditions as if they were transitions from darkness to light. One widely advertised booklet highlighted the experience of a "Baptist Pastor" who had been "loose[ed] from one human prop after another until eventually he received the Pentecostal baptism and launched out in a new life of service for God."[29] Even sawdust trail evangelists like Billy Sunday and Sam Jones fell under the hammer. One combatant dismissed Sunday and Jones as the "white slavers of the religious world," men who trafficked "not in the bodies, but in the souls of humans." In their revivals, it appeared, thousands made professions but few registered anything like a true conversion.[30]

In at least one respect, however, pentecostals proved to be exactly like the mainline Protestants they despised: above all things mortal they feared Roman Catholics. Catholics formed a third large category of largely symbolic foes to be challenged and, if possible, destroyed. Just as pentecostals failed seriously to engage theological liberals, they also failed seriously to engage Roman Catholic spirituality. Augustine was common property, but after him one reads in vain for an appreciative word for any medieval saint, let alone post-Tridentine theologian. Instead, pentecostals summarily linked Catholics with superstition,[31] socialism,[32] criminality,[33] tyranny,[34] congressional corruption,[35] and World War I.[36]

When confronting the specter of Roman Catholicism, pentecostals' weapon of choice was the apostate narrative, the proverbial story of the soul who somehow escaped the clutches of Romanism and somehow lived to tell about it. The tale of Sister Bertha Mackay was more lurid than most but in substance typical. In the spring of 1914 Mackay rehearsed her story for a record-breaking crowd at a Wednesday night prayer meeting in Indianapolis, Indiana. A reporter for the *Christian Evangel* (published in nearby Plainfield) dutifully recorded the sister's remarks. Mackay explained to the eager audience that she had spent five years in a succession of convents. She had never wanted to become a nun but the priests forced her parents on threat of damnation. In these convents she had seen "all the horrors of the Spanish inquisition in full force," including nuns who had their eyes gouged out, tongues cut off, faces smothered, or bodies lacerated by spikes. She personally knew of fifteen babies born to nuns in one convent alone, all of whom were baptized and then tossed into a lime pit. After escaping, Mackay said that twice she had been caught and stoned until presumed dead. Later poisoned by a Jesuit in a Detroit restaurant, she found deliverance by invoking the poison-immunity passage in Mark 16:18—then vomited up enough arsenic to kill ten grown men. The objective facticity of this account does not concern us here. What is relevant is that this story appeared in one of the movement's premier periodicals and was presented as hard news.[37]

One outsider group largely escaped pentecostals' overt condemnation, and that was the Jews. Like most radical evangelicals, Holy Ghost folk uniformly supported Zionism in Palestine[38] and held positive stereotypes about Jews at home. Pentecostals applauded Jews' prosperity[39] and contributions to the professions.[40] The *Christian Evangel* reprinted fundamentalist James Gray's happy prediction that the United States and a restored Israel would soon become "one nation and that Christ will reign over us in Jerusalem."[41] That last point reveals the joker in the deck, however. Jews earned praise partly for their accomplishments but primarily for another reason: because they provided a forum for pentecostals' own triumphant role in the End Times drama.[42] Saints never doubted that Judaism as a *religion* would be extirpated and replaced by Holy Spirit–powered Christianity. Jews who died without embracing Jesus Christ as the sole true Messiah would forever perish as surely as any heathen. That conviction explained why pentecostal zealots sent missionaries to the Jews at home and abroad as avidly as to China or to Africa.[43]

The largely one-way fight between pentecostals and their symbolic opponents persisted throughout the period under scrutiny (and in some quarters persists to the present). What kept it going? Why did believers invest so much time and energy assailing those whom they rarely encountered personally?

Several reasons come to mind. The first might well have been pentecostal leaders' instinctive sense that opposition built character. They understood that good fences made good revivals. That reason leads to a second: outsiders' perceived ability to win converts from the ranks of pentecostals themselves. The key word here is *perceived*. Undoubtedly radical evangelicals posed a very real threat to pentecostals because, for many, that meant nothing more than going home again. But how many fire-baptized souls wandered into Christian Science reading rooms? Or uptown Methodist churches? Or Roman Catholic monasteries?[44] Toward the end of the first generation, we know, two or three leaders jumped ship for other Christian groups.[45] But the aggregate number of defectors likely proved extremely small, as the evidence of self-conscious attrition (as opposed to simply drifting away) remains virtually nil. The key point here is that, regardless of sociological fact, apostolics *believed* that their members were perennially liable to stray into another's arms, and that was all that really mattered.

The third and most important reason for pentecostals' perennial hostility to their symbolic foes stemmed from the satisfaction they gained by separating themselves from error. Primitivists to the bone, saints remained convinced that they had come to possess the truth, the *Whole Truth* (as the Church of God in Christ periodical was titled), without taint of human conditioning. They could not imagine, even for a moment, that their own theological posture might need some therapy. There was nothing especially distinctive about that premise, of course, for many believers had felt the same throughout Christian history. Nor was there anything especially distinctive about pentecostals' additional assumption that their truth applied to all persons at all times and places. That too was a common legacy of the evangelical missionary movement. What gave pentecostals' foreign relations a particularly jagged edge was the additional assumption that the Holy Spirit had made the full gospel message convincing to all. When outsiders did not embrace it, the only possible explanation was willful defiance of God's law and promises. Outsiders had not simply stumbled into error. They deliberately chose it—and deserved to be treated accordingly.

Social Foes

Early pentecostals fell into repeated, protracted, and sometimes physically violent conflicts with the men and women they worked with by day and likely encountered over the backyard fence by night. Our first task is to survey the scope and character of those face-to-face quarrels. The second is to try to understand the reasons for them.

The evidence suggests that converts' trouble with their actual neighbors took three distinct though often overlapping forms. The first consisted of instances in which saints found themselves on the receiving end of unprovoked acts of harassment. (Of course the definition of "provoked" and "unprovoked" very much depended on who was telling the story.) Many such incidents look more like cowardly pranks than real crimes. In those cases rotten eggs seemed the weapon of choice. In Winnipeg, Manitoba, for example, vandals tossed eggs into Zelma Argue's church.[46] In Houston in 1906 rowdies reportedly "chunk[ed]" an Apostolic Faith tent with three-month old grocery eggs.[47] Sometimes, though, more dangerous missiles were used. In Portland, Oregon, snowballs, bottles, and tin cans smashed out every window in Florence Crawford's downtown mission.[48] In San Antonio rocks and tin cans sailing over a backyard fence forced Brothers Overstreet and Burnside to take cover.[49] In Santa Barbara airborne whiskey bottles struck and cut unsuspecting worshipers.[50] In Canalu, Illinois, rowdies threw so much cayenne pepper into a church service that those inside could not breathe.[51] In Athens, Tennessee, a stink bomb broke up a meeting.[52] In Benton, Arkansas, an uninvited goat in the aisle achieved the same effect.[53] In Columbus, Kansas, "hoodlums" threatened to cowhide evangelist Charles Fox Parham if he did not leave town.[54] In Los Angeles, a cowboy sauntered into a Holy Ghost meeting, sat down, drew his six-shooter and dropped it on the floor three times.[55]

These intimidation tales, which represent many others, might leave the impression that harassment rarely involved anything worse than a cut lip or a hurt feeling. But that would be a mistake, for the data suggest that some harassment entailed property destruction and serious injury. At Morehouse, Illinois, for example, thugs severely beat the evangelist Walter Higgins.[56] Elder L. Echols found East Ellway, Georgia, a dangerous place to preach the gospel when two sticks of unexploded dynamite were discovered under his church building and an assailant clubbed him on a local street.[57] In Cleveland, Tennessee, bullets smashed through the windows of A. J. Tomlinson's home.[58]

Just outside Hearne, Texas, twenty-five men savagely beat evangelist F. F. Bosworth on a railroad platform as he was leaving town.[59] C. H. Mason of the Church of God in Christ learned that marauding whites were not the only danger that a black bishop might face in the rural South. On one occasion fellow blacks beat Mason when he tried to admonish them about their bad debts and godless ways.[60] One Brother Burris of the Church of God was stripped naked and lashed thirty times with a whip.[61] Holy Ghost people found themselves especially plagued by arson. Vigilantes torched Nellie Wright's revival tent in Coffeyville, Kansas,[62] and Robert Chisholm's Neshoba Holiness School (Pentecostal Faith) near Union, Mississippi.[63] A Methodist minister in Shoal Creek, North Carolina, distinguished himself by burning down a meetinghouse when the pentecostal pastor started teaching, ironically enough, the necessity of multiple baptisms of fire.[64]

A second form of mundane trouble stemmed from pentecostals' real or perceived interference in other persons' family lives. Outsiders commonly believed that Holy Spirit–filled zealots targeted children, particularly adolescents, for evangelization—and outsiders reacted predictably. When the parents of Ralph Herrill, a student at Charles Parham's Beth-El Faith Home in Topeka, Kansas, heard of visions and tongues in the home, they arranged for a friend to accompany young Ralph out of the institution and back to town.[65] Sometimes such scenes could turn truly nasty. The Quaker pentecostal Levi Lupton apparently made the mistake of concealing Arthur Smith at his Alliance, Ohio, camp meeting. The evidence suggests that Smith's mother thereupon encouraged local toughs to invade the meeting, squirt Lupton and various worshipers with diluted sulfuric acid, and retrieve her child.[66] In Salem, Oregon, a young, Roman Catholic woman adopted M. L. Ryan's radical holiness teachings as he teetered on the precipice of pentecostalism. When the young woman proposed to leave the area with Ryan to attend Pacific Holiness College, an angry crowd, including her family, captured Ryan, horsewhipped him, and drove him out of town. "It became noised abroad," said one editor, "that the preacher was trying to break up the family."[67] On occasion, parents' protective instincts ran so deep that they tried to shield even adult children from the full gospel threat. When one father heard that his grown son had decided to take up preaching on the Holy Ghost circuit, the father angrily tried to break up his first service, arguing that his son had been "hypnotized."[68]

Strain marked other kinds of family relations, not just those between parents and children. On Cape Hatteras, in the late 1930s, for example, one Mrs. Price's conversion to the latter rain movement plunged the family into a crisis. On hearing of his wife's conversion, Mr. Price threw her over the fence and punched an intervening minister in the face, knocking him on his back.

In the meantime a Holy Spirit-filled niece thrust a fork into Mr. Price's back with such force that it had to be removed by Price's son.[69] In the midst of a 1907 Memphis revival, one irate husband physically dragged his wife from the altar and threatened to kill the speaker.[70] At Aquilla, Missouri, local farmers ordered their wives and daughters not to attend a Holy Ghost meeting at a nearby vacant church building. The farmers may have foreseen more than they realized, for the service ended in a mass fistfight between pro- and antipentecostal factions.[71] Common sense tells us that most confrontations over family members were less dramatic. Even so, what stuck in the mind of Howard Goss many years later was the number of times that he had been "threatened by angry mobs or by raging individuals when some member of their family had been converted."[72]

Pentecostals' real or perceived interference with others' family relations became a good deal more complicated when civil authorities concluded that saints were abusing their children. Perhaps few believed a story, published in the *Los Angeles Express* in 1906, that Holy Ghost zealots were contemplating child sacrifices to "appease the wrath of God."[73] Yet the fact that such a claim could be published at all suggests the degree of apprehension the new sect engendered. Sometimes the issue seemed to be simple solicitude by the state for the welfare of minors. At different times and places municipalities passed laws or directives to bar children from attending pentecostal meetings[74] or even to remove them from pentecostal homes.[75] More often, though, the law cracked down on apostolics when they refused medical attention for ailing or injured children. The situation grew especially volatile when these children died. In 1915, for example, Walter Barney, a member of the Church of God in Foster Falls, Virginia, served four months at hard labor for the manslaughter death of his sick child after Barney refused to call a physician or administer medicine.[76]

Infringing on other people's civil rights constituted the third and by far most frequent form of trouble that Holy Ghost folk got themselves into. This behavior took a variety of forms.

We might well begin with the consequences of missionizing: saying what they thought, forcing others to listen—and paying the price. Often it was just a matter of making themselves a nuisance by painting scripture verses on bridges or pestering train passengers with tracts.[77] Sometimes, though, the perceived infringement on the civil rights of others bore serious consequences. Kurt O. Berends shows, for example, that in the village of Jefferson, New Hampshire, the First Fruit Harvesters' relentless attacks on fraternal lodges and established churches in the area culminated in violence in December 1908. Locals, weary of being labeled "harlots and daughters of harlots" by the pentecostals, twice interrupted Harvester services with threats of bloodshed. Soon a vigilante group reportedly numbering 100 demolished the chapel with crowbars and axes, then dynamited the chimney. The Harvester's own periodical, *The Sheaf,* depicted the event as proof that the End Times had come and that Christians should be prepared to die a martyr's death. Secular papers either ignored the bombing or implied that the Harvesters got what they deserved.[78]

Saints' interference with others' ability to earn a living was a more common disturber of civil order. Here we might remember the incident, recounted in an earlier chapter, of the Pasadena rooming house owner who had to appeal to the city council for protection from a Household of God revival next door. There was so much noise at all hours of the day and night—reportedly including "unearthly shrieks and groans"—that the proprietor of the rooming house found it impossible to rent rooms on that side of the building.[79] In Flintstone, Maryland, according to the *Cumberland Evening News,* hooligans unsuccessfully tried to dynamite the home of the Reverend Walter Long, a steel car builder turned Holy Ghost preacher. The reason: "religious agitation got such a hold on a number of men and women that they would not work and thus others were suffering."[80] Still more troubling was pentecostals' perceived tendency to blur the line between inconsiderateness and fraud. In 1913 Sarah E. Cripe of Indianapolis sued the Reverend D. Wesley Myland, founder of Gibeah Bible Institute—popularly known as a "Gliggy Bluk" center—for pressuring her into giving $2,000. Myland insisted that she had donated the money of her own free will. Cripe's attorneys retorted that Myland had extorted the sum by claiming a divine vision in which she would be damned if she did not. Though Cripe eventually dropped the suit, the newspaper publicity undoubtedly helped to perpetuate pentecostals' reputation for unfair dealings.[81] As late as 1948 evangelist Harry Bowley was still boasting that he had put a small-town Missouri circus out of business back in 1909. Even when the mayor had implored him not to do so, presumably to protect the community's economic health, Bowley remembered that he laughed and shot back, "Well, my Lord has it in hand."[82] Enthusiasts often seemed constitutionally unable to empathize with other persons' point of view.

Pentecostals' willingness to disturb the peace of the neighborhood constituted by far the most frequent form of civil rights infringement. Often they were quite explicit—though rarely candid—about this. In Indianapolis, for example, Elder G. T. Haywood said that his tiny band of followers endured "persecutions . . . everywhere" when they started worshipping in a tin-making shop on West Michigan Street. The reason is not hard to figure out. "Night after night," Haywood went on, "songs of praise could be heard floating in the air for several blocks away." After moving to an empty storeroom down the street, the beleaguered band (as they saw themselves) found that they still had to nail boards over the window sashes because they were smashed out by those who came to "mock and jeer." Bricks and rotten eggs pounded the building. Haywood, of course, attributed the trouble to a "bombardment from the enemy," but common sense tells us that the neighbors' sleep, or rather lack of it, was the real issue.[83] Sometimes latter rain folk were not oblivious at all but remarkably, even defiantly, aware of the effects of their actions. Consider Pastor J. A. Wilkerson of Mansfield, Ohio, well known on the revival circuit for shinnying up the main pole of the tent and preaching while holding on with one hand. True to form, he eventually decided to install a public address system on the roof of his church and broadcast the Sunday evening services, along with the extended prayer meetings that followed, for the benefit of the surrounding homes. Despite repeated entreaties from the residents, and then from the sheriff, Wilkerson refused to end the broadcast even at nine P.M. until he was forced to do so by the city authorities.[84]

As this incident suggests, pentecostals' propensity to worship whenever and however they wanted involved municipal authorities in unpleasant ways. In the first blush of the California revival, for example, police arrested four workers in Whittier for agitating their neighbors. "We are charged," proudly wrote the defendants in an apparent jailhouse letter, "with using boisterous language, [and making] unusual noise."[85] That was southern California, where one might expect unbuttoned behavior, but the pattern surfaced elsewhere. When Andrew Urshan—a Persian immigrant and something of an aristocrat in pentecostal circles because of his Presbyterian upbringing—launched a mission in Chicago, he immediately ran into trouble because the noise lasted long past midnight. The city asked him to close the services by 10:00 P.M. but he refused and was arrested. Eventually the group moved to a new site, but the problem persisted. Irate neighbors smashed the windows out of the building and, according to Urshan's own account, drew up petitions "to drive from the neighborhood what they were pleased to call a nuisance."[86] Farther east, in the village of Mount Forest, Ontario, nightly victory meetings on the front lawn of a Mrs. Sharp landed her and guest evangelist Aimee McPherson in a courtroom. The charge: "praising Jesus with a loud voice." We gain a sense of what those nightly events must have been like when we read that Sharp and McPherson persuaded the magistrate to let them go after they "danced around the constable in the Spirit."[87]

Stories of scrapes between exuberant worshipers and local constabularies tapered off after the World War I. Even so, as late as 1928, when the new pastor of an Assemblies of God church in Kansas City arrived in town, the first thing he heard from a member was, "Brother . . . we have been arrested again for too much loud praying."[88] When charged with disturbing the peace pentecostals instinctively retorted that other community activities, such as circuses and skating rinks, made just as much commotion and ran just as late. What they could never see, however, was that their movement threatened to change the social and symbolic order in ways that mere entertainment did not.[89]

Early pentecostals fell into other forms of trouble with the state. (I take up the special—and specially tangled—case of pacifism in a later chapter.) Some of it was principled trouble, intentional controversy aimed to make a public display of their differences from the worldly disorder around them. So it was that on one occasion zealots gave a virtuoso performance of speaking in tongues in a courtroom with the apparent aim of antagonizing the judge and the city attorney.[90] And some of it was unintentional trouble, situations in which saints did not really want conflict with the law but just ran into it. At one time or another they found themselves charged with vagrancy,[91] swindling,[92] and mail fraud.[93] And then there was divine healing—or the lack of it.

Civil authorities repeatedly charged that pentecostal healers promised more than they could deliver, resulting in tragic consequences.[94] The most notorious instances actually involved the prepentecostal, radical evangelical leaders John Alexander Dowie in Chicago and Frank W. Sandford in central Maine. Dowie's offense, magnified no doubt by the hostile curiosity of the emerging medical establishment, was that he established a chain of faith homes that operated without the benefit of physicians or medicine. Authorities arrested Dowie more than 100 times for running a medical facility without a license. Though he was never convicted, he spent considerable money and scores of days in jail and in court fighting the indictments.[95] But Frank W. Sandford took the prize for extremism on all counts. After refusing to allow a child to receive medical attention when it became obvious that the child would (and did) die without it, he was convicted of manslaughter (though later freed by a hung jury).[96] Other Holy Ghost zealots faced charges of one sort or another on other occasions—though they generally benefited from the legal system's disinclination to interfere in grass-roots healing practices.[97]

Why did pentecostals experience so much conflict with the people they met day by day? It is possible, of course, that saints were simply angular folk to begin with, prone to rub neighbors the wrong way. Yet it is risky to assume that any large social movement, numbering tens of thousands, can be explained—or explained away—in terms of some putative personality type. We stand on firmer ground if we look at the cultural assumptions that rewarded some patterns of behavior while discouraging others.

A brief digression may help. In recent years the sources and functions of "collective memory," as it is called, have become something of a cottage industry among social historians. It refers to the highly selective ways that large groups recall their past and shape it for the edification of themselves and their children. The "official" history of the Church of God Mountain Assembly, published in 1954, offers a clear example of the genre. Formally organized in the summer of 1906 at Jellico Creek Church, high up in the Appalachians of eastern Kentucky, this group remained one of the most isolated of pentecostal bodies. Yet in one respect the Mountain Assembly's official story—its collective memory—unfolded exactly as every other pentecostal group's official story. According to the sanctioned account, the Mountain Assembly found itself the victim of seemingly unprovoked physical violence from its neighbors. What crime had Mountain Assembly partisans committed? Receiving the baptism of the Holy Ghost and fire, calling sinners to repent of their ways, and seeking to heal them of their illnesses. And what thanks did they receive? Persecution—mindless, inexplicable persecution. Just as in the days of the apostles, goes the narrative, "many of the ministers and Saints were whipped, and treated cruel, by the enemies of the Church." Indeed in 1907 J. H. Parks nearly lost his life to thugs who invaded his church, armed with knives and pistols. But when Parks rebuked them in the name of the Lord, the would-be assailants "fell out as dead men and left."[98]

This sketch resembles other persecution narratives in a number of ways. Foremost, perhaps, is the presupposition that pentecostals remained innocent of any wrongdoing. Their only offense was that they had tried to save their neighbors from suffering in the present world and damnation in the world to come. Second, that kind of harassment was to be expected because the apostles themselves had suffered in exactly the same way. Third, though the intended victim was duly named, and thus honored, the site of the disturbance and the identity of the perpetrators went unnamed. As a result, independent verification of the details of the incident remains elusive. And finally, the Lord Himself miraculously intervened at the crucial moment. The Lord's act stopped the violence, verified the truthfulness of the pentecostal message, and confirmed the legitimacy of the messengers themselves.

By now we begin to sense why pentecostals experienced so much difficulty with their flesh-and-blood neighbors. In their own minds they represented God's chosen people. As such, they bore a lifesaving message for these final days of history. To oppose them was to oppose God Himself. It proved a heavy burden too, for nothing could be done simply for its own sake. Every thought, gesture, and deed bore a larger significance. One is reminded of the quip, attributed to Stanley Vishnewski, that the Catholic Worker movement consisted of two kinds of people, saints and martyrs. The martyrs were the ones who had to live with the saints.[99] Much of the same could be said of pentecostals, who inadvertently proved that their chosenness—saintliness, if you will—produced more than a few martyrs along the way.

Class Foes

Primitivist instincts shaded into pragmatic ones when early pentecostals turned their attention from theological to social foes—and especially aggregations of social foes—that seemed to be standing in their way. Often behaving more like John Wayne than Saint Paul, they pushed aside the ones they could and blustered at the ones they could not. Though religious motives never entirely disappeared from these confrontations, overall, religion played a subordinate role. The issue was space, social space, and some groups were taking up more than their share.

Saints proved themselves equal opportunity offenders, assailing men and women in a wide range of occupations and professions. Lodge men,[100] "infidel professors,"[101] and venal politicians[102] were especially vulnerable. T. M. Lee, for example, writing on the eve of the Holy Spirit outpouring, revealed a good deal about his own class resentments when he targeted members of secret societies. "How many of the wealthy, bon-ton members of any order," he demanded, "will meet a brother, who is a laboring man and whose hands are hard with the strokes of honest toil, and invite him into his parlor to be entertained by his stylish daughter and society loving wife?"[103] But the elitist sins of all these groups combined seemed minor compared to the infamies of two others: medical doctors and mainline clergymen.

The emergent class of medical doctors took a fierce drubbing. Zion's City's First Apostle, John Alexander Dowie, prefigured the assault in more ways than one. In the 1890s he waged a "Holy War" against "'Doctors, Drugs, and Devils,'" insisting that the most dreaded disease of all was "'*bacillis lunaticus medicus*.'"[104] Dowie's pentecostal progeny occasionally thanked physicians for the good work they did, but not often, especially in the first generation.[105] Storms of resentment typically drowned out any note of appreciation. Though it is hard to know where honest advocacy of divine healing left off and hostility toward seemingly avaricious and incompetent physicians began, clearly there was plenty of both. W. F. Bryant, a founder of the Church of God, spoke for many. "I'd rather die a martyr and do what Jesus says, than to spend all my money for Doctors and then die and the Dr. have to be paid with the money that my wife and children ought to have."[106] Grievances like this one died hard. Fourteen years later Bryant told of sitting down by his wife's side. "With tears in her eyes she said, 'The doctors have gotten all we have and we now owe them over one hundred dollars. Here are my little children ragged and nothing to wear and how will we pay the doctors? I don't know.'"[107] Bryant's overseer, A. J. Tomlinson, simply could not grasp why people would support a druggist or doctor who typically lived in a "beautiful mansion yonder among the trees." Anyone could do the arithmetic, he implied. "As one physician goes up in the scale of wealth a dozen or more families are reduced to poverty."[108]

Early pentecostals might have brushed off the greed and arrogance of the medical profession if they believed that they were getting their money's worth, but they did not. They felt that doctors' recklessness and ineffectiveness made their avarice all the more despicable.[109] China missionary E. May Law triumphantly noted that after seven years of battling fever, dysentery, smallpox, and cholera in South Asia, the missionaries who used doctors lost six patients while those who relied on Jesus alone had lost only one.[110] The Bible, according to founding leader Charles Parham, always associated doctors and drugs with the "vilest sins against God and humanity." After four thousand years of medical bumbling, humans still willingly laid themselves on physicians' altars to be "doped, blistered, bled and dissected." In Parham's judgment, medical science—the "octopus-god Molloch"—had hardly advanced beyond biblical times.[111]

Pentecostals leveled additional charges. Besides greed and ineffectiveness, the arrogance of doctors prevented them from acknowledging the divine healings that took place before their eyes.[112] Given the depth and breadth of saints' antagonism toward this newly powerful class of professionals, it is little wonder that they alternated between attacking doctors and, in bitter exasperation, just making fun of them. "While preaching in the home of the sick woman," quipped John E. Dull of Florence, South Carolina, "in came three men, dressed like the world, well perfumed and starched. I had no idea whether they were doctors, gamblers or preachers."[113]

As it happened, preachers—the mainline denominational variety—took the most abuse of all. Some of that antagonism undoubtedly stemmed from other sources, including honest theological differences and the venerable sectarian sport of ridiculing "hireling preachers" of any stripe. But much of it grew from red-blooded antipathy toward overly refined men in black gowns who made their living by delivering learned but spiritually vacuous expositions. At one point or another apostolics likened mainline sermons to stale bread,[114] "chips and shavings,"[115] "man-made theories,"[116] "cologne bottles,"[117] or "nice, fine, eloquent oration[s]."[118] Many of the attacks carried the sting of overt class antagonism. Aimee McPherson, for example, ridiculed uptown preachers for parading around on their "high horses of earthly knowledge, theology, formality, and ceremonial and clerical dignity, breathing out threatenings against the despised Pentecostal people."[119] A *Household of God* writer, likely its editor William F. Manley, associated Methodist bishops with the anti-Christ, partly because of their dictatorial power, and partly because they forced a man to "pass through their human institutions . . . paying out a good sum for books and then devoting much time to packing his head with human wisdom." The Methodist system elevated "hypocrites, backsliders and nominal professors" over honest Holy Ghost workers.[120] The logo of Manley's periodical said it all: "*Un-denominational and Anti-denominational.*"[121]

Saints satirized mainline preachers and their institutions without mercy. Earlier we noted their contempt for the spiritual and theological bankruptcy of the mainline, here the problem was social. "The churches are very popular affairs," jabbed one wag, "as attested by their palace-like cathedrals, massive organs, their D.D.s, and their large membership of wealthy business men and fashionable women."[122] One of McPherson's supporters similarly defended Sister's ministry by pinpointing the social location of those who opposed her: "hifalutin frock-tails, who orate in the pulpit to swell congregations, who look through one eye-glass and wear silk tomfooleries, envious because of empty benches prevailing."[123] Poking fun, albeit bitter fun, at one's ecclesiastical betters had long been a staple in radical evangelical circles, and remained so among pentecostals. It might be called the "come-uppance" narrative. In this time-honored scenario, the seminary-educated denominational clergyman sensed the vapidness of his message, experienced conversion and Holy Spirit baptism, and then—but only then—displayed a truly empowered ministry. Pentecostals loved to tell of people, especially uptown parsons, who abandoned the mausoleums that passed for churches after they witnessed the vitality of a real Holy Ghost meeting.[124] "Proud, well-dressed preachers come in to 'investigate,'" ran one typical account. "Soon their high looks are replaced with wonder, then conviction comes and very often you will find them in a short time wallowing on the dirty floor, asking God to forgive them and make them as little children."[125]

One account, which described the conversion (or reconversion) in the 1920s of Dr. Charles Price, a Congregational minister in Lodi, California, is worth looking at in some detail. It represents the genre well, and Price, one of the best-known pentecostal preachers of the interwar period, liked to tell it about himself. First printed in the *Sherburn, (Minnesota) Advance-Standard* (aptly subtitled *The Paper with the Punch*), Price reprinted it in his own periodical *Golden Grain*. The narrative portrays the prepentecostal Price as a "sure-enough, blown-in-the-bottle modern social gospel preacher, drawing a nice salary, having a good time and not caring particularly how long school kept." Predictably, Price belonged to the Rotary Club, the Modern Woodmen lodge, and other high-society clubs. Everybody liked him because he was so "broadminded." Yet he resisted when someone invited him to attend a nearby Aimee McPherson meeting. After all, what could she teach a "D.D. like himself"? But under McPherson's preaching Price quickly realized that he was "just a common everyday, six-cylinder sinner with the cutout wide open and heading straight for hell." After experiencing genuine salvation and Holy Spirit baptism, Price discovered a miraculously revitalized ministry—burnished, not incidentally, by even greater prominence. Having abandoned the "social gospel" and the "popularity crowd" for keeps, he now embraced a "simple and humble" ministry that took him into the "largest auditoriums in the United States." There he preached "nightly to many thousands" despite opposition from the press and denominational churches.[126] The accuracy of the biographical details in this narrative are less important than the formal ingredients: the irrelevance of a mainline theological education, the uselessness of respectable social connections, the unexpected wisdom of a plain woman preacher, the superiority of the simple and humble over the learned and complex, the legitimation by mass acclaim, and, finally, opposition from the elite establishment.

To say that pentecostals displayed hostility toward their social betters tells only half the story, however. They also displayed ambivalence, for they shamelessly courted the approval of the very persons they despised, especially college professors. So Memphis pastor L. C. Hall proudly noted that one Holy Ghost meeting was held in the "neighborhood of three large universities. Many attended from these and some of the theologues were baptized."[127] Azusa pioneer A. W. Orwig just as proudly remembered that the mission attracted all types of people, "not a few of them educated and refined."[128] Pastor M. L. Ryan of Oregon let it be known that "[p]rominent officials and state officers" as well as "university students and professors" regularly attended his Salem work.[129] Repeatedly saints turned to learned men from the universities—"unbiased and competent judges" one convert rather incredibly called them—to substantiate the authenticity of the foreign languages given by the Holy Spirit.[130] Yet when things went awry, when the elite scoffed, enthusiasts just as quickly regarded that turn of events as proof that the Lord had chosen "to confound professors and learned people" with the wisdom of the simple.[131] Holy Spirit–filled believers, like most Christians, aspired for Christlike humility in the face of social hierarchy, but envy came easier, and lasted longer.

Political Foes

Besides high-status social groups, Holy Ghost people also resented large institutions and impersonal aggregations that seemed to stand in their way. So they would summarily dismiss the League of Nations as useless at best, a factotum of the Roman Catholic Church and of non-Christian religions at worst.[132] The U.S. government proved just as bad, racing, it seemed, toward outright socialism. Some mythical proletariat might welcome a new economic system as a means for equalizing resources and establishing a level playing field, but not pentecostals. In their minds, socialism meant the confiscation of money and property that they had earned the hard way, through arduous toil. Saints did not tax the public purse, and they did not see why anyone else should either, except in the direst of emergencies.[133]

Big business and big labor also earned pentecostals' contempt, and in equal measure, for business and labor seemed to prey on the vulnerability of ordinary folk like themselves. According to Susan Duncan, a founder of the Rochester Bible Institute, there once was a time when capitalists were content with a net profit of 10 or 20 percent. But no longer. Nowadays these "thieves and extortioners" demanded a 40–100 percent return on their dollar.[134] In the Midwest Charles Parham saw disaster on the horizon, and big business bore much of the responsibility. "If labor is oppressed," he warned, "if men and women are compelled to labor long hours for wages that threaten them with starvation, there will come a time . . . when . . . a reign of terror will ensue."[135] Labor unions proved just as dangerous. "The present, fast-spreading *antichrist spirit* of unscriptural unionism is defying Almighty God," judged Frank W. Sandford at the Holy Ghost and Us Bible School in rural Maine.[136] A thousand miles to the south, the Church of God's General Assembly grudgingly allowed lay members to pay union dues if they had to in order to keep their jobs, but not to attend union meetings. Laboring ministers were not to join a union under any circumstances, job or no job.[137] To some extent pentecostals' visceral distaste for unions was prompted by a hardheaded calculus that unions just did not work. Strikes invariably cost laboring men more money than they gained, argued Bible teacher D. Wesley Myland.[138] Still, there was more to it than that. When zealots said, as they often did, that the union seal denoted the dreaded Mark of the Beast,[139] or that unions portended a "worldwide confederacy against Christ,"[140] they were, to be sure, using theological language to express theological ideas. But they were also using theological language to express smoldering social resentments.

Opposition to ecumenism similarly arose, at least in part, from the same deep-seated distrust of all social conglomerates that blocked mobility. As far as *Bridegroom's Messenger* editor Elizabeth Sexton could see, the ecumenical spirit aimed to amalgamate all sects into a worldwide union, eventually to be "headed and controlled by the Roman Catholic Church."[141] British pentecostals experienced comparable fears. In Hockley, Essex, Frank Peck excoriated ecumenists as impure, "committing spiritual adultery," for they "joined themselves to harlots."[142] Dark clouds billowed on every horizon. Robert J. Craig, pastor of a thriving pentecostal work in San Francisco, shuddered as he looked about and saw the civilized world coalescing into a series of interlocking confederations. The new Women's Enfranchisement League—like Mussolini's pact with the Pope, which aimed to create a "United States of Europe"—portended nothing but ill for all right-thinking believers.[143]

At first glance pentecostals targeted a strange mix of professions and organizations for vituperation: physicians, professors, uptown clergymen, union bosses, corporate capitalists, high government officials, and ecumenists. But they all held something in common. They all threatened, or at least seemed to threaten, believers' aspirations for holding their own fair share of the American dream. Later we shall see that zealots had little sympathy for populism or any other political or social movement that sought a systematic redistribution of society's resources. But when it came to ripping up old social barriers, and making space for new faces on the communal landscape, they proved themselves populists to the core.

Boundaries defined everything. The noble conviction that the Holy Spirit lived within fostered the less noble conviction that saints' own ideas equaled the Holy Spirit's. If a primitivist sense of direct connection to the divine defined one dimension of pentecostals' social relationships, a pragmatic determination to succeed in the rough-and-tumble world of modern America defined another, equally important dimension. The result was not accommodation, as one might expect, but confrontation with the unrightful owners of scarce social resources.

In sum, religious boundaries needed to be rigorously enforced, and social boundaries needed to be smashed. Holy Spirit-filled enthusiasts were too much a part of their fundamentalist heritage to think and behave otherwise. "I am in for war—war to the hilt," declared the Fire-Baptized evangelist B. H. Irwin on the eve of the revival. Then came the knockout punch: "and I just love it."[144] When it came to the hard business of staking out useful religious boundaries, or uprooting useless social boundaries, Holy Spirit–filled saints could have written the fundamentalist script.

12

Society

We must now change perspectives. The preceding chapters have focused on early pentecostals' religious culture—the ideas, symbols, rituals, and institutional practices that expressed their sense of the sacred. Saints' own priorities dictate that order of presentation, for they invariably considered themselves religious beings first, social beings second. But their self-image distorted reality. With few exceptions, first-generation converts interacted with the external environment in countless ways every day of their lives. The necessities of daily existence—making a living, establishing households, educating children, preparing for death—drew believers out of their sacred enclaves and forced them into the world around them. Spiritual aspirations, in other words, never formed more than a single thread in a rich tapestry "of work and rest, of celebration and mourning, of youth and age."[1] These words, which Josef Barton applied to Holy Ghost laborers in the southern highlands in the early twentieth century, applied to most others as well.

The governing problem for this chapter therefore can be stated as a simple question. Who were pentecostals when they were _not_ at church? What can we say about their sex, age, ethnicity, longevity, education, mobility, marital status, and financial condition? More important, how did they compare with other Americans? Still more important, how did they *interpret* their place in the social system?

At first glance charting early pentecostals' social position seems a simple task, refreshingly free of the nuances of belief and ritual that have concerned us so far. But two factors complicate the endeavor. The first is that extensive documentation for saints' mundane social lives simply is not available. In time better records may turn up, but even then we should not expect much. Believers generally failed to keep such data precisely because it looked too much like nose counting—what the folk in the tall-steeple churches uptown did. The 1919 minutes of the interracial Pentecostal Assemblies of the World explicitly stated, for example, that their leaders had not maintained careful records because it was not necessary: "The names of the members are kept on record in heaven."[2] Besides, adherents expected the Lord to return any moment. Under the circumstances, detailed observations about secular affairs mattered little. This paucity of evidence means that we are forced to draw on a variety of sources of uneven quality—usually literary, sometimes material, occasionally quantitative—and patch them together as best we can. The result is not exactly guesswork but it is not exactly hard science either.

The second and more challenging complication is that real or apparent tensions twist through the social data from beginning to end. On one hand pentecostals repeatedly emphasized their own social marginality. For example one Azusa stalwart, likely Clara E. Lum, proudly noted that the Holy Ghost stirring had started among "poor colored and Spanish people." If the Lord had waited for the better people in the established churches to open their hearts, she judged, it never would have happened.[3] India missionary Max Wood Moorhead echoed those views. Moorhead, a white Amherst College dropout, noted that the movement had started among "negroes, poor, lowly, ignorant, and despised . . . because there was no room for it in the modern church."[4] Partisans in other countries agreed. The British monthly *VICTORY!* tersely observed that the "Third Person of the Trinity" had chosen to work through a "few foolish, weak, base, despised nobodies."[5] Surveying the worldwide spread of the movement after a quarter century, one of the first pentecostal historians judged that "evidently the Lord had found the little company at last, outside as always, through whom he could have right of way."[6]

On the other hand pentecostals sometimes went out of their way to stress the respectability of their social placement. To hear them tell the story, the wealthy, the well placed, and the well educated felt very much at home in their meetings. Texas evangelist Howard Goss boasted that some of the "best people of the town" attended his services.[7] Aimee McPherson similarly bragged that her Baltimore revival attracted "many ministers (learned men, with degrees after their names), Jewish Rabbis, medical doctors, and the finest people of the city."[8] Saints never missed a chance to excoriate secular entertainers, but they also never missed a chance to gloat about converts from that strangely intriguing world. "One of the results of the revival [in Copenhagen]," one editor exulted, "was the salvation of a great Danish actress, Anna Lars[s]en . . . Another Danish actress, Anna Lewini, was also saved and filled."[9] Los Angeles' *Upper Room* went further, judging that the Danish revival had started when God converted "two leading actresses."[10] Statements like these undoubtedly said more about status desired than status achieved, but they also showed that adherents did not always see themselves stuck on the bottom rungs of the social ladder.

Visitors' reports about Holy Ghost meetings mirrored this doubleness, this tension between marginality on one hand and respectability on the other. Some spoke of the worshipers' sorry condition, calling them "chiefly poor people,"[11] or mostly "poor [and] ignorant,"[12] or folk who earned their "daily bread . . . at HARD labor during long hours and at inadequate pay."[13] At the same time others emphasized pentecostals' respectability, describing them as "well-dressed, sober folk,"[14] or "well-dressed and decorous-looking,"[15] or "intelligent and respectable."[16] Still others tried to have it both ways, saying that saints were "[m]en and women of all stations in life,"[17] or that some possessed "at least common intelligence and education, while some had years of business experience, in dealing with many kinds of people."[18]

How should we interpret these diverse comments? Granted, none represented disinterested sociological analysis. Insiders' remarks carried a heavy moral message—marginality betokened Christlike humility, respectability betokened sound judgment. Outsiders' remarks carried their own messages of moral disapproval and approval. Still, it would be reckless to disregard all observations as nothing but homilies. The authors clearly intended to say something objectively truthful about their own or their subjects' place in the social system. The most reasonable response, therefore, is to assume that different eyes saw different slices of social reality as time and place dictated.

In this chapter I try to forge an interpretive framework that accounts for both perspectives, both data sets. In brief, I argue that early pentecostals represented a cross section of the American population. That means, first of all, that a minority found themselves stuck at the bottom of the class and status ladder. And though it is risky to draw a one-to-one correlation between social location and worldview for the dispossessed, it is reasonable to assume that some responded by invoking the comforts of elaborate otherworldliness. But representing a cross section of the population also means that a majority occupied the lower-median and median rungs of the social ladder. And though it is just as risky to draw a one-to-one correlation between social location and worldview for the better off, it is reasonable to assume that some responded by embracing the comforts of an elaborate thisworldliness.

Marks of Marginalization

Dregs. Misfits. Drifters. From the beginning outsiders depicted pentecostals largely in such terms. In 1925 the *Nation* called them "Holy Rollers on Shinbone Ridge." In 1932 John Steinbeck's *The Grapes of Wrath* portrayed them as hapless victims of economic collapse. More recently scholars in a variety of disciplines have produced a portrait of personal misfortune and social dysfunction. Robert Mapes Anderson's 1979 study, *Vision of the Disinherited: The Making of American Pentecostalism*, still constitutes the most compelling example of the genre. The cogency of Anderson's analysis, the sophistication of his research methods, and the wealth of his empirical findings make his volume the starting point for any serious examination of early pentecostals' social standing.[19]

Anderson began with Holy Ghost leaders. His group portrait encompassed forty-five principals about whom substantial information existed. Almost all had been born between 1870 and 1885, all achieved prominence before 1914, most before 1909. The portrait was unpromising to say the least. Most were white males from the South or Midwest who had joined the movement before age forty. Three-fourths hailed from farm families. Most had acquired about as much education as the typical American at the turn of the century (though not the typical clergyman), perhaps an elementary or junior high school equivalency. While some were barely literate, others had finished high school or acquired a bit of college. Anderson found one seminary graduate (E. N. Bell), but none who had completed doctoral work in any theological discipline. Economically most had seen their share of hard times. Though a handful were reasonably well off when they converted, none was wealthy or well born. Besides financial insecurity, most had experienced a major personal crisis before affiliating, such as physical abuse by parents, loss of a child, the untimely death of a parent, prolonged illness, or a crippling accident. Most leaders displayed significant mobility, even as adults, changing residence, occupations, or religious affiliations (or all three) several times before taking up Holy Ghost ministry.[20]

What did the rank and file look like? The majority, Anderson argued, were female and youthful, ranging from their late teens to early forties. They were mostly "old stock whites"[21] reared in the South or Midwest. The minority who were not old stock whites included Asians, African Americans, Mexican Americans, American Indians, and non-English speaking Europeans. Nearly all emerged either from rural areas or from small towns with agrarian attitudes. Though many conversions took place in city missions, most converts were recent migrants from farms or small towns. As such, they perpetuated agrarian traditions of "fundamentalism, puritanism and sectarianism."[22] Almost all were either illiterate or barely literate. Many endured chronic unemployment. Those who did find steady work usually ended up in manual trades like carpentry or masonry or toiled in menial roles as cooks, dishwashers, janitors, day laborers, and migrant farm workers.[23]

The mass of early pentecostals thus represented, in Anderson's view, a "crippled and displaced"[24] agrarian and industrial proletariat.[25] More precisely, they proved to be three-time losers. First, they were economically disinherited, the "lowest base of the work force,"[26] the "'honest poor,'"[27] or, "as one Pentecostal put it, 'the "scum" of society.'"[28] Second, they were victims of social disinheritance, their financial plight "exacerbated by their generally low social status."[29] Third, they were culturally disinherited, exhibiting a "deeply-rooted, underlying mood of profound cultural despair."[30] The typical leader might have been slightly better off,[31] but most zealots found themselves "[e]conomically, socially, culturally, and even physically displaced and deprived."[32]

There is much to be said for Anderson's portrait. Without question, poverty, hunger, homelessness, minimal education, and ill health defined the lives of thousands. Page after page of Anderson's work, staggering under the weight of hard-won footnotes, attest to the deprivations they endured.

Additional pages of my own could be added to Anderson's sobering narrative. For example in 1910 W. F. Bryant, a Church of God evangelist in the southern highlands, lamented that the folk he worked with near Hillview, Tennessee, could not come to a service "for want of clothing."[33] Bryant himself traveled from meeting to meeting by train when he had the means and walked when he did not.[34] Another mountain preacher, who scratched out a living by farming a patch of corn, was so poor he owned only a piece of a Bible.[35] Though most of the references to destitution in early pentecostal periodicals refer either to blacks or to Appalachian whites, others knew hard times too. The editor of the *Good Report* in Ottawa, Canada, noted that many letters came from "old people, and those who are poor in this world's goods, and some living in backward localities."[36] The editors of the Azusa *Apostolic Faith* said they gave the paper away because many readers could not afford to buy even a single issue.[37]

Outsiders' scorn aggravated insiders' shame. Nonpentecostals often made clear that they considered saints the rubbish of society. In Alliance, Ohio, for example, one husband sought to win a divorce by telling the judge his wife had attended a pentecostal meeting.[38] In Los Angeles young Myrle Fisher reported that when she received Holy Spirit baptism at the Azusa Mission none of the other children at school the next day would play with her—except, significantly, a lone black girl.[39] Converts struggled not to let such attitudes get the best of them, but it was hard. In a letter to *Gleams of Grace,* published in St. Joseph, Missouri, a Brother Hesse revealed how much such attitudes could hurt: "Some one said: 'The Hesses used to be real decent folks.' But I know we are decent still, I know it."[40] The opprobrium of joining the apostolics sometimes strained family ties to the breaking point. When the youthful Howard Goss declared his new faith, his father, an atheist, ordered Goss "never to darken his doors again."[41] And then we can almost see the tears of hurt and anger as Cora Fritsch, a rookie missionary in China, admitted, "One thing that is very hard for me is, that all the missionaries from different churches look down on us and call us 'Holy Rollers.'"[42] Tough minded these believers may have been, but outsiders' condescending gaze surely took a toll at some deep level.

Given such deprivation, real or perceived, it is hardly surprising that at different times and places saints tried to separate themselves from the environing society. At the most radical extreme stood the small minority who clustered themselves into holy communities geographically roped off from the outside world. The largest and best known were the quasi-pentecostal settlements at Zion City, Illinois, and Shiloh, Maine. Less publicized efforts, also more or less pentecostal, included Thomas Hampton Gourley's communitarian experiment on Lopez Island, Washington,[43] and the White City enterprise near Lucedale, Mississippi.[44] In all of these settings the intent was to prevent needless interactions with strangers, all the way down to raising one's own "eatables."[45]

But since most converts could not afford to remove themselves from the workaday world of farms and factories for an extended stretch of time, many set up temporary sites that served the same isolating function.[46] The Falcon Holiness School in the hamlet of Falcon, North Carolina, for example, proudly stated in its advertising literature that it occupied "a country town, away from the evils of city life."[47] Scores of short- and long-term Bible and missionary training institutes, as well as camp meetings, met at the same time and place each year in secluded settings partly out of desire for the same sort of isolation. Scraps of evidence suggest that saints conducted many of their business dealings only with each other, not outsiders.[48] "God demands separation, absolute and entire," stormed British preacher H. Mogridge. "The defaulter must be dragged to the light, exposed, judged, condemned, and cast out."[49] Then too the teaching of the Blessed Hope, which promised the imminent rapture of pentecostal saints, may have symbolized the separation converts desired but could not practically attain. At the very least, the Blessed Hope reminded believers that the allegiances of Holy Spirit-filled Christians ultimately lay elsewhere.

Still, after surveying the evidence for economic misfortune and social alienation, two problems remain. First, did Holy Ghost religion serve as compensation for the good things pentecostals wanted but could not have? Or did it *dislodge* them from their old commitments and thus open them to new possibilities? Second, may we not reasonably doubt that most pentecostals were seriously disadvantaged to begin with? On the whole their setting offered a life that was, if not plush, at least adequately comfortable. The contours of that social environment—fluid and opportunity filled—now merit scrutiny.

Leaders of Standing

Where did pentecostal leaders fit in the social system of the day? Drawing on Robert Anderson's data, and adding data of our own, it now seems reasonable to say that a few plainly enjoyed upper-middle-class standing, and many others enjoyed at least a solidly middle-class position. It is impossible to determine exactly how large this comparatively comfortable group was, but to call it a conspicuous minority seems reasonable.

A handful were wealthy by anyone's standards. Consider, for example, Carrie Judd Montgomery. Among many enterprises, Montgomery probably won most recognition as the founder and publisher of the monthly *Triumphs of Faith,* which she edited for sixty-five years. Reared in an upper-crust Episcopal family in northern New York, Montgomery used the fortune that her millionaire husband George earned in mining ventures in Mexico to fund a variety of ventures, including orphanages, overseas missions, and divine healing homes. Moreover her easy interaction with mainline Christians of all stripes—Episcopal, Congregational, Methodist, Dutch Reformed—suggests upscale breeding as much as upscale funding.[50] Or again we might consider Joel Adams Wright, a land agent by trade, who organized the First Fruit Harvesters in northern New England in 1897. This radical evangelical group became pentecostal some ten years later. A succession of profitable business transactions enabled Wright to headquarter the group on 135 acres of prime New Hampshire real estate, eventually adding an orphanage and retirement center. About 1917 Wright and his son, J. Elwin, became the sole proprietors of the Tanglewood Hotels, two luxury resorts on the Maine coast catering to those who wanted—according to the advertisements—"the best in comfort and service."[51] Another financial worthy was Richard G. Spurling. In the 1880s Spurling, a founder of the Church of God, owned nearly 1,100 acres in eastern Tennessee at a time when the average freeholder in the state could claim fewer than eighty. One social historian aptly describes Spurling's son, with other early Church of God leaders, as "literate, capable, responsible" and, not incidentally, well fixed.[52] And then there was the Los Angeles healing evangelist, William Doctor Gentry. In 1921 he casually noted that his stock options stood at $100,000—on a $5,000 initial investment. Gentry's stationery letterhead, "In Business for God," may have revealed more than he realized.[53]

Other leaders boasted solid social standing. San Antonio pastor L. C. Hall was the grandson of Alabama governor and U.S. senator Arthur Pendleton Bagby. Hall himself attended the U.S. Military Academy at West Point, Asbury College, Vanderbilt University, and Washington University Law School. A. J. Tomlinson's biographer tells us that Tomlinson was reared in the home of an enterprising Indiana Quaker farmer, a "'go-getter'" who made his mark by building roads and sawmills and investing in railroad stock. W. F. Carothers also comes to mind. Possibly the most prominent pentecostal in the Southwest before World War I, Carothers gained admission to the Texas bar in 1894, managed the Houston Abstract Company, helped found the Houston Real Estate Board, and eventually served as a U.S. commissioner judge. Or we might consider Lilian Yeomans, an influential divine healing evangelist and vitriolic critic of the medical profession. Yeomans, who held an M.D. degree from the University of Michigan, joined John Alexander Dowie's Christian Catholic Apostolic Church in the 1890s and then the pentecostal movement just after the turn of the century. Finis Yoakum, founder of the Pisgah Home in Highland Park, California, a refuge for homeless derelicts, traced another revealing path. Also a physician, Yoakum was teaching at Gross Medical College in Denver and reportedly earning $18,000 a month when he gave up his practice to enter full-time ministry in radical evangelical and, later, pentecostal circles.[54]

Besides significant material comfort, a surprising number of first-generation leaders possessed a respectable formal education beyond high school and sometimes beyond college. The most touted examples include the Assemblies of God chairman E. N. Bell and the Pentecostal Holiness Church editor George Floyd Taylor. They held graduate degrees from the University of Chicago and from the University of North Carolina at Chapel Hill, respectively (though Taylor did not finish until 1931). Nickels John Holmes, a South Carolina educator, attended the University of Edinburgh for three years and practiced law in his home state for fourteen. A list of those who were formally well educated would also include the Southern Baptist scholar A. S. Worrell, a perennial fellow traveler who never quite joined the pentecostal movement but wrote about it sympathetically. Educated at Mercer University, Worrell served as president of Mount Pleasant College in Missouri, edited the *Western Recorder,* later founded and edited the *Gospel Witness,* and achieved lasting distinction as translator of a New Testament version bearing his name. George B. Studd, a scion of English gentry, graduated from Eton College and from Jesus College, Cambridge University. He helped found a number of Los Angeles missions including Peniel Hall, the Azusa Mission, and the Upper Room Mission. In time Studd exhausted his fortune underwriting pentecostal foreign missions. P. C. Nelson, educational architect of Southwestern Assemblies of God College in Waxahachie, Texas, graduated from Denison University and Rochester Theological Seminary, studying under the formidable Baptist theologian Augustus H. Strong. Nelson was serving as pastor of Conley Memorial Baptist Church in Detroit, one of the largest in the city, when he converted to the movement in 1920 and launched a lengthy career as a healing evangelist, author, and educator.[55]

A less-merciful chronicler might extend this list at length, but these vignettes are enough to show that more than a few first-generation leaders found themselves agreeably placed in the social system by virtue of wealth, profession, education, or all three.[56]

The key question is whether these well-positioned men and women typified pentecostal leaders in general. The answer is no—and yes. No, in that few enjoyed the wealth of a Carrie Judd Montgomery, or the social standing of a W. F. Carothers, or the education of an A. S. Worrell. But yes, in that the average leader, initially starting in the lower middle class, evinced a trajectory of insistent upward mobility and personal achievement. The biographical evidence, sketchy though it is, suggests that before joining, most had held modest, white-collar jobs in stores, banks, businesses, newspapers, and law firms, or that they had served as missionaries or pastors in other radical evangelical groups such as the Free Methodists or the Christian and Missionary Alliance. A few went on to college and some even made it into seminary. If we set the social profile of the typical pentecostal leader against the social profile of the average Southern Methodist or Southern Baptist leader, who had no college or seminary degree at all (rather than elite Congregationalists or Episcopalians), pentecostals come off surprisingly well.[57] In brief, most leaders' lives were defined by modestly comfortable circumstances, generally a notch above the stable working class standing of the pentecostal rank and file.[58]

Followers as Typical Americans

Where did rank-and-file believers fit in the social system? The answer can be simply stated. Contrary to stereotype, the typical convert paralleled the demographic and biographical profile of the typical American in most though not quite all respects.

Using 1910 as the benchmark, let us begin by looking at grass-roots converts' demographic profile—the attributes of sex, age, health, and race that marked them by accident of birth.[59] Sex, the ratio of men to women, is the most visible and determinative characteristic. At first glance sex seems an inauspicious place to launch an argument for the typicalness of ordinary believers. In the general population men slightly outnumbered women, while in Holy Ghost churches women formed almost three-fifths of the membership.[60] Nonetheless, the significance of female numerical predominance must be qualified in three respects. First, there was nothing unusual about this pattern, for women outnumbered men in most Protestant churches.[61] Second, in a representative (though not random) study of forty-three virtually anonymous men and women who frequented southern California missions between 1906 and 1916, Cecil M. Robeck found that twenty-three were male and twenty female.[62] Third, it will be recalled that males dominated the movement's public life. The handful of female superstars (McPherson, Woodworth-Etter, Cotton) formed the exceptions that proved the rule. Taken together, these points suggest that males exercised a qualitative presence in Holy Ghost circles that exceeded their numerical minority status.

What about age? Here the correlation between the general and the pentecostal populations breaks down a bit, but in a counterintuitive direction. The average convert was a mature adult, not an emotionally mercurial adolescent, as commonly supposed. Specifically, in 1910 Mr. and Ms. Average American were in their mid-twenties. Mr. and Ms. Average Pentecostal on the other hand were measurably older, in their late thirties or early forties. The evidence for this claim is patchy but consistent. First, the earliest pertinent census data, reported in *Religious Bodies of the United States 1916,* shows that the number of persons over age thirteen in pentecostal churches exceeded the number of persons over age thirteen in the general population by 4 percent.[63] Second, at least two reports by outsiders specifically noted the mature age of the worshipers at Holy Ghost meetings.[64] Whether these reports were typical or atypical awaits further research, but I know of no outsider who found them conspicuously youthful. Third, the Robeck study cited above revealed a median age of forty-three, with a plurality in their thirties. Finally, 71 of 100 key biographical profiles in the *Dictionary of Pentecostal and Charismatic Movements* contain information on subjects' age when they experienced Holy Spirit baptism, which probably came shortly after affiliating with the revival. The median was thirty-eight.[65] To be sure, these individuals were leaders, not followers, so they might have been somewhat older than the rank and file. That qualification aside, the bulk of the evidence suggests that men and women in the prime of life formed the movement's demographic backbone.

What can be said about adherents' health? At the turn of the twentieth century most Americans, once safely past infant diseases, could expect to live into their early sixties—men a year or two less, women a year or two more. At first glance pentecostals seemed less fortunate, for in their testimonies they emphasized the succession of accidents and illnesses that afflicted their lives before converting. But those accounts must be taken with a grain of salt, partly because most wanted to claim a dramatic divine healing experience, and partly because the actuarial evidence frankly tells a different story. Specifically, the 100 biographical articles in the *Dictionary of Pentecostal and Charismatic Movements* noted above show that partisans' median birth and death dates were 1869 and 1943, yielding an average life span of seventy-four years. If health is defined by longevity, then most pentecostals proved remarkably healthy, for they lived a full decade longer than most Americans born in 1869. (Again, these data pertain to leaders, but there is no prima facie reason to assume that leaders lived longer than followers.)

The last demographic feature to be noted is race, by which I simply mean the ratio of blacks to whites. National averages for 1930 must provide the benchmark for comparison since the census failed to ask about race in its 1916 and 1926 religious surveys. In 1930 blacks represented 10 percent of the general population, and 30 percent of the population of the South Atlantic, East South Central, and West South Central states. When the enumerators did ask about race in the religious survey of 1936, they discovered that nationwide about 80 percent of pentecostals were white, about 20 percent black, and a tiny minority interracial. The three southern districts reflected a nearly identical distribution. Robert Anderson rightly notes that the census undoubtedly overlooked many blacks in independent churches and small associations. That said, the statistical evidence suggests that in the 1930s black pentecostals constituted twice the percentage of blacks in the general population, but only two-thirds the percentage in the broadly southern region where the revival found disproportionate support.[66]

We now turn from demographic to biographical characteristics. By biographical characteristics I mean the life features that individuals more or less chose for themselves, including marriage, residence, schooling, and occupation. Again, national and pentecostal patterns consistently approximated each other.

Marital standing is the hardest biographical characteristic to pin down, both for the general population and for pentecostals. For present purposes it suffices to say that according to the 1910 census a majority, probably a substantial majority, of U.S. adults were married. What about pentecostals? The only quantitative data I have discovered come from the Robeck study noted above, which suggest a marriage percentage among Los Angeles partisans of four-fifths.[67] The periodical literature rarely revealed family status at all, but when it did, it seemed to take the normativeness of marriage for granted. Though he himself did not wed until his forties, *Weekly Evangel* editor E. N. Bell felt certain that in "ordinary times" it was best for "young, healthy, capable young men and women to marry."[68] Indeed, another editor cheerfully specified "six good Bible reasons" for marrying, including "a happy home promised."[69] These items intimate that at both the sociological and the prescriptive levels early pentecostals apparently approximated national marriage patterns.

If marital status is the hardest of the biographical factors to pin down, residence is perhaps the easiest. The main point can be easily stated. As late as 1910 the majority of Americans lived essentially rural lives, residing either on a farm or in a town of 2,500 or fewer. Since the 1916 survey of religious bodies did not ask about residence, a research assistant and I addressed this question by combing through the return addresses on letters to the editors of five large-circulation pentecostal periodicals published in different parts of the United States between 1906 and 1910. Predictably, we discovered that a solid majority lived on farms or in small towns.[70] Yet not for long. The 1926 and 1936 surveys of religious bodies (which did ask about residence) showed that by the 1920s a slight majority of Americans had moved from rural to urban areas, and so had pentecostals.[71]

The formal education of the typical American and the typical pentecostal also paralleled each other. In 1910 Mr. and Ms. Average American possessed what might be called a functional education—approximately a middle school equivalency—just enough for most folks to earn a living. On any given day more children wandered the streets than entered the classroom. The school year lasted only 158 days, students missed nearly one-third of their classes, and one-fifth were not enrolled at all. One in twenty reached high school. A variety of literary clues tell us that pentecostal converts replicated the national pattern. To be sure, the primary sources noted virtual illiteracy among some, but those comments almost always referred to the Appalachian region, and even there illiteracy occasioned surprise. The main hint that the revival attracted adherents with at least a functional level of formal education lay in the plenitude and seriousness of the periodical literature. At least seventy (and probably many more) weeklies and monthlies popped into existence during the first decade.[72] A few, like *Bridegroom's Messenger,* featured mostly syrupy testimonials. But for every *Bridegroom's Messenger* there was a *Pentecost,* whose stock-in-trade involved densely argued treatises on the scriptural and theological warrants for the full gospel message. Though most of the early publications fell somewhere between these two publications, more resembled the seriousness of the second than the mawkishness of the first.

We come finally to occupation, the single most reliable indicator of social standing. In 1910 Mr. Average American worked outside the home, Mrs. Average American did not. The typical man toiled as a manual or as a skilled laborer. More precisely, if he was one of ten brothers, four held jobs like his, three farmed, two supported themselves in white collar positions, and one provided some kind of service. Extending the example, a single half-brother would have claimed professional or technical training. These data remind us that until the 1920s and 1930s the social system resembled a pear—thin at the top, wide at the bottom. If we divide the social hierarchy into four status-defined strata, in which the first or bottom stratum represented the truly destitute, the second the stable working class, the third the upwardly mobile middle class, and the fourth or top stratum the upper class of old wealth, we see that a majority of Americans still occupied the second stratum of the work force, the stable working class.[73]

Once again, when it came to employment the mass of pentecostals proved remarkably unremarkable. A small but conspicuous minority were chronically unemployed or locked in menial jobs at the bottom of the employment scale. Conversely a tiny minority at the top qualified as occupational elites—professionals, businessmen, and teachers. But what the evidence mostly reveals is a great body of laborers, craftsmen, artisans, clerks, shopkeepers, and service providers in the second and, to a lesser extent, third strata. For example Robeck's southern California study showed the following configuration (in alphabetical order): attorney, boarding house operator, boilermaker (unemployed), bookkeeper, business owner, carpenter (3), bottle milk worker, day laborer (unemployed), drummer, evangelist (2), foreman, government office manager, janitor, missionary (2), pastor of rescue mission (2), plasterer, seamstress, servant (3), shoemaker, stationary engineer, streetcar conductor, surgeon. In a study of the *Assemblia Cristiana* on the Near North Side of Chicago in 1910, Joseph Colletti discovered that of the eighteen family heads who attended that church, ten worked as artisans or as small business proprietors (grocers, mosaic craftsmen, stonecutters, weavers, and wholesalers).[74] Kurt Berends' analysis of converts in northern New Hampshire in the same period showed that participants were "gainfully employed in the local economy," working as lumbermen, painters, school teachers, construction hands, and real estate agents.[75] Though pentecostals rarely explicitly identified themselves with any labor movement, a 1920 issue of the Oregon *Apostolic Faith* designated itself, "The Workingman's Edition: What It Means to Be a Bible Christian at the Work Bench." The paper featured testimonies from individuals in the following lines: bricklayer, contractor, electrician, logger, miner, pressman, and railroad man.[76] An observer of the first pentecostal church in Britain, the congregation in Kilsyth, Scotland, similarly noted the presence of a coal pitman, an engine driver, a firemen, a policeman, and several miners.[77]

The following entries represent a good faith sampler of the occupations of rank-and-file partisans I encountered while researching this chapter. In most cases the sources either did not name the person or their names hold no historical import. The list excludes leaders and the occupations they held before taking up the ministry. In alphabetical order, the list includes: "a good job," attorney, barber, burglar (!), "business man," business owner, carpenter, cattleman, civil service examiner, cobbler, college professor, college student, cook and servant, cotton mill workers (children), cowboy, farmer, frescoe painter, foundry man, foundry superintendent, fruit wagon owner, grocer, hardware man, logger, lumberjack, milkman, miner, motorman, newsstand owner, physician (2), policeman, realtor, roadhouse owner, rock crusher, school teacher, school principal, soldier, steel car builder, teamster, washwoman. What we see here is a predictable mix of laborers, artisans, service workers, small entrepreneurs and, occasionally, professionals. Taken together, they look very much like a cross section of the labor force of the general population.[78]

Closely related to occupation was financial worth. According to the census, in 1910 the average American worker, all trades, usually male, earned $574 per year (which equaled $10,045 in 1999 purchasing power).[79] To flesh that figure out a bit, if the worker happened to be a school teacher, he brought home less than $500 per year. If he supported himself by farming in the southern states, where about half of pentecostals lived, he made less than $200 per year with board.[80]

These data provide a framework for measuring pentecostals' own financial standing. The upshot is that most, though hardly comfortable by modern standards, lived comfortably by the standards of their own age, and that is the crucial point.[81] Members routinely spoke of raising extraordinary sums of money for missions and other activities. Some of that harvest surely represented a deep sacrifice. Yet missionary Cora Fritsch spoke of traveling from China to Japan via first-class cabin,[82] Elmer M. Walker paid $1,200 for gas, repairs, and food to take his family in a new Model T roadster to the Church of God General Assembly,[83] evangelist Marrion DeViney handily raised $1,700 for missions in a Wednesday night prayer meeting,[84] Vandalia Fry sold her diamond ring for $1,500 to help ship a revival tent to Tulsa,[85] the interracial Pentecostal Assemblies of the World in Indianapolis "lifted" $1,560 in cash and pledges in a single offering for missionaries,[86] a New Jersey congregation garnered $7,500 in a single meeting for Africa missions, and a tiny Bible training school in Rochester, New York, set aside $75,000 in twenty years for world missions.[87] Considering all these data, we begin to catch a whiff of respectability, especially when we remember that the sums were listed in (roughly) 1910 dollars.[88]

Spreading the word to the Lost cost money too, but never, it seemed, too much. Frank Bartleman, who perennially claimed penury, casually remarked at one point that he had personally paid for the printing and distribution of a quarter million tracts he had written.[89] William H. Durham, describing the constituency of his North Avenue Mission in Chicago, underscored their poverty yet boasted that the mission had given hundreds of dollars to the poor—who always seemed to be someone else. At one juncture the little North Avenue group, despite its humble station, managed to pay for the printing and distribution of 30,000 copies of controversial booklets called *Heavenly Messages,*[90] 300,000 copies of Durham's periodical, *Pentecostal Testimony,* as well as a quarter million tracts.[91] He proudly stated that the paper had never been delayed "one moment" for lack of funds, that every helper received a "fair wage every week," and that they owed no one anything.[92]

Indications of the adequate economic standing of most pentecostals emerge in unexpected ways. Except for Appalachian whites and blacks in general, we find few allusions to hunger, and virtually none to homelessness or unemployment.[93] The frequency and apparent ease with which grass-roots believers (not to mention leaders) traveled from state to state and region to region said something about both the material resources and the mental horizons of a decidedly mobile class. The early newspapers overflowed with accounts of pilgrims striking out for Los Angeles' Azusa Mission, or Toronto's Hebden Mission, or any of a score of holy sites on all parts of the continent, and sometimes overseas, without a hint that the journey might pose a serious financial burden. Occasionally zealots spoke of walking because they could not afford other means, but they usually revealed that they used trains or autos to get around exactly as they wished.

With surprising frequency saints admitted to a real measure of financial security. "[M]ost of us have plenty," said editor George Floyd Taylor in the midst of World War I. "We may not have all we want, but we have all we need."[94] Even in the depth of the Great Depression, New York's *Glad Tidings Herald* could say that none of their missionaries had "suffered for anything."[95] Charles Parham, among others, had no use for saints who pretended poverty. He called them "whining evangelists and Christian workers who spend most of their time like paupers—by the wayside, begging piteously, crying out their divers . . . infirmities."[96] Or consider a different kind of example, as spare as it is revealing. In the 1950s patriarch M. M. Pinson decided to type out an autobiographical reflection on his long career preaching on the itinerant circuit. He saw fit first of all to thank the Lord for a full measure of "grit, grace and glory," and then—significantly—to thank the Lord for "some greenbacks that did help me on the way."[97] Pinson's remark appeared almost as an afterthought. And that is precisely why it is credible. Life had dealt him a pretty fair hand after all.

What was true of Pinson was true of Holy Spirit–filled believers in general. If from time to time they had to struggle to make ends meet, they proved no different from most Americans, then or now. This point is critical. Knowing how much money the average recruit had stashed away under the proverbial mattress might be an interesting bit of information in itself, but it becomes historically useful only comparatively, only in the context of time and place. And on that count ordinary pentecostals, like their leaders, scored surprisingly well. They were farmers, artisans, shopkeepers, and service providers with the middle school education and honorable social standing characteristic of those groups. In other times and places they would have been called yeomen, or perhaps plain folk, or perhaps just "salt of the earth types." They possessed little discretionary income but, as the sociologist David Martin said in a somewhat different context, they ate well.[98]

In one additional respect early pentecostals looked like most Americans. In a word, they lived just about everywhere, turning up in significant numbers in all parts of the country (except the Mormon wards of the intermountain

West and the Catholic parishes of Louisiana). Granted, the 1936 *Census of Religious Bodies*—the first to tabulate residential information for pentecostals—showed that Dixie provided the most fertile soil for Holy Ghost conversions if measured as a percentage of regional population.[99] But the 1936 census also showed that a majority of pentecostals lived outside the South if measured absolutely. The majority lived outside the South culturally too. Consider for example saints' headquarters locations. Of the four oldest and largest sects, only one centered itself in the Deep South (Franklin Springs, Georgia), while the other three set up shop along Dixie's northern rim (Cleveland, Tennessee; Memphis, Tennessee; Springfield, Missouri). The main second-rank bodies were located far outside the South in Indianapolis and in Portland, Oregon, while the largest group in Canada made its home in Toronto. After World War I, Aimee McPherson established her sect in downtown Los Angeles. In the interwar years two large breakaway groups ended up in Des Moines and in Brooklyn. Just after World War II, the largest of the Oneness groups established itself in a suburb of St. Louis. When in 1914 J. Roswell Flower, assistant editor of the nationally distributed *Christian Evangel,* casually described the Civil War as the "Great Rebellion," he obviously knew that he was not addressing a preponderantly southern readership.[100]

So where *did* pentecostal readers reside? A complete answer awaits further research, but a preliminary examination of hundreds of notices of meetings, letters to editors, and directories of mission sites printed in five regionally prominent periodicals in the winter and spring of 1907–08 offers hints. Neither rural isolation nor urban congestion seemed to matter much. Nor did climate, economic base, or the presence or absence of minorities.[101] In sum, no aspect of the revival was more striking than its geographical ubiquity. In the early twentieth century it would have been hard to find any definable religious tradition, except Methodists, that presented its face more broadly and in more diverse geographic and social settings.[102]

Normal Americans they were in almost every respect. Moreover, if the reports of visitors to the United States can be trusted, Americans placed an exceptional emphasis on the value of personal autonomy. And so did pentecostals. With the Holy Ghost inside, it was hard to sit still, and even harder to take "No" for an answer.

Personal Autonomy

Objective placement in the social system was one thing, what individuals made of that placement was quite another. To jump ahead in the story, the materials consistently reveal a two-fisted sense of personal autonomy in the face of bounded yet very real economic and social opportunities. Variants of this trait repeatedly emerge in different chapters of this book, sometimes dressed as temperamental independence, sometimes as theological pelagianism, sometimes as cultural aggressiveness. In economic and social matters, saints presented themselves as hard workers, eyes fixed on the far horizon, determined to take care of themselves and their families come what may.

Occupational mobility surfaced as the most conspicuous manifestation of personal autonomy. By occupational mobility I simply mean that pentecostals moved around a lot, usually up, occasionally down, sometimes just over. The bumpy though assertively upward career of A. G. Osterberg exemplifies the pattern. Born of immigrant Swedish parents in Chicago in 1885, Osterberg moved with his parents to Los Angeles just after the turn of the century. Devout Baptists, the Osterbergs used their own home for prayer and Bible study meetings. Soon deciding, however, that their home was not large enough, Osterberg and his father and brother, all finish carpenters by trade, constructed a mission with their own hands and money at the corner of Sixty-eighth and Denver in Los Angeles. Significantly, they called it Full Gospel Assembly. Members of the Assembly asked Osterberg, then all of twenty-four, to serve as pastor. In the meantime he landed a foreman's job at J. V. McNeil Construction Company in Los Angeles, and also served as the superintendent of construction for the Los Angeles school system. Until the 1920s, when he finally gave up lay employment for full-time ministry in Kingsburg, California, Osterberg took great pride in the fact that he, like the Apostle Paul, worked with his hands and his wits during the week and served the Lord as a pastor on the weekend.[103]

The early literature brims with stories of this sort. Though the plot lines in the autobiographies and biographies often look shamelessly self-serving, the main narrative displays remarkable consistency. And what the main narrative depicts, again and again, is a story of men and women of modest birth who proved resourceful, hard working, fired by ideals and, above all, determined to get the job done. This nimbleness drew many into lines that offered substantial control over the organization of their lives. Enthusiasts' repeated statements that they attended worship services until the wee hours of the morning, or all night, or for extended periods during the week suggest a preference for piecework, or fee-for-service tasks.[104] Some may have been out of work, but references to unemployment were so rare one suspects that most simply worked for themselves, by the hour or by the job as they saw fit.[105]

This strong sense of personal autonomy almost suggests the mythology of the frontier West. For example the Oklahoma and California sharecroppers featured in Dan Morgan's study, *Rising in the West,* never doubted that they held their earthly destinies in their own hands. Thinking back to the early

1930s, his informants reported that they worked in the fields, but never considered themselves field hands. Unlike a true proletariat, stuck at the bottom with no hope of escape, Morgan's pentecostals remained convinced they had the stuff to move up and out—and many did too, sometimes becoming quite wealthy.[106] Such individualism produced a hard-nosed rigorism when it came to economic dealings with themselves, with each other, and with outsiders. When Aimee McPherson quipped that she preferred to leave the people below to the Salvation Army, one suspects that she was not entirely joking.[107] Sometimes zealots sounded like hawkers for a Dale Carnegie course. "It is always better to encourage people to do what they can for themselves," one leader averred. "People are pauperized by teaching them . . . to ask the Lord to do for us many things which we ought to do ourselves."[108] Saints did not want to snub the less fortunate, but they saw no need to harm them with gratuitous benevolence either.

Where self-sufficient individualism left off and a go-for-broke aggressiveness began is anyone's guess. Arrell M. Gibson's study of the Tri-State District, the prosperous lead mining region where Kansas, Oklahoma, and Missouri intersect, and where Holy Ghost revivals flourished, illumines this trait. Gibson stressed the risk-taking, swashbuckling character of the miners who populated the area. Saloons, gambling dens, and bawdy houses dotted the streets. Folks conducted fully one-fourth of the week's business between 8:00 P.M. and midnight on Saturday nights. That much was predictable for a wide-open mining town. Less predictable but more important for present purposes were the housing patterns. Over the years the mines proved lucrative, but Gibson found that the miners typically lived in substandard housing. Why? The explanation lay in the character of the men and women involved. They were, he argued, born gamblers. Rather than invest their daily earnings in their homes, they preferred to sink their gains in new stakes, hoping always for the big strike.[109] How many of those miners were pentecostals cannot be known, but a significant crossover seems likely. Charles Parham said that the revival grew rapidly among miners in that region,[110] local newspapers reported a Holy Spirit revival in that area in 1903,[111] and two small but sturdy pentecostal sects (Apostolic Faith and Pentecostal Church of God) eventually headquartered themselves there.

The materials also disclose exceptional geographical mobility, a trait surely related to underlying assumptions about personal autonomy. Saints simply moved around a lot, from town to town and state to state. If standard biographies of the leaders can be trusted, one wonders when they ever slept. A. A. Boddy's fourteen journeys across the Atlantic (along with side trips to Africa, Siberia, and the European Continent), or Aimee McPherson's continual crisscrossing of the United States, or F. M. Britton's legendary walking from town to town over the red clay hills of Georgia found countless parallels in the wanderings of lesser known figures.[112] Young Cora Fritsch's movements represented the pattern well. Barely in her twenties, Fritsch traveled from Portland, Oregon, to the Azusa Mission to receive the baptism experience. In Los Angeles she and a friend received divine instructions to pack their things immediately and "sail to China." Fritsch stayed in China hardly long enough to catch her breath when the Lord sent her on to Korea. Then back to China. On and on in this way the story runs, ending only when an untimely death in 1912 finally stilled her peregrinations.[113]

Pentecostals' geographic restlessness seemed so pronounced that the movement eventually became synonymous with itinerancy. Of course some traveled constantly because they were overseers or traveling preachers by trade. But the autobiographies make clear that the opposite dynamic often dominated: many became overseers or itinerants in the first place because they could not abide the confinement of a settled pastorate for more than a few weeks at a stretch. Some evidently became foreign missionaries for the same reason. Alfred and Lillian Garr wrote that they gladly suffered the loss of their "old Holiness friends" in order to be the first missionaries to herald the pentecostal message in Asia. One can almost feel their expansionist exuberance: "It was like beginning life over, a new ministry . . . not limited to a small fraction of the Holiness people, nor to one country . . . but the 'World our parish.'"[114] Sometimes globe-trotting got out of hand, even by pentecostal standards. Complaints about the needlessly mobile ways of overseas missionaries regularly spiked the editorial columns of the early newspapers. The line dividing the pilgrim soul from the vagrant foot was always a blurry one, especially in the eyes of mainline Protestants proud of their roots.

What proved true of leaders seemingly proved true of ordinary folk too. Though saints reflected national norms in most respects, in this one they differed significantly. According to the 1910 census, nearly nine-tenths of Americans lived either in the state in which they were born or, occasionally, in a contiguous one. The 1916 *Census of Religious Bodies*—the first to take note of pentecostals' existence—did not ask about residence, so there is no systematic way to track their moving patterns. But many bits of evidence intimate geographic restlessness. Robeck discovered, for example, that his forty-three Los Angeles mission habitués had migrated from places as diverse as England, Sweden, Germany, Pennsylvania, Georgia, Manitoba, Texas, and Ohio. None of the forty-three listed Los Angeles as their place of origin or place of permanent destination. More significantly, none turned up in *both* the 1900 and 1910 census for the western region.

Transience proved so widespread that it became a nuisance for those hoping to see things settle down. An advertisement for an Apostolic Faith camp meeting in Baxter Springs, Kansas, offered tents and free food to all accredited workers, but warned: "(Apostolic Bums Need Not Apply)."[115] In Los

Angeles Brother H. Morse scored "Religious Hoboism." "The common thing here in California," he groused, "is to see people . . . come from somewhere and stay a few days in an assembly and before you can get properly acquainted with them, they are talking of taking a trip." Morse may have revealed more than he intended when he added: "If it is not work, it is the hot climate or cold climate, dry climate or wet climate."[116] In England, the Anglican vicar A. A. Boddy urged pentecostal leaders to send the exact addresses of their preaching stations to his newspaper so that others could locate them—"especially," said Boddy, "as people travel so freely now."[117] To outsiders, and even to some insiders, converts' peripatetic ways looked like rootlessness. But most believers knew better. Always looking for the promised land, they were born to keep moving.

Finally, we need to ask whether pentecostals' abiding sense of personal autonomy actually fostered financial prosperity. The answer is: maybe. The testimonies repeatedly spoke of brighter prospects ahead, and almost all of the standard denominational histories note growing affluence in the second and third generations. Nonetheless, the same attributes promoted recklessness, as the shattered empires of the deliverance evangelists in the 1950s and the television preachers in the 1980s attest. Moreover the constant pressure to contribute every penny to the "work" after providing for life's necessities likely took a toll on believers' ability to provide for the long range. Above all, personal autonomy did not necessarily translate into financial, let alone business, acumen. For every entrepreneur who parlayed a nickel into a fortune there undoubtedly was another who parlayed a fortune into a nickel. Pragmatism did not always equal astuteness.

What conclusions, then, does the sociological evidence support? Three seem warranted. First, a small but significant minority of saints perennially struggled against poverty and alienation. Second, a majority—likely a large majority—resembled most Americans, both demographically and biographically. Their leaders seem to have represented the most upwardly mobile segment of the middling class, while their followers seem to have represented the most upwardly mobile segment of the stable working class. Finally, pentecostals—all pentecostals, leaders and followers alike—distinguished themselves on the religious landscape by their jut-jawed stress on personal autonomy. That this attitude promoted occupational and geographical mobility seems clear, economic prosperity less so.

All told, the image that emerges from the social data is one of ready experimentation, a willingness to abandon old options that did not work in favor of fresh ones that did. If such traits once suggested Dodge City, in time they would suggest Silicon Valley.

13

Nation

Since time immemorial, it seems, Christians have struggled with the claims of the civil realm. For every Roger Williams who insisted that the Christian's allegiances resided in the Kingdom of God, there was a John Cotton who insisted with equal conviction that the Christian's life necessarily unfolded in the empire of a Caesar. Whether average pentecostals would have recognized either of those Puritan worthies may be doubted, but they knew the score. As primitivists, saints instinctively identified with Williams's outlook, but as pragmatists, they knew that Cotton's could not be ignored. If political purity called from afar, political realism called from up close. That lesson came dear, however. Converts discovered, as R. Laurence Moore writes about American Catholics, that "[m]eaningful activity in history usually involves exchanging one dilemma for another."[1]

In this chapter I distinguish among state, land, and nation. State represents political and governmental structures, land represents the cultural and emotional symbols associated with place, and nation embraces both. Pentecostals themselves were not especially self-conscious about how they applied those labels, but if we look closely, the concepts they denoted remained clearly distinct.

State

Estrangement ran deep. Like Mormons, Jehovah's Witnesses, and many pacifist sects, early pentecostals determined to separate themselves from the state. But what exactly did that mean? Avoiding voluntary political activity like voting and running for office? Or something more radical, such as civil disobedience? Holy Ghost folk were never very analytical about these matters. But they meant at least this: Christians' fundamental allegiance should never be lodged with the state since the state was an earthly fabrication. Like the Tower of Babel, the state signaled human presumption at best, the enthronement of godlessness, immorality, greed, and violence at worst.

Charles Parham, the first pentecostal leader with anything like a broadly regional following, proved one of the most radical as well. In the summer of
1901, six months after speaking in tongues erupted in his Topeka, Kansas,
Bible school, Parham sponsored "special services" on July 4th. But he went
out of his way to tell a local reporter that the meetings held no patriotic significance whatsoever.[2] As the years passed, Parham consistently resisted any
hint of dual allegiance to the Kingdom of God and that of a Caesar. Long before the outbreak of the war in Europe, he assailed all Christian states, including the United States, for yielding themselves to the "Moloch God, Patriotism, whose doctrine was honor (?)." Their soldiers, he sneered, were "self-
appointed murderers," their governments "imbecile."[3] In Parham's mind,
the Moloch God Patriotism stemmed from other, more fundamental flaws in
American society. In a 1912 sermon symptomatically titled, "The American
Circus," he lampooned the United States as a country of "fine churches and
180,000 licensed saloons," a place where a man could buy a good Bible for
fifteen cents and a bad drink of whiskey for five, a setting where one man was
jailed for stealing a loaf of bread and another placed in Congress for stealing a
railroad.[4] Several years later, when the so-called preparedness debate started
to engulf the American public life, Parham made clear that he would support
no war nor any efforts to prepare for one. He also made clear that his position
grew both from biblical principles of nonviolence and from a conviction that
the United States was not worth fighting for in the first place. Soon, he insisted, "this country will end with a dictator and a final fall . . . in which the
government, the rich and the churches will be on one side and the masses on
the other."[5]

Parham sounded more vitriolic (or at least more colorful) than most, but
other leaders echoed his sentiments. Their critique of the United States took
different forms. Sometimes pentecostals urged Christians to wean themselves
from all earthly powers, including their own. "[T]he things that pertain to
earth should forever lose their hold," said denominational executive Stanley
H. Frodsham on the eve of World War I, "even that natural love for the nation where one happened to be born."[6] More often they argued that the
United States did not deserve Christians' allegiance, as it had shown itself as
vile as any other state. Several days before the country entered the war, for example, the Assemblies of God's *Weekly Evangel* sought to dispel the illusion
that the European conflict pitted Christian nations against each other. Truth
was, no state, including the United States, had ever been Christian. All acted
at the "instigation of Satan."[7] Even in the very midst of the war, H. Musgrave
Reade, in the fiercely independent *Trust*, mustered the courage to charge
that the great spiritual evil of the age was an "immoderate patriotism" that
had come to displace true religion. Indeed, in Reade's mind, "national sec-

tarianism" fanned by an "unscrupulous press" ranked as one of the great delusions of the age.[8] Given this climate of opinion, it is hardly surprising that Quaker pentecostal Levi Lupton would assail Fourth of July celebrations as a waste of God's money.[9]

Democracy too received a blistering critique. To attack the United States of America—the Government centered in Washington, D.C.—was one thing, but to attack democracy—the timeless ideal that underpinned the American experiment—was something else. Yet many apostolics did exactly that. In their minds democracy represented just another political scheme cooked up by humans to serve their prideful interests, no worse perhaps but certainly no better than any other political scheme. One habitué of Los Angeles' Upper Room Mission asserted that democracy equaled the political system predicted and condemned in Daniel. Though Americans idealized democracy, in practice democracy meant rule of the people with God left out, "demagogism and anarchy," governance by children.[10] When Susan Duncan, a founder of the Rochester Bible Institute, read Revelation, she too saw "world powers controlled by popular passion, and what thousands of men call liberty." Unfortunately those masses were sorely deluded. "[D]emocracy will not save the world," Duncan warned. "Republicanism will not bring the Millen[n]ium."[11]

If America today held little hope of redemption, America tomorrow held even less. Holy Ghost writers rarely singled out the United States for special chastisement in God's end-of-time plan of Great Tribulation, but neither did they exempt it. The Rev. H. Pierson King, preaching the "Signs of the Coming of Our Lord" in 1915, spoke for thousands. Christ's imminent return, he declaimed, will serve as an "eternal indictment upon all forms of human rule." The armies and the navies of the earth, along with the international peace movement and its "attendant national follies," will all end up in "God's scrap heap." In sum: "Border lines will be vanished, empires will collapse, thrones will cease and all methods of human government will be eliminated in the new rule of Theocracy."[12] Though pentecostals did not see *themselves* standing in the path of divine judgment (since they expected to be physically raptured from the earth), they saw their own country deservedly falling into the maw of God's awful retribution.

Politics

United States historians agree on few matters, but one point seems to enjoy universal assent: at the turn of the twentieth century millions of earnest citizens found political affairs the most exciting game in town. The presidential elections of this period, running from McKinley's affray with Bryan in 1896 to Wilson's battle with Taft in 1912, still rank among the most fiercely fought contests in American history.

But not for pentecostals. For them, evidence of interest in secular political affairs is scarce at best. Consider for example the simple matter of holding public office. Did any abandon the sawdust trail for the stump circuit? I have discovered none who ran for election, and only two who held jobs that might have involved appointment by an elected official. The first was William B. Holt, an elder in the Church of God in Christ, who apparently worked as a deputy sheriff in California in the late 1910s.[13] The second was evangelist S. Clyde Bailey, who briefly served as police chief of Marion, Illinois, in the late 1920s. Later he thanked God that he had never been elected mayor. His reason is telling: "The devil tried to get me deeper into politics."[14] In time researchers will undoubtedly locate individuals here and there who held elected office, but how many would it take to alter the picture significantly?

If early pentecostals rarely ran for office themselves, did they support those who did? Differently stated, did they get out and work for any organized political party or cause? With two or three minor exceptions, I find almost no evidence that leaders publicly endorsed Democrat, Republican, or Bull Moose candidates. But what about populists in the late nineteenth century, the political movement that supposedly represented the class interests of the men and women who would become pentecostal after the turn of the century? Students of American political history have long noted that popular reform movements of the Gilded Age like Grangers, Socialists, Free Silver Democrats, and the Southern Farmers' Alliance (commonly known as populists) routinely adopted the vocabulary and rituals of revivalist Protestantism.[15] And students of pentecostal history have known for decades that Holy Ghost converts appeared in conspicuous numbers in counties where populist sentiment ran strong.[16] Not surprisingly, some scholars have therefore contended that the pentecostal revival represented a direct expression of populist attitudes,[17] or at least an indirect or parallel expression.[18]

I remain doubtful. At this point the data offer few reasons to believe that pentecostals actively backed political movements of any kind, populist or otherwise. Several leaders—E. M. Walker in North Dakota and A. B. Crumpler and George Floyd Taylor in North Carolina—apparently held populist sympathies at one time, but I find no evidence that their political interests survived their entry into Holy Ghost ranks.[19] We know that in 1911 two Oklahoma Pentecostal Holiness preachers embraced socialist principles, but their fate proved more revealing than their principles. The sect's Annual State Convention, consisting of some fifty brothers and sisters in the Lord, admonished the two men that they must "entirely abandon their doctrine of Socialism as our doctrines are Christ and Him only."[20] Who else? Again, the record remains nearly silent, both for the populism at the turn of the century and for the Progressive Era of the 1910s and 1920s.

If pentecostals did not run for office, or actively support political causes, or make a point to vote in partisan elections, did they at least show interest in the pressing political questions of the day? On the whole the answer is no. In the early periodicals one can easily read through twenty or thirty pages at a stretch without coming up with a single nugget of real-life political commentary. Antitrust regulation, child labor, civil service reform, free silver, immigration quotas, Indian education, lower tariffs, minority justice, progressive taxation, utilities oversight, women's suffrage—all issues that aroused the conscience of other Christian bodies—eluded saints' attention. There were exceptions, to be sure. Levi Lupton deplored sweat factories, capital punishment, and Western imperialism.[21] California evangelist Frank Bartleman protested the decimation of Indians.[22] Oakland preacher J. Narver Gortner addressed California gubernatorial matters in the pulpit.[23] New York City's *Glad Tidings Herald* endorsed Hoover for president because he supported Prohibition.[24] Questions about the morality of the Ku Klux Klan arose from time to time, some defending, some denouncing the Klan.[25] That said, such instances of public policy awareness represent trace elements in the literature. They happened so rarely the modern reader is invariably taken aback when they appear.

Norman Dann's careful sociological study of the chronological, geographic, and thematic coalescence of populist and Wesleyan holiness constituencies in the late-nineteenth and early-twentieth-centuries illumines this problem. Granted, Wesleyan holiness was not the same as pentecostal, but the former helped to spawn the latter, and lacking a comparable study of populists and pentecostals, Dann's work casts valuable light on this understudied question. Using state electoral records as an index of political trends on one side, and holiness periodicals and schools as an index of religious trends on the other, Dann found that the two movements coincided in time but not in space. Specifically, they both rose and fell between 1880 and 1910, but one group won support in one cluster of states while the other group found support in a different cluster. More important, he also discovered that the economic and social concerns that agitated populist spokesmen failed to spark the interest of the editors of holiness periodicals. Indeed, some of those editors emphasized their determination to avoid partisan political questions altogether. Dann concludes that populist agitation might have stimulated the diffusion of holiness religion later on by highlighting the insensitivities of the elite, but there is little evidence of direct crossover.[26]

Did Holy Ghost folk even bother to vote? Here the data reveal a similar pattern of determined otherworldliness. Charles Parham, for example, advised his students not to vote at all.[27] "[W]e have not time to dabble in politics," declared a California periodical (significantly titled *Progress*) excerpted in the pages of Parham's *Apostolic Faith*. "Fighting by sword or ballot arouses all the carnal there is in people."[28] Though there is no way to know for sure, the data intimate that actual practice followed rhetoric. Pentecostal Holiness leader George Floyd Taylor, for example, confided to his diary that he did not vote at all until age twenty seven, only to cast his ballot in 1908 for the Prohibition Party.[29] Edith Blumhofer, Aimee McPherson's scholarly biographer, tells us that McPherson freely advised her followers how to vote on local issues. Yet the more revealing point is that Blumhofer does not specify the content of that advice. One suspects that it was not conspicuous enough in McPherson's life story to merit comment.[30]

We learn a good deal about pentecostals' attitudes toward voting from the Church of God overseer A. J. Tomlinson. Writing in 1913, Tomlinson remembered that back in the late 1880s he had embraced secular politics so fervently that he vowed to emigrate to Australia if his party—the Republicans—lost.[31] In 1892 he even ran for auditor of Hamilton County, Indiana, on the People's Party (populist) ticket.[32] But Tomlinson lost that election, and in his mind it was a good thing too, for he soon experienced salvation and sanctification and renounced politics for keeps. Now finding himself "dead to the world," he determined never to vote for anyone except Jesus.[33] Tomlinson spoke for his people. In 1908 the Church of God's General Assembly authorized its members to cast ballots—but only if they could do so with a "clear conscience."[34] The record implies that very few did. Church of God historian Mickey Crews tells us that according to oral tradition first-generation converts in the southern highlands generally voted Republican. The key point here is not that Appalachian pentecostals voted Republican but rather that Crews gained that information through oral tradition. Evidently mountain saints did not prove sufficiently interested in political activity for their voting preferences to win a place in either the sect's or the region's written historical record.[35]

To be sure, appearances could be deceiving. If outsiders were to glance at the headlines of some of the leading pentecostal periodicals, especially in the 1910s, they might conclude that converts found the war in Europe, Jews in Palestine, and natural disasters everywhere intensely interesting.[36] But close inspection would show that those stories really had nothing to do with actual events. Rather world affairs for pentecostals functioned as biblical antetypes, scenes in a vast cosmic drama planned from the beginning of the time. Prudent Christians studied such events in order to know where they themselves stood in the grand scheme of things, not to come up with constructive policies for the here and now.

On the rare occasions when saints did venture near a public policy problem in its own right, they almost always framed it as a question of private morality. For example the annual General Assemblies of the Church of God repeatedly discussed labor unions. Was it all right to join one? Answer: Not really. Was it permissible to join if one had to in order to work? Answer: One could pay dues but not attend meetings. Was it moral to join if you were a minister? Answer: No.[37] No one, it seems, ever thought to ask if working folk had a class interest of their own. The morality of consenting to the draft constituted the main exception to this pattern of political disengagement, and I examine that debate in the next chapter. Here it suffices to say that pentecostals did not address this issue until it was literally forced on them. Even then, the discussion centered on the righteousness or sinfulness of pentecostal men fighting for their country, not the effectiveness or ineffectiveness of the war itself as an instrument of national policy.

The reasons for pentecostals' disengagement from the political realm are easy to see. One stemmed from a realistic sense of what was feasible. Though they rarely hailed from the lowest strata of society, they were, like most Americans, limited by finite economic and cultural resources. So Holy Ghost folk focused on what they could change: themselves, their families, and their church communities.[38] But such measured realism—pragmatism, if you will—was not the main factor. The main factor was principle, and principle decreed that governance of the state simply fell outside the Christian's proper sphere of concern. In the early decades of the twentieth century committed Christians filled the upper echelons of both political parties, including Secretary of State William Jennings Bryan and Presidents Theodore Roosevelt and Woodrow Wilson. But that hardly mattered. Men and women who felt they had little stake in America or its future simply had no time to worry about the affairs of Caesar.[39]

Reform

The idea that the church ought to support political measures to alleviate physical suffering also found little resonance in pentecostal circles. Though a few supported Prohibition (then regarded as a progressive plan), most did not bother. One Kansas pastor seemed to speak for the majority when he dismissed Prohibition as one of the "clap-trap methods and silly reforms" of the age, pushed, predictably, by "'long-haired preachers and short-haired women.'"[40]

This is not to say that saints remained oblivious to suffering. Compassion ministries flowered. Though hard figures are scarce, the standard denominational histories make clear that saints invested impressive sums of time, effort, and money in orphanages, soup lines, prison ministries, homes for unwed mothers, and famine relief (especially in China). Very much like Salvation Army workers, pentecostals everywhere made serious and concrete efforts to address the deprivation they saw around them. In the early years of the Depression the mostly black United Holy Church in Los Angeles made major efforts to feed the unemployed.[41] So did Aimee McPherson's Angelus Temple.[42] Both worked within a strong regional tradition of compassion ministry. Just after the turn of the century Finis Yoakum, a one-time physician turned Holy Ghost preacher, established Pisgah, a multifaceted rescue mission several miles up the road from Angelus Temple. Pisgah offered more than salvation, too. The little colony's newspaper stated its aims plainly on the front page: "PISGAH Devoted to the Material Welfare, Bodily Healing, Moral Uplift and Spiritual Life of the Stricken in Body, Victim of Drink, Outcast, Cripple, Hungry, Friendless and WHOSOEVER IS IN NEED OF THE WATERS OF LIFE." By its own count Pisgah helped "[o]ver a hundred thousand . . . drunkards and harlots" each year for the better part of two decades.[43]

But we should not be fooled. Early pentecostals' compassion ministries remained local in scope and episodic in duration. Once again, Charles Parham well represented the majority when he boasted that his Divine Healing Mission in Topeka fed a warm meal to 300 poor people on New Year's Day. That was it. A warm meal on a cold day.[44] Though the value of a good lunch for a hungry stomach should not be gainsaid, one looks in vain for any sense that the church bore a special obligation to the poor, let alone that the church ought to support governmental programs that systematically addressed the dislocations that often created poverty in the first place. A Chicago writer spoke for most when he denounced Social Gospelers Walter Rauschenbusch, Washington Gladden, and Lyman Abbott for "meddl[ing] in temporal affairs as if Christ's kingdom were of this world."[45] The same resolute otherworldliness marked pentecostals in England, where evangelist H. Mogridge warned that anyone who sought to import "the social and secular in church fellowship" would not be recognized. "If we are right with God," he explained, "we are right with everybody else, and the secular and the social will look after themselves as a natural consequence."[46]

The commitments revealed and, just as important, not revealed in the correspondence of veteran China missionary W. W. Simpson were symptomatic. It will be recalled that he ranked as one of the brightest stars in the firmament of pentecostal missionary heroes, having labored for the better part of a century in Tibet and northwest China. Without question Simpson was acutely aware of the magnitude of the human suffering he witnessed in those remote regions. During the drought of 1928, he wrote, "I saw crowds of starving people . . . [who] had stripped the bark off the trees as high as they could reach . . . hoping to prolong life a few days longer." In the town of Lanchow he learned of human flesh being sold in restaurants. He observed a small child so crazed with hunger she was gnawing her own fingers.[47] On other occasions he wrote of epidemics "sweeping over the province hurling millions into graves,"[48] ceaseless political turmoil, atrocities committed by occupying Moslem soldiers,[49] native Chinese Christians dying of cold and starvation.[50] It is important to give credit where credit is due. Simpson's orphanages and farming techniques reportedly saved thousands of lives.[51] And he may well have been more sensitive to the nuances of national culture than most Western missionaries, for he advocated indigenous control of missions and sought to avoid imposing Western values.

Yet through it all Simpson remained more interested in the empyrean world beyond than the misery unfolding before his eyes. Year after year he justified virtually every good deed that he or others performed almost solely in terms of its usefulness for spreading the gospel. He made clear that orphanages were established only secondarily to feed and care for destitute children. They were mainly intended to encourage children to accept Christ and experience Holy Spirit baptism.[52] Moslem occupation, cruel as it was, could be sanctioned because it brought a lawful and orderly situation in which the gospel could be preached. Contributions from the United States were desperately needed, not primarily to feed and clothe victims of famine and epidemic, but to "build chapels, support students and send them forth to preach Christ ere too late."[53] Simpson possessed a genuine capacity to suffer with the suffering, yet simultaneously to view their misery as ultimately inconsequential.

What does all this say about the social outlook of Simpson and other pentecostals? Simpson's willingness to favor the welfare of the soul over the needs of the body hardly distinguishes him in Christian missionary history. What sets him apart—not uniquely but at least recognizably—is the ardor, the single-mindedness that structured his salvationist objectives in the face of so much human misery. If Simpson's voluminous correspondence can be taken as a fair index of his thinking, scarcely in fifty-seven years of missionary service did he pause to suppose that famine, epidemic, or civil war might be more important than setting straight nonpentecostal evangelicals on the fine points of doctrine back home,[54] or correctly interpreting the dragon, the Man-Child, and the woman clothed with the sun in Revelation,[55] or recapturing New Testament signs and wonders in twentieth-century China.[56]

In sum, there is virtually no documentary evidence that first-generation converts believed the church bore any obligation to support social gospel efforts to alleviate suffering or injustice. Though compassion ministries existed here and there, they grew from simple human decency, not any sense of identification with the poor as a class nor any feeling that the church ought to press government agencies to help them. The primitivist vision dictated saints' priorities when it came to the social gospel, just as it dictated their priorities when it came to party politics and their identity as citizens of the United States.

Yet early apostolics were too much travelers of the here and now to be able to live all dimensions of their lives according to otherworldly principles. In three respects—race relations, police power, and loyalty to the American land (not the American state)—we see them quietly ignoring their primitivist convictions in order to make a functional life for themselves in modern America. If there was a time to stand firm, there was also, it seemed, a time to bend.

Race

White–black relations among early pentecostals are hard to untangle on any count, but they begin to make at least a little sense if we see them as a process of inexorable accommodation to segregationist or Jim Crow mores in the United States in the early twentieth century. The times were unforgiving. One scholar recently has judged that in the South during the 1890s there was on average three lynchings of African Americans per week.[57] I have discovered no evidence that white saints participated in physical violence against blacks, but there is considerable evidence that they participated in the racist assumptions that made such violence possible. By the same token black pentecostals adjusted themselves, however reluctantly, to these segregationist arrangements. For whites, accommodation was the price of status, for blacks, the price of survival.

Two qualifications are needed. First, it should be recalled that I use the terms *race* and *ethnicity* in a historical sense to refer to the differing social experiences of white and black pentecostals and of culturally Anglo and non-Anglo pentecostals. Second, since the following paragraphs may seem to distribute the blame for accommodation to segregationism evenly between whites and blacks, I wish to stress that this is not my intent. In America racism was first and last the besetting sin of white people, Christians included. Blacks did not escape the moral limitations of the human condition, but as a disempowered minority they remained the victims, not the perpetrators, of race contempt. That said, we proceed with a painful story, albeit one marked by many moments of redemptive transformation.

Here, perhaps more than anywhere else in this book, a brief look at the recent secondary literature is needed. First of all, those materials make clear that the story was never a narrative only of white–black relations. Gaston Espinosa reminds us that other ethnic groups, especially Latinos, complicated the picture in significant ways.[58] Second, since the 1970s several influential studies of early pentecostals' racial notions have advanced what might be called an Edenic model of white–black relations. Though the authors do not agree on all particulars, the general story runs as follows. In the beginning, particularly at Azusa, remarkable harmony prevailed. But soon the snake of white racism struck the movement's heart. As a result, most of the major sects experienced serious racial conflict. It happened in a variety of ways. The Fire-Baptized Holiness Church formally split, the Church of God reorganized itself into racially bounded jurisdictions, and the Pentecostal Assemblies of the World splintered into geographically as well as racially defined bodies. By one reading most whites in the Church of God in Christ (COGIC) departed to form their own fellowship, the Assemblies of God. By another reading the whites who later organized the Assemblies of God shared minor business arrangements with COGIC but little else. Either way, the two largest pentecostal bodies went their own, racially separate ways.[59]

There is considerable truth in the Edenic model. Without question the earliest years saw a remarkable degree of interracial fraternity. Also without question, most pentecostal bodies eventually broke along racial lines or galvanized as virtually all-white or all-black bodies. The separation process was largely completed by World War I among majority white groups and by World War II among majority black ones. The Edenic model also contains a fundamental mistruth, however, for it suggests that the revival moved from racial harmony to disharmony as naturally and as inevitably as night follows day. I see a more complex pattern.

My argument can be stated in three simple propositions. First, throughout the initial generation there was, at the strictly personal level, a great deal of unselfconscious mixing. Whites and blacks routinely came together for worship and fellowship, and often seemed genuinely fond of one another. Second, when whites stopped to think about what was happening, they invariably pulled away, and blacks, by necessity, followed suit. Third, on the whole, pentecostal culture failed to provide a sustained theology of racial reconciliation for whites and blacks alike.[60]

Let us begin on the positive side by noting signs of unselfconscious race mixing in the movement generally. Ample evidence suggests that daily or casual interactions between whites and blacks were hospitable, frequently cordial, sometimes even familial.[61] That pattern marked the first several years and, to a significant extent, prevailed throughout the first generation. As noted in Chapter 6, whites and blacks often worshipped together harmoniously.[62] We know that whites received Holy Spirit baptism in mostly black settings, and vice versa.[63] Blacks spoke in white pulpits with surprising frequency.[64] As a case in point, in 1914 the Church of God in Christ bishop

C. H. Mason, accompanied by a black choir, preached at the organizing meeting of the Assemblies of God in Hot Springs, Arkansas.[65] Mason also preached at the organizing meeting of the white Pentecostal Church of God in Chicago seven years later.[66] When Mason held meetings for whites in Nashville in 1916 and Little Rock in 1919, some 7,000 souls attended each.[67] And whites apparently spoke in black pulpits.[68] Executives of the newly formed Assemblies of God voted to send a representative to the Church of God in Christ's convention in Memphis in the fall of 1914.[69] Such informal exchanges may have taken place often but escaped remark precisely because they seemed so unremarkable.

Over the years journalists, historians, and true believers have repeatedly pointed to the Azusa Street revival as evidence of racial harmony at the outset, and with some reason. The mission's *Apostolic Faith* described whites, blacks, and various "nationalities" worshipping together in harmony. Though primarily descriptive, all of those accounts carry a clear note of approval. The paper also contained several brief but explicitly theological references to racial and ethnic boundaries melting away through the power of Christ's blood,[70] or anticipation of Christ's return,[71] and several more that might be interpreted that way.[72] It should be noted that most of these texts—both the descriptive and the prescriptive—remained untitled and unsigned. That fact suggests that they expressed the views of both editors, William J. Seymour, the black leader of the mission, and Clara E. Lum, the white secretary. Guests too witnessed the racial concord that Seymour and Lum represented. William H. Durham, a white leader from Chicago, visited the mission in February 1907. He left impressed by the "love and unity that prevailed" and the "heavenly sweetness" filling the air.[73] Even Frank Bartleman, who never varnished anything in the interest of public relations, believed that in the beginning the "'color line' was washed away in the blood."[74] The aspiration for racial accord often extended to those who received Holy Ghost baptism at Azusa and then returned home. White North Carolina evangelist G. B. Cashwell spoke of his love and admiration for the Holy Spirit–filled "colored people" in his home state, adding, with manifest conviction, "All the people of God are one here."[75]

Sometimes the strongest indication of racial camaraderie in the movement came from those who reviled pentecostals precisely because of it. Just months after the Azusa revival started, the *Whittier (Calif.) Daily News* deplored local pentecostals' "rank fanaticism." The editor apparently found their mixing of races as objectionable as their noise. "[I]t's none of our concern," he snapped, "if blacks and whites join together and shout themselves into insensibility."[76] So it was in the Midwest, where an interracial water baptismal service in 1907 attracted the hostile attention of the *Indianapolis Star*. After the service, the reporter observed, "White women threw their arms about the dusky necks of negresses . . . [putting] to shame the most accomplished 'park spooning.'"[77] The same notes of alarm rang out in the Northwest. An Oregon newspaper headline spoke volumes: "COLOR LINE OBLITERATED: WHITE AND NEGRO FANATICS HOLD SERVICES: People Living Near Hall . . . Ask Police to Interfere."[78] Outsiders' contempt for pentecostals' interracial meetings actually triggered the separation and reorganization of at least one black denomination. W. E. Fuller reported that his group, the Fire-Baptized Holiness Church of God of the Americas, broke away from the Fire-Baptized Holiness Church (later Pentecostal Holiness Church) in 1908, not because of racial tension within the parent body, but because outsiders threw rocks and sent threatening letters.[79]

David Bundy and David Daniels persuasively argue that the Pentecostal Assemblies of the World (PAW) and the Church of God in Christ (COGIC) sought to maintain their interracial compositions into the 1920s and early 1930s.[80] Though PAW's origins remain obscure, if we use the conventional organization date of 1919, it is evident that whites and blacks constituted roughly equal numbers in the beginning. COGIC in turn had been predominantly though not exclusively black from its prepentecostal origins in the late 1890s. After it became pentecostal in 1907, some whites, such as Memphis pastor L. P. Adams, held conspicuous leadership roles. The sect made its interracial commitments clear in its church manual, published in the heat of World War I. "Many denominations have made distinctions between their colored and white members," the manual said in a section significantly titled "Equal in Power and Authority." But such practices had created many misunderstandings. "The Church of God in Christ recognizes the fact that all believers are one in Christ Jesus and all its members have equal rights. Its Overseers, both colored and white, have equal power and authority in the church."[81] COGIC distinguished itself by making William B. Holt, a blond-haired German, a national officer for nearly two decades, from 1916 to 1933. Indeed by 1926 Holt had risen to the rank of general secretary, just beneath General Overseer C. H. Mason, his bosom friend. Other whites held prominent positions too, including August Feick, general superintendent of the White Churches of God in Christ (the white jurisdiction, or "phase," as he put it, of the parent body).[82] Such arrangements stemmed from principle, not accident.

Having said all this, we also need to say that another, more regressive thread quickly appeared. Azusa Mission pioneer A. G. Osterberg remembered, for example, that in the beginning color meant nothing at the church, but he also remembered that racial tension soon emerged, apparently referring to 1906 and 1908.[83] Another Azusa Mission pioneer, the Englishman

George B. Studd, wrote in his diary of personality clashes, doctrinal disputes, and attrition at Azusa.[84] Though he did not attribute any of these incidents to racial distrust, it is reasonable to assume it played a role. Elsewhere Studd suggested that whites founded the rival Upper Room Mission down the street because blacks had taken over the Azusa Mission and sought to control it—which of course may have been another way of saying that whites wanted to control it.[85] In 1908 W. J. Seymour fell into a bitter, protracted conflict with white co-editor Clara E. Lum over ownership of the mission's periodical and its mailing lists. Soon Seymour's black wife, Jennie Evans Moore, and Lum's white friend, Florence Crawford, were involved. There is no evidence that the dispute started as a racial conflict (indeed a romantic disappointment may have sparked it), but given that two of the main protagonists on one side were black and two on the other side were white, race hardly could have been absent.[86] At Azusa other kinds of tensions emerged. The white evangelist Frank Bartleman, apparently referring to a meeting in 1909 in which he was present, reported that when some "poor, illiterate Mexicans" tried to testify of their baptism experience, the leader "crushed them ruthlessly."[87] Given the changing roster at Azusa, the leader could have been white or black, male or female, but one suspects that for the dispossessed Mexicans that day it was all the same.

Though pentecostals prided themselves on harmony in the Holy Spirit, venerable conventions structured even devotional patterns. Rural Missouri evangelist Walter Higgins recalled, for example, that blacks and whites joyfully worshipped together in his services—yet took care to sit separately.[88] Healing evangelist Maria Woodworth-Etter remembered that whites attending her Louisville, Kentucky, revival in 1888 refused to be seated in the same tent with blacks. Woodworth-Etter held firm: they would worship together or not at all. She recalled: "God came in such wonderful power it was not long till [whites] seemed to forget the color." Not entirely, however. "The altar," Woodworth-Etter continued, seemingly unaware of the irony, "was filled with seekers, white people on one side and colored on the other." This event preceded the pentecostal revival by more than a decade, but she told the story in 1916, and again in 1922, suggesting that the pattern remained as unremarkable as it was unchanged.[89]

Some white pentecostals used theology explicitly to sanction segregation and, by implication, white domination. For example, Texas attorney W. F. Carothers argued that God intended to keep races separate by placing them in different lands. Whites broke God's plan by forcibly resettling blacks in the United States. "[B]ut the Holy Spirit also, in a final effort to preserve the integrity of the races, has intensified the racial impulse. This latter is not prejudice . . . but merely the Lord's own substitute for wholesome geographical bounds of separation." Carothers thus implied that the sin lay not in enslavement but in geographical mixing.[90] Levi Lupton too, though normally progressive on social matters, felt that Africans were "so low on the scale of intellect" that few would be prominent in their native lands within a generation.[91] Among a minority of white pentecostals, talk about Anglo-Saxon superiority in the form of British–Israelite theology cropped up for years.[92] As late as 1929 Assemblies of God general superintendent E. S. Williams urged white and black Holy Spirit–filled believers in the South not to worship together.[93]

Facing a brick wall of white incomprehension at best, and hostility at worst, black pentecostals responded with resignation. By 1914 William J. Seymour reluctantly had come to the conclusion that it was necessary to restrict directors' posts at the Azusa Mission to "people of Color." He amended the Articles of Incorporation accordingly (though at least one white remained a trustee to the end).[94] The following year, in an address to the members of the church, Seymour explained that the group had made this change in order to "keep down race war in the Churches and friction." He attributed the conflict both to whites, who were "causing div[i]sion, and spreading wild fire and fanaticism," and to blacks, who had "caught the disease of this spirit of division also."[95] Seymour made clear that such animosity pained him—and evidently pained some of his white congregants too.[96] Nonetheless, this son of slaves succinctly captured the ambiguity of race relations at the mission when he said it would be carried forward for the "benefit of the colored people of the State of California, but the people of all countries, climes, and nations shall be welcome."[97]

Eventually the ax of racial distrust cleaved two significantly interracial bodies. In 1924 the Pentecostal Assemblies of the World split into mostly white and black denominations, and so they would remain, despite their common insistence on the Oneness of the Godhead. In the late 1920s and early 1930s the Church of God in Christ also became largely black as white leaders departed or were dismissed from their posts (most notably, the national field secretary William B. Holt). The white rank and file drifted into separate white jurisdictions or into the Assemblies of God. By then, David Daniels argues, Bishop Mason himself had found prudential, ethical, and biblical reasons for separation. The fight seemed no longer worth the effort.[98]

Three brief case studies of first-generation leaders—the first two white, the third black—reveal both the complexity of this story and the incapacity of the primitivist impulse to withstand the inclination to accommodate. We begin with the tangled racial attitudes of founder Charles Fox Parham. James R. Goff, Jr., Parham's scholarly biographer, acknowledges that Parham used racial theories to explain the different development of civilizations, yet notes that Parham included all races in God's plan of salvation and therefore felt a special missionary concern for blacks. Though no blacks attended Parham's Bible School in Topeka, he preached to mixed audiences from the outset. Setting up shop in Houston in 1905, Parham observed Jim Crow protocols, yet permitted the black evangelist William J. Seymour to attend his school by listening from an adjacent room. In the rigidly segregationist context of the times, Goff argues, Parham's decision was more paternalistic than racist. Parham also preached alongside Seymour in a joint ministry to the black community in Houston. At least five additional black ministers soon affiliated with Parham's work in Texas, one receiving the title, "Director of the . . . Houston District among his people."[99] Parham helped to fund Seymour's trip to Los Angeles in the winter–spring of 1906.[100] In September 1906 the Azusa *Apostolic Faith* proclaimed Parham to be "God's leader in the Apostolic Faith Movement." Parham returned the favor, saying, "I rejoice in God over you all, my children . . . [W]e are baptized by one Spirit into one body."[101] Goff argues that in this period Parham occupied a "paternalistic middle ground" between the extreme racism of Texas leader W. F. Carothers and the explicitly miscegenistic views of Illinois leader John Alexander Dowie.[102]

But Parham changed. His attitudes toward African Americans hardened dramatically in the fall of 1906 following a rupture in his relation with Seymour. Though that story has been told many times, the details remain murky. It suffices to say that the emotionalism Parham witnessed at Azusa and elsewhere among both white and black pentecostals repulsed him. Seymour's growing prominence undoubtedly added to Parham's dismay. Whatever the exact mix of factors, Parham's *Apostolic Faith* later linked "holy-rolling-dancing-jumping, shaking, jabbering, chattering, wind-sucking and giving vent to meaningless sounds and noises" with the religious practices of southern blacks.[103] Using crude racial slurs, Parham denounced white women who consorted with black men in worship at the Azusa mission, and deplored that white and black men and women knelt together and fell across one another. Such "foolishness," he charged, had followed the Azusa work everywhere.[104] In 1927 Parham publicly praised the reorganized Ku Klux Klan, though he urged its "splendid" leaders to root social reform in a "restoration of the Old Time Religion."[105] Nonetheless, in later years Parham occasionally preached to mixed audiences. Accounts of those meetings suggested that he felt paternalistic appreciation for blacks, Indians, Mexicans, and poor whites who attended them.[106] In 1916 the black songwriter Thoro Harris said that when Parham preached at Harris's Lake Street Mission in Chicago, the people loved the message and the messenger and "look[ed] forward" to his return. Harris described the meetings as a "feast of good things."[107] In the end Parham seemed as unsure of African Americans as they seemed of him.

The knottiness of white pentecostal attitudes toward blacks emerged even more poignantly in the life of healing evangelist F. F. Bosworth—more poignant because he remained oblivious to the irony of his assumptions. Bosworth may have been more representative than Parham precisely because he was a midlevel leader. It will be recalled that in the spring of 1911 a mob savagely beat Bosworth at a rural Texas railway station. He later explained why. Some white saints had been worshipping at a black Holy Ghost camp meeting at Hearne, Texas, a small town 100 miles from Dallas. The whites, impressed by the "spiritual power evident" at the revival, but "not wanting to seek the Baptism at a Colored Alter," asked Bosworth to come and preach to them. Accepting the invitation, Bosworth spoke to separate audiences, one white and one black. On the way back that night a band of "white ruffians" threatened to kill him. They assumed that he intended to break down racial segregation. Bosworth explained that he came to preach to the whites, and that he had "no thought or desire of putting them on a level with anyone." The thugs let him go, but when he sought to leave town the next day, another gang clubbed him with boat oars, presumably for the same reason. Three points are worth noting in this incident. First, white and black pentecostals were worshipping more or less together in the Deep South. Second, outsiders regarded pentecostals a threat to racial mores precisely for that reason. Third, Bosworth unselfconsciously reproduced the white racial prejudices of the day.[108]

Oral evidence suggests that Elder Eddie R. Driver of the Church of God in Christ changed too. When Driver arrived in Los Angeles in 1914, according to Rose Marie McDuff, the racial mixing in apostolic services "amazed" him. The Saint's Home Church, which he soon founded, attracted Elder [A. H.?] Argue, Elder [William F.?] Manley, and an Irish Sister Bridget, all almost certainly white. Aimee McPherson often worshipped at Saint's Home before her own Angelus Temple was built. Members of Saint's Home worshipped at Angelus Temple and vice versa. Nonetheless the harmony eventually dissolved. One member of Saint's Home Church recalled that whites would not accept blacks' leadership. Conversely, McDuff writes, "Other informants made statements to the effect that 'Dad' Driver talked quite 'rough' in regard to some white people, and would often call them names." One witness reported: "People began to leave, because he would talk so bad about them . . . And after a while it began to dawn on the white man as to what he was saying, and he just drove them away." Even so, on other occasions, another informant said, Driver tried to save "not only Black boys but White boys" from going to the "pen."[109] Again, three points should be noted. First, whites and blacks initially moved freely between each others' churches. Second, Driver changed as circumstances changed. Third, interracial fellowship failed the test of time.

I close this section by noting that the editors of pentecostal periodicals—

the men and women who were, in many ways, the movement's working theologians—offered little guidance in race matters. Though the problem needs further research, my reading of a wide span of early pentecostal periodicals, mostly edited by whites, suggests that they remained largely oblivious to such questions. To be sure, descriptive references to interracial worship appeared frequently enough that we may safely assume that a visitor to Holy Ghost meetings in the South or in certain urban areas like Los Angeles or New York probably would have seen a conspicuous minority of black or white faces. But those references did not constitute normative statements about human equality in worldly matters, let alone acceptance of social integration outside the meeting house. Moreover, viewed as a percentage of the whole, they formed a minuscule fraction—a trace element, one might say—of the editors' concerns.

That white editors said little about race is hardly surprising, but black editors seemed equally indifferent. Consider, for example, the *relative* paucity of references to interracial mixing in the pages of the Azusa *Apostolic Faith*. As noted in Chapter 2, twelve of the fourteen extant issues of this important periodical have been digitized. In that corpus, running nearly 210,000 words (perhaps a 400-page book), I find about twenty references to white–black mingling in worship. Though all implied endorsement of interracial fellowship, fewer than half were explicitly prescriptive, and most involved only two or three brief sentences.[110] If we look at the articles that Seymour himself signed (totaling more than 17,000 words), we find that he mentioned race only once, and that was a simple, biblically cadenced statement: "All races, nations, and tongues are receiving the baptism with the Holy Ghost and fire, according to the prophecy of Joel."[111] (In contrast Seymour repeatedly addressed the pentecostal hallmarks of sanctification, healing, Second Coming, and Holy Ghost baptism.) The same pattern of comparative inattention to white-black relations characterized other early periodicals edited by African Americans, including *Whole Truth,* edited by Justus Bowe of the Church of God in Christ, and *Voice in the Wilderness,* edited by G. T. Haywood of the Pentecostal Assemblies of the World. The latter publication in particular seemed almost completely unmindful of such matters.[112] The point here is not that Seymour, Bowe, or Haywood were unaware of race in their personal lives—how could they have been?—but rather that it played a slight role in their theological thinking.[113]

What we see in all this is that for pentecostals, as for most Christians in America, race relations kept getting mixed up. On the one hand ideals of racial mixing, even harmony, constantly renewed their lives. After all, pentecostal whites and blacks shared a common history, a common land, and, above all, a common faith. On the other hand strong pressures toward racial separation, even animosity, intruded. If whites bore the guilt of enslaving fellow Christians, blacks suffered the more onerous burden, imposed by their Christian consciences, of forgiving whites for wrongs inflicted. But on the whole the pentecostal message offered inadequate help to either group. Most whites probably did not think about the problem very much. Most blacks probably *did* think about the problem very much but, with the exceptions noted, did not use the language of the revival to express either their grievances or their aspirations. "Though Holy Spirit baptism implied divine enablement to overcome human frailties," James R. Goff observes, "few seemed clear about its implications or able to accept the radical consequences of its message."[114]

No one should be surprised. Pentecostals were, after all, normal American Christians, subject to all the prejudices and confusions that afflicted most normal American Christians. Pragmatic accommodation to the mores of the age was a survival strategy, not a certificate of moral purity.

Police

Pragmatism proved both a curse and a blessing—a curse because it prevented pentecostals from distancing themselves from contemporary culture when, by their own lights, they should have done so, and a blessing because it helped them come to grips with modern life when the prayer meeting let out. This included the subtle and sometimes not-so-subtle ways that believers embraced the law enforcement power of the nation.

Police officials fared well in pentecostals' estimation because they represented public order. To be sure, saying that partisans generally enjoyed an amicable relationship with the constabulary may strike some as dubious since the movement's literature suggested the opposite. Insiders almost always described themselves as the victims, not the beneficiaries, of government scrutiny.[115] And they had a point, for some law enforcement officials clearly held pentecostals in contempt. "The ignorant class and lawless element are its followers," sneered one Bureau of Investigation (BOI) agent about a Church of God flock he investigated in 1918. The agent went on to report—without a trace of evidence, one should add—that Holy Ghost meetings were "nothing more than whore houses and are responsible for numerous cases of young girls being wronged."[116] Nonetheless, the primary record makes clear that the government protected believers more often than it harassed them. Moreover—and this is the key point—Holy Spirit–filled partisans routinely accepted government assistance, apparently without a second thought.

On most occasions the police tried to guarantee worshipers' safety. Consider for instance the events that transpired on the front steps of the Pythian

Castle in Macon, Georgia, just before Christmas 1911. The Children of God, a pentecostal band consisting of Mercer University professor J. R. Moseley and four female followers, had moved their service to that site when they were kicked out of the First Presbyterian Church. (The group's "peculiar form of worship," sniffed the pastor, did not fall "in line" with the denomination's.) The Pythian Castle meeting ran true to form. According to one press account, "loud shrieks and deep groans" that could be heard blocks away repeatedly punctuated the singing and praying. Yet the police solemnly stood guard, guaranteeing both the company's safety and its right to worship as it pleased so long as no one complained about the noise.[117] Or consider a similar incident in the other corner of the country, the supposedly secular Northwest. For several nights running, said the *Salem (Ore.) Daily Capital Journal,* a "band of young hoodlums" had made a point of harassing the faithful at a local "'Tongues of Fire'" street mission. Things came to a head when one miscreant hurled a rock the size of an inkstand at the preacher, one Mr. Shipley. The latter thereupon decided that his life was in peril. The following morning the Shipleys called at city hall. They received a promise that henceforth the "strong arm of the law would guard the outpouring of the Holy Ghost"—or, as the reporter tellingly put it, the pentecostals would enjoy the "chaperonage of the blue-coated guardians of the city's peace."[118] Similar stories could be related but these are enough to illustrate the pattern of civil solicitude for the rights of all citizens, however "peculiar their form of worship."[119]

Important as this kind of protective oversight was, more serious forms of assistance sometimes were needed—and gladly received. The crack of a sheriff's nightstick administered to ruffians bent on disrupting Holy Ghost meetings echoes throughout the primary accounts. In 1902, when a gang of 106 Methodist and Baptist ruffians and others torched the almost-pentecostal Holiness Church at Camp Creek, North Carolina, they quickly found themselves arrested and "bound to court."[120] And when the black United Holy Church sought to establish a base in Martinsville, West Virginia, and local whites persuaded town authorities to padlock the church door, a quick visit by United Holy bishop J. D. Diggs from Winston Salem, North Carolina, prompted the local sheriff to remove the padlock and issue a public apology.[121]

On at least two occasions the rule of law proved strong enough to protect a trio of pentecostal preachers from the apparent forces of religious intolerance, patriotic zeal, racial prejudice, and BOI power. In the fall of 1918 the BOI pressured two Texas grand juries to indict Church of God in Christ bishop C. H. Mason and two helpers, Henry Kirvin and William B. Holt (Mason and Kirvin were black, Holt white) on charges of conspiracy to obstruct the draft, impersonating government officials, and swindling.[122] In the end, however, both grand juries steadfastly refused to buckle under government pressure and the beleaguered apostolics went free.

Pentecostals almost never acknowledged, except inadvertently, that sometimes the police actually bent the law on their behalf—and at others' expense. In Orlando, Florida, for example, one of Sister McPherson's followers could not fathom why the authorities would try to shut down her tent revival at the "early hour" of 10:00 P.M. When a woman living several blocks away said that she could not sleep because of the noise, Sister dismissed her complaint as selfish. McPherson's supporters resolved the problem, she later boasted, by persuading the mayor to scotch the curfew—thus allowing Sister to preach "straight from the shoulder," often until midnight.[123] Such incidents show that pentecostals would embrace almost any power that wore a uniform or wielded a gavel and proved willing to support their interests. The third General Assembly of the Church of God may have revealed more than it intended when it admonished members to appreciate officers of the law, for they were, after all, "God's ministers."[124] Pentecostals, in other words, not only knew how to play ball, but also knew that it was a good idea to befriend the umpire.

Pilgrim's Pride

A love for the American land provides one more lens for viewing pentecostals' relation to the nation. As noted at the chapter's outset, saints had no use at all for the state, the political entity centered in Washington, D.C. But the true America, the "land of pilgrim's pride," was a quite different matter, for it evoked powerful emotions wrapped, as Abraham Lincoln had said long before, in "mystic chords of memory."

Early pentecostals did not just happen to live in America, they belonged to America, heart and mind. To be sure, examples of that attitude do not crop up everywhere, at least not in the same conspicuous way that healing stories do. But if we look carefully, we can detect barely expressed and perhaps barely expressible feelings of love of country resting quietly in the shaded corners of the texts. Some years before American doughboys started falling in France, a Fourth of July sermon by eighteen-year-old Homer Tomlinson focused on the legacy of the pilgrims and Valley Forge. Afterward, reported the *Evening Light and Church of God Evangel,* the Holy Spirit "seemed to envelop the congregation . . . and not a few wept outright as their bosoms heaved with suppressed emotion."[125] A half-dozen years later, in an essay almost certainly written by A. J. Tomlinson (young Homer's notable father), the *Church of God Evangel* opposed saints' participation in the world war.

The reason was obvious: pentecostal Christians were citizens of the Heavenly City.[126] But the elder Tomlinson also opposed the conflict because the fighting seemed disloyal. *Disloyal?* Disloyal to whom? War preparedness, he made clear, acted as a terrible "iron hand . . . slowly closing in on our own beloved land," a "cruel monster" dragging sons from the parental nest and subjecting them to a foreign struggle.[127]

Others, too, expressed feelings for their land without hesitation. In response to a question about the propriety of saluting the flag, Assemblies of God chairman E. N. Bell responded forthrightly. "Unintentional neglect might be overlooked," he judged, "but a willful refusal would be as good as rejecting the Government of the U.S.A." Honoring the flag did not betoken worship of the nation but only "our love for our country and its flag and an acceptance of its rightful authority."[128] The same surge of loyal feeling surfaced far off in Hong Kong. The diary of youthful Cora Fritsch, an independent faith missionary if ever there was one, revealed scarcely a trace of real-life political consciousness. One reads page after page in vain for any comment on domestic affairs, world affairs, anything at all beyond the urgency of evangelizing the lost. Then without warning we read of her hurrying down to the waterfront one morning to see the Stars and Stripes fluttering above a U.S. ship docked in the harbor. "But when they played the national song at sun down and lowered the flag," she admitted, "I felt something within me thrill. I was so proud I am an American. I love my country more than ever now."[129] So did others. Just after the armistice was signed, an anonymous writer in the Church of God's *Faithful Standard* urged Holy Ghost people to "stand for true Americanism and for the Christian religion with no uncertain sound."[130] One can hardly fail to notice the instinctive, almost automatic way that love of land and love of the full gospel message flowed together.

Photographs of early pentecostal parades and rallies and storefront missions tell their own stories of love of country. Again and again they showed an American flag standing in the background, or off to the side, or squarely up front and center.[131] One particularly memorable image pictures Charles Parham standing with a group of followers on the Carthage, Missouri, courthouse steps, holding small banners bearing the words APOSTOLIC, FAITH, LIFE, UNITY, and VICTORY—along with two oversized American flags on either side. That was 1905, the very year that he had assailed the "Moloch God, Patriotism." Another photograph depicts Aimee McPherson kneeling in front of the Holdrege, Nebraska, civic auditorium in 1919, with six American flags flying overhead while Sister clutches a seventh flag in her right hand—a Bible in her left. Still another shows McPherson, at a 1927 Denver revival, apparently raising a cripple from his sickbed that had been placed on a platform festooned with American flags. It is a fair guess that neither Parham nor McPherson nor any other zealot thought very much about the significance of pairing the symbols of their faith with the symbols of their land. Yet precisely for that reason, those mute sentinels testified to believers' deepest assumptions about the essential sacredness of the land of their birth.

In the end, saints could not distance themselves from love of country any more than other radical evangelicals—or, for that matter, other Americans—could. It would be unfair to say that early pentecostals were Americans first and Christians second, but it would be inaccurate to say that they were Christians first and Americans second. The plain truth is that these pilgrims found themselves occupying the same ground that countless true believers and true citizens before them had occupied. They yearned to make the demands of Christ preeminent, yet the emotional necessity of owning the soil in which they had invested so many years of toil guaranteed that the demands of Christ would have to adjust to the demands of daily life. It was, after all, the land they had inherited from their parents and meant to bequeath to their children. It was, to adapt William B. Yeats's words, the "land of heart's desire." Church of God pioneer W. F. Bryant well knew the rigors of mission work in the Appalachians, but seemed ultimately not to care. "When I . . . let my mind wander back to the hills and mountains of Tennessee," he mused aloud at the 1912 General Assembly, and "as I . . . once more feel and breathe the clear cool air as it comes bounding down the hills, over the deep gullies, through the dark forests, and then out into the open where it bows to the ground the submissive sage-grass, my heart seems to ache with an inexpressible hunger to once more be there."[132] First-generation converts did not often pause quietly to take it all in. But on those rare occasions when they did, they spoke from the heart.

Our story concludes as predictably as it began. For all of their aspirations to heavenly mindedness, in the end early pentecostals showed that they were exactly like most Christians, or at least most American Christians. They revealed that the earthly temptation that most attracted them was not the abuse of sex or money or power, but the lure of a continent "too easily loved."[133] In this respect, as in so many others, they were more thisworldly than they admitted. Deep down they seemed to know that they were, as President Lincoln had said of Americans generally, members of the almost-chosen people, and their country the almost-chosen land.

14

War

For early pentecostals, as for millions of American Christians, World War I seemed more than a military and political struggle. Not at first, but little by little, the War (as I shall simply call it in this chapter) emerged as a moral dilemma of profound dimensions. Everyone knew that obeying Christ was more important than obeying Caesar. But what exactly did that mean? Principled pacifism? Strategic noncooperation? Or could it mean compliance with the just demands of the nation—demands that had, after all, been sanctioned by the Lord Himself? Whatever the answer, one thing remained certain: balancing the claims of Christ against the claims of Caesar would tax saints' conscience in ways they originally scarcely imagined.

Pentecostals' attitudes toward participation in war changed over time. At the turn of the century, in the initial heat of the revival, their first publicly articulated position on war reflected either qualified pacifism or simple indifference. Either way, their noncompliant attitude seemed predictable enough since they were predisposed to feel and think in primitivist categories. But as the fighting escalated on (and under) the high seas, and then in the trenches of Europe, the pressures of surviving in the real world forced adjustments. By the time of U.S. entry into the War in the spring of 1917, a clear pattern of accommodation to the nation's policies had emerged. By the time of the fighting's end in the fall of 1918, that accommodationist pattern had come to dominate—yet never entirely eclipse—the earlier propensities toward noncompliance.

Readers will note that this chapter is structured somewhat differently from most of the previous ones. In the others we have seen that pentecostals' accommodative impulses took hold almost immediately, usually within months if not simultaneously with the revival's beginnings. In this case, however, the accommodative process took considerably longer, perhaps because the stakes of taking and losing life seemed so much higher.

"Washington's Vision"

We begin with a potted morality tale, as bizarre as it is intriguing. Though the incident remains but a minor episode, it succinctly illustrates the knotting of otherworldly ideals and thisworldly calculations in pentecostals' view of their responsibility to the nation in time of war.

It all began with a one-page document widely known as the "Washington Vision," which apparently originated in an 1880 issue of the *National Tribune*, a District of Columbia newspaper published for Civil War veterans.[1] According to the story, one cold afternoon in the winter of 1777 an apparition, a "singularly beautiful female," visited General George Washington in his private quarters at Valley Forge. Repeatedly addressing Washington as "Son of the Republic," the apparition led him through three dreams. In the first, a dark cloud arose from Europe, then swept across the Atlantic and enveloped the American continent. When the cloud receded, it left "villages, towns and cities . . . springing up" everywhere. The second vision involved an "ill-omened spectre" arising from Africa and approaching the American shore. Soon "every town and city" was arrayed against each other. But then a "bright angel" appeared, wearing a "crown of light on which was traced the word 'union,' bearing the American flag." Instantly the nation's inhabitants dropped their weapons and united around the "National standard." In the third vision, "thick, black clouds" emerged from Europe, Africa, and Asia. The clouds shrouded "hordes of armed men" sailing to American shores. These "vast armies" devastated the land. Then the same angel descended from heaven and gave victory to the Americans. Still holding the flag, the angel declared: "While the stars remain, and the heavens send down dew upon the earth, so long shall the Republic last." The people then knelt before the crown bearing the word *Union,* as well as the flag, and uttered "Amen." The apparition then said to Washington: "Let every child of the Republic learn to live for his God, his land and Union." Though the text of the "Vision" did not explicitly say so, the three perils were understood to denote the Revolutionary War, the Civil War, and the impending war in Europe.[2]

The *Christian Evangel* ran the text of the "Vision," titled "The Destiny of Our Nation," on the front page of its October 1914 issue, just after the fighting in France and Belgium had begun. In an accompanying editorial, assistant managing editor J. Roswell Flower lent his own considerable prestige to the "Vision" by acknowledging that General Washington may or may not have actually received a heavenly caller, but the "Vision"'s main points remained valid.[3] The following month the full text of the prophecy reappeared in *Word and Witness*.[4] Writing in the *Weekly Evangel* several months later,

E. T. Slaybaugh gave the document almost canonical status by linking it with the New Testament book of Revelation. "[W]here Washington's vision leaves off," Slaybaugh somberly judged, "John's vision takes up the thread and completes the scene."[5] In 1926 the document showed up once again on the front page of another major pentecostal weekly, the *Pentecostal World*, published in Chicago.[6]

Several aspects of "Washington's Vision" merit comment. Most obvious, perhaps, is its rhetorical structure, which resembles the epiphanies in Daniel, Ezekial, and Revelation. The "Son of the Republic" salutation parallels the Gospels' recurring references to the "Son of Man." The event significantly took place not in a church but in the national holy of holies, Independence Hall. In all three scenarios the Old World harbored the forces of evil, while the New World, or at least the U.S. portion of it, cradled an unmistakably millennial scene of peace, prosperity, and progress. The Lord repeatedly intervened to bless the nation's future, including its continental expansion and urbanization. The promise that the Republic would persist as long as the stars shone and the dew glistened echoed God's covenants with Abraham. Most striking, the secular *National Tribune* printed this covenant-like promise in standard font while the editors of the *Christian Evangel* highlighted it in bold font, along with another angelic assurance that the "whole world united shall not prevail against her [America]." A powerful fantasy it was, not least because this biblical apocalypticism fueled the engine of patriotic fervor without out a trace of self-awareness.

More followed. In an accompanying editorial J. Roswell Flower ruminated, through the lips of an unnamed source, that a "monarchial party" had practically overtaken Congress. That party was the worldwide Jesuit organization and a large class of money grubbers who had subverted "all patriotic, moral and religious questions" in their own interests. The solution? To place in office a "radical American administration which [would] turn the monarchial parties away and administer the government along the patriotic lines of the Fathers of the Nation." Of course Flower did not honestly expect that this reformation would ever take place. True to fundamentalist form, he predicted that the United States—minus Christ's raptured saints—would soon be swept up in the fires of Armageddon to pay for its sins. But Flower could not resist hoping that if Americans repented of their godless ways and truly sought a "work of righteousness" they might lessen or even avert the wrath to come.[7]

Flower's ambivalence about his dual citizenship in the heavenly and in the earthly realms hardly meant that he was confused. It only meant that he was struggling, as countless Christians and loyal citizens before (and after) him, to come to terms with the conflicting demands of split allegiances. His otherworldly impulses told him that he belonged to another kingdom. In principle it really should not have mattered what fate befell the United States since he was, after all, a citizen of a higher Kingdom. History would unfold exactly as predicted by the prophets of old, and the American Republic, like all earthly domains, would fall beneath the juggernaut of divine judgment. Yet Flower, like most American Christians, could never quite bring himself to believe that this grim outcome was inescapably foreordained. The nation's story seemed too full of millennial promise to be consigned to the trash bin of hopeless causes. Surely Americans could save their dear land if—*if*—they would just muster the strength and courage to do so.

One War, Many Plots

Developments in the infant Assemblies of God (AOG) showed with painful clarity how primitivist resistance and pragmatic accommodation fought for the movement's heart as the nation stumbled toward war. I focus on the AOG because it kept better records than any pentecostal sect and permitted a variety of views in its official publications until 1917, when the United States entered the conflict.

Between 1900 and 1914 two attitudes toward Christian involvement in war seemed prevalent among pentecostals who would later influence the AOG's ethos. The first might be thought of as a qualified pacifism. In those very early years a small but vocal number of leaders—including quasi-pentecostal John Alexander Dowie, Charles Parham, Frank Bartleman, Arthur S. Booth-Clibborn, and British-born Stanley H. Frodsham—spoke forcefully against killing on behalf of any nation, including the United States.[8] Their record was not perfectly consistent, however. Of the men named, only Booth-Clibborn maintained an unfailingly pacifist stance, and he never formally affiliated with the fellowship. Dowie's resistance to fighting was selective, as he acknowledged the legitimacy of "war[s] for protection."[9] Parham seemed driven more by an animus against big government than by regard for pacifist principles per se.[10] Bartleman appeared to contemporaries suspiciously sympathetic to the German cause and, in any event, too cranky to be taken entirely seriously.[11] And Frodsham eventually buckled under the cumulative weight of cultural and perhaps denominational pressure to support the nation's policies. Still, except for leaders in the peace church tradition, these early pentecostal writers proved as thoughtful about the issue of war as most American Christians, pacifist or otherwise. They laid out a series of careful rationales for resistance, including New Testament proscriptions against violence, a distaste for the self-aggrandizing motives of earthly governments, and the priority of world evangelization before the Lord's return.[12]

The other attitude toward the nation that turned up among the very earliest pentecostals was not exactly the opposite of pacifism—not, in other words, some version of Just War theory—but simply nothing at all. We might think of it as simple indifference. Except for the handful of writers named above, and perhaps a few others, there is precious little in the primary sources that might count as a serious exposition of the Christian's responsibility to the nation in time of war, or any other time for that matter. (Even the pacifists noted above usually cast their thoughts in starkly otherworldly categories, rarely suggesting that pacifist principles might work positively as a healing force in a broken world.) The best evidence that indifference reigned among most pentecostals who later joined the AOG was that neither of the sect's two main foundational documents said a word about the matter.[13] What that omission most likely means is that the question just did not exist for the majority. Until war engulfed the continent of Europe in the summer of 1914, and the Atlantic shipping lanes the following year, no one thought to forge a systematic response to the problem.[14]

Between 1914 and 1917, however, the nation's political atmosphere changed dramatically, and so did pentecostals' sense of responsible citizenship. The sinking of the *Lusitania* in May 1915 served as a tocsin, and by the spring of 1917 the United States found itself drawn into the conflict. Though many Christians, including Secretary of State William Jennings Bryan, initially opposed American involvement, in time prowar sentiment swept the country, bringing with it the draft, the Espionage and Sedition Acts of 1917 and 1918, anti-German feelings, vigilante groups like the American Protective League, and a mounting sense that pacifism was neither principled nor loyal but cowardly and treasonable. Opinion within the AOG reflected a similar transformation. Peace voices never died out completely, but they did grow increasingly faint. Indifference rapidly turned into a desire to support the government in every way morally possible.[15]

On April 28, 1917, twenty-two days after the United States declared war on Germany, the denomination's executive presbyters sent a resolution concerning combatant military service to all ministers. The resolution began by noting that the Lord Himself had ordained human governments, and affirmed unswerving loyalty to the government of the United States. But it went on to state that the inspired Word of God, which served as the exclusive basis of faith and practice, instructed Christians to seek peace and not to shed blood. The critical concluding sentence of the resolution read: "THEREFORE we, as a body of Christians, while purposing to fulfill all the obligations of loyal citizenship, are nevertheless constrained to declare we cannot conscientiously participate in war and armed resistance which involves the actual destruction of human life."[16] The resolution's immediate purpose was to qualify the sect as a pacifist denomination in the eyes of the government, thus allowing partisans to apply for noncombatant status along with Quakers, Mennonites, and other peace groups.[17]

Efforts to interpret the resolution's meaning for grass-roots members soon followed. On May 19, 1917, one day after Congress passed the Selective Service Act, Chairman J. W. Welch published an article in the *Weekly Evangel* elaborating the resolution's implications. His article marked the beginning of an obviously painful process of backing down from the idealism of the previous month. Welch made three points. First, the resolution was not designed to hinder anyone from taking up arms if their conscience permitted. Second, the resolution aimed to make it legally possible for AOG men to apply for noncombatant status but not exemption from other forms of military service. Third, the denomination would support the government in all ways possible short of direct participation in killing. Welch stressed that applying for noncombatant status should not be taken lightly. Since it entailed "moral and financial responsibilities," it was not an option for someone who wanted simply to escape military service.[18] Welch did not try to explain how killing might be morally permissible for some but not for others, nor did he try to clarify how supportive activities, such as purchasing war bonds, differed from actually pulling a trigger.

In the succeeding months the AOG accommodated the nation's demands bit by bit. After May, no more articles supporting pacifism appeared in official publications. Welch urged all eligible members immediately to register for the draft, which went into effect June 5, 1917. If they could not conscientiously engage in killing they should apply for legal exemption. He did not say what one should do if an application for exemption failed to be accepted.[19] At the next General Council, held in September 1917, officials denounced "so-called" pentecostal preachers who insulted the flag as well as "radicals" who spoke against the government.[20] Toward the end of the year E. N. Bell, now the editor of the *Weekly Evangel,* reaffirmed his group's opposition to killing but also noted that they had never supported complete exemption from military service. "The General Council is not in sympathy with any sort of twisting, shirking or 'slackering' in our duty to our flag," he declared. Bell urged believers to do all they could to "sustain our President in this great conflict."[21]

Viewed from a distance, through much of 1917 the official position of the AOG seemed to balance pacifism with the growing pressure to support the nation's policies. As late as August of that year dissenting voices against involvement in war could still be heard among the senior leaders.[22] But events of 1918 tipped the scales—though never completely—in favor of the patriot side. As support for the war grew in the culture at large, Bell moved in tandem. He sought to do all that he could, within the prescriptive boundaries of the original resolution, to constrict the scope of conscientious objection and to amplify the scope of legitimate military service. Bell opened the new year by arguing that opposition to killing was a personal issue, a matter of individual choice. Far from being normative, it was both inappropriate and unlawful for pacifist Christians to "push" their faith on others. Moreover pentecostals who availed themselves of noncombatant status should prove their gratitude by doing extra service for humankind, for the government, and for God.[23] Bell was on a roll. In the succeeding weeks he encouraged AOG members to buy Liberty Bonds,[24] remember that Jesus paid taxes to the Roman government,[25] and keep in mind that civil authority was ordained by God.[26] Responding perhaps to the plain reality that the government really would enforce the Sedition Act, Bell put teeth into his role as editor of the *Weekly Evangel* and general manager of the Gospel Publishing House. In the summer of 1918 he ordered the destruction of all copies of Frank Bartleman's antiwar broadside, *Present Day Conditions,* which the *Evangel* had printed back in 1915 and later reprinted in tract form.[27] The General Council, meeting in September of 1918, added its own bass notes to the chorus by once again affirming its "unswerving loyalty" to the president. The General Council restated its determination to help "in every way morally possible, consistent with our faith, in bringing the present 'World War' to a successful conclusion."[28]

When peace finally arrived on November 11, 1918, much of the West saw it as a time for mourning sons lost, but not the official voice of the AOG. Two months after the armistice was signed, Bell, soon to be elected chairman for the second time, sought to remove any remorse that pentecostals might feel about the slaughter in the trenches. He pointed out that the morality of slaying depended on motive. If one slew with hatred it was sin, but if one slew on behalf of duly constituted authority it was not sin.[29] Shortly afterward Bell suggested there was no sin in killing if necessary to "rescue those who are being oppressed."[30] Bell's tone seemed unchastened by sorrow for all the death and suffering that had taken place. The moral enormity of spilling so much blood for a "botched civilization," as one critic had put it, seemed to elude him.

How many AOG men and women did E. N. Bell represent? His voice counted in at least two ways. As the best educated man in the denomination, a tireless writer and speaker, and as editor of two high-circulation publications, first *Word and Witness* and then *Weekly Evangel,* he surely exerted considerable influence on rank-and-file opinion. Common sense tells us that the reverse was true too: he surely reflected rank-and-file opinion or he would not have remained in those positions as long as he did. More telling is the fact that he was elected chairman of the denomination on two occasions. There is

no evidence that any elected official within the denomination publicly resisted Bell or his point of view. If Bell did not speak for everyone, he evidently
spoke for most.

Significantly, Aimee McPherson, who closely associated with the AOG for
several years following the war (holding credentials in that body from 1919
to 1922), echoed Bell's attitudes. Though Sister remained more apolitical
than not, she never scrupled about using war themes to make spiritual points.
"Liberty Bonds—'Over There,'" "Modern Warfare—'Over the Top,'" "Red
Cross," and "A Red Cross Hospital atop Calvary's Hill," topped the list of
best-loved sermon titles.[31] Lest anyone doubt it McPherson made clear
where her working sympathies lay. "Practically everywhere one looks," she
declared in the heat of the war, one sees the "need for sacrifice and loyalty at
this trying hour." Duty dictated the purchase of Liberty Bonds. "Sacrifice
and giving are absolutely essential."[32] McPherson knew her audience. The
pages of AOG periodicals carried request after request for prayer for the spiritual and physical safety of mothers' sons fighting overseas. No one requested
prayer for conscientious objectors. One can only assume that they were either
too few to count or that editors screened out such requests, knowing how
most readers would react.[33]

But if Bell and McPherson represented the AOG, did the AOG represent
other pentecostal bodies? The church–state views of only two other sects
have received critical attention, the mostly white Church of God and the
mostly black Church of God in Christ. In each instance the story is somewhat
more tangled than in the case of the AOG but ultimately not much different.
Those narratives can be quickly told.

Mickey Crews's social history of the Church of God suggests that primitivist impulses in general, and pacifist ones in particular, ran deeper and persisted longer in that body than anywhere else in the pentecostal tradition.
The reason may have stemmed from geographical isolation since the Church
of God was strongest in the remote valleys of the southern highlands. But a
more likely reason was the commanding presence of the sect's longtime general overseer, A. J. Tomlinson. It will be recalled that in the 1880s, after an
intense religious conversion, Tomlinson renounced all forms of secular political involvement. That abiding commitment, plus a conviction that the war
dragged mothers' sons into an essentially foreign conflict, led him to maintain a strictly pacifist stance throughout the war years, undoubtedly contrib-
uting to a 1917 General Assembly declaration against members "going to
war."[34] Crews convincingly documents that believers meant what they said
too. A number of Church of God ministers and laymen paid for their pacifist
convictions with harassment at the workplace, Bureau of Investigation (BOI)
intimidation, incarceration and, in one case at least, loss of life.[35]

Even so, close inspection of the Church of God story predictably reveals numerous twists and turns as members struggled to come to grips with the conflicting demands of dual citizenship. Oral tradition holds that in 1916 Church of God folk voted en mass not for the Democrat, Woodrow Wilson, the more pacific of the two candidates, but for the Republican, former New York governor Charles Evans Hughes, who campaigned on a preparedness platform.[36] Moreover Tomlinson clearly did not speak for all. Other leaders, such as Richard G. Spurling, Jr. and William F. Bryant, who predated and for a time rivaled Tomlinson, accepted the necessity of fighting for their country. And apparently so did some of the laity whose views somehow slipped through Tomlinson's editing of the *Church of God Evangel*.[37] Even Tomlinson encouraged all male members properly to register for the draft and apply for exemption through all legal means possible.[38] Moreover the rationale that some Church of God leaders advanced for resisting service sounded as pragmatic as it was primitivist. Members deplored the bungling of European diplomats, the possibility of food rationing, the threat of government censorship, and the sheer waste of time that being at war imposed.[39] Finally and most important, the proscription against war handed down by the General Assembly in 1917 did not stick. It disappeared from the *Minutes* in 1921, reappeared in modified form in 1928 (permitting noncombatant service), then disappeared for good in 1945.[40]

In the Church of God in Christ (COGIC) the old tension between heavenly aspirations and earthly accommodations reappeared in similar ways, although predictably complicated by race. Theodore Kornweibel's painstaking research in BOI files has shown that starting in September 1917, and running through October 1918, the BOI repeatedly investigated Bishop C. H. Mason for conspiracy to obstruct the draft and for seditious statements against the war. Informants claimed that Mason espoused pacifist principles, debunked the war as a fight between rich white men, and insisted that black folk had no quarrel with the Germans. Mason was twice arraigned but never indicted. Nor was he alone. At different times the BOI called in and verbally harassed other Church of God in Christ elders, including William B. Holt. Mason and Holt were actually the lucky ones. In April 1918 irate locals tarred and feathered the Rev. Jesse Payne of Blytheville, Arkansas, for pacifist and pro-German remarks. Nor were the suspicions of the BOI and local citizen groups about the COGIC entirely off base. Though hard documentation that the sect espoused pacifist principles before 1917 remains elusive, strong oral tradition suggests that it, along with other black pentecostal bodies, initially opposed combatant participation in war.[41]

Even so, one of the more remarkable features of this narrative is how carefully Mason and other COGIC spokesmen packaged their pacifism. In August 1917, for example, they drew up a document affirming loyalty to magistrates, civil laws, the flag, the president, and all God-given institutions, though carefully stating that the shedding of blood violated the teachings of Jesus.[42] Some eight months later another elder assured one BOI investigator that neither he nor Mason had ever preached antidraft or antiwar messages.[43] Shortly afterward Mason vouched to the BOI that he had never advised church members to claim conscientious objector exemptions and that he had supported Liberty Bond, War Stamp, and Red Cross efforts.[44] According to later Church of God in Christ documents, on June 23, 1918, Mason preached to a "vast throng" in North Memphis. In a sermon symptomatically titled, "The Kaiser in the Light of the Scriptures," the bishop first complimented President Wilson, then carefully linked the Kaiser, not President Wilson, to the "war beast" of Revelation 13. Most important in the present context was Mason's support for Liberty Bonds. He boasted that he himself had raised more than $3,000 for the cause, hoping for nothing in return except that the "German hordes" would be defeated and driven back over the Rhine.[45] Other members of Mason's group proved that they too were willing to support the use of deadly force if the occasion required. When Elder William B. Holt was jailed in Texas for carrying a gun, Mason explained that Holt had been a deputy sheriff in California (the point presumably being that he was entitled to carry one).[46] Another elder affirmed his support for the Red Cross, adding, "I am now teaching that nations ought to chastise one another."[47]

Short stories with epic dimensions these are, case studies of conscientious men and women struggling to adjust deeply felt convictions to the hard realities of the age. Bell, Tomlinson, and Mason well understood that zealous defense of the full gospel, with no eye for real-life consequences, could destroy the pentecostal faith just as surely as lassitude or cowardice. So it was that at the height of the war, in an essay tellingly called "Days of Perplexity," Tomlinson would lament just how morally complicated things could grow. Refusing to kill was surely virtuous, he observed, but what about all the other ways that Christians like himself had indirectly assisted the war effort? "We are helping to pull the triggers that fire the guns that take the lives of our fellow men," he judged in a moment of painful self-reflection. "We do not want to do this but it is forced upon us." If a military officer should order him to kill another human being, Tomlinson went on, he would have to defy the order and bear the consequences. Nothing surprising there, but the terse simplicity of the next sentence gives pause: "I do not say that others should do so."[48] That qualification—the refusal to universalize an ethical principle—reveals a great deal about the inner dynamics of the subculture. This is my own path, Tomlinson seemed to be saying, but my vision is limited, so I cannot judge others who take other routes.

Only the blindest partisan of the pacifist cause, or for that matter of any cause, could fail to sense the moral distress that Providence had inflicted on Tomlinson's generation. Admitting that war was hell proved easy. Admitting that it was also the incubator of moral perplexities for which Holy Spirit baptism held no easy answers proved very much harder. But that was the conclusion that conscience and experience forced on some of the tradition's most thoughtful members.

15

Destiny

The American experience suggests that religious movements that denude themselves of an extensive past often compensate by providing themselves an extensive future. That certainly was the case for early pentecostals. First-generation converts took pride in their lack of substantial continuity with the historic Christian tradition. In the first book-length survey of the revival's origins, published in 1916, Bennett F. Lawrence boasted that saints made no "serious effort" to trace a historical connection to the primitive church precisely because they did not need one. "The Pentecostal Movement has no such history; it leaps the intervening years crying, 'BACK TO PENTECOST!'"[1] That was the key. The absence of roots, or at least roots in the previous 1,800 years, left the revival free to imagine a future as vast in scope as it was glorious in complexity.

This final chapter moves from principles to implementations. It begins by looking at the formal structure of ideas that informed pentecostals' view of their own and the world's destiny. Radical evangelicals, especially the higher life fundamentalists among them, commonly called that structure "dispensational premillennialism." Pentecostals both presupposed and altered the classic formulation of this eschatological worldview, though in their hands it acquired a new name: "latter rain covenant." The rest of the chapter then seeks to examine the effects of latter rain thinking on daily life. One was a sense of doom just ahead, especially for those who discounted the full gospel message. But another, simultaneous, effect was an exhilarating sense of hope, especially for those who embraced the full gospel message. And this hope prompted saints to a frenzy of expansionist activity.

As before, the old tensions reappear. At first glance pentecostals' view of the future seems overwhelmingly primitivist. The latter rain covenant flowed from otherworldly sources of authority, as did the feelings of doom and hope that it inspired. But when saints got down to the hard business of figuring out exactly how they themselves fit into this grand design, the practical and very human desire to stake out a place for themselves came into play. In a

251

score of ways converts exhibited invincible confidence in their own prospects for religious and perhaps even cultural victory in this present world. For a band of "despised nobodies," as one of their leaders put it, it was a handsome destiny indeed.[2]

Latter Rain

From the beginning pentecostals often called their revival the latter rain movement. Sermons, tracts, books, and song lyrics repeatedly spoke of latter rain falling. Outsiders, too, dubbed Holy Ghost folk "latter rain people." By the 1930s the term had fallen into disuse, but in the 1950s an intensely primitivist—and controversial—renewal movement swept southward from the Canadian prairies, significantly calling itself the Latter Rain. To partisans at the turn of the twentieth century, as well as those in the 1950s, it all seemed wondrously miraculous in origin. But nothing had tumbled from the skies. It all had an earthly history.

The origins of the latter rain concept lay in dispensational premillennialism, one of the most powerful popular intellectual traditions of the late nineteenth century. Several versions of dispensational premillennialism circulated through radical evangelical circles on both sides of the Atlantic. The most common one—especially favored by American higher life fundamentalists—divided human history into seven eras or "dispensations" in which God related to human beings according to distinct sets of rules. The rules were not arbitrary but defined by human responses to God's overtures. Those dispensations typically received the names of Innocency (prefallen Adam), Conscience (fallen Adam), Human Government (Noah), Promise (Abraham), Law (Moses), Grace (Earthly Christ), Kingdom (Heavenly Christ).[3] But things grew complicated when theorists tried to figure out where established Christianity fit into this scheme. Most higher life writers maintained that a "Great Parenthesis," roughly equaling the history of the institutional church, had wedged itself between the dispensation of Grace and the dispensation of the Kingdom. (The Great Parenthesis earned that sobriquet because it resulted from the Jews' free, hence unforeseeable, rejection of Jesus.) The Great Parenthesis meant, among other things, that the Holy Spirit's gifts, initially bestowed on the Day of Pentecost, had terminated with the end of the dispensation of Grace in the early second century. Since God Himself had abolished those supernatural gifts, their reappearance in the twentieth century betokened a human invention at best, a Satanic counterfeit at worst. Of course pentecostals would challenge this conclusion, but that story lies ahead.

For dispensational premillennialists the same logic that structured the past also structured the future. They taught that the Lord was about to return for His saints, unheralded, as a thief in the night. In that moment—in the twinkling of an eye, they said—Christ would literally take His saints from the earth so they would not have to endure the seven years of Tribulation preceding the Battle of Armageddon. They called this event the Rapture or the Blessed Hope. At the height of the Battle of Armageddon the Lord would return to earth with His saints, bind the forces of evil, then rule with His saints throughout the Millennial (or Kingdom) age. At the close of the Millennium the Lord would judge all humans, cast evildoers into the Lake of Fire, and rule forever with the redeemed in the New Heavens and New Earth.

Pentecostals assumed the basic framework of dispensational premillennialism but modified it in three ways. The first modification entailed the flagrantly invidious claim that only Holy Spirit–baptized believers would be taken up in the Rapture. Other Christians might escape hell but they would not escape the persecutions of the Tribulation era. One does not have to be especially cynical to suspect that some powerful sociological motivations were implicit here: in the end pentecostals would be rewarded but their evangelical rivals would not. Still, a number of scriptural warrants for restricting the Rapture to saints came to hand. Both 2 Corinthians 1:22 and Ephesians 4:30 suggested that only those who had been specially sealed by the Holy Spirit qualified as Christ's bride. "Those that are not ready at the rapture will be left to go through the awful tribulation that is coming upon the earth," Azusa founder William J. Seymour warned.[4] Believers' conviction that they alone would escape the Tribulation also found support in the mysterious reference to the "Man-Child" in Revelation 12:5, which they took to refer to themselves.[5]

A second modification involved the conviction that Christ would not return for his bride until all the world had heard the *full* gospel message of salvation, healing, baptism (evidenced by tongues), and the Lord's return. Like many premillennialists, pentecostals proved inconsistent on this score. Sometimes they talked as if the Lord might return as a thief in the night regardless of their efforts,[6] sometimes they suggested the Lord would return when enough people wanted him to,[7] and sometimes they succumbed to the temptation to set specific dates for his return.[8] Typically, however, zealots insisted that the wheels of history would not grind to a halt until, as a writer for the tiny Pentecostal Church of God phrased it, the "gospel harvest" had been readied by the "proclamation of the message of preparation to all the world."[9] In this case the "message of preparation" did not mean the old-fashioned gospel of salvation by repentance and faith in Jesus Christ, but the full gospel message, including supernatural signs and wonders. No insider could have missed the true import of the title of the premier pentecostal missionary organ of the era: *Full Gospel Missionary Herald*. Or as Elmer K. Fisher, the pastor of Los Angeles's Upper Room Mission urged, in these End Times ordinary preaching no longer proved effective. The only kind of preaching that could establish the Lord's Kingdom worldwide, and thus bring back the King, was the full gospel message known and preached only by pentecostals.[10]

The third and by far most important modification of the dispensational scheme entailed a dramatic reconception of the period running from the Day of Pentecost to the present. As noted, dispensationalists called that era the Great Parenthesis because it represented an *interruption* of the divine plan for history. Pentecostals, in contrast, called that same period the Age of the Holy Spirit. They reasoned that it represented not an interruption but a *fulfillment* of the divine plan for history, particularly in its beginning and ending periods.[11] Inspired by the early and latter rain (or early and latter harvest) metaphors in Deuteronomy 11:14, Joel 2:23, and James 5:7, Holy Ghost folk dubbed the miraculous events that took place on the Day of Pentecost the "early rain," and the ones that took place in their own time the "latter rain." The relative absence of miraculous gifts between the second and the twentieth centuries did not mean that God had withdrawn them, as other dispensationalists contended. Rather it only meant that the church's apostasy and disobedience had rendered them unusable for those who were spiritually unfit.[12]

The rationale for this new rendering of history seemed self-evident in the pages of Scripture, at least if one read Scripture through the lens of restorationist literalism. In both the Old and New Testaments, pentecostals held, the Lord had promised to manifest His power first in an early or former rain to prepare the soil for planting, then again in a late or latter rain to prepare the crops for harvest. In the first sustained exposition of Holy Ghost theology, published in 1907, George Floyd Taylor explained that the land of Palestine received "two special rains each year," one in the early spring, enabling the seeds to sprout, and another just before harvest in the fall, enabling the grain to "mature and mellow." Since the Lord had designed Palestine to serve as a "miniature world in itself," its meteorological pattern would be spiritually replicated in the "church at large." Taylor allowed that the latter rain had been "foreshadowed" in the Protestant Reformation, and the holiness revivals of the 1890s qualified as "preliminary showers."[13] But the current movement marked the beginning of the full deluge. An unnamed writer for the Azusa *Apostolic Faith* said it as clearly as anyone. "[The Lord] gave the former rain moderately at Pentecost, and He is going to send upon us in these last days the former and latter rain. There are greater things to be done in these last days of the Holy Ghost."[14]

But how did pentecostals know that *their* revival equaled the true latter rain, the one the theory called for? There had been other white-hot evangelical stirrings in the recent past. What made this one different?

In their hearts saints probably never entertained a moment's doubt about it, but to combat skeptics they had to come up with a reasonable defense. The answers commonly given included the return of the Jews to Palestine, the apostasy of the mainline denominations, ominous political turns like the rise of Bolshevism, growing disobedience to parents, the increase of natural calamities, and the surge of inexplicable astral phenomena (including a perfect rainbow).[15] The 1906 San Francisco earthquake loomed especially large in saints' calculations. California evangelist Frank Ewart noted that in all of "God's great moves nature sympathizes." The natural world convulsed at Sinai and at Calvary and did so again at the Azusa revival in Los Angeles, for in nearby San Francisco an "earthquake of frightful dimensions rocked the physical world."[16] Indeed, the recent incidence of terrifying calamities around the world convinced Rochester Bible Institute teacher Susan A. Duncan that the "dividing line" of history had been crossed and that the church was now entering "the time of the latter rain."[17]

Even so, understanding such social and natural phenomena in this way was more of an afterthought, corroborating documentation at best. The proof, the hard proof, that the current revival betokened the long-predicted latter rain lay elsewhere. To begin with, close students of the Bible knew that miracles marked the beginning and the end of dispensations. "[U]nder identical circumstances God acts identically: His action, in a recurring crisis, cannot deviate from its original perfection," said a British authority on the subject.[18] More important, the kind of miracles that marked the beginning of a dispensation always marked its end. Miraculous gifts of the Holy Ghost had swept the apostolic church, and they were sweeping Holy Spirit–filled churches today. What else could it mean? So when J. W. Welch, an early chairman of the Assemblies of God, witnessed the "glorious manifestations of divine power" in the current revival, he knew that the "last days" had come. Such events proved that "God's time-piece [had] reached the dispensational hour" in which the Lord would "pour out His Spirit in *Latter Rain* significance."[19]

But above all the reappearance of one gift, the gift of tongues, proved to pentecostals that the present revival fulfilled the biblically predicted latter rain. When Rochester's Susan A. Duncan asked, "[How] do I know this is the Latter Rain?," she answered predictably: since tongues was the only sign unique to the Day of Pentecost, its present manifestation showed that the end was near.[20] Influential Oakland editor Carrie Judd Montgomery saw a direct connection between the Day of Pentecost and present events. If tongues introduced the Christian era, she judged, it would be "most natural" to expect tongues to close it.[21] India missionary Minnie F. Abrams similarly avowed that the first two chapters of Acts stood at the "head of this dispensation as beacon lights," demonstrating that it was now possible to receive Holy Spirit baptism with "*The Same Signs that Followed the Apostles.*"[22]

Where did this latter rain concept come from? Historians might reasonably suspect that status motivations played a role, for the scheme secured for pentecostals a pivotal place at the center of God's plan for present and future history. More broadly, the latter rain concept hung thick in the sectarian air pentecostals breathed. For example Mormons, properly and significantly known as Latter-day Saints, had long maintained that they themselves fulfilled biblical latter times prophecies. Though they exercised little if any direct influence on pentecostals, Mormons helped produce the fund of available ideas in the culture. For many years Christian and Missionary Alliance founder A. B. Simpson had been saying that the holiness and divine healing revivals of the late nineteenth and early twentieth centuries betokened the coming of the latter rain. Prominent radical evangelicals like G. Campbell Morgan, A. T. Pierson, and Jesse Penn-Lewis had gone so far as to pinpoint the 1904–1905 Wales revival as the exact fulfillment of the latter rain promised by Joel.[23] Closer home, both John Alexander Dowie's Christian Catholic Apostolic Church in Illinois and Frank W. Sandford's Shiloh movement in Maine also imagined themselves to be direct fulfillments of biblical latter times prophecies. All of this is to say that pentecostals' embrace of the latter rain theory of history required only slight modification of readily available ideas.

To Holy Ghost partisans everything fit together, miraculously so. Given the evidence—calamities, miracles, tongues—no other explanation for current events seemed possible, let alone credible.

Doom

In some ways a sense of imminent catastrophe seemed the most conspicuous result of latter rain thinking. A scarcely definable foreboding of cataclysmic changes soon to come seemed pervasive. In this eerie light life's edges grew sharper and its colors darker. Occurrences that most folks considered ordinary acquired grim meaning.

The sheer ominousness of converts' view of events just ahead immediately arrests our attention. For example the front cover of every copy of the *Everlasting Gospel*, a monthly issued by the quasi-pentecostal healing community in Shiloh, Maine, proclaimed "FOR THE HOUR OF HIS JUDGMENT IS COME . . . THE LAST SOLEMN MESSAGE OF THE AGE . . . 'the day of vengeance of our God.'"[24] And solemn it was too. In the nation's heartland, the Kansas *Apostolic Faith*, edited by Charles F. Parham, the revival's initial theological architect, repeatedly declared that the age of salvation had nearly passed. The "Gospel of the Kingdom [has] spent its force," it warned. "[T]he end draweth nigh . . . [A] reign of terror will ensue."[25] Soon the gutters of the land would splash with blood.[26] Surveying world affairs in the winter of 1916, Memphis pastor L. P. Adams advised his people that the previous year had exceeded all years of human history for the number of wars, earthquakes, famines, pestilence, commotions, and disasters on sea and land. "The background is indeed dark," he warned. "Time is speeding us on, and we stand at the closing of the 6,000 years of the world's history."[27] The passage of weeks darkened Adams's outlook. Six months later he found the prospect of things immediately to come "so tremendously awful before our eyes, that the mind almost staggers."[28] In the midst of the supposedly roaring 1920s, the prominent evangelist William Booth-Clibborn judged that in the preceding decade the human race had witnessed "five different colossal calamities, the greatest each of its kind in all history." Those catastrophes included the world war, the Russian Revolution, global plagues of Spanish flu, worldwide famines, and the earthquake in Kansu, China.[29]

Though the spiritually blind might imagine progress in human affairs, pentecostals perceived deeper forces at work. Students at the Rochester Bible Institute learned, for example, that the present downward course of history would continue, the chasm between the classes and the masses would deepen until nations would burn with the flames of revolution, and science would continue to create weapons accelerating the suicide of the human race.[30] For many years influential periodicals bearing the name *Midnight Cry* streamed from independent presses at both ends of the continent, Seattle and New York City. The same language appeared in England, where the editor of *Confidence* announced that the pentecostal movement sought not only "[t]o bring restoration of the apostolic gifts," but also "[t]o sound the midnight cry."[31]

And then there was the overwhelming feeling of urgency. The very first issue of the Azusa Mission's *Apostolic Faith* said it all: "time is short" (a phrase that would be repeated at least six times in the periodical's pages in the next two years).[32] "But when the trumpet sounds," the mission's leader warned shortly afterward, "it will be too late to prepare."[33] A San Jose, California, evangelist judged the current revival the "last call that the world will receive before He comes."[34] One anonymous zealot stirred a Mississippi meeting by proclaiming, "Jesus is coming," while a cohort shouted out, "Pentecost! Pentecost! Last message! Last Message! Get under the blood! No time to lose!"[35] In the mountains of eastern Tennessee, the second issue of the *Evening Light and Church of God Evangel* trumpeted the same solemn news: "The end is near, and we have no time to parley or reason with the devil."[36]

When World War I swept through Europe the urgency deepened, yet the cessation of fighting in the fall of 1918 brought no lessening of saints' premonition of the nearness of the End. Just days after the signing of the armistice, the *Christian Evangel,* published in the Ozarks, grimly warned that the "real tug of war for the nations . . . is still to come . . . The night cometh when no man can work."[37] In pentecostals' eyes even technology heralded the imminent closing of history. Writing about 1910, evangelist Florence L. Burpee suspected that steam cars and automobiles represented the "chariots" foretold by the prophet Nehemiah as he looked toward the climax of history.[38]

With the nations stumbling toward Armageddon, it is hardly surprising that pentecostals resorted to martial rhetoric to describe their present and future relations with the outside world. A sampling of letters posted to periodical editors reveals deep-seated attitudes: "We are still on the firing line for God . . . in Norwich, Kansas";[39] "This leaves us still in the battle at Seymour";[40] "All the artillery of hell was turned on us."[41] For some, the crisis of the times elicited grim determination: "We are flying our colors and are still in the battle."[42] Hawaii missionaries "H. M. Turney and wife" dutifully reported that they had "opened fire upon the enemy" as soon as they arrived on the island.[43] Still others took the long view. Charles Parham's *Apostolic Faith* advertised their annual convocation in Baxter Springs, Kansas, as a "gathering of the battle scarred heroes of the cross." No wonder they were battle scarred. What the world needed, the paper declared, was men who could "wield the jaw bone and smite the enemies of the cross."[44] Not to be outdone, the 1920 convocation of the black United Holy Church noted that in the preceding year that body had been "victorious in every battle"—yet warned that there was "still much land to be taken, and greater victories to be won."[45] Even Quaker pentecostals took up arms, albeit verbal ones. "[T]he 'sham battle' is over, the real fight is on," wrote one.[46] Against a background of "sharp cannonading," "frequent skirmishes," and "heavy siege[s]," Levi Lupton described his evangelistic forays in language that would have stirred the troops on San Juan Hill.[47]

This military rhetoric undoubtedly flowed from several sources. It represented the climate of the age, a time when the memory of bloody Civil War battles remained fresh enough that delegates to the 1912 Progressive Party nominating convention could sing "Onward Christian Soldiers" and "Battle Hymn of the Republic," bandannas waving. It represented the very real verbal and physical harassment that early pentecostals endured, even if they brought a good measure of it on themselves. And it represented the stock vocabulary of the radical evangelical tradition as a whole. But above all it represented saints' abiding sense of imminent worldwide cataclysm.

Finally, we should note pentecostals' special fascination with the torments of hellfire soon to come—for others. Here we must be careful. There was nothing new about Christians' conjuring up lurid visions of the fate of the lost, and pentecostals' radical evangelical parents certainly contributed their fair share to that fiery imagery. Still, most Holy Ghost writers (with several important exceptions)[48] found this line of speculation especially congenial and applied it to the unredeemed with unflinching ferocity. Many went out of their way to highlight the inevitability of eternal punishment for all non-Christians—by which they really meant all nonevangelical Protestants—in their official statements of faith.[49] Some actually listed it as a doctrine equal in importance to salvation and Holy Spirit baptism.[50] More striking than the official statements, however, were the visions of hell that peppered the early periodicals' pages. The out-of-body experience of Effie Cooper proved typical. "As I looked, oh, horror of horrors, there was an ocean of fire . . . It was so hot there was a vapor looking a little like steam, everywhere. Oh, the misery and suffering. Words utterly fail me."[51] A writer for Portland's *Apostolic Faith*, likely matriarch Florence Crawford herself, similarly described a vision in which she saw a "great lake of fire. O, it was awful! . . . The flames would lap up and fork over. The Lord showed me it was an everlasting lake of fire that would burn with brimstone forever and ever."[52]

The palpable reality of hell flowed from pentecostals' enduring ability to reinforce ideology with ecstasy. Simply put, visions, buttressed with Scripture, functioned as polemical weapons in themselves. Consider Effie Cooper's and Florence Crawford's experiences noted above. For Cooper the out-of-body experience focused on saints' perceived enemies, the mainline preachers, who told their hearers "how joyful heaven is" but never remembered to tell them "how awful hell is."[53] For Crawford the vision targeted rival evangelists who went around deluding the people with the heresy of "'[n]ohellism.'"[54] To be sure, Holy Spirit–filled saints poured an exceptional share of their resources into the evangelization of the lost. But damnation for the recalcitrant never moved very far from the center of their attention either. Speaking particularly of the zealots who joined the quasi-pentecostal community at Shiloh, Maine, Shirley Nelson writes that they found it "easier to cast out demons than learn to live with them."[55] So too other saints sometimes found it easier to consign their real and imagined adversaries to everlasting damnation than to learn to live with them.

And who should be surprised? To pentecostals, anyone with a clear eye and an open mind could see that the world was hurtling toward its doom. Convinced that "a terrific battle" engaged "the hosts of the Almighty, and Satan and the hosts of evil,"[56] saints looked for the imminent fiery end of history with as much certainty as most folk looked for the daily rising and setting of the sun.

Hope

Aimee McPherson probably said more than she realized when she told a reporter, "I only remember the hours when the sun shines."[57] So it was that pentecostals' rhetoric of doom, though real, readily blended into a larger language of hope. If saints lived on the "lip of eternity," as one historian writes, it was an eternity filled with prospects of everlasting new life.[58]

To begin with, Holy Ghost folk knew that Christ would soon reign and they would reign with Him. It is hard to imagine a message better suited to inspire the faithful. "This is a world-wide revival, the last Pentecostal revival to bring our Jesus," proclaimed the premier issue of the Azusa Mission's *Apostolic Faith*. Taken by itself that proclamation might suggest either foreboding or triumphalism. But the next sentence revealed an entirely different sensibility: "The church is taking her last march to meet her beloved."[59] If the pentecostal revival betokened the end of times, it also betokened "the greatest miracle the world has ever seen."[60] A mission in Akron, Ohio, excitedly reported that the "burden of everyone that has received their personal Pentecost is, *'Jesus is coming soon.'*"[61] The Massachusetts weekly *Word and Work* likewise proclaimed that its sole purpose was to spread the "Good News of the Soon Coming of our Lord"—not, it is worth noting, the historic Good News of salvation in Christ, but the Good News of the imminent end of history.[62]

The promise of the Rapture particularly fired saints' imagination. Letter writers repeatedly spoke of their anticipation of being caught up to "meet the Lord in the air."[63] For many the expectation that they literally would be physically whisked off the face of the earth remained an ever-present prospect. No one captured that electric excitement better than the Azusa leader William J. Seymour: "The time is short when our blessed Jesus shall return to this earth, and snatch away His waiting bride."[64] Evangelist Elizabeth Sisson, a delegate to the organizing meeting of the Assemblies of God in 1914, actually left instructions at home about what should be done with her personal effects lest she be "caught up" in the Rapture while away.[65] Basking in the afterglow of the Eighth Annual Convention of the Apostolic Faith Assembly in Indianapolis, Elder G. T. Haywood, leader of that tiny interracial sect, speculated that its next convention might well be held in the New Jerusalem. "Who can tell?"[66] Indeed the 1912 encampment of the Churches of God in Christ in Eureka Springs, Arkansas, could barely proceed for the intensity of the anticipation that they were about "to be caught up to meet Jesus in the air."[67] Enthusiasts routinely closed letters, "Yours waiting for the wedding in the air,"[68] or "Yours in the Coming One."[69] In such a context one can almost feel the same exhilaration one missionary felt as he burst forth with the realization that "we, ourselves, shall never see the grave!"[70] Sometimes anticipation grew so intense it encroached on the fantastic. One preacher looked forward to flying past the atmospheric heaven, past the starry heaven, and on into the "heaven of heavens—the place where God is."[71] What such dreams may have lacked in theological orthodoxy they gained in potency to inspire.

The early periodicals conveyed a sense of thrilling events unfolding nearly too fast to report, like a television newsroom on election night. Under the banner, "Italians and Indians Receive the Holy Ghost," the *Apostolic Faith* announced—one can almost hear the wire service machines clattering in the background—"reports are coming in from nearly every quarter of the globe of how the latter rain is falling."[72] With this framework, social marginality, real or perceived, served less as a limitation than a springboard for action. "However little is our band, and however ignorant and simple are we," declared Mok Lai Chi, pastor of the Apostolic Faith Mission in Hong Kong, "the Lord has been pleased to set us apart, one after another, to go forth proclaiming His soon coming."[73] At the tiny Household of God mission in Pasadena, California, the leader breathlessly told of emissaries—endowed, not incidentally, with the power to raise the dead—fanning out to take the word to Oakland, to Palestine, to India. The Lord's return, he added almost glumly, would be delayed until those distant places had heard the pentecostal message.[74]

Given all that needed to be accomplished, time counted. That plain fact required rigorous husbanding of one's time in order to focus on the task at hand. Scurrying from one mission to another up and down the California coast, evangelist Frank Bartleman dashed off a note to himself: "My time is not my own . . . 'The King's business requires haste.'"[75] So it was everywhere. Overseer A. J. Tomlinson boasted that he worked tirelessly, "at late hours of the night while the millions . . . were taking their rest." He had no choice. "An unseen impelling" had "pressed it" on him.[76] Oral tradition held that Tomlinson habitually ran, not walked, home for lunch just in order to save time.[77] Given the ripeness of the harvest, Tomlinson knew that he "dare[d] not falter" before the task at hand.[78] Indeed a great part of pentecostals' real or perceived asceticism was not asceticism at all but a conviction that conventional habits consumed moments better spent elsewhere. Soda water and chewing gum drew a rebuke from Assemblies of God chairman E. N. Bell, not because they were intrinsically wrong, but because they squandered God's money and wasted precious minutes, turning a saint into a "soda fountain bum or a gum sot."[79]

How then should Holy Spirit–filled Christians spend their time? The answer seemed obvious. "Thrust in now," the Quaker evangelist Levi Lupton exhorted. "First and last and all the time," the true Christian must "bend to the one end—the salvation of men and the hastening of the Lord's return."[80] The problem with the kind of religion that passed itself off for real Christianity in most places, charged Missouri pastor Howard Goss, was that it represented a "defeatist religion." Its message was: "Just do the best you can, and hope for the best after death."[81] Saints wanted none of that. "I am still on the war path," one convert asserted, "with the eternal glow and GO in my soul."[82] In context, the "GO" seemed almost more important than the "glow." Saints were God's agents, and since God remained in charge, they had nothing to lose. As a later era would say, they could afford to go for broke. Indeed they could afford to do nothing else.

Expansionism

These points bring us finally to expansionism, a cluster of actual and desired practices that defined a great deal of daily life.

Here we must be cautious. From time to time converts sang requiem notes. Everyone knew that many brothers and sisters had grown cold and lost their first love. A few had fallen by the wayside altogether. When Chicago fire-eater William H. Durham visited the Los Angeles missions in 1911, he recorded "with grief" that some were "departing from the first order of things."[83] The situation only seemed to grow worse as the years wore on. By 1918 ordinary folks were beginning to remember the "good old camp meeting times of ten years ago . . . when there were hungry souls praying through to God."[84] Those were the words of Brother Pittman, otherwise forgotten by history, writing to the *Pentecostal Holiness Advocate* just after the war to express his foreboding. Pittman was not alone. Soon a cottage industry was born devoted to excoriating the "coldness and indifference among God's baptized saints."[85] Pastor John G. Lake of Houston even wondered whether they were about to witness the "dying of Pentecost as other lesser revelations of God have come to the world, fluttered and sputtered for a few years, and then disappeared?"[86] Looking back from the vantage point of 1927, historian Frank Bartleman growled that the movement looked "like the little chicken who has dropped the worm. It is still running and the other chickens are chasing it. But the worm is gone. We have lost the vision."[87] By 1932 things seemed even worse. New York City pastor Marie Brown lamented that Holy Ghost churches now seemed hardly different from other Protestant churches. Typically spending only five or ten minutes at the altar, and acting as if the Holy Spirit were a "*toy* to be amused with," Brown judged that her confederates had lapsed into "Sleepy Virgin time."[88]

The great irony, of course, was that none of these comments was meant to be taken literally. Seriously yes, literally no. All represented bugle blasts calling the troops to new triumphs. In their hearts pentecostals knew that the Lord had chosen them and them alone to lead a vast movement of global spiritual conquest. What Paul Varg said of evangelical missionaries to China applied to early pentecostals too: "All felt the lure of playing life's role on the world stage."[89] No storefront meeting place seemed too small or too impoverished to send out missionaries to all parts of the continent, even to all parts of the world. "[T]he blessed work is spreading so rapidly," reported a correspondent for the British *Confidence,* "that I suppose there are few large towns where there are not one or more Missions."[90] Within a year of the Azusa Mission's founding in Los Angeles in 1906, native language pentecostal newspapers were thriving in Norway, Germany, China, Japan, Palestine, and Brazil.[91] By 1909 zealots had planted missions in at least fifty foreign countries.[92] The chapter titles of one of the earliest insider historical narratives recounted the movement's global spread: "The Pentecostal Flame in Canada," "The Pentecostal Outpouring in the British Isles," "The Work in Norway and Denmark," "Revival in Russia and Other European Countries," "Showers of Latter Rain in India," "Signs Following in China and Japan," "A Great Pentecostal Outpouring in Central Africa," "The Beginning of a Great Work in Egypt," "The Rain Falls in South America," "God's Visitation in Venezuela."[93]

By any reasonable measure of such things, the rhetoric of global conquest vastly outstripped the reality. But the rhetoric was significant. As early as 1901 a Harvard-trained stalwart at the tiny Shiloh compound in Maine boasted that Shiloh stood as a great "enginery for belting the earth" with "THE TRUTH."[94] Apparently few if any of Charles Parham's Topeka Bible school students carried the pentecostal message overseas, yet he declared that his institution's purpose was to "fit men and women to go to the ends of the earth to preach."[95] Within three years of the Los Angeles revival pentecostal speakers were exulting about the way that the movement had already "circled the globe."[96] One asserted that never in history "did a revival of God fly round the world as this one has."[97] Another impetuously judged that the full gospel message had "stirred the religious world from center to circumference."[98]

This vision, global in aspiration if not in fulfillment, involved multiple forms of triumphalism—including claims of priority of origin, size, and influence. Soon local pentecostal groups all over the country fell into the habit of describing their convocations as the first or the biggest or the best of its kind.[99] Many routinely hailed their local meetings as national or international in scope.[100] Hyperbole reigned. "Mammoth," "immense," and "mighty" became the adjectives of choice to describe everything saints set out to do.[101] The Holy Spirit never moved imperceptibly or slightly but always, it seemed, in a "mighty outpouring"[102] or in a "cyclonic manifestation"[103] or in "mighty shocks of power."[104] A scant twenty-nine months after the first missionaries departed American shores, saints in India started laying plans for a "World's Pentecostal Conference."[105] In 1920 the Chicago-based *Pentecostal Herald* greeted its readers with a six-inch headline on the front page, "WORLD'S GREATEST PENTECOSTAL CONVOCATION: A Nation Wide Union Revival Meeting: Evangelists with World-Wide Reputation will speak."[106] A 1922 unity meeting in St. Louis received billing as "THE GREATEST GATHERING SINCE THE DAYS OF THE APOSTLES."[107] One suspects that few were impressed. They had heard it all before.

From their radical evangelical forebears pentecostals inherited and amplified a variety of techniques for sustaining this kind of global consciousness. One was prayer chains, which bade churches everywhere to pray for the revival's success at exactly the same time of the day and week, preferably from 10:00 A.M. to 3:00 P.M. each Thursday.[108] The inconvenience and unreliability of electronic communication in the early twentieth century may have actually enhanced rather than minimized the sense of world solidarity by forcing partisans to rely on spiritual (and therefore unlimited) linkages of prayer. Zealots also sustained global consciousness through mail networks. The Minute Book of the oldest pentecostal work in Britain, the Church of God in the remote village of Kilsyth, Scotland, reveals a world in itself. The record for December 28, 1908, a page taken almost at random, registered contributions posted to evangelist Levi Lupton in the United States, to missionary Mrs. Cowan in Japan, to orphanage director Pandita Ramabai in India, and to the Quarrier Homes orphanage nearby.[109]

Periodicals constituted by far the most important technique for sustaining national and world consciousness. They created the impression that pentecostals were triumphing everywhere. Holy Ghost papers routinely published long lists of approved—and sometimes disapproved—evangelists, churches, camps, books, and even other periodicals.[110] The papers typically set aside a column or two, or even several pages, for reports from pentecostal outstations in faraway places. Typical was the first page of the January 1909 issue of Portland, Oregon's *Apostolic Faith,* which carried announcements of the activities of fire-baptized workers and missionaries in China, Egypt, Germany, Holland, India, Ireland, New Zealand, Scotland, Sweden, Syria, and the Transvaal—along with letters from missions in various parts of the United States serving non-English speaking constituencies (such as the Finnish mission in San Jose).[111] These accounts normally highlighted the rapid progress of the work, though occasionally admitting delays in the face of the "dense ignorance and superstition of the masses."[112] Correspondents' single-minded focus on the scorecard of converts won, or almost won, helped focus readers' attention on the spiritual needs of the world at large.

This expansionist fervor grew from several sources. One, of course, involved the long tradition of Christian missions, rooted in the Great Commission and other biblical injunctions to spread the Gospel. For some, a sense of social marginality undoubtedly played a role too. Though this mood waxed and waned, in its full moon phase it tempted saints to translate perceptions of immediate misfortune into dreams of long-range fortune. The expansionist momentum in pentecostals' ecstatic experiences also surfaced in testimony accounts of the baptism event. As noted, those accounts sometimes indicated that the Lord had lifted newborn saints into the heavenlies, and from that vantage point they could survey the terrible lostness of the heathen world. Above all, the sense of inevitable global triumph emerged from the feeling of chosenness, the sense that the Holy Spirit had elected to reside within—not metaphorically, but literally, physically within—the believer's human body. When writers on both sides of the Atlantic could, without a trace of irony, describe themselves as "hand-picked fruit,"[113] or as "diamonds" in the Lord's crown,[114] or as "pure gold,"[115] or as the "elite of the Universe,"[116] outsiders knew it was time to seek cover. In one sense pentecostals proved as parochial as the next person, for the world they visualized in experiences of this sort was a world of their own construction. But the more important point is that they soared beyond their immediate self-interests to embrace peoples and cultures not their own.

And who should be surprised? Was not the earth theirs for the taking? Whatever else the pentecostal message meant, it meant Good News—wanted or not—for the rest of humankind. Memphis pastor L. P. Adams captured the joyousness of those prospects with brilliant succinctness. Like many perfectionist Christians before him, Adams felt certain that Scripture proved "our intimate and absolute union with . . . Christ." Unlike many perfectionist Christians, however, he also felt certain that the cash value of that absolute union was that "we shall be like Him"—not far off in the distant future, "but here, and now, as He is, so are we in this world."[117] If that conviction promised the supernatural empowerment of Holy Spirit–filled humans, it also promised that the future belonged to them. A glorious destiny it was, especially for Americans accustomed to thinking expansively.

Epilogue

In this book I have tried to rescue early pentecostals from the shadowy fate that E. P. Thompson once called (in another context) "the enormous condescension of posterity."[1] Too often modern interpreters have looked at the Holy Ghost revival and gone away shaking their heads, wondering how something so shamelessly regressive could have flourished in the sunlit progressivism of the early twentieth century. I have argued, in contrast, that saints seized a timeless formula, as old as the New Testament story of Mary and Martha, and brilliantly put it to modern use.

Early pentecostals' ability to balance the most eye-popping features of the supernatural with the most chest-thumping features of the natural, and to do so without admitting it, gave them a recognizable profile in early-twentieth-century America. To be sure, many Christian groups intimated and sometimes even paralleled those tendencies, but pentecostals made them as starkly explicit as any. Still, the dynamics typically were different. For the others, very often, the modern problem was to find room for the supernatural in a world that seemed adequately explained in alternate ways. For saints, tutored by an ahistorical theology and swept by waves of religious ecstasy, the modern problem was the reverse. It was to distance themselves from the supernatural so that life could go on in a reasonable normal way. But distance themselves they did. And they did it by arming themselves with the conviction that God's Holy Spirit, now living inside their very bodies, made them not only conquerors, but invincible conquerors of the everyday world.

America has changed dramatically since then, and pentecostals have changed with it, but only superficially. At the end of the twentieth century the creative tension—or creative complementarity—between the primitive and the pragmatic persisted as productively as ever. On one hand the theology and worship patterns that energized the movement's inner life survived largely untouched by the secular culture's lapse into moral and epistemological relativism. Biblical inerrancy and wooden literalism hovered as close to the ground at century's end as they did at the beginning. On the whole the challenges posed by Darwin, Marx, and Freud, not to mention more recent icons of the secular academy, remained firmly outside the horizon of pentecostal consciousness. For many partisans homosexuality—to take one of many indices of accommodation to postmodernity—was not an orientation but a sinful choice, and its acceptance, in the words of one denominational position paper, "sentimental credulity."[2] More significant, the longing for vital manifestations of the supernatural gifts of the Holy Spirit flourished with unabated fervor. Holy Ghost periodicals brimmed with stories of stunning healings and supernatural interventions in daily life. In the late 1990s millions—literally, millions—reportedly flocked to the nonstop revival churning at the Brownsville Assembly of God Church in Pensacola, Florida.[3] If one looked in the right places, miracles continued to dance before believers' eyes as frequently and as wondrously as ever.[4]

At the same time, however, latter day enthusiasts rushed to embrace the therapeutic rewards and technological amenities of late-twentieth-century culture with scarcely a second thought. Though a minority still gathered in storefront missions and avoided the trappings of the good life, the majority, especially the white majority, worshiped in carpeted, climate-controlled buildings indistinguishable from the local Southern Baptist church. Adherents propagated their message with state-of-the-art communications technology. Their magazines showed how the Holy Spirit helped believers adjust to the stresses of life in the passing lane. Once-tiny Bible institutes reinvented themselves as accredited colleges, seminaries, and universities. Pentecostals admired the rich and the powerful. Indeed a fair number *were* the rich and the powerful. Presidential candidates of a Republican stripe usually found a warm welcome in precincts thick with pentecostal voters. Saints appeared to dress, work, and play on a par with most middle-class Americans. Sometimes it appeared that the only difference between Holy Spirit–filled Christians and mainline Christians was that the former, though late on the scene, built their programs bigger, better, and more conspicuously.[5]

Viewed as a whole, one is struck by how deeply American the pentecostal movement was, first in its primitivist certitude, and second and perhaps more important in its pragmatic effectiveness. In many ways the revival was as American as apple pie—only more so, as the saying goes. One gains a sense of its true cultural paternity by looking, for example, at William R. Hutchison's and Andrew Walls's perceptive studies of the American missionary movement. In their narratives, the tactics that American missions theorists, especially evangelicals, commonly esteemed as products of sound biblical exegesis, Holy Spirit guidance, and good common sense were the very ones that outsiders commonly viewed as characteristically—and often deplorably—American.[6] This point brings us back to the subjects of this book. Pentecostals' legendary ability to strike out for the remotest corners of the globe, and then to build durable ministries on a shoestring when they got there, suggests that they distinguished themselves on the American evangelical landscape not so much by doing new things as by doing old things in a strikingly dynamic way.

Even so, scholars who have made it their business to survey recent pentecostal-charismatic stirrings worldwide have found many of the same tendencies turning up in other settings.[7] One pundit has quipped that the pentecostal wine, fermented in America, and bottled on the mission field, has been uncorked with dazzling success in the Third World. The basic recipe has varied little: the Holy Spirit, though radically supernatural and radically autonomous, *wants* to save, heal, and supply the Holy Spirit-filled Christian's every need. As the historian Joel Carpenter puts it, "Pentecostals can be unblushingly self-interested in their worldly dealings because they know that God wants them to prosper here."[8] In one sense the world-affirming impulse—the expectation that "something *good* is going to happen to you"—seems to stand in tension with the world-denying impulse. But in another, deeper, sense it clearly does not. The otherworldly legitimates the thisworldly. It says that all things are possible for modern-day saints, no less than for the New Testament ones. It is hard to imagine a formula better suited for a civilization wracked with timeless spiritual needs, yet rapidly opening to the unprecedented possibilities of technological and information-age prosperity.

So we come full circle, back to the first generation, back to that effervescent moment of intense creativity in the American heartland in which the radical evangelical dynamic took a particularly powerful form. In that setting the primitive and the pragmatic impulses thrived as scripted roles, identities that Holy Ghost culture inherited, redefined, adapted, and rendered deeply satisfying, each in its own way. The two attitudes flourished precisely because each was invigorated by being yoked to the other. That combination gave saints the joy of knowing God's Holy Spirit on the inside and, at the same time, the tools for flexibly managing the everyday world on the outside. Lest such an achievement make pentecostals seem more ingenious than plain folk ought to be, we might take refuge once again in the words of Lionel Trilling, who reminds us that the "refinement of our historical sense chiefly means that we keep it properly complicated."[9] It would be an injustice to those earnest partisans to flatten out their lives and make them less creative than they really were.

So it turned out that pentecostals transcended one of the fundamental problems that had engaged the entire history of Christian thought and pastoral concern—what we might call the "Mary and Martha" problem: how to negotiate spiritual and material well being at once. Since God's Holy Spirit did everything, Holy Spirit–filled Christians did nothing. But since Holy Spirit–filled Christians did nothing, they were free to do everything. That conviction, as inspiring as it was ironic, gave saints the two greatest goods that mortal existence had to offer: the life beyond in all its fullness, and the life at hand in all its richness. It was heaven below.

Appendix: U.S. Pentecostal Statistics

The most commonly used, though not necessarily most reliable, index of inclusive membership (hereafter adherence) is the annual review published in the *Yearbook of American and Canadian Churches*. The 2000 edition of this work showed 10,997,706 adherents and 47,091 churches for the twenty largest pentecostal groups in the United States,[1] yielding an average of 234 adherents per church. The Assemblies of God (AOG) and the Church of God Christ (COGIC) were by far the largest. In 2000 the former claimed 2,525,812 adherents and 11,937 churches. The latter claimed 5,499,875 adherents and 15,300 churches. These figures yielded an average of 212 and 359 adherents per church, respectively. In May 2000 the AOG web site claimed 29,000,000 additional "members and adherents" in "Assemblies of God organizations around the world." At the same time the COGIC web site affirmed that COGIC ranked as the "second largest pentecostal group in America," adding that its 1997 membership equaled an "estimated eight million." Whether this figure denoted domestic or domestic and international members combined remained unclear. *Yearbook of American and Canadian Churches 2000,* ed. Eileen W. Lindner (Nashville: Abingdon Press, 2000), pp. 339–351, esp. pp. 340, 342.

Not surprisingly, social surveys have consistently yielded lower (sometimes dramatically lower) figures than denominational self-reports. For example, random telephone sampling of the adult U.S. population in 1990 by the National Survey of Religious Identification, sponsored by the Graduate School of the City University of New York, showed 4,083,000 adherents for the main pentecostal bodies.[2] However the survey may have missed many responders who identified simply as Protestant or "Born Again." Barry A. Kosmin and Seymour P. Lachman, *One Nation under God: Religion in Contemporary American Society* (New York: Harmony Books, 1993), pp. 15–16, 295. Though the sample, involving 113,000 households, made it the largest religion survey since the last U.S. Religious Census in 1936, questions have been raised about the study's statistical value. For one critique and the reply of those involved, see Robert S. Ellwood and Donald E. Miller, "Questions Regarding the CUNY National Survey of Religious Identification," *Journal for the Scientific Study of Religion,* 31 (1992): 94–96, and Barry A. Kosmin and Seymour P. Lachman, "Reply to Comments on the CUNY National Survey of Religious Identification (NSRI)," pp. 97–99.

A survey of 4,001 adult Americans conducted spring 1992 by the Survey Research Center of the University of Akron indicated that 3.6 percent of the interviewees belonged to pentecostal bodies. If we assume a U.S. population of 250 million in 1990 (*Statistical Abstract of the United States: 1999,* p. 868), we derive about 9 million pentecostal adherents, comprising 6,250,000 whites and 2,750,000 blacks. Alternately 4.7 percent or 11,750,000 self-identified as pentecostals, while another 6.6 percent or 16,5000,000 self-identified as charismatics. Curiously about a third who belonged to pentecostal bodies did not self-identify as pentecostal, while many who did self-identify as pentecostal did not belong to pentecostal bodies. Corwin E. Smidt, Lyman A. Kellstedt, John C. Green, and James L. Guth, "The Spirit-Filled Movements in Contemporary America: A Survey Perspective," in *Pentecostal Currents in American Protestantism,* ed. Edith L. Blumhofer, Russell P. Spittler, and Grant Wacker (Urbana: University of Illinois Press, 1999), chap. 6, esp. pp. 113–116.

The University of North Carolina at Chapel Hill *Religious Identity and Influence Survey 1996* was smaller in scope but more detailed than the other two surveys. It showed that 1.7 percent of 2,591 individuals, a statistically random sample of the U.S. population, belonged to historically pentecostal denominations, and another 4.8 percent of the sample self-identified as charismatics. Assuming a U.S. population of 261,000,000 in 1994, the UNC study thus suggested 4,437,000 pentecostal and 12,528,000 charismatic adherents (less 10–11 percent for overlapping of categories). Christian Smith, *Christian America? What Evangelicals Really Want* (Berkeley: University of California Press, 2000), pp. 16–17, 231. Note that the methods used to tabulate pentecostals and charismatics differed, the former being defined by membership, the latter by self-identification.

Notes

Abbreviations

AGUK   Assemblies of God Archives, Mattersey Hall, U.K.

AOG   Flower Pentecostal Heritage Center, Assemblies of God, Springfield, Mo.

ATS   Hannah Whitall Smith Collection, Asbury Theological Seminary, Wilmore, Ky.

COG   Hal Bernard Dixon Jr. Pentecostal Research Center, Church of God, Cleveland, Tenn.

DPCM   *Dictionary of Pentecostal and Charismatic Movements,* ed. Stanley M. Burgess and Gary B. McGee (Grand Rapids: Zondervan Publishing House, 1988).

FTS   DuPlessis Center, Fuller Theological Seminary, Pasadena, Calif.

WCT   Professor William C. Turner private collection, Duke Divinity School.

For the most part the following endnotes specify only directly quoted or cited primary texts. A few of the sources noted—mostly newspapers—come from photocopy collections that lack page numbers. Since there is no practical way to recover them from the originals, for these sources I have written "pna" (page not available) followed by the collection used. For economy, I have omitted beginning and closing ellipses for quoted sentence fragments, though of course scrupulously retaining ellipses for elisions within quotations. In lieu of additional appendices, I have placed most quantitative and tabulated research materials with the Assemblies of God's Flower Pentecostal Heritage Center, which is open to other researchers.

Introduction

1. Arthur T. Pierson, *Forward Movements of the Last Half-Century* (New York: Garland Publishing, 1984, original 1905).
2. Charles Fox Parham, in *Apostolic Faith* [Kans.], April 1925, p. 9.
3. *Oakland Tribune,* December 2, 1889, and *San Francisco Examiner,* January 11, 1890, quoted in Wayne E. Warner, *The Woman Evangelist: The Life and Times of Charismatic Evangelist Maria B. Woodworth-Etter* (Metuchen, N.J.: Scarecrow Press, 1986), pp. 79, 93. For one of numerous sources describing unleashed emotions in the most radical of radical evangelical meetings, see C. B. Jernigan, *Pioneer Days of the Holiness Movement in the Southwest* (Kansas City, Mo.: Pentecostal Nazarene Publishing House, 1919), pp. 151–157.
4. For the conversionist strain in American evangelicalism, see Harry S. Stout, *The Di-*

vine Dramatist: George Whitefield and the Rise of Modern Evangelicalism (Grand Rapids: William B. Eerdmans Publishing Co., 1991), esp. chap. 11; Christine Leigh Heyrman, *Southern Cross: The Beginnings of the Bible Belt* (Chapel Hill: University of North Carolina Press, 1997), esp. Prologue.

5. Donald W. Dayton, *Theological Roots of Pentecostalism* (Grand Rapids: Zondervan Publishing House, 1987), esp. chaps. 3–4; Melvin Dieter, *The Holiness Revival of the Nineteenth Century* (Metuchen, N.J.: Scarecrow Press, 1980).

6. Edith Lydia Waldvogel, "The 'Overcoming Life': A Study in The Reformed Evangelical Origins of Pentecostalism," Ph.D. diss., Harvard University, 1977.

7. Ibid.; Reuben A. Torrey, *What the Bible Teaches* (New York: Fleming Revell, 1898), p. 272.

8. Timothy L. Smith, "Righteousness and Hope: Christian Holiness and the Millennial Vision in America," *American Quarterly,* 31 (1979): 21–45. For an example of the blending of purity and power themes at the grass roots, see the *Constitution and By-Laws and Minutes of the First Session of the North Carolina Holiness Convention* (Goldsboro, N.C.: Nash Brothers, 1899), p. 1: "[We] therefore . . . [affirm] entire sanctification, which is an instantaneous work of grace . . . whereby inbred sin is purged from the believer's heart, and he is endued with power by the baptism of the Holy Ghost and fire."

9. Dayton, *Theological Roots of Pentecostalism,* chap. 5; Robert Bruce Mullin, *Miracles and the Modern Religious Imagination* (New Haven: Yale University Press, 1996), chap. 4; Grant Wacker, "Caring and Curing: The Pentecostal Tradition," in *Caring and Curing: Health and Medicine in the Western Faith Traditions,* ed. Ronald L. Numbers and Darryl W. Amundsen (Baltimore: The Johns Hopkins University Press, reissued 1998, original 1986), pp. 514–538, 579–580.

10. Dayton, *Theological Roots of Pentecostalism,* chap. 6; Timothy P. Weber, *Living in the Shadow of the Second Coming* (New York: Oxford University Press, 1979), chaps. 1–2.

11. Different parts of the institutional infrastructure that undergirded the radical evangelical and then pentecostal traditions are described in all of the secondary works cited above, and are well summarized in Robert Mapes Anderson, *Vision of the Disinherited: The Making of American Pentecostalism* (New York: Oxford University Press, 1979), chap. 2; George M. Marsden, *Fundamentalism and American Culture: The Shaping of Twentieth-Century Evangelicalism, 1870–1925* (New York: Oxford University Press, 1980), esp. chaps. 8 and 11.

12. See, for example, the multiple personal connections revealed in William H. Durham's account of his transcontinental evangelistic travels in *Missionary World,* April 1906, p. 8.

13. Edith L. Blumhofer, *Restoring the Faith: The Assemblies of God, Pentecostalism, and American Culture* (Urbana: University of Illinois Press, 1993), throughout but esp. pp. 4–5, 12–15; Grant Wacker, "Playing for Keeps: The Primitivist Impulse in Early Pentecostalism," in *The American Quest for the Primitive Church,* ed. Richard T. Hughes (Urbana: University of Illinois Press, 1988), pp. 196–219.

14. Iain MacRobert, *The Black Roots and White Racism of Early Pentecostalism in the USA* (London: Macmillan, 1988), chap. 2, esp. p. 31; Cheryl J. Sanders, *Saints in Exile: The Holiness-Pentecostal Experience in African American Religion and Culture* (New York: Oxford University Press, 1996), pp. 6–9.

15. R. Laurence Moore, "Insiders and Outsiders in American Historical Narrative and American History" (1982), in *Religion and American History: A Reader,* ed. Jon

Butler and Harry S. Stout (New York: Oxford University Press, 1998), pp. 198–221; Stephen J. Stein, "Religious Innovation at the Edges," in *Perspectives on American Religion and Culture,* ed. Peter W. Williams (Malden, Mass.: Blackwell Publishers, 1999), pp. 22–33.

16. Grant Wacker, "The Holy Spirit and the Spirit of the Age in American Protestantism, 1880–1910," *Journal of American History,* 72 (1985): 45–62.

17. See, for example, Tony Ladd and James Mathisen, *Muscular Christianity: Evangelical Protestants and the Development of American Sport* (Grand Rapids: Baker Books, 1999), chaps. 1–2; James H. Moorhead, *World without End: Mainstream American Protestant Visions of the Last Things, 1880–1925* (Bloomington: Indiana University Press, 1999), esp. chap. 4; T. J. Lears, *No Place of Grace: Antimodernism and the Transformation of American Culture, 1880–1920* (New York: Pantheon Books, 1981).

18. Roger Glenn Robins, "Plainfolk Modernist: The Radical Holiness World of A. J. Tomlinson," Ph.D. diss., Duke University, 1999, part 1.

19. See, for example, B. F. Lawrence, *The Apostolic Faith Restored* (St. Louis: Gospel Publishing House, 1916), chaps. 5–7.

20. *Tongues of Fire,* June 15, 1898, pp. 92–94; James R. Goff, Jr., *Fields White unto Harvest: Charles F. Parham and the Missionary Origins of Pentecostalism* (Fayetteville: University of Arkansas Press, 1988), pp. 72–74.

21. Reliable figures on the movement's size in the early years of the century are hard to come by, to say the least. In 1908, in the first attempt to construct a historical overview, India missionary Max Wood Moorhead estimated 50,000 adherents in the United States alone. The following year Memphis pastor L. P. Adams said that 50,000 had received Holy Spirit baptism (presumably meaning at least that many had affiliated). The next year Arthur S. Booth-Clibborn, a thoughtful and widely traveled early leader, put the figure at 60,000–80,000 fully committed members, plus another 20,000–40,000 active supporters worldwide. In 1912 the Ottawa-based *Good Report* claimed 100,000 adherents. In 1936 the U.S. Bureau of the Census listed 356,329 members for twenty-six known pentecostal sects. Given pentecostals' propensity to worship in homes and nondescript meeting houses, the actual number probably was greater. Moorhead, in *Cloud of Witnesses,* November 1908, p. 16; L. P. Adams, in *Present Truth,* December 1909, p. 1; Booth-Clibborn, in *Confidence,* August 1910, p. 182; *Good Report,* no month (vol. 1, no. 3), 1912, p. 5. Census figures come from Anderson, *Vision of the Disinherited,* p. 117.

22. Gaston Espinosa, "Borderland Religion: Los Angeles and the Origins of the Latino Pentecostal Movement in the U.S., Mexico, and Puerto Rico, 1900–1945," Ph.D. diss., University of California Santa Barbara, 1999, pp. 95–96, and chap. 3.

23. I have briefly traced the genealogy of these and other pentecostal bodies in "Pentecostalism," in *Encyclopedia of the American Religious Experience,* ed. Charles H. Lippy and Peter W. Williams (New York: Scribner's, 1988), vol. 2, pp. 933–945. For a fuller account of the literature, and some discussion of areas of historiographic rethinking, see Augustus Cerillo, Jr., and Grant Wacker, "Bibliography and Historiography of Pentecostalism in the United States," *New International Dictionary of the Pentecostal and Charismatic Movements,* ed. Stanley Burgess (Grand Rapids: Harper Collins Zondervan, forthcoming 2001), by title.

24. J. Gordon Melton, "The Pentecostal Family," *Encyclopedia of American Religions,* 4th ed. (Detroit: Gale Research, 1993), pp. 77–84, 401–478. Melton lists 210

pentecostal groups, and an additional 25 in his 1994 *Fourth Edition Supplement,* pp. 17–24.

25. For details, see the Appendix.

26. The classic text is Henry Pitney Van Dusen, "The Third Force in Christendom," *Life,* June 8, 1958, pp. 113–124. See also the essays by Albert Frederick Schenkel, Nancy L. Eisland, Frederick W. Jordan, and Helen Lee Turner in *Pentecostal Currents in American Protestantism,* ed. Edith L. Blumhofer, Russell P. Spittler, and Grant Wacker (Urbana: University of Illinois Press, 1999).

27. *Christian Century,* January 18, 1978, p. 35; Vinson Synan, "Pentecostalism: William Seymour," *Christian History,* no. 65 (Winter 2000): 17.

28. R. Marie Griffith, *God's Daughters: Evangelical Women and the Power of Submission* (Berkeley: University of California Press, 1997); Donald E. Miller, *Reinventing American Protestantism: Christianity in the New Millennium* (Berkeley: University of California Press, 1997); Richard Quebedeaux, "Conservative and Charismatic Developments of the Later Twentieth Century," in *Encyclopedia of the American Religious Experience,* vol. 2, pp. 963–976.

29. For pentecostal versus charismatic views of tongues, see Richard Quebedeaux, *The New Charismatics II* (San Francisco: Harper & Row, 1983), pp. 157–158. For the theological commonalities and distinctions between the two, see Russell P. Spittler, "Theological Style among Pentecostals and Charismatics," in *Doing Theology in Today's World: Essays in Honor of Kenneth S. Kantzer,* ed. John D. Woodbridge and Thomas Edward McComiskey (Grand Rapids: Zondervan Publishing House, 1991), pp. 291–320.

30. The Gallup poll is analyzed in Kenneth S. Kantzer, "The Charismatics among Us," *Christianity Today,* February 22, 1980, pp. 24–29. But contrast these robust figures with lower ones in the sociological surveys described in the Appendix.

31. Harvey Cox, *Fire from Heaven: The Rise of Pentecostal Spirituality and the Reshaping of Religion in the Twenty-First Century* (Reading, Mass.: Addison-Wesley Publishing Co., 1995); David Martin, *Tongues of Fire: The Explosion of Protestantism in Latin America* (Oxford: Basil Blackwell, 1990); Vinson Synan, *The Holiness-Pentecostal Tradition: Charismatic Movements in the Twentieth Century,* 2nd ed. (Grand Rapids: William B. Eerdmans Publishing Co., 1997; original 1971), chaps. 10–14.

32. David B. Barratt and Todd M. Johnson, "Annual Statistical Table on Global Mission: 2001," *International Bulletin of Missionary Research,* 25 (January 2001): 25. Presumably this figure partly overlaps the 650 million "Great Commission Christians" also listed. Many pentecostals are Catholics, but there is no clear way to sort them out. Statistician Peter Brierley listed 88 million pentecostals worldwide in 1990, apparently distinguishing pentecostals from charismatics. Peter Brierley and Heather Wraight, *Atlas of World Christianity: 2000 Years* (Nashville: Thomas Nelson, 1998), pp. 4, 13. Richard Shaull and Waldo Cesar cite studies that suggest that at the end of the 1990s pentecostals in Brazil alone numbered 15–20 million, equaling 10–20 percent of the population. Shaull and Cesar, *Pentecostalism and the Future of the Christian Churches: Promises, Limitations, Challenges* (Grand Rapids: William B. Eerdmans Publishing Co., 2000), p. 9.

33. Charles Edwin Jones, *A Guide to the Study of the Holiness Movement* (Metuchen, N.J.: Scarecrow Press, 1974); *A Guide to the Study of the Pentecostal Movement* (Metuchen, N.J.: Scarecrow Press, 1983); *Black Holiness: A Guide to the Study of Black Participation in Wesleyan Perfectionist and Glossolalic Pentecostal Movements* (Metuchen, N.J.:

Scarecrow Press, 1987); *The Charismatic Movement: A Guide to the Study of Neo-Pentecostalism with Emphasis on Anglo-American Sources* (Metuchen, N.J.: Scarecrow Press, 1995).

34. Cerillo and Wacker, "Bibliography and Historiography," in *New International Dictionary,* by title.

35. Lionel Trilling, *The Liberal Imagination: Essays on Literature and Society* (New York: Doubleday Anchor, reissued 1953, original 1950), p. 200.

36. Anderson, *Vision of the Disinherited,* p. 229.

37. See, for example, R. Laurence Moore, *Religious Outsiders and the Making of Americans* (New York: Oxford University Press, 1986), pp. 140–144. I owe my appreciation for the power of this position to Josef Barton's brilliant social history essay, "Pentecostals and Rural Society: The Highland South, 1890–1940," paper, American Academy of Religion, 1980, Dallas, Tex.

38. Harold Bloom, *The American Religion: The Emergence of the Post-Christian Nation* (New York: Simon and Schuster, 1992), chap. 10, esp. p. 177. The theoretical underpinnings of the three approaches are limned, respectively, in Gary Schwartz, *Sect Ideologies and Social Status* (Chicago: University of Chicago Press, 1970), esp. pp. 39–55; Luther P. Gerlach and Virginia H. Hine, *People, Power, Change: Movements of Social Transformation* (Indianapolis: Bobbs-Merrill Co., 1970), esp. chap. 8; R. Stephen Warner, "Work in Progress toward a New Paradigm for the Sociological Study of Religion in the United States," *American Journal of Sociology,* 98 (March 1993): 1044–93.

39. Conversation with Wheaton College professor James Mathisen, March 1993.

40. A. J. Tomlinson, in [Church of God] *General Assembly Minutes 1906–1914* (Cleveland, Tenn.: White Wing Publishing House, 1992), 1913, p. 163.

41. A. J. Tomlinson, in *Evening Light and Church of God Evangel,* July 1, 1910, p. 1. I call this periodical a fortnightly, though it sometimes came out more or less frequently.

42. Martha Wing Robinson, "Diary," October 30, 1907, p. 78, typed version, AOG.

43. Martha Wing Robinson excerpted in Gordon P. Gardiner, *Radiant Glory: The Life of Martha Wing Robinson,* 2nd ed. ([New York: Bread of Life], 1970, original 1962), p. 223.

44. Ibid., p. 241.

45. Pearl S. Buck, *The Exile* (New York: John Day, 1936), p. 58. See also R. Laurence Moore, *Selling God: American Religion in the Marketplace of Culture* (New York: Oxford University Press, 1994).

46. For the mannerly tone of mainline Protestant preaching in the early twentieth century see, for example, Edwin Scott Gaustad, "The Pulpit and the Pews," in *Between the Times: The Travail of the Protestant Establishment in America, 1900–1960,* ed. William R. Hutchison (Cambridge: Cambridge University Press, 1989), pp. 21–47, esp. p. 27. One gains a sense of the real or perceived innocuousness of the mainline church in *Church Sociables and Entertainments* (New York: Doubleday, Page & Co., 1906), including chapters on "A 'Lemon Squeeze'" and "A Popcorn Sociable," and in Harold Frederic's classic novel *The Damnation of Theron Ware,* first published in 1896. In contrast, Ann Taves notes the historical distinctiveness of some of the key pentecostal teachings and practices, observing that they were "strikingly different from anything that we have seen in the Methodist camp-meeting tradition." Taves, *Fits, Trances, and Visions: Experiencing Religion and Explaining Experience from Wes-*

ley to James (Princeton: Princeton University Press, 1999), pp. 332–334, quotation p. 332. For the view held by many outsiders that saints fell into extremism on all fronts, see my "Travail of a Broken Family: Evangelical Responses to Pentecostalism in America, 1906–1916," *Journal of Ecclesiastical History*, 47 (July 1996): 505–528.

47. Ralph E. Hone, "Should Women Preach?" *Grace and Truth*, February 1939: 36, quoted in Margaret Lamberts Bendroth, *Fundamentalism and Gender, 1875 to the Present* (New Haven: Yale University Press, 1993), p. 82.

48. These groups included A. J. Tomlinson and his followers in the Southern Highlands between 1900 and 1907, Levi R. Lupton and his followers in northeastern Ohio between 1904 and 1907, John Alexander Dowie and his followers in the Chicago area between 1900 and 1907, and Frank W. Sandford and his followers in southeastern Maine between 1890 and 1905. The first two eventually embraced the movement, and the third and fourth virtually did, for they bore all of the earmarks of pentecostals, including divine healing and, in Sanford's case, occasional tongues.

49. See for example David Martin, *A General Theory of Secularization* (New York: Harper & Row, 1978), esp. chap. 2; N. J. Demerath III, "Rational Paradigms, A-Rational Religion, and the Debate over Secularization," *Journal for the Scientific Study of Religion*, 34 (March 1995): 105–112, esp. 110.

50. Peter Brown, *Religion and Society in the Age of Saint Augustine* (New York: Harper & Row, 1972), p. 21.

1. Temperament

1. Perry Miller, *The New England Mind: The Seventeenth Century* (New York: Macmillan, reissued 1954, original 1939), "mood" p. 5, "The Augustinian Strain of Piety" is the title of chap. 1.

2. G. K. Chesterton, *Orthodoxy: A Personal Philosophy* (London: Fontana Books, 1961, original 1908), p. 79.

3. *Apostolic Faith* [Calif.], June–September 1907, p. 3, possibly taken from *Christian Missionary Alliance* without full citation.

4. *Apostolic Faith* [Calif.], January 1907, p. 1.

5. Addie A. Knowlton, in *New Acts*, June 1907, p. 8.

6. Frank Bartleman, *Azusa Street: The Roots of Modern-Day Pentecost*, ed. Vinson Synan (Plainfield, N.J.: Logos International, 1980, original [differently titled] 1925), p. 21.

7. Ardell K. Mead, *Apostolic Faith* [Calif.], November 1906, p. 3; A. A. Boddy, quoting "a working-man," *Christian* [U.K.], August 1, 1907, pna, AGUK; Mrs. Hebden, *Promise*, May 1907, p. 2.

8. *Word and Work*, May 1910, p. 14; *Apostolic Faith* [Calif.] , December 1906, p. 3; A. G. Osterberg, "Second Tape," typescript of interview March 17, 1966, by Jerry Jensen and Jonathan Perkins, p. 6, AOG.

9. A. R. Haughawout, in *Apostolic Faith* [Kans.], June 1914, p. 3.

10. J. M. Vawter, in *New Acts*, August 16, 1906, p. 6.

11. Howard A. Goss, *The Winds of God: The Story of the Early Pentecostal Days (1901–1914) in the Life of Howard A. Goss, as Told by Ethel E. Goss* (New York: Comet Press Books, 1958), p. 78.

12. G. F. Taylor, in *Advocate of Holiness*, February 21, 1918, p. 1.

13. *Church of God Evangel*, February 24, 1917, p. 1.

14. *Bridal Call*, June 1917, pp. 1–2.

15. George Floyd Taylor, "Diary," August 27, 1908, North Carolina State History Archives, Raleigh, N.C. Taylor's concern for his baby son's health occasioned the first quotation (through "Glory!"), his desire to know the inner meaning of the Song of Solomon occasioned the second. Taylor kept this diary for the years 1896, 1901, and 1908.

16. Walter J. Higgins, *Pioneering in Pentecost: My Experiences of 46 Years in the Ministry* (Bostonia, Calif.: n.p., 1958), p. 36.

17. James and June Glover Marshall, "R. G. Spurling Jr.: The Origins of the Church of God," *Reflections . . . Church of God Heritage,* Winter 1990, p. 3.

18. *In Memoriam of Mrs. Cora Fritsch Faulkner Pentecostal Missionary, Hongkong—South China,* [1912], AOG.

19. *Glad Tidings* [SF], July 1928, p. 10.

20. Ibid., May 1926, p. 8.

21. *Showers of Blessings* [U.K.], no. 8, [about 1910], p. 9.

22. Goss, *Winds of God,* p. 136.

23. *Christian Evangel,* October 17, 1914, p. 2.

24. H. D. McMinn, in *Church of God Evangel,* April 4, 1914, p. 6.

25. *Pentecostal Evangel,* November 1, 1919, p. 5.

26. Lewi Petrus, *Urkristna kraftkallor* (1926), quoted in Nils Bloch-Hoell, *The Pentecostal Movement: Its Origin, Development, and Distinctive Character* (New York: Humanities Press, 1964; Norwegian original, 1956), p. 103. I owe the larger point about certitude to Bloch-Hoell's fine work.

27. A. S. Worrell, in *Gospel Witness,* September 1906, p. 25.

28. Aimee Semple McPherson, *The Story of My Life,* ed. Raymond L. Cox (Waco: Word Books, 1973), p. 16.

29. E. N. Bell, in *Christian Evangel,* in August 10, 1918, p. 1. Bell graduated from Stetson University, attended Southern Baptist Seminary in Louisville for two years, and received a B.D. degree from the University of Chicago Divinity School. Richard A. Lewis, "E. N. Bell—A Voice of Restraint in an Era of Controversy," *Enrichment: A Journal for Pentecostal Ministry* (Fall 1999): 49.

30. E. N. Bell, in *Word and Witness,* August 20, 1912, p. 3.

31. See, for example, *Pentecostal Latter Rain,* October 1928, p. 12, for the story of a ten-year-old girl who experienced Holy Spirit baptism on Sunday, was killed in a car wreck on Thursday, and buried on Saturday. "Many were stirred to seek God because of this sad incident."

32. Levi Lupton, in *New Acts,* April 26, 1906, p. 1.

33. Lee Thornburg, in *New Acts,* June 21, 1906, p. 8.

34. [E. K. Fisher], in *Upper Room,* January 1911, p. 1.

35. Charles W. Conn, *Like a Mighty Army: A History of the Church of God: 1888–1976,* rev. ed. (Cleveland, Tenn.: Pathway Press, 1977, original 1955), p. xxvii.

36. Suggested by Timothy P. Weber, *Living in the Shadow of the Second Coming* (New York: Oxford University Press, 1979), p. 62.

37. W. A. Cramer, in *New Acts,* June 1907, p. 4.

38. Higgins, *Pioneering in Pentecost,* p. 15.

39. Max Wood Moorhead, in *Cloud of Witnesses to Pentecost in India,* November 1908, p. 18.

40. Charles F. Parham, in *Apostolic Faith* [Kans.], April 1913, p. 15.

41. "A sister," as rendered in *Apostolic Faith* [Calif.], November 1906, p. 4.

42. See, for example, Bartleman, *Azusa Street,* p. 5; *Latter Rain Evangel,* August 1910, p. 15.

43. See, for example, T. M. Jeffreys, in *Upper Room,* July 1910, p. 3; R. B. Kirkland, *"Speaking with Tongues": Evidence and Gift,* (New York: n.p., 1925), p. 52.

44. *Pasadena Daily News,* July 3, 1906, p. 1.

45. Ibid., July 13, 1906, p. 12.

46. Ibid., July 18, 1906, p. 12.

47. Frank Sandford, in *Tongues of Fire,* December 1 and 15, 1900, p. 199.

48. *Everlasting Gospel* [Maine], July 1, 1903, p. 19.

49. *Apostolic Evangel,* August 23, 1916, p. 4.

50. *Church of God Evangel,* April 11, 1914, p. 3. I owe the main point of the paragraph to Weber, *Living,* p. 62.

51. *From Ballroom to Brothel,* Standard Bearer tract no. 9, advertised in *Standard Bearer,* May 1924, p. 8.

52. Elizabeth Sisson (1895), quoted in Wayne E. Warner, *The Woman Evangelist: The Life and Times of Charismatic Evangelist Maria B. Woodworth-Etter* (Metuchen, N.J.: Scarecrow Press, 1986), p. 109.

53. Sarah E. Parham, in *Apostolic Faith* [Kans.], March 1913, p. 2.

54. *Apostolic Faith* [Calif.], November 1906, p. 4. The vision was attributed to Brother Thomas Junk, based on a story in *Household of God,* issue unspecified.

55. Carrie Judd Montgomery, "Date Book for 1909," March 13, AOG.

56. Alvin Price, "The Pentecostal Gospel Comes to the Outer Banks of North Carolina," typed, 1980, p. 2, AOG.

57. Gordon Lindsay, *John Alexander Dowie: A Life Story of Trials, Tragedies and Triumphs* (Dallas: Christ for the Nations, 1980, original [differently titled] 1951), pp. 232–233.

58. See, for example, William Hamner Piper, in *Latter Rain Evangel,* March 1909, pp. 18–22; B. Freeman Lawrence, in *Pentecost,* April 1910, p. 5; Ralph Riggs, in *Trust,* January 1915, pp. 12–17; F. F. Bosworth, in *Exploits of Faith,* April 1929, pp. 1–6.

59. F. F. Bosworth, *Christ the Healer: Sermons on Divine Healing* (n.p., 1924), pp. 98–99.

60. Though Kenyon formally distanced himself from New Thought and Christian Science, his early career entwined with New Thought readings, teachers, and institutions. Dale H. Simmons, *E. W. Kenyon and the Postbellum Pursuit of Peace, Power, and Plenty* (Lanham, Md.: Scarecrow Press, 1997).

61. E. W. Kenyon, *Jesus the Healer* (1943), p. 20, quoted in Charles Farah, Jr., "A Critical Analysis: The 'Roots and Fruits' of Faith-Formula Theology," *Pneuma: Journal of the Society for Pentecostal Studies,* 13 (1981): 6.

62. Maria B. Woodworth-Etter, *Divine Healing: Health for Body, Soul and Spirit* (Indianapolis: n.p., about 1920), first sentence p. 1, second p. 2.

63. Carrie Judd Montgomery, *Faith's Reckonings,* tract, about 1920, p. 9.

64. Henry Proctor, F.R. S.L., in *Trust,* May–June 1930, p. 15.

65. Edith Shaw, in *Trust,* June–July 1915, fever p. 17, prayed p. 16, lie p. 17.

66. Anecdote related by the daughter, Mildred Edwards, in *Trust,* February 1915, p. 13.

67. Lilian B. Yeomans, M.D., *Health and Healing* (Springfield, Mo.: Gospel Publishing House, 1973, original [differently titled] 1938), pp. 33–34, 56.

68. For examples of the anxiety felt, see letters from E. S. Akins and Nancy J. Lawson, in

Evening Light and Church of God Evangel, August 1, 1910, p. 8; Charles S. Price, *The Real Faith* (Plainfield, N.J.: Logos International, 1972, original 1940), pp. 7–8. For outsiders' attacks on this score, see Rowland V. Bingham, *The Bible and the Body, or Healing in the Scripture* (Toronto: Evangelical Publishers, 1921), Preface; C. E. Putnam, *Modern Religio-Healing: Man's Theories or God's Words?* (Chicago: C. E. Putnam, 1924), pp. 157–159. I examine radical evangelicals' attacks on pentecostals' healing practices in *Travail of a Broken Family: Evangelical Responses to the Emergence of Pentecostalism* (forthcoming).

69. See, for example, *Pentecost,* August 1908, p. 1, which claimed that an enraged physician deliberately rebroke an arm healed by prayer.

70. See, for example, testimonials by Kate Hubbard-Peckham and W. S. Peckham, in *Leaves of Healing,* April 13, 1901, pp. 770–772. Of the hundreds I have seen, none states that there had been no healing at all, but many, perhaps a majority, refer to partial healing, or relapses of illness, and the spiritual rewards of perseverance without medicines or physicians.

71. Gordon Lindsay, *John Alexander Dowie: A Life Story of Trials, Tragedies and Triumphs* (Dallas: Christ for the Nations, Inc., 1980), pp. 214–218; Farah, "Critical Analysis," p. 4, and *From the Pinnacle of the Temple: Faith vs. Presumption?* (Plainfield, N.J.: Logos International, n.d.), pp. 53–54, 121–122.

72. E. N. Bell, *Questions and Answers* (Springfield, Mo.: [Gospel Publishing House], 1923), pp. 56–57, 82; F. M. Britton, *Pentecostal Truths* (Royston, Ga.: Publishing House of the Pentecostal Holiness Church, [1919]), pp. 92–93.

73. See the testimony columns of virtually any issue of *Apostolic Faith* [Calif.], *Apostolic Faith* [Ore.], *Triumphs of Faith,* or *Bridegroom's Messenger.*

74. Grant Wacker, "Caring and Curing: The Pentecostal Tradition," in *Caring and Curing: Health and Medicine in the Western Faith Traditions,* ed. Ronald L. Numbers and Darryl W. Amundsen (Baltimore: The Johns Hopkins University Press, reissued 1998, original 1986), pp. 528–529; Bruce Barron, *The Health and Wealth Gospel* (Downers Grove, Ill.: Intervarsity Press, 1987).

75. Wright quoted in Elizabeth Evans, *The Wright Vision: The Story of the New England Fellowship* (1991), p. 2, quoted in Kurt O. Berends, "A Divided Harvest: Alice Belle Garrigus, Joel Adams Wright, and Early New England Pentecostalism," M.A. thesis, Wheaton College Graduate School, May 1993, p. 51.

76. Timothy L. Smith, *Called unto Holiness—The Story of the Nazarenes: The Formative Years* (Kansas City, Mo.: Nazarene Publishing House, 1962), p. 37.

77. A. J. Tomlinson, in *Evening Light and Church of God Evangel,* June 15, 1910, p. 2.

78. David Lee Floyd interviewed by Wayne E. Warner, February 26, 1981, transcript 1, p. 8, AOG.

79. Frank Bartleman, *Distilled Dew* (Los Angeles: Frank Bartleman, 1934), p. 2.

80. Goss, *Winds of God,* p. 154.

81. *Preamble and Resolution of Constitution,* printed in *1922 General Convention Minutes,* quoted in Larry Martin, *In the Beginning: Readings on the Origins of the Twentieth Century Pentecostal Revival and the Birth of the Pentecostal Church of God* (Duncan, Okla.: Christian Life Books, 1994), p. 125. In 1922 this body changed its name to Pentecostal Church of God.

82. George C. Brinkman, in *Pentecostal Herald,* January 1920, p. 1, quoted in Martin, *In the Beginning,* p. 68.

83. [Charles Fox Parham], *The Life of Charles F. Parham: Founder of the Apostolic Faith*

Movement, compiled by His Wife [Sarah E. Parham] (New York: Garland Publishing, 1985, original 1930), p. 14.

84. *Apostolic Faith* [Houston], October 1908, p. 2; *Midnight Cry* [Wash.], November 1907, p. 2; *Pentecost,* April–May 1909, p. 4; *Seattle Post Intelligencer,* August 29, 1907, p. 6, and September 3, 1907, p. 4. There is no evidence that Ryan knew a word of Japanese, which made his venture to Japan all the more audacious.

85. Elizabeth R. Wheaton, *Prisons and Prayer or a Labor of Love* (Tabor, Iowa: Charles M. Kelley, 1906), p. 29.

86. Ibid., Preface, pp. 25–26. Wheaton emphasized that no church or organization supported her national and international prison ministry. Instead, the driving power stemmed from "an angel band, a Christ love, great charity"—and, significantly— "force of character that knew not fear where duty called" (p. 35, by her brother Emanuel Ryder, whose words she approvingly reproduced).

87. *Apostolic Faith* [Calif.], October 1906, p. 2, for quotation.

88. A. J. Tomlinson, *The Last Great Conflict* (New York: Garland Publishing, 1985, original 1913), pp. 38, 69.

89. Goss, *Winds of God,* p. 65.

90. Ibid., p. 17, regarding Parham.

91. Lewiston, Maine, newspaper reporter describing Frank W. Sandford, quoted in Shirley Nelson, *Fair, Clear, and Terrible: The Story of Shiloh, Maine* (Latham, N.Y.: British American Publishing, 1989), p. 78.

92. E. S. Williams, tape-recorded interview by Wayne Warner, 1979, and by unnamed interviewer, 1977, AOG, describing Florence Crawford.

93. Goss, *Winds of God,* p. 73.

94. *Apostolic Messenger,* February–March 1908, p. 2[?].

95. *Pentecost,* August 1909, p. 6.

96. E. N. Bell, in *Word and Witness,* December 20, 1912, p. 2.

97. *Diary of A. J. Tomlinson,* ed. Homer A. Tomlinson (Queens Village, N.Y.: Church of God, World Headquarters, 1955), vol. 3, pp. 104–105.

98. Plunkitt quoted in James West Davidson et al., *Nation of Nations: A Narrative History of the American Republic* (1994), p. 689, quoted in Roger Glenn Robins, "Plainfolk Modernist: The Radical Holiness World of A. J. Tomlinson," Ph.D. diss., Duke University, 1999, p. 47. Robins's reference applied to the larger radical evangelical-pentecostal subculture.

99. Aimee Semple McPherson, *This Is That: Personal Experiences Sermons and Writings* (New York: Garland Publishing, 1985, original 1919), pp. 112–115, quotation p. 112.

100. Advertisement in *Bridal Call,* July 1917, p. 3.

101. Quoted in David L. Clark, "Miracles for a Dime: From Chatauqua Tent to Radio Station with Sister Aimee," *California History,* Winter 1978–1979, p. 363.

102. Marcus Bach, *They Have Found a Faith* (1946), quoted in Vinson Synan, *The Holiness-Pentecostal Tradition: Charismatic Movements in the Twentieth Century,* 2nd ed. (Grand Rapids: William B. Eerdmans Publishing Co., 1997), p. 201.

103. K. G. Ormiston, in *Bridal Call Foursquare,* January 1925, p. 24; "And They are Still Heralding the Message," [Four Square] *Advance,* undated article in AOG file on McPherson Radio, p. 10. McPherson's station started broadcasting in February 1924.

104. "Still Heralding the Message," p. 10.

105. McPherson quoted in Erik Barnouw, *A History of Broadcasting in the United States,* vol. I, *A Tower in Babel: To 1933* (1966), p. 180, quoted in George H. Douglas, *The Early Days of Radio Broadcasting* (Jefferson, N.C.: McFarland & Co., 1987), p. 94.

106. *Apostolic Faith* [Kans.], February 1913, p. 8.

107. A. E. Street, in *Intercessory Missionary,* June 1907, p. 36.

2. Tongues

1. The quotation comes from Roger Glenn Robins, "Plainfolk Modernist: The Radical Holiness World of A. J. Tomlinson," Ph.D. diss., Duke University, 1999, p. 53. The literature on glossolalia, theologically rendered as speaking in tongues, is immense. Many of the classic scholarly essays on the subject—exegetical, theological, histori-cal, psychological, and sociological—have been conveniently collected in Watson E. Mills, *Speaking in Tongues: A Guide to Research on Glossolalia* (Grand Rapids: William B. Eerdmans Publishing Co., 1986). See especially Mills's survey of the literature, chap. 2. The social science literature in particular receives thorough description and evaluation in H. Newton Malony and A. Adams Lovekin, *Glossolalia: Behavioral Sci-ence Perspectives on Speaking in Tongues* (New York: Oxford University Press, 1985). Most relevant to the present study is chap. 6, "States of Consciousness." Though I reached my interpretation of the physiological and cultural integration of tongues mainly by reading early primary accounts, my conclusions seem consistent with theirs. See esp. pp. 112, 261–262.

2. A. J. Tomlinson, *The Last Great Conflict* (New York: Garland Publishing, 1985, orig-inal 1913), pp. 210–214.

3. "Journal of Happenings: The Diary of A. J. Tomlinson," typed, January 13, 1908, COG.

4. Tomlinson, *Last Great Conflict,* pp. 210–214.

5. Cook, in *Apostolic Faith* [Calif.], November 1906, p. 2. For biographical details see *DPCM.*

6. William H. Durham, in *Pentecostal Testimony,* 2:3 (Summer 1912?): 3–4. Italicized excerpt from Durham, in *Apostolic Faith* [Calif.], February–March 1907, p. 4.

7. T. B. Barratt, in *Apostolic Faith* [Calif.], December 1906, p. 3. The sentences begin-ning "On November 15" and "Eventually he asked" in B. F. Lawrence, *The Apostolic Faith Restored* (St. Louis: Gospel Publishing House, 1916), p. 107.

8. A. A. Boddy, report about Jennie Moore, in *Confidence,* October 1912, p. 233.

9. John G. Lake, untitled, undated sermon apparently referring to events in April 1908, in *John G. Lake—Apostle to Africa,* comp. Gordon Lindsay (Dallas: Christ for the Na-tions, 1981), quotations on pp. 18, 22.

10. Aimee Semple McPherson, *The Story of My Life,* ed. Raymond L. Cox (Waco: Word Books, 1973), p. 30.

11. Howard A. Goss, *The Winds of God: The Story of the Early Pentecostal Days (1901–1914) in the Life of Howard A. Goss, as Told by Ethel E. Goss* (New York: Comet Press Books, 1958), p. 44.

12. McPherson, *Story of My Life,* p. 30.

13. Jenny Moore, in *Apostolic Faith* [Calif.], May 1907, p. 3.

14. See, for example, Gotfred E. Stephan, in *Christian Evangel,* August 1, 1914, p. 1; Joel Adams Wright, in *Sheaf of the First Fruits,* May 1913, pp. 12–13, quoted in Kurt O. Berends, "A Divided Harvest: Alice Belle Garrigus, Joel Adams Wright, and Early

New England Pentecostalism," M.A. thesis, Wheaton College Graduate School, May 1993, p. 44.

15. See, for example, F. F. Bosworth, in *Word and Witness,* December 20, 1912, p. 1; Tomlinson, *Last Great Conflict,* p. 213.

16. Mary P. Perkins, in *Apostolic Faith* [Calif.], November 1906, p. 1.

17. *Apostolic Faith* [Calif.], September 1906, p. 3.

18. Ella M. Goff, in *Apostolic Messenger,* published in Winnipeg by A. H. Argue, reprinted without full citation in *Apostolic Faith* [Calif.] June 1908 p. 4. Argue's connection was significant, given his reputation for restraint.

19. Reported by A. S. Copley regarding a Toronto revival, in *Apostolic Faith* [Calif.], January 1907, p. 4.

20. Jenny Moore, in *Apostolic Faith* [Calif.], May 1907, p. 3. For similar events at the Altamont Bible Institute near Greenville, S.C., see N. J. Holmes and Wife, *Life Sketches and Sermons* (Royston, Ga.: Press of the Pentecostal Holiness Church, [1909]–1920), pp. 154, 156.

21. Margaret Gill, in *Apostolic Faith* [Calif.], February–March 1907, p. 8 for poetry; Gotfred E. Stephan, in *Christian Evangel,* August 1, 1914, p. 1 for rhyming.

22. *Diary of A. J. Tomlinson,* ed. Homer A. Tomlinson (Queens Village, N.Y.: Church of God, World Headquarters, 1949), vol. 1, p. 79.

23. Abbie Cress, in *Evening Light and Church of God Evangel,* July 15, 1910, p. 7.

24. See, for example, Levi Lupton, in *New Acts,* April 1907, p. 2; *Apostolic Faith* [Calif.], September 1906, p. 1; Holmes and Wife, *Life Sketches and Sermons,* pp. 147, 181; Lucillia J. Cornelius, *The Pioneer: History of the Church of God in Christ* (n.p., 1975), p. 13, regarding early experience of Bishop C. H. Mason; photo of Agnes Ozman's Holy Spirit grapholalia in James R. Goff, Jr., *Fields White unto Harvest: Charles F. Parham and the Missionary Origins of Pentecostalism* (Fayetteville: University of Arkansas Press, 1988), illus. 4, following p. 144. But see *Apostolic Faith* [Calif.], September 1907, p. 2, for a cautionary note about the lack of scriptural warrant for writing in tongues (grapholalia).

25. Carrie Judd Montgomery, *A Year with the Comforter,* early tract (n.p., n.d.), p. 11.

26. A. S. Copley, in *Apostolic Faith* [Calif.], January 1907, p. 4.

27. William F. Manley, in *Household of God,* September 1906, p. 7.

28. Frank F. Ewart, *The Phenomenon of Pentecost: A History of the Latter Rain* (Houston: Herald Publishing House, 1947), p. 40.

29. *Trust,* April 1915, p. 11.

30. "Unearthly" and "ravishing" in W. H. Durham, in *Apostolic Faith* [Calif.], February–March 1907, p. 4; *Triumphs of Faith,* May 1908, p. 102; E. K. Fisher, in *Upper Room,* August 1909, p. 2.

31. Most notably, Tomlinson, "Journal of Happenings," January 13, 1908, COG; Church of God, Kilsyth, Scotland, *Minute Book,* "Special Minute" following March 8, 1909; Walter J. Higgins, *Pioneering in Pentecost. My Experiences of 46 Years in the Ministry* (Bostonia, Calif.: published by author, 1958), p. 13; Aimee Semple McPherson, *This Is That: Personal Experiences Sermons and Writings* (New York: Garland Publishing, 1985, original 1919), Preface; Holmes and Wife, *Life Sketches and Sermons,* p. 168.

32. [Charles Fox Parham], *The Life of Charles F. Parham: Founder of the Apostolic Faith Movement,* compiled by his wife [Sarah E. Parham] (New York: Garland Publishing, 1985, original 1930), p. 53; Rachel A. Sizelove, *A Sparkling Fountain for the Whole Earth* (Long Beach, Calif.: n.p., n.d.), p. 6.

33. *Word and Work,* May 1910, p. 141; Levi Lupton, in *New Acts,* February 1907, p. 3.

34. About 1914 Arthur S. Booth-Clibborn, a knowledgeable contemporary, offered a "careful estimate" that 70,000 spoke in tongues and another 70,000 affiliated themselves with the revival but did not speak in tongues. C. W. Shumway, "A Study of 'The Gift of Tongues,'" A.B. thesis, University of Southern California, 1914, p. 191. For recent estimates, see Corwin E. Smidt, Lyman A. Kellstedt, John C. Green, and James L. Guth, "The Spirit-Filled Movements in Contemporary America: A Survey Perspective," in *Pentecostal Currents in American Protestantism,* ed. Edith L. Blumhofer, Russell P. Spittler, and Grant Wacker (Urbana: University of Illinois Press, 1999), p. 116.

35. J. G. Campbell, in *Apostolic Faith* [Goose Creek, Tex.], May 1921, pp. 2–3.

36. Charles Parham, in *Apostolic Faith* [Kans.], January 1912, p. 7.

37. *Faithful Standard,* October 1922, p. 15.

38. Gary B. McGee, "Latter Rain Falling in the East: Early-Twentieth-Century Pentecostalism in India and the Debate over Speaking in Tongues," *Church History: Studies in Christianity and Culture,* 68 (September 1999): 656–659, 664.

39. Elizabeth V. Baker and Co-Workers, *Chronicles of a Faith Life* (New York: Garland Publishing, 1984, original 1915–1916), p. 141. Carrie Judd Montgomery, another influential editor, also resisted the initial evidence teaching at first. Baker and Montgomery soon reversed themselves. For Montgomery, see Jeanette Storms, "Carrie Judd Montgomery: 'The Little General,'" in *Portraits of a Generation: Early Pentecostal Leaders,* ed. James R. Goff, Jr. and Grant Wacker (forthcoming).

40. *Diary of A. J. Tomlinson,* vol. 3, p. 49, for June 14, 1907; "Journal of Happenings," typed, June 14, 1907, COG.

41. A. J. Tomlinson, *Answering the Call of God* (Cleveland, Tenn.: White Wing Publishing House, [1913]), pp. 10, 15; "Journal of Happenings," typed, January 13, 1908, COG (the former gives a date of January 12, the latter January 13).

42. *Church of God Evangel,* August 15, 1910, p. 3. Even then, Tomlinson and three associates simply listed baptism with tongues as one of twenty-five teachings held by the Church of God.

43. See, for example, Albert Norton, in *Triumphs of Faith,* September 1909, p. 199. For a classic statement in pentecostal circles of the Holy Spirit's substantive priority, see Ralph M. Riggs, *The Spirit Himself* (Springfield, Mo.: Gospel Publishing House, 1949).

44. I derived these figures by searching for the following words: coming, sanctification, sanctifying, healing, restored, saved, salvation, tongues, and baptism. I counted "coming" only when it referred to the Lord's advent, "restored" only when it referred to healing, and I discounted references to water baptism or linkages to the word *tongues* in the same sentence (as in "baptism with the Holy Ghost with tongues"). The first twelve issues of *Apostolic Faith* [Calif.] (September 1906–January 1908) are available online at www.umdl.umich.edu/moa/moa_search.html. The first thirteen issues (September 1906–May 1908) are conveniently compiled in *Azusa Street [P]apers: A Reprint of The Apostolic Faith Mission Publications, Los Angeles, California (1906–1908), William J. Seymour, Editor* (Foley, Ala.: Together in the Harvest Publications, 1997). The fourteenth issue is available at AOG. A fifteenth issue, apparently published in the autumn of 1908, has never been located. For details on the paper's tangled publication history, see Grant Wacker, "Who Edited the Azusa Mission *Apostolic Faith* Papers?" *Assemblies of God Heritage,* forthcoming.

45. *Apostolic Faith* [Calif.] claimed a circulation of 40,000 in February–March 1907, p. 2. Among other sources, I infer the periodical's breadth of influence from Clara Lum, in *Bridegroom's Messenger*, December 1, 1907, p. 1; and Wayne E. Warner's Introduction to *Azusa Street [P]apers*, pp. 4–8.

46. M. L. Ryan, in *Chinese Recorder*, May 1915, p. 322.

47. [Parham], *Life of Charles F. Parham*, p. 52; Grant Wacker, "Are the Golden Oldies Still Worth Playing? Reflections on History Writing among Early Pentecostals," *Pneuma: Journal of the Society for Pentecostal Studies*, 8 (Fall 1986): 95–96.

48. It is conventionally assumed that William J. Seymour edited the periodical. However the paper never named Seymour—or anyone else—as editor because, it said, "we want Christ exalted" (January 1908, p. 2). In fact, the evidence leaves numerous clues that Seymour exercised general oversight while Clara E. Lum, a white woman, with office experience elsewhere, ran the day-to-day operations. For these reasons I consistently call Seymour and Lum co-editors, which I believe reflects the actual arrangement. For details, see Wacker, "Who Edited the Azusa *Apostolic Faith* Papers?"

49. W. J. Seymour, in *Apostolic Faith* [Calif.], September 1906, p. 1.

50. A. E. Street, in *Intercessory Missionary*, June 1907, pp. 37, 38.

51. Albert Norton, *Faith Work in India*, July 10, 1907, p. 1. Elsewhere (p. 7) Norton acknowledged that tongues were "incidental." In the rapidly galvanizing pentecostal orthodoxy, incidental did not mean optional but symptomatic of deeper spiritual realities. That distinction commonly proved too subtle—or too tortured—for their evangelical foes.

52. Tomlinson, *Last Great Conflict*, p. 17.

53. *Voice in the Wilderness*, no. 22, probably 1918, p. 2.

54. For representative, very early examples drawn from a variety of social locations, see, in chronological order, Thomas G. Atteberry, in *Apostolic Truth* [Calif.], December 1906, p. 3; W. H. Durham, in *Apostolic Faith* [Calif.], February–March 1907, p. 4; *Cloud of Witnesses*, September 1907, p. 46; *Confidence*, January 1909, pp. 14–15; J. H. King, in *Apostolic Messenger* [Manitoba], February–March, 1908, p. 1; Church of God, Kilsyth, Scotland, *Minute Book*, March 24, 1909; Elmer K. Fisher, in *Upper Room*, June 1909, p. 3; C. R. Curtis, in *Evening Light and Church of God Evangel*, March 1, 1910, pp. 6–7; William Black, in *Good Report*, November 1913, p. 2; Holmes and Wife, *Life Sketches and Sermons*, pp. 138–141.

55. Pentecostals tirelessly reiterated the biblical basis for their initial evidence doctrine. For one example, as clear as it was succinct, see G. F. Taylor, in *Pentecostal Holiness Advocate*, January 31, 1918, pp. 4–5, an exposition of the denomination's *Basis of Union*. Taylor's final sentence captured a thousand others: "We believe that other evidences [of Holy Spirit baptism] will closely follow; but that the first one is the speaking in tongues as the Spirit gives utterance" (p. 5).

56. Edith L. Blumhofer, *Restoring the Faith: The Assemblies of God, Pentecostalism, and American Culture* (Urbana: University of Illinois Press, 1993), pp. 135–137.

57. For Seymour's dramatically different earlier and later views, compare W. J. Seymour, in *Apostolic Faith*, September 1906, p. 1, with W. J. Seymour, *The Doctrines and Discipline of the Azusa Street Apostolic Faith Mission of Los Angeles, Calif., 1915*, pp. 8, 23, 40, 51–52, esp. Preface.

58. W. B. Godbey, *Six Tracts by W. B. Godbey*, ed. Donald W. Dayton (New York: Garland Publishing, 1985), containing, with five other booklets, *Tongue Movement, Satanic* (1918), p. 24.

59. Reader Harris, in *Tongues of Fire* [U.K.], January 1908, p. 7.

60. *Burning Bush,* September 19, 1907, p. 7.

61. W. E. Shepard, in *Herald of Holiness,* August 6, 1919, p. 4.

62. August Youngren, in *Free Methodist,* June 16, 1908, p. 379.

63. Alma White, *The Story of My Life and the Pillar of Fire* (Zarephath, N.J.: Pillar of Fire, 1935), vol. 5, p. 46.

64. *Topeka Daily Capital,* July 5, 1901, p. 3.

65. Sir Robert Anderson, *Spirit Manifestations and "The Gift of Tongues,"* 4th ed. (New York: Loizeaux Brothers, 1909), pp. 23, 24.

66. Shumway, "A Study of 'The Gift of Tongues,'" p. 1.

67. Pentecostals who held to the initial evidence teaching (which is to say, the vast majority by 1910) left at least two common forms of tongues speech curiously uncategorized: tongues as a devotional prayer language uttered in private, and tongues as a praise language uttered in public. I suspect that these forms remained (and remain) uncategorized because no doctrinal dispute arose to force clarification.

68. The label "missionary tongues" is mine, not early pentecostals'. The latter almost always referred to a specific language (such as German or Turkish), though rarely to a dialect (such as Mandarin). Also they never used the words *glossolalia* or *xenolalia.* Probably they simply did not know them. After World War II, with the rise of the charismatic movement, pentecostal theologians and biblical scholars started to use both terms, but very tentatively, undoubtedly sensing that both labels were needlessly pedantic and potentially reductionistic.

69. See, for example, Jesse Penn-Lewis, in *Christian Patriot,* October 1905, p. 6. More broadly, see Gary B. McGee, "Looking for a 'Short-Cut' to Language Preparation: Radical Evangelicals, Missions, and the Gift of Tongues," *International Bulletin of Missionary Research,* forthcoming.

70. Parham maintained to the end of his life in 1928 that all true glossolalia equaled xenolalia.

71. Though the evidence remains sparse, I draw this interpretation from three sources. First, the earliest converts repeatedly specified the various languages in which they spoke. Second, the first sustained exposition of pentecostal thought, penned by theologian George Floyd Taylor in 1907, echoed Parham's position. Finally, there is some but on the whole remarkably little evidence that missionaries tried to test their xenolalic gifts before departing for the mission field, suggesting that they presupposed they could speak the vernacular when they arrived. G. F. Taylor, *The Spirit and the Bride,* published with other documents as *Three Early Pentecostal Tracts,* ed. Donald W. Dayton (New York: Garland Publishing, 1985, original 1907), pp. 52, 62–63, 104–105. Though most pentecostal leaders soon dropped the idea that tongues always involved actual languages, Woodworth-Etter (like Parham) apparently persisted to the end. M. B. Woodworth-Etter, *Signs and Wonders: God Wrought in the Ministry for Forty Years* (Indianapolis: published by author, 1916), p. 117. At least one stalwart argued that he possessed the gift of aurolalia: the ability to understand (though not speak) an unstudied foreign language. Finis Yoakum, in *Latter Rain Evangel,* February 1909, p. 13.

72. See *Apostolic Faith* [Calif.], Warner edition, numerous index entries for "Gift of Languages," and "Glossolalia: As an Identifiable Language," pp. 72–73. For additional examples representing a variety of geographic regions and social locations, see (in chronological order): Agnes N. O[zman] LaBerge, *What God Hath Wrought: Life*

and Work of Mrs. Agnes N. O. LaBerge (New York: Garland Publishing, 1985, original 1920), p. 32, regarding a January 2, 1901 experience; Carrie Judd Montgomery, in *Triumphs of Faith,* December 1906, pp. 248 ff.; Levi Lupton, in *New Acts,* April 1907, p. 2; Mrs. Phillips, in *Promise,* June 1907, p. 4; *Apostolic Faith* [Ore.], July–August 1908, p. 1; *Upper Room,* June 1909, p. 9; Baker and Co-Workers, *Chronicles of a Faith Life,* p. 139. The list could be extended almost indefinitely.

73. A. W. Frodsham, in *Confidence,* June 1911, p. 139.

74. See Robert Mapes Anderson, *Vision of the Disinherited: The Making of American Pentecostalism* (New York: Oxford University Press, 1979), p. 90. According to Frederick G. Henke, Southern Baptist missionary S. C. Todd, writing in *Baptist Argus* (Louisville, Ky.), January 23, 1908, reported eighteen different instances of pentecostal missionaries who thought they had received the gift of missionary tongues in India, China, and Japan, but none was able to demonstrate it on arrival. Todd said he had to take one pentecostal couple into his home to keep them from starving. Henke, "The Gift of Tongues and Related Phenomena at the Present Day," *American Journal of Theology,* 13 (1909): 206; J. C. Vanzandt, *Speaking in Tongues* (Portland, Ore.: published by author, 1926, original 1911), pp. 45–47.

75. See, for example, *Apostolic Faith* [Ore.], July–August 1908, p. 1; *New Acts,* April 1907, p. 2.

76. *Apostolic Faith* [Calif.], November 1906, p. 4.

77. J. E. Simmons, in *Word and Witness,* January 20, 1914, p. 1.

78. *Apostolic Faith* [Calif.], November 1906, p. 2.

79. George B. Studd, in *Upper Room,* November 1910, p. 1.

80. Josie Ellis, in *Apostolic Light,* August 28, 1907, p. 3.

81. George E. Berg, in *Apostolic Faith* [Calif.], February–March 1907, p. 8.

82. Letter from Harriet Shimer in Carrie Judd Montgomery, *Speaking in Tongues,* tract, 1917.

83. Albert Norton, in *Triumphs of Faith,* January 1908, p. 14.

84. Sopel [Sophie?] Hansen, in *Bridegroom's Messenger,* May 15, 1911, p. 3, states that the event took place on July 16, but that probably was an error since the two other accounts cited below say July 26.

85. Sophie Hansen, in *Triumphs of Faith,* June 1916, p. 142, reprinted in *Word and Work,* May 1922, p. 10, and in *Pentecostal Times,* n.d., no. 12, Adelaide, Australia, p. 16.

86. Sophie Hansen, in *Bridegroom's Messenger,* October 1921, p. 3. Given pentecostals' casual documentation habits, it is possible that this 1921 article actually preceded the 1919 autobiographical sermon.

87. George Hansen, in *Pentecostal Evangel,* December 22, 1917, p. 11. Two years later Harold E. Hansen, another China missionary, apparently unrelated, wrote that the missionary who possessed the Chinese language was George's wife, not his. The point is that Sophie's reputation for missionary tongues persisted. *Pentecostal Evangel,* March 8, 1919, p. 10.

88. An important qualification here is "at length." Converts reported hearing short formulaic phrases like "O, Lord, open the mouth . . . O, Lord, open the heart" in their natal language. See, for example, Albert Norton, in *Intercessory Missionary,* June 1907, p. 44, reprinted from *Trust* without full citation.

89. Shumway, "A Study of 'The Gift of Tongues,'" p. 43.

90. Cyril Williams discusses xenoglossy at length, offering additional examples from the

pentecostal tradition, the nonpentecostal Christian tradition, and the non-Christian tradition. Finding naturalistic explanations of xenoglossy sufficient to explain most but not all of the evidence, he tentatively suggests something like a "hereditary genetic memory." Cyril G. Williams, *Tongues of the Spirit: A Study of Pentecostal Glossolalia and Related Phenomena* (Cardiff: University of Wales Press, 1981), pp. 180–189.

91. Taylor, *Spirit and the Bride*, p. 104.

92. G. W. Hall, in *Intercessory Missionary*, January 1908, p. 62. At the other corner of the country, see A. E. Rojahn, in *Apostolic Light*, August 28, 1907, p. 3.

93. Robert Atchison, in *New Acts*, July–August 1907, p. 4.

94. Carrie Judd Montgomery, "Date Book for 1909," April 11, 1909, AOG.

95. Ibid., January 2, 1909.

96. *Minutes of the General Council of the Assemblies of God . . . 1917*, p. 22.

97. Fred Merian, in *Full Gospel Missionary Herald*, January 1922, p. 16.

98. William A. Ward, "The Trailblazer: Dr. A. G. Garr," typed, n.d., p. 9, AOG. Though Garr was one of the most important early pentecostal leaders, the autobiographical and biographical materials remain sketchy and inconsistent. My discussion is based on Ward and the following texts listed in chronological order: *Apostolic Faith* [Calif.], September 1906, p. 4; A. G. Garr and Wife, in *Apostolic Faith* [Calif.], October 1906, p. 2; Mary Johnson, *Apostolic Faith* [Calif.], February–March 1907, p. 1; Mrs. A. G. Garr, *Pentecostal Power* [Calcutta, India], March 1907, pp. 1–2; Sister A. G. Garr, *Apostolic Faith* [Calif.], April 1907, p. 1; Bro. and Sister A. G. Garr, *Apostolic Faith* [Calif.], June–September 1907, p. 1; Mrs. Lillian Garr, *Apostolic Faith* [Calif.], June–September 1907, p. 4; Alfred G. Garr, *Cloud of Witnesses to Pentecost in India*, September 1907, p. 40; *Apostolic Faith* [Calif.], October 1907–January 1908, p. 1; S. C. Todd, "Narrative of Facts," January 1908, reprinted in Vanzandt, *Speaking in Tongues*, pp. 45–47; A. G. Garr, *Cloud of Witnesses to Pentecost in India*, August 1909, p. 10; Lillian Garr, in *Bridegroom's Messenger*, July 15, 1911, p. 4; A. G. Garr, *Latter Rain Evangel*, July 1914, p. 18; Shumway, "A Study of 'The Gift of Tongues,'" pp. 44–45; Arthur S. Paynter, *Moody Church News*, September 1923, pp. 96–119; Ewart, *Phenomenon of Pentecost*, p. 47; A. G. Osterberg, "Reel #4," typed interview, interviewer not named, undated [probably 1966], p. 6, AOG.

99. [A.] G. Garr to A. A. Boddy, March 15, 1908, in *Confidence*, May 1908, Special Supplement, p. 2.

100. Mabel E. Archibald, in *Baptist Missionary Review*, May 1907, pp. 219–220. The pentecostal trio may have been Louise Condit, Lucy M. Leatherman, and Andrew Johnson. *Apostolic Faith*, [Calif.], September 1906, p. 4.

101. Though no pentecostal sect ever officially repudiated xenolalia, individuals occasionally did, at least as a means for overseas evangelization. See, for example, Cora Harris MacIlravy, in *El Bethel*, January–February 1914, pp. 15–16.

102. For affirmations of xenolalia by recent pentecostals, see Ralph W. Harris, *Spoken by the Spirit* (Springfield, Mo.: Gospel Publishing House, 1973), and Wayne Warner, *Touched by the Fire* (Plainfield, N.J.: Logos International, 1978), chaps. 22, 24. Such works form a minuscule fraction of the literature, however.

103. For affirmation of relatively frequent glossolalia in Christian history, see George H. Williams and Edith Waldvogel [Blumhofer], "A History of Speaking in Tongues and Related Gifts," in *The Charismatic Movement* (Grand Rapids: William B. Eerdmans Publishing Co., 1975), chap. 4, summarized p. 104. Both Leigh Eric Schmidt and

Ann Taves imply that tongues erupted occasionally but, on the whole, rarely among nineteenth-century Protestants in America. Schmidt, *Hearing Things: Religion, Illusion, and the American Enlightenment* (Cambridge, Mass.: Harvard University Press, forthcoming); Taves, *Fits, Trances, and Visions: Experiencing Religion and Explaining Experience from Wesley to James* (Princeton: Princeton University Press, 1999), pp. 113, 157. Taves's astute analysis of the different ways that pentecostals interpreted their own and others' baptism-tongues experiences came to my attention too late to be incorporated in this chapter. But the distinction she draws between Wesleyan and Edwardsean outlooks seems to approximate the distinction I draw between primitivist and pragmatic ones. See pp. 328–341, esp. p. 328.

104. For the difficulty of knowing what ancient references to strange speech really denoted, see Stuart D. Currie, "'Speaking in Tongues': Early Evidence Outside the New Testament," *Interpretation,* 19 (1965): 274–294; Frank W. Beare, "Speaking with Tongues: A Critical Survey of the New Testament Evidence," *Journal of Biblical Literature,* 83 (1964): 229–246, esp. p. 246; D. Moody Smith, "Glossolalia and Other Spiritual Gifts in New Testament Perspective," *Interpretation,* 28 (1974): 316–317.

105. For Irvingites, see "Mrs. Oliphant," *The Life of Edward Irving* (London: Hurst & Blackett, 1862), vol. 2, pp. 196–199, 206–209, 432–433. For Mormons, see *Book of Mormon,* Book of Moroni 10: 18–19; Leonard J. Arrington and Davis Bitton, *The Mormon Experience: A History of the Latter-day Saints* (New York: Alfred A. Knopf, 1979), pp. 40, 47, 87, 213. For psychics, see Albert LeBaron [pseud. for William James], "A Case of Psychic Automatism, Including 'Speaking in Tongues,'" *Proceedings of the Society for Psychical Research,* 12 (1896–1897): 277.

106. Ann Braude, *Radical Spirits: Spiritualism and Women's Rights in Nineteenth-Century America* (Boston: Beacon Press, 1989), pp. 87–90, 97–98.

107. For the classic argument by a social scientist for the physiological origin of tongues, see Felicitas D. Goodman, *Speaking in Tongues: A Cross-Cultural Study of Glossolalia* (Chicago: University of Chicago Press, 1972).

108. Frank Bartleman, *Azusa Street: The Roots of Modern-Day Pentecost,* ed. Vinson Synan (Plainfield, N.J.: Logos International, 1980, original [differently titled] 1925), p. 125.

109. Goss, *Winds of God,* p. 95.

110. *Pasadena Daily News,* July 5, 1906, p. 1.

111. *Apostolic Faith* [Kans.], February 1914, p. 9.

112. A. J. Tomlinson, in *Faithful Standard,* September 1922, p. 2.

113. Ibid., p. 1.

114. Albert Norton, in *Triumphs of Faith,* September 1909, p. 198; Tomlinson, *Last Great Conflict,* p. 210; Ardell K. Mead, in *Apostolic Faith* [Calif.], November 1906, p. 3; A. A. Boddy, quoting "a working-man," in *Christian* [U.K.], August 1, 1907, pna, AGUK; [Ellen] Hebden, in *Promise,* May 1907, p. 2.

115. Gotfred E. Stephan, in *Christian Evangel,* August 1, 1914, p. 1; Jackson White, in *Apostolic Herald,* April 1909, p. 4.

116. John G. Lake, "Transcription of John Lake's Diary," apparently referring to October 1907, typed, p. 2, AOG.

117. For the classic argument by a social scientist for the cultural origin of tongues, see William J. Samarin, *Tongues of Men and Angels: The Religious Language of Pentecost-*

alism (New York: Macmillan, 1972), and also Dale B. Martin, "Tongues of Angels and Other Status Indicators," *Journal of the American Academy of Religion,* 59 (1991): 547–589, esp. p. 556.

118. Anonymous, *Way of Faith,* July 29, 1896, p. 5, quoted in Robins, "Plainfolk Modernist," p. 256.

119. [Joseph Hillery King], *Yet Speaketh: Memoirs of the Late Bishop Joseph H. King* (Franklin Springs, Ga.: Publishing House of the Pentecostal Holiness Church, 1949), p. 38.

120. Vinson Synan, Introduction to Frank Bartleman, *Azusa Street,* p. xiii. Context implies Pennsylvania.

121. [Maria Woodworth-Etter], *Life, Work and Experience of Maria Beulah Woodworth* (St. Louis: for author by Commercial Printing Co., 1894), p. 12.

122. Elizabeth Sisson, in *Latter Rain Evangel,* May 1909, p. 10.

123. Ibid., pp. 6–9.

124. *Word and Witness,* June 20, 1913, p. 7.

125. A. L. Knudson, in *Glad Tidings* [SF], August 1927, p. 3.

126. Anna Larssen, in *Upper Room,* July 1910, p. 8.

127. Henry G. Tuthill, in *Faithful Standard,* July 1922, p. 6.

3. Testimony

1. Peter Iver Kaufman, "Historians and Human Behavior: Biography as Therapy," *Clio,* 18 (1989): 180.

2. W. A. Heath, in *Apostolic Faith* [Calif.], February–March 1907, p. 8.

3. Frank Bartleman, *Distilled Dew* (Los Angeles: Frank Bartleman, 1934), p. 3.

4. See, for example, the testimony of E. C. B. [Ernest Charles William Boul], in *Showers of Blessings,* no. 11 [1913], p. 12.

5. A. A. Boddy, in *Confidence,* February 1914, pp. 23–26.

6. "Brother C. H. Mason's Testimony of His Baptism of the Holy Ghost and Fire," reprinted without full citation in Lucillia J. Cornelius, *The Pioneer: History of the Church of God in Christ* (n.p., 1975), p. 13; Ithiel C. Clemmons, *Bishop C. H. Mason and the Roots of the Church of God in Christ* (Bakersfield, Calif.: Pneuma Life Publishing, 1996), p. 5.

7. For a case study of the dense networks of personal relationships that carried the pentecostal message from neighborhood to neighborhood, see Edith L. Blumhofer, "Networks on the Margins and the Emergence of Pentecostalism in Chicago, 1906–1912," forthcoming in *Religion in Urban America,* ed. Virginia Brereton and Mark Wilhelm.

8. See, for example, Helen Innes Wannenmacher, in *"Pentecost in My Soul": Explorations in the Meaning of Pentecostal Experience in the Early Assemblies of God,* ed. Edith L. Blumhofer (Springfield, Mo: Gospel Publishing House, 1989), pp. 181–182.

9. B. H. Irwin, in *Triumphs of Faith,* May 1907, pp. 114–116.

10. Agnes N. [Ozman] LaBerge, "History of the Pentecostal Movement from January 1, 1901," typed, p. 2, AOG.

11. *Missionaeren,* January 3, 1907, p. 6, quoted in Nils Bloch-Hoell, *The Pentecostal Movement: Its Origin, Development, and Distinctive Character* (New York: Humanities Press, 1964, Norwegian original 1956), p. 193, n. 31; Mrs. P. M. La Burge [Agnes Ozman LaBerge], testimony, August 1915, quoted in M. B. Woodworth-

Etter, *Signs and Wonders: God Wrought in the Ministry for Forty Years* (Indianapolis: published by author, 1916), p. 432. Though both sources are open to other readings, I believe that these two, taken together, confirm mine.

12. I owe this point to Nancy Ammerman, *Bible Believers: Fundamentalists in the Modern World* (New Brunswick: Rutgers University Press, 1987), p. 156.

13. W. H. Piper, in *Latter Rain Evangel,* January 1910, p. 2.

14. Carl O'Guin, typed transcript of interview by Wayne Warner, 1983, p. 2, AOG.

15. J. H. King, in *Cloud of Witnesses to Pentecost in India,* September 1907, p. 49.

16. C. Beruldsen, in *Confidence,* April 1908, pp. 11–12.

17. Norman Jones, review of *Prayer, Despair, and Drama: Elizabethan Introspection,* by Peter Iver Kaufman, *Church History: Studies in Christianity and Culture,* 67 (September 1998): 592.

18. Frank F. Ewart, *The Phenomenon of Pentecost: A History of the Latter Rain* (Houston: Herald Publishing House, 1947), p. 6.

19. See, for example, the testimonials of T. B. Barratt, in *Cloud of Witnesses to Pentecost in India,* March 1908, pp. 19–21; E. N. Bell: *Question and Answers* (Springfield, Mo.: [Gospel Publishing House], 1923), p. ix; A. A. Boddy, *"Pentecost at Sunderland": A Vicar's Testimony* (Sunderland, England: published by author, May 1909), p. 9; G. B. Studd, in *Confidence,* May 1911, p. 116; G. B. Cashwell, in *Apostolic Faith* [Calif.], October 1906, p. 3; Mother Wheaton, in *Apostolic Faith* [Calif.] December 1906, p. 2.

20. To say that the testimonies "never ended there" is of course hyperbole. One interviewee admitted to me that she had prayed for the experience daily for eighty years without success. Significantly, her story never saw print.

21. A. C. Knight, in *Pentecostal Holiness Advocate,* February 28, 1918, p. 5.

22. Ewart, *Phenomenon of Pentecost,* p. 5.

23. *Apostolic Faith* [Calif.], February–March 1907, p. 6.

24. See, for example, Eula Wilson, in *Apostolic Faith* [Calif.], July–September 1907, p. 4. Robert Mapes Anderson, *Vision of the Disinherited: The Making of American Pentecostalism* (New York: Oxford University Press, 1979), lists additional instances, p. 264, n. 46.

25. *Flames of Fire,* October 1911, p. 1.

26. Ardell K. Mead, in *Apostolic Faith* [Calif.], November 1906, p. 3.

27. Ibid., p. 3.

28. Samuel J. Mead, in *Apostolic Faith* [Calif.], February–March 1907, p. 5; "Mead, Samuel and Ardell," *DPCM,* by title; Frederick W. Faber, "There's a Wideness in God's Mercy" (1854), *The United Methodist Hymnal* (Nashville: United Methodist Publishing House, 1989), p. 121.

29. Mattie Mason, in *Christian Evangel,* November 15, 1913, p. 8.

30. Reanie Hancock, in *Pentecostal Holiness Advocate,* January 10, 1918, p. 9.

31. Lilah Peppers, in *Pentecostal Holiness Advocate,* January 10, 1918, p. 3.

32. E. M. T. and R. B., in *Christian Evangel,* February 8, 1919, p. 15.

33. D. E. Pittman, in *Pentecostal Holiness Advocate,* April 18, 1918, p. 13.

34. Russell E. Richey, *Early American Methodism* (Bloomington: Indiana University Press, 1991), p. 103.

35. J. E. French, "This Is Like Heaven to Me," 1931, in *Assembly Songs* (Springfield, Mo.: Gospel Publishing House, about 1955), p. 39.

36. Ewart, *Phenomenon of Pentecost,* p. 6.

37. Carrie Judd Montgomery, "Date Book for 1909," January 4.

38. David Faulkner, in *Pentecostal Holiness Advocate*, April 11, 1918, p. 10.

39. John Coxe, in *Grace and Truth*, September 1918, p. 3.

40. Maria Boddy regarding her husband J. T. Boddy's baptismlike experience, apparently subsequent to the initial one, in *New Acts*, February 1907, p. 4. Pentecostals frequently described baptism and subsequent baptismlike experiences in virtually identical language.

41. Howard A. Goss, *The Winds of God: The Story of the Early Pentecostal Days (1901–1914) in the Life of Howard A. Goss, as Told by Ethel E. Goss* (New York: Comet Press Books, 1958), p. 39. See Gotfred E. Stephan, in *Christian Evangel*, August l, 1914, p. 1, for a rare description of pain associated with Holy Ghost baptism.

42. Harriett Gravelle, in *Upper Room*, January 1910, pp. 7–8, quotation p. 8. The first event may have been a prepentecostal sanctification experience.

43. See, for example, M. M. Pinson, "Sketch of the Life and Ministry of Mack M. Pinson," typed, 1949, p. 13, AOG; C. H. Stockdick, letter to Sarah Parham, in [Charles Fox Parham], *The Life of Charles F. Parham: Founder of the Apostolic Faith Movement*, compiled by His Wife [Sarah E. Parham] (New York: Garland Publishing, 1985, original 1930), p. 442.

44. *Midnight Cry* [N.Y.], March–April 1911, p. 4, for the Glad Tidings Hall Apostolic Faith Mission in New York; *Showers of Blessings*, January 1910, p. 5, for the Apostolic Faith in Britain; *Upper Room*, June 1909, p. 4, for the Upper Room Mission in Los Angeles; *Apostolic Messenger*, February–March 1908, p. 2, for Calvary Temple, Winnipeg, premier church of Pentecostal Assemblies of Canada.

45. Stockdick, in [Parham], *Life of Charles F. Parham*, p. 442.

46. Boddy, *"Pentecost at Sunderland,"* pp. 15–16; T. B. Barratt, *The Truth about the Pentecostal Revival*, pamphlet, about 1908, p. 7.

47. John G. Lake, "Transcription of John Lake's Diary," typed, apparently referring to some time in October 1907, p. 8, AOG.

48. F. C. Morton, in *Evening Light and Church of God Evangel*, May 15, 1910, p. 5.

49. Brother Lee, in *Apostolic Faith* [Calif.], November 1906, p. 4.

50. Though recent social scientific studies are hardly unanimous on this point, many, perhaps a majority, have challenged the older assumption that the tongues experience should be linked with psychopathology. See, for example, Cyril G. Williams, *Tongues of the Spirit: A Study of Pentecostal Glossolalia and Related Phenomena* (Cardiff: University of Wales Press, 1981), p. 129; H. Newton Malony and A. Adams Lovekin, *Glossolalia: Behavioral Science Perspectives on Speaking in Tongues* (New York: Oxford University Press, 1985), chap. 5, esp. p. 93.

51. Jonathan Perkins, in *Pentecostal Evangel*, March 22, 1924, pp. 6–7, as quoted in Anderson, *Vision of the Disinherited*, p. 123.

52. A. G. Osterberg, "reel #3," typed interview by Jerry Jensen, March 22, 1966, p. 10, AOG.

53. A. W. Webber, in *Apostolic Faith* [Kans.], May 1944, p. 11.

54. *Apostolic Faith* [Calif.], September 1906, throughout; *Latter Rain Evangel*, October, 1908, p. 1; *Pentecost*, August 1908, p. 1; Nanie Hughes, in *Evening Light and Church of God Evangel*, March 1, 1910, p. 8.

55. Only two issues of this periodical survive. The other one, dated November 19, 1906, was published in Salem, Oregon.

56. E. J. Page, in *Apostolic Light*, August 28, 1907, p. 1.

57. [Eula Wilson], in *Apostolic Light,* August 28, 1907, p. 2.

58. W. F. Carothers, in *Word and Witness,* June 20, 1913, p. 4.

59. Amanda Smith, in *Pentecost,* March 1, 1910, p. 3.

60. Elizabeth V. Baker and Co-Workers, *Chronicles of a Faith Life* (New York: Garland Publishing, 1984, original 1915–1916), p. 137.

61. Walter Brack, in *Pentecostal Holiness Advocate* January 10, 1918, p. 3.

62. A. D. Bayer, *Pentecostal Holiness Advocate,* February 21, 1918, p. 9.

63. B. E. Warren, "Joy Unspeakable," in *Echoes of Victory,* ed. Mr. and Mrs. L. R. Keys (Chicago: Thoro Harris, about 1925), no. 204.

64. Hall quoted (in composite citation) in Gary Don McElhany, "The South Aflame: A History of the Assemblies of God in the Gulf Region, 1901–1940," Ph.D. diss., Mississippi State University, 1996, p. 34.

65. Ralph M. Riggs, in *Trust,* March 1918, p. 11.

66. *Apostolic Faith* [Kans.], January 1916, p. 1.

4. Authority

1. "Preamble and Resolution of Constitution," *Minutes of the General Council of the Assemblies of God . . . 1914,* p. 4.

2. *Midnight Cry* [N.Y.], March–April 1911, p. 4, and *Apostolic Faith* [Calif.], February–March 1907, p. 1. Though these carpentry metaphors marked Masonic literature too, I have discovered no evidence of direct crossover.

3. [Editor E. N. Bell], in *Word and Witness,* May 1915, p. 2. Bell's immediate concern was the meaning of the biblical phrase, "In the name of Jesus Christ," but his larger point was God's versus "man's theory" about this or any other subject.

4. Levi Lupton, in *New Acts,* November 2, 1905, p. 2.

5. E. N. Bell, in *Christian Evangel,* June 29, 1918, p. 9.

6. W. R. Rush, in *Pentecostal Herald,* August 1918, p. 4.

7. W. J. S. [William J. Seymour], in *Apostolic Faith* [Calif.], January 1908, p. 3.

8. Pentecostals readily disallowed prophetic claims when they seemed unbiblical. See, for example, *Elbethel,* 1914, no. 3, p. 15; *Good Report,* January 1, 1914, p. 3; A. G. Garr, in *Word and Witness,* April 20, 1914, p. 3.

9. Lawrence Catley, Azusa eyewitness, said that devotees never consulted commentaries since they knew the Holy Spirit would guide them in reading the Bible. Wayne E. Warner, *The Woman Evangelist: The Life and Times of Charismatic Evangelist Maria B. Woodworth-Etter* (Metuchen, N.J.: Scarecrow Press, 1986), p. 183, n. 2.

10. *Tongues of Fire,* December 1 and 15, 1900, p. 197.

11. Joseph Hutchinson, in *Apostolic Faith* [Kans.], April 1913, p. 7.

12. Advertisement, in *Glad Tidings* [SF], May 1927, p. 9.

13. B. F. Lawrence, *The Apostolic Faith Restored* (St. Louis: Gospel Publishing House, 1916), p. 13.

14. Frank Bartleman, *Azusa Street: The Roots of Modern-Day Pentecost,* ed. Vinson Synan (Plainfield, N.J.: Logos International, 1980, original [differently titled] 1925), p. 75.

15. R. E. Winsett, *Evening Light* (n.p., n.d.), in *Readings in Pentecostal History,* comp. Cecil M. Robeck, Jr. (Pasadena, Calif.: Fuller Theological Seminary, 1986), p. 132.

16. *New York American,* December 3, 1906, reprinted in Nils Bloch-Hoell, *The Pentecostal Movement: Its Origin, Development, and Distinctive Character* (New York: Humanities Press, 1964; Norwegian original 1956), pp. 49–51, quotation p. 50.

17. See, for example, *Apostolic Faith* [Calif.], May 1907, p. 2; advertisement, in *Golden Grain,* September 1926, p. 1; [Charles Fox Parham], *The Life of Charles F. Parham: Founder of the Apostolic Faith Movement,* compiled by His Wife [Sarah E. Parham] (Garland Publishing, N.Y.: 1985, original 1930), p. 53.

18. Levi Lupton, in *New Acts,* October 5, 1905, p. 6.

19. Shirley Nelson and Rudy Nelson, "Tongues of Fire: Frank Sandford of Shiloh, Maine," in *Portraits of a Generation: Early Pentecostal Leaders,* ed. James R. Goff, Jr. and Grant Wacker (forthcoming).

20. *Diary of A. J. Tomlinson,* ed. Homer A. Tomlinson (Queens Village, N.Y.: Church of God, World Headquarters, 1955), vol. 3, p. 13.

21. See, for example, the advertisement in *Apostolic Faith* [Kans.], undated tear sheet, AOG, probably June 1912, p. 12, for Twelfth Annual National Campmeeting preceded by a ten-day fast (that is, no lunch), extendible to forty days for those who preferred it.

22. See, for example, *Apostolic Faith* [Calif.], November 1906, p. 1. "Came through" is not quoted here but the phrase represented pentecostals' common way of describing the baptism process.

23. Gordon P. Gardiner, *Radiant Glory: The Life of Martha Wing Robinson,* 2nd ed. ([New York: Bread of Life], 1970, original 1962), p. 170.

24. [Christian] Schoonmaker, in *Weekly Evangel,* January 12, 1918, p. 6.

25. [Parham], *Life of Charles F. Parham,* pp. 52–53, 60–61, quotation p. 52.

26. Lilian Thistlethwaite, "The Wonderful History of the Latter Rain," reprinted in ibid., p. 60.

27. A. A. Boddy, in *Confidence,* December 1912, p. 282.

28. William H. Piper, "Prefatory," to D. Wesley Myland, *The Latter Rain Covenant and Pentecostal Power,* published with other documents as *Three Early Pentecostal Tracts,* ed. Donald W. Dayton (New York: Garland Publishing, 1985, original 1910), Preface.

29. Russell P. Spittler, "Scripture and the Theological Enterprise," in *The Use of the Bible in Theology: Evangelical Options,* ed. Robert K. Johnston (Atlanta: John Knox Press, 1985), p. 63.

30. *Minutes of the General Council of the Assemblies of God . . . 1914,* p. 4. The first "Statement of Fundamental Truths Approved by the General Council of the Assemblies of God," October 1916, similarly affirmed in its initial article: "The Bible is the inspired Word of God, a revelation from God to man, the infallible rule of faith and conduct, and is superior to conscience and reason, but not contrary to reason." Ibid., *1916,* p. 10.

31. B. H. Irwin, in *Live Coals of Fire,* October 13, 1899, p. 2, quoted in James R. Goff, Jr., "Pentecostal Millenarianism: The Development of Premillennial Orthodoxy, 1909–1943," *Ozark Historical Review,* 12 (1983): 19.

32. D. W. Kerr, in *Weekly Evangel,* December 16, 1916, p. 3.

33. *Church of God Evangel,* March 14, 1914, p. 7.

34. D. M. Panton, in *Word and Witness,* May 1915, p. 5.

35. *Glad Tidings* [SF], October 1925, p. 8.

36. Florence L. Burpee, "The Second Coming of the Lord," *Word and Work,* undated photocopy, about 1910 by internal evidence, p. 368, AOG.

37. R. J. Craig, in *Glad Tidings* [SF], December 1929, p. 14.

38. *Apostolic Faith* [Calif.], January 1907, p. 2.

39. *Apostolic Faith* [Ore.], January 1909, p. 3.
40. Compare Secretary [J. Roswell] Flower, in *Word and Witness,* June 1915, p. 1, with *Minutes* of North Cleveland, Tenn., Church of God, July 1, 1911, COG.
41. *Apostolic Faith* [Calif.], October 1907–January 1908, p. 2. The writer probably was William J. Seymour, or at least one who spoke for him, because the author described the mission's policy.
42. Probably pastor Robert J. Craig, in *Glad Tidings* [SF], December 1929, p. 14.
43. E. T. Slaybaugh, in *Weekly Evangel,* May 15, 1915, p. 3.
44. For snake-handling and related practices, see Robert Mapes Anderson, *Vision of the Disinherited: The Making of American Pentecostalism* (New York: Oxford University Press, 1979), pp. 92–96; Dennis Covington, *Salvation on Sand Mountain: Snake Handling and Redemption in Southern Appalachia* (Reading, Mass.: Addison-Wesley, 1995).
45. G. F. Taylor, *The Spirit and the Bride,* published with other documents as *Three Early Pentecostal Tracts,* ed. Donald W. Dayton (New York: Garland Publishing, 1985, original 1907), p. 42.
46. W. W. Simpson, in *Cloud of Witnesses to Pentecost in India,* July 1910, p. 23.
47. Edward Armstrong, in *Victorious Gospel,* Early Spring 1915, p. 1.
48. *Trust,* March 1916, p. 14.
49. Charles F. Parham, *A Voice Crying in the Wilderness* (Baxter Springs, Kans.: Apostolic Faith Bible College, rev. and repr. 1944[?], 2nd ed. 1910, original 1902), p. 13.
50. See, for example, J. G. Bourmon, in *Apostolic Faith* [Calif.], January 1907, p. 4.
51. For example, *Voice in the Wilderness* editor G. T. Haywood advertised his own book, *The Revelation of the Ages,* by insisting that it was not a "mere piece of guesswork, or fancy imagination," but stood in "perfect harmony with the word of God." *Voice in the Wilderness,* no. 22, probably 1918, p. 2.
52. Mark A. Noll, "Common Sense Traditions and American Evangelical Thought," *American Quarterly,* 37 (Summer 1985): 216–238.
53. R. A. Torrey, *What the Bible Teaches* (New York: Fleming H. Revell Co., 1898), p. 1. For the broader context, see George M. Marsden, *Fundamentalism and American Culture: The Shaping of Twentieth-Century Evangelicalism: 1870–1925* (New York: Oxford University Press 1980), chap. 6, esp. pp. 60–61.
54. Charles Parham, in *Apostolic Faith* [Kans.], October 1912, p. 8.
55. All of these periodicals are housed at AOG or in my possession, except *Truth for the Times,* which is mentioned in *Latter Rain Evangel,* October 1912, p. 24.
56. W. W. Simpson, in *Pentecostal Evangel,* June 6, 1925, p. 10; personal communication from Daniel H. Bays, professor of Chinese history, University of Kansas, June 6, 2000.
57. William Welch, in *Midnight Cry* [Wash.], November 1907, p. 1.
58. *Church of God Evangel,* March 10, 1917, p. l.
59. *Apostolic Faith* [Calif.], September 1906, p. 2.
60. Ibid., December 1906, p. 1.
61. W. J. Seymour, in *Apostolic Faith* [Calif.], October 1907–January 1908, p. 3.
62. Elmer K. Fisher, in *Upper Room,* August 1909, p. 2.
63. Mrs. W. H. Finley, in *Apostolic Faith* [Kans.], May 1912, pp. 8–9.
64. Morton W. Plummer, in *Word and Work,* May 1912, p. 103.
65. Taylor, *Spirit and the Bride,* p. 132.

66. The growth of internal dissension and the numerous groups that resulted from it are compactly surveyed in John Thomas Nichol, *Pentecostalism* (New York: Harper & Row, 1966), chaps. 7–9.

67. For Seymour versus Durham, see Bartleman, *Azusa Street*, pp. 151, 155–156.

68. For Parham versus Durham, see Edith Lydia Waldvogel [Blumhofer], "The 'Overcoming Life': A Study in the Reformed Evangelical Origins of Pentecostalism" (Ph.D. diss., Harvard University, 1977), pp. 187–188, and Edith L. Blumhofer, "The Finished Work of Calvary: William H. Durham and a Doctrinal Controversy," *Assemblies of God Heritage*, Fall 1983, pp. 9–10.

69. J. C. Siebert, in *Apostolic Faith* [Kans.], August 1913, pp. 14–16, quotation p. 14.

70. For King versus McPherson, see Vinson Synan, *The Old-Time Power* (Franklin Springs, Ga.: Advocate Press, 1973), p. 139; [Joseph Hillery King], *Yet Speaketh: Memoirs of the Late Bishop Joseph H. King* (Franklin Springs, Ga.: Publishing House of the Pentecostal Holiness Church, 1949), p. 133.

71. B. L. Fitzpatrick, in *Voice in the Wilderness*, vol. 2, no. 13, probably 1923, p. 9. I infer the author's identity and the location of the scene from the context.

72. *Voice in the Wilderness*, vol. 2, no. not legible, probably late 1920, p. 2 (business identification page), author not named but almost certainly editor G. T. Haywood.

73. For grass-roots examples of bitter intrachurch wrangling, see Paul Haven Walker, *Paths of a Pioneer: Life Story of Paul Haven Walker: My Call and Redemption* (Cleveland, Tenn.: n.p., 1970), pp. 60, 87, 136.

74. E. N. Bell, in *Weekly Evangel*, March 10, 1917, p. 9.

75. Bartleman, *Azusa Street*, p. 101.

76. Ibid., p. 143.

77. T. B. Barratt, in *Confidence*, March 1911, p. 63.

78. A. A. Boddy, in *Confidence*, November 1912, p. 247. Boddy was referring to George B. Studd, one of the famed Cambridge Seven.

79. [King], *Yet Speaketh*, p. 333.

80. Frank F. Ewart, *The Phenomenon of Pentecost: A History of the Latter Rain* (Houston: Herald Publishing House, 1947), p. 106.

81. For example, D. C. O. Opperman preached about Holy Ghost baptism for two years before receiving it himself. "Diary," January 13, 1908, AOG.

82. [King], *Yet Speaketh*, p. 118.

83. A. J. Tomlinson, in *Samson's Foxes*, May 1902, p. 1.

84. Ivan Panin, in *Glad Tidings* [SF], November 1926, p. 1, reprinted from the *New York Sun* without full citation.

85. See, for example, "Magic Numerology," in *Confidence*, January 1911, p. 15; "The Great Pyramid and the Coming of the Lord," and accompanying chart, in *Midnight Cry* [Wash.], March–April 1908, p. 5; Levi Lupton, in *New Acts*, June 14, 1906, p. 6; *Pentecostal Herald*, June 1, 1922, p. 1, a dispensational chart with ten ages; and *Pentecostal Herald*, October 1, 1922, p. 1, a dispensational chart that most unusually specifies dates: Rapture in 1927, Armageddon in 1941.

86. A. J. Tomlinson, in *Church of God Evangel*, May 2, 1914, p. 3.

87. Probably editor Cora Harris MacIlravy, *Elbethel*, no. 3, 1913, p. 15; A. G. Garr, in *Word and Witness*, April 20, 1914, p. 3.

88. A 1909 tract titled *A Message from God*, by Chicago pastor W. H. D. [William H. Durham], represented a typical communication. The penultimate paragraph of the

six-page document reads: "My people, hearken unto My words, for My heart yearns for thee, for thou hast drifted, and thy feet have wandered from the path of humility. Turn thou, turn thou, My children, and set thy faces as a flint, for My grace is sufficient." Hand-dated August 1, 1909, AOG.

89. See, for example, the reminiscence of Mrs. Rothrock, reproduced in [Parham], *Life of Charles F. Parham,* pp. 115–116; *Topeka State Journal,* January 9, 1901, and *Topeka Daily Capitol,* January 6, 1901, reproduced in Lyle Murphy, "Beginning at Topeka," *Calvary Review,* 8 (Spring 1974): 5.

90. N. N. Harriman, in *Everlasting Gospel* [Maine], March 17–30, 1901, p. 119.

91. Bell (1914), quoted in Edith L. Blumhofer, *The Assemblies of God: A Chapter in the Story of American Pentecostalism* (Springfield, Mo.: Gospel Publishing House, 1989), vol. 1, p. 209.

92. In principle the gift of prophecy and the gift of interpretation of tongues should have held equal status, since both embodied the Holy Spirit's thoughts rendered in vernacular speech. In practice, however, pentecostals emphasized prophecy relatively little and the interpretation of tongues a great deal. It is easy to see why. Prophecy was common in the Christian tradition; tongues and the interpretation of tongues were not.

93. [Durham], *Message from God,* p. 1. See also the tongues-translated message of Mrs. I. S. Grant in *New Acts,* April 1907, p. 2: "Jesus is coming. GET READY."

94. See, for example, Levi Lupton, in *New Acts,* April 1907, p. 2; *Bridal Call,* June 1919, pp. 5–8; *Promise,* February 1909, p. 3.

95. W. M. Allison, in *Apostolic Faith* [Kans.], December 25, 1910, p. 7.

96. See, regarding Martha Wing Robinson, Gordon P. Gardiner, *Radiant Glory: The Life of Martha Wing Robinson,* 2nd ed. ([New York: Bread of Life], 1970, original 1962), lodging p. 126, travel schedules p. 214, keys p. 173, packing bags p. 266.

97. Charles Parham, in *Apostolic Faith* [Kans.], November 1913, pp. 5–6.

98. *Apostolic Messenger* [Cambridge, Mass.], December 1920, p. 12.

99. Church of God [of Apostolic Faith] founding meeting *Minutes* by J. W. Ledbetter, February 10, 1911, Slocumb, Ala., AOG.

100. For Myland's Gibeah Bible School in Plainfield, Ind., see Alice Reynolds Flower, *Grace for Grace* (Springfield, Mo.: by author, [1961]), pp. 56–57.

101. T. M. Jeffreys, in *Confidence,* June 1910, quoted in *Upper Room,* July 1910, p. 8.

102. William H. Durham, in *Gospel Witness,* undated, likely January 1914, p. 14.

103. [Church of God] *General Assembly Minutes 1906–1914* (Cleveland, Tenn.: White Wing Publishing House, 1992), 1914, p. 271.

104. *Word and Witness,* April 20, 1914, p. 1.

105. *Apostolic Faith* [Calif.], September 1906, p. 1.

106. Ibid., p. 4.

107. M. B. Woodworth-Etter, *Signs and Wonders: God Wrought in the Ministry for Forty Years* (Indianapolis: published by author, 1916), p. 273.

108. Most of the early periodicals carried a doctrinal statement of some sort on the inside front cover or on the ownership page.

109. Edgar C. Steinberg, in *Voice in the Wilderness,* vol. 2, no. not legible, probably late 1920s, p. 4[?] ("Foreign-Missionary-News" page), AOG.

110. Carl O'Guin, typed transcript of interview by Wayne Warner, 1983, p. 8, AOG.

111. A. S. Copley, in *Way of Faith,* July 23, 1908, p. 5.

112. *Voice in the Wilderness,* vol. 2, no. not legible, probably late 1920, p. 15.
113. I have created this scenario from the following unsigned news items in Ryan's periodical, *Apostolic Light,* August 28, 1907: "The Farewell," "The Address of Missionaries," "Bound for the Orient," all on p. 1; untitled news item, p. 3, col. 1.
114. Almost certainly editor M. L. Ryan, in *Apostolic Light,* August 28, 1907, p. 2.
115. Almost certainly editor M. L. Ryan, in *Apostolic Light,* November 19, 1906, p. 3.
116. V. P. Simmons, in *Triumphs of Faith,* October 1908, p. 222.
117. S. D. Kinne, in *Household of God,* May 1909, p. 13.

5. Cosmos

1. Nils Bloch-Hoell, *The Pentecostal Movement: Its Origin, Development, and Distinctive Character* (New York: Humanities Press, 1964; Norwegian original 1956), p. 109. I owe the main point of this paragraph to Bloch-Hoell's perceptive work. More broadly, Bloch-Hoell has helped me think about pentecostals' cosmology in cultural rather than strictly theological terms.
2. David A. Reed, "Origins and Development of Theology of Oneness," Ph.D. diss., Boston University, 1978; Fred J. Foster, *"Think It Not Strange": A History of the Oneness Movement* (St. Louis: Pentecostal Publishing House, 1965).
3. G. T. Haywood, *Voice in the Wilderness,* no. 22, probably 1918, p. 1. See the numerous testimonials on the same page exemplifying the linkage among water baptism, Holy Spirit baptism, and tongues.
4. William R. Hutchison, *The Modernist Impulse in American Protestantism* (Cambridge: Harvard University Press, 1976), chaps. 3–4, Appendices A and B for breadth of influence of new theological ideas.
5. See, for example, Carrie Judd Montgomery, *God's Word about Witchcraft and Other Kindred Errors,* tract, n.d., p. 4.
6. *Upper Room,* January 1910, p. 3.
7. Shirley Nelson, *Fair, Clear and Terrible: The Story of Shiloh, Maine* (Latham, N.Y.: British American Publishing, 1989), pp. 125–128, quotation p. 126.
8. *Triumphs of Faith,* December 1908, p. 287.
9. J. S. Talley, in *Present Truth,* February 1910, p. 7.
10. W. H. Cossum, in *Upper Room,* July 1910, p. 3, reprinted without full citation from *Latter Rain Evangel.*
11. Arthur Booth-Clibborn, in *Confidence,* reprinted without full citation in *Upper Room,* July 1910, p. 1.
12. *Apostolic Faith* [Ore.], January 1909, p. 3.
13. J. W. Hutchins poem on cover of *Apostolic Faith* [Kans.], September 1905, p. 1.
14. T. K. Leonard, in *Word and Witness,* July 20, 1914, p. 3.
15. Anonymous account in editorial, *Upper Room,* June 1910, p. 4.
16. Lyrics quoted without citation in Edith L. Blumhofer, *The Assemblies of God: A Chapter in the Story of American Pentecostalism* (Springfield, Mo.: Gospel Publishing House, 1989), vol. 1, p. 154.
17. M. B. Woodworth-Etter, *Signs and Wonders God Wrought in the Ministry of Forty Years* (Indianapolis: published by author, 1916), p. 28.
18. "A Cloud of Glory," *Voice in the Wilderness,* July 1910, pna, AOG, apparently referring to a recent meeting at the Apostolic Assembly in Indianapolis; Howard A. Goss,

The Winds of God: The Story of the Early Pentecostal Days (1901–1914) in the Life of Howard A. Goss, as Told by Ethel E. Goss (New York: Comet Press Books, 1958), p. 124, regarding North Avenue Mission in Chicago.

19. *Apostolic Faith* [Ore.], January 1909, p. 4, regarding a "recent revival" in Cleveland, Tennessee.

20. Dean Peck, *Walking in the Spirit, Words of Life—A Tract for Each Week* (Framingham, Mass.: Christian Workers Union, September 18, 1926), no. 826, p. 1.

21. Harold Horton, *The Gifts of the Spirit* (Springfield, Mo.: Gospel Publishing House, 1975, original 1934), pp. 193–194.

22. Frederick G. Henke, "The Gift of Tongues and Related Phenomena at the Present Day," *American Journal of Theology*, 13 (1909): 198, 204.

23. M. L. Ryan, *Polk County (Dallas, Ore.) Observer,* December 28, 1906, p. 1, cited in M. Cecil Robeck, "Florence Crawford and the Apostolic Faith Movement," in *Portraits of a Generation: Early Pentecostal Leaders,* ed. James R. Goff, Jr. and Grant Wacker (forthcoming).

24. Joel Adams Wright, *Sheaf of the First Fruits,* May 1913, pp. 12–13, quoted in Kurt O. Berends, "A Divided Harvest: Alice Belle Garrigus, Joel Adams Wright, and Early New England Pentecostalism," M.A. thesis, Wheaton College Graduate School, 1993, p. 44.

25. *Showers of Blessings,* August–September, 1910, p. 5.

26. First-generation diaries and personal reminiscences brim with references to the Holy Spirit being "grieved" for unknown reasons. See, for example, Jacob Mueller, "Diary," March 7, 1921; George B. Studd, "Diary," December 6, 1908; Charles Fox Parham, letter to "Friends in the Lord," June 11, 1908, AOG; William H. Piper, *Latter Rain Evangel,* October 1908, pp. 4–5. The list of such examples could be extended at length. I have excluded the numerous references to the Holy Spirit being grieved for explicable reasons.

27. Robert Hume Reed, in *Voice in the Wilderness,* no. 19, probably 1916, p. 1.

28. Gordon P. Gardiner, *Radiant Glory: The Life of Martha Wing Robinson,* 2nd ed. (New York: Bread of Life, 1970, original 1962), pp. 186–187.

29. Agnes N. O[zman] LaBerge, *What God Hath Wrought: Life and Work of Mrs. Agnes N. O. LaBerge* (New York: Garland Publishing, 1985, original 1920), p. 60.

30. Mary Bryant, in *Church of God Evangel,* January 24, 1914, p. 7.

31. Agnes Ozman, in *Apostolic Faith* [Tex.], October 1908, p. 2.

32. *Apostolic Faith* [Kans.], August 1913, pp. 4–7, quotations on p. 5, reprinted without full citation from the *Christian.*

33. Alice Reynolds Flower, *Grace for Grace* (Springfield, Mo.: published by author, [1961]), p. 57.

34. A. C. Dixon, in *Pentecostal Herald,* January 1, 1922, p. 1. Dixon, a prominent fundamentalist, was not pentecostal, but this pentecostal periodical let him speak on their behalf.

35. John G. Lake, "Transcription of John Lake's Diary," quoting with approval a Mrs. Dockrall, December 19, 1910, typed, p. 23, AOG.

36. L. P. Adams, in *Grace and Truth,* June 1916, p. 1.

37. *Trust,* August 1918, p. 11.

38. Charles Fox Parham, in *Apostolic Faith* [Kans.], August 1912, p. 4 for herds, and S. D. Kinne, in *Household of God,* November 1907, p. 13 for buildings.

39. Alice M. Reynolds, in *Pentecost,* April–May 1909, p. 11, and [Joseph Hillery King],

Yet Speaketh: Memoirs of the Late Bishop Joseph H. King (Franklin Springs, Ga.: Publishing House of the Pentecostal Holiness Church, 1949), pp. 131–132.

40. *Trust,* August 1918, p. 11.

41. *Apostolic Faith* [Kans.], August 1913, p. 5, reprinted from the *Christian.*

42. A. J. Tomlinson, *The Last Great Conflict* (New York: Garland Publishing, 1985, original 1913), p. 204.

43. *Latter Rain Evangel,* December 1908, pp. 8–9.

44. *Apostolic Faith* [Kans.], August 1913, p. 4.

45. Ibid., p. 4.

46. Frank Bartleman, *Azusa Street: The Roots of Modern-Day Pentecost,* ed. Vinson Synan (Plainfield, N.J.: Logos International, 1980, original [differently titled] 1925), p. 121.

47. *Apostolic Faith* [Kans.], August 1913, pp. 4–7, quotation p. 7, taken without full citation from the *Christian,* pp. 4–7.

48. *Apostolic Faith* [Kans.], August 1913, pp. 5–7, p. 5 for demons, p. 6 for holiness. Elsewhere *Apostolic Faith* denounced "fleshly disorder" in Holy Ghost meetings, and suggested that spirits caused it. *Apostolic Faith* [Kans.], September 1912, p. 8.

49. [Charles Fox Parham], *The Life of Charles F. Parham: Founder of the Apostolic Faith Movement,* compiled by His Wife [Sarah E. Parham] (New York: Garland Publishing, 1985, original 1930), p. 87, regarding his wife Sarah.

50. G. B. S. [Studd], in *Upper Room,* November 1910, p. 3.

51. John G. Lake, "Transcription of John Lake's Diary," November 29, 1910, typed, p. 11, AOG.

52. George Floyd Taylor, "Diary," May 4, 1908, North Carolina State History Archives, Raleigh, N.C.

53. [King], *Yet Speaketh,* pp. 131–132.

54. Morton W. Plummer, in *Word and Work,* May 1910, p. 134.

55. J. E. Sawders, in *Apostolic Faith* [Calif.], February–March 1907, p. 3; *Apostolic Faith* [Calif.], September 1906, p. 1; *New Acts,* February 1907, p. 4; Goss, *Winds of God,* p. 31.

56. Catherine Albanese, *Nature Religion in America* (Chicago: University of Chicago Press, 1990), pp. 8–12.

57. Robert A. Brown, in *Latter Rain Evangel,* July 1929, p. 6.

58. W. W. Hall, in *Word and Work,* February 1924, p. 15.

59. *Upper Room,* September–October 1910, p. 3.

60. *Llanelly (Wales) Mercury,* July 16, 1914, pna, AGUK.

61. A. A. Boddy, in *Confidence,* July 1916, p. 115.

62. *Apostolic Faith* [Calif.], December 1906, p. 4.

63. *Trust,* July 1917, p. 15.

64. See, for example, *Apostolic Faith* [Calif.], September 1906, p. 1; *Tongue of Fire,* September 1907, p. 2; Kittie Wood Kumarakulasinghe, *Free Methodist,* December 17, 1907, p. 811; *Latter Rain Evangel,* May 1909, p. 6; *Glad Tidings* [SF], February 1926, p. 1.

65. *Word and Witness,* October 20, 1913, p. 1.

66. Berends, "Divided Harvest," p. 71.

67. John G. Lake, "Transcription of John Lake's Diary," November 29, 1910, typed, p. 11, AOG.

68. Howard A. Goss, in B. F. Lawrence, *Apostolic Faith Restored* (St. Louis: Gospel Pub-

lishing House, 1916), p. 66 for Farrow. See *Apostolic Faith* [Calif.], January 1907, p. 4, and G. F. Taylor, *The Spirit and the Bride,* published with other documents as *Three Early Pentecostal Tracts,* ed. Donald W. Dayton (New York: Garland Publishing, 1985, original 1907), pp. 39, 44, for other cases of Holy Ghost power transmitted by touch.

69. Vinney McNall, in *Apostolic Faith* [Calif.], February–March 1907, p. 6; *Word and Work,* March 1912, p. 81; *Apostolic Faith* [Ore.], October 1909, p. 3: letter from Newport News, Va.: "When I got the handkerchief [in the mail], I had a bad sore throat . . . I laid the handkerchief on my neck and my throat jumped and throbbed and was healed before I knew it."

70. Bloch-Hoell, *Pentecostal Movement,* p. 229.

71. *Apostolic Faith* [Ore.], no. 21, about 1913, p. 3; *Weekly Evangel,* February 12, 1916, p. 11; D. Fisher, in *Upper Room,* July 1910, p. 1; *Upper Room,* July 1910, September–October 1910, p. 4, regarding Toronto's *Promise.*

72. *Apostolic Faith* [Ore.], January 1909, p. 1.

73. N. N. Harriman, *Everlasting Gospel* [Maine], January 29–February 2, 1901, p. 51.

74. Florence Crawford, in *Apostolic Faith* [Calif.], October [1907]–January 1908, p. 4.

75. Bartleman, *Azusa Street,* p. 134.

76. S. S. Craig, in *Trust,* October 1913, pp. 8–9, first quotation p. 8, second and third p. 9.

77. Robinson excerpted in Gardiner, *Radiant Glory,* p. 147.

78. E. N. Bell, in *Christian Evangel,* June 29, 1918, p. 9.

79. S. D. Kinne, in *Household of God,* November 1907, p. 13.

80. W. J. S. [William J. Seymour], in *Apostolic Faith* [Calif.], May 1908, p. 2.

81. Finis Yoakum, in *Latter Rain Evangel,* June 1912, pp. 7–8.

82. *Confidence,* October 1914, p. 185.

83. Shirley Nelson's astute remarks on Frank W. Sandford in *Fair, Clear and Terrible,* pp. 120–121, prompted me to think about the double image problem.

84. Bartleman, *Azusa Street,* p. 122.

85. *Upper Room,* August 1910, p. 8, taken without full citation from *Trust.*

86. Hannah Whitall Smith, *The Christian's Secret of a Happy Life,* published with another document as *The Devotional Writings of Robert Pearsall Smith and Hannah Whitall Smith,* ed. Donald W. Dayton, rev. ed. (New York: Garland Publishing, 1984, original 1885), first quotation p. 61, second p. 243.

87. Fannie E. Bolton, "Not I, but Christ," in *Songs for the King's Business,* ed. Franklin Edson Belden (Chicago: F. G. Fisher & Glad Tidings Publishing, 1909), no. 69.

88. *Upper Room,* August 1910, p. 8, taken without full citation from *Trust.*

89. William McDonald, "Coming to the Cross," in *Songs for the King's Business,* no. 379.

90. Charles Fox Parham, in *Apostolic Faith* [Kans.], June 1912, pp. 7–9, quotation p. 7.

91. Robinson excerpted in Gardiner, *Radiant Glory,* p. 232.

92. Goss, *Winds of God,* p. 111.

93. Cora Harris MacIlravy, *Elbethel,* no. 14, about 1922, p. 1.

94. A. A. Boddy, in *Confidence,* November 1912, pp. 251.

95. See, for example, Bartleman, *Azusa Street,* p. 41, and Glenn A. Cook, *The Azusa Street Mission* (Los Angeles: published by author, perhaps 1910 for pp. 1–3, perhaps 1914 for p. 4), p. 2.

96. Cook, *Azusa Street Meeting,* p. 4.

97. [King], *Yet Speaketh,* pp. 127–128, which contains a reference to a camp meeting disrupter, identified in the AOG copy (apparently by J. Roswell Flower) as Cook.

6. Worship

1. Christine Leigh Heyrman, *Southern Cross: The Beginnings of the Bible Belt* (Chapel Hill: University of North Carolina Press, 1997), chap. 1; John H. Wigger, *Taking Heaven by Storm: Methodism and the Rise of Popular Christianity in America* (New York: Oxford University Press, 1998), chap. 5.

2. Frank Bartleman, *Azusa Street: The Roots of Modern-Day Pentecost,* ed. Vinson Synan (Plainfield, N.J.: Logos International, 1980, original [differently titled] 1925), p. 82.

3. David Edwin Harrell, Jr., *All Things Are Possible: The Healing and Charismatic Revivals in Modern America* (Bloomington: Indiana University Press, 1975), p. 6.

4. Jacob Mueller, "Diary," entry for September 20, 1921, AOG.

5. Donald Gee, in 1932, quoted by Nils Bloch-Hoell, *The Pentecostal Movement: Its Origin, Development, and Distinctive Character* (New York: Humanities Press, 1964, Norwegian original 1956), p. 161.

6. I have adapted this phrase from Ann Rowe Seaman, *Swaggart: The Unauthorized Biography of an American Evangelist* (New York: Continuum, 1999), p. 16.

7. One suspects that many reporters and academics attended Holy Ghost meetings because they expected to see eye-popping behavior and, sure enough, found what they were looking for. See, for example, Allene M. Sumner, "The Holy Rollers on Shin Bone Ridge," *Nation,* July 29, 1925, pp. 137–138; "The 'Tongue' Movement," *Independent,* June 10, 1909, pp. 1286–1289; Duncan Aikman, "The Holy Rollers," *American Mercury,* 15 (October 1928): 180–191. Some of the most sensational descriptions of pentecostal worship behavior were penned not by outsiders but by rival pentecostals seeking to discredit competitors. See, for example, the attacks by Charles Parham on William J. Seymour in *Apostolic Faith* [Kans.], December 1912, pp. 4–5, and K. Brower, in *Apostolic Faith* [Kans.], May 1912, pp. 10–11. Other unfavorable descriptions came from apostates for whom the pentecostal fruit had turned bitter. See, for example, Mabel Collins, quoted at length in "The False 'Gift of Tongues,'" *Literary Digest,* January 9, 1909, pp. 560–587, and John R. Elsom, *Pentecostalism versus the Bible, or the Tongues Movement and Why I Left It* (Los Angeles: Wetzel Publishing, 1937), pp. 21, 36, 45.

8. Samuel J. Riggins, quoted in *Topeka Daily Capitol,* January 6, 1901, quoted in Lyle Murphy, "Beginning at Topeka," *Calvary Review,* 8 (Spring 1974): 4.

9. *Los Angeles Times,* April 18, 1906, sec. 2, p. 1, FTS.

10. *Los Angeles Daily Times,* July 23, 1906, p. 7, FTS.

11. *Daily Oregon (Salem) Statesman,* November 20, 1906, p. 6, AOG.

12. *New York American,* December 3, 1906, reprinted in Bloch-Hoell, *Pentecostal Movement,* p. 49.

13. J. B. Keeling, in *Birmingham Age-Herald,* June 23, 1907, p. 27, AOG.

14. Dispatch sent from Des Moines, Iowa, to *Birmingham Age-Herald,* printed in the issue of June 23, 1907, p. 27, AOG.

15. *Alliance (Ohio) Daily Review,* June [21 or 29; conflicting dates shown], 1907, probably p. 1, AOG.

16. C. E. McPherson, *Life of Levi R. Lupton* (Alliance, Ohio: published by author, 1911), p. 154.

17. Frederick Henke, "The Gift of Tongues and Related Phenomena at the Present Day," *American Journal of Theology,* 13 (April 1909): 193–206, quotation p. 197.

18. Doremus A. Hayes, *The Gift of Tongues* (Cincinnati: Jennings & Graham, 1913), p. 86.

19. *Ottumwa (Iowa) Courier,* September 3, 1912, pna, date not legible, but another item on the same page bears a byline date of September 3, AOG.

20. *Bridgeport Herald,* June 15, 1913, p. 23. The reporter referred to himself with a masculine pronoun. AOG.

21. C. W. Shumway, "A Study of 'The Gift of Tongues,'" A.B. thesis, University of Southern California, 1914, pp. 67–68.

22. Jules Bois, "The New Religions of America," *Forum,* 73 (February 1925): 145–155, 150–151.

23. A. A. Boddy, in *Confidence,* December 1914, p. 226.

24. *Morning Leader,* November 1907, ATS.

25. Tearsheet of a Welsh newspaper, title, date, page not legible, AGUK.

26. *Bedford (U.K.) Daily Chronicle* June 10, 1910, pna, ATS.

27. *Peckham (U.K.) Morning Leader,* April 2, 1908, pna, ATS.

28. *Chicago Daily News,* January 14, 1908, reprinted in *Assemblies of God Heritage,* Winter 1982–83, pp. 1, 5.

29. See, for example, 2:00 P.M. to 1:00 A.M.: *Apostolic Faith* [Calif.], February–March 1907, p. 3; 5:00 A.M.: *Apostolic Faith* [Calif.], June 1907, p. 19; all night: Walter J. Higgins, *Pioneering in Pentecost. My Experiences of 46 Years in the Ministry* (Bostonia, Calif.: n.p., 1958), p. 30; no regard for time: *Daily Echo and Times (U.K.),* October 4, 1907, pna, ATS; ten hours: *Word and Witness,* October 20, 1913, p. 3.

30. A. G. Osterberg, "Second tape," typescript of interview by Jerry Jensen and Jonathan Perkins, March 17, 1966, p. 6, AOG.

31. Belfry: A. G. Garr, in Thomas R. Nickel, *Azusa Street Outpouring* (Hanford, Calif.: Great Commission International, 1979, original 1956), p. 13; porch: *Apostolic Faith* [Calif.], October 1907–January 1908, p. 2; shoveling coal: *Apostolic Faith* [Calif.], February–March, 1907, p. 5; coal pile at work: *Confidence,* April 1908, p. 9; phone and in bed: Zelma Argue, *Contending for the Faith,* 2nd ed. (Winnipeg: Messenger of God Publishing House, 1928, original 1923), p. 52; dishes: W. A. Cramer, in *New Acts,* June 1907, p. 4.

32. Streetcars: Bartleman, *Azusa Street,* p. 51; trains: *Apostolic Faith* [Calif.], December 1906, p. 1; depots: *Apostolic Faith* [Calif.], October 1906, p. 3, and Agnes N. O[zman] LaBerge, *What God Hath Wrought: Life and Work of Mrs. Agnes N. O. LaBerge* (New York: Garland Publishing, 1985, original 1920), p. 66; saloon: Higgins, *Pioneering in Pentecost,* p. 26; open field: F. M. Britton, *Pentecostal Truth* (Royston, Ga.: Publishing House of the Pentecostal Holiness Church, [1919]), p. 225; street corners: *Apostolic Faith* [Calif.], September 1906, p. 4.

33. Goss, *Winds of God,* pp. 124–125.

34. *Diary of A. J. Tomlinson,* ed. Homer A. Tomlinson (Queens Village, N.Y.: Church of God, World Headquarters, 1949), vol. 1, p. 36 for Chattanooga, p. 46 for Cleveland.

35. Alice Garrigus, in Stanley H. Frodsham, *"With Signs Following": The Story of the Latter-Day Pentecostal Revival* (Springfield, Mo.: Gospel Publishing House, 1926), p. 65.

36. For a sampler of secular newspaper articles showing women playing a conspicuous role in worship services, see *Atlanta Journal,* April 12, 1914; *Ottumwa (Iowa) Daily Review,* August 12, 1912, p. 1; *Salem (Oregon) Daily Oregon Statesman,* November 20, 1906, p. 6; *Los Angeles Herald,* December 4, 1906, p. 6; *Los Angeles Herald,* February 4, 1907, p. 2; *Houston Chronicle,* August 13, 1905, *Kansas City "P. D.,"* [*Post Dispatch?*] January 25, 1901, all AOG.

37. A research assistant and I surveyed eighteen periodicals, representing a broad range

of geographic and social locations. We examined one issue in each of fifteen titles and two issues in three titles (because of their special importance or representativeness). Twelve issues appeared between 1906–10, nine between 1914–23. These 21 issues contained 180 references to meetings. Of these, 131 provided sex-specific information about participants. Males took a prominent role 84 times; women 62 times. However, if we exclude the *Apostolic Faith* [Ore.] (edited, perhaps ironically, by a woman, Florence Crawford), the figures move toward parity: 62 men, 56 women. Prominent role meant taking an active, speaking place in the meeting in which others apparently listened. We did not include references to the leaders of meetings. A full tabulation of our findings is housed at AOG.

38. Henry L. Fisher, "Diary," April 23, 1922, WCT.
39. Brother Rosa, in *Apostolic Faith* [Calif.], October 1906, p. 1.
40. T. B. Barratt, excerpted in B. F. Lawrence, *The Apostolic Faith Restored* (St. Louis: Gospel Publishing House, 1916), p. 107.
41. See, for example, LaBerge, *What God Hath Wrought*, pp. 52, 54, 89; Higgins, *Pioneering in Pentecost*, p. 35; Aimee Semple McPherson, *This Is That: Personal Experiences Sermons and Writings* (New York: Garland Publishing, 1985, original 1919), p. 161; Dan Morgan, *Rising in the West: The True Story of an "Okie" Family from the Great Depression through the Reagan Years* (New York: Alfred A. Knopf, 1992), p. 45.
42. G. B. Cashwell, in *Apostolic Faith* [Calif.], October 1906, p. 3.
43. Ibid., January 1907, p. 1.
44. Ibid., May 1907, p. 1.
45. C. H. Mason, *Whole Truth*, October 1911, p. 2.
46. A. A. Boddy, in *Confidence*, September 1912, p. 209.
47. See, for example, healings: Max Wood Moorhead, in *Apostolic Faith* [Calif.], September 1907, p. 4; xenolalia and admonishing strangers: R. J. Scott, in *Apostolic Faith* [Calif.], February–March 1907, p. 7; singing in tongues: *Apostolic Faith* [Calif.], June 1907, p. 1; preaching: *Apostolic Faith* [Calif.], April 1907, p. 4; leading revivals: *Apostolic Faith* [Calif.], October 1906, p. 3; prophecy: L. P. Adams, in *Present Truth*, December 1909, p. 3.
48. *Glad Tidings*, 1924, probably p. 1, lead article. Born in 1912, Utley achieved national notoriety as the "world's youngest evangelist." Utley barnstormed across the United States in the 1920s, speaking in pentecostal and quasi-pentecostal churches, including John Roach Straton's Calvary Baptist Church in New York City. Uldine Utley, *Why I Am a Preacher* (New York: Fleming H. Revell Co., 1931). Other important child evangelists included Violet Van Gundy and Little David Walker. For the former, see Wayne Warner, "A Child in the Pulpit," *Assemblies of God Heritage*, Spring 1996, pp. 3, 16–17; for the latter, J. A. Hewitt, *DPCM*, by title.
49. Ida Robinson, daughter of Bishop Ida B. Robinson, memorial speech, 1991, quoted in Harold Dean Trulear, "The Mother as Symbolic Presence: Ida B. Robinson and the Mt. Sinai Holy Church," in *Portraits of a Generation: Early Pentecostal Leaders*, ed. James R. Goff, Jr. and Grant Wacker (forthcoming).
50. Tomlinson, *Diary of A. J. Tomlinson*, vol. 3, p. 38.
51. N. J. Holmes and Wife, *Life Sketches and Sermons* (Royston, Ga.: Press of the Pentecostal Holiness Church, [1909]–1920), p. 147.
52. LaBerge, *What God Hath Wrought*, p. 48.
53. [Charles Fox Parham], *The Life of Charles F. Parham: Founder of the Apostolic Faith Movement*, compiled by His Wife [Sarah E. Parham] (New York: Garland Publishing, 1985, original 1930), p. 169.

54. Charles Parham, in *Apostolic Faith* [Kans.], September 1912, p. 9. Charles Shumway apparently witnessed one of Parham's meetings and came away believing that his proved more restrained than most. Shumway, "A Study of 'The Gift of Tongues,'" p. 69.

55. Probably E. N. Bell, in *Word and Witness,* May 20, 1914, p. 3.

56. Elizabeth V. Baker and Co-Workers, *Chronicles of a Faith Life* (New York: Garland Publishing, 1985, original 1915–1916), p. 149.

57. See, for example, *Apostolic Faith* [Calif.], May 1907, p. 3.

58. Probably A. A. Boddy, in *Confidence,* April 1908, p. 10; Church of God, Kilsyth, Scotland, *Minute Book,* March 3, 1909; E. C. B. [Ernest Charles William Boul], *Showers of Blessings,* no. 11, 1913, pna, AGUK; C. Donald, *Should Believers Plead the Blood Rapidly to Speak with Tongues?* tract, n.p., internal reference to 1910, AGUK.

59. T. B. Barratt, in *Confidence,* August 1909, p. 187.

60. P. M. Stokeley, in *Word and Witness,* August 20, 1913, p. 2.

61. T. B. Barratt, in *Confidence,* August 1909, p. 187; Charles F. Parham, in *Apostolic Faith* [Kans.], December 25, 1910, pp. 2–3; E. N. Bell, in *Christian Evangel,* February 8, 1919, p. 5.

62. *Weekly Evangel,* January 8, 1916, p. 11, speaking for W. F. Carothers.

63. Specifics are hard to come by since this was not the kind of information pentecostals wanted to preserve in print. Nonetheless, the oral tradition resonates with instances. Interview, Wayne E. Warner, Archivist, Assemblies of God, July 21, 1997.

64. Probably William F. Manley, in *Household of God,* reprinted in *Evening Light and Church of God Evangel,* March 1, 1910, p. 4.

65. *Confidence,* February 1909, p. 44.

66. The order of service I have described is a composite impression garnered from reading scores of accounts. For representative descriptions, see *The United Holy Church of America 24th Annual Convocation . . . 1918,* pp. 6–10, WCT; *Confidence,* September 1909, p. 212; *Apostolic Faith* [Calif.], February–March 1907, p. 4; M. M. Pinson, "Sketch of the Life and Ministry of Mack M. Pinson," typed, 1949, p. 13, AOG; *South Wales Press,* July 15, 1914, pna, AGUK; Henke, "Gift of Tongues," pp. 196–197.

67. *Minutes of the General Council of the Assemblies of God . . . 1916,* p. 11, *Minutes of the General Council of the Assemblies of God . . . 1917,* p. 21.

68. A. J. Tomlinson, in *Faithful Standard,* September 1922, p. 2.

69. LaBerge, *What God Hath Wrought,* p. 48.

70. See, for example, J. R. Conler, in *Apostolic Faith* [Calif.], January 1908, p. 1; Florence Crawford, in *Apostolic Faith* [Calif.], April 1907, p. 4; J. E. Sawders, in *Apostolic Faith* [Calif.], February–March 1907, p. 3.

71. Bartleman, *Azusa Street,* p. 70; [Joseph Hillery King], *Yet Speaketh: Memoirs of the Late Bishop Joseph H. King* (Franklin Springs, Ga.: Publishing House of the Pentecostal Holiness Church, 1949), pp. 131–132; Shirley Nelson, *Fair, Clear and Terrible: The Story of Shiloh, Maine,* (Latham, N.Y.: British American Publishing, 1989), p. 114.

72. See also Revelation 4:9; Deuteronomy 9:25; and 1 Kings 18:39.

73. I have not located a description of this practice in the early sources, although there are numerous references to inspired dancing. My grandmother told me that when she entered the pentecostal movement in the 1920s in South Dakota, glory marches were common.

74. "Journal of Happenings: The Diary of A. J. Tomlinson," August 4, 1909, COG. Glory marches probably played a prominent role in black pentecostal churches since they resembled the ring shout of slave Christianity. See, for example, C. Eric Lincoln and Lawrence H. Mamiya, *The Black Church in the African American Experience* (Durham: Duke University Press, 1990), pp. 352–354.

75. *Promise*, May 1907, pp. 2–3.

76. Walking on knees: McPherson, *This Is That*, p. 111; whole congregation on knees: *Daily Echo and Times*, October 4 1907, pna, ATS; George Floyd Taylor, "Diary," December 31, 1908, North Carolina State History Archives, Raleigh, N.C.

77. *Minutes of the Church of God of Alabama and Florida,* February 10, 1911, AOG.

78. *Apostolic Faith* [Kans.], December 1914, p. 4, reprinted from *Orders and Regulations for Field Officers, Salvation Army,* chap. 4, sec. 2, p. 51.

79. *Word and Witness,* June 20, 1913, p. 6.

80. *Confidence,* November 1911, pp. 255–256.

81. Though Bartleman recognized music's prominence, he curiously missed its value. Bartleman, *Azusa Street*, p. 57.

82. Mrs. Floyd T. Nichols (Ellene Ellison), undated, unaddressed typed letter, probably 1950s, AOG.

83. David Martin, *Tongues of Fire: The Explosion of Protestantism in Latin America* (Cambridge, Mass.: Basil Blackwell, 1990), pp. 168, 44.

84. See, for example, W. H. Durham, in *Apostolic Faith* [Calif.], February–March 1907, p. 4; *Triumphs of Faith,* May 1908, p. 102; E. K. Fisher, in *Upper Room,* August 1909, p. 2.

85. See, for example, news item symptomatically titled, "Revival Scenes: Weird Chants and Frenzied Appeals," regarding a meeting in Sunderland, England, in *Sunderland (U.K.) Daily Chronicle,* October 8, 1907, pna, ATS.

86. H. E. Calvert, "The Life of William Burton McCafferty," typed, 1952, [pp. 7–8], AOG.

87. Ernest S. Williams, in *Pentecostal Evangel,* August 19, 1951, p. 4.

88. G. T. Neal, in *Gospel Trumpet,* January 31, 1907, p. 74.

89. See, for example, *Trust,* December 1916, p. 16; *Confidence,* May 1908, p. 20; *Confidence,* June 1911, p. 139; *Promise,* February 1909, p. 4; *Showers of Blessings,* January 1910, p. 5; William H. Durham, in *Word and Work,* May 1910, pp. 153–156.

90. Hilda Reeder, *Voice in the Wilderness,* vol. 3, no. 6, probably April 1932, p. 2.

91. David D. Hall, *Worlds of Wonder, Days of Judgment* (New York: Alfred A. Knopf, 1989), p. 161.

92. See, for example, *Word and Witness,* May 1915, p. 2, for an attack on people who read the Sunday newspaper "steeped, filled with its worldliness" rather than the Bible, and for reading "light novel[s]."

93. See, for example, Morgan, *Rising in the West,* pp. 187–189.

7. Rhetoric

1. The Stone Church in Chicago is a notable exception.

2. "This is what I saw: A plain, bare mission hall, with bare floors, wooden benches, a few chairs, and a table. At the table a man kneeling—a strong, rugged man his head bowed; before him an open Bible." Special Correspondent, Sunderland Sunday night, *Sunderland (U.K.) Daily Chronicle,* October 7, 1907, pna, ATS. Lack of heat

and flooring: Walter J. Higgins, *Pioneering in Pentecost* (Bostonia, Calif.: published by author, 1958), p. 37; broken glass: Desmond W. Cartwright, *The Great Evangelists: The Lives of George and Stephen Jeffreys* (Hants, U.K.: Marshall Pickering, 1986), p. 45; messiness: *South Wales Press,* July 15, 1914, pna; obscurity: A. W. Frodsham, *Confidence,* June 1911, p. 139, and A. A. Boddy, *Confidence,* April 1913, p. 69; *Overcoming Life,* January 1909, for back page photo of Cantrel's (?) Assembly Hall in London.

3. *Apostolic Faith* [Calif.], September 1906, pp. 3, 1.

4. Stanley Frodsham, in *Victory!,* no. 13, about 1911, p. 3.

5. See, for example, A. A. Boddy, in *Confidence,* November 1912, pp. 248 and 256, regarding Pisgah and Pisgah Gardens, Calif.; Shirley Nelson, *Fair, Clear and Terrible: The Story of Shiloh, Maine* (Latham, N.Y.: British American Publishing, 1989), p. 70, regarding tabernacle at Shiloh; Levi Lupton, in *New Acts,* February 15, 1906, p. 4, regarding prayer room of the World Evangelization Company.

6. See, for example, the advertisement for a "Pentecostal Upper Room," Courthouse Square, Indianapolis, run by Brother Thomas C. Davis, in *Voice in the Wilderness,* vol. 2, no. not legible, probably late 1920, p. 5. Such notices typified hundreds.

7. The evangelist W. B. McCafferty, for example, led a 1910[?] Fort Worth revival in an old dance pavilion. Or again, in 1907 George and Cora Barney, leaders of the First Fruit Harvesters, purchased an old tavern in Grafton, New Hampshire. They promptly turned it into a pentecostal meeting hall called, significantly, El Nathan, "'God given.'" For McCafferty, see *The Life of William B. McCafferty,* recorded by H. E. Calvert, typed, 1952, n.p., AOG; for Barney, see Kurt O. Berends, "Social Variables and Community Response," in *Pentecostal Currents in American Protestantism,* ed. Edith L. Blumhofer, Russell P. Spittler, and Grant Wacker (Urbana: University of Illinois Press, 1999), p. 74.

8. For preaching protocols, see M. M. Pinson, "Sketch of the Life and Ministry of Mack M. Pinson," typed, 1949, p. 13, AOG; *Apostolic Faith* [Calif.], February–March 1907, p. 4; *Confidence,* September 1909, p. 212; *Confidence,* August 1909, p. 173; George B. Studd, "Diary," Sunday, May 10, 1908, AOG; E. S. Williams, in *Pentecostal Evangel,* August 1951, pp. 3–4.

9. Frank Ewart, *The Phenomenon of Pentecost: A History of the Latter Rain* (Houston: Herald Publishing House, 1947), p. 77; *Diary of A. J. Tomlinson,* ed. Homer A. Tomlinson (Queens Village, N.Y.: Church of God, World Headquarters, 1949), vol. 1, p. 75.

10. Frank Bartleman, *Azusa Street: The Roots of Modern-Day Pentecost,* ed. Vinson Synan (Plainfield, N.J.: Logos International, 1980, original [differently titled] 1925), pp. 41, 80, 155.

11. All excerpts reprinted in *Assemblies of God Heritage,* Fall 1984, p. 9.

12. Charles F. Parham, *A Voice Crying in the Wilderness,* rev. 2nd ed. (Baxter Springs, Kans.: Apostolic Faith Bible College, 1944[?], original 1902), Preface; and [Charles Fox Parham], *The Life of Charles F. Parham: Founder of the Apostolic Faith Movement,* compiled by His Wife [Sarah E. Parham] (New York: Garland Publishing, 1985, original 1930), p. 18.

13. M. B. Woodworth-Etter, *Signs and Wonders: God Wrought in the Ministry for Forty Years* (Indianapolis: published by author, 1916), p. 33. In this quotation Woodworth-Etter was referring to a specific occasion, but clearly it represented her general practice.

14. Levi Lupton, in *New Acts,* July 26, 1906, p. 4. Current observers of the pentecostal movement in Latin America highlight the preachers' incessant motion and elaborate gesture repertoire, emphasizing their effectiveness in holding the audience's attention. David Martin, *Tongues of Fire: The Explosion of Protestantism in Latin America* (Oxford: Basil Blackwell, 1990), p. 178.

15. Sarah Comstock, "Aimee Semple McPherson, Prima Donna of Revivalism," *Harper's Monthly Magazine,* December 1927, pp. 16–17.

16. Ibid., pp. 16–18.

17. Ann Rowe Seaman, *Swaggart: The Unauthorized Biography of an American Evangelist* (New York: Continuum, 1999), p. 35.

18. *Kansas City Journal,* February 1901, quoted in James R. Goff, Jr., *Fields White unto Harvest: Charles F. Parham and the Missionary Origins of Pentecostalism* (Fayetteville: University of Arkansas Press, 1988), p. 82.

19. Goff, *Fields White unto Harvest,* p. 150.

20. Probably pastor and editor Robert H. Brown, in *Midnight Cry* [N.Y.], March–April 1911, p. 8.

21. Scribbled letter to Elim headquarters, posted from Banbridge, dated only "Friday," tucked in a packet of letters from the mid-1920s, AGUK.

22. Russell E. Richey, *Early American Methodism* (Bloomington: Indiana University Press, 1991), p. 82.

23. *Los Angeles Herald,* November 12, 1906, p. 8.

24. Logo of *Bridal Call,* for example October 1918 issue, inside front cover.

25. *Apostolic Faith* [Calif.], May 1907, p. 3.

26. A. J. Tomlinson, in *Evening Light and Church of God Evangel,* July 1, 1910, p. 1.

27. *Latter Rain Evangel,* October 1908, pp. 7–10.

28. Frank Bartleman, *Distilled Dew* (Los Angeles: Frank Bartleman, 1934), p. 10.

29. Homer L. Cox, in *New Acts,* August 9, 1906, p. 4.

30. *Apostolic Faith* [Kans.], December–January 1912–13, p. 10.

31. Almost certainly editor Charles F. Parham, in *Apostolic Faith* [Kans.], January 1916, p. 6.

32. A. B. Crumpler, in *Holiness Advocate,* April 1, 1904, p. 4.

33. Parham, *Voice Crying in the Wilderness,* p. 66.

34. A. B. Simpson, in *Triumphs of Faith,* January 1908, p. 21.

35. Story related by Raymond Young, in *Full Gospel Missionary Herald,* July 1925, p. 19.

36. S. A. Jamieson, in *Pentecostal Evangel,* August 26, 1939, p. 3, inset. The quip appeared posthumously; Jamieson died in 1933.

37. Albert Weaver, in *Pentecostal Evangel,* July 13, 1929, p. 2.

38. Carl O'Guin, typed transcript of interview by Wayne Warner, 1983, p. 48, AOG.

39. Charles Parham, in *Apostolic Faith* [Kans.], November 1913, p. 13.

40. *Midnight Cry* [Wash.], May 1908, p. 4. This issue, like many pentecostal periodicals, bore no editor's name because everyone believed that the Holy Ghost performed that task. I assume Welch's role because the December 1907 issue listed him as the person to whom communications should be sent.

41. This was a full-page advertisement, probably printed in L. P. Adams' *Present Truth,* from context about 1915. It shows p. 4 at the top, but no date, AOG.

42. Photocopies of flyers in AOG. None carries a date. Most appear to be from the 1920s and 1930s.

43. Advertisement in *Pentecostal Herald,* June 1920, p. 1.

44. Undated flyer in AOG.

45. Frank M. Boyd, in *Pentecostal Evangel,* June 15, 1929, p. 5.

46. George Floyd Taylor, "Diary," North Carolina State History Archives, Raleigh, N.C. See, for example, the poignant entry for August 25, 1908.

47. [Joseph Hillery King], *Yet Speaketh: Memoirs of the Late Bishop Joseph H. King* (Franklin Springs, Ga.: Publishing House of the Pentecostal Holiness Church, 1949), p. 328.

8. Customs

1. D. W. Bebbington, *Evangelicalism in Modern Britain: A History from the 1730s to the 1980s* (London: Unwin Hyman, 1989), chap. 5, esp. pp. 175–176.

2. C. T. Studd excerpted in Norman P. Grubb, *C. T. Studd: Cricketer and Pioneer* (London: Religious Tract Society, 1934, original 1933), quotations through "heroism" p. 163, through "service" p. 164.

3. *Minutes of the General Council of the Assemblies of God . . . 1914,* p. 6.

4. Mickey Crews, *The Church of God: A Social History* (Knoxville: University of Tennessee Press, 1990), pp. 52–55.

5. See, for example, coffee: Milton Grotz, *Eat and Drink to the Glory of God, Christian Workers Union Words of Life,* tract, 1914, and G. A. Cook, in *Apostolic Faith* [Calif.], January 1907, p. 1; soft drinks: *Pentecostal Evangel,* August 28, 1926, p. 4; chewing gum, picture shows, and Coca-Cola: *Church of God Evangel,* February 10, 1917, p. 1; pork: *Apostolic Faith* [Calif.], October 1906, p. 2, and J. H. Kellogg, reprinted in *Latter Rain Evangel,* May 1909, p. 1; meat: *Christian Evangel,* November 14, 1914, page number illegible; pharmaceuticals: Milton Grotz, *Healing: God's Law of Health, Christian Workers Union Words of Life,* tract, 1913.

6. See, for example, L. P. Adams, in *Present Truth,* December 1909, p. 6; Albert Norton, in *Triumphs of Faith,* September 1909, pp. 195–200.

7. C. W. Shumway, "A Study of 'The Gift of Tongues,'" A.B. thesis, University of Southern California, 1914, p. 166. Presumably, fasting for extended periods meant living on soup or gruel, not complete absence of food.

8. Ibid., p. 175.

9. See, for example, Henry L. Fisher, "Diary," March 3 and May 19, 1922, WCT.

10. *Confidence,* December 1910, p. 278. *Confidence* noted this event in order to condemn it.

11. David D. Hall, *Worlds of Wonder, Days of Judgment* (New York: Alfred A. Knopf, 1989), p. 171.

12. Aimee Semple McPherson, *This Is That: Personal Experiences Sermons and Writings* (New York: Garland Publishing, 1985, original 1919), p. 41.

13. Martha Wing Robinson "Diary," typed, June 8, 1907, p. 21, AOG.

14. Minutes, Church of God, Alamo, Tex., April 24, 1932, COG.

15. Elizabeth Timmermann, in *Pentecostal Herald,* March 1917, p. 3.

16. C. M. Padgett, in *Church of God Evangel,* October 13, 1917, p. 2.

17. *Lytham (U.K.) Times,* April 18, 1913, pna, AGUK.

18. [Church of God] *General Assembly Minutes 1906–1914* (Cleveland, Tenn.: White Wing Publishing House, 1992), 1913, pp. 212–213.

19. A. A. Boddy, in *Confidence,* reprinted without full citation in *Upper Room,* June 1910, p. 1.

20. Carrie Judd Montgomery, *The Power of the Tongue,* tract, no publication data, p. 2.

21. See, for example, *Confidence,* April 1908, p. 13; *Word and Witness,* May 1915, p. 2; *Church of God Evangel,* March 17, 1917, p. 1.

22. See, for example, McPherson, *This Is That,* p. 38; Zelma Argue, *Contending for the Faith,* 2nd rev. ed. (Winnipeg: Messenger of God Publishing House, 1928, original 1923), pp. 8–11; *Apostolic Faith* [Calif.], January 1908, p. 3; classical violin: Gordon P. Gardiner, *Radiant Glory: The Life of Martha Wing Robinson,* 2nd ed. (New York: Bread of Life, 1970, original 1962), p. 92.

23. Reported by A. A. Boddy in *Confidence,* April–June 1920, p. 26.

24. E. S. Williams, in *Pentecostal Evangel,* July 20, 1929, p. 9.

25. A. W. Orwig, in *Bridegroom's Messenger,* November–December 1919, p. 4.

26. Howard A. Goss, *The Winds of God: The Story of the Early Pentecostal Days (1901–1914) in the Life of Howard A. Goss, as Told by Ethel E. Goss* (New York: Comet Press Books, 1958), p. 38.

27. *Word and Witness,* June 20, 1913, p. 2.

28. *Apostolic Faith* [Calif.], September 1907, p. 2.

29. Neckties: Harold Dean Trulear, "The Mother as Symbolic Presence: Ida B. Robinson and the Mt. Sinai Holy Church," in *Portraits of a Generation: Early Pentecostal Leaders,* ed. James R. Goff, Jr. and Grant Wacker (forthcoming); sports attire: *Apostolic Faith* [Kans.], January 1913, p. 5.

30. *Apostolic Faith* [Kans.], May 1913, p. 15, quoting remarks of Lutheran pastor J. H. Keller.

31. Mattie Lemons, in *Evangel,* August 9, 1914, p. 5, quoted in Crews, *Church of God,* p. 56.

32. *Peniel Advocate,* August 1929, p. 3.

33. Levi Lupton, in *New Acts,* October 5, 1905, p. 7. The quotation purportedly came from Charles G. Finney.

34. Charles Parham, in *Apostolic Faith* [Kans.], December 1912, pp. 4–5.

35. Probably editor E. N. Bell, in *Word and Witness,* October 20, 1912, p. 3. The antipentecostal *Burning Bush* identified Parham's sin as "Sodomy." *Burning Bush,* September 19, 1907, pp. 5–7, quotation p. 7. Other evidence suggests that in 1907 Parham was arrested though not tried for an "unnatural offense." San Antonio [Tex.] *Light,* July 19, 1907, p. l; see also July 24, 1907, p. 2; *Houston Chronicle,* July 21, 1907, p. 14. But see James R. Goff, Jr., *Fields White unto Harvest: Charles F. Parham and the Missionary Origins of Pentecostalism* (Fayetteville: University of Arkansas Press, 1988), pp. 136–142, 223–228, esp. p. 141 for a qualifying perspective.

36. *Apostolic Faith* [Calif.], September 1907, p. 2; *Apostolic Faith* [Calif.], October–January 1908, p. 2; *Apostolic Faith* [Ore.], January 1909, p. 3; *Household of God,* March 1910, p. 12; *Apostolic Faith* [Kans.], February 1913, p. 8; *Elbethel,* 1: 5 (1915): 14. *Good Report,* 1: 3 (1912): 5, denied any "recognized leader" endorsed free love.

37. For details, see Grant Wacker, *Travail of a Broken Family: Evangelical Responses to the Emergence of Pentecostalism* (forthcoming).

38. John Steinbeck, *The Grapes of Wrath* (New York: Penguin Books, 1992), p. 22.

39. James Baldwin, *Go Tell It on the Mountain* (New York: Dell Publishing, 1952), pp. 12, 137.

40. Unfriendly reviews include Terrence Rafferty, "Mud," *New Yorker,* December 2, 1991, pp. 156–159; Richard Alleva, "Obsession Overreaches," *Commonweal,* December 20, 1991, pp. 748–750; David Ansen, "The Horror, the Horror," *Newsweek,*

November 25, 1991, p. 56. The quotation comes from Stanley Kauffmann, "Southern Discomfort," *New Republic,* December 9, 1991, p. 28.

41. For an astute analysis of *The Apostle,* which argues, among other things, that the protagonist was more holiness Baptist than pentecostal, see Conrad Ostwalt, "The Apostle," in *Church History: Studies in Christianity and Culture,* 68 (September 1999): 666–673.

42. Charles Parham specified towns where free love was taught in pentecostal circles: Chicago, Detroit, Fort Worth, Los Angeles, and Wichita; activities in Eureka Springs and Oakland gave the appearance of inappropriate familiarity between the sexes. *Apostolic Faith* [Kans.], December 1912, pp. 4–5. None of the other accounts I have seen provide any locale at all.

43. For "excess," see John Alexander Dowie, *The Sermons of John Alexander Dowie: Champion of the Faith,* comp. and ed. Gordon Lindsay (Dallas: Christ for the Nations, reprinted 1979, original date not shown), p. 101; *Upper Room,* August 1909, p. 3.

44. Earnest Hanson, in *Apostolic Witness and Missionary Advocate,* May 1909, p. 7.

45. E. K. Fisher, in *Upper Room,* August 1909, p. 3, reprinted without full citation from *Confidence.*

46. Probably W. H. Giles, editor, in *Glad Tidings* [Los Angeles], vol. 1, no. 4 [1916 by internal evidence], p. 10.

47. See, for example, Harvey McAlister, in *Good Report,* September 1, 1913, p. 2; W. J. Seymour, in *Apostolic Faith* [Calif.], January 1908, p. 3; *Apostolic Faith* [Calif.], January 1907, p. 3; Charles B. Ebey, in *Free Methodist,* May 7, 1907, p. 296.

48. E. N. Bell, in *Word and Witness,* January 20, 1914, p. 2.

49. Thomas Myerscough, in *Confidence,* October 1913, p. 203. See also A. A. Boddy, in *Confidence,* June 1909, p. 139; W. J. S. [William J. Seymour], in *Apostolic Faith* [Calif.], January 1908, p. 3, who pointed out that there was a "natural use for a wife, which is not lust."

50. For a sampler of proscriptions, see baseball: O. B. Ong, in *New Acts,* August 9, 1906, p. 5; Christmas trees and valentines: Joel Adams Wright, in Kurt O. Berends, "A Divided Harvest: Alice Belle Garrigus, Joel Adams Wright, and Early New England Pentecostalism," M.A. thesis, Wheaton College Graduate School, 1993, p. 43; automobile riding and visiting relatives on Sundays, loitering on street corners, big dinners, and ice cream: "Report of the Committee on Public Morals," in *Pentecostal Holiness Advocate,* December 13, 1917, p. 7; boating, zoos, roller coasters, scenic railroad rides, and bowling: Levi Lupton, in *New Acts,* August 23, 1906, p. 2; idle conversation on the telephone: *Glad Tidings Herald,* July 1931, p. 8; picnics: Minutes, Church of God, Lyra, Tex., July 8, 1917, COG, and Morris E. Golder, *The Life and Works of Bishop Garfield Thomas Haywood (1880–1931)* (n.p., 1977), pp. 13, 29; roller skating: *Philadelphia Public Ledger,* August 16, 1918, p. 16; skating rinks and nickelodian shows: [Church of God] *General Assembly Minutes,* 1908, p. 51; crossword puzzles: *Pentecostal Evangel,* March 7, 1925, p. 5.

51. Minutes of the North Cleveland, Tenn., Church of God, April 12, 1911, for quotation. For other examples of discipline for misbehavior, see Minutes, North Cleveland, Tenn., Church of God, October 28, 1911; January 6, 1912; April 6, 1912; April 7, 1913; May 31, 1913; July 7, 1913, October 6, 1913; April 5, 1915; Minutes, Lyra, Tex., Church of God, July 8, 1917; Minutes, Alamo, Tex., Church of God, March 2, 1932; April 24, 1932, COG.

52. A. C. Holland, in *Apostolic Evangel,* August 23, 1916, p. 4.

53. E. May Law, in *Pentecostal Mission Work in South China: An Appeal for Missions* (Falcon, N.C.: Falcon Publishing Co., [1916]), p. 19.

54. Levi Lupton, in *New Acts,* July 26, 1906, p. 1.

55. A. W. Burpee, in *Word and Work,* September 28, 1918, p. 11.

56. *Gold Tried in the Fire,* April 1913, p. 4.

57. Scribbled letter to Elim headquarters, posted from Banbridge (England?), dated "Friday," tucked in a packet of letters from the mid-1920s, AGUK.

58. Max Wood Moorhead, in *Apostolic Faith* [Calif.], September 1907, p. 4, taken without full citation from *Cloud of Witnesses to Pentecost in India.*

59. Goss, *Winds of God,* p. 111.

60. H. W. Schermer, in *Apostolic Faith* [Kans.], January 1914, vanity and chunks p. 10, flirtations p. 11.

61. J. J. D. Hall, *The Cook-Stove Apostasy,* tract, reprinted in *Weekly Evangel,* March 24, 1917, p. 9.

62. W. F. Carothers, *Church Government* (Houston: n.p., October 1909), p. 53.

63. *Apostolic Faith* [Kans.], September 1913, p. 8.

64. "Journal of Happenings: The Diary of A. J. Tomlinson," typed, March 8, 1901—April 15, 1901, quotation April 15, COG.

65. Goss, *Winds of God,* p. 70.

66. Levi Lupton, in *New Acts,* February 8, 1906, p. 2.

67. See, for example, *Promise,* February 1909, p. 3; A. G. Garr, in *Latter Rain Evangel,* July 1914, pp. 18–19; George Hansen, in *Latter Rain Evangel,* September 1914, p. 19.

68. *Apostolic Faith* [Calif.], September 1906, p. 3.

69. Max Wood Moorhead, in *Cloud of Witnesses to Pentecost in India,* November 1908, p. 16; *Showers of Blessings,* January 1910, p. 5; E. S. Williams, in *Pentecostal Evangel,* August 26, 1951, pp. 4–5.

70. See, for example, *Midnight Cry* [N.Y.], March–April 1911, p. 4; *Apostolic Faith* [Ore.], no. 21 [about 1913], p. 2; Levi Lupton, in *New Acts,* March 22, 1906, p. 1; *Showers of Blessings,* January 1910, p. 5.

71. *Apostolic Faith* [Ore.], no. 21 [about 1913], p. 2.

72. Goss, *Winds of God,* p. 98. In *Apostolic Faith* [Tex.], May 1911 p. 1, Daniel C. O. Opperman said that at the Dallas Interstate Camp Meeting attenders could pay for meals and cots as the Holy Spirit directed, but they would have to bring their own "pillow, lamp, washpan, soap, towel, comb, song book, Bible, etc."

73. David Lee Floyd, interview by Wayne Warner, February 26, 1981, transcript no. 1, p. 20, AOG.

74. See George B. Studd, "Diary," February 2, 1908, and May 10, 1908, AOG; A. G. Osterberg, "reel #4," typed, interviewer unnamed, undated [probably 1966], p. 5, AOG. "We keep no account books here, the Lord keeps the records. We do not publish the names of donors, but the Lord knows who they are." *Apostolic Faith* [Calif.], November 1906, p. 3.

75. Levi Lupton, in *New Acts,* September 27, 1906, p. 4. For a contrary point of view by a pentecostal leader, see *Christian Evangel,* October 19, 1918, p. 5, probably by E. N. Bell.

76. *Apostolic Faith* [Ore.], no. 18 [about 1912], p. 2.

77. *Apostolic Faith* [Calif.], October 1906, p. 4.

78. W. J. Seymour to Brother Carothers, July 12, 1906, reprinted in *Readings in Pentecostal History,* comp. Cecil M. Robeck, Jr. (Pasadena: Fuller Theological Seminary, 1987), p. 45; William W. Menzies, *Anointed to Serve: The Story of the Assemblies of God* (Springfield, Mo.: Gospel Publishing House, 1971), vol. 1, p. 82. Seymour: "I want you to please send it [my credentials] to me so I can have to show to get rates."

79. *Apostolic Faith* [Kans.], September 1912, p. 9; W. B. Brogan, in *Apostolic Faith* [Kans.], May 1914, p. 16.

80. Levi Lupton, in *New Acts,* July 1905, pp. 5–6.

81. *Apostolic Faith* [Calif.], December 1906, p. 1.

82. "Autobiography," Hattie McConnell, typed, pp. 6–7, AOG.

83. *Apostolic Faith* [Kans.], March 1912, p. 9; Walter J. Higgins, *Pioneering in Pentecost: My Experiences of 46 Years in the Ministry* (Bostonia, Calif.: n.p., 1958), p. 20; Victor G. Plymire, "Autobiography," typed, throughout, AOG.

84. Britton, *Pentecostal Truth,* chap. 23, pp. 217–255, first quotation p. 243, second p. 226.

85. Hazel Brewer, in *Church of God Evangel,* June 25, 1962, p. 4, quoted in Crews, *Church of God,* p. 60.

86. Advertisement, in *Faithful Standard,* May 1922, p. 12.

87. Edith Blumhofer, "Life on Faith Lines: Faith Homes and Early Pentecostal Values," *Assemblies of God Heritage,* Summer 1990, pp. 10–12, 22.

88. Donald Gee, *Bonnington Toll: The Story of a First Pastorate* (London: Victory Press, 1943), p. 20.

89. J. H. Black, in *Apostolic Faith* [Kans.], May 1912, p. 12.

90. See also *Apostolic Faith* [Kans.], June 1914, p. 15; *Word and Witness,* August 20, 1912, p. 1.

91. Goss, *Winds of God,* p. 129. On the other hand some early pentecostals did not permit clapping, p. 112.

92. Dan Morgan, *Rising in the West: The True Story of an "Okie" Family from the Great Depression through the Reagan Years* (New York: Alfred A. Knopf, 1992), p. 122.

93. Edith L. Blumhofer, *The Assemblies of God: A Chapter in the Story of American Pentecostalism* (Springfield, Mo.: Gospel Publishing House, 1989), vol. 1, p. 69.

94. For example Glad Tidings Tabernacle in New York City held three services on Sunday—at 10:30 A.M., 3:00 P.M., and 8:00 P.M., plus a service at 8:00 P.M. Tuesday through Friday, plus a healing meeting at 3:00 P.M. on Wednesday and a special children's service at 4:00 P.M. on Friday. *Midnight Cry* [N.Y.], March–April 1911, p. 4.

95. George B. Studd, "Diary," January 19, 1908–December 7, 1908, AOG.

96. John E. Mars and Wife, in *Promise,* May 1907, p. 4.

97. See, for example, *Apostolic Faith* [Kans.], May 1912, p. 12.

98. [Church of God] *General Assembly Minutes,* 1913, pp. 168–169.

99. David Martin perceptively argues that the pentecostal revival in contemporary Latin America—and by implication the tradition as a whole—fits into a longer and larger Methodistic tradition that perennially esteemed seriousness over frivolity. Martin, *Tongues of Fire: The Explosion of Protestantism in Latin America.* (Cambridge, Mass.: Basil Blackwell, 1990), pp. 38–39, 92.

100. Raymond T. Richey, *Helps to Young and Old* (Houston: United Prayer and Workers League, 1979, original 1922), especially pp. 7–8.

101. *Pentecostal Evangel,* March 7, 1925, p. 5.

102. E. N. Bell, *Questions,* p. 107; see also p. 105.

103. *Good Report,* November 1, 1913, p. 1.
104. *Glad Tidings* [SF], July 1926, p. 4. See *Pentecostal Evangel,* March 7, 1925, p. 9, for a typical day at Central Bible Institute in Springfield, Mo.
105. *Apostolic Faith* [Calif.], October 1907–January 1908, p. 2.
106. W. J. Seymour, in *Apostolic Faith* [Calif.], October 1907–January 1908, p. 3.
107. John G. Lake, in *Upper Room,* June 1909, p. 2.
108. Charles E. Robinson, in *Pentecostal Evangel,* September 21, 1929, p. 7.
109. *New Acts,* December 14, 1905, p. 8.
110. E. N. Bell, in *Word and Witness,* March 20, 1914, p. 3.
111. L. P. Adams, in *Grace and Truth,* September 1915, p. 3; October 1915, p. 4; December 1915, pp. 1, 3.
112. Advertisement, in *Christian Evangel,* October 24, 1914, p. 2.
113. *Glad Tidings* [SF], November 1929, p. 16.
114. *Voice in the Wilderness,* vol. 2, no. not legible, about 1920, p. 6, AOG.
115. R. E. Winsett to J. Kamerer, Gospel Publishing House manager, July 16, 1934, AOG.
116. Almost certainly editor Charles Parham, in *Apostolic Faith* [Kans.], December 1912, p. 11; see also *Apostolic Faith* [Kans.], September 1913, p. 8.
117. K. [H.?] W. Schermer, supplement to *Apostolic Faith* [Kans.], January 1912, no page shown.
118. George B. Studd, "Diary," February 4, 1908, AOG.
119. Detailed in Wacker, *Travail of a Broken Family* (forthcoming).
120. M. M. Pinson, in *Victorious Gospel,* Early Spring 1915, p. 2.
121. *Apostolic Faith* [Kans.], September 1905, p. 13.
122. *Weekly Evangel,* February 23, 1918, p. 9.
123. *Latter Rain Evangel,* October 1908, p. 1.
124. Ibid., January 1911, p. 14.
125. W. J. Seymour, *The Doctrines and Discipline of the Azusa Street Apostolic Faith Mission of Los Angeles, Calif. . . . 1915* (n.p., n.d.), p. 51.
126. Arthur L. Slocum, "What God Hath Wrought," pamphlet, pp. 12–13, no publication data (about 1915), AOG.
127. Elizabeth V. Baker and Co-Workers, *Chronicles of a Faith Life* (New York: Garland Publishing, 1985, original 1915–1916), p. 81.
128. Ibid., p. 109.
129. Ibid., p. 114.
130. Thomas Hezmalhalch, in *Apostolic Faith* [Calif.], January 1907, p. 3.
131. A. J. Tomlinson, in *Evangelical Visitor,* March 1, 1906, p. 15.

9. Leaders

1. Aimee Semple McPherson, *This Is That: Personal Experiences Sermons and Writings* (New York: Garland Publishing, 1985, original 1919), p. 635.
2. *Apostolic Faith* [Calif.], October 1906, p. 4. The writer was arguing for the revival's directly supernatural origin—to my mind, the same as ahistoricity.
3. M. L. Ryan, in *Chinese Recorder,* May 1915, p. 323.
4. W. J. S. [William J. Seymour], in *Apostolic Faith* [Calif.], June–September 1907, p. 3.
5. *Minutes of the General Council of the Assemblies of God . . . 1914,* Introduction [p. 2].
6. Elizabeth V. Baker and Co-Workers, *Chronicles of a Faith Life* (New York: Garland

Publishing, 1985, original 1915–1916), p. 134. Baker was referring to the 1904–1905 Wales revival, but clearly the comment applied more broadly.

7. *Pentecost,* November 1908, p. 3.

8. *Latter Rain Evangel,* October 1908, p. 1.

9. [Church of God] *General Assembly Minutes 1906–1914* (Cleveland, Tenn.: White Wing Publishing House, 1992), 1908, p. 55.

10. A. J. Tomlinson, as rendered in ibid., 1912, p. 135.

11. [W. O.] Hutchinson, *Showers of Blessings,* no. 14 [about 1912], p. 4.

12. *Apostolic Faith* [Calif.], November 1906, p. 1.

13. W. M. Collins, in *Upper Room,* October–November 1909, p. 8.

14. See, for example, Frank Bartleman, *Pentecost or No Pentecost* (no publication data, likely 1928), tract, pna, FTS; J. H. King, in *Live Coals of Fire,* February 9, 1900, p. 3. At this point *Live Coals* was virtually pentecostal.

15. For the "standard" historical accounts of these and other groups, see Augustus Cerillo, Jr. and Grant Wacker, "Bibliography and Historiography of Pentecostalism in the United States," *New International Dictionary of the Pentecostal and Charismatic Movements,* ed. Stanley Burgess (Grand Rapids: Harper Collins Zondervan, forthcoming 2001), by title.

16. This paragraph and the next one draw very directly from Edith L. Blumhofer, *Aimee Semple McPherson: Everybody's Sister* (Grand Rapids: William B. Eerdmans Publishing Co., 1993), and Daniel Mark Epstein, *Sister Aimee: The Life of Aimee Semple McPherson* (New York: Harcourt Brace Jovanovich, 1993). See especially pp. 2–3, 6, 161, 174 in Blumhofer, and pp. 146, 156, and 438 in Epstein.

17. *San Francisco Examiner,* January 11, 1890, quoted in Wayne E. Warner, *The Woman Evangelist: The Life and Times of Charismatic Evangelist Maria B. Woodworth-Etter* (Metuchen, N.J.: Scarecrow Press, 1986), p. 93, n. 5. See also pp. 51, 149, and contemporary press coverage reprinted in appendices.

18. See, for example, *Good Report,* August 1, 1913, p. 1.

19. Dolly Dugdale to "The Editors," undated typed letter, probably 1920s, AOG.

20. Wayne E. Warner, introduction to *The Essential Smith Wigglesworth,* ed. Wayne E. Warner and Joyce Lee (Ann Arbor: Servant Publications, 1999).

21. Systematic information about Mason remains elusive. I base my claim for his prominence in both white and black circles on J. O. Patterson et al., *History and Formative Years of the Church of God in Christ with Excerpts from the Life and Works of Its Founder—Bishop C. H. Mason* (Memphis: Church of God in Christ Publishing House, 1969), p. 23; Theodore Kornweibel, Jr., "Bishop C. H. Mason and the Church of God in Christ during World War I: The Perils of Conscientious Objection," *Southern Studies: An Interdisciplinary Journal of the South,* 26 (Fall 1987): pp. 261–281; David D. Daniels, "Charles Harrison Mason and the Interracial Impulse of Early Pentecostalism," in *Portraits of a Generation: Early Pentecostal Leaders,* ed. James R. Goff, Jr. and Grant Wacker (forthcoming).

22. Roger Glenn Robins, "Plainfolk Modernist: The Radical Holiness World of A. J. Tomlinson," Ph.D. diss., Duke University, 1999, chap. 5.

23. See, for example, W. F. Carothers, *Church Government* (Houston: n.p., October 1909), pp. 9, 16.

24. For biographical data on the persons mentioned in this paragraph, see *DPCM,* by title. For Larssen and Pennington, who are not in *DPCM,* see Nils Bloch-Hoell, *The Pentecostal Movement: Its Origin, Development, and Distinctive Character* (New

York: Humanities Press, 1964, Norwegian original 1956), pp. 179–180, and Wayne Warner, "'From the Footlights to the Light of the Cross,' The Story of Evangelist Edith Mae Pennington," *Assemblies of God Heritage,* Winter 1987–88, pp. 6–9, 20.

25. Frank F. Ewart, *The Phenomenon of Pentecost: A History of the Latter Rain* (Houston: Herald Publishing House, 1947), p. 54.

26. Full page advertisement in *Faithful Standard,* August 1922, back cover [p. 26].

27. *Diary of A. B. Simpson, 1907, 1912, 1915,* May 1907, August 9, 1907, September 12, 1907, September 13, 1907, and esp. October 6, 1912, AOG. Admittedly, Simpson's language is elliptical, but taken together there can be little doubt that he sought all the gifts of the Spirit, including tongues if the Lord willed it.

28. Though many partisans learned to speak in tongues with minimal effort, many others—probably a large minority—struggled for weeks, months, or even years to acquire the gift, including some of the most prominent of first-generation leaders. For example T. B. Barratt sought continually for five days, *Cloud of Witnesses to Pentecost in India,* March 1908, pp. 19–21; E. N. Bell tarried for eleven months, *Question and Answers* (Springfield, Mo.: n.p., 1923), p. ix; A. A. Boddy received Holy Spirit baptism in March, tongues December 2, *Pentecost at Sunderland: A Vicar's Testimony* (Sunderland, England: published by author, May 1909), p. 9; G. B. Studd struggled for three years, *Confidence,* May 1911, p. 116; Howard A. Goss sought it for seven months, Howard A. Goss, *The Winds of God: The Story of the Early Pentecostal Days (1901–1914) in the Life of Howard A. Goss, as Told by Ethel E. Goss* (New York: Comet Press Books, 1958), pp. 42–44. *Apostolic Faith* [Calif.] December 1906, p. 2, spoke of noted biblical scholar A. S. Worrell "tarrying" for the baptism along with well-known prison worker, Mother [Elizabeth] Wheaton.

29. T. B. Barratt, in *Cloud of Witnesses to Pentecost in India,* March 1908, p. 24.

30. Besides the account in *Cloud of Witnesses,* ibid., see *Living Truths,* December 1906, pp. 737–738, and "When the Fire Fell," pamphlet, partly reprinted in B. F. Lawrence, *The Apostolic Faith Restored* (St. Louis: Gospel Publishing House, 1916), pp. 107–109.

31. Howard Goss, quoted in Lawrence, *Apostolic Faith Restored,* p. 66.

32. Martha Wing Robinson, "Diary," July 27, 1907, p. 46 typed version, AOG.

33. Gordon P. Gardiner, *Radiant Glory: The Life of Martha Wing Robinson,* 2nd ed. (New York: Bread of Life, 1970, original 1962), p. 196.

34. Shirley Nelson, *Fair Clear and Terrible: The Story of Shiloh, Maine* (Latham, N.Y.: British American Publishing, 1989), p. 67, and Lilian Thistlethwaite, "The Wonderful History of the Latter Rain," reprinted in [Charles Parham], *The Life of Charles F. Parham: Founder of the Apostolic Faith Movement,* compiled by His Wife [Sarah E. Parham] (New York: Garland Publishing, 1985, original 1930), p. 58.

35. Alice Reynolds Flower, *Grace for Grace* (Springfield, Mo.: published by author, [1961]), p. 56.

36. Andrew L. Fraser, in *Weekly Evangel,* February 12, 1916, p. 9.

37. Lewis Wilson, "Bible Institutes, Colleges, Universities," *DPCM,* by title.

38. William H. Durham, in *Gospel Witness,* January 1914[?], p. 5, AOG.

39. Allene M. Sumner, "The Holy Rollers on Shin Bone Ridge," *Nation,* July 29, 1925, p. 138. The theological identity of the people Sumner observed is not certain, but the term *holy rollers* commonly denoted pentecostals.

40. T. K. Leonard, in *Word and Witness,* August 20, 1914, p. 4.

41. O. B. Ong, in *New Acts,* August 9, 1906, p. 5.

42. *Showers of Blessings,* January 1910, p. 4. Several sentences of this paragraph are based on Wilson, "Bible Institutes," *DPCM,* by title.

43. A. C. Holland, in *Apostolic Evangel,* August 23, 1916, p. 2.

44. See, for example, *Apostolic Faith* [Calif.], December 1906, p. 3, which referred to a "Bible school up at the Azusa St. Mission."

45. *Minutes of the General Council of the Assemblies of God . . . 1917,* p. 19.

46. The development of educational institutions within each of the main pentecostal denominations forms a recurring theme in the standard denominational surveys. After World War II virtually all pentecostal groups imposed educational standards for prospective clergy, so that by the 1990s some college training had become requisite for ordination, in practice if not always on paper. For a concise, excellent survey of pentecostal education institutions and philosophies, see Wilson, "Bible Institutes," *DPCM,* by title.

47. William W. Menzies, "Developing Educational Institutions," *Assemblies of God Heritage,* Summer 1983, p. 3 for the first figure; I surmise at least twenty substantial educational enterprises existed by 1930 from the denominational histories mentioned above. By 1990 more than one hundred existed in the United States and three hundred abroad. Wilson, "Bible Institutes," *DPCM,* p. 58.

48. See, for example, the course notes of Ralph M. Riggs from Rochester Bible Institute, AOG.

49. J. Kevin Butcher, "The Holiness and Pentecostal Labors of David Wesley Myland, 1890–1918," M.A. thesis, Dallas Theological Seminary, 1983.

50. Morris E. Golder, *The Life and Works of Bishop Garfield Thomas Haywood (1880–1931)* (n.p., 1977), p. 5; Paul D. Dugas, *The Life and Writings of Elder G. T. Haywood* (Portland, Ore.: Apostolic Book Publishers, 1968), esp. pp. 24, 28; David Bundy, "G. T. Haywood: Religion for Urban Realities," in *Portraits of a Generation: Early Pentecostal Leaders,* ed. James R. Goff, Jr. and Grant Wacker (forthcoming 2001).

51. William C. Turner, Jr., "The United Holy Church of America: A Study in Black Holiness Pentecostalism," Ph.D. diss., Duke University, 1984, p. 105.

52. I have patched together these biographical details from W. W. Simpson, in *Pentecostal Evangel,* June 6, 1925, p. 10; February 13, 1926, p. 10; March 21, 1931, p. 10; December 31, 1950, p. 9; Edith L. Blumhofer, *"Pentecost in My Soul": Explorations in the Meaning of Pentecostal Experience in the Early Assemblies of God* (Springfield, Mo.: Gospel Publishing House, 1989), pp. 237–238; *DPCM,* by title; personal communication from Gary B. McGee, Assemblies of God mission historian, June 5, 2000, and from Wayne Warner, AOG archivist, June 6, 2000.

53. I owe this insight to Russell Congleton, a doctoral student in the Graduate Program in Religion at Duke University.

54. William G. McLoughlin, "Aimee Semple McPherson: 'Your Sister in the King's Glad Service,'" *Journal of Popular Culture,* 1 (Winter 1967): 194.

55. Frank Bartleman, *Azusa Street: The Roots of Modern-Day Pentecost,* ed. Vinson Synan (Plainfield, N.J.: Logos International, 1980, original [differently titled] 1925), p. 1.

56. John G. Lake, in *Overcoming Life,* April 1909, p. 8.

57. This extensive literature is summarized in R. Stephen Warner, "Work in Progress toward a New Paradigm for the Sociological Study of Religion in the United States," *American Journal of Sociology,* 98 (March 1993): 1044–93.

58. David Martin, *Tongues of Fire: the Explosion of Protestantism in Latin America* (Cambridge, Mass.: Basil Blackwell, 1990), p. 108.

59. Martin, *Tongues of Fire*, p. 287.

60. John Alexander Dowie, in *Leaves of Healing*, September 18, 1904, p. 799; Rolvix Harlan, *John Alexander Dowie and the Christian Catholic Apostolic Church in Zion* (Evansville, Wis.: Press of R. M. Antes, 1906), p. 68.

61. Frank W. Sandford, in *Everlasting Gospel* [Maine], January 1, 1901, p. 2.

62. Ibid., November 12, 1901, p. 312.

63. Ibid., January 8–15, 1901, p. 22.

64. R. E. Gleason, in *Everlasting Gospel* [Maine], July 1, 1903, p. 20.

65. For Dowie see, for example, *Apostolic Faith* [Kans.], January 1, 1900, p. 7, which advertised a Dowie exposé by H. H. Gilchrist entitled *Dr. Dowie before the Court of Public Opinion*. For Sandford see, for example, *Apostolic Faith* [Calif.], December 1906, p. 1.

66. Edith L. Blumhofer, "The Christian Catholic Apostolic Church and the Apostolic Faith: A Study in the 1906 Pentecostal Revival," in *Charismatic Experiences in History*, ed. Cecil M. Robeck, Jr. (Peabody, Mass.: Hendrickson Publishers, 1985), pp. 135–139, and Shirley and Rudy Nelson, "Tongues of Fire: Frank Sandford of Shiloh, Maine," in *Portraits of a Generation*. Though the Nelsons and I both recognize disjunction between Shiloh and pentecostalism, what they see as intrinsic incompatibility I view as self-conscious rejection by pentecostals of a movement gone awry.

67. A. J. Tomlinson, in [Church of God] *General Assembly Minutes*, 1913, p. 199.

68. Ibid., p. 265.

69. Roger Glenn Robins, "Plainfolk Modernist: The Radical Holiness World of A. J. Tomlinson," Ph.D. diss., Duke University, 1999, Epilogue.

10. Women

1. See, for example, Letha Scanzoni and Susan Setta, "Women in Evangelical, Holiness and Pentecostal Traditions," in *Women and Religion in America, 1900–1968*, ed. Rosemary Radford Reuther and Rosemary Skinner Keller (San Francisco: Harper & Row, 1986), vol. 3, pp. 223–265; Margaret Lamberts Bendroth, *Fundamentalism and Gender, 1875 to the Present* (New Haven: Yale University Press, 1993), p. 4. The present chapter does not purport to analyze gender, which would involve both male and female roles and the way that each sex imaged the other in order to construct itself.

2. Edith L. Blumhofer. "A Confused Legacy: Reflections of Evangelical Attitudes toward Ministering Women in the Past Century," *Fides et Historia*, 22 (Winter–Spring 1990): 49–61; David Grant Roebuck, "Limiting Liberty: The Church of God and Women Ministers, 1886–1996," Ph.D. diss., Vanderbilt University, 1977, throughout.

3. Mother Cotton, in *Message of the Apostolic Faith*, April 1939, pp. 1–3.

4. A. J. Gordon, in *Missionary Review of the World*, December 1894, pp. 911, 917, 916. Yet Gordon resisted women's ordination, basing that resistance "in nature itself."

5. Howard N. Kenyon, "An Analysis of Ethical Issues in the History of the Assemblies of God," Ph.D. diss., Baylor University, 1988, pp. 194, 198, 202. By 1920 women accounted for 61 percent and 66 percent of Assemblies of God missionaries in China and India, respectively. Gary B. McGee, "Saving Souls or Saving Lives? The Tension between Ministries of Word and Deed in Assemblies of God Missiology," *Paraclete*, 28 (1994): 12.

6. [A. J. Tomlinson], "Brief History of the Church That Is Now Recognized as the Church of God," prepended to *Book of Minutes: A Compiled History of the Work of the General Assemblies of the Church of God,* comp. and ed. by L. Howard Juillerat and Minnie Hayes (Cleveland, Tenn.: Church of God Publishing House, 1922), p. 9. The attending women are listed by name. Even if this record is inaccurate or, more likely, this group not the lineal precursor of the Church of God, as claimed, it little matters, for the Church of God happily positioned women at the beginning of its history.

7. [Church of God] *General Assembly Minutes 1906–1914* (Cleveland, Tenn.: White Wing Publishing House, 1992), 1906, p. 19.

8. Edith L. Blumhofer, *Aimee Semple McPherson: Everybody's Sister* (Grand Rapids: William B. Eerdmans Publishing Co., 1993), p. 361. One congregation was served by a group of LIFE Bible College students, which presumably included females. Understanding women's role among early black pentecostal women is hampered by lack of hard data. One rare source is the minutes of the *United Holy Church of America 24th Annual Convocation . . . 1918,* WCT, which listed sixty-nine ordained ministers, including three women. Yet a large majority of the sect's forty-two named missionaries were women (based on female given names or the prefix "Mrs."), and women routinely preached alongside men, with or without formal ordination, and apparently without consciousness of the need for it (pp. 3–6). Still, women never served as senior pastors in the largest black group, the Church of God in Christ.

9. For bibliographic data on women in early pentecostalism, see Augustus Cerillo, Jr. and Grant Wacker, "Bibliography and Historiography of Pentecostalism in the United States," *New International Dictionary of the Pentecostal and Charismatic Movements,* ed. Stanley Burgess (Grand Rapids: Harper Collins Zondervan, forthcoming 2001), by title.

10. I compiled these figures from *Religious Bodies: 1916* (Washington, D.C.: Department of Commerce, Bureau of the Census, 1919), Table 60; *Religious Bodies: 1926* (Washington, D.C.: Department of Commerce, Bureau of the Census, 1930), Table 13; *Religious Bodies: 1936* (Washington, D.C.: Department of Commerce, Bureau of the Census, 1941), Table 23. The method of reporting varied, involving either the actual number of male and female members or the ratio of males versus females. See also Mickey Crews, *The Church of God: A Social History* (Knoxville: University of Tennessee Press, 1990), p. 17, who argues for a two-to-one female predominance in the Church of God, based on recent interviews.

11. See, for example, documents dated October 2, 1907, October 4, 1907, and June 10, 1910, ATS, apparently from the *Sunderland [U.K.] Daily Chronicle.*

12. Grant Wacker, *Travail of a Broken Family: Evangelical Responses to the Emergence of Pentecostalism* (forthcoming); Reader Harris, *Tongues of Fire,* January 1909, p. 6.

13. Alice Reynolds Flower, taped interview, interviewer unnamed, January 1977, AOG.

14. See, for example, Cheryl Townsend Gilkes, "'Together and in Harness': Women's Traditions in the Sanctified Church," *Signs: Journal of Women in Culture and Society,* 10 (Summer 1985): 678–699, esp. p. 686.

15. See, for example, Donald G. Mathews, *Religion in the Old South* (Chicago: University of Chicago Press, 1977), pp. 120–123, and Christine Leigh Heyrman, *Southern Cross: The Beginnings of the Bible Belt* (Chapel Hill: University of North Carolina Press, 1997), chap. 4, esp. pp. 211–213.

16. William Booth-Clibborn, *A Call to the Dust and Ashes* (Little Rock: First Southern Bible Conference, November 1922), pp. 2–3.

17. See, for example, [Church of God] *General Assembly Minutes,* 1911, p. 101. Pentecostals' holiness Wesleyan forebearers certainly permitted male weeping in worship, but I do not gain a sense from the literature that they made it a normative expectation as pentecostals did.

18. Like most creation stories, this one likely mixed myth and fact. Grant Wacker, "Are the Golden Oldies Still Worth Playing? Reflections on History Writing among Early Pentecostals," *Pneuma: Journal of the Society for Pentecostal Studies,* 8 (Fall 1986): 95–96.

19. Agnes N. O[zman] LaBerge, *What God Hath Wrought: Life and Work of Mrs. Agnes N. O. LaBerge* (New York: Garland Publishing, 1985, original 1920), pp. 33–53 and following. For the weather in Topeka, see Lyle Murphy, "Beginning at Topeka," *Calvary Review,* 8 (Spring 1974): 2, 4.

20. For biographical data on Burgess (later Burgess Brown), see *"Pentecost in My Soul": Explorations in the Meaning of Pentecostal Experience in the Early Assemblies of God,* ed. Edith L. Blumhofer (Springfield, Mo.: Gospel Publishing House, 1989), pp. 191–209; for Farrow, see *DPCM,* by title.

21. *Apostolic Faith* [Calif.], December 1906, p. 1.

22. Mrs. Jesse Reed, in *Trust,* August 1915, p. 18. I surmise Rochester owing to *Trust's* publication site.

23. Howard A. Goss, *The Winds of God: The Story of the Early Pentecostal Days (1901–1914) in the Life of Howard A. Goss, as Told by Ethel E. Goss* (New York: Comet Press Books, 1958), p. 29.

24. *Gleams of Grace,* July 1922, p. 1.

25. *Apostolic Faith* [Calif.], October 1906, p. 3.

26. [Halcy O. Tomlinson], *Our Sister Halcy: This Is Her Own Personal Journal Written When She Was Fifteen 1906–1907* (Cleveland: Tenn., White Wing Publishing, 1974, written 1906–1907), p. 18. The second ellipsis is in the original.

27. Aimee Semple McPherson, *The Story of My Life,* ed. Raymond L. Cox (Waco: Word Books, 1973), p. 27.

28. Aimee Semple McPherson, *This Is That: Personal Experiences Sermons and Writings* (New York: Garland Publishing, 1985, original 1919), pp. 102, 103.

29. Florence Crawford, in *Apostolic Faith* [Calif.], October 1906, p. 3.

30. E[lizabeth] Sisson, in *Triumphs of Faith,* October 1908, p. 231. As a child my grandmother attended Sisson's meetings in Newark, N.J. She told me of Sisson's volubility and inclination to twirl on the platform, petticoats flying.

31. *Apostolic Faith* [Calif.], January 1908, p. 2.

32. Stephen Merritt, in *Midnight Cry* [N.Y.], March 1919, p. 5.

33. For one of many instances in Parham's writings, see Charles F. Parham, *A Voice Crying in the Wilderness,* 2nd ed. (Baxter Springs, Kans.: Apostolic Faith Bible College, 1910, original 1902), p. 31.

34. Elizabeth V. Baker and Co-Workers, *Chronicles of a Faith Life* (New York: Garland Publishing, 1985, original 1915–1916), p. 21.

35. All quotations from M. B. Woodworth-Etter, *Signs and Wonders: God Wrought in the Ministry for Forty Years* (Indianapolis: published by author, 1916), pp. 27–28. In these passages Woodworth-Etter apparently was referring to a series of experiences in 1879–80.

36. Estelle B. Freedman, "The New Woman: Changing Views of Women in the 1920s," *Journal of American History,* 61 (September 1974): 372–393.

37. Bendroth, *Fundamentalism and Gender,* p. 7; Scanzoni and Setta, "Women in Evangelical, Holiness and Pentecostal Traditions," pp. 232–233.

38. Harvey Cox, *Fire from Heaven: The Rise of Pentecostal Spirituality and the Reshaping of Religion in the Twenty-first Century* (Reading, Mass.: Addison-Wesley Publishing Co., 1995), pp. 197–198.

39. *Minutes of the General Council of the Assemblies of God . . . 1914,* pp. 3, 7.

40. *Combined Minutes of the General Council of the Assemblies of God . . . April 2–12, 1914 . . . November 15–29, 1914,* p. 9.

41. *Minutes of the General Council of the Assemblies of God . . . 1916,* p. 9.

42. *Minutes of the General Council of the Assemblies of God . . . 1917,* pp. 5, 9, quoted words p. 9.

43. *Minutes of the General Council of the Assemblies of God . . . 1918,* pp. 13–26.

44. *Combined Minutes of the General Council of the Assemblies of God . . . 1914–1920,* p. 9.

45. *Minutes of the General Council of the Assemblies of God . . . 1919,* p. 7.

46. *Minutes of the General Council of the Assemblies of God . . . 1920,* p. 48.

47. Stanley Frodsham to Robert C. Cunningham, July 20, 1963, esp. p. 4, AOG.

48. Undated general letter from Credential Committee, Executive Office, General Council, to "Dear Sister," AOG. Kenyon dates this document probably prior to June 1923, "Analysis of Ethical Issues," p. 201, n. 82.

49. Alice Flower and E. S. Williams, taped interview, interviewer not named, 1977, AOG. Flower described herself but implied her experience was typical.

50. *Minutes [of the General Council of the Assemblies of God] 1931,* p. 18.

51. *Minutes of the General Council [of the Assemblies of God] . . . 1935,* pp. 112, 111. To be fair, in 1931 the Council had said that officers of the General Council were to be "men of mature experience and ability." *Minutes [of the General Council of the Assemblies of God] 1931,* p. 12. Though one assumes that all clergy, both officers and nonofficers, were to be persons of maturity, it is significant that the Council made that expectation explicit only when speaking of female candidates.

52. Crews, *Church of God,* pp. 93–100; Roebuck, "Limiting Liberty," pp. 6–63.

53. Lincoln and Mamiya, *Black Church,* pp. 210, 275, 287–288; J. O. Patterson et al., *History and Formative Years of the Church of God in Christ with Excerpts from the Life and Works of Its Founder—Bishop C. H. Mason* (Memphis: Church of God in Christ Publishing House, 1969), p. 68; Gilkes, "'Together and in Harness,'" pp. 684–686, 697. Lacking explicit documentation either way, I infer that Church of God in Christ elders barred women's ordination from the outset, based on Seymour's pattern described below, and the likelihood that Seymour mentored Church of God in Christ founder C. H. Mason.

54. *Minute Book and Ministerial Record Of the Pentecostal Assemblies of the World,* 1918 and 1919, partly reprinted in James L. Tyson, *The Early Pentecostal Revival: History of Twentieth-Century Pentecostals and the Pentecostal Assemblies of the World, 1901–1930* (Hazelwood, Mo.: Word Aflame Press, 1992), p. 292.

55. *Minute Book . . . Pentecostal Assemblies of the World,* 1919 and 1920, partly reprinted in Tyson, *Early Pentecostal Revival,* p. 296.

56. Mary Arthur, Mary Barnes, Emma Cotton, Florence Crawford, Julia Delk, Alice Flower, Elmira Jeffries, Minnie Kennedy, Mary Moise, Virginia Moss, Ida Robinson, and Elizabeth R. Wheaton are a few that readily come to mind.

57. A. Reuben Hartwick, "Pentecost Comes to the Northeast," *Assemblies of God Heritage,* Spring 1990, p. 5.

58. The last point needs minor qualification. McPherson sometimes shared the platform with her daughter and mother and on Friday nights with female Bible institute students learning to preach. Blumhofer, *Aimee Semple McPherson,* pp. 362–363.

59. Eleanor Frey to J. R. Evans, September 3, 1928, reprinted in "Selected Letters of Mae [Eleanor] Frey," comp. Edith L. Blumhofer, *Pneuma: The Journal of the Society for Pentecostal Studies,* 17 (Spring 1995), p. 77.

60. Ibid., p. 78.

61. J. R. Evans to Eleanor Frey, September 14, 1928, in Blumhofer, "Selected Letters," p. 79.

62. Frey's husband died in the fall of 1928. Frey held a position as supply pastor in Watertown, New York, 1938–40, but otherwise worked as an itinerant evangelist until her death in 1954. Telephone interview with Wayne E. Warner, archivist, AOG, May 23, 1994.

63. Eleanor Frey to J. R. Evans, December 15, 1928, in Blumhofer, "Selected Letters," p. 81.

64. W. F. Carothers, *Church Government* (Houston: n.p., October 1909), p. 44.

65. Ibid., pp. 44–47. Carothers actually proved more progressive than he seemed. He said that women should be banned from public participation only when the church was transacting business, and implied that those occasions were infrequent (p. 47). Also he scored any man who would maltreat a woman. Still, the issues remained tangled. Why was maltreating a woman bad? Because "[t]he glory of the man is the woman, if he abuse her where is his glory?" (p. 45).

66. Ibid., p. 44.

67. E. N. Bell, in *Christian Evangel,* August 15, 1914, p. 2.

68. Compare E. N. Bell, in *Word and Witness,* January 20, 1914, p. 2, with E. N. Bell, in *Christian Evangel,* June 14, 1919, p. 5. Bell at first seemed to preclude female priestly functions without exception, but later seemed to allow for it.

69. A. J. Tomlinson, *The Last Great Conflict* (New York: Garland Publishing, 1985, original 1913), p. 59; *Church of God Evangel,* April 25, 1914, pp. 1–3, probably by Tomlinson; W. J. Seymour, *The Doctrines and Discipline of the Azusa Street Apostolic Faith Mission of Los Angeles, Cal.* (n.p., 1915), p. 91.

70. Frank Bartleman, *Azusa Street,* p. 22; H. W. Schermer, in *Apostolic Faith* [Kans.], February 1913, p. 5.

71. H. W. Schermer, in *Apostolic Faith* [Kans.], April 1913, p. 3.

72. E. N. Bell, *Questions and Answers,* p. 107. See also ibid., p. 105.

73. *Midnight Cry* [Wash.], May 1908, p. 2. This issue of the *Midnight Cry* [Wash.], like many pentecostal periodicals, bore no editor's name. I assume Welch edited it because the December 1907 issue listed him as the person to whom communications should be sent.

74. George Floyd Taylor, in *Pentecostal Holiness Advocate,* November 15, 1917, p. 16.

75. G. T. Haywood, *Voice in the Wilderness,* no. 19, about 1917, pna.

76. *Apostolic Faith* [Calif.], January 1908, p. 2.

77. *Word and Witness,* November 20, 1913, p. 1, and E. N. Bell, in *Word and Witness,* January 20, 1914, p. 2.

78. M[ax] Freimark, in *Glad Tidings* [SF], January 1927, p. 7.

79. For woman's rebellious thoughts, see F. W. Sandford, in *Everlasting Gospel* [Maine],

September 1, 1901, p. 241; for both quotations, see F. Sandford and Eliza Leger, tract, quoted without full citation in Shirley Nelson, *Fair Clear and Terrible: The Story of Shiloh, Maine* (Latham, N.Y.: British American Publishing, 1989), p. 146.

80. Carl C. Walker, in *Walker's Gospel Messenger,* October 6, 1923, pna (editorial page), AOG.

81. T. DeWitt Talmage, a nonpentecostal evangelical, approvingly quoted in *Glad Tidings Herald,* September 1928, p. 8.

82. H. W. Schermer, in *Apostolic Faith* [Kans.], January 1914, first quotation p. 10, second p. 11.

83. *Apostolic Faith* [Kans.], May 1913, p. 15, quoting remarks of Lutheran pastor J. H. Keller.

84. Mrs. E. C. Broyles, in *Glad Tidings Herald,* October 1930, p. 5. Male licentiousness did not escape condemnation entirely, however. Even in the mountains of Georgia, warned one observer, little girls dared not walk to public school because of the "sex vice among little boys." *Word and Work,* September 24, 1921, p. 15.

85. *Pentecostal Rescue Journal,* January 1911, p. 2. I know of no other copies of this periodical. Charles Edwin Jones cites it as pentecostal in his comprehensive *Guide to the Study of the Pentecostal Movement* (Metuchen, N.J.: Scarecrow Press, 1974), item no. 1853.

86. *Christian Standard,* reprinted without full citation in *Holiness Advocate,* July 15, 1903, p. 6.

87. Frank Bartleman, *Flapper Evangelism: Headed for Hell* (Los Angeles: published by author, [about 1920]), tract [p. 8].

88. Ibid., [p. 7].

89. Ibid., [p. 3].

90. Ibid., [pp. 4–6].

91. Ibid., [p. 4].

92. Ibid., [p. 5].

93. Ibid. Bartleman saw many "decent women" but rued their silence [p. 4].

94. Some women I have listed may have been ordained for ministry in one form or another (such as Brown) but none, as far as I can tell, were ordained as elders with full ministerial privileges, and none explicitly challenged the proscription against women in eldership or administrative positions.

95. Mary McClintock Fulkerson, *Changing the Subject: Women's Discourses and Feminist Theology* (Minneapolis: Fortress Press, 1994), p. 293.

96. *Year Book of the 35th Annual Convocation of The United Holy Church of America, Inc . . . 1929,* p. 66, WCT.

97. Daniel Mark Epstein, *Sister Aimee: The Life of Aimee Semple McPherson* (New York: Harcourt Brace Jovanovich, 1993), pp. 217–218; Blumhofer, *Aimee Semple McPherson,* p. 333. On counsel, McPherson countersued her second husband, Harold McPherson, for desertion.

98. Maria Woodworth-Etter, *DPCM,* by title. This article, by Wayne E. Warner, is expanded in Warner's full biography of Woodworth-Etter, *The Woman Evangelist: The Life and Times of Charismatic Evangelist Maria B. Woodworth-Etter* (Metuchen, N.J.: Scarecrow Press, 1986), p. 140.

99. John Wright Follette, a Bible institute and camp meeting teacher of some note, is the only male leader I know of who never married. C. H. Mason and J. H. King, leaders

respectively of the Church of God in Christ and of the Pentecostal Holiness Church, experienced early divorces. On principle, both remained single until their first spouses died.

100. Carothers, *Church Government*, p. 45; Bartleman, *Flapper Evangelism*, p. 3.
101. *Apostolic Faith* [Calif.], June–September 1907, p. 1.
102. David Martin, *Tongues of Fire: The Explosion of Protestantism in Latin America* (Cambridge, Mass.: Basil Blackwell, 1990), p. 234.
103. Efraim Sandblom, in *Cloud of Witnesses to Pentecost in India,* March 1908, p. 35.
104. For these tensions in early-twentieth-century fundamentalism, see Bendroth, *Fundamentalism and Gender,* and Michael S. Hamilton, "Women, Public Ministry, and American Fundamentalism, 1920–1950," *Religion and American Culture,* 3 (Summer 1993): 171–196.
105. Scanzoni and Setta, "Women in Evangelical, Holiness, and Pentecostal Traditions," 226–229; Margaret M. Poloma, *The Assemblies of God at the Crossroads: Charisma and Institutional Dilemmas* (Knoxville: University of Tennessee Press, 1989), p. 103.

11. Boundaries

1. Robert Mapes Anderson, *Vision of the Disinherited: The Making of American Pentecostalism* (New York: Oxford University Press, 1979), p. 222.
2. *Apostolic Faith* [Calif.], September 1906, p. 3.
3. Ibid., January 1907, p. 2.
4. Ibid., October [1907]–January 1908, p. 2.
5. *Herald of the Church: An Advocate of the Scriptural Unity of the People of God in One Body,* June 1925.
6. *Apostolic Faith* [Calif.], January 1907, p. 2.
7. E. K. Fisher, in *Upper Room,* August 1909, p. 3.
8. *Herald of the Church,* June 1925, p. 2. According to this source, unity conferences were held in the fall of 1922, 1923, and 1924. The first meaningful effort by pentecostals to forge an ecumenical organization among themselves was the Pentecostal Fellowship of North America, formed in 1948. Even then, none of the black or Oneness bodies was invited to join. John Thomas Nichol, *Pentecostalism* (New York: Harper & Row, 1966), pp. 4, 216–218. This body abolished itself in 1994. At that time pentecostals created a new one—called Pentecostal and Charismatic Churches of North America—which included the historically African-American but not Oneness groups. For international efforts, see Nils Bloch-Hoell, *The Pentecostal Movement: Its Origin, Development, and Distinctive Character* (New York: Humanities Press, 1964, Norwegian original 1956), p. 92.
9. Anderson, *Vision of the Disinherited,* pp. 183–188.
10. Grant Wacker, *Travail of a Broken Family: Evangelical Responses to the Emergence of Pentecostalism* (forthcoming).
11. See, for example, *Trust,* October 1919, p. 12.
12. See, for example, Minnie F. Abrams, in *Word and Work,* May 1910, pp. 138–141; Levi Lupton, in *New Acts,* December 7, 1905, p. 6; Carrie Judd Montgomery, in *God's Word about Witchcraft and Kindred Errors,* tract, about 1910, p. 4; *The United Holy Church of America 24th Annual Convocation . . . 1918,* p. 8, WCT; J. O. Patterson et al., *History and Formative Years of the Church of God in Christ with Ex-*

cerpts from the Life and Works of Its Founder—Bishop C. H. Mason (Memphis: Church of God in Christ Publishing House, 1969), p. 1; John G. Lake, "The Spirit of God," 1915, and "Spiritualism," 1923, typed sermons, AOG; *Trust,* October 1919, p. 12.

13. See, for example, Abbie C. Morrow, *Christian Science,* a Christian Workers Union tract, dated 1899 but circulated among pentecostals; Elmer K. Fisher, in *Upper Room,* January 1911, p. 4; *The Masterpiece of Satan,* Evangel Tracts No. Four, about 1915; Delbert S. Bachman, *Why I Left Christian Science for Pentecost and What I Gained* (Quakertown, Pa.: Quakertown Free Press, 1927).

14. *Latter Rain Evangel,* February 1920, pp. 20–22.

15. S. D. Kinne, in *Household of God,* May 1909, p. 14; Florence Burpee, in *Word and Work,* September 24, 1921, p. 14; A. A. Boddy, in *Confidence,* December 1914, p. 280.

16. *Apostolic Faith* [Kans.], April 1913, p. 8.

17. Charles Fox Parham, in *Apostolic Faith* [Kans.], January 1, 1900, p. 6; Herbert and Lillie Buffum, in *Gold Tried in the Fire,* December 1910, p. 4.

18. See, for example, Elmer K. Fisher, in *Upper Room,* August 1909, p. 3; Levi Lupton, in *New Acts,* June 14, 1906, p. 6.

19. H. Mogridge, *Lytham (U.K.) Times,* March 27, 1914, reprint of a sermon, pna, AGUK.

20. C. H. Fredericks, in *Apostolic Faith* [Kans.], November 1912, p. 9.

21. Ibid., June 1912, p. 3.

22. H. W. Schermer, in *Apostolic Faith* [Kans.], January 1914, pp. 10–11.

23. Abbie C. Morrow, in *Church Amusements,* Words of Life Tract No. 357, 1915.

24. John Roach Straton approvingly quoted in *Worldliness in the Present Day Church,* Words of Life Tract No. 641, 1922.

25. *New Acts,* November 23, 1905, p. 7.

26. J. N. Hoover, in *Pentecostal Evangel,* December 7, 1929, p. 7.

27. Bertha Pinkham Dixon, in *Triumphs of Faith,* May 1908, p. 116. For a potpourri of attacks on liberalism in the mainline church, see Effie Cooper, in *Glad Tidings* [SF], March 1928, p. 9; *Golden Grain,* February 1927, pp. 30–31; Oswald J. Smith, in *Exploits of Faith,* May 1928, pp. 4–7 (Smith was not pentecostal but *Exploits* was).

28. See, for example, Samuel J. Mead, in *Apostolic Faith* [Kans.], February–March 1907, p. 5; Jacob Mueller, "Diary," January 30, 1921, AOG; *Promise,* February 1909, p. 4; W. R. Bunyard, in *Apostolic Faith* [Kans.], December 25, 1918, p. 6; Joseph Hutchinson, in *Apostolic Faith* [Kans.], February 1913, pp. 1–4; A. A. Boddy, *Pentecost at Sunderland: A Vicar's Testimony* (Sunderland, U.K.: n.p., May 1909), p. 15.

29. Advertisement in *Christian Evangel,* October 10, 1914, p. 2.

30. *Apostolic Faith* [Kans.], January 1916, p. 6.

31. Harriet Gravelle, in *Upper Room,* January 1910, pp. 7–8.

32. E. N. Bell, in *Weekly Evangel,* February 2, 1918, p. 8.

33. *Apostolic Faith* [Calif.], September 1906, p. 2.

34. Levi Lupton, in *New Acts,* June 28, 1906, p. 4.

35. J. R. F. [J. Roswell Flower], in *Christian Evangel,* October 10, 1914, p. 2.

36. J. G. Campbell, in *Apostolic Faith* [Kans.], February 1915, p. 14.

37. Sister Bertha Mackay, public remarks as reported in *Christian Evangel,* May 9, 1914, p. 4. The correspondent likely was J. Roswell Flower, the managing editor.

38. Baron Porcelli, in *Pentecostal Herald,* January 4, 1922, p. 3; W. H. Cossum, in *Latter Rain Evangel,* May 1910, p. 3; Levi Lupton, in *New Acts,* September 20, 1906, p. 6.

39. John Lewis Shuler, in *Pentecostal Herald,* December 15, 1922, p. 1.

40. Levi Lupton, in *New Acts,* July 19, 1906, p. 2.

41. *Christian Evangel,* October 31, 1914, p. 2.

42. See, for example, *Apostolic Faith* [Calif.], February–March 1907, p. 6.

43. See, for example, Florence I. Bush and Mother, in *Word and Work,* tear sheet, likely March 1917, p. 134, AOG; Lucy Leatherman, in *Household of God,* December 1908, pp. 5–6; James Gray, in *Christian Evangel,* October 17, 1914, p. 2.

44. Frank Bartleman, *Azusa Street: The Roots of Modern-Day Pentecost,* ed. Vinson Synan (Plainfield, N.J.: Logos International, 1980, original [differently titled] 1925), p. 48; Howard A. Goss, *The Winds of God: The Story of the Early Pentecostal Days (1901–1914) in the Life of Howard A. Goss, as Told by Ethel E. Goss* (New York: Comet Press Books, 1958), p. 31; *Book of Minutes . . . The Church of God* (Cleveland, Tenn.: Church of God Publishing House, 1917), p. 296; Gaston Espinosa, "Borderland Religion: Los Angeles and the Origins of the Latino Pentecostal Movement in the U.S., Mexico, and Puerto Rico, 1900–1945," Ph.D. diss., University of California Santa Barbara, 1999, p. 93.

45. Two well-known attacks by pentecostal apostates included Jonathan Elsworth Perkins, *Pentecostalism on the Washboard* (Fort Worth: published by author, n.d. [probably mid-1930s]), and John R. Elsom, *Pentecostalism versus the Bible, or The Tongues Movement and Why I Left It* (Los Angeles: Wetzel Publishing Co., 1937).

46. Zelma Argue, *A Vision and a Vow or the Vision and Vow of a Canadian Maiden: The Story of My Mother's Life* (Springfield, Mo.: Gospel Publishing House, n.d.), p. 42.

47. *Houston Chronicle,* October 5, 1906, p. 8.

48. *Apostolic Faith* [Ore.], July–August 1908, p. 3.

49. *Good Report,* August 1, 1913, p. 1.

50. *Apostolic Faith* [Kans.], September 1907, p. 1.

51. Walter J. Higgins, *Pioneering in Pentecost. My Experiences of 46 Years in the Ministry* (Bostonia, Calif., n.p., 1958), pp. 27–28.

52. A. J. Tomlinson, *Diary of A. J. Tomlinson,* ed. Homer A. Tomlinson (Queens Village, N.Y.: Church of God, World Headquarters, 1949), vol. 1, p. 113. From the context I infer Athens, Tennessee, not Georgia.

53. Higgins, *Pioneering in Pentecost,* p. 41.

54. Charles Fox Parham, in *Apostolic Faith* [Kans.], September 1905, p. 4.

55. *Apostolic Faith* [Calif.], February–March 1907, p. 3. The context suggests that this was a recent, local incident. The cowboy converted before the meeting was over.

56. Higgins, *Pioneering in Pentecost,* p. 31.

57. L. Echols, in *Word and Witness,* June 20, 1913, p. 5.

58. Tomlinson, *Diary of A. J. Tomlinson,* vol. 1, p. 64.

59. "Beating in Texas follows Ministry to Blacks: F. F. Bosworth's 1911 Letter to His Mother," reprinted in *Assemblies of God Heritage,* Summer 1986, pp. 5, 14.

60. Patterson, *History and Formative Years of the Church of God in Christ,* p. 23.

61. Mickey Crews, *The Church of God: A Social History* (Knoxville: University of Tennessee Press, 1990), p. 17, citing an interview with Nora Jones, daughter of W. F. Bryant.

62. *Weekly Evangel,* January 19, 1918, p. 14.

63. Edith L. Blumhofer, *The Assemblies of God: A Chapter in the Story of American Pentecostalism* (Springfield, Mo.: Gospel Publishing House, 1989), vol. 1, p. 205.

64. *Methodist Advocate Journal* of Chattanooga and Knoxville, Tenn., August 9, 1900,

p. 1. The worshipers may have been Wesleyan holiness, not pentecostal, though almost certainly moving from the former to the latter.

65. James R. Goff, Jr., *Fields White unto Harvest: Charles F. Parham and the Missionary Origins of Pentecostalism* (Fayetteville: University of Arkansas Press, 1988), p. 80.

66. *Free Methodist*, July 2, 1907, p. 417. The article implies that Smith's mother instigated the incident in order to retrieve her child. See C. E. McPherson, *Life of Levi R. Lupton* (Alliance, Ohio: published by author, 1911), p. 53, for a somewhat different rendering of what was probably the same incident.

67. Levi Lupton, describing the incident, in *New Acts*, January 11, 1906, p. 7.

68. Higgins, *Pioneering in Pentecost*, p. 16. Higgins told this story about his father and himself.

69. Alvin Price, "The Pentecostal Gospel Comes to the Outer Banks of North Carolina," typed, 1980, p. 8, AOG. Alvin Price wrote of his parents, whose names, I assume, were Price. I also assume the date of the incident from the context.

70. G. B. Cashwell, in *Apostolic Faith* [Calif.], May 1907, p. 1.

71. Higgins, *Pioneering in Pentecost*, pp. 48–50.

72. Goss, *Winds of God*, p. 87.

73. *Los Angeles Express*, July 20, 1906, p. 1.

74. See, for example, M. B. Woodworth-Etter, *Signs and Wonders: God Wrought in the Ministry for Forty Years* (Indianapolis: published by author, 1916), p. 429, and Wayne E. Warner, *The Woman Evangelist: The Life and Times of Charismatic Evangelist Maria B. Woodworth-Etter* (Metuchen, N.J.: Scarecrow Press, 1986), p. 234; *Birmingham Age-Herald*, June 23, 1907, p. 27.

75. *Apostolic Faith* [Ore.], December 1908, p. 4.

76. Crews, *Church of God*, pp. 74–75.

77. Vinson Synan, introduction to Bartleman, *Azusa Street*, p. xiv, and Bartleman, *Azusa Street*, p. 51.

78. Kurt O. Berends, "Social Variables and Community Response," in *Pentecostal Currents in American Protestantism*, ed. Edith L. Blumhofer, Russell P. Spittler, and Grant Wacker (Urbana: University of Illinois Press, 1999), pp. 81–83.

79. *Pasadena Daily News*, July 3, 1906, p. 1, also July 9, 1906 and July 13, 1906; *Los Angeles Express*, July 13, 1906, p. 15.

80. "Preacher Tells of Attempt to Dynamite His Home," typed transcript apparently from *Cumberland (Md.) Evening News*, May 28, 1921, p. 2, AOG.

81. *Plainfield (Ind.) Friday Caller*, January 1913, p. 1.

82. Harry E. Bowley, "The Great Ozark Mountains Revival," *Assemblies of God Heritage*, Summer 1982, p. 1, reprinted from the *Pentecostal Evangel*, June 12 and 19, 1948.

83. Morris E. Golder, *The Life and Works of Bishop Garfield Thomas Haywood (1880–1931)* (n.p., 1977), pp. 31–32, 37, quoting G. T. Haywood, *Brief History of Christ Temple Church*, written December 1924, no further citation.

84. Paul C. Taylor, "Interesting, Humorous, Exciting, and Spiritually Uplifting Experiences of the Early Days of the Pentecostal Movement," typed, no date, AOG, pp. 12–13.

85. *Apostolic Faith* [Calif.], November 1906, p. 1.

86. Andrew D. Urshan, *The Story of My Life* (St. Louis: Gospel Publishing House, [1916]), pp. 45–46, 50.

87. Aimee Semple McPherson, *This Is That: Personal Experiences Sermons and Writings* (New York: Garland Publishing, 1985, original 1919), pp. 113–114, 258–260.

88. Leatha Perkins Dahlgren to Wayne Warner, October 23, 1994, AOG.

89. I owe this insight to George Waldrep, "From the 'Rebel Carpenter of Nazareth' to the Ku Klux Klan: Race, Religion, and Rebellion in Sowela, 1900–1930," seminar paper, Department of History, Duke University, undated, p. 13.

90. "A Worker," in *Apostolic Faith* [Calif.], December 1906, p. 3.

91. Theodore Kornweibel, Jr., "Bishop C. H. Mason and the Church of God in Christ during World War I: The Perils of Conscientious Objection," *Southern Studies*, 26 (Fall 1987): 278.

92. Ibid., pp. 277–278; Warner, *The Woman Evangelist*, pp. 216, 231–232.

93. *Word and Witness*, December 20, 1913, p. 2.

94. Crews, *Church of God*, pp. 74–78; Vinson Synan, *The Old-Time Power* (Franklin Springs, Ga.: Advocate Press, 1973), p. 166.

95. Grant Wacker, "Marching to Zion: The Functions of Faith in a Modern Utopian Community," *Church History*, 54 (1985): 496–511.

96. Shirley Nelson, *Fair Clear and Terrible: The Story of Shiloh, Maine* (Latham, N.Y.: British American Publishing, 1989), pp. 242, 256.

97. Crews, *Church of God*, pp. 75–78. I know of two instances in which pentecostals were charged with homicide for slaying adults. One involved stomping the demons out of a woman's body until she died, the other involved deliberate choking to symbolize the death of sin. For the first, see P. C. Nelson, *Does Christ Heal Today: Messages of Faith, Hope and Cheer for the Afflicted* (Enid, Okla.: Southwestern Press, 1941), Appendix p. V [letter "V"]; for the second, see "Grand Jury to Hear Story of Inez-Cult Slaying Today . . ." unidentified newspaper tear sheet dated April 3, 1933, ascribed to a West Virginia border town, AOG.

98. Luther Gibson, *History of the Church of God Mountain Assembly* (n.p., 1954), p. 6.

99. Stanley Vishnewski quoted in Martin E. Marty, *Modern American Religion*, vol. 2, *The Noise of Conflict: 1919–1941* (Chicago: University of Chicago Press, 1991), p. 338.

100. [Church of God] *General Assembly Minutes 1906–1914* (Cleveland, Tenn.: White Wing Publishing House, 1992), 1908, p. 43; *Minutes of North Cleveland Church of God*, July 7, 1913, p. 74, COG; Berends, "Social Variables," p. 78.

101. Seeley D. Kinne, in *Evening Light and Church of God Evangel*, March 15, 1910, p. 5, taken without full citation from *Household of God*.

102. Charles Parham: "The average politician . . . does not know whether Christ was crucified on Calvary or shot at Bunker Hill" (1914), quoted in Edith L. Blumhofer, *The Assemblies of God: A Chapter in the Story of American Pentecostalism* (Springfield, Mo.: Gospel Publishing House, 1989), vol. 1, p. 424, n. 18.

103. T. M. Lee, in *Holiness Advocate*, April 15, 1902, p. 1.

104. First and second quotations from Gordon Lindsay, *John Alexander Dowie: A Life Story of Trials, Tragedies, and Triumphs* (Dallas: Christ for the Nations, 1980, original 1951), p. 162; third quotation from [John Alexander Dowie], in *Leaves of Healing*, June 14, 1895, p. 563.

105. See, for example, B. F. Lawrence, *The Apostolic Faith Restored* (Saint Louis: Gospel Publishing House, 1916), p. 15; J. B. Bell, M.D., in *Triumphs of Faith*, June 1907, pp. 132–133.

106. [Church of God] *General Assembly Minutes 1906–1914* (Cleveland, Tenn.: White Wing Publishing House, 1992), 1907, p. 37.

107. [W. F. Bryant, p. 6], in *Faithful Standard*, September 1922, p. 20.

108. A. J. Tomlinson, *The Last Great Conflict* (New York: Garland Publishing Co., 1985, original 1913), pp. 80, 82.

109. Fannie F. Rowe, in *Standard Bearer*, no. 62, about 1920, no page shown; Margaret Small, in *New Acts*, April 5, 1906, p. 8.

110. E. May Law, *Pentecostal Mission Work in South China: An Appeal for Missions* (Falcon, N.C.: Falcon Publishing Co., [1916]), pp. 35–36.

111. Charles F. Parham, *A Voice Crying in the Wilderness*, 2nd ed. (Baxter Springs, Kans.: Apostolic Faith Bible College, 1910, original 1902), p. 41.

112. Testimony of Mrs. Lethia Long, in *Pentecost*, August 1908, cover story. See *Apostolic Faith* [Tex.], May 1911, p. 4, for a typical instance in which a physician was "dumbfounded" in the face of a divine healing miracle.

113. John E. Dull, in *Live Coals of Fire*, January 12, 1900, p. 3.

114. D. Wesley Myland, *The Latter Rain Covenant and Pentecostal Power*, published with other documents as *Three Early Pentecostal Tracts*, ed. Donald W. Dayton (New York: Garland Publishing, 1985, original 1910), p. 57.

115. *Apostolic Faith* [Calif.], October 1906, p. 3.

116. L. P. Adams, in *Present Truth*, December 1909, p. 5.

117. Homer L. Cox, in *New Acts*, May 24, 1906, p. 3.

118. W. J. S. [William J. Seymour], *Apostolic Faith* [Calif.], June–September 1907, p. 3.

119. Aimee Semple McPherson, *This Is That*, pp. 461–462. The context suggests that McPherson had mainline clergy uppermost in mind.

120. Probably William F. Manley, in *Household of God*, September 1906, p. 1.

121. *Household of God*, September 1906, logo on p. 8.

122. H. W. Schermer, in *Apostolic Faith* [Kans.], March 1913, p. 5.

123. Unnamed Orlando, Fla., newspaper reporter, excerpted in McPherson, *This Is That*, p. 170.

124. Pearl Bowen, in *Apostolic Faith* [Calif.], January 1907, p. 1.

125. Ibid., September 1906, p. 1.

126. Manford Evans, *Sherburn (Minn.) Advance-Standard*, reprinted without full citation in *Golden Grain*, October 1926, pp. 22–23.

127. L. C. Hall, in *Living Waters*, excerpted in Frank Ewart, *The Phenomenon of Pentecost: A History of the Latter Rain* (Houston: Herald Publishing House, 1947), p. 96.

128. A. W. Orwig quoted in Stanley H. Frodsham, *"With Signs Following": The Story of the Latter-Day Pentecostal Revival* (Springfield, Mo.: Gospel Publishing House, 1926), p. 31.

129. M. L. Ryan, in *Apostolic Faith* [Calif.], December 1906, p. 3.

130. Mrs. J. M. Dulaney quoted in [Charles Fox Parham], *The Life of Charles F. Parham: Founder of the Apostolic Faith Movement*, compiled by His Wife [Sarah E. Parham] (New York: Garland Publishing, 1985, original 1930), p. 116.

131. *Banner of Truth*, quoted without full citation in *Apostolic Faith* [Calif.] April 1907, p. 4.

132. *Midnight Cry* [N.Y.], March 1919, p. 4; *Bridegroom's Messenger*, May 1920, p. 1; ibid., September 1919, p. 4.

133. *Apostolic Faith* [Kans.], January 1914, p. 3; Dan Morgan, *Rising in the West: The True Story of an "Okie" Family from the Great Depression through the Reagan Years* (New York: Alfred A. Knopf, 1992), p. 220.

134. *Trust*, November 1920, p. 12.

135. Charles Parham, in *Apostolic Faith* [Kans.], March 1913, pp. 8–9, quotation p. 9.

136. Frank W. Sandford, in *Everlasting Gospel* [Maine], November 1–December 31, 1902, p. 501.

137. Crews, *Church of God*, p. 65.

138. Myland, *Latter Rain,* p. 115.
139. Daniel Mark Epstein, *Sister Aimee: The Life of Aimee Semple McPherson* (New York: Harcourt, Brace, Jovanovich, 1993), p. 165.
140. George Floyd Taylor, in *Pentecostal Holiness Advocate,* March 28, 1918, p. 13.
141. Sexton quoted in Frank Peck, in *Apostolic Faith* [Kans.], February 1915, pp. 11–13, quotation p. 13.
142. Ibid., p. 12.
143. Robert S. Craig, in *Glad Tidings,* May 1927, pp. 6–7.
144. B. H. Irwin, in *Way of Faith,* July 8, 1896, p. 1, quoted in Roger Glenn Robins, "Plainfolk Modernist: The Radical Holiness World of A. J. Tomlinson," Ph.D. diss., Duke University, 1999, p. 67.

12. Society

1. Josef Barton, "Pentecostals and Rural Society: The Highland South, 1890–1940" (paper presented at the annual meeting of the American Academy of Religion, Dallas, Tex., 1980), p. 3.
2. Morris E. Golder, *History of the Pentecostal Assemblies of the World* (Indianapolis: n.p., 1973), p. 34, quoting without full citation a pamphlet written by Sister Hilda Reeder about 1940.
3. *Apostolic Faith* [Calif.], November 1906, p. 1. I infer Clara Lum's hand from the reference to letters and office, which she oversaw. She was here quoting with approval a "leading Methodist layman of Los Angeles."
4. Max Wood Moorhead, in *Cloud of Witnesses to Pentecost in India,* November 1908, p. 15.
5. *VICTORY!,* April 1909, p. 1.
6. Frank Bartleman, *Azusa Street: The Roots of Modern-Day Pentecost,* ed. Vinson Synan (Plainfield, N.J.: Logos International, 1980, original [differently titled] 1925), p. 43.
7. Howard A. Goss, *The Winds of God: The Story of the Early Pentecostal Days (1901–1914) in the Life of Howard A. Goss, as Told by Ethel E. Goss* (New York: Comet Press Books, 1958), p. 80.
8. McPherson quoted in William G. McLoughlin, "Aimee Semple McPherson: 'Your Sister in the King's Glad Service,'" *Journal of Popular Culture,* 1(Winter 1967): 205.
9. Stanley H. Frodsham, *"With Signs Following": The Story of the Latter-Day Pentecostal Revival* (Springfield, MO.: Gospel Publishing House, 1926), to ellipsis p. 83, following ellipsis p. 84.
10. *Upper Room,* March 1910, p. 3, probably referring to the same persons Frodsham named. The article may have been taken from a letter by T. B. Barratt.
11. *Lytham (U.K.) Times,* June 12, 1914 (regarding a conference at Sunderland), pna AGUK.
12. *Confidence,* August 15, 1908, p. 11.
13. W. F. Carothers, in *Word and Witness,* September 1915, p. 8. As an attorney Carother's social position distanced him from the rank and file, so for this purpose I consider him an outside observer.
14. Unidentified tear sheet from a British newspaper, ATS, dated November 26, 1907, referring to a gathering in Shrewsbury.
15. Unidentified tear sheet from a British newspaper, ATS, dated June 10, 1910, probably *Sunderland (U.K.) Daily Echo.*

16. Doremus A. Hayes, *The Gift of Tongues* (Cincinnati: Jennings & Graham, 1913), p. 87. Hayes also said that he observed a fair number of laborers and an "unusual proportion of middle-aged and elderly, fleshy women."

17. Unidentified tear sheet from a British newspaper, ATS, dated 1904, likely an incorrect reference to a 1907 Shropshire revival.

18. "Interest in Meetings Continues to Grow," Yellville, Marion County, Arkansas [newspaper title not shown], February 10, 1911, pna, AOG.

19. Allene M. Sumner, "The Holy Rollers on Shin Bone Ridge," *Nation,* July 29, 1925, pp. 137–138; Robert Mapes Anderson, *Vision of the Disinherited: The Making of American Pentecostalism* (New York: Oxford University Press, 1979). I summarize the progression of historical monographs that set the stage for Anderson's work in "Taking Another Look at the *Vision of the Disinherited,*" *Religious Studies Review,* 8 (January 1982): 15–22. See also Augustus Cerillo, Jr. and Grant Wacker, "Bibliography and Historiography of Pentecostalism in the United States," *New International Dictionary of the Pentecostal and Charismatic Movements,* ed. Stanley Burgess (Grand Rapids: Harper Collins Zondervan, forthcoming 2001), by title.

20. Anderson, *Vision of the Disinherited,* chap. 6, esp. pp. 100–110, 291–295.

21. Ibid., p. 114.

22. Ibid., p. 135.

23. Ibid., chap. 7, summarized on pp. 135–136.

24. Ibid., p. 226.

25. Ibid., p. 136.

26. Ibid., p. 225.

27. Ibid., p. 114.

28. Ibid.

29. Ibid., p. 226.

30. Ibid., p. 224.

31. Ibid., p. 113.

32. Ibid., p. 136.

33. W. F. Bryant, in *Evening Light and Church of God Evangel,* March 1, 1910, p. 8.

34. W. F. Bryant, in *Triumphs of Faith,* October 1911, pp. 228–229.

35. J. B. Mitchell, in *Triumphs of Faith,* August 1907, pp. 173–174. See also *Evening Light and Church of God Evangel,* July 1, 1910, p. 4, which speaks of a group unable to raise the $175 needed to replace a meetinghouse torched by arsonists.

36. R. E. McAlister, *Good Report,* January 1914, p. 16.

37. *Apostolic Faith* [Calif.], December 1906, p. 2.

38. *Alliance (Ohio) Daily Review,* June 30, 1908, p. 14.

39. Interview with Stanley Horton, son of Myrle Fisher, August 16, 1996, Springfield, Mo.

40. Brother Hesse, in *Gleams of Grace,* July 1922, p. 3.

41. Goss, *Winds of God,* p. 81. Goss's father later joined the pentecostal movement.

42. Cora Fritsch, September 18, 1907, in *Letters from Cora,* typed, comp. Homer and Alice Fritsch, 1987, AOG.

43. James R. Goff, Jr., "Thomas Hampton Gourley: Testing the Boundaries of American Pentecostalism," in *Portraits of a Generation: Early Pentecostal Leaders,* ed. James R. Goff, Jr. and Grant Wacker (forthcoming).

44. *Word and Work,* November 1918, p. 14.

45. Ibid.

46. See, for example, J. Elwin Wright, in *Word and Work,* February 1912, p. 57; Alice Reynolds Flower, *Grace for Grace* (Springfield, Mo.: published by author, [1961]), p. 44.

47. *Apostolic Evangel,* August 23, 1916, p. 4.

48. See, for example, *Year Book of the 35th Annual Convocation of the United Holy Church of America, Inc. . . . 1929,* p. 15, WCT; Henry L. Fisher "Diary," March 14, 1922, WCT; *Word and Witness,* October 1915, p. 3.

49. H. Mogridge, *Lytham (U.K.) Times,* April 18, 1913, pna, AGUK.

50. For George Montgomery, see Jennifer Stock, "George S. Montgomery: Businessman for the Gospel," *Assemblies of God Heritage,* part 1, Spring 1989, pp. 4–5, 17–18, part 2, Summer 1989, pp. 12–14, 20. For Carrie Judd Montgomery's economic-social-educational standing, see her "Date Book for 1909," especially noting the spare eloquence of her obviously well-tutored writing style.

51. Tanglewood Hotels stationery shared by Professor Kurt O. Berends, Calvin College. See also Kurt O. Berends, "A Divided Harvest: Alice Belle Garrigus, Joel Adams Wright, and Early New England Pentecostalism," M.A. thesis, Wheaton College Graduate School, 1993, pp. 51–54, and related research notes. The George Barney family, friends of the Wrights and stalwarts in the New England revival, owned the 345-acre Breezynook Farm outside Canaan, New Hampshire, reputedly the largest in the region. Kurt O. Berends, "Social Variables and Community Response," in *Pentecostal Currents in American Protestantism,* ed. Edith L. Blumhofer, Russell P. Spittler, and Grant Wacker (Urbana: University of Illinois Press, 1999), p. 73.

52. Mickey Crews, *The Church of God: A Social History* (Knoxville: University of Tennessee Press, 1990), p. 6.

53. William Doctor Gentry to Arthur G. Osterberg, September 2, 1921 (envelope date), AOG.

54. For Hall, see Gary Don McElhany, "The South Aflame: A History of the Assemblies of God in the Gulf Region, 1901–1940," Ph.D. diss., Mississippi State, 1996, pp. 33–34. Hall withdrew from West Point after a few months and it is not clear that he graduated from any of the other schools listed. For Tomlinson, see Roger Glenn Robins, "Plainfolk Modernist: The Radical Holiness World of A. J. Tomlinson," Ph.D. diss., Duke University, 1999, p. 152. My sentence closely follows Robins's. For Carothers, Yeomans, and Yoakum, see *DPCM,* by title.

55. For Bell, see Richard A. Lewis, "E. N. Bell—A Voice of Restraint in an Era of Controversy," *Enrichment: A Journal for Pentecostal Ministry,* (Fall 1999): 49; for Taylor, see *DPCM,* and below; for Holmes, see Charles E. Bradshaw, *Profiles of Faith* (Franklin Springs, Ga.: Advocate Press, 1984), p. 106, and N. J. Holmes and Wife, *Life Sketches and Sermons* (Royston, Ga.: Press of the Pentecostal Holiness Church, [1909]-1920), pp. 54–58; for Worrell, Studd, and Nelson, see *DPCM,* by title. University of North Carolina, Chapel Hill, records show that Taylor received his B.A. in 1928 and M.A. in history in 1931.

56. Other first-generation leaders who either graduated from established colleges or evinced significant college training included Minnie Abrams, Paul Bettex, Harold A. Baker, Frank Boyd, R. B. Chisholm, A. S. Copley, Susan Easton, W. I. Evans, John Wright Follette, Andrew L. Fraser, A. G. Garr, Alice Bell Garrigus, J. Narver Gortner, Thomas Hindle, Charles Hodges, Willis C. Hoover, Fred Hornshuh, S. A. Jamieson, Alice E. Luce, J. B. Mitchell, Max Wood Moorhead, J. Rufus Moseley, Albert Norton, Francisco Olazabel, D. C. O. Opperman, William H. Piper, Charles Hamilton

Pridgeon, William E. Schliemann, Adolf Gunnar Vingren, and Lilian B. Yeomans. For biographical details on each, see Grant Wacker, *Heaven Below* research file, AOG.

57. Conrad Cherry, *Hurrying toward Zion: Universities, Divinity Schools, and American Protestantism* (Bloomington: Indiana University Press, 1995), pp. 130, 187. Cherry's data suggest that even in the elite traditions ordinands had experienced a significant loss of social status by the early twentieth century. In 1934 the number of ministers in twenty-three denominations holding both college and seminary degrees totaled 22 percent, only a college degree 16 percent, only a seminary degree 12 percent, and no degree 49 percent. Among Southern Methodists and Southern Baptists, who provided the main talent pool for pentecostals, 63 percent and 65 percent, respectively, held no degree at all. Mark A. May, *The Education of American Ministers*, vol. 2, *The Profession of the Ministry* (New York: Institute of Social and Religious Research, 1934), pp. 14, 84, 79.

58. See, for example, the biographical sketches of seventeen leaders, prefixed to each autobiographical document, in *"Pentecost in My Soul": Explorations in the Meaning of Pentecostal Experience in the Early Assemblies of God,* ed. Edith L. Blumhofer (Springfield, Mo.: Gospel Publishing House, 1989); Anderson, *Vision of the Disinherited*, pp. 100–103. See also the occupations for the individuals listed in Grant Wacker, "Occupational Profiles," *Heaven Below* research file, AOG.

59. Wherever reasonably possible I have combined the relevant data for 1910 in the following list.

Population: 92m.

Age (median): males, 25; females, 24.

Adults (percent over age 13): 87.

Longevity: at birth 1910, 50 years (includes infant mortality); age 10 in 1910, 61 years (excludes infant mortality); age 24 in 1910, 63 years (excludes infant mortality).

Marital status of adults: males, 54 percent; females, 56 percent. NB: the actual percentage almost certainly proved much higher, since (1) the Census defined adults as persons over fourteen and (2) the median marriage age for females was 22, males 25.

Nativity: foreign born, 15 percent; foreign parentage, 18 percent; mixed parentage, 9 percent.

Race/ethnicity 1930: U.S: white, 89 percent; black, 10 percent; other, 2 percent. South Atlantic: 28 percent black. East South Central region: 27 percent black. West South Central: 19 percent black.

Residence: rural, 50m; urban, 42m.

Provenance: birth state, 78 percent; state contiguous to birth state, 10 percent; state not contiguous to birth state, 11 percent.

Occupation: manual labor, 38 percent; farming, 31 percent; white collar, 21 percent; service, 10 percent; professional and technical, 5 percent.

Earnings: all: $575. Federal employees (executive), $1,100; ministers, $800; railroads, street railways, $680; miners, $560; public school teachers, $490; farm labor, $340; farm labor in South Atlantic, East South Central, and West South Central Census Regions, $190. Average family income 1901: $651.

Education expenditures: not available for 1910. For the next closest census period,

1917 to 1919: average family with at least one child: reading materials, $11; education, $8.

Educational attainment: high school graduates, 9 percent; illiterates, 8 percent. School year length, 158 days; days attended, 113; percentage of persons 5–17 years old enrolled in a school, 79.4 percent.

Services: electricity, 16 percent of dwelling units; telephone, 82 per 1,000 population, including residences and businesses.

Historical Statistics of the United States: Colonial Times to 1970 (Washington, D.C.: U.S. Department of Commerce, Bureau of the Census, 1975), parts 1 and 2; U.S. Department of Commerce, Bureau of the Census, *Fifteenth Census of the United States: 1930* (Washington, D.C.: Government Printing Office, 1933), vol. 2, p. 46. Figures are rounded to the nearest whole. Because of overlaps and differences in enumeration procedures, percentages do not always add up to 100 and totals do not always cross reference exactly. "Years of Life Expected at Birth," compiled by National Center for Health Statistics, in *The World Almanac and Book of Facts 1992* (New York: World Almanac, 1992), p. 956. Life expectancy after infant mortality is factored out is taken from *The 1992 Information Please Almanac* (Boston: Houghton Mifflin, 1992), p. 817.

60. In 1916 women constituted the following membership percentages in three identifiably pentecostal groups: Assemblies of God, 59.1 percent; Apostolic Faith Movement, 53.5 percent; Pentecostal Holiness Church, 61.4 percent. The weighted average equals 59 percent. *Religious Bodies 1916* (Washington D.C.: Department of Commerce, Bureau of the Census, 1919), pp. 142–146.

61. Ann Braude, "Women's History *Is* American Religious History," in *Retelling U.S. Religious History,* ed. Thomas A. Tweed (Berkeley: University of California Press, 1997), p. 88.

62. Robeck, a historian at Fuller Seminary, has used census figures, tax registers, and estate records to track the demographic profiles of some 500 pentecostals who frequented the Los Angeles area missions between 1906 and 1916. He and student researchers analyzed the sample of forty-three, cited here, in 1986. These and other results are forthcoming in a major study of early pentecostals in Southern California.

63. The Assemblies of God average for 6,700 adherents was 92.6 percent adults, Apostolic Faith average for 2,200 adherents was 71.6 percent adults, Pentecostal Holiness Church average for 5,400 adherents was 95.7 percent adults. The weighted average for 14,300 pentecostal adherents equaled 91 percent adults. *Religious Bodies 1916* (Washington, D.C.: Department of Commerce, Bureau of the Census, 1919), part 2, pp. 36–38.

64. Hayes, *The Gift of Tongues,* p. 86.

65. I selected 100 subjects in the *DPCM* on the basis of prominence within the movement. A research assistant and I then noted sex, birth date, place of birth, cause of death, marital status, education, main occupation in the church, secular occupation before joining the movement, travel distinctives, originating denomination, theological distinctives, claim of missionary tongues (xenolalia), illness/healings, miscellaneous distinctives, date of Holy Spirit baptism, place of Holy Spirit baptism, and conversion experience. We reduced the key data to computer-readable spread sheets. See Wacker, *DPCM* data base, *Heaven Below* research file, AOG.

66. The national percentages for pentecostals were 78.4 percent white, 17.7 percent

black, and 3.9 percent interracial. The southern district percentages were 77 percent white, 19.6 percent black, and 0.03 percent interracial. I have drawn these figures from Anderson's compilations of twenty-six pentecostal denominations in the 1936 *Religious Bodies of the United States.* Anderson, *Vision of the Disinherited,* p. 118, 125, 169. (Neither Anderson nor I tried to adjust for the small number of separately organized blacks in the mostly white groups, nor whites in mostly black groups.) The Robeck study suggests a somewhat higher percentage of blacks in the southern California missions (of thirty-five whose race could be determined, there were eight blacks and twenty-seven whites, yielding 29 percent overall). This finding may mean that the percentage of blacks was greater in 1910 than in 1936, or that Los Angeles was atypical, or both. In any event, Robeck's figures still challenge the conventional notion that the revival in southern California and elsewhere involved mostly African Americans.

67. The marital status of thirty-three of Robeck's forty-three subjects can be determined with certainty: twenty-five were married, seven were single, and one was a widower. The status of the other ten remain unknown, although several probably were or had been married, given clues such as a reference to an adult live-in son.

68. E. N. Bell, in *Weekly Evangel,* January 26, 1918, p. 7.

69. Probably editor Ernest Hanson, in *Apostolic Witness,* January 1909, p. 5.

70. We examined *Word and Work* (Russell, Mass.), January–March 1908, nos. 1–3; *Bridegroom's Messenger* (Atlanta), November 1, 1907, January 1–March 1, 1908, nos. 5–9; *Apostolic Faith* (Los Angeles), October 1907–May 1908, nos. 11–13; *Apostolic Faith* (Portland, Ore.), July–December 1908, nos. 15–17; *Pentecost* (Indianapolis), January–February 1909, no. 5; and *Pentecost* (Kansas City, Mo.), April–July 1909, nos. 6–8. Wacker, "Residence Patterns," *Heaven Below* research file, AOG.

71. From the 1936 census, Anderson calculated the urban–rural distribution of twenty-six pentecostal denominations in 1936 as urban 62.4, rural 37.6. Anderson, *Vision of the Disinherited,* pp. 168–169.

72. As early as the summer of 1908 Oregon's *Apostolic Faith* spoke of ten pentecostal papers in the United States and "other lands." *Apostolic Faith,* July–August 1908, p. 1. I count roughly seventy pentecostal periodicals published in the United States between 1900 and 1930 (roughly, owing to splits and mergers) in Charles Edwin Jones, *A Guide to the Study of the Pentecostal Movement* (Metuchen, N.J.: Scarecrow Press, 1983).

73. Besides the census data in note 59, see Thomas J. Schlereth, *Victorian America: Transformations in Everyday Life* (New York: Harper Collins Publishers, 1991), pp. 29, 34–35, 78, 80, and Gary B. Nash et al., *The American People: Creating a Nation and a Society,* 3rd ed., vol. 2, *Since 1865,* (New York: Harper Collins College Publishers, 1994), pp. 621–622.

74. Joe Colletti, "Sociological Study of Italian Pentecostals in Chicago, 1900–1930" (paper presented to the 16th annual meeting of the Society for Pentecostal Studies, Costa Mesa, Calif., 1986), p. 8.

75. Kurt O. Berends, "A Mixed Harvest: The First Fruit Harvesters' Ministry in Rural New England" (paper presented to Pentecostal Currents in the American Church conference, Fuller Theological Seminary, Pasadena, Calif., March 1994), p. 25.

76. *Apostolic Faith* [Ore.], no. 45 [about 1910], p. 1.

77. *Confidence,* April 1908, p. 9.

78. For data, see Wacker, "Occupations Profile," *Heaven Below* research file, AOG.

79. The $10,045 figure assumes a Consumer Price Index multiplier of 17.5. Bureau of Labor Statistics web site, www.bls.gov, extracted February 21, 2000, pp. 1–3. The Bureau's figures only go back to 1913. My extrapolation to 1910 is based on the formula in John J. McCusker, "How Much Is That in Real Money?" *Proceedings of the American Antiquarian Society,* 101 (1992): 313–314.

80. Besides census data, see Schlereth, *Victorian America,* pp. 78, 80.

81. Again consider Robeck's forty-three subjects (including twelve couples). Four owned their homes, one free of mortgage. Another apparently owned a boarding house. Two claimed boarders, and another listed a live-in servant. The surgeon identified himself as the Chief Operating Surgeon at the General Hospital of Los Angeles. The business owner and the seamstress quit their jobs, suggesting backup financial security. Many of the jobs listed required either extended training or measurable capital outlay.

82. Fritsch, *Letters from Cora,* January 7, 1909.

83. Paul Haven Walker, *Paths of a Pioneer: Life Story of Paul Haven Walker: My Call and Redemption* (Cleveland, Tenn.: n.p., 1970), pp. 73–77.

84. Marrion DeViney, in *Christian Evangel,* October 31, 1914, p. 2.

85. Bob Burke, *Like a Prairie Fire: A History of the Assemblies of God in Oklahoma* (Oklahoma City: Oklahoma District Council of the Assemblies of God, 1994), p. 23.

86. *Voice in the Wilderness,* vol. 2, no. not legible, probably late 1920, pp. 6 and 15, undoubtedly referring to the same event.

87. Gary B. McGee, "Three Notable Women in Pentecostal Ministry," *Assemblies of God Heritage,* Spring 1985, p. 5.

88. George B. Studd recorded in his diary that his wealthy brother Cecil gave the Azusa mission £1,500 pounds in February 1908 to clear the mortgage. Studd, "Diary," February 2, 1908, AOG.

89. Bartleman, *Azusa Street,* p. 95.

90. William H. Durham, in *Word and Work,* May 1910, p. 156.

91. *Pentecostal Testimony,* January 1912, p. 15.

92. [William H. Durham by internal evidence], in *Pentecostal Testimony,* July 1, 1910, p. 11.

93. Archie P. Gaylord, for example, noted that at one point he had been out of work, "very hard up," and short of food, but hastened to add that he preferred to turn down a job rather than join a labor union. *Apostolic Faith* [Ore.], July–August 1908, p. 4.

94. G. F. Taylor, in *Pentecostal Holiness Advocate,* February 21, 1918, p. 1.

95. *Glad Tidings Herald,* November 1932, p. 4.

96. Charles Parham, in *Apostolic Faith* [Kans.], September 1905, p. 5.

97. M. M. Pinson, "Sketch of the Life and Ministry of Mack M. Pinson," typed, 1949, p. 16, AOG.

98. David Martin, *Tongues of Fire: The Explosion of Protestantism in Latin America.* (Cambridge, Mass.: Basil Blackwell, 1990), p. 34. It should be acknowledged that the average value of pentecostal edifices ran far below the average for all bodies— roughly 10 percent. Yet that fact is hardly surprising—or symptomatic—since saints, having withdrawn from or been kicked out of their parent bodies, almost always had to start from scratch. *Religious Bodies: 1936* (Washington, D.C.: Government Printing Office, 1941), Table 14, pp. 104–115.

99. In 1936, 49 percent (156,422) of pentecostals lived in the South, 51 percent (164,384) outside the South, as defined by the census. *Religious Bodies: 1936* (Washington, D.C.: Department of Commerce, Bureau of the Census, 1941), Table 13.

100. J. R. F[lower]., in *Christian Evangel,* October 10, 1914, p. 1.

101. These included *Word and Work,* published in Worcester, Mass., *Bridegroom's Messenger,* published in Atlanta, *Pentecost,* published in Kansas City, Mo., *Apostolic Faith,* published in Los Angeles, and *Apostolic Faith,* published in Portland, Ore. See also the far-flung sites listed in "Apostolic Faith Directory," in *Apostolic Faith* [Tex.], October 1908, p. 5, and the similar directory in *Confidence,* July 15, 1908, p. 7.

102. In his study of the seventeen-state southern region before World War II, Robert F. Martin found few social differences between counties that did and did not contain a strong pentecostal presence. Martin, "The Early Years of American Pentecostalism, 1900–1940: Survey of a Social Movement," Ph.D. diss., University of North Carolina at Chapel Hill, 1975, esp. pp. 150–151. Martin's interpretation of the data differs somewhat from mine.

103. "A Brief summary of Life of Arthur George Osterberg, Prepared from his diary and notes by his son, Dean Osterberg, August 1990," and "Arthur George Osterberg," both typed, AOG.

104. See, for example, William H. Durham, in *Word and Work,* May 1910, p. 154; A. W. Frodsham, in *Confidence,* June 1911, p. 139; Walter J. Higgins, *Pioneering in Pentecost. My Experiences of 46 Years in the Ministry* (Bostonia, Calif.: no publisher, 1958), p. 30; *Word and Work,* May 1910, p. 141; Morris E. Golder, *The Life and Works of Bishop Garfield Thomas Haywood (1880–1931)* (n.p., 1977), p. 32.

105. The social historian Josef Barton discerns striking occupational and geographical churning among pentecostal laborers in the southern highlands (and in Detroit factories in the 1930s). David Martin similarly notes that modern pentecostals in Chile gravitate toward jobs that involved significant physical mobility, such as porters, salespersons, and night watchmen. Barton, "Pentecostals and Rural Society"; Martin, *Tongues of Fire,* p. 79.

106. Dan Morgan, *Rising in the West: The True Story of an "Okie" Family from the Great Depression through the Reagan Years* (New York: Alfred A. Knopf, 1992), pp. 106, 110–112; see also pp. 163–170.

107. McPherson quoted in Daniel Epstein, *Sister Aimee: The Life of Aimee Semple McPherson* (New York: Harcourt Brace Jovanovich, 1993), p. 330, and in Edith L. Blumhofer, *Aimee Semple McPherson: Everybody's Sister* (Grand Rapids: William B. Eerdmans Publishing Co., 1993), p. 382.

108. *Living Water,* reprinted without full citation in *Triumphs of Faith,* June, 1908, p. 123.

109. Arrell M. Gibson, *Wilderness Bonanza: The Tri-State District of Missouri, Kansas, and Oklahoma* (Norman: University of Oklahoma Press, 1972), chap. 15, esp. pp. 252, 256.

110. *Apostolic Faith* [Kans.], July 1912, p. 3.

111. James R. Goff, Jr., *Fields White unto Harvest: Charles F. Parham and the Missionary Origins of Pentecostalism* (Fayetteville: University of Arkansas Press, 1988), pp. 91–93.

112. See, for example, F. M. Britton, *Pentecostal Truths* (Royston, Ga.: Publishing House of the Pentecostal Holiness Church, [1919]), throughout, esp. chap. 23.

113. Fritsch, *Letters from Cora,* see especially July 13, 1908.

114. Alfred and Lillian Garr, quoted in B. F. Lawrence, *The Apostolic Faith Restored* (St. Louis: Gospel Publishing House, 1916), p. 98.
115. *Apostolic Faith* [Kans.], July 1912, p. 12.
116. H. Morse, in *Good Report,* August 1, 1913, p. 2. The *Good Report* itself moved from Ottawa to Los Angeles, probably in the spring of 1913. *Word and Witness,* June 20, 1913, p. 8.
117. A. A. Boddy, in *Confidence,* May 1911, p. 111.

13. Nation

1. R. Laurence Moore, *Religious Outsiders and the Making of Americans* (New York: Oxford University Press, 1986), p. 69.
2. *Topeka Daily Capital,* July 5, 1901, p. 3.
3. Charles Fox Parham, in *Apostolic Faith* [Kans.], September 1905, p. 7.
4. Ibid., March 1912, p. 2.
5. [Charles Fox Parham], *The Life of Charles F. Parham: Founder of the Apostolic Faith Movement,* compiled by His Wife [Sarah E. Parham] (New York: Garland Publishing, 1985, original 1930), p. 274.
6. Stanley H. Frodsham, in *Word and Witness,* October 1915, p. 3.
7. Reprint of a tract by Leonard Newby, from Southsea, England, in *Weekly Evangel,* April 10, 1917, p. 1.
8. H. Musgrave Reade, in *Trust,* November 1917, pp. 7–13, all quotations p. 13.
9. Levi Lupton, in *New Acts,* July 5, 1906, p. 8.
10. Horace Houlding, in *Upper Room,* June 1910, p. 4.
11. Probably by Susan A. Duncan, an editor, in *Trust,* September 1918, p. 13.
12. H. Pierson King, in *Trust,* October 1915, p. 13.
13. Theodore Kornweibel, Jr., "Bishop C. H. Mason and the Church of God in Christ during World War I: The Perils of Conscientious Objection," *Southern Studies: An Interdisciplinary Journal of the South,* 26 (Fall 1987): 273–274.
14. S. Clyde Bailey, *Pioneer Marvels of Faith: Wonderful Forty-Six Years of Experience* (Morristown, Tenn.: published by author, [about 1955]), p. 15.
15. See, for example, Peter H. Argersinger, "Pentecostal Politics in Kansas," *Kansas Quarterly,* 1 (1969): 24–35; Rhys H. Williams and Susan M. Alexander, "Religious Rhetoric in American Populism: Civil Religion as Movement Ideology," *Journal for the Scientific Study of Religion,* 33 (March 1994): 1–15.
16. Mickey Crews, *The Church of God: A Social History* (Knoxville: University of Tennessee Press, 1990), pp. 1–3; James R. Goff, Jr., *Fields White unto Harvest, Charles F. Parham and the Missionary Origins of Pentecostalism* (Fayetteville: University of Arkansas Press, 1988), p. 234, n. 39.
17. Vinson Synan, *The Holiness-Pentecostal Tradition: Charismatic Movements in the Twentieth Century,* 2nd ed. (Grand Rapids: William B. Eerdmans Publishing Co., 1997, original 1971), pp. 42–43, esp. p. 43, n. 53.
18. Crews, *Church of God,* p. 2. James R. Goff notes the geographic coincidence but adds that Parham himself "steered clear of political involvement." *Fields White unto Harvest,* p. 156.
19. For Walker, see Paul H. Walker, *Paths of a Pioneer* (Cleveland, Tenn.: n.p., 1970) pp. 15, 19, 170; for Crumpler, see *The Caucasian,* August 27, 1896, p. 3; for Taylor,

see *The Caucasian,* March 10, 1898, p. 4. I owe the Walker reference to Darrin Rodgers.

20. *Reports of the Oklahoma State Convention, Pentecostal Holiness Church* (Oklahoma City, 1911), p. 2. For the larger context see James Scott Bissett, "Agrarian Socialism in America: Marx and Jesus in the Oklahoma Countryside," Ph.D. diss, Duke University, 1989, p. 120.

21. Lupton assailed sweat factories in *New Acts,* July 12, 1906, p. 8; capital punishment in ibid., March 1, 1906, p. 7; imperialism in ibid., March 22, 1906, p. 6.

22. Augustus Cerillo, Jr., "Frank Bartleman: Pentecostal 'Lone Ranger' and Social Critic," in *Portraits of a Generation: Early Pentecostal Leaders,* ed. James R. Goff, Jr. and Grant Wacker (forthcoming).

23. Gortner attacked muckraker Upton Sinclair, who was running for governor on a Socialist ticket, and the then current governor for winking at a mob lynching in San Jose. Wayne Warner, "The Pentecostal Methodist: J. Narver Gortner" *Assemblies of God Heritage,* Summer 1988, p. 13; and interview with Warner, August 9, 1996, AOG.

24. *Glad Tidings Herald,* November 1932, p. 4.

25. The issues included but also transcended white racism. Some saints endorsed the Klan because it appeared to support a range of traditional American values, while some opposed the Klan because it seemed a sign of the Last Days and because the Klan opposed them. For support, see A. B. Cox, "Sketches from a sermon in the largest Pentecostal Assembly in the [C]ity," about November 1923; May E. Fray [Frey ?] to Brother [J. W.] Welch, June 9, 1925, Klan file, AOG. For opposition, see *Assemblies of God Arkansas District Council Minutes,* 1924, p. 12; and J. W. Welch to Mrs. Lewis Schlemmer, October 25, 1923, AOG and Klan file, AOG; Walter J. Higgins, *Pioneering in Pentecost. My Experiences of 46 Years in the Ministry* (Bostonia, Calif.: n.p., 1958), p. 76; Synan, *The Holiness-Pentecostal Tradition,* p. 182; Dan Morgan, *Rising in the West: The True Story of an "Okie" Family from the Great Depression through the Reagan Years* (New York: Alfred A. Knopf, 1992), p. 119.

26. Norman Kingsford Dann, "Concurrent Social Movements: A Study of the Interrelationships between Populist Politics and Holiness Religion," Ph.D. dissertation, Syracuse University, 1974, pp. 16–20, 56, 60, 77–78. Some of Dann's Wesleyan holiness periodicals and schools later became pentecostal.

27. C. W. Shumway, "A Study of 'The Gift of Tongues,'" A.B. thesis, University of Southern California, 1914, p. 166.

28. *Progress* [Perris, Calif.], quoted without full citation in *Apostolic Faith* [Kans.], March 1912, p. 2.

29. George Floyd Taylor, "Diary," May 26, 1908, North Carolina State History Archives, Raleigh, N.C.

30. Edith L. Blumhofer, *Aimee Semple McPherson: Everybody's Sister* (Grand Rapids: William B. Eerdmans Publishing Co., 1993), p. 265.

31. A. J. Tomlinson, *Answering the Call of God* (Cleveland, Tenn.: White Wing Publishing House, [1913]), p. 4, and Roger Glenn Robins, "Plainfolk Modernist: The Radical Holiness World of A. J. Tomlinson," Ph.D. diss., Duke University, 1999, p. 176 for Republican Party identification.

32. *Hamilton County (Ind.) Ledger,* October 28, 1892, pna, AOG; Robins, "Plainfolk Modernist," p. 225.

33. Tomlinson, *Answering the Call of God,* pp. 9–10, quotation p. 10.

34. [Church of God] *General Assembly Minutes 1906–1914* (Cleveland, Tenn.: White Wing Publishing House, 1992), 1908, p. 43.

35. Crews, *Church of God,* pp. 109–10, 192, n. 4. Deborah McCauley's fine historical ethnography of Appalachian pentecostalism significantly says nothing at all about politics, social reform, or the Social Gospel. McCauley, *Appalachian Mountain Religion: A History* (Urbana: University of Illinois Press, 1995), chaps. 13, 17, 19.

36. To test this assertion, I tabulated the content of the first twenty issues of the *Pentecostal Evangel* for 1925. The cover stories and the lead articles proved overwhelmingly devotional or doctrinal in nature. Other articles broke down as follows: Palestine 52, international antisemitism 21, domestic antisemitism 4, war 16, everything else (such as Nazism, communism, and famine) totaled 105.

37. Crews, *Church of God,* p. 65.

38. See, for example, D. Wesley Myland, *The Latter Rain Covenant and Pentecostal Power,* published with other documents as *Three Early Pentecostal Tracts,* ed. Donald W. Dayton (New York: Garland Publishing, 1985, original 1910), pp. 114–115.

39. In an excellent survey of recent scholarship, Randall J. Stephens reaches similar conclusions about pentecostals' noninterest in worldly political matters, though he stresses the role of premillennialism more than I do. Stephens, "The Convergence of Populism, Religion, and the Holiness-Pentecostal Movements: A Review of the Historical Literature," *Fides et Historia: Journal of the Conference on Faith and History,* 32 (Winter/Spring 2000): 62–64.

40. H. W. Schermer, in *Apostolic Faith* [Kans.], October 1913, pp. 15–17.

41. William C. Turner, Jr., "The United Holy Church of America: A Study in African-American Holiness Pentecostalism," Ph.D. diss., Duke University, 1984, p. 91.

42. David Clark, "Miracles for a Dime," *California History* (Winter 1978–79): 354–363, 361–362.

43. *Pisgah,* January 1915, front page, and April 6, 1918, p. 2. Finis Yoakum's ephemeral compassion ministry received brief description in Robert V. Hine, *California's Utopian Colonies* (San Marino, Calif.: Huntington Library, 1953), pp. 153–154.

44. Charles Fox Parham, in *Apostolic Faith* [Kans.], January 1900, p. 7.

45. Carl J. Johnson, in *Pentecostal Herald,* January 1, 1922, p. 4, apparently a reprint from one Dr. Sandt of the *Lutheran.* See also *Latter Rain Evangel,* March 1919, p. 23.

46. H. Mogridge, interview in *Lytham (U.K.) Times,* October 7, 1910, pna, AGUK.

47. W. W. Simpson, "Contending for the Faith," typed, pp. 67–68, AOG. The article did not specify the child's sex. I am guessing female as demographically more likely.

48. Ibid.

49. W. W. Simpson, in *Pentecostal Evangel,* September 15, 1923, p. 13.

50. W. W. Simpson, letter to wife, November 25, 1947, AOG.

51. W. W. Simpson, in *Pentecostal Evangel,* March 31, 1921, p. 10.

52. Ibid., January 5, 1918, p. 10; March 31, 1921, p. 10; September 15, 1923, p. 13; February 13, 1926, p. 10; March 21, 1931, p. 11, among many.

53. W. W. Simpson, letter to wife, November 25, 1947, AOG.

54. W. W. Simpson, in *Weekly Evangel,* July 14, 1917, pp. 2–6.

55. W. W. Simpson to N. J. Gortner, September 22, 1950. AOG.

56. W. W. Simpson to A. B. Simpson, October, about 1915, AOG.

57. Thomas J. Schlereth, *Victorian America: Transformations in Everyday Life* (New York: Harper Collins Publishers, 1991), p. 265.

58. Gaston Espinosa, "Borderland Religion: Los Angeles and the Origins of the Latino Pentecostal Movement in the U.S., Mexico, and Puerto Rico, 1900–1945," Ph. D. dissertation, University of California Santa Barbara 1999.

59. For a fuller description and critique of the Edenic model, see Augustus Cerillo, Jr. and Grant Wacker, "Bibliography and Historiography of Pentecostalism in the United States," *New International Dictionary of the Pentecostal and Charismatic Movements,* ed. Stanley Burgess (Grand Rapids: Harper Collins Zondervan, forthcoming 2001), by title. The best survey of black pentecostals (and their relations with whites) remains Vinson Synan, *The Holiness-Pentecostal Tradition: Charismatic Movements in the Twentieth Century,* 2nd ed. (Grand Rapids: William B. Eerdmans Publishing Co., 1997, original 1971), chap. 9.

60. My thinking about the complexity of pentecostal race relations is informed by Gary Don McElhany, "The South Aflame: A History of the Assemblies of God in the Gulf Region, 1901–1940," Ph.D. diss., Mississippi State University, 1996, throughout, partly summarized pp. 287–289.

61. Agnes N. O[zman] LaBerge, *What God Hath Wrought: Life and Work of Mrs. Agnes N. O. LaBerge* (New York: Garland Publishing, 1985, original 1920), pp. 52, 89; Morgan, *Rising in the West,* pp. 45, 121.

62. See, for example, LaBerge, *What God Hath Wrought,* p. 54; Aimee Semple McPherson, *This Is That: Personal Experiences Sermons and Writings* (New York: Garland Publishing, 1985, original 1919), p. 161; Carrie Judd Montgomery, "Date Book for 1909," July 14 and November 16; "Dipped in Mississippi," *Pioneer Press* [St. Paul, Minn.], July 4, 1915, pna, AOG.

63. Carrie M. Pool to Zelma Argue, November 18, 1956 (regarding whites receiving baptism at Bonnie Brae Street presumably in 1906), in *Pentecostal Evangel Files,* AOG; G. B. Cashwell, in *Apostolic Faith* [Calif.], January 1907, p. 1; A. A. Boddy, in *Confidence,* September 1912, p. 209; B. H. Irwin, tear sheet in AOG, bearing the handwritten source and date at the top: *Apostolic Faith,* February or May 1911.

64. See, for example, *Year Book of the 35th Annual Convocation of the United Holy Church of America, Inc. . . . 1929,* p. 15, WCT; Henry L. Fisher, "Diary," entry for September 27, 1922, WCT; *Good Report,* September 1, 1913, p. 2.

65. Vinson Synan, "The Quiet Rise of Black Pentecostals," *Charisma,* June 1986, p. 50.

66. Larry Martin, *In the Beginning: Readings on the Origins of the Twentieth Century Pentecostal Revival and the Birth of the Pentecostal Church of God* (Duncan, Okla.: Christian Life Books, 1994), p. 88.

67. J. O. Patterson et al., *History and Formative Years of the Church of God in Christ with Excerpts from the Life and Works of Its Founder—Bishop C. H. Mason* (Memphis, Tenn.: Church of God in Christ Publishing House, 1969), p. 23.

68. *Year Book of the 35th Annual Convocation of The United Holy Church of America, Inc, . . . 1929,* p. 15, WCT; George Floyd Taylor, "Diary," June 7, 1908, N.C. State History Archives.

69. *Minutes, Executive Presbytery, Assemblies of God,* November 21–25, 1914, pp. 22, 28.

70. "The Blood of Jesus Christ . . . makes all races and nations into one common family in the Lord and makes them all satisfied to be one." *Apostolic Faith* [Calif.], April 1907, p. 3.

71. "One token of the Lord's coming is that He is melting all races and nations together, and they are filled with the power and glory of God." Ibid., February–March 1907, p. 7.

72. "Pentecost makes us love Jesus more and love our brothers more. It brings us all into one common family." Ibid., May 1908, p. 3. "Tongues are one of the signs that go with every baptized person, but it is not the real evidence of the baptism in the every day life. Your life must measure with the fruits of the Spirit. If you get angry, or speak evil, or backbite . . . you have not the baptism with the Holy Spirit." Ibid., June–September 1907, p. 2.

73. William H. Durham, in *Apostolic Faith* [Calif.], February–March 1907, p. 4.

74. Frank Bartleman, *Azusa Street: The Roots of Modern-Day Pentecost*, ed. Vinson Synan (Plainfield, N.J.: Logos International, 1980, original [differently titled] 1925), p. 54, apparently referring to June 1906, when the Azusa revival began in earnest.

75. G. B. Cashwell, in *Apostolic Faith* [Calif.], January 1907, p. 1. See also the issue of May 1907, p. 1, where Cashwell speaks with similar warmth of Bishop Mason.

76. *Whittier (Calif.) Daily News,* September 8, 1906, p. 2, quoted in Cecil M. Robeck, "Outreach to Whittier," forthcoming part of book on pentecostals in California.

77. *Indianapolis Star,* June 16, 1907, p. 10, quoted in David Bundy, "G. T. Haywood: Religion for Urban Realities," in *Portraits of a Generation: Early Pentecostal Leaders,* ed. James R. Goff, Jr. and Grant Wacker (forthcoming).

78. *Portland (Ore.), Oregonian,* December 31, 1906, p. 4, AOG.

79. David Morgan, "N. J. Holmes and the Origins of Pentecostalism," *South Carolina History Magazine,* 84 (July 1983): 150.

80. David Bundy, "G. T. Haywood: Religion for Urban Realities," and David D. Daniels, "Charles Harrison Mason and the Interracial Impulse of Early Pentecostalism," in *Portraits of a Generation: Early Pentecostal Leaders,* ed. James R. Goff, Jr., and Grant Wacker (forthcoming).

81. *A Brief Historical and Doctrinal Statement and Rules for Government of the Church of God in Christ,* comp. William B. Holt (n.p., n.d.), p. 9, quoted in Daniels, "Charles Harrison Mason," and partly quoted without bibliographic data in David D. Daniels, "They Had a Dream," *Christian History,* no. 58 (Spring 1998): 21. Daniels dates the document to about 1917.

82. For Holt, see *Year Book of the Church of God in Christ . . . 1926,* comp. Lillian Brooks Coffey (Chicago: n.p., [1927?]), p. 125, AOG; August Feick to General Council of the Assemblies of God, April 6, 1926, AOG. For personal details on Holt, see Joe Maxwell, "Building the Church (of God in Christ)," *Christianity Today,* April 8, 1996, p. 26.

83. A. G. Osterberg, typescript of interview March 22, 1966, by Jerry Jensen, "reel #3," p. 21, and A. G. Osterberg, typed interview March 17, 1966, by Jerry Jensen and Jonathan Perkins, "Second tape," p. 5, both AOG.

84. George B. Studd, "Diary," February 1, 2, 4, 23, May 10, and December 6, 1908, AOG. References to conflict and attrition at other missions in the area appeared in the entries for May 8, July 7, July ß17. All references come from the handwritten original, which differs from the typed version, AOG.

85. George B. Studd, in *Confidence,* August 15, 1908, p. 10. See also Bartleman, *Azusa Street,* pp. 83–84.

86. For a closer look at these events, see Grant Wacker, "Who Edited the Azusa Mission *Apostolic Faith* Papers?" *Assemblies of God Heritage,* forthcoming. See also Cecil M. Robeck, "Seymour, William Joseph," by title, in *New International Dictionary;* Ithiel C. Clemmons, *Bishop C. H. Mason and the Roots of the Church of God in Christ* (Bakersfield, Calif.: Pneuma Life Publishing, 1996), p. 50.

87. Bartleman, *Azusa Street,* p. 145.

88. Higgins, *Pioneering in Pentecost,* p. 35.

89. M. B. Woodworth-Etter, *Signs and Wonders: God Wrought in the Ministry for Forty Years* (Indianapolis: published by author, 1916), p. 101; *Marvels and Miracles* (Indianapolis: published by author, 1922), pp. 57–59.

90. W. F. Carothers, in *Weekly Evangel,* August 14, 1915, p. 2.

91. Levi Lupton, in *New Acts,* May 1905, p. 1.

92. See, for example, *Everlasting Gospel* [Maine], July 8, 1902, p. 421; *Tongue of Fire,* January 1907, p. 1; *Confidence,* September 1911, p. 209; Charles F. Parham, *A Voice Crying in the Wilderness,* 2nd ed. (Baxter Springs, Kans.: Apostolic Faith Bible College, 1910, original 1902), Preface. But some pentecostals resisted British–Israelite teaching. See, for example, Myland, *Latter Rain Covenant,* p. 80; *Pentecostal Herald,* March 1917, p. 2.

93. E. S. Williams, in *Pentecostal Evangel,* July 20, 1929, p. 9.

94. "Constitution of Apostolic Faith Mission," 1914, Articles C, F, G, in W. J. Seymour, *The Doctrines and Discipline of the Azusa Street Apostolic Faith Mission of Los Angeles, Calif. 1915,* pp. 47–50, quotation p. 49. The white leader was Louis Osterberg, named on the first (1907) and last (1931) "legally filed list of Trustees," though not on the 1914 list. The mission was torn down in 1931. Douglas J. Nelson, "For Such A Time as This: The Story of Bishop William J. Seymour and the Azusa Street Revival: A Search for Pentecostal/Charismatic Roots," Ph.D. diss., University of Birmingham, 1981, pp. 263–264, 288.

95. Seymour, "Apostolic Address," in *Doctrines,* p. 12.

96. "Some of our white brethren and sisters have never left us in all the division . . . We love our white brethrens and sisters and welcome them." Ibid., p. 13.

97. Seymour, "Amended Articles," ibid., p. 47.

98. *Minutes of the General Assembly,* 1928, and December 5, 1933, cited in Daniels, "Charles Harrison Mason"; see Daniels, "They Had a Dream," p. 20, and photo p. 20. See also Clemmons, *Bishop C. H. Mason,* p. 98.

99. Goff, *Fields White unto Harvest,* p. 108. I derive five black associates by adding the three listed on p. 108 (R. A. Hall, W. M. Viney, and M. H. Robinson) with the two listed on p. 112 (Lucy Farrow and J. A. Warren).

100. Ibid., p. 111.

101. Endorsement and Parham's response in the same paragraph of *Apostolic Faith* [Calif.], September 1906, p. 1. Almost certainly the endorsement was written by Seymour or carried his approval since it appeared in the first column of the first issue of the paper. A blurb in the October issue described Parham as "a brother who is full of divine love" (p. 3).

102. Goff, *Fields White unto Harvest,* pp. 108–112.

103. Almost certainly editor Charles F. Parham, in *Apostolic Faith* [Kans.], October 1912, p. 6. See also Parham, *Everlasting Gospel,* p. 118.

104. Charles F. Parham, in *Apostolic Faith* [Kans.], December 1912, p. 4. See also Parham, *Everlasting Gospel,* p. 72, and *Apostolic Faith* [Kans.], May 1913, p. 14, almost certainly by Parham.

105. Charles F. Parham, *Apostolic Faith* [Kans.], March 1927, p. 5; Goff, *Fields White unto Harvest,* p. 157.

106. [Parham], *Life of Charles F. Parham,* pp. 246, 302.

107. Thoro Harris, in *Everlasting Gospel* [Kans.], April 1916, pp. 12–13, quotations p. 13.

Significantly, Sarah Parham reprinted the core of this letter in [Parham], *Life of Charles F. Parham,* p. 263.

108. I have pieced together this account from F. F. Bosworth, *Bosworth's Life Story* (Toronto: Alliance Book Room, n.d.), pp. 12–14, and F. F. Bosworth, letter to "Mother and All," August 21, 1911, both AOG. "Spiritual power" and "ruffians" from *Life Story,* pp. 12 and 13, "Colored Alter" and "no thought" from letter, pp. 2 and 4. See also the slightly edited version of the letter in *Assemblies of God Heritage,* Summer 1983, pp. 5, 14, and the slightly different rendering in *Latter Rain Evangel,* October 1912, p. 14.

109. Rose Marie McDuff, "The Ethnohistory of Saint's Home Church of God in Christ, Los Angeles, California," M.A. thesis, California State University, Sacramento, 1972, pp. 20–44, McDuff for "amazed" p. 20; M. Driver for Argue, Manley, Bridget, p. 33; McDuff for "call them names," p. 43; unidentified informants for white resistance to black leadership and for "drove them away," both p. 43, and for "pen," p. 44. See also Clemmons, *Bishop C. H. Mason,* p. 190, n. 20.

110. Based on word searches for the following terms or variations thereof: African, black, colored, Egyptian, Ethiopian, family, Negro, race, Soudanese, white, Zulu. I say "about" twenty references, since two or three passages are ambiguous and actually might allude to cases of segregated worship.

   The question of ethnicity or nationality is more complex. The Azusa *Apostolic Faith* contains scores of ethnic references (Armenian, Chinese, Creek, Dane, and so forth). A few (about six) explicitly endorse multi-ethnic worship, a small minority (about twenty-four) describe instances of multi-ethnic worship, and sizable minority (about thirty-nine) serve as geographic labels. Most (about one hundred) appear in a missions context, usually specifying a miraculous foreign language received or promised. To be sure, such passages imply a universal rather than tribal conception of the full gospel message. But whether they also imply social equality is, to put it mildly, more problematic.

   In tabulating both racial and ethnic references, I counted multiple uses of the keyed terms in a single passage as one. Conversely I did not count passing or rhetorical or nonracial/ethnic iterations (for example, colored policeman, Adam's family, run a race). Also I did not count the two dozen references to Jews, which almost always depicted them as biblical characters, eschatological actors, or subjects of evangelism. I have deposited a breakdown of this research at AOG.

111. W. J. E. [W. J. S.?], *Apostolic Faith* [Calif.], January 1907, p. 2. It also should be said that *Apostolic Faith* tersely disassociated itself from the eighth day creation idea. Parham had taught that marriage between pre-Adamic humans, who had been *created* on the sixth day, and Adamic humans, who had been *formed* on the eighth day, somehow led to the deadly intermarriage of whites, blacks, and "reds" in modern America. The unnamed writer may have meant to distance the paper from these invidious ideas, or may have simply believed that Parham's notion was exegetically preposterous. *Apostolic Faith* [Calif.], December 1906, p. 1; Charles F. Parham, *The Everlasting Gospel,* rev. ed. (Baxter Springs, Kan.: Apostolic Faith Bible College, 1920[?], original 1911), p. 3.

112. I have located one issue of *Whole Truth* and nine complete or partial issues of *Voice in the Wilderness* published before 1930. The former contains three brief references, without comment, to pentecostal whites and blacks working or worshipping together. C. H. Mason, *Whole Truth,* October 1911, p. 2, L. V. Smith, p. 3. The latter,

which runs for several thousand tiny-print words, includes one reference to whites and blacks, and that involves an End Time event of mysterious meaning. C. H. Saylors, *Voice in the Wilderness,* no. 24, 1913 or 1918 [illegible], p. 1. I may have missed references owing to the unreadable condition of parts of text. Professor David Bundy of Christian Theological Seminary recently discovered these documents and generously shared them with me.

113. It is conceivable that both white and black editors held strongly principled views on race reconciliation but reluctantly chose not to publicize them for fear of reprisals from outsiders. That interpretation seems dubious, however, since those same men and women proved eager to assail other conventions of mainline churches and middle class society, often at high cost to themselves and their cohorts, including ostracism, verbal abuse, and sometimes even physical violence.

114. James R. Goff, Jr., personal communication, May 2000.

115. See, for example, *Word and Witness,* July 20, 1914, p. 1.

116. D. S. Vinn, BOI report, in Crews, *Church of God,* p. 119. The BOI became the Federal Bureau of Investigation (FBI) in 1935.

117. Photocopy of single, unidentified newspaper page from Macon, Georgia, hand-dated December 25, 1911, pna, AOG.

118. *Salem (Ore.) Daily Capital Journal,* November 14, 1906, pna, AOG.

119. See, for example, Hattie McConnell, "Autobiography," unpaginated typescript, AOG; *Houston Chronicle,* October 5, 1906, p. 8, AOG; Wayne E. Warner, *The Woman Evangelist: The Life and Times of Charismatic Evangelist Maria B. Woodworth-Etter* (Methuchen, N.J.: Scarecrow Press, 1986), pp. 88–92; J. Wesley Jones, "The Night God Stopped the Angry Mob," *Assemblies of God Heritage,* Spring 1983, p. 6.

120. W. F. Bryant, in *Faithful Standard,* September 1922, p. 20.

121. Elder R. K. Diggs, son of late Bishop J. D. Diggs, of United Holy Church of America, interview by William C. Turner, December 7, 1982, WCT.

122. Kornweibel, "Bishop C. H. Mason," pp. 276–278.

123. McPherson, *This Is That,* pp. 168–170. McPherson approvingly reproduced both quotations by a friendly reporter, p. 170.

124. [Church of God] *General Assembly Minutes 1906–1914* (Cleveland, Tenn.: White Wing Publishing, 1992), 1908, p. 43.

125. *Evening Light and Church of God Evangel,* July 15, 1910, p. 1.

126. *Church of God Evangel,* February 24, 1917, p. 1.

127. A. J. Tomlinson (1916), quoted in Crews, *Church of God,* p. 111.

128. E. N. Bell, in *Christian Evangel,* July 12, 1919, p. 5.

129. Cora Fritsch, December 26, 1909, in *Letters from Cora,* comp. Homer and Alice Fritsch, typed, 1987, AOG.

130. *Faithful Standard,* April 1922, p. 12.

131. See the large collection of photographs of early pentecostal events and sites in AOG, many of which feature an American flag. McPherson's *Bridal Call* (with variant names) routinely carried American flags on the front cover. See, for example, *Bridal Call Foursquare,* February 1933, bedecked with a flag, an eagle, and photographs of George Washington and Abraham Lincoln framing a center photograph of McPherson.

132. W. F. Bryant, in [Church of God] *General Assembly Minutes 1906–1914* (Cleveland, Tenn.: White Wing Publishing House, 1992), 1912, p. 128.

133. Suggested by Moore, *Religious Outsiders,* pp. 65, 69, quotation p. 69.

14. War

1. "Washington's Dream," subtitled "Washington's Vision," *National Tribune,* December 1880, p. 1.
2. *Christian Evangel,* October 10, 1914, p. 1.
3. J. Roswell Flower, in *Christian Evangel,* October 10, 1914, p. 2.
4. No copy of the November 1914 *Word and Witness* survives, but in the *Weekly Evangel,* May 15, 1915, p. 3, E. T. Slaybaugh said that the text had appeared in that issue.
5. E. T. Slaybaugh, in *Weekly Evangel,* May 15, 1915, p. 3. Slaybaugh found the last episode of the "Vision" to be "synonymous" with Revelation 6:4.
6. *Pentecostal World,* July 1, 1926, p. 1.
7. J. R. F. [J. Roswell Flower], in *Christian Evangel,* October 10, 1914, p. 2, and the editorial introduction to the "Vision" on p. 1.
8. For recent secondary literature on early pentecostal pacifism, see Augustus Cerillo, Jr. and Grant Wacker, "Bibliography and Historiography of Pentecostalism in the United States," *New International Dictionary of the Pentecostal and Charismatic Movements,* ed. Stanley Burgess (Grand Rapids: Harper Collins Zondervan, forthcoming 2001), by title. My interpretation runs closer to the older, prerevisionist literature which (for different reasons) minimized the breadth and depth of pacifism in the tradition.
9. John Alexander Dowie, in *Leaves of Healing,* Sept 24, 1904, p. 805, quoted in Howard N. Kenyon, "An Analysis of Ethical Issues in the History of the Assemblies of God," Ph.D. diss., Baylor University, 1988, p. 286.
10. See, for example, [Charles Fox Parham], *The Life of Charles F. Parham: Founder of the Apostolic Faith Movement,* compiled by His Wife [Sarah E. Parham] (New York: Garland Publishing, 1985, original 1930), p. 274, and Parham, *Apostolic Faith* [Kans.] September 1905, p. 7.
11. Frank Bartleman, in *Weekly Evangel,* July 10, 1915, p. 3. The perceived intemperance of Bartleman's remarks prompted J. Roswell Flower, secretary-treasurer of the young denomination, officially to apologize for them the following month, in *Weekly Evangel,* August 14, 1915, p. 2.
12. The theological tenets of early pentecostal pacifism are astutely analyzed in Murray W. Dempster, "Reassessing the Moral Rhetoric of Early American Pentecostal Pacifism," *Crux,* 26 (March 1990): 23–36.
13. See "Preamble and Resolution of Constitution," drawn up at the time of organization in 1914, and the "Statement of Fundamental Truths," drawn up two years later, in *Minutes of the General Council of the Assemblies of God . . . 1914,* p. 4, and *Minutes of the General Council of the Assemblies of God . . . 1916,* pp. 10–13.
14. Roger Robins, "A Chronology of Peace: Attitudes toward War and Peace in the Assemblies of God: 1914–1918," *Pneuma: Journal of the Society for Pentecostal Studies,* 6 (Spring 1984): 3.
15. For this and the following paragraphs pertaining to the debate in the Assemblies of God, I am particularly indebted to Kenyon "Analysis of Ethical Issues," and to Edith L. Blumhofer, *The Assemblies of God: A Chapter in the Story of American Pentecostalism* (Springfield, Mo.: Gospel Publishing House, 1989), vol. 1, pp. 343–355.
16. Resolution printed in *Weekly Evangel,* August 4, 1917, p. 6.
17. Congress required that the declaration of pacifist principles be recorded by May 18, 1917. Kenyon, "Analysis of Ethical Issues," p. 308.

18. *Weekly Evangel,* May 19, 1917, p. 8.

19. *Weekly Evangel,* June 30, 1917, p. 8. Welch's name appeared at the top of the editorial staff column, but the young office editor, J. Roswell Flower, probably wrote the actual words.

20. *Minutes of the General Council of the Assemblies of God . . . 1917,* pp. 17–18.

21. E. N. Bell, in *Weekly Evangel,* November 24, 1917, p. 8.

22. See, for example, Stanley H. Frodsham, in *Weekly Evangel,* August 4, 1917, p. 6.

23. E. N. Bell, in *Weekly Evangel,* January 5, 1918, p. 4.

24. Ibid., January 26, 1918, p. 9.

25. Ibid., February 23, 1918, p. 6.

26. *Christian Evangel,* June 1, 1918, p. 8, probably by editor E. N. Bell, speaking for S. A. Jamieson and A. P. Collins.

27. E. N. Bell, in *Christian Evangel,* August 24, 1918, p. 4; Frank Bartleman, in *Weekly Evangel,* June 5, 1915, p. 3.

28. *Minutes of the General Council of the Assemblies of God . . . 1918,* p. 9.

29. E. N. Bell, in *Christian Evangel,* October 19, 1918, p. 5.

30. Ibid., January 11, 1919, p. 5.

31. Aimee Semple McPherson, *This Is That: Personal Experiences Sermons and Writings* (New York: Garland Publishing, 1985, original 1919), pp. 344–367 for the first three titles, *Bridal Call,* May 1919, p. 16, for the fourth.

32. McPherson, *This Is That,* p. 344.

33. See, for example, the prayer requests in *Christian Evangel,* October 5, 1918, p. 15.

34. A. J. Tomlinson, *The Last Great Conflict* (New York: Garland Publishing, 1985, original 1913), p. 209, and Mickey Crews, *The Church of God: A Social History* (Knoxville: University of Tennessee Press, 1990), p. 116.

35. Crews, *Church of God,* pp. 117–121.

36. Ibid., pp. 110, 192, n. 4.

37. Ibid., pp. 123, 125.

38. Ibid., pp. 115–116.

39. Ibid., pp. 110–114.

40. Ibid., p. 193, n. 29.

41. Besides COGIC, Kornweibel lists the following black pentecostal or sanctified groups as pacifist during World War I: Pentecostal Assemblies of the World, Churches of the Living God, Church of God and Saints in Christ, and (black) Church of Christ congregations. Theodore Kornweibel, Jr., "Bishop C. H. Mason and the Church of God in Christ during World War I: The Perils of Conscientious Objection," *Southern Studies,* 26 (Fall 1987): 275.

42. Kornweibel, "Bishop C. H. Mason," p. 269.

43. Ibid.

44. Ibid., p. 270.

45. Elder C. H. Mason, "The Kaiser in the Light of the Scriptures," portions transcribed by William B. Holt, reprinted in J. O. Patterson et al., *History and Formative Years of the Church of God in Christ with Excerpts from the Life and Works of Its Founder—Bishop C. H. Mason* (Memphis, Tenn.: Church of God in Christ Publishing House, 1969), pp. 26–28.

46. Kornweibel, "Bishop C. H. Mason," pp. 273–74.

47. Henry Kirvin, July 1918, quoted in Kornweibel, "Bishop C. H. Mason," p. 274.

48. A. J. Tomlinson, 1918, quoted in Crews, *Church of God,* p. 117.

15. Destiny

1. B. F. Lawrence, *The Apostolic Faith Restored* (St. Louis: Gospel Publishing House, 1916), p. 12.
2. *Victory!*, April 1909, p. 1.
3. *The Scofield Reference Bible* (New York: Oxford University Press, 1945, original 1909), p. 5, n. 5.
4. W. J. S. [William J. Seymour], in *Apostolic Faith* [Calif.], January 1907, p. 2; see also Charles Parham, in *Apostolic Faith* [Kans.], June 1915, pp. 1–3; G. T. H[aywood], in *Voice in the Wilderness*, no 19, probably 1916, p. 5.
5. *Upper Room*, May 1910, p. 8.
6. William H. Piper, *Latter Rain Evangel*, April 1909, p. 13; Vernon G. Gortner, *Full Gospel Missionary Herald*, October 1922, p. 3.
7. *Christian Evangel*, August 24, 1918, p. 1, headline: "An Appeal to the Pentecostal People throughout the World to Observe Sunday, Nov. 3rd and Monday, Nov. 4, 1918 in United Prayer Inviting Jesus, Our Heavenly Bridegroom, to Come Back."
8. See, for example, *Weekly Evangel*, April 21, 1917, p. 4, letter from Mrs. Clarence Shreffler setting September 1917 as the date of the Lord's return.
9. John Lewis Shuler, in *Pentecostal Herald*, December 1, 1922, p. 1.
10. E. K. Fisher, in *Upper Room*, February 1910, pp. 1–2.
11. See, for example, C. H. Fredericks, *Apostolic Faith* [Kans.], October 1912, p. 7.
12. D. Wesley Myland, *The Latter Rain Covenant and Pentecostal Power,* published with other documents as *Three Early Pentecostal Tracts,* ed. Donald W. Dayton (New York: Garland Publishing, 1985, original 1910), pp. 97–107. The continuities and differences between conventional and pentecostal versions of dispensational premillennialism received systematic exposition in Frank M. Boyd, *Ages and Dispensations* (Springfield, Mo.: Gospel Publishing House [1955]), especially p. 46.
13. G. F. Taylor, *The Spirit and the Bride,* published with other documents as *Three Early Pentecostal Tracts,* ed. Donald W. Dayton (New York: Garland Publishing, 1985, original 1907), pp. 90–91.
14. *Apostolic Faith* [Calif.], September 1906, p. 4.
15. See, for example, *Samson's Foxes,* January 1901, p. 6; A. E. Stuernagel, in *Glad Tidings* [SF], August 1927, pp. 2, 11. For the rainbow, see C. M. Carraway, in *Weekly Evangel*, January 19, 1918, p. 13.
16. Frank Ewart, *The Phenomenon of Pentecost: A History of the Latter Rain* (Houston: Herald Publishing House, 1947), p. 18.
17. S[usan] A. Duncan, *The Early and the Latter Rain* (Rochester, N.Y.: Elim Publishing House, [about 1910]), pp. 7–8.
18. D. M. Panton, in *Trust,* September 1915, p. 16. Panton was a British holiness premillennialist author of note. Though not pentecostal himself, saints freely quoted and reprinted his works.
19. J. W. Welch, "Introduction," to Lawrence, *Apostolic Faith Restored*.
20. Susan A. Duncan, in *Word and Work,* August 1910, p. 239, quoted in D. William Faupel, "The Function of 'Models' in the Interpretation of Pentecostal Thought," *Pneuma: Journal of the Society for Pentecostal Studies,* 2 (1980): 68.
21. Carrie Judd Montgomery, *The Latter Rain,* tract, no publication data.
22. Minnie F. Abrams, in *Word and Work,* May 1910, p. 138.
23. D. William Faupel, *The Everlasting Gospel: The Significance of Eschatology in the Development of Pentecostal Thought* (Sheffield: Sheffield Academic Press, 1996), p. 188.

24. See almost any issue. This one is taken from January 1, 1901, p. 1, full caps from logo under the title, remainder from frontispiece.

25. First quotation is from *Apostolic Faith* [Kans.], January 1916, p. 1, second from March 1913, p. 9, both unsigned but almost certainly by editor Charles Parham.

26. Ibid., September 1914, p. 2.

27. L. P. Adams, in *Grace and Truth,* January 1916, p. 2.

28. Ibid., June 1916, p. 1.

29. William Booth-Clibborn, in *Glad Tidings* [SF], April 1927, pp. 2–3.

30. R. S. Craig, in *Trust,* November 1915, p. 15.

31. A. A. Boddy, in *Confidence,* April 1913, p. 74.

32. *Apostolic Faith* [Calif.], September 1906, p. 1.

33. W. J. S. [William J. Seymour], *Apostolic Faith* [Calif.], January 1907, p. 2.

34. H. M. Turney, in *Apostolic Faith* [Calif.], January 1907, p. 1.

35. Reported in *Present Truth,* December 1909, p. 7.

36. Almost certainly editor A. J. Tomlinson, in *Evening Light and Church of God Evangel,* March 15, 1910, p. 1,

37. E. N. Bell, in *Christian Evangel,* December 14, 1918, p. 1.

38. Florence L. Burpee, "The Second Coming of The Lord," *Word and Work,* undated photocopy [about 1910 by internal evidence], p. 368, AOG.

39. Mrs. G. F. Patton and Miss Dora E. Preston, in *Apostolic Faith* [Kans.], April 1925, p. 17.

40. J. H. Bennett, in *Christian Evangel,* May 9, 1914, p. 8.

41. M. B. Woodworth-Etter, *Acts of the Holy Ghost* (Dallas: John F. Worley Printing, [1912]), p. 171.

42. W. E. Krise, *Apostolic Faith* [Kans.], February 1913, p. 16.

43. H. M. Turney and Wife, in *Apostolic Faith* [Calif.], February–March 1907, p. 1.

44. *Apostolic Faith* [Kans.], August 1927, first quotation p. 3, second p. 4, almost certainly by editor Charles Parham.

45. *Minutes of the 26th Annual Convocation of the United Holy Church of America, Inc . . . 1920,* p. 1.

46. Lillian Thistlethwaite, in *Apostolic Faith* [Kans.], November 1912, p. 4. Thistlethwaite's father was Quaker. Lacking contrary evidence, I assume she was too.

47. Levi Lupton, in *New Acts,* August 9, 1906, p. 6.

48. Charles Parham and his immediate followers were the main advocates of conditional immortality. Charles H. Pridgeon and his Pittsburgh Bible Institute taught a modified universalism (hell's duration is limited). Robert Mapes Anderson, *Vision of the Disinherited: The Making of American Pentecostalism* (New York: Oxford University Press, 1979), p. 159. British theologian Donald Gee and American editor Carrie Judd Montgomery may have privately embraced universalist views of some sort. For Gee, see A. E. Saxby's handwritten list of universalists at AGUK; for Montgomery, see her "Date Book for 1909," June 4 and 9, AOG. Oral tradition holds that George B. Studd of Los Angeles mission fame did too.

49. See, for example, "WHAT THE MOVEMENT TEACHES," in *Apostolic Faith* [Tex.], October 1908, pp. 6–7, esp. p. 7; W. J. Seymour, *The Doctrines and Discipline of the Azusa Street Apostolic Faith Mission of Los Angeles, Calif. 1915* (n.p., n.d.), p. 54; *Showers of Blessings,* May 1915, p. 9.

50. See, for example, L. P. Adams, in *Grace and Truth,* June 1916, p. 3, for doctrinal emphases with key Bible proof texts.

51. Effie Cooper, in *Glad Tidings* [SF], March 1928, p. 9.

52. Probably editor Florence Crawford, in *Apostolic Faith* [Ore.], September 1908, p. 3.

53. Effie Cooper, in *Glad Tidings* [SF], March 1928, p. 9.

54. Probably editor Florence Crawford, in *Apostolic Faith* [Ore.], September 1908, p. 3.

55. Shirley Nelson, *Fair Clear and Terrible: The Story of Shiloh, Maine* (Latham, N.Y.: British American Publishing, 1989), p. 429.

56. Seeley D. Kinne, in *Evening Light and Church of God Evangel,* March 15, 1910, p. 4.

57. Aimee Semple McPherson, quoted in William G. McLoughlin, "Aimee Semple McPherson: 'Your Sister in the King's Glad Service,'" *Journal of Popular Culture* (Winter 1967): 193–217, quotation p. 214.

58. Roger Glenn Robins, "Plainfolk Modernist: The Radical Holiness World of A. J. Tomlinson," Ph.D. diss., Duke University, 1999, p. 298.

59. *Apostolic Faith* [Calif.], September 1906, p. 4.

60. Ibid., October 1907, p. 1.

61. Pearl Brown, posted from Akron, in *Apostolic Faith* [Calif.], January 1907, p. 1.

62. Advertisement for *Word and Work,* in *Bridal Call,* April 1918, p. 2.

63. *Apostolic Faith* [Calif.], October 1907, p. 1.

64. Brother [William J.] Seymour, in *Apostolic Faith* [Calif.], June–September 1907, p. 4.

65. *Minutes of the General Council of the Assemblies of God . . . 1917,* p. 20.

66. G. T. H[aywood], in *Voice in the Wilderness,* no. 22, probably 1918, p. 4.

67. *Word and Witness,* August 20, 1912, p. 1.

68. A. W. Orwig, in *New Acts,* July–August 1907, p. 6.

69. Addie A. Knowlton, in *New Acts,* June 1907, p. 8.

70. Tom Hezmalhalch, in *Apostolic Faith* [Calif.], June–September 1907, p. 4.

71. A. J. Tomlinson, in [Church of God] *General Assembly Minutes 1906–1914* (Cleveland, Tenn.: White Wing Publishing House, 1992), 1912, p. 142.

72. *Apostolic Faith* [Calif.], May 1908, p. 4.

73. Mok Lai Chi, in *Pentecostal Truths,* April 1909, p. 2.

74. William F. Manley, in *Household of God,* September 1906, pp. 6–9.

75. Frank Bartleman, *Azusa Street: The Roots of Modern-Day Pentecost,* ed. Vinson Synan (Plainfield, N.J.: Logos International, 1980, original [differently titled] 1925), p. 47.

76. A. J. Tomlinson, *The Last Great Conflict* (New York: Garland Publishing Co., 1985, original 1913), p. viii.

77. Robins, "Plainfolk Modernist," p. 395.

78. A. J. Tomlinson, in *Evening Light and Church of God Evangel,* March 1, 1910, p. 1.

79. E. N. Bell, in *Christian Evangel,* June 29, 1918, p. 9.

80. Levi Lupton, in *New Acts,* December 14, 1905, p. 1, and in *New Acts,* June 1905, p. 7.

81. Howard A. Goss, *The Winds of God: The Story of the Early Pentecostal Days (1901–1914) in the Life of Howard A. Goss, as Told by Ethel E. Goss* (New York: Comet Press Books, 1958), p. 149.

82. Elizabeth Lee, in *New Acts,* March 8, 1906, p. 6.

83. William Durham, in *Pentecostal Testimony,* January 1912, p. 8.

84. Brother Pittman, *Pentecostal Holiness Advocate,* April 18, 1918, p. 13.

85. Mrs. R. G. Staple, in *Believing and Receiving or Doubting and Retreating,* Christian Workers Union tract, June 1923, p. 1.

86. John G. Lake to Charles Parham, March 24, 1927, p. 3, AOG.

87. Frank Bartleman, *Pentecost or No Pentecost,* tract, 1928, p. 2.

88. Mrs. Robert A. Brown, in *Glad Tidings Herald,* November 1932, p. 2.

89. Paul Varg, *Missionaries, Chinese, and Diplomats: The American Protestant Mission-ary Movement in China, 1890–1952* (Princeton: Princeton University Press, 1958), p. 56.

90. George A. Murray, in *Confidence,* July 1908, p. 7.

91. *Apostolic Faith* [Ore.], July–August 1908, p. 1; *Apostolic Faith* [Tex.], October 1908, p. 2.

92. Faupel, *Everlasting Gospel,* p. 15, n. 6.

93. Stanley H. Frodsham, *"With Signs Following": The Story of the Latter-Day Pentecostal Revival* (Springfield, Mo.: Gospel Publishing House, 1926). These chapter titles represent the tone and content of others, which I have omitted.

94. N. H. Harriman, in *Everlasting Gospel,* March 31, 1901, p. 136.

95. [Charles Fox Parham], *The Life of Charles F. Parham: Founder of the Apostolic Faith Movement,* compiled by His Wife [Sarah E. Parham] (Garland Publishing, N.Y.: 1985, original 1930), p. 51.

96. *Apostolic Faith* [Ore.], July–August 1908, p. 1; William H. Piper, in *Latter Rain Evangel,* March 1909, p. 7.

97. *Upper Room,* June 1909, p. 5.

98. J. W. Welch, "Introduction," to Lawrence, *Apostolic Faith Restored,* p. 7.

99. See, for example, *Apostolic Faith* [Kans.], January 1913, p. 11; L. P. Adams, in *Grace and Truth,* October 1915, p. 3.

100. For one of countless examples, see *Weekly Evangel,* March 30, 1918, p. 8, advertisement for the second "WORLD WIDE MISSIONARY CONFERENCE."

101. See, for example, *Apostolic Faith* [Kans.], June 1925, p. 1; *Apostolic Faith* [Kans.], April 1928, p. 8; L. P. Adams, in *Present Truth,* December 1909, p. 1.

102. Sister [Ellen] Hebden, in *Apostolic Faith* [Calif.], April 1907, p. 1.

103. Bartleman, *Azusa Street,* p. 125.

104. John G. Lake, "Transcription of John Lake's Diary," apparently referring to October 1907, typed, p. 2, AOG.

105. Max Wood Moorhead, *Cloud of Witnesses to Pentecost in India,* November, 1908, p. 24.

106. *Pentecostal Herald,* June 1920, p. 1.

107. *Word and Work,* September 1922, p. 10.

108. See, for example, *Minutes of the General Council . . . Nov, 15, 1914,* printed in *Christian Evangel,* November 1914, p. 3.

109. Church of God, Kilsyth, Scotland, *Minute Book,* December 28, 1908.

110. See, for example, *Confidence,* July 1908, p. 7; *Apostolic Faith* [Tex.], October 1908, p. 5.

111. See, for example, monthly column on "PENTECOST OVER THE GLOBE," in *Apostolic Faith* [Ore.] January 1909, p. 1.

112. Edith E. Baugh and B. C. Lu from India in *Trust,* June–July 1915, p. 25.

113. *Latter Rain Evangel,* October 1908, p. 9.

114. Mrs. J[ulia?] W. Hutchins, in *Apostolic Faith* [Kans.], September 1905, p. 1.

115. *Apostolic Faith* [Ore.], January 1909, p. 2.

116. T. M. Jeffreys, in *Confidence,* quoted in *Upper Room,* July 1910, p. 8.

117. L. P. Adams, in *Grace and Truth,* June 1916, p. 2.

Epilogue

1. E. P. Thompson, *The Making of the English Working Class* (New York: Random House, 1966), p. 12.

2. This statement partly stems from my sampling of recent pentecostal periodicals and television preachers, and from Mark A. Shibley, *Resurgent Evangelicalism in the United States: Mapping Cultural Change since 1970* (Columbia: University of South Carolina Press, 1996), pp. 20, 123–124, and Christian Smith, *Christian America? What Evangelicals Really Want* (Berkeley: University of California Press, 2000), pp. 211–218. The quotation comes from [Assemblies of God] *Where We Stand* (Springfield, Mo.: Gospel Publishing House, 1990), p. 122. Smith's data may refer to homosexual practice rather than orientation, though the language is not clear. Although the Assemblies of God position paper speaks of homosexual "behavior" and "practice," on the whole it seems not to draw a distinction between behavior and orientation, stating repeatedly that "homosexuality is sin" (pp. 117–123).

3. Hal Donaldson, "Brownsville: Three Years Later," *Pentecostal Evangel,* July 19, 1998, p. 8, and Rick Bragg, "A Years-Long Revival Draws the Multitudes," *New York Times,* May 27, 1997, pp. A1, A12.

4. Margaret Poloma, *The Assemblies of God at the Crossroads: Charisma and Institutional Dilemmas* (Knoxville: University of Tennessee Press, 1989), chap. 9, esp. p. 161.

5. Edith L. Blumhofer, *Restoring the Faith: The Assemblies of God, Pentecostalism, and American Culture* (Urbana: University of Illinois Press, 1993), chap. 11, esp. pp. 254–260; Harvey Cox, *Fire from Heaven: The Rise of Pentecostal Spirituality and the Reshaping of Religion in the Twenty-first Century* (Reading, Mass.: Addison-Wesley Publishing Co., 1995), pp. 272–273, 287–297; Mickey Crews, *The Church of God: A Social History* (Knoxville: University of Tennessee Press, 1990), esp. chap. 7; Grant Wacker, "Caring and Curing: The Pentecostal Tradition," in *Caring and Curing: Health and Medicine in the Western Faith Traditions,* ed. by Ronald L. Numbers and Darryl W. Amundsen (New York: Macmillan, 1986), pp. 527–531; Vinson Synan, *The Holiness-Pentecostal Tradition: Charismatic Movements in the Twentieth Century,* 2nd ed. (Grand Rapids: William B. Eerdmans Publishing Co., 1997), pp. 220–223. For a one-sided though telling expose of pentecostals' relentless pursuit of the good life, see Robert Johnson, "Heavenly Gifts," *Wall Street Journal,* December 11, 1990, p. 1. Actually, none of this should be surprising. Recent surveys have suggested that, contrary to stereotype, speaking in tongues and related activities are *positively* correlated with higher levels of education and wealth. See, for example, Poloma, *Assemblies of God,* pp. 48–49; William J. Samarin, *Tongues of Men and Angels: The Religious Language of Pentecostalism* (New York: Macmillan, 1972), p. 213; Luther P. Gerlach and Virginia H. Hine, *People, Power, Change: Movements of Social Transformation* (Indianapolis: Bobbs-Merrill, 1970), pp. 4–5; H. Newton Malony, "Debunking Some of the Myths about Glossolalia," *Journal for the Scientific Study of Religion,* 34 (1982): 144–148.

6. William R. Hutchison, *Errand to the World: American Protestant Thought and Foreign Missions* (Chicago: University of Chicago Press, 1987), pp. 125–138; Andrew F. Walls, "The American Dimension of the Missionary Movement," in *Earthen Vessels: American Evangelicals and Foreign Missions, 1880–1980,* ed. Joel Carpenter and Wilbert Shenk (Grand Rapids: William B. Eerdmans Publishing Co., 1990), pp. 1–25.

7. See, for example, Cox, *Fire from Heaven,* chaps. 9–12; Paul Gifford, *African Christianity: Its Public Role* (Bloomington: Indiana University Press, 1998); David Martin, *Tongues of Fire: The Explosion of Protestantism in Latin America* (Oxford: Basil Blackwell, 1990), Richard Shaull and Waldo Cesar, *Pentecostalism and the Future of the Christian Churches: Promise, Limitations, Challenges* (Grand Rapids: William B. Eerdmans Publishing Co., 2000); David Maxwell, *Christians and Chiefs in Zimbabwe: A Social History of the Hwesa People* (Westport, Conn.: Praeger, 1999); Everett A. Wilson, "Sanguine Saints: Pentecostalism in El Salvador," *Church History,* 52 (June 1983): 186–198, and "The Central American Evangelicals: From Protest to Pragmatism," *International Review of Mission,* 77 (January 1988): 94–106.

8. Joel Carpenter, letter to Grant Wacker, June 13, 2000.

9. Lionel Trilling, *The Liberal Imagination: Essays on Literature and Society* (New York: Doubleday Anchor, 1953), p. 183.

Appendix

1. Denominations enumerated: Apostolic Faith Mission Church of God, Apostolic Faith Mission of Portland, Oregon, Apostolic Overcoming Holy Catholic Church of God, Inc., Assemblies of God, Church of God (Cleveland, Tenn.), Church of God in Christ, Church of God Mountain Assembly, Inc., Church of God of Prophecy, Congregational Holiness Church, Inc., Elim Fellowship, Full Gospel Assemblies International, International Church of the Foursquare Gospel, International Pentecostal Church of Christ, International Pentecostal Holiness Church, Open Bible Standard Churches, Inc., Pentecostal Assemblies of the World, Pentecostal Church of God, Inc., Pentecostal Fire-Baptized Holiness Church, Pentecostal Free Will Baptist Church, Inc., and United Pentecostal Church International. I based this list on my own sense of the pentecostal landscape and denominational self-descriptions in the *Yearbook.* Since those descriptions were sometimes terse or vague, the list should be considered an approximation. One also should note that the mostly Latino Apostolic Assembly of the Faith in Christ Jesus, not listed in the *Yearbook* at all, may number 100,000 in the United States alone.

2. The data base included respondents who self-identified as Pentecostal, Assemblies of God, Apostolic, Charismatic, Full Gospel, Church of God in Christ, Foursquare, and Open Bible. It did not include 442,000 adherents of the "Church of God," since several nonpentecostal Wesleyan holiness bodies also used that name.

Index

Abrams, Minnie F., 41, 175, 256
Absolutism, moral, 23–25
Adams, L. P., 91, 138, 229, 257, 265
Adventists, Seventh-day, 4, 155
African American pentecostals, 65, 104–105, 153, 206–207, 226–235. *See also* Church of God in Christ; Pentecostal Assemblies of the World; Race relations
Albanese, Catherine, 93
Anderson, Robert Mapes, 177, 179, 199–201, 202, 207
Angelus Temple, 145, 168, 224, 233. *See also* McPherson, Aimee Semple
Anti-intellectualism, alleged, 31. *See also* Education
Apocalypticism. *See* Lord's soon return
Apostolic Assembly of the Faith in Christ Jesus, 7
Apostolic Evangel, 152. *See also* Holland, A. C.
Apostolic Faith (California), 37, 42, 45, 46, 66, 74, 77, 80, 126, 144, 163, 172, 176, 178, 201, 228, 232, 234, 254, 257, 260, 261. *See also* Azusa Street; Lum, Clara E.; Seymour, William J.
Apostolic Faith (Goose Creek, Texas), 41. *See also* Campbell, J. G.
Apostolic Faith (Kansas), 109, 117, 125, 129, 139, 171, 173, 181, 222, 232, 256–257, 258. *See also* Parham, Charles Fox
Apostolic Faith (Oregon), 74, 259
Apostolic Faith (Oregon), The, 76, 131, 145, 160, 175, 209, 264. *See also* Crawford, Florence
Apostolic Faith (Texas-Arkansas), 179
Apostolic Faith (Tri-State District of Kansas, Oklahoma, Missouri), 214
Apostolic Faith Church (England and Wales), 143. *See also* Hutchinson, William Oliver
Apostolic Faith Mission (Hong Kong), 261

Apostolic Faith Mission (Los Angeles), 43, 74. See also *Apostolic Faith;* Azusa Street; Seymour, William J.
Apostolic Light, 30, 66, 86. *See also* Ryan, M. L.
Archibald, Mabel E., 50
Argue, A. H., 31, 233
Argue, Zelma, 184
Asberry, Richard, 159
Ashcroft, John, 7
Assemblia Christiana, 209
Assemblies of God: Trinitarian controversy, 6, 28, 147; size, 7; tongues, 43, 48; Bible, 70; "Statement of Fundamental Truths," 85; food restrictions, 122; leadership, 142; education, 152; women ministers, 160, 165–167, 168, 169; internal friction, 179; World War I, 218, 243–247; race relations, 227, 228, 231; mentioned, 29, 82, 83, 95, 106–107, 109, 119, 136, 142, 145, 154, 170, 188, 204, 231, 237, 255, 261
Atonement, 3, 26, 88. *See also* Divine healing; Jesus-centrism
Autonomy, personal, 212–216. *See also* Independence of temperament
Azusa Street revival and Mission: beginnings, 6; place of conversion(s), 37, 39, 49, 132, 201, 215; creedal statement, 77; doctrinal controversies, 79; interpreting the Holy Spirit, 83; worship, 100; race relations, 104, 105, 227, 228, 230, 232; physical setting, 112; dress, 125; finances, 131; scholarship on, 159; alleged ecumenism, 178, 194; mentioned, 24, 25, 36, 65, 78, 80, 99, 103, 123, 137, 139, 160, 162, 163, 194, 198, 204, 211, 229, 255, 260, 263. See also *Apostolic Faith;* Seymour, William J.
Azusa Temple, 174. *See also* Cotton, Emma

Bagby, Arthur Pendleton, 203

Bailey, S. Clyde, 220

Baker, Elizabeth V.: tongues, 41, regularization of worship, 107; finances, 140; call to preach, 164, mentioned, 67, 143, 175. *See also* Rochester Bible and Missionary Training Institute

Baldwin, James, 126

Baptism by immersion, 41, 110

Baptists, 1, 6, 28, 64, 169, 181, 205, 213

Barnes, Mary Mother, 31

Barney, Walter, 186

Barratt, T. B., 37, 39, 79, 104, 148–149

Barrett, David W., 8

Bartleman, Frank: revival beginnings, 19; independence of temperament, 28–29; experience of Holy Spirit, 52, 55; doctrinal disunity, 79; Holiness fanaticism, 100; and singing, 109; preaching, 113, 117; prayer, 154; historian, 159; women ministers, 173–174; patriarchy, 176; finances, 210; race relations, 228, 230, war, 243, 246; Lord's soon return, 261; revival decline, 262; mentioned, 92, 94, 96, 221

Barton, Josef, 197

Bell, E. N.: absolutism, 22; stamina, 31; authority of Holy Spirit; 82; regularization of worship, 106; on women's dress, 136, 171; finances, 137; leadership, 145, 147; women ministers, 170; education, 200, 204; love of country, 238; World War I, 245–247, 249; food restrictions, 261; mentioned, 95, 207. See also *Weekly Evangel; Word and Witness*

Berends, Kurt O., 186, 209

Berg, George E., 46

Beruldsen, C., 61

Beth-el Faith Home, 185. *See also* Parham, Charles Fox

Bethel Missionary Society and Bible School, 168, 174

Bible: authority, 11, 70–76; interpretation, 72–76, 150–151; precedent for miracles, 93–94; women in ministry, 170, 171, 175–176; Lord's soon return, 254

Bible training schools, 150–151, 152, 168, 175, 202, 267

Black pentecostals. *See* African American pentecostals

Blackstone, William E., 3

Blessed Truth, 28, 76

Blumhofer, Edith L., 134, 222

Boddy, A. A., 59, 73, 79, 97, 104, 214, 216. See also *Confidence*

Bois, Jules, 102

Bonnie Brae house, 123. *See also* Azusa Street

Booth, Catherine, 88, 159

Booth-Clibborn, Arthur S., 88, 89, 147, 243

Booth-Clibborn, William E., 162, 257

Bosworth, F. F., 26, 43, 185, 233

Bowe, Justus, 234

Bowley, Harry E., 118–119, 187

Boyd, Frank M., 119–120

Bresee, Phineas, 118

Bridal Call, 116. *See also* McPherson, Aimee Semple

Bridegroom's Messenger, 41, 46, 47, 147, 195, 208. *See also* Sexton, Elizabeth

Brinkman, George S., 80. See also *Pentecostal Herald*

Britton, F. M., 133, 138, 214

Brooks, Eugene, 12. *See also* Zion Faith Home

Brown, Marie, 162, 174, 262. *See also* Glad Tidings Tabernacle

Brown, Peter, 17

Brown, Robert H., 115. *See also* Glad Tidings Tabernacle

Brownsville Assembly of God Church, 267

Brumback, Carl, 142

Bryan, William Jennings, 219, 223, 244

Bryant, Mary, 90

Bryant, W. F., 191–192, 201, 239, 248

Buffum, Herbert and Lillian, 129, 135

Bundy, David, 229

Burbank Hall, 100

Burgess, Marie. *See* Brown, Marie

Burning Bush, 49. *See also* Garr, Alfred G.

Burpee, A. W., 129

Burpee, Florence L., 258

Campbell, J. G., 41. See also *Apostolic Faith* (Goose Creek, Texas)

Camp meeting revivals, 135–136, 202

Carothers, W. F.: rewards of pentecostalism, 67; *Church Government*, 130; women ministers, 169–170; patriarchy, 176; public prominence, 203–204; race relations, 230–231, 232

Carpenter, Joel, 268

Cashwell, G. B., 35, 94, 104, 132, 228

Central Bible Institute, 150

Chi, Mok Lai, 261

Children, 105, 185, 186

Christian and Missionary Alliance, 1, 3, 148, 152, 154, 179, 205, 256. *See also* Simpson, A. B.

Christian Catholic Apostolic Church, 155, 204, 256. *See also* Dowie, John Alexander

Christian Evangel, 21, 182, 212, 241, 242, 258

Christian Scientists, 4, 155, 180

Christian Union, 160. *See also* Church of God, The (Cleveland, Tennessee)

Christian Worker's Union, 77

Church Government, 130. *See also* Carothers, W. F.

Church of God (Britain), 264

Church of God, The (Cleveland, Tennessee): adoption of pentecostalism, 6; size, 7; tenets, 41; inspiration of Holy Spirit, 83; leadership, 143; women, 160, 167–168; labor, 195, 223; voting, 222; race relations, 227; World War I, 247, 248; mentioned, 20, 23, 65, 123, 125, 147, 156, 171, 185, 186, 191, 201, 203, 210, 222, 235, 238, 239. *See also* Spurling, Richard G., Jr.; Tomlinson, A. J.

Church of God Evangel, 25, 77, 237, 248

Church of God in Christ: adoption of pentecostalism, 6; size, 7; *Whole Truth,* 76; women, 167–168; race relations, 227, 228, 229, 231; World War I, 248–249; mentioned, 41, 59, 104, 138, 145, 147, 159, 185, 220, 233, 234, 236. *See also* Mason, C. H.

Church of God Mountain Assembly, 190

Church of God of Prophecy, The, 76

Churches of Christ, 4

Churches of God (Winebrenner), 146

Churches of God in Christ, 76, 229, 260. *See also* Assemblies of God; Church of God in Christ; *Truth*

Clark, Vern, 7

Colletti, Joseph, 209

Common sense realism, 75

Confidence, 50, 109, 257, 263. *See also* Boddy, A. A.

Congregationalists, 203, 205

Conn, Charles W., 23

Conversion, 6, 29–30, 58–59. *See also* Holy Ghost baptism; Salvation

Cook, Glenn A., 36–37, 97–98

Copley, A. S., 80, 143

Cotton, Emma, 159, 205. *See also* Azusa Temple

Cox, Harvey, 165

Cox, Homer L., 117

Craig, Mary, 150

Craig, Robert J., 150, 196

Craig, S. S., 95

Crawford, Florence: apocalypticism, 94, 259; leadership, 145; prominence, 147; founder of The Apostolic Faith, 160, 163; Lum-Seymour controversy, 230; mentioned, 175, 184

Crews, Mickey, 222, 247

Crumpler, A. B., 117, 220

Cullis, Charles, 3

Daniels, David, 229, 231

Dann, Norman, 221

Delk, Julia, 175

Democratic Party, 220, 248

Diggs, J. D., 236

Disciples of Christ, 118

Dispensational premillennialism. *See* Lord's soon return

Divine healing: four-fold gospel, 1–3; atonement-healing idea, 3, 26; anti–medical establishment, 15, 191–192, 204; prevailing prayer, 26–28; enduement of power, 59, 62; Holy Ghost baptism, 65–67; demons, 92; mediums, 94; leadership criteria, 149; legal controversies, 189; mentioned, 41, 42, 100, 104, 234, 253

Doctrine: correct doctrine, 76–81; controversies, 78–79, 85. *See also* Trinitarian controversy

Dowie, John Alexander: decline, 155–156; legal difficulties, 189; anti–medical establishment, 191; myscegenation, 232; war, 243; Lord's soon return, 256; mentioned, 3, 204. *See also* Christian Catholic Apostolic Church; Zion City

Draper, Minnie T., 174

Driver, Eddie R., 233

Duncan, Susan, 195, 219, 255

Durham, William H.: absolutism, 22; sanctification controversy, 78; preaching, 115, 120; Bible training school, 151; finances, 210; Azusa race relations, 228; revival's decline, 262; mentioned, 103

Easton, Susan C., 175

Ecumenism, 178

Education: attitude toward, 144; Bible training colleges, 150, 152; leadership criteria, 151–153; background, 200, 203–205, 208

Elbethel Faith Home, 97. *See also* MacIlravy, Cora Harris

Elim. *See* Rochester Bible and Missionary Training Institute

Ellis, William T., 102
Episcopalians, 7, 203, 205
Espinosa, Gaston, 226
Evans, J. R., 169
Evans, W. I., 150
Evening Light and Church of God Evangel,
   66, 257. *See also* Tomlinson, A. J.
Everlasting Gospel, 256. *See also* Shiloh
Ewart, Frank, 50, 61, 79, 147, 255
Experience, authority of, 84–88

Faithful Standard, 41, 134, 238. *See also*
   Church of God, The (Cleveland,
   Tennessee)
Faith homes, 3, 134, 189
Falcon Holiness School, 202
Farrow, Lucy F., 38, 94, 149, 159, 162
Feick, August, 229
Finney, Charles G., 2, 74
Fire-Baptized Holiness Church, 1, 73, 80,
   133, 227. *See also* Irwin, B. H.; King,
   J. H.; Pentecostal Holiness Church
Fire-Baptized Holiness Church of God of the
   Americas, 229. *See also* Fire-Baptized
   Holiness Church; Fuller, W. E.
First Fruit Harvesters, 28, 186–187, 203. *See*
   also Wright, Joel Adams
Fisher, Elmer K., 77, 127, 178, 254. *See also*
   Upper Room Mission
Fisher, Henry L., 104, 123. *See also* United
   Holy Church
Flower, J. Roswell, 212, 241–243. See also
   Christian Evangel
Floyd, David Lee, 28–29
Four-fold gospel, 1–3, 77
Fraser, Andrew L., 150
Fredericks, C. H., 180–181
Freimark, Max, 172
Frey, Eleanor, 169–170
Fritsch, Cora, 21, 201, 210, 215, 238
Frodsham, A. W., 45
Frodsham, Stanley H., 218, 243
Fulkerson, Mary McClintock, 175
Fuller, W. E., 229. *See also* Fire-Baptized
   Holiness Church of God of the Americas
Full Gospel Business Men's Fellowship
   International, 7
Full Gospel Missionary Herald, 254

Garr, Alfred G., 49–50, 51, 79, 215
Garr, Lillian Anderson, 49–50, 215
Garrigus, Alice Belle, 94, 103, 175
Gee, Donald, 100, 134
Gentry, William Doctor, 203

Gibeah Bible School, 73, 150, 187. *See also*
   Myland, D. Wesley
Gibson, Arrell M., 214
Glad Tidings (Los Angeles), 127
Glad Tidings (San Francisco), 56
Glad Tidings Bible Institute, 136, 150
Glad Tidings Herald, 211, 221
Glad Tidings Tabernacle, 93, 162, 174
Gleams of Grace, 201
Glossolalia. *See* Tongues
Godbey, W. D., 75
God's Newspapers, 81. See also *Yellow Books*
Goff, James R., Jr., 231, 235
Golden Grain, 193
Gold Tried in the Fire, 76, 129. *See also*
   Buffum, Herbert and Lillian
Good Report, 136, 201
Gordon, A. J., 159–160
Gortner, J. Narver, 221
Gospel Witness, 204. *See also* Worrell, A. S.
Goss, Howard: independence of
   temperament, 29; alleged anti-
   intellectualism, 31; Holy Ghost baptism,
   39; tongues, 52; sin, 97; women's dress,
   124; levity, 129; music, 135; threats
   against, 186; elite following, 198; critique
   of defeatist religion, 262; mentioned, 21,
   103, 130, 201
Gourley, Thomas Hampton, 202
Grace and Truth, 76, 138. *See also* Adams,
   L. P.
Gravelle, Harriet, 64
Gray, James, 182

Hall, David D., 111, 123
Hall, L. C., 68, 147, 194, 203
Hansen, Sophie, 46–47
Harrell, David Edwin, 100
Harriman, Nathan N., 82, 94
Harris, Thoro, 135, 232
Hays, Doremus A., 101
Haywood, G. T.: tongues, 43; Jesus-centrism,
   88; conflicts, 118, 187–188; leadership,
   145; intellect, 152–153; women ministers,
   172; race relations, 234; mentioned, 110.
   See also Pentecostal Assemblies of the
   World; *Voice in the Wilderness*
Healing. *See* Divine healing
Hebden Mission, 211
Hedge, Mrs. L. M., 163
Henke, Frederick, 101
Herald of the Church: An Advocate of the
   Scriptural Unity of the People of God in One
   Body, 178

Herrill, Ralph, 185
Hezmalhalch, Thomas, 140
Higgins, Walter, 20, 23, 184, 230
Higher life fundamentalists (Keswick), 2, 3, 4, 179, 252
Holiness Advocate, 173
Holiness Church, 104, 117
Holiness Wesleyans. *See* Wesleyan holiness
Holland, A. C., 152. See also *Apostolic Evangel*
Holmes, Nickels John, 106, 204
Holmes Bible and Missionary Institute, 106. *See also* Holmes, Nickels John
Holt, William B., 220, 229, 231, 236, 248, 249
Holy Ghost and Us. *See* Shiloh
Holy Ghost baptism: four-fold gospel, 1, 2; order of salvation, 5–6, 29, 58; assurance of salvation, 22, 62; source of power, 62–63; rewards, 63–68; healing, 65–67; purity of doctrine, 77; mentioned, 103, 234, 253. *See also* Holy Spirit; Salvation; Tongues
Holy Spirit: authority of, 14, 70, 81–84; view of, 89–91; worship, 103–108; preaching, 113–114; leader(-lessness), 141–144; Biblical interpretation, 150–151; women ministers, 162–165, 169, 171. *See also* Holy Ghost baptism
Hoover, Herbert, 33, 221
Hoover, J. N., 181
Household of God, 24, 187, 261. *See also* Manley, William F.; Post, A. H.
Household of God, 192. *See also* Manley, William F.
Human nature, doctrine of, 95–98
Hutchins, Julia, 159
Hutchinson, William Oliver, 143. *See also* Apostolic Faith Church
Hutchison, William R., 267

Independence of temperament, 28–34. *See also* Autonomy, personal
Intercessory Missionary, 34, 43. *See also* Street, A. E.
International Church of the Foursquare Gospel, 6, 7, 145, 160, 169. *See also* McPherson, Aimee Semple
International Pentecostal Holiness Church, 7
Irvingites, 51
Irwin, B. H., 60, 73, 196. *See also* Fire-Baptized Holiness Church

Jamieson, S. A., 117
Jeffreys, Stephen, 124

Jehovah's Witnesses, 4, 180, 217
Jesus-centrism, 87–89
Jews, 155, 182–183
Johnson, Todd M., 8
Jones, Charles Edwin, 8
Jones, Sam, 181–182

Kaufman, Peter I., 59
Kenyon, E. W., 26
Kerr, D. W., 73
Keswick. *See* Higher life fundamentalists
King, J. H.: leadership, 6, 145; sanctification, 54–55; conversion to pentecostalism, 61, 80; doctrinal controversies, 78, 79, 80; preaching, 120. *See also* Fire-Baptized Holiness Church; Pentecostal Holiness Church
Kinne, S. D., 95, 180
Kirvin, Henry, 236
Kornweibel, Theodore, 248
Kuhlman, Kathryn, 33, 158
Ku Klux Klan, 221, 232

Laberge, Agnes Ozman. *See* Ozman, Agnes
Lake, John G., 38, 54, 64, 91, 94, 137, 154, 262
Larssen, Anna, 56, 147, 198
Latino pentecostals, 7, 226–227
Latter-day Saints, 4, 51, 127, 155, 180, 217, 256
Latter Rain (renewal movement), 152
Latter Rain Evangel, 66, 91, 116, 139, 143. *See also* Piper, William H.
Law, E. May, 128–129, 192
Lawrence, Bennett F., 159, 251
Leaders: Holy Spirit directed, 141–144; vs. clergy, 142; titles, 143–144; egalitarianism, 144; prominence, 145–148; Holy Spirit gifts, 148–149; education, 151–153; organizational skills, 153–154; pragmatism, 155–157
Leatherman, Lucy, 38
Lee, Edward S., 159
Lee, Owen, 39
Lee, T. M., 191
Leith, Scotland, 134
Leonard, T. C., 117–118, 151–152
Letters from Jesus, 81
Liberalism, theological, 4, 181
Lord's soon return: four-fold gospel, 1, 2, 3; dispensational premillennialism, 251–256; sense of doom, 256–259; sense of hope, 260–262; mentioned 23, 41, 42, 115, 198, 202, 219, 222, 228, 234

Lum, Clara E., 43, 172, 198, 228, 230. See also *Apostolic Faith*

Lupton, Levi R.: view of Bible, 71; on women's dress, 125; finances, 130, 132, 137; education, 152; theological liberalism, 181; external conflict, 181, 185, 258; separation from state, 219; social progressivism, 221; race relations, 231; Lord's soon return, 258, 261–262; mentioned, 101

Lutherans, 7, 181

MacIlravy, Cora Harris, 97. *See also* Elbethel Faith Home

Mahler, Thomas, 83–84

Manley, William F., 192, 233. *See also* Household of God

Martin, David, 155, 211

Marty, Martin E., 179

Mason, C. H.: leadership, 6, 145; Holy Ghost baptism, 59; race relations, 104, 227–228, 229, 231, 236; prominence, 146–147; violence against, 185; World War I, 248–249. *See also* Church of God in Christ

Mathisen, James, 10

McCafferty, Burt, 110

McConnell, Hattie and John, 132

McDuff, Rose Marie, 233

McPherson, Aimee Semple: founder of International Church of the Foursquare Gospel, 6, 77; life sketch, 32–33, 145; Kall Four Square Gospel, 33; sanctification controversy, 78; preaching, 114–115, 120, 167, 192; Holy Spirit directed, 141–142; prominence, 145; kidnapping controversy, 145; leadership, 154; women ministers, 160, 163, 168; social class, 198, 214; mobility, 214; voting, 222; race relations, 233; love of country, 238–239; World War I, 247; mentioned, 9, 16, 22, 39, 115–116, 123, 126, 134, 158, 169, 175, 188, 193, 194, 205, 212, 224, 237, 260

Mead, Ardella and Samuel, 62–63

Mennonites, 1, 245

Merian, Fred and Lillian, 48

Merritt, Stephen, 164

Methodists, 1, 28, 30, 63, 99, 104, 115, 118, 133, 192–193, 203, 205

Midnight Cry, 76, 118, 172. *See also* Welch, William

Miller, Perry, 18

Mims, W. P., 118–119

Miracles: resurrections, 15, 62, 67, 88, 261; signs and wonders, 22–23, 92–95; prevailing prayer, 25–28; biblical motifs, 93–94; mediums, 94; Lord's soon return, 253, 254, 255, 256; recent pentecostalism, 267; mentioned, 11, 15, 94. *See also* Divine healing

Missionary Bands of the World, 1

Missionary Review of the World, 3. *See also* Pierson, A. T.

Mission impulse: missionary tongues 48, 86; heroes, 147; universality of full gospel, 183; urgency, 261; expansionism, 263–265, 267–268; mentioned, 215. *See also* Tongues: missionary; Pentecostalism, global

Modernism. *See* Liberalism

Mogridge, H., 180, 202, 224

Montgomery, Carrie Judd: prayer and healing, 26, missionary tongues, 46, 48; Holy Ghost baptism, 63; wealth, 203; Lord's soon return, 255; mentioned, 117, 124. See also *Triumphs of Faith*

Moore, Jenny Evans, 39, 230. *See also* Seymour, William J.

Moore, R. Laurence, 217

Moorhead, Max Wood, 198

Morality, practical: traditional restrictions, 122, 128–129; food and drink, 122–123, 133, 134, 137, 261; speech, 123–124; reading, 124; music, 124; dress, 124–125, 133, 136; sexual behaviors, 125–128; recreational activities, 128–130, 133, 134, 136; finances, 130–133, 137–140; rejection of medical care, 133, 137

Morgan, Dan, 135, 213

Morgan, G. Campbell, 256

Mormons. *See* Latter-day Saints

Morrow, Abbie C., 181

Moseley, J. R., 236

Moss, Virginia E., 175

Mount Sinai Holy Church of America, 160, 167. *See also* Robinson, Ida

Mueller, George, 122, 130

Mueller, Jacob, 100

Music, 109, 124, 135. *See also* Worship

Myland, D. Wesley, 73, 80, 150, 152–153, 187, 195

Nazarenes, 118

Nelson, P. C., 150, 204

Nelson, Shirley, 259

Neshoba Holiness School (Pentecostal Faith), 185

New Acts, 22, 139. *See also* Lupton, Levi R.

New Thought, 26, 180. *See also* Kenyon, E. W.
Nickel, Thomas R., 159
North Avenue Mission (Chicago), 37, 101, 103, 210
Norton, Albert, 43, 46

O'Guin, Carl, 61
Oneida Perfectionists, 15, 127
Oneness pentecostals, 6, 7, 16, 28, 82, 85, 88, 118, 147, 153, 212, 168. *See also* Pentecostal Assemblies of the World; Trinitarian controversy
Orwig, A. W., 194
Osterberg, A. G., 50, 65, 103, 213, 229
Ozman, Agnes: Holy Ghost baptism, 60, 72, 106, 108 (Laberge), 123; Holy Spirit, 90–91; preaching, 162

Page, E. J., 66–67
Palmer, Phoebe, 2, 159, 165
Panin, Ivan, 80–81
Parham, Charles Fox: founder, 5; tongues and Holy Ghost baptism, 5, 23, 41, 42, 45; absolutism, 23; conditional immortality, 30, 41; independence of temperament, 30; healing, 66; Biblical interpretation, 75; sanctification, 78; prophet, 97; worship, 106; preaching, 113, 115, 120; humor, 118; emotionalism, 125, 127; faith, 131, 138–139; Bible school, 150; scholarship regarding, 159; women preachers, 164; threats against, 184; business and labor, 195; finances, 211; separation from state, 218; voting, 221–222; charity, 224; race relations, 231–232; conflict with Seymour, 232; love of country, 238–239; war, 243; mentioned, 9, 53, 72, 80, 90, 91, 100, 106, 117, 123, 134, 149, 173, 180, 185, 214, 256, 258, 263
Parham, Sarah, 25
Patriotism, 237–239. *See also* State; World War I
Payne, Jesse, 248
Peck, Frank, 195
Peniel Bible Institute, 125
Peniel Hall, 204
Pennington, Edith Mae, 134, 147
Penn-Lewis, Jesse, 159, 256
Pentecost, 66, 208. *See also* Copley, A. S.
Pentecostal, as label, 15–16
Pentecostal Assemblies of the U.S.A., 29
Pentecostal Assemblies of the World: Trinitarian controversy and founding, 6, 7;

absolutism, 78; authority of experience, 85; leadership of G. T. Haywood, 145, 153; women ministers, 168, 172; finances, 210; race relations, 227, 229, 231; mentioned, 110, 138, 197–198, 234. *See also* Oneness pentecostals
Pentecostal Church of God, 214, 228, 253
Pentecostal Herald, 264
Pentecostal Holiness Advocate, 68, 172, 262. *See also* Taylor, George Floyd
Pentecostal Holiness Church: adoption of pentecostalism, 6; internal strife, 79, 120; on socialism, 220; mentioned, 20, 54, 61, 78, 120, 133, 145, 152, 204, 222. *See also* King, J. H.; Taylor, George Floyd
Pentecostalism, global, 10, 102, 262–266, 268. *See also* Mission impulse
Pentecostalism, interpretations of, 10, 60, 142, 266
Pentecostalism, recent, 7–8, 165, 266–268
Pentecostal Missionary Union, 83
Pentecostal Rescue Journal, 173
Pentecostal Testimony, 210. *See also* Durham, William H.
Pentecostal World, 242
Pentecostals, conflicts: 17, 177–196, 259. *See also* State
Pentecostals, social demographics: marginality, 198, 199–202, 216; middle and upper class, 198–199, 202–205, 216; education, 200, 203–205, 208; sex, 205; age, 206; health, 206; race, 206–207; marital status, 207; rural vs. urban, 207–208; employment, 208–209; financial status, 209–211, 216; geographical location, 211–212; mobility, 213–216
Pentecost Evangel, 113, 137
Perfectionists, Oberlin, 2, 3, 4
Periodicals: role, 29; titles, 76, 257; race, 233–234; native language, 263; global reach, 265
Perkins, Jonathan, 65
Petrus, Lewi, 22
Pierson, A. T., 3, 256
Piety, 19–21
Pillar of Fire, 1
Pinson, M. M., 139, 211
Piper, William H., 61, 73, 116
Pisgah Home and Gardens, 97, 204, 224. *See also* Yoakum, Finis
Plymire, Victor, 147
Plymouth Brethren, 3, 181
Politics. *See* State
Portland, Oregon, 160, 163, 184, 212, 215

Post, A. H., 24
Prayer, prevailing, 25–28, 264
Preaching: Holy Spirit directed, 113–114; talent and style, 114–120; women, 162–165; critique of mainline preachers, 192–193. *See also* Worship
Presbyterians,1, 6
Price, Charles S., 193–194
Prohibition, 221, 223

Race relations: egalitarianism of Holy Ghost baptism, 65, 144, and worship, 103–105; progressive attitudes, 165, 227–229; scholarship on, 226–227; accomodationist attitudes, 229–231; case studies, 231–233; theology of race relations (paucity of), 233–235
Ramabai, Pandita, 46, 140, 264
Rauschenbusch, Walter, 224
Reade, H. Musgrave, 218
Red Cross, 247, 249
Reeder, Hilda, 110–111
Reform, 220–221, 223–226
Reformed tradition, 6
Republican Party, 220, 222, 248, 267
Restorationism, 3–4, 71–72
Richey, Raymond T., 136
Richey, Russell E., 63, 115
Riggs, Ralph M., 68
Robeck, Cecil M., 205, 206, 207, 209, 215
Roberts, Oral, 7, 33, 145, 158
Robertson, Pat, 33
Robins, Roger, 32
Robinson, Charles E., 137. See also *Pentecost Evangel*
Robinson, Ida, 147, 160. *See also* Mount Sinai Holy Church of America
Robinson, Martha Wing: pragmatism, 12–13, 14; experience of Holy Spirit, 72, 90, 97; on sin, 95; leadership, 149–150; mentioned, 123, 175
Rochester Bible and Missionary Training Institute, 41, 143, 150, 168, 195, 219, 255, 257. *See also* Baker, Elizabeth V.
Roebuck, David G., 167
Roman Catholics, 4, 7, 39, 179, 182, 195, 217
Rosa, Adolph, 104
Ryan, M. L., 30, 42, 66, 85–86, 90, 142, 185, 194. See also *Apostolic Light*

Saints Home Church, 233. *See also* Driver, Eddie R.

Salvation, assurance of, 61–62
Salvation, order of, 5–6, 29, 40
Salvation, personal, 1–2, 40, 42, 253
Salvation Army, 181, 214, 224
Samson's Foxes, 130. *See also* Tomlinson, A. J.
Sanctification: and Holy Ghost baptism, 2, 43, 54–55; order of salvation, 29, 58; mentioned, 42, 78, 234
Sandford, Frank W.: autocracy, 24–25; Bible training school, 150; downfall, 155–156; and legal problems, 156, 189; patriarchy, 172; Lord's soon return, 256; mentioned, 5, 195. *See also* Shiloh
Satan, view of, 91–92
Schermer, H. W., 129, 171, 181
Schoonmaker, Christian, 72
Seaman, Ann Rowe, 115
Second Coming. *See* Lord's soon return
Semple, Robert, 32
Sexton, Elizabeth, 175, 195. See also *Bridegroom's Messenger*
Seymour, William J.: adoption of pentecostalism, 6; necessity of tongues, 43–44; authority of Bible, 71; purity of doctrine, 77; sanctification controversy, 78; finances, 140; leadership of Holy Spirit, 142–143; scholarship on, 159; race relations, 228, 230, 231, 234; conflict with Lum, 230; and Parham, 232; Lord's soon return, 253, 260; mentioned, 7, 97–98, 131. See also *Apostolic Faith;* Azusa Street
Sheaf, The, 187. *See also* First Fruit Harvesters
Shiloh (Holy Ghost and Us): Durham, Maine, 5, 24, 71, 76, 82, 88, 91, 94, 150, 156, 172, 189, 195, 256, 263; conflicts, 24–25; Bible, 71; restorationism, 72; founding, 156; patriarchy, 172; separation from society, 202; Lord's soon return, 256; mentioned, 1, 5, 76, 82, 91, 94, 195, 259, 263. *See also* Sandford, Frank W.
Shumway, Charles William, 44, 47, 102
Simpson, A. B., 3, 27, 77, 148, 256. *See also* Christian and Missionary Alliance
Simpson, W. W., 75, 153–154, 224–225
Sisson, Elizabeth, 25, 55, 166, 175, 260
Slaybaugh, E. T., 242
Slocum, Arthur L., 140
Smale, Joseph, 159
Smith, Amanda Berry, 159
Smith, Arthur, 185
Smith, Hannah Whitall, 96, 159
Smith, Mabel, 53
Smith, Timothy L., 28

Society of Friends, 1, 30, 118, 181, 186, 245, 258. *See also* Lupton, Levi R.

Southern Bible Conference, 162

Southwestern Bible Institute, 150, 204

Spencer, Ivan Q., 150

Spiritualists, 4, 51, 92, 180

Spurling, Richard G., 203

Spurling, Richard G., Jr., 20, 203, 248

State: separation from, 217–219; politics, 220–223; law enforcement, 235–237, 247, 248–249. *See also* Patriotism; World War I

Steinbeck, John, 126, 199

Steinberg, Edgar, 85

Stereotypes, 125–128

Stone Church, 116, 132. *See also* Piper, William H.

Street, A. E., 33, 43. See also *Intercessory Missionary*

Studd, C. T., 121–122, 135

Studd, George B., 46, 135, 139, 204, 230

Sunday, Billy, 101, 117, 181–182

Supernatural beings, view of, 91–92

Swaggart, Jimmy, 33, 115

Taylor, F. W., 136

Taylor, George Floyd: piety, 20; tongues, 74; doctrine, 92; itinerancy, 120; women ministers, 172; education, 204; finances, 211; Lord's soon return, 254; mentioned, 220, 222. *See also* Pentecostal Holiness Church

Terry, Neely, 159

Thompson, E. P., 266

Tomlinson, A. J.: founder of Church of God, 6; primitivism, 11, 14; independence of temperament, 28–29, 31; stamina, 32; tongues and Holy Ghost baptism, 35–36, 41, 43, 56; doctrine, 81; Holy Spirit and worship, 106, 108, 109; finances, 130, 140; leadership, 143, 145, 147, 156–157; women ministers, 171; doctors, 192; background, 203, 222; politics, 222; World War I, 238, 247–248, 249; Lord's soon return, 261; mentioned, 72, 80, 103, 116, 124, 163, 184, 250

Tomlinson, Halcy, 163

Tomlinson, Homer, 237

Tongues: sign of Holy Ghost baptism, 5–6, 40–44, 74, 80, 86; recent pentecostals, 7; autobiographical experiences of, 35–40; sign-gift doctrine, 44; missionary, 45–51, 108; scholarly interpretations, 51–58; sources of, 52–55; Biblical basis, 74–75; interpretation, 82–84; human medium, 94; regularization, 107; tongues singing, 110; leadership criteria, 148–149

Tongues of Fire, 71. *See also* Shiloh

Torrey, Reuben A., 2, 75

Trasher, Lillian, 147, 175

Trinitarian controversy, 6, 28, 79, 85, 88, 118, 147. *See also* Jesus-centrism; Oneness pentecostals

Triumphs of Faith, 46, 117, 124, 203. *See also* Montgomery, Carrie Judd

Trust, 76, 218

Truth, 76. *See also* Churches of God in Christ; *Whole Truth*

Truth Bible School, 76, 154

Union Holiness Mission, 101

United Brethren, 146, 181

United Holy Church, 104, 123, 160, 175, 224, 236, 258. *See also* Fisher, Henry L.

United Pentecostal Church, 6, 7

Upper Room Mission, 22, 46, 77, 96, 178, 198, 204, 219, 230, 254. *See also* Fisher, Elmer K.

Urshan, Andrew, 80, 188

Utley, Uldine, 105

Valdez, A. C., 159

Varg, Paul, 263

VICTORY!, 198

Vishnewski, Stanley, 190

Vision of the Disinherited: The Making of American Pentecostalism, 199–201. See also Anderson, Robert Mapes

Voice in the Wilderness, 43, 85, 118, 234. *See also* Haywood, G. T.

Walker, Elmer M., 210, 220

Walker's Gospel Messenger, 172

Walls, Andrew, 267

"Washington's Vision," 241

Way of Faith, 96

Weekly Evangel, 78, 139, 207, 218, 241, 245, 246. *See also* Bell, E. N.

Welch, J. W., 167, 245, 255

Welch, William, 118, 172. See also *Midnight Cry*

Wesleyan holiness, 2, 3, 4–5, 6, 25, 179, 221

Western Recorder, 204. *See also* Worrell, A. S.

Wheaton, Mother Elizabeth R., 31

White City, Mississippi, 202

Whole Truth, 41, 76, 183, 234. *See also* Church of God in Christ

Wigglesworth, Smith, 94, 146
Wilkerson, J. A., 188
Williams, E. S., 231
Wilson, Eula, 67
Wilson, Woodrow, 220, 223, 248, 249
Winnipeg, Canada, 80, 184
Winsett, R. E., 138
Women: egalitarianism of revival, 103–104, 144; dress, 125, 134, 171, 173–174; faith homes, 134; scholarship regarding, 158–159, 176; preachers and ministers, 159–165; predominance, 159–162, 205; feminine imagery, 161–162; restrictions against, 165–176; assertion vs. compliance, 174–176
Women's Aglow, 7
Woodworth-Etter, Maria: emotionalism of services, 1, 3, 101–102; faith and healing, 26; authority of Holy Spirit, 26, 84, 114, 164; anointing, 55; healing evangelist, 66; sanctification controversy, 78; preaching, 114, 164; prominence, 146; race relations, 230; mentioned, 9, 169, 175, 205
Word and Witness, 31, 106, 109, 125, 172, 241, 246. *See also* Bell, E. N.
Word and Work, 260

World War I, 20, 218, 222, 237–238, 240–250
Worrell, A. S., 148, 204
Worship: Spirit-filled, 99–103, 105–108; egalitarianism, 103–105; regularization, 105–111; prophecy and interpretation, 107; music, 109–110, 135; frequency, 110, 135; physical setting, 112–113; preaching, 113–120; source of external conflict, 187–189; recent, 267
Wright, J. Elwin, 203
Wright, Joel Adams, 28, 90, 203

Xenolalia. *See* Tongues: missionary

Yellow Books, 81–82
Yeomans, Lilian B., 27, 175, 204
Yoakum, Finis, 97, 204, 224. *See also* Pisgah Home and Gardens

Zion (Providence, Rhode Island), 168
Zion City, Illinois, 3, 12, 15, 155–156, 175, 191, 202. *See also* Dowie, John Alexander
Zion Faith Home, 12, 72, 149, 175. *See also* Brooks, Eugene; Robinson, Martha Wing
Zionism, 182